AF779931

Economic Development in the Digital Economy Era

Economic Development in the Digital Economy Era

Guest Editor

Weixin Yang

MDPI

Basel • Beijing • Wuhan • Barcelona • Belgrade • Novi Sad • Cluj • Manchester

Guest Editor
Weixin Yang
Business School
University of Shanghai for
Science and Technology
Shanghai
China

Editorial Office
MDPI AG
Grosspeteranlage 5
4052 Basel, Switzerland

This is a reprint of the Special Issue, published open access by the journal *Economies* (ISSN 2227-7099), freely accessible at: https://www.mdpi.com/journal/economies/special_issues/080P45E5H8.

For citation purposes, cite each article independently as indicated on the article page online and as indicated below:

Lastname, Firstname, Firstname Lastname, and Firstname Lastname. Article Title. *Journal Name* **Year**, *Volume Number*, Page Range.

ISBN 978-3-7258-7410-1 (Hbk)
ISBN 978-3-7258-7411-8 (PDF)
https://doi.org/10.3390/books978-3-7258-7411-8

© 2026 by the authors. Articles in this reprint are Open Access and distributed under the Creative Commons Attribution (CC BY) license. The reprint as a whole is distributed by MDPI under the terms and conditions of the Creative Commons Attribution-NonCommercial-NoDerivs (CC BY-NC-ND) license (https://creativecommons.org/licenses/by-nc-nd/4.0/).

Contents

About the Editor . . . . **vii**

Preface . . . . **ix**

Weixin Yang, Chen Zhu and Yunpeng Yang
Does Urban Digital Construction Promote Economic Growth? Evidence from China
Reprinted from: *Economies* **2024**, *12*, 59, https://doi.org/10.3390/economies12030059 . . . . . . **1**

Irina Korgun and Altin Hoti
Dynamics of Bilateral Digital Trade: The Case of a Korea–EU Digital Partnership
Reprinted from: *Economies* **2023**, *11*, 248, https://doi.org/10.3390/economies11100248 . . . . . . **33**

Mónica González Morales and José Antonio Cavero Rubio
Impact of Digitalization of Sales on the Profitability of the Restaurant Industry during COVID-19
Reprinted from: *Economies* **2023**, *11*, 283, https://doi.org/10.3390/economies11110283 . . . . . . **47**

Jingke Gao, Wenxiao Zhou, Jinhua Cheng and Ziyuan Liu
Digital Economy Development, Common Prosperity, and Carbon Emissions: An Empirical Study in China
Reprinted from: *Economies* **2024**, *12*, 120, https://doi.org/10.3390/economies12050120 . . . . . . **63**

Jose Carlos Montes Ninaquispe, Alberto Luis Pantaleón Santa María, Diego Alejandro Ludeña Jugo, William Teófilo Castro Muñoz, Juan Cesar Farias Rodriguez, Billy Heinrich Maco Elera and Kelly Cristina Vasquez Huatay
Peruvian Agro-Exports' Competitiveness: An Assessment of the Export Development of Its Main Products
Reprinted from: *Economies* **2024**, *12*, 156, https://doi.org/10.3390/economies12060156 . . . . . . **83**

Ying Chen, Haiyan Ma and Tianyi Zhou
Learn from Whom? An Empirical Study of Enterprise Digital Mimetic Isomorphism under the Institutional Environment
Reprinted from: *Economies* **2024**, *12*, 243, https://doi.org/10.3390/economies12090243 . . . . . . **99**

Jarmila Horváthová and Martina Mokrišová
The Use of the Data Envelopment Analysis–Malmquist Approach to Measure the Performance of Digital Transformation in EU Countries
Reprinted from: *Economies* **2024**, *12*, 291, https://doi.org/10.3390/economies12110291 . . . . . . **118**

Ozcan Ozturk
The Impact of AI on International Trade: Opportunities and Challenges
Reprinted from: *Economies* **2024**, *12*, 298, https://doi.org/10.3390/economies12110298 . . . . . . **138**

Brian Tavonga Mazorodze
The Impact of Trade Openness and ICT on Technical Efficiency of Township Economies in South Africa
Reprinted from: *Economies* **2025**, *13*, 125, https://doi.org/10.3390/economies13050125 . . . . . . **151**

Roman Chinoracky, Natalia Stalmasekova, Radovan Madlenak and Lucia Madlenakova
Are Nations Ready for Digital Transformation? A Macroeconomic Perspective Through the Lens of Education Quality
Reprinted from: *Economies* **2025**, *13*, 152, https://doi.org/10.3390/economies13060152 . . . . . . **173**

Fadi Ghosn, Mohamad Zreik, Hala Koleilat Al Dilby, Caroline Dib Kassably Fakhry and Fida Ragheb Hassanein
Tokenomics and Digital Economy in China: Analyzing the Influence of Blockchain Technology Integration on Traditional Business Models
Reprinted from: *Economies* **2025**, *13*, 189, https://doi.org/10.3390/economies13070189 . . . . . . **195**

Shanqiang Zheng and Yaodong Zhou
Digital Transformation and Competitive Advantage in Manufacturing: The Role of Business Model Innovation
Reprinted from: *Economies* **2025**, *13*, 209, https://doi.org/10.3390/economies13070209 . . . . . . **209**

Yunsong Xu and Qian Ao
Digital Transformation, New Quality Productive Forces, and Corporate Environmental Investment: Empirical Evidence from Chinese A-Share Listed Companies
Reprinted from: *Economies* **2025**, *13*, 236, https://doi.org/10.3390/economies13080236 . . . . . . **237**

About the Editor

Weixin Yang

Weixin Yang received his Ph.D. in Economics from Shanghai Academy of Social Sciences. He is currently teaching at University of Shanghai for Science and Technology. He has published over 100 papers, book chapters, and conference proceedings. He has also been invited as a reviewer and academic editor of well-known journals. His main research interests are digital economy and sustainable development.

Preface

I am pleased to present "Economic Development in the Digital Economy Era," a Special Issue that brings together thirteen research contributions exploring the transformative impact of digital technologies on economic development across diverse contexts. As digitalization reshapes industries, markets, and societies worldwide, understanding how economies can harness these transformations for sustainable and inclusive growth has become a pressing concern for scholars, policymakers, and practitioners alike.

This collection addresses critical questions at the intersection of digital transformation and economic development. The scope encompasses corporate digital strategies and business model innovation, artificial intelligence applications in international trade, blockchain and tokenomics integration in traditional industries, workforce readiness for automation, and the environmental implications of digital economy advancement. The geographical coverage spans multiple regions, including China, the European Union, South Korea, South Africa, Peru, and OECD countries, reflecting the global nature of digital transformation challenges and opportunities. Through both firm-level analyses and macroeconomic perspectives, the contributions examine how digital technologies influence competitiveness, sustainability, and development trajectories in varied institutional environments.

The motivation for compiling this work stems from the recognition that developing and developed economies face distinct yet interconnected challenges in navigating digital transformation. While advanced economies grapple with automation-induced labor market disruptions and digital infrastructure optimization, emerging economies seek pathways to leverage digitalization for accelerating development and narrowing the gap with industrialized nations. This collection aims to provide evidence-based insights that illuminate both universal patterns and context-specific dynamics in the digital economy era.

This work is addressed to researchers in economics, management, and information systems; policymakers designing digital economy strategies and industrial policies; business practitioners implementing digital transformation initiatives; and students seeking to understand the complex relationships between technological change and economic development.

I extend my sincere gratitude to all contributing authors whose rigorous research made this publication possible. I also express my appreciation to the anonymous reviewers who provided constructive feedback that strengthened each contribution. Special thanks are due to the editorial team at *Economies* for their professional support and guidance throughout the publication process. I hope this collection serves as a valuable resource for advancing both scholarly understanding and practical approaches to economic development in an increasingly digital world.

Weixin Yang
Guest Editor

economies

MDPI

Article

Does Urban Digital Construction Promote Economic Growth? Evidence from China

Weixin Yang [1,*], Chen Zhu [1] and Yunpeng Yang [2,*]

[1] Business School, University of Shanghai for Science and Technology, Shanghai 200093, China
[2] Antai College of Economics and Management, Shanghai Jiao Tong University, Shanghai 200030, China
* Correspondence: iamywx@outlook.com (W.Y.); yang_yunpeng@outlook.com (Y.Y.)

Abstract: In order to explore the causal relationship between the level of urban digital construction and urban economic growth, this paper takes 280 cities in China as the research object and constructs a comprehensive indicator evaluation system covering digital infrastructure, overall economic level, innovation development level, digital industry development status, and ecological environment conditions. Using the entropy method to weigh various indicators, this paper has obtained the evaluation results of the digital construction level of each city from 2011 to 2021. Furthermore, a panel data regression model is used to empirically analyze the impact of urban digital construction level on urban economic growth. The results show that for every 1% increase in the level of urban digital construction, the GDP will increase by 0.974. Through the above research, we hope to further enrich the theoretical and empirical research in the field of the digital economy, provide a scientific and reasonable method for quantitatively evaluating the level of urban digital construction, and provide decision-making references for improving the level of urban digital construction and promoting sustainable urban development.

Keywords: digital construction; urban development; economic growth; evaluation index system

1. Introduction

The digital economy represents a novel economic paradigm in human history, succeeding agriculture and industry (Laitsou et al. 2020; Williamson 2022; Yang et al. 2023d). In the course of social production, the digital economy places data resources as a crucial production factor, utilizing modern information networks for various socio-economic activities, continuously optimizing production efficiency, and enhancing development quality through the progressive advancement of information and communication technology (Allcott et al. 2022; Fernandes et al. 2023; Jemiluyi and Jeke 2023; Jensen 2007). Consequently, the digital economy not only profoundly alters the developmental patterns of traditional production processes but also exerts a far-reaching impact on various facets of the socio-economic domain (Beraja et al. 2023a; Cahyadi and Magda 2021; Karle et al. 2020; Loebbing 2022; Maresova et al. 2018). With the continual progress and widespread adoption of digital technologies, the digital economy has emerged as a key driver and strategic advantage for global economic development (Costinot and Werning 2023; Korgun and Hoti 2023; Mpofu 2022; Mpofu and Mhlanga 2022).

China stands as one of the global leaders in digital economy development, boasting robust digital infrastructure and policy environments, dynamic digital enterprises and innovators (Supari and Anton 2022), and a massive user base (Maresova et al. 2018; Travkina et al. 2022; Yang et al. 2023c). According to statistics from the China Cyberspace Administration, the total volume of China's digital economy reached CNY 50.2 trillion in 2022, constituting 41.5% of the nation's GDP. China's digital economy not only holds a leading position globally in terms of scale but also continuously elevates its quality, giving rise to a cadre of internationally competitive and influential digital platforms, products, and services (Chen and Yang 2023; Karle et al. 2020; Travkina et al. 2022).

Urban areas serve as crucial carriers and settings for the development of the digital economy, representing primary arenas for the application and innovation of digital technologies (Liu et al. 2023; Ogujiuba and Mngometulu 2022). The level of urban digitalization reflects a city's capacity and effectiveness in leveraging digital technologies to drive economic and social development. It also influences a city's competitiveness and attractiveness on regional, national, and global scales (Einav et al. 2018; Lefatsa et al. 2021; Li and Camerer 2022). Therefore, evaluating the level of digitalization in Chinese cities and its impact on urban economic development holds significant importance for uncovering patterns in urban digital development, promoting digital transformation and upgrading, and enhancing overall urban capabilities.

However, there is currently a lack of a systematic and scientific evaluation framework for the level of digitalization in Chinese cities. Existing studies have mostly focused on singular aspects or domains of the digital economy (Ren et al. 2023; Yang et al. 2022), failing to comprehensively capture the multidimensional, multilevel, and multifaceted characteristics and effects of urban digitalization. Additionally, the relationship between the level of urban digitalization and urban economic development lacks sufficient theoretical and empirical support, making it challenging to reveal the mechanisms and extent of the impact of urban digitalization on urban economic growth.

Therefore, this paper first establishes a comprehensive evaluation index system for the level of digitalization in Chinese cities. Employing the entropy weighting method, we evaluate the digitalization level of 280 cities in China from 2011 to 2021 across five dimensions: urban digital infrastructure, overall economic level, innovation development level, digital industry development status, and ecological environment conditions. Building upon this foundation, a measurement model for urban digitalization levels is further developed for empirical analysis, aiming to explore the actual impact of the level of urban digital construction on economic growth. Our research findings indicate that for every 1% increase in the level of urban digitalization, the Gross Domestic Product (GDP) rises by 0.974 percentage points.

Specifically, this paper contributes in the following ways: By constructing a comprehensive evaluation index system for urban digitalization that covers five dimensions: digital infrastructure, overall economic level, innovation development level, digital industry development status, and ecological environment conditions. The application of the entropy weighting method to these indicators enriches theoretical research in the field of digital economic development. Utilizing data from 280 Chinese cities during the period 2011–2021, this paper calculates scores for each city across the five dimensions using the established index system. The results provide a summary of the achievements in digitalization for each city, offering a quantitative basis for further enhancing digitalization levels and a timely narrowing of the "digital divide" between different cities. Through empirical analysis, this paper quantifies the impact of digitalization on economic growth. The results show a significant positive effect of urban digitalization on its own economic growth. Through a series of robustness tests, this result is proven reliable, contributing not only to empirical research in the field of digital economic development but also to adding new content to the literature of urban economics.

This paper comprises six sections. Section 2 reviews the relevant literature. Section 3 constructs the index system and comprehensively evaluates the digitalization levels of various cities. Sections 4 and 5 empirically analyze the impact of urban digitalization on economic growth. Section 6 concludes the entire paper and proposes policy recommendations.

2. Literature Review

2.1. Urban Digital Construction

The concept of urban digitalization emerged in the early 1980s. Scholars, focusing on urban development in France, introduced the concept of the "Wired City", asserting that it represents a fundamental prototype that cities should embody under the digital economic paradigm. In the Wired City, the government invests in digital infrastructure, continuously improving urban network construction and user terminals to achieve high-quality citywide communication. Building on this, the academic community explored the convenience of information brought about by urban networking, giving rise to the theory of "urban informatization" (Avgerou 1991; Knox and Castells 1995). This theory posits that modern information technologies, represented by network communication, will significantly reshape urban planning and layout, exerting profound effects on the future development of major cities worldwide. Subsequently, developed Western countries successively formulated and implemented digital development strategies centered on cities, such as the "Information Superhighway" (Kettinger 1994) and the "Digital Earth". These strategies aimed to propel the overall digitization of the national economy through the digital transformation and development of major cities.

Considering the digital development strategies proposed by Western developed countries' governments and academia, the core objective is to implement the informatization and digitization of the entire national economy at the city level, realizing urban informatization and digitization (Goloshchapova et al. 2023; Kettinger 1994; Maresova et al. 2018). Specifically, it involves applying information network technologies, predominantly represented by the Internet, and digital technologies to the daily production and life of cities (Chen et al. 2023; Marshall 2023). This integration allows various sectors of the urban economy to merge with digital elements, ultimately achieving comprehensive penetration of digital elements into urban construction and development. The goal is to promote the networked and digitally intelligent development of the entire city. In this process, the digital development strategies of Western countries consider the efficient and rational allocation of urban information resources as a fundamental prerequisite. They seek to promptly integrate existing technologies and the latest achievements of informatization and digitization into various aspects of urban production, consumption, distribution, and exchange. This approach aims to facilitate citizens' lives, achieve sustained economic growth, and comprehensively upgrade digitization in areas such as urban economic development, ecological conservation, citizen living, and public services, ultimately realizing sustainable urban development (ElMassah and Mohieldin 2020; Goloshchapova et al. 2023; Veretennikova and Selezneva 2023).

2.2. Digital Technology in Urban Digital Construction

From a technological perspective, urban digital development strategies are rooted in digital information systems comprised of computers, databases, and urban communication networks. These strategies integrate advanced digital technologies of the time, such as broadband networks, satellite remote sensing and positioning systems, geographic information collection and analysis systems, and virtual reality, into urban construction (Graham 2002; Malecki 2003; Yang et al. 2022). With the continuous advancement of digital technology, emerging technologies like mobile internet, big data, blockchain, and artificial intelligence have been incorporated into urban digital development strategies. This integration not only transforms data elements in the urban construction process but also further promotes digital technology innovation through urban development (Acemoglu and Restrepo 2022; Calvano et al. 2020). In the fields of planning and public services, urban digital development strategies provide a quantitative basis for decision-making in city management through the collection and detection of basic information, enhancing the scientific nature and operational efficiency of urban decision-making through technological means (Masik et al. 2021; Nochta et al. 2021).

Domestic scholars have also conducted in-depth research on digital technology in urban digital construction (Deng et al. 2022; Wang et al. 2022; Yang et al. 2024; Zhang et al. 2022b). They propose that to achieve digital transformation and development, cities should first improve their digital infrastructure, and then increase investment in research and development and application in the digital field. Constructing a unified and comprehensive urban informatization platform, and achieving digital integration in various fields, such as economy, trade, finance, shipping, technology, and culture, through efficient and secure digital entry points (Liu et al. 2023; Yang et al. 2023c, 2023d). Other scholars point out that in the process of urban digital development, it is crucial to deeply understand the key points of the combination of digital technology and the inherent characteristics of the city. This promotes the comprehensive and in-depth integration of digital technology into various areas of urban development, construction, public services, ecological protection, and factory utilization, ensuring that residents can benefit from digital welfare, and ultimately achieving sustainable urban development through digitization.

2.3. The Level of Urban Digital Construction and Economic Growth

The measurement methods and indicators of the level of urban digital construction are an important basis for research on the urban digital economy. In recent years, domestic and foreign scholars have proposed a variety of measurement methods and indicators for urban digitalization levels from different dimensions and perspectives, mainly including:

1. Measurement dimensions and indicators of the level of urban digital construction. Generally speaking, scholars have examined the level of urban digital construction from aspects such as digital infrastructure (Cong et al. 2022; Ndubuisi et al. 2021), digital economy (Popkova and Gulzat 2020; Wang et al. 2022), digital government (Castro and Lopes 2022; Lin et al. 2021; Pedrosa et al. 2020), and digital ecology (Pauliuk et al. 2022; Peng and Tao 2022). Meanwhile, indicators involving digital innovation elements (Cheng and Wang 2022; Ramdani et al. 2022), digital infrastructure (Lan and Zhu 2023; Sotolongo 2023), core digital industries (Ariffin and Ahmad 2021; Zhu and Chen 2022), and digital convergence applications (Borowiecki et al. 2021; Mitrović 2020) have also been considered. These indicators have both commonalities and differences, reflecting the multidimensionality and complexity of urban digital construction.
2. Measurement methods and technologies for urban digital construction. Scholars have used different measurement methods and techniques, such as the index method (Alderete 2020; Ren et al. 2022), factor analysis method (García-Vandewalle García et al. 2023; Zhang et al. 2022c), cluster analysis method (Xia et al. 2022; Zheng et al. 2020), structural equation model (Nicolas et al. 2020; Wang et al. 2021), data envelopment analysis method (Cao et al. 2022; Kutty et al. 2022), gray correlation analysis method (Sun and Zhang 2020), etc. In addition, some studies have also tried to use new technologies, such as big data (Atitallah et al. 2020; Zhang et al. 2022a), cloud computing (Jiang 2020; Kaginalkar et al. 2021), and machine learning (Austin et al. 2020; Li et al. 2022; Zekić-Sušac et al. 2021), to improve the measurement accuracy and real-time performance of urban digital construction.
3. The relationship between urban digital construction and economic growth. A number of scholars have discussed the correlation or causality between the level of urban digital construction and economic growth, arguing that the former has positive effects on the latter (Guo et al. 2023; Zhu and Chen 2022). At the same time, other scholars have pointed out that the relationship between urban digital construction and economic growth is not a simple linear relationship (Huang et al. 2023; Liu et al. 2022).

General Secretary Xi Jinping of China places a high priority on the digital economy, explicitly urging in the 20th Central Committee report to "accelerate the development of the digital economy and promote deep integration between the digital economy and the real economy". Nationwide, there has been a warm response to the important directives of the General Secretary, with active participation in urban digital transformation and a continuous enhancement of the diversity of digital cities based on their unique characteristics. Scholars have studied the development of the digital economy in key cities, such as Beijing, Shanghai, Guangzhou, Shenzhen, and Hangzhou, and believe that each city has distinctive characteristics in digital transformation. For instance, Beijing aggregates a large amount of high-quality high-end data resources, Shanghai possesses advanced digital industries and a superior business environment, Guangzhou has significant potential in industrial digitization, Shenzhen has advantages in the construction of new smart cities, and Hangzhou is home to leading enterprises in the Chinese digital industry. As long as these key cities fully leverage their advantages and closely integrate traditional industries with digital industries the prospects for their digital development are promising (Yang et al. 2023a).

According to research by Chinese scholars, the core of building digital cities is, in fact, a large-scale system engineering that covers the entire process of urban informatization. It involves every aspect of city operation, not only including economic and industrial digitization, digital governance, digitalization of people's livelihoods, medical and health informatization, digital ecology, and digital government but also impacting the comprehensive development of the entire city. It is of great significance for regional and national development, contributing to enhancing urban competitiveness and sustainability. The digital transformation of cities is not only an essential part of digital government governance and construction but also a consideration in various aspects such as social production and exchange, ecological environment, etc. Digitalization is a key factor in economic digital transformation. Only through the collection, integration, and application of data, continuous innovation in technological development, and improvement of comprehensive processing capabilities can it be integrated into various aspects of economic operation, service optimization, and industrial structure upgrading, taking China's economy to new development heights. In the process of government digital transformation, digital analysis is a key point. Digital governance requires the government to assess the implementation effects of policies and citizens' opinions and suggestions through data analysis, continuously accept feedback, and promptly improve various policies, allowing the government to better serve the vast population. Additionally, the digital transformation of cities should be human-centered, a key focus mentioned in the current digital strategies of most countries or regions (Allcott et al. 2020; Barwick et al. 2023). The ultimate goal of urban digital construction is to benefit citizens, ensuring peaceful and progressive social development. Therefore, urban digital construction needs to prioritize citizen welfare, providing more efficient public services to the general public through digital applications, digital government, and other channels.

The above domestic and international research provides a comprehensive analysis of the strengths and weaknesses of digital economic development, summarizing experiences in national and urban digital development. However, there are still some shortcomings: On one hand, existing research tends to lean towards qualitative analysis, lacking in-depth quantitative analysis and cross-sectional comparisons of specific countries and cities in building a digital economy. On the other hand, while many scholars, especially those focusing on China's advanced cities, have paid considerable attention to the recent digital construction and transformation, the research often revolves around digital technology and draws on international experiences. It fails to tightly integrate theoretical research, quantitative analysis, and urban characteristics, leading to a lack of a comprehensive evaluation of China's urban digital economic development level.

To address these gaps, our research strives for a more balanced approach by incorporating both evaluation index systems and empirical analysis. Through the above efforts, we strive to further arouse interest in the digital economy among readers and related academic journals around the world. At present, the digital economy has become an important driving force and strategic advantage for global economic development. Countries are actively promoting digital transformation and upgrading, and are exploring the deep integration of digital technology with economic and social development. As one of the global leaders in the digital economy, China has a strong digital infrastructure and policy environment, active digital enterprises and innovators, and a large user group. Its experience and results in urban digital construction provide a good example and reference for the world. Therefore, the research content of this paper can arouse the interest of readers and related academic journals around the world, especially those who pay attention to the development trends and dynamics of the digital economy, seek digital development opportunities and challenges, or hope to cooperate and communicate with China in the digital field. By providing them with valuable information and perspectives, we hope to further enhance their understanding of China's urban digital construction and promote international digital economic cooperation and exchanges.

3. Methodology

Building upon the previous analysis, this section will first establish the evaluation index system for the level of urban digital construction. Subsequently, the entropy weight method will be applied to assign weights to each indicator, thereby deriving a comprehensive score for the evaluation of the level of digital construction in various cities across China.

3.1. Factors Influencing the Level of Urban Digital Construction

When assessing the level of urban digital construction, it is crucial to base the evaluation on the digital development goals of the city, considering various factors such as the foundational elements of urban digital development, the objective conditions and subjective goals of the construction entities, and the information required to construct the evaluation system. Specifically, this includes the following: in the process of constructing the evaluation index system for the level of urban digital construction, the first consideration should be given to various foundational elements of building a digital city. Given the multitude of basic elements used to assess the level of urban digital construction, this paper, based on the actual situation of Chinese cities, has chosen the most relevant core foundational indicators. In the evaluation of the level of urban digital construction, the objective conditions and subjective goals of the construction entities are additional crucial factors in constructing the evaluation index system. This mainly includes the digital development level of the construction entities, digital output, and goals for the development of the digital industry. When constructing the evaluation index system for urban digital construction, attention should be given to the theoretical validity of the selected indicators and the various data information that needs to be collected and organized. Adjustments and improvements should be made based on actual circumstances, continuously refining and perfecting the index system.

3.1.1. Primary Indicators

Based on the principles of constructing the evaluation index system (detailed principles in Appendix A) and a thorough analysis of the theory and practice of urban digitization, this paper determines five primary indicators for the urban digital construction index system: urban digital infrastructure, overall economic level, innovation development level, digital industry development status, and ecological environment status.

Urban Digital Infrastructure: In the process of urban digital transformation, digital infrastructure is an essential element. It serves as the material carrier for economic activities in the international digital economy hub and is a necessary condition for its rapid development (Chen et al. 2023; Graham 2002; Masik et al. 2021; Nochta et al. 2021). Therefore, digital infrastructure, including networks, communication facilities, and digital platforms, has become a prerequisite for supporting the construction of digital cities.

Overall Economic Level of the City: The overall economic level is a crucial reflection of the city's comprehensive strength and is closely tied to the process of building a digital city (Ali 2017; Li and Camerer 2022). As China enters the high-quality development stage, the continuously improving overall economic level of cities provides robust support and guarantees for digital construction. Conversely, digital construction can enhance the overall economic level by improving economic structures, operating modes, and development environments.

Innovation Development Level: As technological innovation becomes a national strategy, a city's innovation capability has become a vital aspect of digital development (Beraja et al. 2023b; Wang et al. 2022; Zhang et al. 2022b). In a report on digital economic development by the State Council, independent innovation in key digital technologies is emphasized as an inexhaustible driving force for urban digital construction and digital economic development. Therefore, the innovation development level is considered a primary indicator to measure the progress of a city's digital construction.

Digital Industry Development Status: The development status of the digital industry is a crucial indicator of the level of urban digital construction and a driving force for digital economic development (Deng et al. 2022; Hills et al. 2019; Jensen 2007; Mpofu and Mhlanga 2022). Currently, the digital industry has become a strategic pillar industry of the national economy, exerting a strong driving force on various industries. Assessing the development of the digital industry as a primary indicator can effectively measure the key achievements in digital city construction.

Ecological Environment Status: General Secretary Xi Jinping has profoundly revealed the inherent mechanism and dialectical relationship between technology and the environment, emphasizing the need to rely on technological innovation to solve green development problems. Improving the urban ecological environment and promoting green development will create enormous development space for urban construction and generate numerous new economic growth points (Deng et al. 2022; Wang et al. 2022; Zhang et al. 2022b). Therefore, this paper considers the ecological environment status as a primary indicator for evaluating digital city construction.

3.1.2. Secondary Indicators

Based on the practical experience of digital city construction in China, this paper conducts a detailed analysis of the connotations of the primary indicators mentioned above. Following the construction principles mentioned earlier, specific secondary indicators are selected for each primary indicator.

Under the Primary Indicator of Urban Digital Infrastructure: Telecom Service Revenue (X_1), Number of Mobile Phone Users (X_2), and Number of Internet Broadband Access Users (X_3). These three secondary indicators measure the fundamental and pioneering industries supporting and reflecting the development of the digital economy. A high level of digital development in a city will require telecom operators to provide more services to support its development, and it is precisely because of demand that telecom operators will implement more telecom services in a city, so the telecom operators in a city with a higher level of digital development will provide more services and generate more telecom revenue (Harwit 2004). Judging from the actual situation in China, areas with higher levels of digital development generally have a wider range of telecom services, which means that their telecom income will be higher than in other cities (Peng and Dan 2023). Therefore, a city's telecom service revenue can reflect the size and activity of the city's digital service market, thereby measuring the city's digital construction level. Moreover, the number of mobile phone users and internet broadband access users reflects the development status of digital platforms, portraying the level of informatization in the city.

Under the Primary Indicator of Overall Economic Level of the City: Per Capita Regional Gross Domestic Product (X_4), Regional Gross Domestic Product Growth Rate (X_5), and Proportion of Urban Construction Land to City Area (X_6). These three secondary indicators reflect the economic development achievements and speed of the city, representing the overall economic level of the city in terms of quantity and quality. The proportion of urban construction land to city area also reflects the city's economic development level from the perspective of urbanization.

As far as the "Proportion of Urban Construction Land to City Area" indicator is concerned, this indicator reflects the city's land utilization rate (Han et al. 2020). If the indicator is higher, it means that the scale, density, and shape of the city are more conducive to the spread and application of digital technology and the construction and maintenance of digital infrastructure, thus providing better physical conditions for urban digitalization. In addition, the higher the indicator, the more concentrated the urban population, industries, and services are, the stronger the economic vitality and social demand, and the stronger the demand for and consumption of digital technology, digital industry, and digital services (Chen et al. 2020; Xia et al. 2020). Finally, this indicator also reflects the challenges faced by urban governance. The higher the indicator, the more likely the city will hope to improve its governance efficiency and quality through the improvement of the digitalization level.

Therefore, it will be more interested in digital technology, digital industry, and digital services (Peng et al. 2022).

Under the Primary Indicator of Innovation Development Level: Innovation Index Calculated Based on the Number of Invention Patents (X_7), and Expenditure on Science and Technology (X_8). The number of invention patents is an important indicator for measuring a city's innovation capability, while expenditure on science and technology reflects the government's investment in stimulating innovation. The total GDPs of major Chinese cities such as Beijing and Shanghai are very high. Although their expenditure on science and technology is very high, the relative proportion of GDP spent in these areas is still small, and the relative ratio may not accurately characterize the real impact of science and technology spending. Therefore, here we do not use relative indicators such as the ratio of the expenditure on science and technology to the city's GDP, etc.

Under the Primary Indicator of Digital Industry Development Status: Proportion of Employees in the Tertiary Industry (X_9), Number of Employees in the Information Transmission, Software, and Information Technology Services Industry (X_{10}), Proportion of the Tertiary Industry to GDP (X_{11}), and Peking University Digital Inclusive Finance Index (X_{12}). These secondary indicators are selected as there is currently no specific indicator for the digital economic industry in the statistical data from official sources such as the National Bureau of Statistics and various yearbooks. The Peking University Digital Inclusive Finance Index provides a convenient channel for evaluating the development of the digital economy.

Under the Primary Indicator of Ecological Environment Status: Greening Coverage Rate of the Built-up Area (X_{13}), Number of Green Patents Applied (X_{14}), Carbon Dioxide Emissions (X_{15}), and Industrial Sulfur Dioxide Emissions (X_{16}). These four secondary indicators reflect the city's ecological greening level, the combination of digital technology and green development, and the city's low-carbon development level in terms of carbon dioxide emissions and industrial sulfur dioxide emissions. Although the relationship between urban digital construction and emission is not simple, in general, the two aspects are related and therefore influence the status of the ecological environment. Positive views are also held on the relationship between the two (Lee et al. 2022; Lu et al. 2021; Qi et al. 2022; Wu et al. 2023; Yang et al. 2023b). As for X_{13}, by using digital technology combined with environmental informatization to detect the city's ecosystem, the city's environmental management can be accurately achieved. The development of this form has not yet been specifically reflected in China's urban data, but the development of smart city construction can be reflected through other indicators. The greening coverage of built-up areas reflects the greening level of the city and reflects the green development of the city. It is a key factor that needs to be considered for digital development and becoming a smart city.

3.2. *Construction of the Evaluation Index System*

3.2.1. Indicator System

This article comprehensively considers the current state of digital economic development in China, drawing on both domestic and international experiences in constructing indicator systems. Simultaneously, based on the essence of digital cities and existing research outcomes, this article involved the selection of indicators from five dimensions: urban digital infrastructure, overall economic level, innovation and development level, digital industry development status, and urban ecological environment conditions. The result is the construction of the Urban Digitalization Development Evaluation Indicator System, as presented in Table 1.

Table 1. Urban Digitalization Development Evaluation Indicator System.

Primary Indicator	Secondary Indicator	Unit	Indicator Type
Digital Infrastructure	Telecommunication Revenue (X_1)	CNY	Positive
	End-of-Year Mobile Phone Users (X_2)	10,000 Households	Positive
	Internet Broadband Access Users (X_3)	10,000 Households	Positive
Overall Economic Level	Per Capita Regional GDP (X_4)	CNY	Positive
	GDP Growth Rate (X_5)	%	Positive
	Urban Construction Land as a Percentage of Municipal Area (X_6)	%	Positive
Innovation Development Level	Innovation Index (X_7)	/	Positive
	Expenditure on Science and Technology (X_8)	CNY	Positive
Digital Industry Development Status	Proportion of Tertiary Industry Employees (X_9)	%	Positive
	Employees in Information Transmission, Software, and Information Technology Services (X_{10})	10,000 People	Positive
	Proportion of Tertiary Industry in GDP (X_{11})	%	Positive
	Digital Inclusive Finance Index (X_{12})	/	Positive
Ecological Environment Conditions	Greening Coverage of Built-up Areas (X_{13})	%	Positive
	Number of Green Patents Applied (X_{14})	Units	Positive
	Industrial Sulfur Dioxide Emissions (X_{15})	10,000 Tons	Negative
	Carbon Dioxide Emissions (X_{16})	10,000 Tons	Negative

3.2.2. Data Sources

After calculating the objective weights of various indicators using the entropy method (see Appendix B), this study further computes the comprehensive evaluation scores for the level of digitalization development in various cities in China (see Table A1). Considering the continuity of the data and based on academic conventions, the research focuses on cities in mainland China during the period from 2011 to 2021 (excluding Hong Kong, the Macau Special Administrative Region, and Taiwan Province).

The data for each city's indicators during the research period are sourced from official statistical data on China's urban digitalization process. These include the annual "China Statistical Yearbook", "China City Statistical Yearbook", and "China Science and Technology Statistical Yearbook", as well as various provincial and municipal statistical yearbooks. Additionally, this study refers to digital economy research reports compiled and released by institutions such as the National Internet Information Office, the Informationization Research Department of the National Information Center, and the China Academy of Information and Communications Technology. From these sources, data on relevant indicators were collected for 297 cities nationwide.

For the initially obtained indicator data, careful screening was conducted. Considering that this study primarily investigates the development level of China's urban digital economy, cities with fewer than 2 years of data or those with discontinued or unreported statistics, including 17 cities such as Bijie City, Bozhou City, and Qamdo City, were excluded. Regarding the remaining data with occasional missing values for certain indicators in individual years, interpolation was employed to fit the gaps. As a result, data on relevant indicators for 280 Chinese cities from 2011 to 2021 were obtained.

4. Results

4.1. Evaluation Results

Based on the aforementioned entropy method, this study first calculates the weights of various indicators, as shown in Table 2:

Table 2. Weights of indicators.

Primary Indicator	Primary Indicator Weight	Secondary Indicator	Secondary Indicator Weight
		Telecommunication Revenue (X_1)	0.0446
Digital Infrastructure	0.1692	End-of-Year Mobile Phone Users (X_2)	0.0607
		Internet Broadband Access Users (X_3)	0.0638
Overall Economic Level	0.1227	Per Capita Regional GDP (X_4)	0.0578
		GDP Growth Rate (X_5)	0.0274
		Urban Construction Land as a Percentage of Municipal Area (X_6)	0.0376
Innovation Development	0.2228	Innovation Index (X_7)	0.1833
		Expenditure on Science and Technology (X_8)	0.0395
Digital Industry Development Status	0.2890	Proportion of Tertiary Industry Employees (X_9)	0.0605
		Employees in Information Transmission, Software, and Information Technology Services (X_{10})	0.0468
		Proportion of Tertiary Industry in GDP (X_{11})	0.0734
		Digital Inclusive Finance Index (X_{12})	0.1084
Ecological Environment Conditions	0.1963	Greening Coverage of Built-up Areas (X_{13})	0.0149
		Number of Green Patents Applied (X_{14})	0.0698
		Industrial Sulfur Dioxide Emissions (X_{15})	0.0620
		Carbon Dioxide Emissions (X_{16})	0.0495

Based on the comprehensive evaluation results mentioned above, this study further calculates the average scores of the digital construction level for each city in China from 2011 to 2021. Figure 1 presents the top ten and bottom ten cities based on the average scores.

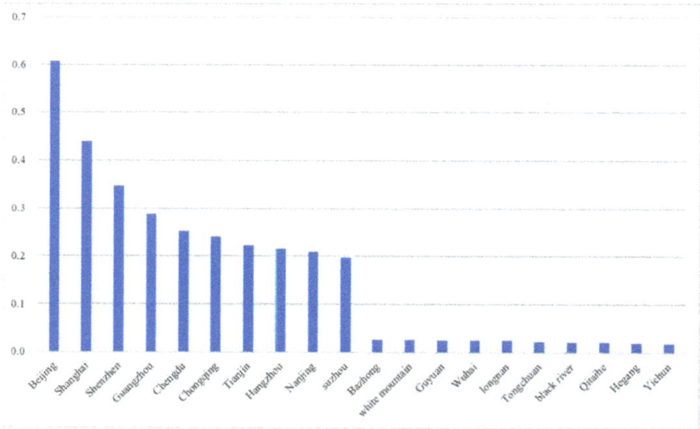

Figure 1. Average scores of digital construction level in Chinese cities (2011–2021).

From the figure, it is evident that cities such as Beijing, Shanghai, Shenzhen, and Guangzhou have consistently led in digital construction throughout the observation period. This indicates that economically developed cities generally prioritize digital economy development and that their digital construction processes are in a phase of rapid advancement. However, there is a significant gap in the level of digital construction between leading cities, like Beijing, Shanghai, Shenzhen, and Guangzhou, and cities with lower rankings such as Hegang and Yichun. This suggests that without timely measures to achieve a synchronized improvement in the national urban digital development level, a "digital divide" between different cities may emerge and gradually deepen.

4.2. Model Specification

Based on the computed results in the previous sections, this study, following existing research and considering the characteristics of urban digital development, takes the regional gross domestic product (GDP) as the core dependent variable. Simultaneously, the comprehensive evaluation score of the digital construction level, calculated earlier, serves as the core explanatory variable. By constructing a panel data regression model, this study empirically analyzes the causal relationship between urban digital construction level and urban economic growth.

In the model selection process, the Hausman test was initially conducted, and the results indicated that a fixed-effects model is more suitable for this study. Additionally, adopting fixed effects for both years and cities aligns better with the practical aspects of this research. Therefore, this study ultimately constructs the fixed-effects model as shown in Equation (1):

$$lnGDP_{it} = \alpha_0 + \beta Digcity_{it} + \gamma X_{it} + \lambda_t + \mu_i + \varepsilon_{it} \quad (1)$$

where i and t represent cities and years, respectively. The dependent variable $lnGDP_{it}$ is the natural logarithm of the regional gross domestic product for each city. The core explanatory variable $Digcity_{it}$ is the comprehensive evaluation score of the digital construction level for each city. X_{it} is the vector of control variables. λ_t and μ_i represent the year fixed effects and city fixed effects, covering time factors unaffected by city-specific differences and city-specific factors unaffected by the passage of time. β is the regression coefficient of interest, reflecting the impact of the urban digital construction level on urban economic development. ε_{it} is the error term.

4.3. Variable Selection

Dependent Variable: The natural logarithm of the regional gross domestic product (GDP) for each city is selected as the dependent variable for empirical analysis. Regional GDP is a crucial indicator for measuring economic growth, and using the natural logarithm of GDP as the dependent variable helps capture the causal relationship between urban digital construction level and urban economic development.

Core Explanatory Variable: The core explanatory variable is the comprehensive evaluation score of the digital construction level for each city. Calculated based on the previously constructed indicator system and evaluation method, it covers the digital construction level reflected by 5 primary indicators and 16 secondary indicators.

Control Variables: The control variables in this econometric model mainly include the natural logarithms of the end-of-period number of employees in urban units (A_1), the number of industrial enterprises above a designated size (A_2), the natural logarithm of fixed asset investment (A_3), and the natural logarithm of public budget expenditure (A_4). The selection of these control variables aims to control, to the greatest extent possible, the impact of urban unit employees, large-scale industrial enterprises, and fixed asset investment on regional GDP. This helps reflect the extent to which the urban digital construction level affects urban economic development.

Descriptive statistics for all variables are provided in Table A2.

4.4. Empirical Results and Analysis

Based on the variable specifications and data sources mentioned above, the econometric model represented by Equation (8) was used to obtain the benchmark regression results for the impact of urban digital construction on regional economic growth, as shown in Table 3. Columns (1) and (5) present the OLS regression results without and with control variables, respectively. Columns (3) and (7) further control for year and city fixed effects. According to the overall results of the benchmark regression, the coefficients of the dependent variable are significantly positive, with most being statistically significant at the 1% level. This result further confirms the calculation results of the indicator evaluation system mentioned earlier, indicating that the level of urban digital construction plays a crucial and significant role in driving and promoting economic development.

Table 3. Benchmark regression results.

	(1)	(2)	(3)	(4)	(5)	(6)	(7)	(8)
	OLS	**2SLS**	**OLS**	**2SLS**	**OLS**	**2SLS**	**OLS**	**2SLS**
				Second stage				
Digcity	6.2341 *** (77.3740)	9.1571 *** (56.6460)	2.1390 *** (16.6791)	1.661 *** (2.6093)	1.2632 *** (11.3900)	2.4478 *** (7.0686)	1.1058 *** (6.1547)	2.5731 *** (11.3978)
A_1					0.4711 *** (26.5348)	0.3929 *** (13.8294)	0.1267 * (1.7031)	0.1282 *** (2.9278)
A_2					0.2316 *** (15.5896)	0.2489 *** (18.4672)	0.3256 *** (5.4253)	0.3459 *** (11.3756)
A_3					0.2045 *** (9.7338)	0.1365 *** (5.7467)	0.1555 *** (4.8843)	0.1152 *** (4.5678)
A_4					−0.0405 (−0.7668)	−0.0564 (−1.0448)	−0.0279 (−0.5815)	−0.0347 (−0.6778)
_cons	4.3292 *** (106.9652)	2.9199 *** (36.9279)	6.3037 *** (101.9463)	6.5344 *** (21.2872)	0.2034 (0.7590)	0.9447 *** (3.2521)	1.6907 *** (4.1097)	3.1551 *** (8.5837)
N	3080	3080	3080	3080	3080	3080	3080	3080
R^2	0.5519		0.8590		0.1618		0.2643	
year	No	No	Yes	Yes	Yes	Yes	Yes	Yes
city	No	No	Yes	Yes	Yes	Yes	Yes	Yes
				First stage				
X_{10}		0.0729 *** (55.2808)		0.0242 *** (7.7671)		0.0403 *** (15.6866)		0.0151 *** (5.2663)
R^2		0.4306		0.1537		0.8512		0.1377
F Statistic on IV		1534.468		60.328		246.070		27.734

Note: *, **, *** indicate significance levels at 10%, 5%, and 1%, respectively.

In the context of urban digitization, for every 1 percentage point increase in the digitization process, the regional gross domestic product (GDP) is expected to increase by 1.1058 percentage points. Similarly, a 1 percentage point increase in the proportion of urban employed persons to the total workforce leads to a 0.1267 percentage point increase in regional GDP. The presence of a 1 percentage point higher value in the number of industrial enterprises above a certain scale corresponds to a 0.3256 percentage point increase in regional GDP. Additionally, a 1 percentage point rise in fixed asset investment is associated with a 0.1555 percentage point increase in regional GDP. Conversely, a 1 percentage point increase in public budget expenditure results in a decrease of 0.0279 percentage points in regional GDP.

Regarding the controlled variables, the regression results suggest that the number of year-end urban employed persons, the number of industrial enterprises above a certain scale, fixed asset investment, and public budget expenditure all have positive impacts on urban regional GDP. The underlying mechanisms can be elucidated as follows: Year-End Urban Employed Persons: This variable reflects the employment and urbanization status of the city. When both the employment rate and urbanization rate are at higher levels, the overall production level of the city tends to be higher. Output increases continuously with the improvement of productivity. Number of Industrial Enterprises above a Certain Scale: These enterprises essentially constitute a crucial source of urban regional GDP. An increase in the number of industrial enterprises results in an elevation of industrial GDP, consequently leading to an overall increase in urban regional GDP. Fixed Asset Investment: This variable has consistently been a significant factor influencing regional GDP. An increase in fixed asset investment indicates a rise in current and future inputs for driving economic development. This not only generates a current increase in regional GDP but also enhances long-term production output, thereby creating a dual-increase effect. Public Budget Expenditure: From a fiscal perspective, public budget expenditure reflects the city's spending situation. An increase in public budget expenditure indicates a greater financial outlay by the city. However, this may not necessarily exert a very strong stimulating effect on driving urban economic development.

5. Test and Analysis

5.1. Endogeneity Test

Endogeneity is an indispensable consideration in empirical research. In the empirical analysis of this paper, although the impact of urban digitalization on regional economic growth is significant, there exists a theoretical bidirectional causal relationship between the two factors. Additionally, there are numerous factors influencing urban regional GDP, leading to the inevitable presence of omitted variable issues in regression analysis. Therefore, this paper further employs the instrumental variable (IV) approach to examine potential endogeneity issues in the aforementioned empirical analysis.

The chosen instrumental variable in this study is the number of employees in the information transmission, software, and information technology services industry. This variable simultaneously satisfies the requirements of relevance and exogeneity for instrumental variables. On one hand, the mentioned industry is a core sector of the digital economy, and the number of employees in this industry is a crucial indicator considered in constructing the urban digitalization process index system. Hence, it is closely related to the digitalization processes in various cities, meeting the relevance requirement for instrumental variables. On the other hand, based on principles of macroeconomics, regional GDP is composed of consumption, investment, government purchases, and net exports. The variation in the number of employees in the information transmission, software, and information technology services industry mainly stems from the expansion and contraction of the industry itself, lacking a direct connection with regional GDP. Furthermore, as one of the indicators measuring the digital information industry, the number of employees in this sector can only influence regional GDP through the development of urban digitalization processes. Therefore, it has no direct or indirect relationship with potential factors affecting regional GDP (residual terms in the regression), meeting the exogeneity requirement for instrumental variables.

From the results in Table 3, it is evident that the coefficient of urban digitalization processes on regional GDP remains significantly positive, consistent with the earlier findings. Simultaneously, the instrumental variable undergoes overidentification and weak instrumental variable tests, where the F-statistic value exceeds 10 with a p-value of 0.000. Furthermore, the Hausman test yields a p-value of 0.000, rejecting the null hypothesis that all explanatory variables are exogenous, indicating the need for instrumental variable correction. These results affirm the credibility of selecting the number of employees in the information transmission, software, and information technology services industry as the instrumental variable for urban digitalization processes in this study.

5.2. Robustness Test

5.2.1. Substitution of Core Explanatory Variable

Despite the significant empirical results obtained in the previous analysis and the passing of endogeneity tests using instrumental variables, it is essential to conduct a robustness test to ensure the accuracy of the empirical findings. Based on the weight scores of the indicator system in Table 2, this paper reorganized the primary and secondary indicators according to their weighted scores, resulting in the ranking of indicator weights, as shown in Table A3.

Due to the higher weights assigned to indicators in the objective weighted scores, indicating their greater reference value and importance for urban digitalization, this paper, considering the characteristics of digital city development, selected the highest-weighted secondary indicators in Table A3 as the core explanatory variables for the robustness test. These include the Digital Inclusive Finance Index (X_{12}), Innovation Index (X_7), Green Patent Applications (X_{14}), and the Number of Internet Broadband Access Users (X_3). Detailed test results can be found in Tables A4 and A5.

In both tables, it is observed that the impact coefficients of the core explanatory variables are consistently positive at the 1% significance level. The Digital Inclusive Finance Index, as an effective indicator of digital economic development, plays a crucial role in narrowing regional economic development gaps and promoting economic growth. The increase in the Innovation Index is significant for innovative development, serving as a key driver of economic progress. The positive impact of Green Patent Applications on regional GDP contributes to the advancement of both ecology and technology, fostering sustainable productivity. The increase in the number of internet broadband access users reflects the economic development strength of the region, making it a significant factor in the regression results. The robustness test, employing these core explanatory variables, reaffirms the reliability and stability of the empirical results, providing additional confidence in the findings.

5.2.2. Substitution of Control Variables

According to the evaluation indicator system, this paper subsequently selected the natural logarithm of year-end mobile phone users (X_2), the natural logarithm of per capita regional GDP (X_4), the proportion of urban construction land to municipal area (X_6), the proportion of tertiary industry employees (X_9), and the natural logarithm of carbon dioxide emissions (X_{16}) as control variables, replacing the original set of control variables. The regression results after substituting control variables can be found in Tables A6 and A7.

In the overall benchmark regression results, the coefficients of each control variable are significantly positive at the 1% significance level. This further confirms the calculation results of the indicator evaluation system mentioned earlier.

5.2.3. Selection of Different Study Periods

As mentioned earlier, China's digital economy has undergone three main stages of development. Currently, with the digital economy entering the third stage of intelligent development, the country has clearly defined the overall planning and guiding principles for digital economic development at the top-level design, making it an important national strategy. Since 2015, China has continuously formulated and released development strategies and implementation plans in the field of the digital economy, aiming to elevate it to new heights. The term "digital economy" officially appeared in Premier Li Keqiang's government work report in 2017. Since then, many core indicators of the digital economy have had clear measurements and statistics. Accordingly, this paper chose three different research periods, 2011–2014, 2015–2016, and 2017–2021, to test the robustness of aforementioned empirical results further. Detailed test results can be found in Table A8.

From the table, it can be observed that the coefficients of the core explanatory variables are significantly positive at the 1% level, and other variables also exhibit good levels of significance. When using data from the period 2017–2021 for testing, the coefficient significantly increases, indicating that the digital economy has become a crucial driver of economic development in China. This demonstrates that the regression results after selecting different study periods remain consistent with the earlier empirical analysis results, confirming that the empirical analysis of this paper has passed this robustness test.

5.3. Heterogeneity Analysis

As mentioned earlier, there is a significant "digital divide" phenomenon in the development of China's digital economy among different cities and even substantial regional disparities in overall economic development. Considering the imbalance in resource endowments and economic development among different regions, this section divides China's provinces into three major regions: East, Central, and West. A panel fixed-effects model is employed to conduct heterogeneity analysis, exploring whether there are differences in the level of digital construction among regions.

The regional division in China began in 1986, officially announced during the Fourth Session of the Sixth National People's Congress as part of the "Seventh Five-Year Plan". The

National Development and Reform Commission explained that the division into East, Central, and West is a policy-based rather than a geographical-based distinction. Specifically, the East includes 11 provinces (municipalities): Beijing, Tianjin, Hebei, Liaoning, Shanghai, Jiangsu, Zhejiang, Fujian, Shandong, Guangdong, and Hainan. The Central region comprises 10 provinces (autonomous regions): Shanxi, Inner Mongolia, Jilin, Heilongjiang, Anhui, Jiangxi, Henan, Hubei, Hunan, and Guangxi. The West includes 10 provinces (autonomous regions): Sichuan, Guizhou, Yunnan, Tibet, Shaanxi, Gansu, Qinghai, Ningxia, Chongqing, and Xinjiang.

In this heterogeneity test, two main components are considered. First, the impact of the level of digital construction on regional GDP is regressed across the East, Central, and West regions to examine whether there are significant differences between the different regions. Second, the evaluation scores of digital constructions are used as the dependent variable, regressed against high-weighted core indicators separately for each region to investigate whether there are regional differences in digital construction in various cities. Table 4 reports the results of the heterogeneity analysis obtained by regressing the comprehensive evaluation score of digital construction (Digcity) as the core explanatory variable against regional GDP in different regions.

Table 4. Heterogeneity analysis results of the impact of digital construction evaluation scores on regional GDP.

	(1)	(2)	(3)
	Eastern Region	**Central Region**	**Western Region**
Digcity	1.6365 *** (5.4042)	0.9483 *** (3.0052)	0.3897 (1.0557)
A_1	0.1855 (1.5284)	0.0330 (0.3179)	0.0587 (0.6051)
A_2	0.2555 *** (4.1380)	0.3663 *** (4.6102)	0.4053 *** (4.5466)
A_3	0.1573 *** (3.5028)	0.1542 *** (2.8417)	0.2130 *** (3.1969)
A_4	−0.0118 (−0.2270)	−0.1311 (−1.3708)	−0.0075 (−0.0667)
_cons	1.7770 *** (2.7238)	1.9547 *** (2.9582)	0.6454 (0.7373)
N	1133	902	1045
R^2	0.3447	0.2931	0.2016
year	Yes	Yes	Yes
province	Yes	Yes	Yes

Note: *, **, *** indicate significance levels at 10%, 5%, and 1%, respectively.

From the table, it is evident that only in the Eastern and Central regions do the digital constructions of cities have a significant positive impact on regional GDP. One possible reason for this is that the digitalization process in the Western region is still in a developmental stage requiring the sustained expansion of investments, and its input–output ratio has not achieved the same favorable outcomes as in the Central and Eastern regions.

Subsequently, this study employs the Digital Inclusive Finance Index (X_{12}), Innovation Index (X_7), Green Patent Applications (X_{14}), and Internet Broadband Access Users (X_3) as core explanatory variables. These are regressed against the evaluation scores of digital constructions in different regions to obtain results for heterogeneity analysis. The detailed findings of the tests can be found in Tables A9–A12.

In the regressions involving the Digital Inclusive Finance Index, Innovation Index, and Internet Broadband Access Users, the coefficients for all three regions are positive and statistically significant at the 1% level. This implies that there are no significant differences among the three regions concerning the impact of green development on the digital economy.

However, in the results obtained with Green Patent Applications as the core explanatory variable, only the coefficient for the Eastern region is statistically significant at the 1% level (please refer to Table A11). This suggests regional differences in the development process of urban digital construction in China. Due to the higher level of digital industry development in the Eastern region compared to the Central and Western regions, the impact of Green Patent Applications on driving the digital construction process is more pronounced in the East. In the Central and Western regions, where the digital economy and industry development are relatively lagging, its driving effect still needs further manifestation.

6. Conclusions

Based on the data of 280 cities in China from 2011 to 2021, this paper constructs a comprehensive evaluation index system for the level of urban digital construction, uses the entropy method to weigh various indicators, and obtains the evaluation results of the digital construction level of each city. On this basis, this paper further uses a panel data regression model to empirically analyze the impact of the urban digital construction level on urban economic growth. The main conclusions are as follows.

6.1. Theoretical Conclusions

First, from a theoretical perspective, this paper comprehensively considers the various aspects of urban digital construction from the five dimensions of digital infrastructure, overall economic level, innovation development level, digital industry development status, and ecological environment conditions, and constructs a systematic evaluation index system to provide a feasible method for the quantitative evaluation of the level of urban digital construction (please refer to Tables 1 and 2). Moreover, an econometric model based on the causal relationship between the level of digital construction and economic growth is developed (please refer to Section 4.2), which empirically tests the impact of urban digital construction on urban economic growth, providing new evidence for theoretical research on urban digital construction.

6.2. Practical Conclusions

Secondly, at the practical level, the results of the empirical analysis show that the level of urban digital construction has a significant positive role in promoting economic growth, and these results have passed a series of robustness tests, proving their reliability. Specifically, every 1% increase in a city's digital construction level will increase its GDP by 0.974. This result shows that urban digital construction is an important way to promote urban economic growth and an effective means to enhance a city's comprehensive competitiveness. This paper also found that there are large differences in the level of digital construction between different cities, indicating that the imbalance of urban digital construction is still prominent.

6.3. Social Conclusions

Finally, in terms of social value, this research has important social value and policy significance. On the one hand, it provides a scientific tool for evaluating and monitoring the level of urban digital construction. It can help the government and all sectors of society understand the status quo and trends of urban digital construction, identify problems and deficiencies in a timely manner, formulate reasonable goals and measures, and promote urban digitalization and the healthy development of construction. On the other hand, it provides a strong basis for promoting the coordinated development of urban digital construction and economic growth. It can help the government and all sectors of society to fully understand the important role of digital construction in urban development, increase investment and support for digital construction, optimize the environment and mechanisms of digital construction, stimulate the vitality and innovation of digital construction, and achieve a positive interaction between urban digital construction and economic growth.

6.4. Policy Recommendations

Based on the research conclusions, the following policy recommendations are put forward:

Firstly, enhance the construction of urban digital infrastructure. Digital infrastructure is a prerequisite for the transformation of urban digitization and a crucial driving force for improving the level of urban digitization and enhancing economic growth efficiency. Therefore, investments in digital infrastructure, including broadband networks, cloud computing, the Internet of Things (IoT), and big data, should be increased to achieve the deep integration of digital infrastructure with other areas of the city.

Secondly, support the improvement of urban innovation development. Innovation is the core driving force for urban development and a key element in promoting urban digital transformation. Therefore, efforts should be made to strengthen the research and application of cutting-edge technologies such as artificial intelligence, blockchain, and digital twins. Additionally, fostering and attracting innovative digital enterprises and talents, and constructing and perfecting innovation ecosystems and service platforms, will stimulate innovation vitality and drive the high-quality development of the urban economy.

Thirdly, narrow the "digital divide" between cities in different regions. To address the imbalance in regional development, it is essential to promote the sharing and connectivity of digital resources among cities. Moreover, cities in the eastern region should actively share their successful experiences in digital transformation to assist cities in the central and western regions in improving their digital construction levels. The central government can establish special funds to support the digital construction of cities in the central and western regions, thereby promoting balanced regional development and further narrowing the "digital divide".

Lastly, ensure a talent pool for digital construction. To meet the development needs of the digital economy, cities should comprehensively enhance the digital skills and literacy of citizens. The government can establish special funds to support schools and enterprises in offering digital skills courses and training programs. Simultaneously, through policy guidance, various sectors of society should be encouraged to actively participate in the promotion of digital education.

There are still some shortcomings in this research, as follows:

On the one hand, the evaluation index system for urban digital construction can be further improved. Due to limitations in data availability, when constructing an evaluation index system for urban digital construction, this paper does not cover all aspects of urban digital construction. Future research can further enrich and optimize the urban digital construction evaluation index system based on the updating and improvement of data, making it more scientific and comprehensive.

On the other hand, urban digital construction is a dynamic process, and the level and effect of urban digital construction may also change over time. Future research can consider introducing methods such as panel threshold models and panel cointegration models to analyze the dynamics of urban digital construction to reveal the deeper laws and mechanisms of urban digital construction.

Author Contributions: Conceptualization, C.Z. and W.Y.; methodology, C.Z.; software, W.Y.; validation, C.Z., W.Y. and Y.Y.; formal analysis, C.Z.; data curation, C.Z.; writing—original draft preparation, C.Z., W.Y. and Y.Y.; writing—review and editing, W.Y. and Y.Y.; visualization, C.Z.; supervision, W.Y. and Y.Y.; project administration, W.Y. and Y.Y.; funding acquisition, W.Y. and Y.Y. All the authors contributed equally to this work. All authors have read and agreed to the published version of the manuscript.

Funding: This research was funded by the Project of Shanghai Philosophy and Social Science Planning (2021BGL014, 2021EJB006), the Shanghai Soft Science Research Program (23692104400), the National Natural Science Foundation of China (72241431, 72031006), the Major Projects on Philosophy and Social Science Research of the Ministry of Education of the People's Republic of China (20JZD010), the Humanities Young Talent Cultivation Program at Shanghai Jiao Tong University (2023QN004), the Startup Fund for Young Faculty at Shanghai Jiao Tong University (SFYF at SJTU), and the Shangli Chenxi Social Science Special Project of University of Shanghai for Science and Technology (22SLCX-ZD-010). We gratefully acknowledge the above financial support.

Institutional Review Board Statement: Not applicable.

Informed Consent Statement: Not applicable.

Data Availability Statement: The data used in this paper are all from the statistical data officially released by China and have been explained in Section 3.2.2.

Conflicts of Interest: The authors declare no conflicts of interest.

Appendix A. Principles for Constructing an Evaluation Indicator System

In conducting an empirical analysis of urban digitalization, it is imperative to quantitatively compare the digitalization levels of various cities based on a set of indicators. Given the plethora of available indicators, each possessing distinct attributes, adherence to the following principles is essential to ensure the effectiveness and objectivity of the evaluation indicator system:

Comprehensive Principle of Indicator Selection: The selection of indicators should comprehensively consider the primary influencing factors across various aspects of the digital city construction process. This entails constructing a relatively comprehensive evaluation indicator system that provides a scientific basis for analyzing and assessing the status of urban digitalization. As digital city construction encompasses multiple domains, including urban infrastructure, economic development, and public governance, it is crucial to integrate considerations from these domains and their influencing factors when selecting indicators, thereby constructing a comprehensive indicator system.

Relevance Principle of Indicator Selection: In evaluating the digitalization level of urban development, it is imperative to deeply understand its essence and influencing factors. Indicators should be selected based on their relevance to reflect the essence and influencing factors of urban digitalization accurately. Through the specific meanings embedded in each indicator concerning digital development, an objective assessment of the urban digitalization level can be achieved.

Accessibility Principle of Indicator Selection: The selection of indicators must consider their accessibility, meaning they should be easily obtainable during the research process and amenable to quantification or standardization. This ensures the comparability of data. The factors influencing the digital transformation of urban development encompass both quantitative and qualitative indicators, necessitating relevant processing to effectively apply these indicators to the evaluation system. In selecting indicators, efforts should be made to utilize primary data obtained through authoritative channels, such as the National Bureau of Statistics, official city websites, and statistical yearbooks. Moreover, there should be a conscious effort to minimize the selection of qualitative indicators to enhance the efficiency and practicality of constructing the evaluation indicator system.

Scientific Principle of Indicator Selection: As the evaluation indicator system is a judgment criterion constructed by integrating theory and practice, the selection of indicators should not only focus on objective realities but also adhere to corresponding theoretical requirements. It is crucial to strike a balance between theory and practice, selecting indicators that achieve internal consistency in theoretical logic and grasp the essential characteristics of urban digitalization in practice. This ensures that a comprehensive reflection of the essence and development status of urban digitalization is reached.

Appendix B. Empowerment Methodology

Building upon the construction of the evaluation indicator system for urban digitalization, this paper will further determine the computational weights for each indicator. In terms of empowerment methodology, this study employs the entropy method for measurement analysis to obtain the weights of each indicator. Subsequently, this enables the calculation of comprehensive scores for the digitalization construction evaluation of each city. This approach facilitates an objective comparison of the digitalization construction levels across different cities.

The entropy method is an objective empowerment technique that utilizes scientific computational procedures to objectively assign weights to each indicator. This approach mitigates the subjective biases introduced by human factors, ensuring a higher level of accuracy, credibility, and reliability in the evaluation process. The application of the entropy method enhances the reliability of the evaluation results by providing an unbiased and scientifically grounded approach to determining the weights of various indicators.

Table A1. Comprehensive evaluation scores of digitalization level in 280 Chinese cities from 2011 to 2021.

	2011	2012	2013	2014	2015	2016	2017	2018	2019	2020	2021
Ankang	0.3384	0.3540	0.3644	0.3729	0.3950	0.4198	0.4599	0.4510	0.4729	0.4333	0.4734
Anqing	0.3750	0.4103	0.4324	0.4496	0.4908	0.5250	0.5731	0.5497	0.5827	0.5970	0.6266
Anshun	0.2962	0.3378	0.3633	0.4001	0.4303	0.4607	0.4874	0.4987	0.4996	0.5008	0.5478
Anyang	0.3807	0.3997	0.4196	0.4352	0.4650	0.4916	0.5289	0.5368	0.5528	0.5503	0.5631
Anshan	0.4556	0.4672	0.4925	0.4983	0.5154	0.5270	0.5484	0.5538	0.5584	0.5578	0.5639
Bayannur	0.2868	0.2996	0.3242	0.3492	0.3730	0.4127	0.4413	0.4231	0.4615	0.4768	0.5022
Bazhong	0.2645	0.2958	0.3142	0.3477	0.3807	0.4079	0.4208	0.4105	0.4390	0.4290	0.4409
Baicheng	0.2916	0.3177	0.3449	0.3517	0.3702	0.3978	0.4596	0.4293	0.4532	0.4603	0.4927
Baishan	0.3282	0.3290	0.3433	0.3519	0.3661	0.3992	0.4096	0.4262	0.4523	0.4458	0.4730
Baiyin	0.2440	0.3044	0.3292	0.3546	0.3697	0.4096	0.4641	0.4427	0.4603	0.4702	0.4952
Baise	0.3074	0.3159	0.3263	0.3609	0.3900	0.4336	0.4821	0.4615	0.4931	0.5170	0.5478
Bengbu	0.3958	0.4257	0.4494	0.4735	0.5029	0.5456	0.5657	0.5783	0.5948	0.6033	0.6243
Baotou	0.4103	0.4425	0.4624	0.4833	0.4989	0.5368	0.5663	0.5543	0.5731	0.5894	0.6145
Baoji	0.3763	0.4301	0.4384	0.4621	0.4836	0.5030	0.5393	0.5455	0.5659	0.5832	0.5992
Baoding	0.4526	0.4824	0.4937	0.5143	0.5356	0.5618	0.6111	0.6163	0.6506	0.6630	0.6961
Baoshan	0.2527	0.2806	0.3017	0.3209	0.3509	0.3682	0.4184	0.4093	0.4550	0.4714	0.4978
Beihai	0.3496	0.3817	0.4051	0.4216	0.4461	0.4719	0.5343	0.5147	0.5305	0.5393	0.5603
Beijing	0.7583	0.7899	0.8304	0.8407	0.8592	0.8738	0.8920	0.9082	0.9389	0.9306	0.9334
Benxi	0.3560	0.3683	0.3955	0.4140	0.4299	0.4324	0.4607	0.4439	0.4572	0.4769	0.5027
Binzhou	0.3281	0.3403	0.3659	0.3627	0.3797	0.4020	0.4332	0.4280	0.4535	0.4766	0.5014
Cangzhou	0.3594	0.3777	0.3993	0.4124	0.4353	0.4504	0.5144	0.4913	0.5128	0.5292	0.4977
Changde	0.3822	0.4159	0.4384	0.4645	0.4918	0.5226	0.5449	0.5662	0.5986	0.6325	0.5954
Changchun	0.5131	0.5562	0.5642	0.5699	0.6039	0.6305	0.6429	0.6618	0.6719	0.6851	0.7038
Changsha	0.5628	0.6092	0.6284	0.6337	0.6688	0.6975	0.7347	0.7471	0.7745	0.7853	0.7633
Changzhi	0.3518	0.3945	0.3990	0.4207	0.4474	0.4730	0.5147	0.5111	0.5373	0.4753	0.4899
Changzhou	0.4079	0.4354	0.4744	0.4678	0.4854	0.5059	0.5045	0.5299	0.5495	0.5700	0.5486
Chaoyang	0.3285	0.3461	0.3669	0.3922	0.4068	0.4401	0.4677	0.4649	0.4878	0.5077	0.4788
Chaozhou	0.3272	0.3416	0.3481	0.3761	0.3719	0.3927	0.3858	0.4074	0.4275	0.4464	0.4243
Chenzhou	0.3091	0.3343	0.3623	0.3754	0.3953	0.4146	0.4465	0.4555	0.4742	0.4817	0.4597
Chengdu	0.5945	0.6269	0.6843	0.6873	0.7299	0.7551	0.7657	0.7902	0.8237	0.8597	0.8296
Chengde	0.3530	0.3841	0.4025	0.4163	0.4434	0.4720	0.5075	0.5074	0.5269	0.5506	0.5228
Chizhou	0.2679	0.3070	0.3185	0.3225	0.3564	0.3835	0.3708	0.3929	0.4158	0.4357	0.4666
Chifeng	0.3502	0.3688	0.3970	0.4125	0.4369	0.4551	0.4759	0.4972	0.5131	0.5066	0.5295
Chongqing	0.5642	0.5826	0.6209	0.6435	0.6726	0.6852	0.7099	0.7109	0.7572	0.7360	0.7548
Chongzuo	0.2351	0.2644	0.3020	0.3494	0.3857	0.4275	0.4629	0.4664	0.4859	0.4898	0.5086
Chuzhou	0.3144	0.3432	0.3609	0.3837	0.4004	0.4204	0.4455	0.4599	0.4700	0.4718	0.5005
Dazhou	0.2803	0.3127	0.3120	0.3278	0.3460	0.3715	0.4216	0.3997	0.4275	0.4136	0.4051
Dalian	0.5562	0.5845	0.6112	0.6090	0.6315	0.6540	0.6893	0.6921	0.7019	0.7071	0.7267
Daqing	0.4195	0.4426	0.4799	0.4664	0.4834	0.5105	0.5302	0.5233	0.5365	0.5507	0.5721
Datong	0.3589	0.4006	0.4205	0.4297	0.4591	0.4759	0.5124	0.5130	0.5377	0.5575	0.5791

Table A1. *Cont.*

	2011	2012	2013	2014	2015	2016	2017	2018	2019	2020	2021
Dandong	0.3934	0.4150	0.4238	0.4344	0.4464	0.4772	0.5219	0.5076	0.5243	0.5390	0.5708
Deyang	0.3711	0.4402	0.4403	0.4593	0.4862	0.5119	0.5631	0.5504	0.5687	0.5343	0.5511
Dezhou	0.3212	0.3592	0.3784	0.3836	0.3978	0.4223	0.4518	0.4497	0.4741	0.4483	0.4812
Dingxi	0.2702	0.3051	0.3285	0.3451	0.3708	0.3950	0.4351	0.4325	0.4633	0.4215	0.4879
Dongguan	0.5479	0.5810	0.6062	0.5976	0.6256	0.6382	0.6756	0.6858	0.7090	0.6635	0.6921
Dongying	0.4049	0.4469	0.4635	0.4775	0.4967	0.5028	0.5332	0.5375	0.5602	0.5327	0.5623
Ordos	0.3707	0.3978	0.4193	0.4303	0.4546	0.4674	0.5250	0.5103	0.5236	0.4719	0.5024
Ezhou	0.2324	0.2677	0.2872	0.2938	0.3125	0.3438	0.3708	0.3771	0.4022	0.3640	0.3878
Fangchenggang	0.2399	0.2980	0.3166	0.3589	0.3766	0.3906	0.4279	0.4168	0.4624	0.4314	0.4574
Foshan	0.5394	0.5611	0.5781	0.5830	0.6081	0.6172	0.6622	0.6762	0.7045	0.6671	0.7112
Fuzhou	0.4098	0.4433	0.4657	0.4757	0.5003	0.5059	0.5602	0.5499	0.5605	0.5747	0.5922
Fushun	0.3805	0.4072	0.4184	0.4302	0.4565	0.4459	0.4843	0.4811	0.4845	0.4979	0.5241
Fuzhou	0.2722	0.2969	0.3135	0.3248	0.3483	0.3576	0.4058	0.4169	0.4371	0.5402	0.5804
Fuxin	0.3244	0.3583	0.3722	0.3921	0.4051	0.4356	0.4701	0.4704	0.4953	0.4989	0.5080
Fuyang	0.3607	0.4057	0.4377	0.4315	0.4755	0.5091	0.5501	0.5467	0.5842	0.6107	0.6340
Ganzhou	0.3266	0.3607	0.3704	0.3877	0.4117	0.4382	0.4756	0.4800	0.5046	0.5141	0.5390
Guyuan	0.2268	0.2573	0.2783	0.2903	0.3173	0.3451	0.3879	0.3739	0.4150	0.4331	0.4728
Guang'an	0.2965	0.3306	0.3426	0.3672	0.4035	0.4230	0.4343	0.4294	0.4654	0.4707	0.4957
Guangyuan	0.3227	0.3457	0.3688	0.3856	0.4077	0.4386	0.4672	0.4624	0.4760	0.4741	0.5014
Guangzhou	0.6994	0.7224	0.7717	0.7595	0.7738	0.8015	0.8238	0.8432	0.8634	0.8782	0.8991
Guigang	0.2889	0.3376	0.3654	0.3805	0.4043	0.4312	0.4845	0.4762	0.5296	0.5300	0.4942
Guiyang	0.4905	0.5259	0.5664	0.5798	0.5983	0.6165	0.6476	0.6574	0.6775	0.6960	0.6698
Guilin	0.4325	0.4634	0.4836	0.4956	0.5137	0.5446	0.5842	0.5784	0.6192	0.6349	0.6124
Harbin	0.5731	0.5814	0.6336	0.6188	0.6456	0.6682	0.6972	0.6916	0.7212	0.7320	0.7083
Haikou	0.5132	0.5366	0.5824	0.5843	0.6075	0.6274	0.6595	0.6559	0.6838	0.6918	0.6727
Handan	0.4258	0.4617	0.4618	0.4803	0.5111	0.5249	0.5646	0.5556	0.5815	0.6067	0.5767
Hanzhong	0.3410	0.3761	0.4058	0.4107	0.4381	0.4649	0.4872	0.4881	0.5073	0.5128	0.5030
Hangzhou	0.6302	0.6597	0.6910	0.6889	0.7211	0.7456	0.7668	0.7731	0.8015	0.8205	0.7912
Hefei	0.5149	0.5406	0.5729	0.5886	0.6297	0.6654	0.7053	0.7099	0.7509	0.7275	0.7570
Hechi	0.2471	0.3044	0.3349	0.3662	0.4004	0.4482	0.4824	0.4750	0.4906	0.5031	0.5239
Heyuan	0.3166	0.3344	0.3775	0.4000	0.4277	0.4600	0.4972	0.5179	0.5416	0.5601	0.5892
Heze	0.4014	0.4285	0.4569	0.4600	0.4887	0.5175	0.5452	0.5437	0.5775	0.6020	0.6199
Hezhou	0.2464	0.2804	0.2941	0.3208	0.3354	0.3667	0.3980	0.4013	0.4116	0.4114	0.4377
Hebi	0.2707	0.3006	0.3364	0.3545	0.3592	0.3935	0.4354	0.4517	0.4765	0.4938	0.5221
Hegang	0.2318	0.2648	0.2873	0.2669	0.2968	0.3206	0.3483	0.3420	0.3731	0.3817	0.4141
Heihe	0.2297	0.2585	0.2952	0.3018	0.3057	0.3605	0.4058	0.3778	0.3924	0.4036	0.4453
Hengshui	0.3772	0.4063	0.4199	0.4352	0.4608	0.4967	0.5566	0.5425	0.5722	0.5825	0.6023
Hengyang	0.3803	0.4118	0.4429	0.4641	0.4825	0.5126	0.5625	0.5755	0.5996	0.6145	0.5984
Hohhot	0.4660	0.5083	0.5518	0.5563	0.5747	0.6032	0.6215	0.6413	0.6735	0.6299	0.6613
Huludao	0.3388	0.3844	0.3867	0.3967	0.4084	0.4389	0.4770	0.4780	0.4912	0.4340	0.4746
Huzhou	0.3543	0.3810	0.4112	0.4226	0.4295	0.4506	0.4758	0.4923	0.5019	0.4636	0.4869
Huaihua	0.3526	0.3964	0.4248	0.4341	0.4606	0.4915	0.5570	0.5410	0.5718	0.5243	0.5715
Huai'an	0.4195	0.4509	0.4898	0.4891	0.5066	0.5385	0.5608	0.5861	0.6191	0.5915	0.6330
Huaibei	0.3063	0.3437	0.3745	0.3926	0.4174	0.4557	0.4846	0.4841	0.5220	0.5131	0.5418
Huainan	0.3160	0.3604	0.3868	0.4035	0.4422	0.4786	0.5093	0.5113	0.5464	0.5157	0.5384
Huanggang	0.3228	0.3724	0.4016	0.4138	0.4401	0.4688	0.5192	0.5179	0.5568	0.5038	0.5592
Huangshan	0.3867	0.4121	0.4419	0.4514	0.4769	0.4936	0.5316	0.5345	0.5556	0.5745	0.6034
Huangshi	0.3315	0.3693	0.4001	0.4200	0.4379	0.4686	0.5023	0.5046	0.5444	0.5524	0.6104
Huizhou	0.3602	0.3874	0.4290	0.4309	0.4479	0.4630	0.4729	0.4820	0.5008	0.5142	0.5435
Jixi	0.3057	0.3271	0.3622	0.3525	0.3755	0.3883	0.4047	0.4281	0.4571	0.4496	0.5111
Ji'an	0.3304	0.3626	0.3839	0.3966	0.4144	0.4411	0.4848	0.4953	0.5179	0.5354	0.5734
Jilin	0.4229	0.4383	0.4679	0.4775	0.4932	0.5043	0.5353	0.5393	0.5473	0.5481	0.5569
Jinan	0.5655	0.5906	0.6312	0.6483	0.6716	0.6890	0.7108	0.7262	0.7630	0.7611	0.7348
Jining	0.4170	0.4463	0.4762	0.5016	0.5211	0.5439	0.5701	0.5705	0.5975	0.6317	0.6164
Jiamusi	0.3269	0.3546	0.4077	0.4028	0.4128	0.4235	0.4897	0.4257	0.4547	0.4762	0.4729
Jiaxing	0.4423	0.4727	0.5016	0.5117	0.5360	0.5538	0.5864	0.5965	0.6435	0.6296	0.6562
Jiayuguan	0.2239	0.2514	0.2754	0.3331	0.3379	0.3837	0.3963	0.4044	0.4238	0.3442	0.3774
Jiangmen	0.4014	0.4339	0.4670	0.4980	0.5071	0.5273	0.5488	0.5694	0.5935	0.5863	0.6088

Table A1. *Cont.*

	2011	2012	2013	2014	2015	2016	2017	2018	2019	2020	2021
Jiaozuo	0.3902	0.4104	0.4376	0.4592	0.4851	0.5223	0.5356	0.5555	0.5848	0.5302	0.5580
Jieyang	0.4119	0.4341	0.4356	0.4511	0.4662	0.4903	0.5035	0.5529	0.5970	0.5582	0.5853
Jinchang	0.2131	0.2465	0.2608	0.2955	0.3127	0.3574	0.3534	0.3772	0.4179	0.3960	0.4300
Jinhua	0.4611	0.4875	0.5254	0.5307	0.5571	0.5754	0.5960	0.6187	0.6556	0.6528	0.6932
Jinzhou	0.3435	0.3533	0.3776	0.3949	0.4029	0.4115	0.4431	0.4510	0.4901	0.4278	0.4521
Jincheng	0.3402	0.3600	0.3815	0.4048	0.4305	0.4586	0.4995	0.4970	0.5279	0.5013	0.5289
Jinzhong	0.3636	0.3672	0.3985	0.4179	0.4450	0.4822	0.4840	0.4972	0.5286	0.5355	0.5572
Jingmen	0.3266	0.3408	0.3799	0.3962	0.4197	0.4449	0.4658	0.5030	0.5255	0.5360	0.5756
Jingzhou	0.3095	0.3242	0.3547	0.3595	0.3867	0.4155	0.4483	0.4437	0.4664	0.4649	0.5026
Jingdezhen	0.3193	0.3446	0.3921	0.4018	0.4295	0.4545	0.5056	0.4856	0.5250	0.5185	0.5555
Jiujiang	0.3540	0.3653	0.4091	0.4268	0.4656	0.4843	0.5425	0.5239	0.5505	0.5784	0.6074
Jiuquan	0.3109	0.3227	0.3463	0.3497	0.3850	0.4223	0.4656	0.4670	0.4764	0.4705	0.4941
Kaifeng	0.3752	0.3728	0.4137	0.4305	0.4640	0.4857	0.5326	0.5358	0.5569	0.5715	0.6040
Karamay	0.2831	0.3187	0.3337	0.3533	0.3895	0.4146	0.4386	0.4409	0.4617	0.4713	0.4784
Kunming	0.4843	0.5345	0.5583	0.5820	0.5995	0.6177	0.6541	0.6495	0.6819	0.7155	0.7365
Laibin	0.2629	0.3099	0.3107	0.3546	0.3805	0.4238	0.4656	0.4615	0.4714	0.4585	0.4796
Laiwu	0.2309	0.2852	0.2910	0.3093	0.3194	0.3459	0.3598	0.3737	0.4166	0.4382	0.4557
Lanzhou	0.3639	0.4008	0.4223	0.4469	0.4664	0.4962	0.5203	0.5170	0.5319	0.5333	0.5473
Langfang	0.4204	0.4628	0.4803	0.5087	0.5409	0.5696	0.6289	0.6099	0.6324	0.6426	0.6626
Leshan	0.3418	0.3794	0.3882	0.4170	0.4376	0.4667	0.5049	0.5067	0.5184	0.5249	0.5431
Lijiang	0.2558	0.2984	0.3282	0.3453	0.3820	0.4077	0.4657	0.4341	0.4646	0.4658	0.4865
Lishui	0.3996	0.4353	0.4568	0.4784	0.5044	0.5353	0.5688	0.5712	0.5902	0.6063	0.6286
Lianyungang	0.4320	0.4720	0.5029	0.4931	0.5196	0.5476	0.5799	0.5751	0.6056	0.6166	0.6550
Liaoyang	0.3520	0.3713	0.3918	0.4076	0.4201	0.4540	0.4543	0.4516	0.4702	0.4855	0.4988
Liaoyuan	0.3037	0.3364	0.3365	0.3340	0.3611	0.3800	0.4008	0.4015	0.4267	0.4521	0.4869
Liaocheng	0.3977	0.4356	0.4819	0.4604	0.4887	0.5222	0.5344	0.5411	0.5637	0.5760	0.5985
Lincang	0.2523	0.2933	0.3067	0.3068	0.3477	0.3846	0.4290	0.4247	0.4587	0.4682	0.4915
Linfen	0.3598	0.3910	0.4045	0.4236	0.4477	0.4797	0.5385	0.5096	0.5105	0.5255	0.5455
Linyi	0.4508	0.4860	0.5075	0.5207	0.5409	0.5667	0.5984	0.5926	0.6094	0.6374	0.6522
Liuzhou	0.3291	0.3784	0.3777	0.3970	0.4177	0.4404	0.4579	0.4434	0.4482	0.4546	0.4668
Lu'an	0.3872	0.4193	0.4352	0.4558	0.5003	0.5253	0.5582	0.5753	0.6068	0.6306	0.6484
Liupanshui	0.2639	0.2946	0.3370	0.3611	0.3987	0.4282	0.4676	0.4588	0.4747	0.4792	0.5031
Longyan	0.3573	0.3989	0.4317	0.4604	0.4878	0.5229	0.5457	0.5477	0.5679	0.5767	0.5976
Longnan	0.2078	0.2358	0.2731	0.3066	0.3418	0.3600	0.4114	0.3534	0.4378	0.4637	0.4922
Loudi	0.3569	0.3939	0.3929	0.4069	0.4235	0.4475	0.5027	0.4972	0.5230	0.5391	0.5576
Luzhou	0.2676	0.3060	0.3195	0.3405	0.3639	0.3868	0.4305	0.4202	0.4358	0.4377	0.4596
Luoyang	0.4422	0.4835	0.5124	0.5420	0.5610	0.5935	0.6438	0.6441	0.6580	0.6694	0.6918
Luohe	0.2831	0.3163	0.3485	0.3643	0.3602	0.3908	0.4228	0.4295	0.5165	0.5435	0.5795
Luliang	0.3093	0.3610	0.3566	0.3668	0.3890	0.4174	0.4808	0.4600	0.4854	0.4843	0.5234
Ma'anshan	0.3628	0.4100	0.4385	0.4419	0.4748	0.5300	0.5607	0.5651	0.5894	0.6077	0.6342
Maoming	0.3564	0.4001	0.4329	0.4447	0.4715	0.4942	0.5180	0.5299	0.5588	0.5597	0.5927
Meishan	0.3291	0.3639	0.3841	0.3981	0.4178	0.4552	0.4963	0.5004	0.5175	0.5221	0.5568
Meizhou	0.3244	0.3428	0.3456	0.3687	0.3877	0.3899	0.4215	0.4418	0.4763	0.4218	0.4453
Mianyang	0.4151	0.4481	0.4690	0.4864	0.5143	0.5510	0.5998	0.6083	0.6174	0.6035	0.6235
Mudanjiang	0.3677	0.3772	0.4373	0.4128	0.4259	0.4515	0.4938	0.4930	0.5168	0.5149	0.5591
Nanchang	0.4798	0.5170	0.5456	0.5549	0.5688	0.6009	0.6496	0.6527	0.6770	0.6789	0.7162
Nanchong	0.3683	0.3871	0.4044	0.4133	0.4375	0.4706	0.5525	0.5219	0.5288	0.5474	0.5618
Nanjing	0.6066	0.6380	0.6945	0.6878	0.7117	0.7466	0.7763	0.7927	0.8214	0.8393	0.8634
Nanning	0.5101	0.5385	0.5507	0.5735	0.5979	0.6224	0.6575	0.6633	0.6894	0.6954	0.7183
Nanping	0.3680	0.3950	0.4207	0.4394	0.4727	0.4867	0.5075	0.5166	0.5419	0.5600	0.5919
Nantong	0.4933	0.5257	0.5486	0.5501	0.5734	0.6033	0.6444	0.6526	0.6749	0.6970	0.7301
Nanyang	0.3856	0.4205	0.4404	0.4733	0.4989	0.5365	0.5919	0.5969	0.6265	0.6313	0.6610
Neijiang	0.2912	0.3248	0.3269	0.3550	0.3799	0.4099	0.4793	0.4757	0.5033	0.4733	0.5173
Ningbo	0.5395	0.5804	0.6110	0.6238	0.6472	0.6655	0.7010	0.6983	0.7315	0.7016	0.7281
Ningde	0.3886	0.4094	0.4382	0.4432	0.4608	0.4896	0.5362	0.5267	0.5621	0.5326	0.5574
Panzhihua	0.3395	0.3829	0.3901	0.4255	0.4433	0.4711	0.5105	0.5025	0.5248	0.4863	0.5022
Panjin	0.3420	0.3734	0.3790	0.4021	0.4105	0.4244	0.4707	0.4578	0.4802	0.4556	0.4730
Pingdingshan	0.3552	0.3832	0.4100	0.4426	0.4396	0.4911	0.5299	0.5175	0.5555	0.5253	0.5577

Table A1. *Cont.*

	2011	2012	2013	2014	2015	2016	2017	2018	2019	2020	2021
Pingliang	0.2040	0.2559	0.2726	0.3212	0.3301	0.3837	0.4499	0.4050	0.4531	0.4289	0.4598
Pingxiang	0.3051	0.3458	0.3628	0.3761	0.3909	0.4314	0.4754	0.4793	0.5029	0.4712	0.4942
Putian	0.3404	0.4001	0.4172	0.4428	0.4658	0.5055	0.5375	0.5191	0.5639	0.5856	0.5632
Puyang	0.3278	0.3718	0.3997	0.4265	0.4437	0.5084	0.5409	0.5146	0.5550	0.5665	0.5484
Qitaihe	0.2122	0.2642	0.2908	0.2866	0.3023	0.3356	0.3679	0.3513	0.3705	0.3897	0.3691
Qiqihar	0.4233	0.4308	0.4855	0.4960	0.4889	0.5267	0.5759	0.5359	0.5553	0.5660	0.5510
Qinzhou	0.2674	0.3019	0.3056	0.3377	0.3440	0.3788	0.4027	0.3904	0.4204	0.4384	0.4084
Qinhuangdao	0.4248	0.4667	0.4823	0.4960	0.5124	0.5603	0.5804	0.5657	0.5885	0.6090	0.5826
Qingdao	0.5417	0.5867	0.6208	0.6572	0.6579	0.6997	0.7295	0.7293	0.7595	0.7798	0.7611
Qingyuan	0.3217	0.3808	0.4053	0.4144	0.4435	0.4768	0.5129	0.5152	0.5479	0.5694	0.5431
Qingyang	0.3036	0.3237	0.3023	0.3420	0.3625	0.3946	0.4399	0.4227	0.4585	0.4795	0.4620
Quzhou	0.3209	0.3428	0.3661	0.3767	0.4013	0.4244	0.4511	0.4534	0.4765	0.4867	0.5096
Qujing	0.3053	0.3259	0.3730	0.3806	0.4029	0.4441	0.4874	0.4596	0.4975	0.5230	0.5582
Quanzhou	0.3754	0.4049	0.4350	0.4265	0.4513	0.4787	0.5023	0.5083	0.5179	0.5207	0.5365
Sunshine	0.3691	0.4036	0.4235	0.4418	0.4606	0.4912	0.5176	0.5205	0.5448	0.5706	0.5989
Sanmenxia	0.3231	0.3612	0.3891	0.4142	0.4330	0.4503	0.4751	0.4688	0.5094	0.5225	0.5469
Sanming	0.3620	0.4003	0.4202	0.4303	0.4589	0.4881	0.5163	0.5100	0.5245	0.5331	0.5547
Sanya	0.4046	0.4147	0.4467	0.4482	0.4766	0.5054	0.5115	0.5267	0.5590	0.5666	0.5952
Xiamen	0.5189	0.5613	0.5969	0.6043	0.6352	0.6685	0.6871	0.7156	0.7401	0.7604	0.7797
Shantou	0.4460	0.4717	0.4943	0.4918	0.5233	0.5410	0.5582	0.5592	0.5922	0.6008	0.6349
Shanwei	0.3135	0.3470	0.3663	0.3606	0.3903	0.4105	0.4479	0.4731	0.5129	0.4827	0.5148
Shangluo	0.2729	0.3073	0.3193	0.3168	0.3496	0.3777	0.4017	0.4159	0.4458	0.4612	0.4492
Shangqiu	0.3551	0.3958	0.4016	0.4157	0.4506	0.4782	0.5121	0.5257	0.5570	0.5633	0.5477
Shanghai	0.6848	0.7219	0.7889	0.7749	0.8080	0.7881	0.8566	0.8739	0.9168	0.9221	0.8839
Shangrao	0.3445	0.3816	0.4013	0.4108	0.4488	0.4309	0.5166	0.5099	0.5402	0.5590	0.5355
Shaoguan	0.3595	0.3933	0.4199	0.4520	0.4636	0.4645	0.5320	0.5345	0.5441	0.5432	0.5339
Shaoyang	0.3511	0.3837	0.4091	0.4290	0.4371	0.4403	0.5152	0.5118	0.5482	0.5674	0.5492
Shaoxing	0.4727	0.5116	0.5302	0.5447	0.5632	0.5611	0.6236	0.6297	0.6522	0.6720	0.6453
Shenzhen	0.6819	0.7367	0.7712	0.7778	0.7945	0.7886	0.8434	0.8605	0.8855	0.8955	0.8568
Shenyang	0.5566	0.5924	0.6081	0.6133	0.6268	0.6308	0.6799	0.6889	0.7163	0.6843	0.7110
Shiyan	0.3517	0.3922	0.4299	0.4330	0.4460	0.4519	0.5152	0.5265	0.5604	0.5632	0.6003
Shijiazhuang	0.4992	0.5413	0.5729	0.5799	0.5960	0.5990	0.6740	0.6697	0.6936	0.7143	0.7314
Shizuishan	0.2770	0.3265	0.3335	0.3371	0.3525	0.3870	0.4179	0.4312	0.4562	0.4741	0.4894
Shuangyashan	0.2767	0.2984	0.3413	0.3458	0.3607	0.3874	0.4260	0.3818	0.4078	0.4136	0.4495
Shuozhou	0.2594	0.2925	0.3081	0.3222	0.3140	0.3599	0.4006	0.3798	0.3863	0.3925	0.4245
Siping	0.3369	0.3725	0.3816	0.4184	0.4132	0.4409	0.4713	0.4824	0.4962	0.4995	0.5335
Matsubara	0.3167	0.3473	0.3567	0.3654	0.3754	0.4140	0.4319	0.4410	0.4465	0.4626	0.4960
Suzhou	0.4423	0.4780	0.5260	0.5109	0.5184	0.5446	0.5631	0.5797	0.5986	0.6135	0.6346
Suizhou	0.2766	0.3012	0.3292	0.3410	0.3538	0.3763	0.4227	0.4156	0.3996	0.3807	0.4195
Suining	0.3119	0.3731	0.3637	0.3917	0.4138	0.4420	0.4774	0.4930	0.4724	0.4482	0.4662
Taizhou	0.3788	0.4125	0.4317	0.4452	0.4547	0.4786	0.5039	0.5074	0.5022	0.4839	0.4659
Taiyuan	0.5155	0.5521	0.5750	0.5955	0.6160	0.6457	0.6667	0.6887	0.7024	0.6610	0.6851
Taian	0.4130	0.4470	0.4741	0.4928	0.5114	0.5388	0.5620	0.5670	0.5835	0.5496	0.5666
Taizhou	0.3710	0.4032	0.4077	0.4072	0.4266	0.4592	0.4817	0.4818	0.4779	0.4763	0.5035
Tangshan	0.4538	0.4821	0.4864	0.5017	0.5290	0.5506	0.5710	0.5836	0.5826	0.5786	0.5997
Tianjin	0.5849	0.6235	0.6432	0.6536	0.7008	0.7211	0.7349	0.7462	0.7597	0.7604	0.7692
Tianshui	0.3130	0.3520	0.3682	0.4121	0.4319	0.4549	0.4796	0.4672	0.4815	0.4698	0.4836
Tieling	0.3302	0.3683	0.3747	0.3898	0.4009	0.4217	0.4769	0.4521	0.4747	0.4442	0.4635
Tonghua	0.3647	0.3926	0.4150	0.4054	0.4228	0.4325	0.4973	0.4920	0.5181	0.5247	0.5708
Tongliao	0.3282	0.3601	0.3682	0.3970	0.4265	0.4334	0.4576	0.4660	0.4829	0.4937	0.5286
Tongchuan	0.2299	0.2510	0.2634	0.2826	0.2975	0.3288	0.3536	0.3703	0.4036	0.4232	0.4018
Tongling	0.2827	0.3526	0.3808	0.4063	0.4180	0.4605	0.4849	0.4892	0.5079	0.5398	0.5076
Weihai	0.4127	0.4571	0.4856	0.5082	0.5253	0.5522	0.5675	0.5816	0.6030	0.6164	0.5949
Weifang	0.4450	0.5071	0.5410	0.5531	0.5747	0.5931	0.6189	0.6276	0.6490	0.6708	0.6523
Weinan	0.3475	0.4005	0.4112	0.4251	0.4384	0.4671	0.4941	0.4920	0.5057	0.5344	0.5638
Wenzhou	0.4061	0.4417	0.4696	0.4738	0.4908	0.5237	0.5391	0.5522	0.5520	0.5844	0.6092
Wuhai	0.2736	0.3088	0.3308	0.3508	0.3592	0.3913	0.4005	0.4153	0.4384	0.4420	0.4565

Table A1. *Cont.*

	2011	2012	2013	2014	2015	2016	2017	2018	2019	2020	2021
Ulanqab	0.2690	0.3436	0.3540	0.3667	0.3906	0.4148	0.4457	0.4403	0.4509	0.4521	0.4742
Urumqi	0.5052	0.5238	0.5562	0.5608	0.5855	0.6123	0.6302	0.6489	0.6734	0.6791	0.7000
Wuxi	0.5535	0.5884	0.6338	0.6238	0.6409	0.6740	0.7030	0.7122	0.7340	0.7506	0.7792
Wuhu	0.4206	0.4622	0.4895	0.5090	0.5487	0.5689	0.6084	0.6265	0.6411	0.6570	0.6851
Wuhong	0.2519	0.2956	0.3204	0.3291	0.3612	0.3751	0.3943	0.4348	0.4658	0.4742	0.4987
Wuzhou	0.2824	0.3123	0.3260	0.3147	0.3547	0.3694	0.4064	0.4116	0.4220	0.4392	0.4499
Wuhan	0.5906	0.6225	0.6640	0.6756	0.6978	0.7253	0.7467	0.7690	0.7932	0.7939	0.8291
Wuwei	0.2829	0.2840	0.2873	0.3233	0.3549	0.3863	0.4193	0.4317	0.4581	0.4749	0.4871
Xi'an	0.5987	0.6214	0.6690	0.6768	0.6986	0.7323	0.7562	0.7686	0.7894	0.8028	0.8248
Xining	0.3988	0.4261	0.4533	0.4641	0.5016	0.5203	0.5724	0.5763	0.6089	0.6153	0.5968
Xianning	0.3319	0.3506	0.3844	0.4058	0.4318	0.4563	0.4638	0.5154	0.5388	0.4835	0.5177
Xianyang	0.4076	0.4330	0.4529	0.4534	0.4718	0.4978	0.5450	0.5483	0.5719	0.5837	0.5654
Xiangtan	0.3926	0.4104	0.4413	0.4851	0.5012	0.5225	0.5351	0.5545	0.5825	0.6046	0.5789
Xiaogan	0.3389	0.3691	0.4013	0.4193	0.4397	0.4654	0.5058	0.5179	0.5543	0.5604	0.5575
Xinzhou	0.2842	0.3074	0.3205	0.3348	0.3452	0.3671	0.4026	0.3853	0.4136	0.4190	0.4117
Xinxiang	0.4064	0.4410	0.4486	0.4688	0.5005	0.5355	0.5878	0.5847	0.6118	0.6273	0.6111
Xinyu	0.2960	0.3367	0.3476	0.3824	0.4086	0.4348	0.4462	0.4656	0.4943	0.5081	0.4811
Xinyang	0.3464	0.3836	0.3942	0.4169	0.4396	0.4908	0.5010	0.5175	0.5439	0.5638	0.5971
Xingtai	0.3811	0.4082	0.4143	0.4336	0.4642	0.4920	0.5414	0.5544	0.5751	0.5939	0.6150
Suqian	0.3788	0.4172	0.4334	0.4437	0.4652	0.4957	0.5343	0.5422	0.5766	0.6190	0.6699
Suzhou	0.2848	0.3195	0.3251	0.3706	0.4001	0.3991	0.4494	0.4326	0.4610	0.5879	0.6211
Xuzhou	0.3814	0.4175	0.4467	0.4353	0.4454	0.4644	0.5042	0.5125	0.5423	0.5655	0.5968
Xuchang	0.3657	0.4068	0.4199	0.4483	0.4772	0.4944	0.5420	0.5458	0.5779	0.6127	0.6444
Xuancheng	0.3686	0.4054	0.4298	0.4329	0.4595	0.4826	0.5199	0.5328	0.5525	0.5582	0.6016
Ya'an	0.3011	0.3523	0.3631	0.3921	0.4162	0.4313	0.4853	0.4822	0.5151	0.5151	0.5488
Yantai	0.4572	0.5015	0.5281	0.5510	0.5785	0.5953	0.6341	0.6306	0.6590	0.6755	0.7048
Yan'an	0.2754	0.3176	0.3249	0.3528	0.3857	0.4081	0.4827	0.4635	0.4688	0.4719	0.5139
Yancheng	0.4335	0.4684	0.4971	0.4991	0.5249	0.5503	0.5960	0.6151	0.6578	0.6851	0.7205
Yangzhou	0.3621	0.3975	0.4174	0.4170	0.4370	0.4574	0.4971	0.4922	0.5159	0.5367	0.5569
Yangjiang	0.3201	0.3537	0.3723	0.3866	0.4126	0.4274	0.4581	0.4828	0.5040	0.5165	0.5320
Yangquan	0.2945	0.3378	0.3502	0.3699	0.3915	0.4198	0.4511	0.4558	0.4888	0.5097	0.5269
Yichun	0.2092	0.2526	0.2745	0.2410	0.2755	0.2759	0.3014	0.3042	0.3319	0.3476	0.3814
Yibin	0.3277	0.3596	0.3789	0.4120	0.4374	0.4656	0.5158	0.4993	0.5301	0.5452	0.5620
Yichang	0.3875	0.4470	0.4596	0.5044	0.5014	0.5418	0.5619	0.5763	0.5998	0.5977	0.6408
Yichun	0.2684	0.3014	0.3150	0.3426	0.3582	0.3839	0.4131	0.4412	0.4656	0.3672	0.3495
Yiyang	0.3428	0.3811	0.3970	0.4283	0.4418	0.4734	0.5115	0.5306	0.5451	0.5583	0.5824
Yinchuan	0.3904	0.4369	0.4674	0.5169	0.5311	0.5419	0.5820	0.5779	0.6058	0.5693	0.5896
Yingtan	0.2657	0.3249	0.3366	0.3672	0.3806	0.4161	0.4701	0.4463	0.4773	0.4266	0.4583
Yingkou	0.3908	0.4248	0.4394	0.4566	0.4676	0.4654	0.5320	0.5023	0.5298	0.4975	0.5133
Yongzhou	0.2933	0.3251	0.3341	0.3580	0.3714	0.3891	0.4369	0.4327	0.4607	0.4178	0.4385
Yulin	0.3303	0.3663	0.3801	0.3981	0.4133	0.4328	0.4654	0.4745	0.4964	0.4958	0.5279
Yulin	0.3440	0.3842	0.3947	0.4032	0.4449	0.4514	0.5288	0.5251	0.5371	0.5091	0.5335
Yuxi	0.3396	0.3704	0.3946	0.4036	0.4399	0.4497	0.4588	0.4739	0.5328	0.5152	0.5441
Yueyang	0.3937	0.4311	0.4578	0.4591	0.4951	0.5036	0.5684	0.5441	0.5879	0.5677	0.5960
Yunfu	0.3000	0.3240	0.3396	0.3476	0.4141	0.4183	0.4521	0.4581	0.4997	0.4807	0.5099
Yuncheng	0.3796	0.3990	0.4277	0.4283	0.4621	0.4809	0.5689	0.5179	0.5611	0.5530	0.5679
Zaozhuang	0.3818	0.4063	0.4326	0.4445	0.4678	0.4747	0.5021	0.5267	0.5450	0.5681	0.5949
Zhanjiang	0.4193	0.4470	0.4708	0.4807	0.5131	0.5324	0.5591	0.5491	0.5694	0.5867	0.6030
Zhangjiajie	0.3267	0.3606	0.3742	0.3957	0.4251	0.4448	0.4923	0.4926	0.5169	0.5152	0.5287
Zhangjiakou	0.3778	0.4036	0.4297	0.4350	0.4672	0.4925	0.5253	0.5327	0.5509	0.5655	0.5842
Zhangye	0.2767	0.3057	0.3267	0.3407	0.3862	0.4107	0.4551	0.4631	0.4791	0.4888	0.5069
Zhangzhou	0.3413	0.3697	0.3920	0.3902	0.4127	0.4352	0.4719	0.4752	0.4878	0.4848	0.4964
Zhaotong	0.2681	0.2893	0.3216	0.3342	0.3712	0.3900	0.4406	0.4292	0.4703	0.4340	0.4648
Zhaoqing	0.4132	0.4518	0.4671	0.4737	0.4840	0.4895	0.5527	0.5670	0.5820	0.5641	0.5997
Zhenjiang	0.4502	0.5023	0.5460	0.5369	0.5701	0.5989	0.6431	0.6332	0.6652	0.6327	0.6616
Zhengzhou	0.4195	0.4522	0.4728	0.4920	0.5206	0.5461	0.5846	0.5880	0.6345	0.6051	0.6256
Zhongshan	0.4755	0.5104	0.5400	0.5395	0.5646	0.5880	0.6268	0.6397	0.6496	0.5805	0.6059
Zhongwei	0.2126	0.2547	0.3011	0.3149	0.3364	0.3729	0.4114	0.4193	0.4384	0.3980	0.4227

Table A1. *Cont.*

	2011	2012	2013	2014	2015	2016	2017	2018	2019	2020	2021
Zhoushan	0.4125	0.4402	0.4823	0.5260	0.5463	0.5645	0.5880	0.5867	0.6019	0.6149	0.6242
Zhoukou	0.3661	0.3773	0.4042	0.4157	0.4477	0.4798	0.5272	0.5304	0.5600	0.5562	0.5906
Zhuhai	0.4748	0.5029	0.5593	0.5686	0.5976	0.6338	0.6689	0.6834	0.7141	0.7258	0.7500
Zhuzhou	0.4150	0.4471	0.4831	0.4924	0.5157	0.5419	0.5815	0.5922	0.6098	0.5941	0.6121
Zhumadian	0.3530	0.3614	0.3986	0.4183	0.4404	0.4759	0.5170	0.5345	0.5497	0.5599	0.5816
Ziyang	0.3227	0.3398	0.3518	0.3789	0.4105	0.4192	0.4553	0.4676	0.4937	0.5091	0.5237
Zibo	0.4473	0.4747	0.5039	0.5191	0.5416	0.5667	0.5922	0.5930	0.6136	0.6366	0.6683
Zigong	0.3521	0.3987	0.4029	0.4221	0.4383	0.4690	0.5223	0.5288	0.5473	0.5500	0.5655
Zunyi	0.3976	0.4251	0.4428	0.4682	0.4897	0.5171	0.5590	0.5740	0.5803	0.5851	0.6096

Table A2. Descriptive statistics for all variables.

Variable	Specific Name	Sample Size	Mean	Median	Standard Deviation	Minimum	Variable
$lnGDP$	Natural logarithm of regional gross domestic product	3080	7.335	7.244	0.978	5.033	10.133
$Digcity$	Comprehensive evaluation score for urban digitalization construction level	3080	0.482	0.472	0.117	0.204	0.939
A_1	Natural logarithm of the number of urban employed persons at the end of the year	3080	3.633	3.553	0.857	1.867	6.583
A_2	Natural logarithm of the number of industrial enterprises above a designated scale	3080	6.584	6.583	1.099	3.367	9.243
A_3	Natural logarithm of fixed asset investment	3080	16.382	16.411	0.982	12.352	18.651
A_4	Natural logarithm of public budget expenditure	3080	13.451	13.383	1.351	10.121	17.522
X_1	Natural logarithm of telecommunications service revenue	3080	12.521	12.432	0.976	9.667	15.582
X_2	Natural logarithm of year-end mobile phone users	3080	5.840	5.814	0.782	3.871	8.210
X_3	Natural logarithm of broadband access users	3080	4.257	4.220	0.932	1.938	6.662
X_4	Natural logarithm of per capita regional gross domestic product	3080	10.782	10.763	0.572	9.289	12.151
X_5	Regional gross domestic product growth rate	3080	8.048	8.100	3.767	−6.630	17.882
X_6	Proportion of urban construction land to urban area	3080	0.087	0.056	0.094	0.002	0.591
X_7	Natural logarithm of innovation index	3080	1.202	1.021	1.873	−3.316	6.727
X_8	Natural logarithm of scientific and technological expenditures	3080	11.451	11.582	1.464	6.690	15.441
X_9	Proportion of employees in the tertiary industry	3080	0.553	0.549	0.143	0.186	0.935
X_{10}	Natural logarithm of the number of information transmission employees	3080	8.361	8.206	1.128	5.278	12.853
X_{11}	Proportion of the tertiary industry in GDP	3080	0.430	0.425	0.105	0.192	0.773
X_{12}	Natural logarithm of the inclusive financial index	3080	5.140	5.280	0.539	3.461	5.914
X_{13}	Greening coverage rate of built-up areas	3080	0.400	0.410	0.0700	0.004	0.610

Table A2. *Cont.*

Variable	Specific Name	Sample Size	Mean	Median	Standard Deviation	Minimum	Variable
X_{14}	Natural logarithm of the number of green patents applied	3080	5.397	5.286	1.704	1.386	10.062
X_{15}	Natural logarithm of industrial sulfur dioxide emissions	3080	9.748	9.813	1.424	5.165	13.291
X_{16}	Natural logarithm of carbon dioxide emissions	3080	3.206	3.229	0.819	0.269	5.628

Table A3. Weighted ranking results of the indicator system.

Primary Indicator	Primary Indicator Weight	Secondary Indicator	Secondary Indicator Weight
Digital Industry Development	0.2890	Digital Inclusive Finance Index (X_{12})	0.1084
		Share of GDP from Tertiary Industry (X_{11})	0.0734
		Share of Employees in Tertiary Industry (X_9)	0.0605
		Number of Employees in Information Transmission, Software, and Information Technology Services Industry (X_{10})	0.0468
Innovation Development	0.2228	Innovation Index (X_7)	0.1833
		Expenditure on Science and Technology (X_8)	0.0395
Ecological Environment	0.1963	Green Patent Applications (X_{14})	0.0698
		Industrial Sulfur Dioxide Emissions (X_{15})	0.0620
		Carbon Dioxide Emissions (X_{16})	0.0495
		Greening Coverage in Built-up Areas (X_{13})	0.0149
Digital Infrastructure	0.1692	Number of Internet Broadband Access Users (X_3)	0.0638
		Number of Year-End Mobile Phone Users (X_2)	0.0607
		Telecom Service Revenue (X_1)	0.0446
Overall Economic Level	0.1227	Per Capita Regional Gross Domestic Product (X_4)	0.0578
		Share of Urban Construction Land in City Area (X_6)	0.0376
		Regional Gross Domestic Product Growth Rate (X_5)	0.0274

Table A4. Regression results after substituting core explanatory variable (1).

	(1)		(2)
X_{12}	0.0013 *** (10.6225)	X_7	0.0011 *** (3.7116)
A_1	0.1197 (1.5530)	A_1	0.0039 (0.0748)
A_2	0.3499 *** (5.8491)	A_2	0.3173 *** (4.8955)
A_3	0.1086 *** (4.1733)	A_3	0.2373 *** (7.7841)
A_4	−0.0295 (−0.6280)	A_4	−0.0059 (−0.1080)
_cons	2.6095 *** (6.1966)	*_cons*	1.3016 *** (3.0794)
N	3080	N	3080
R^2	0.2887	R^2	0.2339
year	Yes	*year*	Yes
province	Yes	*province*	Yes

Note: *, **, *** indicate significance levels at 10%, 5%, and 1%, respectively.

Table A5. Regression results after substituting core explanatory variable (2).

	(1)		(2)
X_{14}	0.0876 *** (6.6464)	X_3	0.1720 *** (7.0706)
A_1	0.1199 * (1.6894)	A_1	0.1093 (1.5761)
A_2	0.3310 *** (5.5094)	A_2	0.3238 *** (5.1393)
A_3	0.1601 *** (5.3580)	A_3	0.1523 *** (5.1776)
A_4	−0.0322 (−0.6762)	A_4	−0.0244 (−0.5167)
_cons	1.6767 *** (4.3927)	_cons	1.6128 *** (4.1936)
N	3080	N	3080
R^2	0.2671	R^2	0.2742
year	Yes	year	Yes
province	Yes	province	Yes

Note: *, **, *** indicate significance levels at 10%, 5%, and 1%, respectively.

Table A6. Regression results after substituting control variables (1).

	(1)	(2)		(3)	(4)
	OLS	FE		OLS	FE
X_{12}	−0.0009 *** (−8.3109)	0.0009 ** (2.3026)	X_7	0.0004 *** (4.3492)	0.0011 *** (3.4512)
X_2	0.9245 *** (80.8594)	0.3710 *** (3.3180)	X_2	0.9117 *** (72.7184)	0.4179 *** (4.9920)
X_4	0.5932 *** (30.3937)	0.1623 (1.4927)	X_4	0.5147 *** (30.7941)	0.2371 *** (3.2996)
X_6	0.2483 *** (2.8505)	0.2321 (1.4826)	X_6	0.2910 *** (3.1625)	0.1901 (1.1640)
X_9	−0.2476 *** (−4.1135)	0.0827 (0.7608)	X_9	−0.4618 *** (−8.0245)	0.2464 ** (1.9933)
X_{16}	−0.0002 (−0.6576)	−0.0006 ** (−2.0142)	X_{16}	−0.0008 *** (−2.8606)	−0.0006 ** (−2.0194)
_cons	−4.1775 *** (−20.8858)	3.1980 ** (2.4630)	_cons	−3.3022 *** (−17.5792)	2.1338 *** (4.7796)
N	3080	3080	N	3080	3080
R^2	0.8478	0.1994	R^2	0.8424	0.1605
year		Yes	year		Yes
province		Yes	province		Yes

Note: *, **, *** indicate significance levels at 10%, 5%, and 1%, respectively.

Table A7. Regression results after substituting control variables (2).

	(1) OLS	(2) FE		(3) OLS	(4) FE
X_{14}	0.0543 *** (5.6654)	0.0600 *** (3.0428)	X_3	0.0257 (1.2430)	0.1038 *** (2.7783)
X_2	0.8533 *** (48.8034)	0.3979 *** (4.2964)	X_2	0.8924 *** (36.0008)	0.3529 *** (3.4955)
X_4	0.4513 *** (21.5562)	0.1967 ** (2.2444)	X_4	0.5158 *** (30.3988)	0.2098 ** (2.4923)
X_6	0.2425 *** (2.7628)	0.2095 (1.3224)	X_6	0.3050 *** (3.4538)	0.2037 (1.2193)
X_9	−0.4643 *** (−8.9126)	0.1881 * (1.7234)	X_9	−0.4298 *** (−8.2462)	0.2407 ** (2.2437)

Table A7. *Cont.*

	(1) OLS	(2) FE		(3) OLS	(4) FE
X_{16}	−0.0006 **	−0.0005 *	X_{16}	−0.0005 *	−0.0005
	(−1.9650)	(−1.6661)		(−1.7526)	(−1.6494)
_cons	−2.5531 ***	2.4542 ***	*_cons*	−3.3201 ***	2.4274 ***
	(−10.6642)	(3.2569)		(−17.0138)	(2.9353)
N	3080	3080	*N*	3080	3080
R^2	0.8475	0.1961	R^2	0.8451	0.1956
year		Yes	*year*		Yes
province		Yes	*province*		Yes

Note: *, **, *** indicate significance levels at 10%, 5%, and 1%, respectively.

Table A8. Regression results for different study periods.

	(1) 2011–2014	(2) 2015–2016	(3) 2017–2019
Digcity	1.8980 ***	1.1949 ***	6.4258 ***
	(6.8811)	(6.2388)	(9.1206)
A_1	0.0830 ***	0.0764 **	−0.0694
	(2.9329)	(2.1217)	(−0.2515)
A_2	0.1342 ***	0.0139	0.3222 ***
	(3.3146)	(0.3357)	(2.7555)
A_3	0.1468 ***	0.2851 ***	0.2638 ***
	(3.2753)	(8.2147)	(4.0602)
A_4	−0.0010	−0.0004	−0.0720
	(−0.0570)	(−0.0196)	(−0.6570)
_cons	2.8846 ***	1.7660 ***	−2.2119
	(5.6273)	(4.1280)	(−1.3027)
N	1120	560	1400
R^2	0.8258	0.7535	0.2225
year	Yes	Yes	Yes
province	Yes	Yes	Yes

Note: *, **, *** indicate significance levels at 10%, 5%, and 1%, respectively.

Table A9. Heterogeneity analysis results of the impact of the digital inclusive finance index on the evaluation score of digital construction level.

	(1) Eastern Region	(2) Central Region	(3) Western Region
X_{12}	0.0007 ***	0.0007 ***	0.0007 ***
	(47.1090)	(42.3459)	(34.3354)
X_2	0.0295 ***	0.0250 ***	0.0402 ***
	(8.5098)	(5.7935)	(5.2229)
X_4	0.0292 ***	0.0254 ***	0.0386 ***
	(9.9885)	(6.5593)	(10.2636)
X_6	0.0166	0.0475 ***	−0.0019
	(1.2896)	(2.6597)	(−0.1585)
X_9	0.0872 ***	0.0973 ***	0.0583 ***
	(8.4477)	(8.3861)	(4.4240)
X_{16}	−0.0002 ***	−0.0002 ***	−0.0002 ***
	(−12.6247)	(−12.7052)	(−6.6956)
_cons	−0.1493 ***	−0.1538 ***	−0.3241 ***
	(−4.0432)	(−3.5815)	(−6.2566)
N	1133	902	1045
R^2	0.9690	0.9621	0.9636
year	Yes	Yes	Yes
province	Yes	Yes	Yes

Note: *, **, *** indicate significance levels at 10%, 5%, and 1%, respectively.

Table A10. Heterogeneity analysis results of the impact of the innovation index on the evaluation score of digital construction level.

	(1) Eastern Region	(2) Central Region	(3) Western Region
X_7	0.0002 *** (3.4412)	0.0004 *** (4.7666)	0.0004 *** (3.0753)
X_2	0.1506 *** (8.4374)	0.0998 *** (6.5165)	0.1154 *** (4.2326)
X_4	0.1234 *** (11.3885)	0.1276 *** (10.3195)	0.1303 *** (8.3331)
X_6	0.0287 (0.5805)	0.0283 (1.1475)	−0.0023 (−0.0729)
X_9	0.2866 *** (7.6280)	0.2762 *** (6.5969)	0.3014 *** (6.6740)
X_{16}	−0.0000 (−0.8860)	−0.0001 ** (−2.2779)	−0.0001 *** (−2.6809)
_cons	−1.9027 *** (−17.6202)	−1.6284 *** (−18.3844)	−1.7308 *** (−17.3274)
N	1133	902	1045
R^2	0.7968	0.7833	0.8155
year	Yes	Yes	Yes
province	Yes	Yes	Yes

Note: *, **, *** indicate significance levels at 10%, 5%, and 1%, respectively.

Table A11. Heterogeneity analysis results of the impact of the number of green patent applications on the evaluation score of digital construction level.

	(1) Eastern Region	(2) Central Region	(3) Western Region
X_{14}	0.0868 *** (3.5842)	0.0377 (1.5787)	0.0606 (1.1979)
X_2	0.4476 ** (2.2487)	0.4453 *** (4.2659)	0.3224 *** (2.6310)
X_4	0.2011 * (1.7422)	0.1338 (1.1016)	0.2215 (1.2168)
X_6	0.6408 *** (3.2960)	0.0407 (0.1034)	−0.2401 (−0.9046)
X_9	0.2268 (1.4889)	0.3697 ** (2.1621)	−0.0964 (−0.5085)
X_{16}	−0.0005 (−1.3527)	0.0005 (1.1370)	−0.0012 * (−1.7670)
_cons	2.1460 * (1.6678)	2.5651 *** (2.9145)	2.7647 * (1.8200)
N	1133	902	1045
R^2	0.8725	0.8873	0.8997
year	Yes	Yes	Yes
province	Yes	Yes	Yes

Note: *, **, *** indicate significance levels at 10%, 5%, and 1%, respectively.

Table A12. Heterogeneity analysis results of the impact of the number of internet broadband access users on the evaluation score of digital construction level.

	(1) Eastern Region	(2) Central Region	(3) Western Region
X_3	0.0750 *** (9.0329)	0.0684 *** (12.1247)	0.0722 *** (8.0962)
X_2	0.0118 (0.6528)	0.0327 *** (3.2975)	0.0386 * (1.7426)

Table A12. *Cont.*

	(1) Eastern Region	(2) Central Region	(3) Western Region
X_4	0.0718 ***	0.0740 ***	0.0858 ***
	(6.4117)	(8.4245)	(7.9130)
X_6	0.0017	0.0203	−0.0254
	(0.0349)	(1.0269)	(−1.0370)
X_9	0.2389 ***	0.1728 ***	0.2289 ***
	(7.3876)	(7.9236)	(7.1152)
X_{16}	−0.0001 ***	−0.0002 ***	−0.0001 ***
	(−3.4111)	(−4.8939)	(−2.6988)
_cons	−0.8112 ***	−0.8846 ***	−1.0806 ***
	(−4.6713)	(−8.8349)	(−9.8263)
N	1133	902	1045
R^2	0.8382	0.8927	0.8820
year	Yes	Yes	Yes
province	Yes	Yes	Yes

Note: *, **, *** indicate significance levels at 10%, 5%, and 1%, respectively.

References

Acemoglu, Daron, and Pascual Restrepo. 2022. Tasks, Automation, and the Rise in U.S. Wage Inequality. *Econometrica* 90: 1973–2016. [CrossRef]

Alderete, María Verónica. 2020. Exploring the Smart City Indexes and the Role of Macro Factors for Measuring Cities Smartness. *Social Indicators Research* 147: 567–89. [CrossRef]

Ali, Muhammad. 2017. Determinants of Related and Unrelated Export Diversification. *Economies* 5: 50. [CrossRef]

Allcott, Hunt, Luca Braghieri, Sarah Eichmeyer, and Matthew Gentzkow. 2020. The Welfare Effects of Social Media. *American Economic Review* 110: 629–76. [CrossRef]

Allcott, Hunt, Matthew Gentzkow, and Lena Song. 2022. Digital Addiction. *American Economic Review* 112: 2424–63. [CrossRef]

Ariffin, Khairul Akram Zainol, and Faris Hanif Ahmad. 2021. Indicators for maturity and readiness for digital forensic investigation in era of industrial revolution 4.0. *Computers & Security* 105: 102237. [CrossRef]

Atitallah, Safa Ben, Maha Driss, Wadii Boulila, and Henda Ben Ghézala. 2020. Leveraging Deep Learning and IoT big data analytics to support the smart cities development: Review and future directions. *Computer Science Review* 38: 100303. [CrossRef]

Austin, Mark, Parastoo Delgoshaei, Maria Coelho, and Mohammad Heidarinejad. 2020. Architecting Smart City Digital Twins: Combined Semantic Model and Machine Learning Approach. *Journal of Management in Engineering* 36: 04020026. [CrossRef]

Avgerou, Chrisanthi. 1991. The Informational City: Information Technology Economic Restructuring and the Urban Regional Process. *European Journal of Information Systems* 1: 76–77. [CrossRef]

Barwick, Panle Jia, Yanyan Liu, Eleonora Patacchini, and Qi Wu. 2023. Information, Mobile Communication, and Referral Effects. *American Economic Review* 113: 1170–207. [CrossRef]

Beraja, Martin, Andrew Kao, David Y. Yang, and Noam Yuchtman. 2023a. AI-tocracy. *The Quarterly Journal of Economics* 138: 1349–402. [CrossRef]

Beraja, Martin, David Y. Yang, and Noam Yuchtman. 2023b. Data-intensive Innovation and the State: Evidence from AI Firms in China. *The Review of Economic Studies* 90: 1701–23. [CrossRef]

Borowiecki, Ryszard, Barbara Siuta-Tokarska, Jolanta Maroń, Marcin Suder, Agnieszka Thier, and Katarzyna Żmija. 2021. Developing Digital Economy and Society in the Light of the Issue of Digital Convergence of the Markets in the European Union Countries. *Energies* 14: 2717. [CrossRef]

Cahyadi, Afriyadi, and Róbert Magda. 2021. Digital Leadership in the Economies of the G20 Countries: A Secondary Research. *Economies* 9: 32. [CrossRef]

Calvano, Emilio, Giacomo Calzolari, Vincenzo Denicolò, and Sergio Pastorello. 2020. Artificial Intelligence, Algorithmic Pricing, and Collusion. *American Economic Review* 110: 3267–97. [CrossRef]

Cao, Lingling, Huawei Niu, and Yifeng Wang. 2022. Utility analysis of digital villages to empower balanced urban-rural development based on the three-stage DEA-Malmquist model. *PLoS ONE* 17: e0270952. [CrossRef] [PubMed]

Castro, Conceição, and Cristina Lopes. 2022. Digital Government and Sustainable Development. *Journal of the Knowledge Economy* 13: 880–903. [CrossRef]

Chen, Bin, Chen Lin, Peng Gong, and Jiafu An. 2023. Optimize urban shade using digital twins of cities. *Nature* 622: 242. [CrossRef]

Chen, Kunqiu, Hualou Long, Liuwen Liao, Shuangshuang Tu, and Tingting Li. 2020. Land use transitions and urban-rural integrated development: Theoretical framework and China's evidence. *Land Use Policy* 92: 104465. [CrossRef]

Chen, Nan, and Yunpeng Yang. 2023. The Role of Influencers in Live Streaming E-Commerce: Influencer Trust, Attachment, and Consumer Purchase Intention. *Journal of Theoretical and Applied Electronic Commerce Research* 18: 1601–18. [CrossRef]

Cheng, Cong, and Limin Wang. 2022. How companies configure digital innovation attributes for business model innovation? A configurational view. *Technovation* 112: 102398. [CrossRef]

Cong, Xuhui, Sai Wang, Liang Wang, Jonas Šaparauskas, Jarosław Górecki, and Miroslaw J. Skibniewski. 2022. Allocation Efficiency Measurement and Spatio-Temporal Differences Analysis of Digital Infrastructure: The Case of China's Shandong Province. *Systems* 10: 205. [CrossRef]

Costinot, Arnaud, and Iván Werning. 2023. Robots, Trade, and Luddism: A Sufficient Statistic Approach to Optimal Technology Regulation. *The Review of Economic Studies* 90: 2261–91. [CrossRef]

Deng, Haiyan, Ge Bai, Zhiyang Shen, and Lanqi Xia. 2022. Digital economy and its spatial effect on green productivity gains in manufacturing: Evidence from China. *Journal of Cleaner Production* 378: 134539. [CrossRef]

Einav, Liran, Chiara Farronato, Jonathan Levin, and Neel Sundaresan. 2018. Auctions versus Posted Prices in Online Markets. *Journal of Political Economy* 126: 178–215. [CrossRef]

ElMassah, Suzanna, and Mahmoud Mohieldin. 2020. Digital transformation and localizing the Sustainable Development Goals (SDGs). *Ecological Economics* 169: 106490. [CrossRef]

Fernandes, Catarina, Rui Pires, and Maria-Ceu Gaspar Alves. 2023. Digital Entrepreneurship and Sustainability: The State of the Art and Research Agenda. *Economies* 11: 3. [CrossRef]

García-Vandewalle García, José Manuel, Marina García-Carmona, Juan Manuel Trujillo Torres, and Pablo Moya Fernández. 2023. Analysis of digital competence of educators (DigCompEdu) in teacher trainees: The context of Melilla, Spain. *Technology, Knowledge and Learning* 28: 585–612. [CrossRef]

Goloshchapova, Tatiana, Vladimir Yamashev, Natalia Skornichenko, and Wadim Strielkowski. 2023. E-Government as a Key to the Economic Prosperity and Sustainable Development in the Post-COVID Era. *Economies* 11: 112. [CrossRef]

Graham, Stephen. 2002. Bridging Urban Digital Divides? Urban Polarisation and Information and Communications Technologies (ICTs). *Urban Studies* 39: 33–56. [CrossRef]

Guo, Bingnan, Yu Wang, Hao Zhang, Chunyan Liang, Yu Feng, and Feng Hu. 2023. Impact of the digital economy on high-quality urban economic development: Evidence from Chinese cities. *Economic Modelling* 120: 106194. [CrossRef]

Han, Wenjing, Xiaoling Zhang, and Xian Zheng. 2020. Land use regulation and urban land value: Evidence from China. *Land Use Policy* 92: 104432. [CrossRef]

Harwit, Eric. 2004. Spreading Telecommunications to Developing Areas in China: Telephones, the Internet and the Digital Divide. *The China Quarterly* 180: 1010–30. [CrossRef]

Hills, Gage, Christian Lau, Andrew Wright, Samuel Fuller, Mindy D. Bishop, Tathagata Srimani, Pritpal Kanhaiya, Rebecca Ho, Aya Amer, Yosi Stein, and et al. 2019. Modern microprocessor built from complementary carbon nanotube transistors. *Nature* 572: 595–602. [CrossRef] [PubMed]

Huang, Jie, Huali Jin, Xuhui Ding, and Aihua Zhang. 2023. A Study on the Spatial Correlation Effects of Digital Economy Development in China from a Non-Linear Perspective. *Systems* 11: 63. [CrossRef]

Jemiluyi, Olufunmilayo Olayemi, and Leward Jeke. 2023. How Catalytic Is Digital Technology in the Nexus between Migrants' Remittance and Financial Development in Sub-Saharan African Countries? *Economies* 11: 74. [CrossRef]

Jensen, Robert. 2007. The Digital Provide: Information (Technology), Market Performance, and Welfare in the South Indian Fisheries Sector. *The Quarterly Journal of Economics* 122: 879–924. [CrossRef]

Jiang, Dingfu. 2020. The construction of smart city information system based on the Internet of Things and cloud computing. *Computer Communications* 150: 158–66. [CrossRef]

Kaginalkar, Akshara, Shamita Kumar, Prashant Gargava, and Dev Niyogi. 2021. Review of urban computing in air quality management as smart city service: An integrated IoT, AI, and cloud technology perspective. *Urban Climate* 39: 100972. [CrossRef]

Karle, Heiko, Martin Peitz, and Markus Reisinger. 2020. Segmentation versus Agglomeration: Competition between Platforms with Competitive Sellers. *Journal of Political Economy* 128: 2329–74. [CrossRef]

Kettinger, William J. 1994. National infrastructure diffusion and the U.S. information super highway. *Information & Management* 27: 357–68. [CrossRef]

Knox, Paul L., and M. Castells. 1995. The Informational City. Information Technology, Economic Restructuring, and the Urban-Regional Process. *The Geographical Journal* 161: 94. [CrossRef]

Korgun, Irina, and Altin Hoti. 2023. Dynamics of Bilateral Digital Trade: The Case of a Korea–EU Digital Partnership. *Economies* 11: 248. [CrossRef]

Kutty, Adeeb A., Murat Kucukvar, Galal M. Abdella, Muhammet Enis Bulak, and Nuri Cihat Onat. 2022. Sustainability Performance of European Smart Cities: A Novel DEA Approach with Double Frontiers. *Sustainable Cities and Society* 81: 103777. [CrossRef]

Laitsou, Eleni, Antonios Kargas, and Dimitris Varoutas. 2020. Digital Competitiveness in the European Union Era: The Greek Case. *Economies* 8: 85. [CrossRef]

Lan, Mudan, and Yuke Zhu. 2023. Digital infrastructure construction, carbon total factor productivity, and carbon rebound effect. *Environmental Science and Pollution Research* 30: 88968–85. [CrossRef] [PubMed]

Lee, Chien-Chiang, Ying Yuan, and Huwei Wen. 2022. Can digital economy alleviate CO_2 emissions in the transport sector? Evidence from provincial panel data in China. *Natural Resources Forum* 46: 289–310. [CrossRef]

Lefatsa, Palesa Milliscent, Kin Sibanda, and Rufaro Garidzirai. 2021. The Relationship between Financial Development and Energy Consumption in South Africa. *Economies* 9: 158. [CrossRef]

Li, Xiaomin, and Colin F. Camerer. 2022. Predictable effects of visual salience in experimental decisions and games. *The Quarterly Journal of Economics* 137: 1849–900. [CrossRef]
Li, Xiaoming, Hao Liu, Weixi Wang, Ye Zheng, Haibin Lv, and Zhihan Lv. 2022. Big data analysis of the Internet of Things in the digital twins of smart city based on deep learning. *Future Generation Computer Systems* 128: 167–77. [CrossRef]
Lin, Jiesen, Lemuria Carter, and Dapeng Liu. 2021. Privacy concerns and digital government: Exploring citizen willingness to adopt the COVIDSafe app. *European Journal of Information Systems* 30: 1–14. [CrossRef]
Liu, Jing, Chin-Hong Puah, Mohammad Affendy Arip, and Meng-Chang Jong. 2023. Impacts of Digital Financial Inclusion on Urban–Rural Income Disparity: A Comparative Research of the Eastern and Western Regions in China. *Economies* 11: 282. [CrossRef]
Liu, Tinghua, Mengyuan Hu, Ehsan Elahi, and Xiao Liu. 2022. Does digital finance affect the quality of economic growth? Analysis based on Chinese city data. *Frontiers in Environmental Science* 10: 951420. [CrossRef]
Loebbing, Jonas. 2022. An Elementary Theory of Directed Technical Change and Wage Inequality. *The Review of Economic Studies* 89: 411–51. [CrossRef]
Lu, Sha, Yiyun Zhao, Zhouqi Chen, Mengke Dou, Qingchun Zhang, and Weixin Yang. 2021. Association between Atrial Fibrillation Incidence and Temperatures, Wind Scale and Air Quality: An Exploratory Study for Shanghai and Kunming. *Sustainability* 13: 5247. [CrossRef]
Malecki, Edward J. 2003. Digital development in rural areas: Potentials and pitfalls. *Journal of Rural Studies* 19: 201–14. [CrossRef]
Maresova, Petra, Ivan Soukal, Libuse Svobodova, Martina Hedvicakova, Ehsan Javanmardi, Ali Selamat, and Ondrej Krejcar. 2018. Consequences of Industry 4.0 in Business and Economics. *Economies* 6: 46. [CrossRef]
Marshall, Will. 2023. Governance: A Pugwash council for the digital age. *Nature* 621: 691. [CrossRef]
Masik, Grzegorz, Iwona Sagan, and James W. Scott. 2021. Smart City strategies and new urban development policies in the Polish context. *Cities* 108: 102970. [CrossRef]
Mitrović, Đorđe. 2020. Measuring the efficiency of digital convergence. *Economics Letters* 188: 108982. [CrossRef]
Mpofu, Favourate Y. 2022. Taxation of the Digital Economy and Direct Digital Service Taxes: Opportunities, Challenges, and Implications for African Countries. *Economies* 10: 219. [CrossRef]
Mpofu, Favourate Y., and David Mhlanga. 2022. Digital Financial Inclusion, Digital Financial Services Tax and Financial Inclusion in the Fourth Industrial Revolution Era in Africa. *Economies* 10: 184. [CrossRef]
Ndubuisi, Gideon, Chuks Otioma, and Godsway Korku Tetteh. 2021. Digital infrastructure and employment in services: Evidence from Sub-Saharan African countries. *Telecommunications Policy* 45: 102153. [CrossRef]
Nicolas, Clément, Jinwoo Kim, and Seokho Chi. 2020. Quantifying the dynamic effects of smart city development enablers using structural equation modeling. *Sustainable Cities and Society* 53: 101916. [CrossRef]
Nochta, T., L. Wan, J. M. Schooling, and A. K. Parlikad. 2021. A Socio-Technical Perspective on Urban Analytics: The Case of City-Scale Digital Twins. *Journal of Urban Technology* 28: 263–87. [CrossRef]
Ogujiuba, Kanayo, and Ntombifuthi Mngometulu. 2022. Does Social Investment Influence Poverty and Economic Growth in South Africa: A Cointegration Analysis? *Economies* 10: 226. [CrossRef]
Pauliuk, Stefan, Maximilian Koslowski, Kavya Madhu, Simon Schulte, and Sebastian Kilchert. 2022. Co-design of digital transformation and sustainable development strategies—What socio-metabolic and industrial ecology research can contribute. *Journal of Cleaner Production* 343: 130997. [CrossRef]
Pedrosa, Glauco Vitor, Ricardo A. D. Kosloski, Vitor G. De Menezes, Gabriela Y. Iwama, Wander C. M. P. Da Silva, and Rejane M. Da C. Figueiredo. 2020. A Systematic Review of Indicators for Evaluating the Effectiveness of Digital Public Services. *Information* 11: 472. [CrossRef]
Peng, Weibin, Liuqing Fang, and Xiaojing Lin. 2022. *Digital Governance for Smart City and Future Community Building: From Concept to Application*. Singapore: Springer Nature, pp. 41–67.
Peng, Yongzhang, and Changqi Tao. 2022. Can digital transformation promote enterprise performance?—From the perspective of public policy and innovation. *Journal of Innovation & Knowledge* 7: 100198. [CrossRef]
Peng, Zhuangzhuang, and Ting Dan. 2023. Digital dividend or digital divide? Digital economy and urban-rural income inequality in China. *Telecommunications Policy* 47: 102616. [CrossRef]
Popkova, Elena G., and Kantoro Gulzat. 2020. *Contradiction of the Digital Economy: Public Well-Being vs. Cyber Threats*. Cham: Springer International Publishing, pp. 112–24.
Qi, Guangzhi, Zhibao Wang, Zhixiu Wang, and Lijie Wei. 2022. Has Industrial Upgrading Improved Air Pollution?—Evidence from China's Digital Economy. *Sustainability* 14: 8967. [CrossRef]
Ramdani, Boumediene, Siddhartha Raja, and Marina Kayumova. 2022. Digital innovation in SMEs: A systematic review, synthesis and research agenda. *Information Technology for Development* 28: 56–80. [CrossRef]
Ren, Shuming, Lianqing Li, Yueqi Han, Yu Hao, and Haitao Wu. 2022. The emerging driving force of inclusive green growth: Does digital economy agglomeration work? *Business Strategy and the Environment* 31: 1656–78. [CrossRef]
Ren, Xiaohang, Gudian Zeng, and Giray Gozgor. 2023. How does digital finance affect industrial structure upgrading? Evidence from Chinese prefecture-level cities. *Journal of Environmental Management* 330: 117125. [CrossRef] [PubMed]
Sotolongo, Marisa. 2023. Defining environmental justice communities: Evaluating digital infrastructure in Southeastern states for Justice40 benefits allocation. *Applied Geography* 158: 103057. [CrossRef]

Sun, Minglin, and Jian Zhang. 2020. Research on the application of block chain big data platform in the construction of new smart city for low carbon emission and green environment. *Computer Communications* 149: 332–42. [CrossRef]

Supari, Supari, and Hendranata Anton. 2022. The Impact of the National Economic Recovery Program and Digitalization on MSME Resilience during the COVID-19 Pandemic: A Case Study of Bank Rakyat Indonesia. *Economies* 10: 160. [CrossRef]

Travkina, Elena Vladimirovna, Alim Borisovich Fiapshev, and Marianna Tolevna Belova. 2022. Stablecoin-Based Digital Trading and Investment Platforms and Their Potential in Overcoming Sanctions Restrictions. *Economies* 10: 246. [CrossRef]

Veretennikova, Anna Y., and Daria A. Selezneva. 2023. Development of Regulatory Strategies in the Sharing Economy: The Application of Game Theory. *Economies* 11: 298. [CrossRef]

Wang, Di, Tao Zhou, and Mengmeng Wang. 2021. Information and communication technology (ICT), digital divide and urbanization: Evidence from Chinese cities. *Technology in Society* 64: 101516. [CrossRef]

Wang, Jianda, Kangyin Dong, Xiucheng Dong, and Farhad Taghizadeh-Hesary. 2022. Assessing the digital economy and its carbon-mitigation effects: The case of China. *Energy Economics* 113: 106198. [CrossRef]

Williamson, Stephen. 2022. Central Bank Digital Currency: Welfare and Policy Implications. *Journal of Political Economy* 130: 2829–61. [CrossRef]

Wu, Liu, Xiaowen Wan, Atif Jahanger, Mengyi Li, Muntasir Murshed, and Daniel Balsalobre-Lorente. 2023. Does the digital economy reduce air pollution in China? A perspective from industrial agglomeration. *Energy Reports* 9: 3625–41. [CrossRef]

Xia, Chang, Anthony Gar-On Yeh, and Anqi Zhang. 2020. Analyzing spatial relationships between urban land use intensity and urban vitality at street block level: A case study of five Chinese megacities. *Landscape and Urban Planning* 193: 103669. [CrossRef]

Xia, Haishan, Zishuo Liu, Maria Efremochkina, Xiaotong Liu, and Chunxiang Lin. 2022. Study on city digital twin technologies for sustainable smart city design: A review and bibliometric analysis of geographic information system and building information modeling integration. *Sustainable Cities and Society* 84: 104009. [CrossRef]

Yang, Lifan, Jiatian Dong, and Weixin Yang. 2024. Analysis of Regional Competitiveness of China's Cross-Border E-Commerce. *Sustainability* 16: 1007. [CrossRef]

Yang, Weixin, Lingying Pan, and Qinyi Ding. 2023a. Dynamic analysis of natural gas substitution for crude oil: Scenario simulation and quantitative evaluation. *Energy* 282: 128764. [CrossRef]

Yang, Weixin, Yue Hu, Qinyi Ding, Hao Gao, and Lingguang Li. 2023b. Comprehensive Evaluation and Comparative Analysis of the Green Development Level of Provinces in Eastern and Western China. *Sustainability* 15: 3965. [CrossRef]

Yang, Yunpeng, Hongmin Chen, and Hejun Liang. 2023c. Did New Retail Enhance Enterprise Competition during the COVID-19 Pandemic? An Empirical Analysis of Operating Efficiency. *Journal of Theoretical and Applied Electronic Commerce Research* 18: 352–71. [CrossRef]

Yang, Yunpeng, Nan Chen, and Hongmin Chen. 2023d. The Digital Platform, Enterprise Digital Transformation, and Enterprise Performance of Cross-Border E-Commerce—From the Perspective of Digital Transformation and Data Elements. *Journal of Theoretical and Applied Electronic Commerce Research* 18: 777–94. [CrossRef]

Yang, Zhen, Weijun Gao, Qing Han, Liyan Qi, Yajie Cui, and Yuqing Chen. 2022. Digitalization and carbon emissions: How does digital city construction affect china's carbon emission reduction? *Sustainable Cities and Society* 87: 104201. [CrossRef]

Zekić-Sušac, Marijana, Saša Mitrović, and Adela Has. 2021. Machine learning based system for managing energy efficiency of public sector as an approach towards smart cities. *International Journal of Information Management* 58: 102074. [CrossRef]

Zhang, Dan, Loogeok. G. Pee, Shan L. Pan, and Lili Cui. 2022a. Big data analytics, resource orchestration, and digital sustainability: A case study of smart city development. *Government Information Quarterly* 39: 101626. [CrossRef]

Zhang, Jinning, Yanwei Lyu, Yutao Li, and Yong Geng. 2022b. Digital economy: An innovation driving factor for low-carbon development. *Environmental Impact Assessment Review* 96: 106821. [CrossRef]

Zhang, Wei, Xuemeng Liu, Die Wang, and Jianping Zhou. 2022c. Digital economy and carbon emission performance: Evidence at China's city level. *Energy Policy* 165: 112927. [CrossRef]

Zheng, Chuanjun, Jingfeng Yuan, Lei Zhu, Yajing Zhang, and Qiuhu Shao. 2020. From digital to sustainable: A scientometric review of smart city literature between 1990 and 2019. *Journal of Cleaner Production* 258: 120689. [CrossRef]

Zhu, Wenjing, and Jianjun Chen. 2022. The spatial analysis of digital economy and urban development: A case study in Hangzhou, China. *Cities* 123: 103563. [CrossRef]

Disclaimer/Publisher's Note: The statements, opinions and data contained in all publications are solely those of the individual author(s) and contributor(s) and not of MDPI and/or the editor(s). MDPI and/or the editor(s) disclaim responsibility for any injury to people or property resulting from any ideas, methods, instructions or products referred to in the content.

economies
MDPI

Perspective

Dynamics of Bilateral Digital Trade: The Case of a Korea–EU Digital Partnership

Irina Korgun [1,2] **and Altin Hoti** [3,*]

1 EU Center, Hankuk University of Foreign Studies, Seoul 02450, Republic of Korea
2 The Institute of Economics, Moscow 117218, Russia
3 College of Engineering and Technology, American University of Middle East, Kuwait
* Correspondence: altin.hoti@aum.edu.kw

Abstract: The rapid growth of digital trade has had a profound impact on global economies, revolutionizing trading practices and facilitating trade expansion. The purpose of this paper is to explore the digital partnership between Korea and the European Union (EU) and its implications for their shared agenda in digital trade to theorize the dynamics of digital trade. A case study method is used to explore trade between Korea and the EU with in-depth descriptive analysis. Digital trade-flow statistics were analyzed to develop the case for Korea and EU digital trade and derive implications for both countries. The findings were generalized by discussing the relevant literature and data from other countries to identify the wider implications. The analysis was focused on the areas of information and communication technology and e-commerce. The findings suggest uncovered trade imbalances, such as Korea's surplus of ICT goods exports and the EU's dominant position in online trade. There is an influence of supply chain dynamics, specifically the presence of Korean manufacturers' production units in countries like Vietnam, and the same dynamics have shaped Korea's actual place in the supply of ICT goods to the European market. While the digital partnership was established to align regulatory frameworks and foster trust, transparency, and harmonization in the digital domain, it has failed to adequately reflect the importance of digital trade. Although both sides are motivated to collaborate on the harmonization of digital trade rules, there have been instances where the partners' interests diverge. It is concluded that some political and economic factors may hinder the effectiveness of the digital partnership, unless concrete measures that go beyond traditional bilateral policymaking approaches are implemented. It is therefore recommended to emphasize the need to enhance the efficacy of the digital partnership by taking bolder actions to develop digital trade.

Keywords: digital trade; digital partnership; online trade

1. Background

The transformation to digitalized trade is one of the most prominent trends in today's global economy. This transformation accelerates trade expansion, revolutionizes trading practices and the types of products exchanged, lowers costs, and facilitates broader participation of small- and medium-sized enterprises (SMEs) in international trade (WTO 2018; López González and Ferencz 2018). Consequently, digital trade plays a vital role in the overall digital transition of economies towards development.

By definition, "digitalization is changing what and how we trade" (López González and Jouanjean 2017, p. 24). The scope of digital trade is, however, wide, and the definition of digital trade remains fluid due to the rapid ever-evolving nature of technology and trading platforms. Presently, there seems to be a general consensus to accept the OECD's definition of digital trade, which encompasses digitally enabled transactions involving the trade of goods and services. The goods and services can be delivered either digitally or physically, and may involve consumers, firms, and governments in the digital trade ecosystem.[1] Digital trade is also referred to as e-commerce or online trading.

Global digital trade has experienced substantial growth and, in absolute terms, reached USD 5.1 trillion in 2018 (López González et al. 2023). Furthermore, the rate of growth in digital trade has consistently exceeded that of non-digital trade by at least 30% (Jaax et al. 2023). Thus, there is a high likelihood that digital trade will continue to occupy a larger share of the market than conventional trade.

In spite of the growing importance of digitally enabled trade among various nations, there have been few discussions on (i) exploring the dynamics of such a bilateral trades, and (ii) implications of the same for their common agenda, even though recent studies have emphasized the importance of research on digital trade (Burri and Polanco 2020; Fayyaz 2019; Ferracane et al. 2018; Lund and Manyika 2016; Rachel et al. 2021; Tarantilis et al. 2015). This paper, therefore, aimed to contribute to the ongoing discussions surrounding digital trade by analyzing trends in bilateral digital trade between Korea and the EU as a focal case, to understand and theorize about the dynamics of digital trade. In this study, we sought to understand how these trends align with the goals set forth in the ambitious digital partnership agreement reached in 2022 and discuss how the effectiveness of the partnership can be enhanced. This study is important because "as global data flows and digital technologies transform international trade, governments and regulators have to determine how to benefit from these developments while maintaining the integrity of their domestic regulations" (Meltzer 2019, p. 523).

Many governments are also intensifying their efforts to establish appropriate regulations at both the national and international levels, and studies in this area will have implications for the same. Some countries are coordinating their actions to prepare effectively for the digital transformation. For instance, the digital partnership between Korea and the EU serves as a case study of such collaborative efforts. Both Korea and the EU have established robust regulatory frameworks and standards for digital trade. By aligning their regulations and standards, Korea and the EU can promote trust, transparency, and harmonization in digital trade, facilitating cross-border transactions.

Both Korea and the EU are renowned for their technological advancements and innovation. They have strong digital infrastructure, widespread internet connectivity, and high rates of technology adoption among their populations. These factors create a conducive environment for digital trade to flourish. Additionally, both Korea and the EU possess strong comparative advantages in manufacturing industries, including sectors like electronics, automobiles, machinery, and pharmaceuticals, among others. The integration of digital technologies with traditional manufacturing processes is an important factor behind digital trade development, enabling the production and export of high-tech digital goods and also other services, thus challenging traditional regimes (Azmeh et al. 2020).

2. Methods and Material

This study was a single embedded case study of Korea and the EU. Case studies are popular for understanding single or multiple instances of a phenomenon in more depth (Yin 2017). This case study was established through four main sections. The first section estimated different components of digital trade between Korea and the EU. Drawing on data from sources such as UNCTAD, TiVA, and the Korean statistical service, it uncovered the imbalanced nature of these trade flows. The second section examined the digital partnership and the reasons for Korea and the EU to conclude it. It revealed that the current global environment, characterized by conflicts and disputes, encourages alliances in the digital space, and analyzed the limitations that hinder the progress of the digital partnerships. Section four discussed ways to enhance the impact of the partnership. The connected elements caused the emergence of a novel framework of theory development from a case study (Eisenhardt 1989).

3. Results

3.1. Trends in Digital Trade between Korea and the EU

The analysis of digital trade flows is complicated by the lack of comprehensive and comparable statistics in this field (López González et al. 2023). However, the Digital Economy Report 2019 (UNCTAD 2019)[2] offers a valuable framework for understanding the key components of digital trade. The report identified three interconnected layers of the digital economy to enable digital trading. According to the report, digital trade is enabled through core infrastructural components. These include the trade of semiconductors, computers, telecommunication devices, and digital infrastructure such as the Internet and fiber-optic cables. These infrastructure elements are essential for the digital trade of products and services to occur between Korea and the EU. Secondly, the report identified the digital and information technology sectors which produce key products and services relying on core digital technologies, such as digital platforms, mobile applications, and payment services. These soft resources operationalize and support the overall running digital ecosystem. Thirdly, the digitalization of important service sectors like finance, media, tourism, and transportation play a significant role in the broader scope of digital trade (UNCTAD 2019).

Based on these considerations and the levels of the digital ecosystem, it is possible to identify several indicators that provide insights into the state of digital trade between Korea and the EU. These indicators include trade in information and communication technology (ICT) goods, e-commerce conducted through online platforms, and trade in ICT services, financial services, and others. However, due to data availability, this section will focus on discussing the trade in ICT goods and e-commerce.

Korea and the EU share a vital economic partnership, with Korea being the EU's 9th largest export destination for goods, and the EU serving as Korea's 3rd largest export market. The EU–Korea Free Trade Agreement (FTA) has established a solid foundation for economic cooperation and has become a strategic pillar of their partnership over the years (Chung and Lee 2019). Both parties play significant roles in global digital trade in distinct ways. Korea is a major producer of ICT products and has a rapidly growing e-commerce market, which ranks as the 6th largest in the world. On the other hand, the EU is a strong regulatory power, spearheading forward-looking laws and mechanisms to ensure the safety of people's data online. These contrasting strengths enable both countries to complement each other in their biliteral trade.

Digitalized trade has significant potential in terms of both size and growth. Traditional trade between Korea and the EU has also experienced steady but slow growth since the implementation of the KOREU FTA in 2011 (Grübler and Reiter 2021; European Commission 2020). As per the UNCTAD data for the last 10 years, the total trade volume increased from USD 94.5 billion in 2011 to USD 130 billion in 2021, marking a 37% total or a 3.7% p.a. increase. The trade in ICT goods between Korea and the EU reached USD 9.8 billion in 2021, with Korea maintaining a substantial surplus, as its exports to the EU amounted to USD 7.1 billion, while imports reached USD 2.7 billion. In 2021, Korea ranked as the 7th largest supplier of ICT goods to the EU, following China, Vietnam, Taiwan, the USA, Malaysia, and Ireland (Figure 1).

The relatively low volume of Korea's ICT shipments to the EU may appear surprisingly small considering Korea's position as one of the world's top electronics producers. However, there is a caveat to national-level data, as they are based on the country-of-origin rule and do not account for the international nature of manufacturing. It is important to consider that a significant portion of trade in global value chains is managed by multinational corporations. Korea is home to several major ICT manufacturers who have sophisticated systems of production dispersed across various jurisdictions. Therefore, Korea's actual participation in the EU's imports of ICT products could be more significant than what is shown in the country-level data. In other words, Korean electronics producers may supply ICT goods to the EU from production units located in countries other than Korea. In this context, Vietnam deserves closer examination. This point is elaborated to understand Korean digital trade in the context of production transferring to Vietnam.

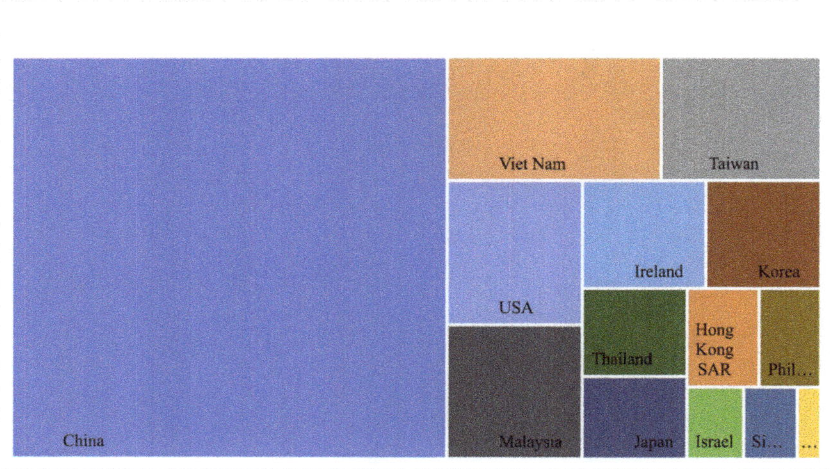

Figure 1. EU sources of ICT imports. Source: constructed by authors based on (UNCTADstat n.d.).

As Figure 2 shows, the decline in Korea's ICT exports to the EU in the late 2000s coincided with a steady increase in Vietnam's exports of ICT products to the EU. In 2012, there was a turning point, where Vietnam's ICT exports surpassed Korea's in terms of value. By 2020, Vietnam was shipping four times the value of ICT products to the EU compared to Korea.

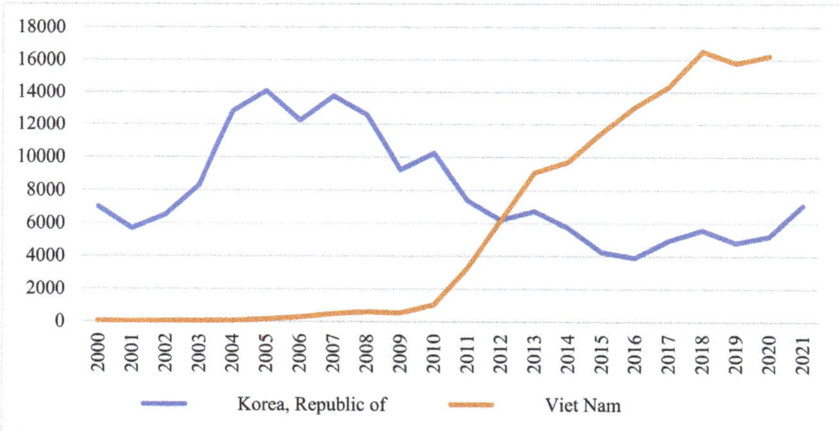

Figure 2. Korea and Vietnam ICT exports to the EU 2000–2021, USD million. Source: constructed by authors based on (UNCTADstat n.d.).

This change was not a coincidence. Korean electronics manufacturers began relocating from China after the Global Financial Crisis, primarily due to concerns over rising labor costs. Samsung Electronics, for instance, commenced production in Vietnam in 2009, and subsequently launched one of the largest manufacturing facilities in the country. Vietnam became a crucial manufacturing platform for a wide range of Samsung products, including smartphones, tablets, smartwatches, and basic mobile phones. As of June 2018, Samsung was producing 1 billion devices in Vietnam. The rise of Vietnam's electronics exports can be attributed to the influence of Korean conglomerates like Samsung.[3] The impact of Samsung on the Southeast Asian economy remains significant, with the company accounting for 25% of Vietnam's total exports and 80% of its electronics exports in 2020[4]. Other Korean producers, such as SK Hynix[5], have also established a presence in Vietnam and have the potential to export to the EU from there.

When considering this aspect of the global value chain in electronics, the actual volume of ICT goods shipped by Korean companies to the EU is considerably larger than what is reflected in macro-level statistical data at the national level. Consequently, Korea may rank as the 4th or even 3rd major source of ICT products for the EU, taking into account these supply chain dynamics.

The composition of Korea's ICT exports to the EU is heavily concentrated on electronic components, accounting for 60% of the total ICT shipment volume in 2021. The next most significant categories are computers and peripheral equipment (12.12%) and a miscellaneous category (12.26%). In relation to Vietnam, it is important to note that 92.5% of Vietnam's ICT exports to the EU in 2020 consisted of electronic components. These figures suggest that components produced by Korean manufacturers in Vietnam are being sent to assembly and manufacturing facilities located within the EU for the final stages of production, along with high numbers of assembled products. This hypothesis was supported by a recent study conducted by the Korean Institute of Economic Policy (KIEP). Their expert examined the impact of the KOREU FTA on Korea's exports to the EU and concluded that the FTA stimulated Korean exports to East European countries such as Hungary, Slovakia, and Poland, where Korean conglomerates have established factories for the European market.

In contrast, Korea's imports of ICT products from Europe have remained relatively unchanged over the past two decades (Figure 3). There was a slight increase in the imported value in 2021, but it is uncertain whether this indicates the start of an upward trend or not. The minimal change in import flows implies that, in real terms (adjusted for inflation), Korea's imports of ICT from the EU have stagnated.

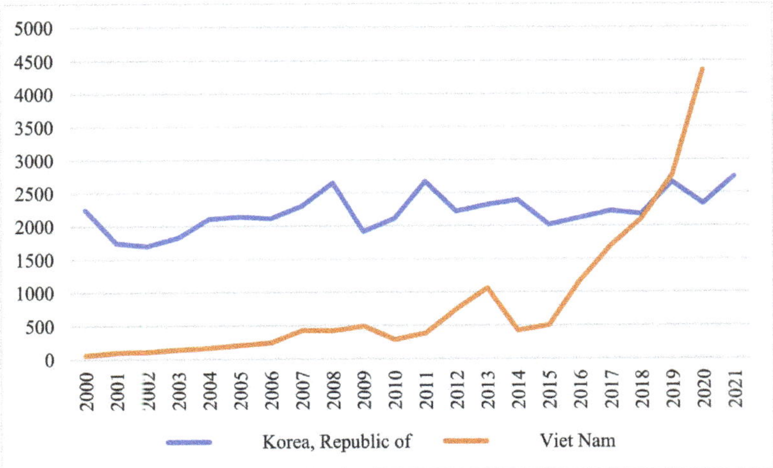

Figure 3. Korea and Vietnam's import of ICT from the EU. Source: constructed by authors based on (UNCTADstat n.d.).

Unsurprisingly, Vietnam has experienced a significant increase in its imports of ICT products from the EU, particularly during the period of 2015–2020 (Figure 3). However, available data do not allow us to determine whether this growth was partially driven by Korean companies. Vietnam does not provide detailed trade data, and Korean multinationals do not disclose their component sources, as they often follow a vertically integrated production approach. Nevertheless, it is plausible that the presence of Samsung has influenced ICT imports from other countries, including the EU. Local Vietnamese manufacturers may be attempting to enter the production sector, either as subcontractors for Samsung or in an effort to develop their own capabilities in this industry.

In the upcoming years, the significance of Vietnam within Samsung's value chain is expected to continue growing. Samsung is expanding its manufacturing of semiconductor parts in Vietnam and is currently constructing a research center in Hanoi.[6]

However, it is important to acknowledge that the growing relationship between Korean businesses and Vietnam may not necessarily result in a stronger trade relationship between Vietnam and the EU. Both Korea and Vietnam represent a small share of the EU's exports of ICT products. As illustrated in Figure 4, the majority of the EU's ICT exports in 2021 were directed towards China, the United States, Ireland, Singapore, Hong Kong, and Taiwan. These countries hold a more significant position as destinations for the EU's ICT exports.

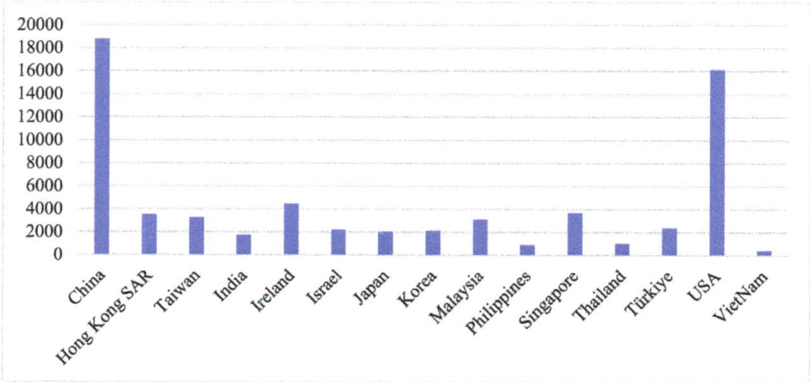

Figure 4. EU's major destinations of ICT exports. Source: constructed by authors based on (UNCTADstat n.d.).

3.2. State of e-Commerce/Online Trade in Goods

Online trade in goods between Korea and the EU has undergone significant growth with certain asymmetries. According to Korean sources, the estimated volume of online trade between the two regions has reached 850 million euros[7]. This represents a substantial increase of 6.4 times compared to 2014, when data collection began. From 2016 to 2019, the growth rates ranged from 30% to 36%. However, the COVID-19 pandemic had an impact, with growth rates falling to 15.7% in 2020, 8.2% in 2021, and declining to negative figures in 2022 at −0.02%. Nonetheless, as economies recover from the pandemic's adverse effects, there is a generally positive outlook for e-commerce.

The e-commerce trade flows between Korea and the EU exhibit an asymmetry, with more than 90% of the bilateral trade volume consisting of Korea's purchases from the EU. In 2022, Koreans purchased EUR 836.6 million worth of European goods through online platforms, while Korean sales amounted to a mere EUR 13.3 million. The COVID-19 pandemic appears to have impacted Korean sales to the EU more significantly than Korean purchases from the EU. In 2020, Korean sales were at EUR 30 million, which decreased to EUR 13.3 million in 2022. On the other hand, purchases increased from EUR 768.3 million to EUR 836.6 million. These differing dynamics may be explained by the varying income elasticities of the products being sold and purchased online.

According to the data presented in Table 1, clothing and fashion, as well as audiovisual equipment, account for 34.29% and 29.53% of Korean sales, respectively. In contrast, Korean purchases are predominantly focused on clothing and fashion, making up 63.38% of all online purchases in 2022. European clothing and fashion products typically belong to higher-priced categories, and demand for these products tends to occur among those with higher income elasticity and therefore higher expected earnings in Korea. The literature suggests that if elasticity is a factor, the goods are more likely to be luxury items (Tarantilis et al. 2015). Additionally, despite increasing prices, reports have indicated that there was strong demand for upscale European brands in Korea during the pandemic, driven by revenge consumption and consumer preferences.

Table 1. Structure of Korea–EU online trade by category in 2022.

	Korean Sales	Korean Purchases
Computers and periphery	17.02%	0.19%
Home appliances and electronics	0.06%	3.53%
Software	0.00%	0.06%
Books	5.01%	0.85%
Office appliances	0.30%	0.16%
Audio, visual equipment	29.53%	0.14%
Clothing and fashion	34.29%	63.38%
Sports and leisure	3.50%	1.43%
Cosmetics	6.63%	4.94%
Children's clothes	0.28%	0.56%
Food	0.08%	14.71%
Agricultural products	0.00%	0.00%
Lifestyle goods and goods for automobiles	0.29%	4.57%
Other	3.00%	5.49%

Source: Korea Statistical Information Service (2023). Retrieved from https://kosis.kr (accessed on 12 April 2023).

In 2022, Korean online sales to the EU accounted for approximately 1% of Korea's total online sales. Korea's imports from the EU represented 21% of all online imports by Korea during the same year. From Korea's perspective, this is an unbalanced structure of bilateral trade that contributes to the overall trade deficit in the country's trade with the EU. In 2021, the trade deficit stood at 2.5 billion USD.

Several observations regarding the state of Korea–EU digital trade can be made based on the discussion above:

- Trade volumes in major components of the digital trade between the partners are modest compared to the strategic level of cooperation.
- Korea's exports of ICT goods to the EU have maintained a substantial surplus, while imports have remained relatively unchanged. The actual volumes of ICT goods shipped by Korean companies to the EU may be larger than reflected in national-level data due to the international nature of manufacturing.
- Korean companies may supply ICT goods to the EU from their production units located in countries other than Korea, emphasizing the importance of considering supply chain dynamics.
- Trade volumes in ICT are much larger than volumes of e-commerce, although the latter has shown a rapid pace of expansion.
- E-commerce trade flows between Korea and the EU exhibit an asymmetry, with Korea's purchases from the EU dominating the bilateral trade volume. The COVID-19 pandemic had a more significant impact on Korean sales to the EU than Korean purchases from the EU.
- E-commerce imports from the EU are one of the contributors to Korea's total trade deficit with EU; this is an important issue for Korea, which for many decades has pursued a mercantilist trade policy. Potentially, this deficit may diminish the appetite, from Korea's side, to bring Korea–EU online trade to a new level if Korea does not see opportunities for counterbalance.

4. Digital Partnership between Korea and the EU: Common and Divergent Interests

Digital trade will play a crucial role in shaping the future of economic relations between the EU and Korea. This potential could, however, be constrained by externalities such as excessive taxation. Therefore, bilateral trade must be addressed strategically to avoid the impact of such externalities. If not addressed through strategic and purposeful actions, digital trade may fall behind other dimensions of Korea–EU cooperation. To foster digital trade, both parties should harness the potential of the recently launched Digital Partnership. This section provides an overview of the key points in this partnership, including the driving forces behind it and its hindering factors.

The Digital Partnership between Korea and the EU was officially established on 28 November 2022. This agreement serves as a framework to enhance bilateral cooperation on digital technology-related issues. According to a communique released by Korea's Ministry of Science and ICT, under the partnership, Korea and the EU plan to join efforts on 11 topics, which include the following: Collaborative Research, Semiconductors, High Performance Computing (HPC) & Quantum Technologies, Cybersecurity & Trust, Beyond 5G/6G, Skills, Mobility & Digital inclusion, Artificial Intelligence, Online & Digital Platform Cooperation, Data-Related Laws and Systems, Digital Identity & Trust Services, and Digital Trade.[8] Additionally, the partners have agreed to organize a ROK–EU forum for semiconductor researchers to facilitate regular discussions on the latest research trends and design, while also establishing mechanisms to address supply chain disruptions.

Several key factors are driving the collaboration between Korea and the EU in the digital realm. Firstly, the escalating conflict between the US and China is reshaping international trade and trade governance (Hopewell 2020). The disruption of technological supply chains, which will be hard to avoid (Witt 2020), could adversely affect other dependent actors, like Korea and the EU. Secondly, security concerns and safety issues in the largely unregulated digital space present serious challenges that demand joint efforts. Thirdly, the rapid pace and concentrated nature of digital technology development can lead to a significant accumulation of competitive advantage in the hands of a limited number of countries. Joint collaboration can ensure mutually beneficial sharing of technologies.

The outlined reasons highlight why Korea and the EU are natural partners for cooperation, as both parties would bear substantial costs in the event of a US–China conflict[9]. Moreover, the proliferation of digital technology creates new vulnerabilities when data is misused, making it imperative for partners to join forces in a collective effort. Additionally, the extent to which the US is willing to share advanced technologies with its allies remains uncertain. Thus, it is crucial for Korea and the EU to take necessary action and prepare for potential risks to avoid growing dependency and insecurity.

In the current multipolar world order, alliances and partnerships are vital for policymaking, geopolitical longevity, and maintaining the balance of power in the digital realm. While the EU possesses strong credibility in enforcing rules beyond its borders, it requires support from other countries to establish global standards in emerging digital domains (Cervi 2022; Bradford 2015). Korea is a partner that shares many of the EU's concerns.

The rapid digitalization of international trade and its benefits has incentivized closer cooperation between the EU and Korea, prompting the formation of a partnership. Many believe that digitalizing trade will enhance efficiency, productivity, and inclusivity by providing more opportunities for small businesses to engage in international trade and streamline trade processes by reducing paperwork and disseminating technologies.

Considering the significance of issues around digital trade, it is surprising that the agreement's text only touches briefly on the topic of digital trade itself. Digital trade is explicitly mentioned when referring to paperless trading, data flow, and online consumer protection. However, the overall framing remains vague, calling for "deeper discussions" on the matter, and the need for a "set of digital trade principles."[10]

The limited treatment of digital trade in the Korea–EU Digital Partnership contrasts with the treatment of digital trade in cooperation with other countries. For example, the EU's approach to partnerships with India and the US includes bilateral councils on trade and digital technologies[11], with the purpose of establishing a direct link between the development of relevant technologies and their practical application. Korea has taken a proactive approach to advancing digital trade at the regional level[12]. A good example of such efforts is the RCEP (Regional Comprehensive Economic Partnership), which includes a chapter on digital trade. Additionally, Korea is active in promoting digital trade rules as part of the global digital agenda. The cautious approach to digital trade that both Korea and the EU have taken in the bilateral digital partnership might be a sign of divergent views on the matter.

One Partnership, Different Dreams?

Within the realm of digital cooperation, the partnership between Korea and the EU showcases a blend of collaborative and competitive dynamics. Despite shared interests in the digital agenda, each side is propelled by their respective national priorities, a classic force behind outward policy actions according to realism theory. It is, however, not unusual that major economies such as the US and China, despite having political differences, realize the highest volume of trade (Gao 2018). Various factors influence competitiveness, including the pursuit of European digital autonomy, Korea's strategy to assert a stronger position as a regional and global rule maker, the US's active engagement with Korea on digital matters, and intra-regional integration.

The concept of European digital autonomy and sovereignty has gained significant prominence within the EU's digital strategy (Broeders et al. 2023), aligning with its broader pursuit of strategic autonomy (Tocci 2021). Initially, disagreement with the US on China, which was once regarded as a potential 5G technology provider for the European market, spurred the EU to actively seek collaborations with alternative partners, including Korea. Disruptions in semiconductor supplies during the COVID-19 lockdowns exposed the vulnerability and excessive reliance of the EU on a limited number of sources for digital technologies. Consequently, efforts to fortify supply chain security have been reinvigorated and intensified by the EU. As part of this strategy, the EU aims to capture a minimum of 20% of global chip production by 2030, up from their current 10%.[13]

Korea, a major producer of ICT technologies, places less emphasis on digital sovereignty and self-sufficiency. Instead, its primary focus lies in preserving and expanding its competitive advantage in digital technology production. While the goals of Korea and the EU may not necessarily contradict each other, there may be limitations to the extent of cooperation they are willing to pursue in sharing information on key technology developments. Large Korean companies, chaebols, have pursued a strategy of techno-nationalism, which appreciates S&T in terms of national interests (Hee-Je Bak 2014; H.-S. Kim et al. 2010) and tries trying to maintain maximum control over production processes to avoid technology leaks.

One of Korea's main motivations for entering into a digital partnership with the EU was to elevate its position as a rule-maker and transform it into a 'leading country in the digital era, rather than staying stagnant as a fast-follower' (Chennery 2023). President Yoon's own words were: 'to ensure the legitimacy and sustainability of the digital order, it is necessary to guarantee fair opportunities through digital rights'.[14] The EU is widely recognized as a powerhouse in generating various rules and integrating them into international norms, and the Digital Partnership with the EU will help Korea to increase its credibility as a provider of norms for the digital age. To achieve this goal, Korea must collaborate with the EU, a recognized leader in international rulemaking, to enhance the accountability, ethics, and social value of its initiatives (Bennett and Raab 2020).

The EU is not the sole economy seeking cooperation with Korea in the realm of digital technologies. The United States is also actively pursuing multifaceted engagement with Korea in the digital sector. The US has adopted an assertive approach by leveraging its strategic alliance with Korea, Japan, and Taiwan in the Chip4 Alliance (Lee 2022). Additionally, Korea's reliance on US manufacturing technology for semiconductor development is being exploited to limit exports to China and pivot production to the US.

While the US is interested in bringing the EU onboard with its plan to restrict the spread of high-end technologies to non-alliance countries, its willingness to share the full benefits with the EU remains questionable. The US is utilizing all available tools at its disposal, including granting more visas and opportunities to live and work in the US, to attract Korean specialists. If the Korea–EU digital partnership fails to provide clearly defined benefits, its potential impact may be limited to the domains of security and privacy.

Another factor that will shape whether the Korea–EU digital partnership is successful is intra-regional integration. Asia, specifically the Asia-Pacific region, remains a central priority for Korea's economic strategy. Countries other than China are also projected to become major consumers of Korean goods and are viewed as alternatives to China for manufacturing platforms. Consequently, Korea may have a reduced appetite for deepening digital cooperation with the EU until it has solidified its position within the region. On the other hand, the EU also has its own commercial interests and is aiming to enhance its competitive advantages in the Asia-Pacific region. Thus, there may come a point in the future where the interests of the EU and Korea in the Asian theater could potentially conflict with each other.

5. The Way Forward for the Korea–EU Digital Partnership

To enhance the impact of the Korea–EU digital partnership and promote digital trade, there are several aspects that need to be taken into consideration. The development of digital trade relies on the balanced progress of various elements (Table 2), including connectivity, payments, digital skills, logistics, and digital policy and regulation. Thus far, the focus of the digital partnership has primarily been on digital policy and regulation. While regulatory harmonization is crucial for establishing a level playing field, it is equally important to strengthen other elements to maximize the outcomes of policy measures.

Table 2. Main pillars of the digital economy.

Name of Pillar	Details
Connectivity	Affordable, reliable, and high-quality broadband internet access
Payment infrastructure	Safe and secure digital payment services that facilitate electronic transactions both domestically and overseas
Digital skills	Basic digital and data literacy skills, specialized skills to benefit from digital innovation
Logistics	E-commerce/digital trade is particularly dependent on well-regulated, widely available, and cost-effective logistics services, given high demand for delivery of goods
Digital policy and regulation	Policies cover a wide range of areas, from data privacy and cybersecurity to consumer protection. Regional coordination of such policies is desirable

Source: created by authors.

Connectivity, synergies in payment systems, and efficient logistics are all significant factors that contribute to the success of digital partnerships (Burri and Polanco 2020; Ferracane et al. 2018). Tuning these elements will play a vital role in ensuring seamless integration and cooperation between Korea and the EU. By prioritizing the development and improvement of these aspects, the digital partnership will be able to operate more effectively and yield greater benefits for both parties involved.

The active involvement of businesses is crucial for advancing the Korea–EU digital partnership. Without the participation of businesses, the partnership's impact will be limited. To ensure business engagement, it is necessary to provide tangible and significant benefits, as well as establish transparent mechanisms for administering these benefits. Linking the partnership to the EU's Chip act would further amplify its impact.

The EU needs to offer specific benefits that incentivize Korean companies to engage in collaborative activities. Presently, Korean businesses are primarily focused on strengthening their presence in countries such as Slovakia, Poland, and Hungary. The recent visit of the first deputy minister for industry to Hungary, leading a large delegation of businesses, indicated Seoul's keen interest in advancing bilateral ties in trade and investment. This suggests that Korea prefers nonbinding commitments.

The digital partnership should be open to the participation of other interested countries. Similar to the free and open Indo-Pacific strategy in geopolitics, the EU and Korea could promote an open and secure digital economy in the Indo-Pacific region, engaging with other significant players such as Vietnam, Thailand, Malaysia, and Indonesia. This approach would allow for capitalizing on existing geopolitical realities and align the changing economic landscape with geopolitical shifts. Facilitating regional harmonization of regulations in the early stages of digital trade development will create more opportunities to enhance efficiency and reduce costs. Any future adjustments would require additional resources and result in lost time.

Korea and the EU should collaborate actively to advance the digital economy and digital trade in Southeast Asia. By joining forces, they could work towards developing necessary infrastructure, introducing consumer protection policies, reducing barriers, and harmonizing regulations. This collaborative approach will help prevent unnecessary competition and resource wastage between the two entities.

The EU should not solely rely on its regulatory power when engaging with South Korea. It needs guiding principles that go beyond traditional patterns of bilateral cooperation. There is significant potential in establishing mechanisms to identify investment opportunities for European stakeholders in South Korea's startup ecosystem. This could contribute to overcoming the dominance of chaebol-controlled financial markets in the country. European agencies could collaborate with the Korea Institute of Startup and Entrepreneurship Development and the ROK Ministry of SMEs and Startups to design investment programs tailored to the Korean market. This would provide an advantage to the EU in terms of lower production costs and scale efficiency, as the Korean market has achieved sufficient economies of scale.

Another initiative that could benefit the partnership would be to give young Koreans opportunities to work in the European technology sector. However, there would be competition with the US, which is looking at attracting Korean talent.

6. Conclusions

This paper has discussed issues of digital partnership between Korea and the EU and the state of digital trade as an important element of this partnership. It has highlighted that both Korea and the EU have rationales to cooperate with each other. It also draws attention to the fact the current state of digital trade is small and unbalanced, which is a sign of existing divergence between core national priorities within the partnership. If this divergence remains unaddressed, it will affect the outcomes of the partnership. We have suggested areas that could be considered to maximize the impact of cooperation. We argued that the partnership should engage other actors (like businesses) through mechanisms that would outline benefits from closer cooperation in a clearer way. Bringing in other regional players that are important for the smooth operation of value chains will enhance the partnership's effectiveness. Synchronization of regulation at an early stage will optimize costs in the longer term, allowing for a more productive multi-level partnership. Mechanisms that go beyond traditional bilateral policy toolkits are needed for the new digital era. In future, the Korean–EU case could be replicated to generalize the findings into other jurisdictions.

Author Contributions: Conceptualization—I.K.; methodology—I.K., A.H.; validation—A.H.; investigation—A.H.; resources—I.K.; writing—original draft preparation I.K.; writing—review and editing A.H.; visualization I.K.; project administration—A.H. All authors have read and agreed to the published version of the manuscript.

Funding: Irina Korgun received Funding from The Korea Foundation's Fellowship For Field Research.

Informed Consent Statement: Informed consent was obtained from all subjects involved in the study.

Data Availability Statement: Data for this research were sources from official statistics portals, data sources are indicated under graphic materials.

Conflicts of Interest: The authors declare no conflict of interest.

Notes

1 OECD. Official web-site. The impact of digitalisation on trade. https://www.oecd.org/trade/topics/digital-trade/ (accessed on 10 April 2023).

2 Viettonkin Consulting (2022). The effect Samsung has on the economy of Vietnam. https://www.viettonkinconsulting.com/general/the-effect-samsung-has-on-the-economy-of-vietnam/ (accessed on 18 May 2023).

3 Contribution from Samsung to the economy is still "unknown", or in other words, the regulatory agencies are not able to calculate the contribution. Official information on the financial situation is published by Samsung Vietnam on its website, citing the Financial Statements of the parent corporation in South Korea, and stating that the first three quarters of 2019 revenue and operating profit reached USD 51–53 billion and USD 6.4–6.6 billion, respectively. There are no separate financial statements for the Vietnam market, which is Samsung's largest global production base. //Vietnam Credit (2020). Samsung: Driver of Vietnam's Economic Growth? Retrieved from https://vietnamcredit.com.vn/news/samsung-driver-of-vietnams-economic-growth_13481 (accessed on 18 May 2023); Business Korea (2019). Samsung Electronics Accounts for 28% of Vietnam's GDP. Retrieved from http://www.businesskorea.co.kr/news/articleView.html?idxno=29966 (accessed on 18 May 2023).

4 Korea IT News (2022). Hana Micron, to hire 3000 employees at a new plant in Vietnam… Improving OSAT business. Retrieved from https://english.etnews.com/20220525200003 (accessed on 18 May 2023).

5 The electronics giant also has six plants in the country and is building a new research and development center in the capital Hanoi.//Vietnam Briefing (2022). Vietnam's Semiconductor Industry: Samsung Makes Further Inroads. Retrieved from https://www.vietnam-briefing.com/news/vietnams-semiconductor-industry-samsung-makes-further-inroads.html/ (accessed on 18 May 2023).

6 Korea Statistical Information Service (2023). Retrieved from https://kosis.kr/ (accessed on 12 April 2023).

7 Official web-site of the Korea Ministry of Science and ICT (2023). Retrieved from https://www.msit.go.kr (accessed on 18 April 2023).

8 CEIAS Insights (2022). Korea-Europe relations: How to reach the full potential of the strategic partnership? Retrieved from https://ceias.eu/korea-europe-relations-how-to-reach-the-full-potential-of-the-strategic-partnership/ (accessed on 28 April 2023)

9 Text of 'ROK-EU Digital Partnership'. Retrieved from https://www.msit.go.kr (accessed: 21 April 2023).

10 EU-India: new Trade and Technology Council to lead on digital transformation, green technologies and trade. Retrieved from https://ec.europa.eu/commission/presscorner/detail/en/IP_23_596 (accessed on 18 May 2023); EU-US Trade and Technology Council. Retrieved from https://commission.europa.eu/strategy-and-policy/priorities-2019-2024/stronger-europe-world/eu-us-trade-and-technology-council_en (accessed on 12 June 2023).

11 Korea Herald (2023). South Korea joins world's 1st digital trade pact to boost exchange. June 9. Retrieved from https://www.koreaherald.com/view.php?ud=20230609000457 (accessed on 15 June 2023).

12 Delotte (2022). A new dawn for European chips. Retrieved from https://www2.deloitte.com/uk/en/insights/industry/technology/semiconductor-chip-shortage-supply-chain.html (accessed on 8 May 2023).

13 Aju Daily (2023). S. Korea to set new standards and guidelines on copyrights of AI-generated content. Retrieved from https://www.ajudaily.com/view/20230503104752108 (accessed on 1 June 2023).

14 Nikkei (2023). U.S. urges Seoul not to fill China gaps if Beijing bans Micron chips. April 24. Retrieved from https://asia.nikkei.com/Business/Tech/Semiconductors/U.S.-urges-Seoul-not-to-fill-China-gaps-if-Beijing-bans-Micron-chips (accessed on 2 May 2023).

References

Azmeh, Shamel, Christopher Foster, and Jaime Echavarri. 2020. The international trade regime and the quest for free digital trade. *International Studies Review* 22: 671–92. [CrossRef]

Bak, Hee-Je. 2014. The Politics of Technoscience in Korea: From State Policy to Social Movement. *East Asian Science, Technology and Society: An International Journal* 8: 159–74. [CrossRef]

Bennett, Colin J., and Charles D. Raab. 2020. Revisiting the governance of privacy: Contemporary policy instruments in global perspective. *Regulation & Governance* 14: 447–64. [CrossRef]

Bradford, Anu. 2015. Exporting standards: The externalization of the EU's regulatory power via markets. *International Review of Law and Economics* 42: 158–73. [CrossRef]

Broeders, Dennis, Fabio Cristiano, and Monica Kaminska. 2023. In Search of Digital Sovereignty and Strategic Autonomy: Normative Power Europe to the Test of Its Geopolitical Ambitions. *JCMS: Journal of Common Market Studies* 61: 1261–80. [CrossRef]

Burri, Mirs, and Rodrigo Polanco. 2020. Digital Trade Provisions in Preferential Trade Agreements: Introducing a New Dataset. *Journal of International Economic Law* 23: 187–220. [CrossRef]

Cervi, Giullio Vittorio. 2022. Why and How Does the EU Rule Global Digital Policy: An Empirical Analysis of EU Regulatory Influence in Data Protection Laws. *DISO* 1: 18. [CrossRef]

Chennery, Philip. 2023. The Missing Piece of the EU-ROK Digital Partnership: Development Cooperation in ASEAN. *EIAS*. March 31. Available online: https://eias.org/policy-briefs/the-missing-piece-of-the-eu-rok-digital-partnership-development-cooperation-in-asean/ (accessed on 5 May 2023).

Chung, Sae Wong, and Jae-Sung Lee. 2019. Building the pillars of the EU-South Korea strategic partnership. *Asia Europe Journal* 17: 327–40. [CrossRef]

Eisenhardt, Kathleen M. 1989. Building Theories from Case Study Research. *Academy of Management Review* 14: 532–50. [CrossRef]

European Commission, Directorate-General for Trade. 2020. Evaluation of the Implementation of the Free Trade Agreement between the EU and Its Member States and the Republic of Korea—Final Report, Publications Office. Available online: https://data.europa.eu/doi/10.2781/897452 (accessed on 20 April 2023).

Fayyaz, Saeed. 2019. A review on measuring digital trade & e-commerce as new economic statistics products. *Statistika* 99: 57–68.

Ferracane, Martina Francesca, Hosuk Lee-Makiyama, and Erik van der Marel. 2018. Digital Trade Restrictiveness Index. *European Center for International Political Economy, April.* Available online: https://ecipe.org/wp-content/uploads/2018/05/DTRI_FINAL.pdf (accessed on 20 April 2023).

Gao, Henry. 2018. Digital or trade? The contrasting approaches of China and US to digital trade. *Journal of International Economic Law* 21: 297–321. [CrossRef]

Grübler, Julia, and Oliver Reiter. 2021. Non-tariff trade policy in the context of deep trade integration: An ex-post gravity model application to the EU-South Korea agreement. *East Asian Economic Review* 25: 33–71. [CrossRef]

Hopewell, K. 2020. *Clash of Powers: US-China Rivalry in Global Trade Governance.* Cambridge: Cambridge University Press. [CrossRef]

Jaax, Alexander, Sébastien Miroudot, and Elisabeth van Lieshout. 2023. *Deglobalisation? The Reorganisation of Global Value Chains in a Changing World.* OECD Trade Policy Papers. No. 272. Paris: OECD Publishing. [CrossRef]

Kim, Hwan-Suk, Dong Kwang Kim, Hye-Sun Cho, Jin-hee Park, and Hee-Je Bak. 2010. *Hangook-eui gwahakja-sa-hoe: Yuksa, Goojo, Sahoe-hwa 한국의 과학자사회: 역사, 구조, 사회화 (Korean Scientific Community: History, Structure, and Socialization).* Seoul: KungRee.

Lee, Jeung-Eun. 2022. Why South Korea Needs to Be a Global Player. *Carnegie Endowment.* Available online: https://carnegieendowment.org/2022/11/22/why-south-korea-needs-to-be-global-player-pub-88421 (accessed on 10 June 2023).

López González, Javier, and Janos Ferencz. 2018. *Digital Trade and Market Openness.* OECD Trade Policy Papers. No. 217. Paris: OECD Publishing. [CrossRef]

López González, Javier, and Marie-Agnes Jouanjean. 2017. Digital Trade: Developing a Framework for Analysis. OECD Trade Policy Papers, 205, 24. Available online: https://ideas.repec.org/p/oec/traaab/205-en.html (accessed on 12 April 2023).

López González, Javier, Silvia Sorescu, and Pinar Kaynak. 2023. *Of Bytes and Trade: Quantifying the Impact of Digitalisation on Trade.* OECD Trade Policy Papers. No. 273. Paris: OECD Publishing. [CrossRef]

Lund, Susan, and James Manyika. 2016. How Digital Trade Is Transforming Globalisation. International Centre for Trade and Sustainable Development. Available online: www.ictsd.org (accessed on 13 April 2023).

Meltzer, Joshua P. 2019. Governing Digital Trade. *World Trade Review* 18: S23–S48. [CrossRef]

Rachel, F. Fefer, Shayerah I. Akhtar, and Michael D. Sutherland. 2021. Digital Trade and U.S. Trade Policy. *Congressional Research Service*, 1–53. Available online: https://crsreports.congress.gov (accessed on 22 April 2023).

Tarantilis, Filippos, Kostas Athanasakis, Dimitris Zavras, Athanassios Vozikis, and Ioannis Kyriopoulos. 2015. Estimates of price and income elasticity in Greece. Greek debt crisis transforming cigarettes into a luxury good: An econometric approach. *BMJ Open* 5: e004748. [CrossRef] [PubMed]

Tocci, Nathalie. 2021. European Strategic Autonomy: What It Is, Why We Need It, How to Achieve It. Istituto Affari Internazionali Papers and Articles. Available online: https://www.iai.it/en/pubblicazioni/european-strategic-autonomy-what-it-why-we-need-it-how-achieve-it (accessed on 18 May 2023).

UNCTAD. 2019. *Digital Economy Report 2019: Value Creation and Capture: Implications for Developing Countries.* Geneva: United Nations, p. 172. Available online: https://unctad.org/publication/digital-economy-report-2019 (accessed on 20 April 2023).

UNCTADstat. n.d. Statistical Platform of UNCTAD. Available online: https://unctadstat.unctad.org/EN/ (accessed on 15 April 2023).

Witt, Michael A. 2020. Prepare for the U.S. and China to Decouple. Harvard Business Review. Available online: https://hbr.org/2020/06/prepare-for-the-u-s-and-china-to-decouple (accessed on 18 April 2023).

WTO. 2018. World Trade Report 2018. The Future of World Trade: How Digital Technologies Are Transforming Global Commerce. Available online: https://www.wto.org/english/res_e/publications_e/world_trade_report18_e.pdf (accessed on 20 April 2023).
Yin, Robert K. 2017. *Case Study Research and Applications: Design and Methods*, 6th ed. Thousand Oaks: SAGE Publications, Inc. 352p.

Disclaimer/Publisher's Note: The statements, opinions and data contained in all publications are solely those of the individual author(s) and contributor(s) and not of MDPI and/or the editor(s). MDPI and/or the editor(s) disclaim responsibility for any injury to people or property resulting from any ideas, methods, instructions or products referred to in the content.

economies

MDPI

Article

Impact of Digitalization of Sales on the Profitability of the Restaurant Industry during COVID-19

Mónica González Morales * and José Antonio Cavero Rubio

Department of Economics and Financial Studies, Miguel Hernandez University, 03202 Elche, Spain; cavero@umh.es
* Correspondence: monica.gonzalezm@umh.es

Abstract: The COVID-19 pandemic had a severe impact on the restaurant industry. Temporary shutdowns and seating capacity restrictions led to a sharp drop in sales. In this scenario, digitalization emerged as a crucial strategy for business survival, offering opportunities to increase restaurants' competitiveness and revenues. This study examines the financial profitability of restaurants during 2020, comparing establishments with digital sales tools to those without. Multiple linear regression results indicate that liquidity, sales growth, restaurant size, and having a website directly influenced profitability. In addition, restaurants with their own online ordering and home delivery services or associated with delivery platforms experienced lower profitability losses. These findings contribute to our understanding of the role of digitalization in the restaurant sector during the pandemic, providing valuable practical and theoretical implications for the industry in similar contexts.

Keywords: restaurant sector; digitalization; home delivery; profitability

1. Introduction

The COVID-19 pandemic had a profound economic impact on the majority of the production sectors, including the food service industry, which has a substantial influence on the Gross Domestic Product (GDP). The measures enforced by countries to control the spread of the pandemic limited companies' activity and led to serious financial imbalances, even undermining the viability of many of them (Kim et al. 2020; Hu and Zhang 2021). Restaurants, classified as non-essential establishments with high social interaction, faced operational challenges in 2020, having to shut down and reduce seating capacity. Changes in consumer habits, driven by concerns about contagion risks, led to a decline in eating out (Liu and Kim 2021). Globally, the number of consumers who chose the traditional option of eating at a restaurant decreased by 30% globally between February 2019 and 2022 (Statista 2022a).

To survive the unprecedented health and economic crisis caused by COVID-19, businesses needed to embrace digitalization. Innovations and digital tools became crucial in developing competitive advantages that ensure profitability and resilience in the face of market turmoil (Schwertner 2017; Bouwman et al. 2018). Electronic commerce emerged as a leading trend, allowing companies to connect with consumers while ensuring social distancing and compliance with pandemic regulations (Dannenberg et al. 2020). Establishing an online sales channel became a vital tool for businesses to withstand the crisis and its economic impact (Kim et al. 2020; Türkes et al. 2021).

In this regard, the global market for restaurant online ordering and home delivery services experienced significant qualitative growth in 2020. Turnover increased from USD 157.34 billion in 2019 to USD 232.33 billion in 2020, with an annual growth rate of 26.45% in 2021 (Statista 2023). It was estimated that in 2022, global revenue from online sales for the restaurant industry would reach USD 325.44 billion and will continue growing at an annual rate of 6.71%, forecasting a turnover of USD 450.30 billion in 2027 (Statista 2023). In Spain, this industry witnessed remarkable sales growth between 2015 and 2018, with revenue exceeding 420 million euros in 2019. During the pandemic in 2020, revenue surpassed 1018.92 million euros, and in the first three quarters of 2022 alone, restaurant online sales generated revenue of 1267.61 million euros (Statista 2022b).

Beyond the impact that the pandemic has had on the market growth of online orders and home delivery, the digitalization of sales channels presents restaurant businesses with opportunities to expand their competitive advantages (Ma et al. 2021). This technology has been shown to increase companies' productivity, minimize errors, reduce costs (Kimes 2011; See-Kwong et al. 2017; Niu et al. 2021; Türkes et al. 2021), improve customers' user experience (Gavilán et al. 2021), and foster customer loyalty (Kim et al. 2019).

However, while there is consensus that online sales should be included in a comprehensive restaurant offering to ensure continuity and growth, companies must address several issues to maximize the usefulness of this sales channel (Liu and Kim 2021). Factors such as increased packaging and transport costs, delivery platform commissions, delivery errors, and the substitution effect of traditional sales can negatively impact business earnings and profitability (Collison 2020; Ma et al. 2021; Chen et al. 2022). The aim of this study is to contribute to the understanding of how the digitalization of the sales channel has affected the financial performance of businesses in the restaurant sector in the context of the COVID-19 pandemic. For this purpose, this study analyses the financial performance of restaurant companies during the challenging year of 2020, distinguishing between those with digital sales tools and those without. Specifically, three categories are established: having a website, minimal digitalization requirement; having an online ordering system and own home delivery services; and having an online ordering system and home delivery services through any of the delivery platforms.

The case study focuses on restaurant establishments in the Valencian Community, one of Spain's territorial divisions. Spain was chosen due to its high tourism rates, ranking as the second most visited country by international tourists in 2019 (World Tourism Organization 2020). The restaurant sector contributes significantly to the national GDP, representing around 5.5% until 2020 (Statista 2023). Spain was also one of the European states most affected by the pandemic and the strict measures enforced by the authorities had a strong impact on restaurant establishments. The Valencian Community, known for its tourism activity, relies on the restaurant sector as a significant contributor to its economy, with tourism representing 15.7% of the region's GDP in 2019, and the restaurant industry accounting for more than 6% (Hostelería de España 2021). In 2020, it had more than 30,000 establishments (bars and restaurants), positioning itself as the third Spanish region with the most dining venues (Hostelería de España 2021). However, it is important to note that, during 2020, due to the COVID-19 pandemic, tourist activities plummeted dramatically in most destinations, including the Valencian Community. During this period, international tourism in the region experienced a steep year-on-year decline of 73.1%, and domestic tourism fell by 51.6%. However, internal tourism within the Community saw a much more moderate reduction of 26.6% (Exceltur 2021). Therefore, in the context of our research, local residents and proximity tourism played a crucial role in sustaining and stimulating the restaurant industry in 2020 (IvieLAB 2021).

To verify the relationship between companies' financial performance and the digitalization of sales channels, a multiple linear regression is performed where the dependent variable is Return on Assets (ROA). The results show that liquidity, sales variance, restaurant size and having a website had a direct and positive impact on restaurants' profitability. Similarly, restaurants with their own online ordering and home delivery services or through delivery platforms presented a lower loss in profitability.

2. Review of the Literature and Hypotheses

2.1. Digitalization and Financial Performance

Digital transformation is a global trend that is spreading throughout all economic sectors (Zhai et al. 2022). By implementing technology in the value creation processes, companies are trying to adapt to the changes and impacts taking place in the business environment (Vial 2019). By doing so, they seek to maintain their competitive advantages or to develop new advantages that allow them to set themselves apart from their competitors (Schwertner 2017; Bouwman et al. 2018) and to guarantee the continuity of their business (Türkes et al. 2021). This transformation is intrinsically linked to dynamic capability theory, which argues that organisations that are able to identify and adjust their capabilities to changing environments are more likely to succeed (Teece et al. 1997).

From an economic perspective, different studies agree that digital transformation contributes to improving companies' profitability. In this sense, based on an analysis of business services, Ribeiro-Navarrete et al. (2021) conclude that the business use of social networks and training in digital tools improve the profitability of organizations. Fernández-Portillo et al. (2022) analysed a sample of Spanish companies and found that there is a direct and positive relation between a company's digitalization and its financial performance, with adequate innovation management acting as moderating variable. The results of the studies by Peng and Tao (2022) and Zhai et al. (2022), whose studies are based on a sample of listed Chinese companies, are in the same line. These authors determined that digital transformation directly and indirectly improves business performance: directly, because it increases return on assets and return on equity; and indirectly, because it reduces costs, increases operation efficiency, and contributes to the success of innovation.

Although it is one of the sectors most lagging behind (Tan and Netessine 2019), the restaurant sector is also immersed in the digital transformation of all its business processes (Collins et al. 2017). Digital tools provide support to the internal processes of restaurant businesses linked to the so called back of house activities (BOH), such as logistical management, human resources, and the finance/accounting area, and the external processes linked to front of house activities (FOH), which involve customer relations (Alt 2021).

FOH digitalization processes, especially digital marketing and online ordering and home delivery services, can have a positive impact on restaurants' profitability. The compilation and analysis of client data and their ordering habits can contribute to marketing strategies and together with home delivery services offer a new business opportunity, additional revenue and a stronger financial performance (Türkes et al. 2021). In addition, as described in the literature, if the digital tools used to provide these services are well implemented and integrated into a company's operations, they also offer other numerous benefits (Kimes 2008). They can attract new buyers, increase business efficiency, reduce mistakes in orders and improve customer relations management and profitability (Kimes 2011; See-Kwong et al. 2017; Niu et al. 2021; Türkes et al. 2021). In addition, these tools contribute to enhancing customer experience because customers benefit from the ease and convenience of online ordering and home delivery services, which contributes to an increase in their satisfaction and loyalty (Kimes 2011; Gavilán et al. 2021).

Nevertheless, these types of services also present some challenges. They could simply result in the cannibalization of traditional sales rather than an increase in demand. Customers could substitute physical purchases for online shopping without there being an increase in either sales or financial performance (Collison 2020; Chen et al. 2022). Likewise, the profit margins and profitability of companies could decrease due to higher costs involved in an online ordering system and home delivery (Kimes 2011; Chen et al. 2022; Niu et al. 2021). Incremental costs occur, although with differences, whether a restaurant invests in its own website, fleet of vehicles and delivery staff or whether it must pay commission to delivery platforms. Another risk, as See-Kwong et al. (2017) point out, is that restaurants lose control of the food once handed over to the delivery person and the desired level of quality could be compromised, which could consequently affect customer satisfaction, sales and profitability.

Therefore, although different empirical studies show a positive relationship between online ordering technologies and the sales growth of restaurants (Liu and Kim 2021; Tan and Netessine 2019), the truth is that this relationship is not always so evident and neither is it clear if it directly relates to a higher profitability for companies. The relationship between the digitalization of restaurant sales channels and their financial performance is an aspect that has not been studied in depth. One study of note, by Collison (2020), analyses a sample of visa transactions made in the United States between card owners and restaurants with home delivery services. Although the study data reveals an increase in the revenue of restaurants that offer these services, it also reflects lower profitability. For their part, Van Veldhoven et al. (2021) analyse the financial performance of a sample of Belgians who offer online ordering through an external platform. They determine that restaurants' liquidity increases but there is no significant evidence that profitability and solvency also improve. The theoretical model by Ma et al. (2021) determines that although in practice the introduction of online ordering and home delivery can initially increase sales and revenue there are other factors, such as the cannibalization of sales and the restaurants' capacity to meet the demand from all the distribution channels, that influence the individual profitability of each establishment, making it difficult to determine their effect on economic and financial indicators.

2.2. Digitalization of the Restaurant Industry during COVID-19 and Financial Performance

During the most restrictive stage of the pandemic, providing online access for clients to place their orders and collect their food from the premises or by home delivery was crucial for the sustainability of many businesses. In the digital era, not being on the internet can mean a company does not exist for certain clients or users and consequently a loss of potential revenue and profitability. In this regard, the study by Han et al. (2023) based on the theory of customer acquisition marketing and the theory of uses and gratification, shows that restaurant revenues increase as their digital visibility increases. In the context of the pandemic, Brewer and Sebby (2021) also found that restaurant consumers' purchase intentions were positively influenced by the visual presentation of menus on websites.

Corporate websites are a basic tool in the digitalization process of companies and fundamental for digital communication (García-García et al. 2021). As Saleem et al. (2022) concluded in their research, a quality corporate website with clear, concise, engaging and relevant content for the audience positively influences consumers' purchasing decisions and consequently benefits the financial performance of the business. This digital tool enables customers to find out about the company, its products and services, production processes and any information that it is interested in making public (Lowry et al. 2014). It also makes it easier for customers to communicate with the company, and they can make suggestions or comments that could be useful for improving organizational performance. Websites are also a very valuable information channel for conducting personalized marketing actions (Kimes 2011; Safari et al. 2015), which, as a result of their impact on client satisfaction and loyalty, can influence restaurants' profitability (Kim et al. 2019). Singh et al. (2022) empirically tested the effect of using various digital marketing tools in the restaurant sector and found that they have a positive relationship with the competitiveness of businesses. Therefore, in light of the previous literature, the following hypothesis is proposed:

Hypothesis 1. *Corporate websites positively influenced the financial performance of restaurants during COVID-19.*

As well as having a corporate website, online ordering and home delivery services have also established themselves as effective tools to reach a larger number of consumers in a cost-effective way (Ray et al. 2019), and they were key for restaurant businesses during the pandemic. As stated by some studies (Yang et al. 2020; Türkes et al. 2021), these services allowed restaurants to continue generating revenue, cover some of their fixed costs and ensure a portion of their profitability during periods of mandatory closure and restricted operating hours. Huang and Siao (2023) explored the impact of implementing online ordering and delivery services in restaurants during the COVID-19 pandemic, concluding that these services can improve both the financial and non-financial performance of establishments. Similarly, Kim et al. (2021) demonstrated that the adoption of digital channels had a positive impact on restaurant sales in China, regardless of the restrictions imposed by the city's location. Likewise, Neise et al. (2021) highlighted that during the initial months of the lockdown in Germany, delivery and takeout services were the most relevant factors that explained the resilience of restaurants. Moreover, once the restrictions were lifted, and restaurants were able to reopen, the reduction in seating capacity and consumers' fear of contagion meant a substantial decrease in the influx of consumers on the premises. In this context, the demand for online ordering and home delivery services continued to be an important source of revenue for restaurants (Kim et al. 2021; Gavilán et al. 2021; Hu and Zhang 2021).

In recent years, an increasing number of restaurants have developed their own websites to allow customers to place orders directly through this channel (Yeo et al. 2017). However, whether due to operational or financial considerations, many restaurants choose to outsource these services through digital delivery platforms (See-Kwong et al. 2017), such as Deliveroo, Glovo, Just Eat, or Uber Eats. Both options have potential advantages and disadvantages. On the one hand, restaurants with in-house online ordering and home delivery services must bear the fixed and operational costs of this infrastructure, which can potentially impact their profitability (Collison 2020). However, as highlighted by Du et al. (2023), providing these services autonomously allows them to have greater control over the process, including service quality, delivery time and customer relationships, which can increase consumers' purchase intent and benefits.

On the other hand, the qualitative research by See-Kwong et al. (2017) suggests that restaurant managers believe that marketing investments and delivery services provided by large delivery platforms enhance the visibility and reach of restaurants, helping them attract more customers and generate higher revenue. According to the study by Kim et al. (2021), restaurants offering services through China's main food delivery platform benefited from the COVID-19 crisis, experiencing an increase in average monthly sales in the first quarter of 2020 compared to the same period in 2019. Nevertheless, as noted by See-Kwong et al. (2017), the commissions charged by these platforms for each order can negatively impact the profitability of restaurants, which already have very tight profit margins. This reduction in profitability particularly affects smaller restaurants as they have limited negotiation power with the platforms (Ji et al. 2022).

Additionally, Tao et al. (2020) highlight the issue of restaurants losing control over service quality when using these platforms, a concern that can also have a negative impact on sales and profitability. However, Mhlanga (2022) measured the impact of these platforms on restaurants in two South African cities and determined that they do not influence meal prices or restaurant profitability. The study by Niu et al. (2021) concludes that the choice between using in-house infrastructure or delivery platforms depends on a restaurant's ability to adjust prices to cover the cost of the service, whether in-house or outsourced. It also suggests that a restaurant prefers to use its own logistics when there is a high potential for online sales. Conversely, they will outsource services when online sales are minimal. Therefore, based on the mixed results of previous research, we posit the following hypotheses:

Hypothesis 2. *In-house online ordering and home delivery services influenced the financial performance of restaurants during COVID-19.*

Hypothesis 3. *Online ordering and delivery services through external platforms influenced the financial performance of restaurants during COVID-19.*

3. Methodology

3.1. Sample Selection and Data

The first step in this study was to determine the target population. In a primary selection process, the restaurants were selected in exactly the same way as in the study by Lado-Sestayo et al. (2016), using the database of the Iberian Balance Sheet Analysis System (SABI).

SABI is a widely used database by researchers, offering a 25-year historical dataset of accounting, economic and financial information for 2,900,000 Spanish companies. As a result, the restaurant establishments examined in this study are limited to those with a legal structure as corporations. These companies are required to submit their annual reports to the Commercial Registry, making their information publicly available. The restaurant establishments which were operated by individual entrepreneurs do not have accounting, economic and financial information in the database; therefore they were not included in the analysis.

The variable used for the search was code I.5610: "Restaurants and mobile food service activities" from the statistical classification of economic activities in the European Community (NACE). To conduct the search and obtain the list of restaurant establishments, the year 2020 was selected, as it was the worst year of the COVID-19 crisis when restaurants experienced mandatory closures for extended periods. Once they were allowed to reopen, they had to cope with strict seating capacity restrictions. Subsequently, as a search filter, the Valencian Community was included. This region is a significant driver of tourism and the economy in Spain. According to data from the National Statistics Institute, in 2019, tourism contributed 12.6% to the national GDP, employing 12.5% of the employed population. The restaurant sector contributed 5.5% to the national GDP, representing approximately 7.9% of employment across all sectors. In the Valencian Community, tourism accounted for 15.7% of the region's GDP and 15.8% of employment (Exceltur 2021). The restaurant sector generated 6.8% of the Valencian Community's GDP and employed 9.7% of the population.

As shown in Table 1, the total number of restaurant establishments in 2020 amounted to 63,997. After excluding the restaurants whose database information was insufficient, incomplete or did not meet the requirements for analysis, the population was 8494.

Table 1. Restaurant population selection process.

Search Criterion	N° of Excluded Restaurants	N° of Valid Restaurants
Code NACE I.5610		63,997
Geographic area: Valencian Community	54,329	8668
Unreliable accounting reports	47	8621
Incomplete accounting data	86	8535
Incoherent accounting data	41	8494

Once the population was established, a simple random sample was taken from the total number of restaurant businesses that belong to the Valencian Community, with a confidence level of 95% and a sample error of 1%. The number of restaurants to be studied as a result of this random sampling was 1503. Subsequently, the financial information from the balance sheet and income statement of these selected restaurants for the 2020 fiscal year was collected.

This study aims to determine the effect of digitalization on the profitability of restaurant businesses during the pandemic according to the three hypotheses established. Thus, the next step was to classify the establishments with respect to their digitalization situation and the mode of service they used to confront the situation caused by the pandemic.

First, the restaurant establishments were classified according to whether they had a website. In this respect, it is assumed that having a website corresponds to a basic level of digitalization, which is the first classification category. Having a website allowed clients to consult information corresponding to the menu, whether the establishment was closed or not, opening hours, how to place an order, whether they could collect from the establishment or if home delivery was possible. Second, companies were divided according to whether an order could be placed online instead of using other alternatives, such as in person or by telephone, and whether the establishment had its own delivery service.

Finally, companies were segmented into a third category, which included establishments integrated into any of the numerous external food ordering and delivery platforms like Glovo, Just-Eat or Deliveroo.

The information consulted to make the above classifications was mainly available on the restaurant websites themselves, home delivery platforms, web portals like Tripadivsor, the Fork, Bookeat, Restaurantes.com, and social networks like Facebook or Instagram. Table 2 presents the number of restaurants that are grouped under each of the classifications according to their digitalization category.

Table 2. Distribution of restaurants by type of digital service.

Variables		Companies	%
Website (WEB)	No	556	36.99%
	Yes	947	63.01%
Website + own delivery service (WODS)	No	1390	92.48%
	Yes	113	7.52%
Delivery Platforms (DF)	No	1272	84.63%
	Yes	231	15.37%
Pooled sample		1503	100.00%

Note: The % symbol indicates the percentage of restaurants within each category.

3.2. Variables

In reference to the studies by Chen (2010), Cavero-Rubio and Amorós-Martínez (2020), Nguyen and Nguyen (2020) and Van Veldhoven et al. (2021) Return on Assets (ROA) has been chosen as the dependent variable to measure financial performance. According to these authors, ROA is the variable usually used to measure financial performance in research, and many researchers see it as a stable variable and more indicative of an organization's financial performance.

The independent variables included in this study are indebtedness, liquidity and sales variance (Xu and Jin 2022; Opstad et al. 2022). Firstly, an excessive level of debt can decrease a company's profitability when their financial costs increase (Nguyen and Nguyen 2020; Opstad et al. 2022). However, it is also possible that a moderate level of indebtedness may improve profitability as it permits a company to finance investment projects at a lower cost than if they were to only use their own resources (Margaritis and Psillaki 2010).

Secondly, COVID-19 caused restaurant establishments to be hit by a serious liquidity crisis due to the severe loss of revenue they sustained (Dube et al. 2021). In particular, in the case of the restaurant sector, which was vulnerable during the pandemic, having liquidity was crucial (Nguyen et al. 2021). Not only did restaurants need to cover operational and financial costs, but they also required sufficient resources to adapt their installations and processes to health protocols and invest in digital tools and online sales channels that would help increase their income and profitability. Apart from this, restaurants with insufficient liquidity could find themselves being forced into taking drastic measures like selling assets or resorting to loans, which could negatively affect their profitability. Therefore, the adequate management of liquidity is fundamental for small and medium companies, as is the case of most restaurants (Lakatos 2020), and it is crucial to improve long-term business profitability (Zimon and Tarighi 2021; Kumar 2022).

According to Markman and Gartner (2002), business growth is the basis for achieving competitive advantages and increasing profitability. Sales variance is a good measure of business growth (Fareed et al. 2016) and maintains a close link to profitability (Mun and Jang 2015; Fareed et al. 2016). Generally, the more sales increase, the greater the likelihood that profitability will increase. Nevertheless, although different studies suggest that there is a positive relation between sales variance and business performance (Lee 2014; Fareed et al. 2016), other researchers have found that this relation is negative

(Reid 1995; Jang and Park 2011) or that the relation between both variables is not significant (Markman and Gartner 2002).

As size influences a company's capacity to adapt to changes and make the most of the benefits from digitalization (Buer et al. 2021), the size of the restaurant businesses has been selected as the control variable and is measured as the natural logarithm of all their assets. This is a factor that can also positively influence profitability because of the economies of scale and the advantage of having more market power (Mun and Jang 2015). However, in the case of labour-intensive industries such as the restaurant sector, it is possible that there are diseconomies of scale and that smaller-size companies may be more profitable, as shown in the results of the study by Opstad et al. (2022).

Table 3 shows the definition and description of the variables considered in this study.

Table 3. Definition and description of the variables.

Variable	Description
Return on Assets (ROA)	Earnings before interests and taxes (EBIT)/Total assets
Indebtedness (DEBT)	(Current liabilities + Long-term liabilities)/Net Worth
Liquidity (LIQ)	Current assets/Current Liabilities
Sales growth (SGROW)	(Sales year^{t} − Sales year^{t-1})/(Sales year^{t-1});
SIZE	Natural logarithm of total assets
Website (WEB)	Yes = 1 if the restaurant business has a website No = 0 otherwise
Website + own delivery service (WODS)	Yes = 1 if the restaurant business has a website and own home delivery No = 0 otherwise
Delivery Platform Service (DPS)	Yes = 1 if the restaurant uses external online ordering platforms and home delivery No = 0 otherwise

3.3. *Models and Estimation Method*

In line with Lucas and Ramires (2022) and Opstad et al. (2022), a multivariate analysis is performed to contrast the proposed hypotheses. It uses a linear regression approach, which is one of the most commonly used models in multivariate statistical analysis (Lederer and Lederer 2022). Linear regression allows the examination of the specific effects of one variable on another while controlling for the effects of other variables. Using the established hypotheses, the objective is to verify whether the effects of the pandemic crisis on sales growth (SGROW), liquidity (LIQ) and indebtedness (DEBT) imply a higher financial performance by restaurants according to the three different digitalization categories established.

Given that the aim of this study is to determine whether restaurants' profitability was conditioned by the digitalization of their operations, it is necessary to introduce a new effect on the model that will include these three interactions. In line with Hardy (1993) and Aiken et al. (1991), to determine the effects of digitalization, the product of WEB, WODS and DPS with the explanatory (LIQ, DEBT, SGROW) and control (SIZE) variables is added to the model. In this way, the β coefficients of the interactions represent the effect of sales growth, liquidity, indebtedness and size on ROA for restaurants with a website, with a website + own delivery service or integrated into a delivery platform.

Given that the interactions only affect digitalized restaurants, to determine the total effect of the explanatory variables on their performance, the β coefficients of the interactions are added to or subtracted from the β coefficients of all the individual values of LIQ, DEBT, SGROW and SIZE.

Thus, for restaurant i in year t, the defined equation for WEB is as follows:

$$ROAit = \alpha_0 + \beta_1 LIQ_{it} + \beta_2 DEBT_{it} + \beta_3 SGROW_{it} + \beta_4 SIZE_{it} + \beta_5 WEB + \beta_6 WEB \times LIQ_{it} + \beta_7 WEB \times DEBT_{it} + \beta_8 WEB \times SGROW_{it} + \beta_9 WEB \times SIZE_{it} + e_{it}$$

For restaurant i at year t the defined equation for WODS is as follows:

$$ROAit = \alpha_0 + \beta_1 LIQ_{it} + \beta_2 DEBT_{it} + \beta_3 SGROW_{it} + \beta_4 SIZE_{it} + \beta_5 WODS + \beta_6 WODS \times LIQ_{it} + \beta_7 WODS \times DEBT_{it} + \beta_8 WODS \times SGROW_{it} + \beta_9 WODS \times SIZE_{it} + e_{it}$$

And, for restaurant i at year t the defined equation for DPS is as follows:

$$ROAit = \alpha_0 + \beta_1 LIQ_{it} + \beta_2 DEBT_{it} + \beta_3 SGROW_{it} + \beta_4 SIZE_{it} + \beta_5 DPS + \beta_6 DPS \times LIQ_{it} + \beta_7 DPS \times DEBT_{it} + \beta_8\ DPS \times SGROW_{it} + \beta_9 DPS \times SIZE_{it} + e_{it}$$

To measure the intensity of association between the model's variables, Pearson's correlation analysis is carried out. As the Pearson correlation coefficients (untabulated) between variables do not exceed the rule of thumb level (0.80), and the Variance Inflation Factors (VIF) and condition indices (untabulated) for the independent variables are less than 4 and 10, respectively, we can assert that multicollinearity is unlikely to be an issue of concern (Menard 2002; Kleinbaum et al. 1998).

4. Results

4.1. Descriptive Statistics

Tables 4 and 5 summarize the descriptive statistics for the liquidity, indebtedness, profitability and sales growth ratios for the restaurant companies in the sample. In Table 4, the statistics are presented for the entire sample, whereas in Table 5, they are presented separately for each of the established digitalization categories along with the results of the Student's t-test.

Table 4. Descriptive Statistics. Pooled Sample.

Ratio	Mean	Median	Std. dv
LIQ	1.76	1.22	1.86
DEBT	2.41	1.43	2.62
ROA %	−4.77	−1.97	15.89
SGROW %	−34.10	−33.42	21.58

Table 5. Descriptive statistics. Mean Differences. T-Student test.

Variables	Ratio	Yes			No			Difference T-Student Test
		Mean	Median	Std. dev.	Mean	Median	Std. dev.	
WEB	LIQ	1.76	1.23	1.65	1.45	0.96	1.61	0.31 ***
	DEBT	4.65	1.78	7.89	5.34	1.32	2.28	−0.70 *
	ROA %	−5.65	−1.04	19.29	−11.63	−6.71	24.02	5.98 ***
	SGROW %	−32.70	−32.77	19.66	−34.67	−33.17	18.92	1.98 **
WODS	LIQ	1.65	1.23	1.52	1.63	1.10	0.92	0.02
	DEBT	4.77	2.18	6.91	4.89	1.71	8.36	−0.12
	ROA %	−1.38	0.91	18.90	−8.36	−3.47	21.44	6.98 ***
	SGROW %	−25.43	−24.49	23.55	−34.32	−33.66	19.18	8.89 ***
DPS	LIQ	1.81	1.26	1.75	1.62	1.09	1.62	0.19 **
	DEBT	4.36	2.05	5.80	4.81	1.68	8.31	−0.45
	ROA %	−4.08	−0.57	18.97	−8.52	−3.48	21.67	4.43 ***
	SGROW %	−28.58	−31.43	20.56	−34.44	−33.32	19.18	5.86 ***

Note: * $p < 0.05$, ** $p < 0.01$, *** $p < 0.001$.

As shown in Table 5, in 2020, having a corporate website was a competitive advantage for restaurants. Establishments with their own website averaged higher liquidity (+0.31), lower indebtedness (−0.7), reduced profitability loss (+5.98) and a smaller decrease in sales (+1.98) compared to those without this digital tool. Statistically significant differences were observed between both groups for all ratios. Similar results are also found for restaurants that have a website and offer their own home delivery service compared to those that do not provide this option to consumers. In this case, while there were no statistically significant differences in liquidity and indebtedness, significant variations were observed in profitability and sales growth. Although both groups had negative mean values for the last two variables, they were less unfavourable in restaurants with a website and their own delivery service, with profitability and sales growth at −1.38% and −25.43%, respectively, as opposed to −11.63% and −34.67% for restaurants without this technology. In the same way, all the ratio values of restaurants integrated into delivery platforms are better than those that do not have this form of e-commerce, and, except for indebtedness, all the differences are statistically significant.

4.2. Multivariate Analysis

To test the hypotheses established and to analyse how the restaurants' financial indicators and the level of digitalization of sales channels affected ROA during COVID-19, three regression models are proposed. These three models (Table 6) are differentiated by the dichotomous variables included in each one and their interaction with the predictor variables. The dichotomous variables included in the regression models are the first model (1) WEB, the second model (2) WODS, and the third model (3) DPS. The adjusted R2 suggests that all the models have an adequate goodness-of-fit for the sample data.

Table 6. Regression analysis results.

Variables	(1)	(2)	(3)
	ROA	ROA	ROA
Intercept	−0.212 (−4.416) ***		−0.096 (−1.318)
LIQ	0.017 (4.766) ***	0.013 (6.052) ***	0.007 (3.249) ***
SGROW	0.287 (13.332) ***	0.304 (15.140) ***	0.318 (13.852) ***
SIZE	0.040 (4.330) ***	0.057 (6.771) ***	0.031 (3.519) ***
WEB	0.072 (4.744) ***		
WEB × LIQ	−0.011 (−2.313) **		
WEB × DEBT	−0.005 (−2.008) **		
WODS × SGROW		−0.093 (−1.717) **	
DPS × DEBT			−0.011 (−3.292) ***
DPS × SGROW			−0.097 (−2.462) ***
N	1503	1503	1503
Adj. R^2	0.220	0.203	0.203

Note: * $p < 0.05$, ** $p < 0.01$, *** $p < 0.001$.

As shown in Table 6, the results across all models consistently highlight the positive influence of liquidity, sales growth, and size on restaurant financial performance during the pandemic. Greater liquidity can help restaurants cope better with economic challenges posed by COVID-19, such as a decrease in sales. It provides a financial cushion to sustain operations and meet obligations during difficult periods, ultimately leading to improved performance. Moreover, size can also help them more effectively address economic challenges, establishing itself as a strategic advantage that enhances their profitability.

Regarding the effects of digitalization tools, in model (1), it can be observed that having a website had a positive effect (+0.072) on profitability, proving hypothesis 1. However, efficient liquidity management is essential to increase profitability (Aktas et al. 2015), and it is possible that restaurants with websites may not be managing it effectively. This is highlighted by the negative β coefficient for the WEB × LIQ interaction (−0.011), which indicates that the positive influence of liquidity on the ROA of restaurants is moderated when they have their own website (0.017 − 0.011 = 0.006). Moreover, as the WEB × DEBT (−0.005) interaction indicates, the higher the indebtedness of restaurants with this digital tool, the more their financial performance decreases.

Model (2) shows that having a website and own home delivery service leads to an improvement in financial performance for restaurants during COVID-19. The interaction with sales growth (WODS × SGROW= −0.093) implies a favourable effect for restaurants with this digitalization characteristic. This is so because the negative coefficient value of this interaction reduces the positive coefficient value of SGROW on ROA (0.304 − 0.093 = 0.211). In this way, the low coefficient value for digitalized restaurants on the negative value of SGROW during the 2020 financial year implies a lower negative impact on financial performance. Consequently, hypothesis 2 is confirmed.

Finally, model (3) shows that having online ordering and delivery services using a platform positively influences restaurant profitability. Therefore, hypothesis 3 is confirmed. Similar to model (2), the impact of the decline in sales during the COVID-19 pandemic on the profitability of restaurants with this technology is reduced, as the interaction DPS × SGROW (−0.097) implies a lower coefficient value for SGROW (0.318 − 0.097 = 0.221). Conversely, as indicated by the significance of the interaction DPS × DEBT (−0.011), the level of indebtedness of establishments with this system of ordering and home delivery negatively affects ROA.

5. Discussion and Conclusions

In this study, we analysed the financial performance of restaurants during 2020, a very critical year for this sector from an operational perspective since it became vulnerable due to the different restrictions and regulations enforced by the government to control the spread of COVID-19. Research has been carried out into how a combination of economic variables and variables of the digitalization of sales channels influence restaurants' ROA.

In line with previous studies (Shaharuddin et al. 2021; Lucas and Ramires 2022; Opstad et al. 2022), this study shows that liquidity is a key determinant of the financial performance of restaurants. However, the reduction in sales, the weight of fixed costs, and additional expenses related to safety and protection measures against the virus led to serious liquidity problems for companies (Hao et al. 2022). This was particularly the case in the restaurant industry, which in comparison to other industries, is characterised by having structural liquidity deficits (Mun and Jang 2015). Nonetheless, liquidity was crucial for restaurants during the pandemic so they could maintain operations and afford the investments required for adapting businesses to government restrictions and requirements. For example, establishing a home delivery service would allow them to continue to generate revenue and profitability. In fact, for some researchers, during periods of uncertainty and crisis, investment opportunities open up for companies that can turn out to be more profitable than in ordinary periods (Zimon and Tarighi 2021). Nevertheless, as previous studies have noted (Mun and Jang 2015; Chambers and Cifter 2022), there is an optimal level of liquidity, and an excess of liquidity can be detrimental to business performance, given that maintaining idle assets incurs opportunity costs. In this sense, the results suggest that it is likely that in the face of economic uncertainty, the restaurants with a website, whose mean liquidity values were significantly higher than the rest of the restaurants, could have maintained idle financial resources and renounced making investments that could have generated greater profitability for the company.

Furthermore, the results show that the indebtedness of restaurants does not affect their profitability, aligning with the findings of Jung et al. (2019). In the context of the COVID-19 crisis, this may be partly explained by government support measures for businesses, which included debt restructurings and deferments. However, the results indicate that in restaurants adhering to delivery platforms, indebtedness did have a negative impact on their financial results. According to the results of Nguyen and Nguyen (2020) and Opstad et al. (2022), because these restaurants perhaps did not use debt for profitable investments, the cost of debt led to a decline in their revenues and profitability.

Regarding sales growth, in line with the findings of Mun and Jang (2015), this study found that it positively influences the financial performance of restaurants. This effect is even more pronounced for restaurants with online ordering and home delivery services, whether they have their own infrastructure or use a delivery platform. As stated by Kumar and Ayedee (2021) in their study, the pandemic led to the adoption of e-commerce, enabling businesses to adapt to consumer needs, resulting in increased sales and revenue. Despite the potential decrease in restaurants' profit margins due to the implementation of this technology (Li et al. 2020; Ma et al. 2021), during certain periods in 2020, it possibly represented the only source of revenue for these establishments.

Finally, similarly to previous research within the restaurant industry (Hsu and Jang 2009; Sun and Kim 2013), this study has identified a positive relationship between restaurant size and financial performance. This relationship may be partially explained by the ability to leverage economies of scale (Gschwandtner and Hirsch 2018) and reduce operational expenses, particularly those related to the cost of food, which directly impact business profitability (Mun and Jang 2015). On the other hand, larger restaurants can access greater financial support to cope with unexpected situations like the COVID-19 pandemic to the detriment of smaller restaurants, which are more sensitive to the negative effects of operational interruptions (Wieczorek-Kosmala 2021).

6. Theoretical and Practical Implications

This study contributes to enriching the existing literature on the digitalization of sales channels and its impact on the financial performance of restaurants in crisis contexts like the COVID-19 pandemic. Furthermore, it enhances the understanding of the factors that can affect the resilience of restaurants, emphasizing the significance of liquidity and business size in the effective adaptation of these establishments to crises like the COVID-19 pandemic.

From a theoretical perspective, this study emphasizes the importance of agility in business management, a fundamental concept within the theory of dynamic capability. Our research highlights how digital sales channels have become essential components that enable restaurants to adjust their strategies and operations swiftly and effectively in times of crisis. This not only allows them to survive but also to maintain and strengthen their competitive advantage, resulting in improved financial performance. The study also underscores the significance of liquidity management, indebtedness and sales in the context of the digitalization of sales channels, as they play a crucial role in enhancing the profitability of restaurants.

Furthermore, the findings of this study have clear practical implications for both restaurant managers and public policymakers. They can be useful for restaurant managers to make informed decisions regarding their finances and marketing strategies during periods of market instability and turbulence. In this regard, this study provides empirical evidence that, in a time marked by restrictions on dining in restaurants, online orders and home delivery services offered restaurants an opportunity for growth and resilience development while also contributing to enhanced profitability. Additionally, it suggests that maintaining an appropriate liquidity balance and having a larger business size may be crucial for safeguarding profitability during times of complexity and uncertainty. The findings also highlight the importance of directing debt towards profitable investments, as its impact on profitability may vary depending on the sales model of the business.

For policymakers, this study provides evidence of the importance of providing liquidity to smaller and more vulnerable businesses in the context of severe economic shocks. This may be through direct grants or credit lines, but it is essential that support measures are designed in a way that is easy to access, quick to implement and simple to process, which will allow restaurants to cope with financial difficulties and continue to operate. Moreover, given the importance of digitalization in improving the resilience and competitiveness of businesses in a constantly changing economic environment, funds aimed at boosting digital transformation in the sector are essential. In this regard, the importance of the Next Generation EU funds, approved by the European Council to help all Member States to repair the economic and social damage caused by the pandemic, should be highlighted. The appropriate and efficient allocation of these resources will be essential to maximise this drive towards recovery and sustainable growth of the restaurant industry in the digital age.

7. Limitations and Future Lines of Research

Although this study provides significant findings, it is true that it also has some limitations. Firstly, the study sample of restaurant establishments corresponds to a region in Spain, which, although it is the third region with the highest number of registered restaurants and bars, is not a random sample of all the restaurants in the country. Future research could extend the study to a national and international level to obtain more generalizable results. Secondly, the information about the degree of digitalization of restaurants was obtained from different websites, social networks and delivery platforms. However, no qualitative research has been carried out on the quality of these services. Future research could address this subject to evaluate how far better online ordering and home delivery practices influenced the commercial success of restaurants and their profitability during the pandemic. Thirdly, this study has considered a limited number of variables; in future studies, it would be of interest to introduce other explanatory and control variables that influence restaurants' capacity to deal with a crisis like COVID-19 and their financial performance in general.

Author Contributions: All authors contributed equally to this work. All authors have read and agreed to the published version of the manuscript.

Funding: This research received no external funding.

Informed Consent Statement: Not applicable.

Data Availability Statement: Data are available upon reasonable request.

Conflicts of Interest: The authors declare no conflict of interest.

References

Aiken, Leona S., Stephen G. West, and Raymond R. Reno. 1991. *Multiple Regression: Testing and Interpreting Interactions*. Thousand Oaks: Sage.

Aktas, Nihat, Ettore Croci, and Dimitris Petmezas. 2015. Is working capital management value-enhancing? Evidence from firm performance and investments. *Journal of Corporate Finance* 30: 98–113. [CrossRef]

Alt, Rainer. 2021. Digital transformation in the restaurant industry: Current developments and implications. *Journal of Smart Tourism* 1: 69–74. [CrossRef]

Bouwman, Harry, Shahrokh Nikou, Francisco J. Molina-Castillo, and Mark de Reuver. 2018. The impact of digitalization on business models. *Digital Policy, Regulation and Governance* 20: 105–24. [CrossRef]

Brewer, Prawannarat, and Angela G. Sebby. 2021. The effect of online restaurant menus on consumers' purchase intentions during the COVID-19 pandemic. *International Journal of Hospitality Management* 94: 102777. [CrossRef]

Buer, Sven-Vegard, Jo Wessel Strandhagen, Marco Semini, and Jan Ola Strandhagen. 2021. The digitalization of manufacturing: Investigating the impact of production environment and company size. *Journal of Manufacturing Technology Management* 32: 621–45. [CrossRef]

Cavero-Rubio, José Antonio, and Aracelí Amorós-Martínez. 2020. Environmental certification and Spanish hotels' performance in the 2008 financial crisis. *Journal of Sustainable Tourism* 28: 771–96. [CrossRef]

Chambers, Nurgul, and Atilla Cifter. 2022. Working capital management and firm performance in the hospitality and tourism industry. *International Journal of Hospitality Management* 102: 103144. [CrossRef]

Chen, Manlu, Ming Hu, and Jianfu Wang. 2022. Food delivery service and restaurant: Friend or foe? *Management Sciencie* 68: 6539–51. [CrossRef]

Chen, Ming-Hsiang. 2010. The economy, tourism growth and corporate performance in the Taiwanese hotel industry. *Tourism Management* 31: 665–75. [CrossRef]

Collins, Galen R., Cihan Cobanoglu, Anil Bilgihan, and Katerina Berezina. 2017. *Hospitality Information Technology: Learning How to Use It*, 8th ed. Dubuque: Kendall/Hunt.

Collison, Jack. 2020. *The Impact of Online Food Delivery Services on Restaurant Sales*. Stanford: Department of Economics, Stanford University.
Dannenberg, Peter, Martina Fuchs, Tim Riedler, and Cathrin Wiedemann. 2020. Digital transition by COVID-19 pandemic? The German food online retail. *Tijdschrift voor Economische en Sociale Geografie* 111: 543–60. [CrossRef]
Du, Zhong, Zhi-Ping Fan, and Fenghao Sun. 2023. O2O dual-channel sales: Choices of pricing policy and delivery mode for a restaurant. *International Journal of Production Economics* 257: 108766. [CrossRef]
Dube, Kaitano, Godwell Nhamo, and David Chikodzi. 2021. COVID-19 cripples global restaurant and hospitality industry. *Current Issues in Tourism* 24: 1487–90. [CrossRef]
Exceltur. 2021. Estudio del Impacto Económico del Turismo Sobre la Economía y el Empleo de la Comunitat Valenciana. Available online: https://www.exceltur.org/wp-content/uploads/2023/01/Impactur-Co.Valenciana-2021-Documento.pdf (accessed on 17 July 2023).
Fareed, Zeeshan, Zahid Ali, Farrukh Shahzad, Muhammad Imran Nazir, and Assad Ullah. 2016. Determinants of profitability: Evidence from power and energy sector. *Studia Universitatis Babes-Bolyai Oeconomica* 61: 59–78. [CrossRef]
Fernández-Portillo, Antonio, Manuel Almodóvar-González, Mari Cruz Sánchez-Escobedo, and José Luis Coca-Pérez. 2022. The role of innovation in the relationship between digitalisation and economic and financial performance. A company-level research. *European Research on Management and Business Economics* 28: 100190. [CrossRef]
García-García, Maria, María Victoria Carrillo-Durán, and Jose Maia. 2021. The maturity of corporate websites as a digital communication channel in Portuguese SMEs' process of adopting e-commerce. *Sustainability* 13: 11972. [CrossRef]
Gavilán, Diana, Adela Balderas-Cejudo, Susana Fernández-Lores, and Gema Martinez-Navarro. 2021. Innovation in online food delivery: Learnings from COVID-19. *International Journal of Gastronomy and Food Science* 24: 100330. [CrossRef]
Gschwandtner, Adelina, and Stefan Hirsch. 2018. What drives firm profitability? A comparison of the US and EU food processing industry. *The Manchester School* 86: 390–416. [CrossRef]
Han, Wenjia, Ozgur Ozdemir, and Shivam Agarwal. 2023. Linking social media marketing to restaurant performance–the moderating role of advertising expenditure. *Journal of Hospitality and Tourism Insights. ahead-of-print*. [CrossRef]
Hao, Zezhong, Xiuwu Zhang, and Jiangying Wei. 2022. Research on the effect of enterprise financial flexibility on sustainable innovation. *Journal of Innovation & Knowledge* 7: 100184. [CrossRef]
Hardy, Melissa A. 1993. *Regression with Dummy Variables*. Thousand Oaks: Sage, vol. 93.
Hostelería de España. 2021. Anuario de la hostelería de España 2021. Available online: https://www.hosteleriayturismociudadreal.es/wp-content/uploads/2021/12/ANUARIO-HOSTELERIA-2021-digital.pdf (accessed on 15 July 2023).
Hsu, Li-Tzang, and SooCheong Jang. 2009. Effects of restaurant franchising: Does an optimal franchise proportion exist? *International Journal of Hospitality Management* 28: 204–11. [CrossRef]
Hu, Shiwei, and Yuyao Zhang. 2021. COVID-19 pandemic and firm performance: Cross-country evidence. *International Review of Economics & Finance* 74: 365–72. [CrossRef]
Huang, Shiu-Li, and Huei-Ru Siao. 2023. Factors Affecting the Implementation of Online Food Delivery and Its Impact on Restaurant Performance during the COVID-19 Pandemic. *Sustainability* 15: 12147. [CrossRef]
IvieLAB. 2021. Impacto Económico de la COVID-19 en la Comunitat Valenciana: Desagregación por Ramas de Actividad. Available online: https://www.ivie.es/es_ES/ptproyecto/ivielab-impacto-economico-la-covid-19-la-comunitat-valeciana-desagregacion-ramas-actividad/ (accessed on 29 October 2023).
Jang, SooCheong, and Kwangmin Park. 2011. Inter-relationship between firm growth and profitability. *International Journal of Hospitality Management* 30: 1027–35. [CrossRef]
Ji, Xu, Xuerong Li, and Shouyang Wang. 2022. Balance between Profit and Fairness: Regulation of Online Food Delivery (OFD) Platforms. Available online: https://ssrn.com/abstract=4485895 (accessed on 30 October 2023).
Jung, SoYeon, Toni Repetti, Hyun Kyung Grace Chatfield, Michael Dalbor, and Robert Chatfield. 2019. Internationalization and accounting-based risk in the restaurant industry. *Journal of Hospitality and Tourism Management* 41: 148–55. [CrossRef]
Kim, Eojina, Liang Tang, and Robert Bosselman. 2019. Customer perceptions of innovativeness: An accelerator for value co-creation. *Journal of Hospitality & Tourism Research* 43: 807–38. [CrossRef]
Kim, Jaewook, Jewoo Kim, and Yiqi Wang. 2021. Uncertainty risks and strategic reaction of restaurant firms amid COVID-19: Evidence from China. *International Journal of Hospitality Management* 92: 102752. [CrossRef]
Kim, Jaewook, Jewoo Kim, Seul Ki Lee, and Liang Rebecca Tang. 2020. Effects of epidemic disease outbreaks on financial performance of restaurants: Event study method approach. *Journal of Hospitality and Tourism Management* 43: 32–41. [CrossRef]
Kimes, Sheryl E. 2008. The role of technology in restaurant revenue management. *Cornell Hospitality Quarterly* 49: 297–309. [CrossRef]
Kimes, Sheryl E. 2011. The current state of online food ordering in the US restaurant industry. *Cornell Hospitality Report* 11: 6–18.
Kleinbaum, David G., Lawrence L. Kupper, Azhar Nizam, and Eli S. Rosenberg. 1998. The Method of Maximum Likelihood. In *Applied Regression Analysis and Other Multivariable Methods*. Pacific Grove: Duxbury Press.
Kumar, Anuj, and Nishu Ayedee. 2021. Technology Adoption: A Solution for SMEs to overcome problems during COVID-19. *Forthcoming, Academy of Marketing Studies Journal* 25: 1–16.
Kumar, Pradip. 2022. Liquidity management: An empirical study. *International Business & Economics Studies* 4: 74–87. [CrossRef]
Lado-Sestayo, Ruben, Luis Otero-Gonzalez, Milagros Vivel-Búa, and Onofre Martorell-Cunill. 2016. Impact of location on profitability in the Spanish hotel sector. *Tourism Management* 52: 405–15. [CrossRef]

Lakatos, Vilmos. 2020. Controlling tools for decision-making in micro, small and medium-sized enterprises. *Annals of Faculty of Economics* 1: 192–203.

Lederer, Johannes, and Johannes Lederer. 2022. Linear Regression. In *Fundamentals of High-Dimensional Statistics: With Exercises and R Labs*. Cham: Springer, pp. 37–79.

Lee, Sanghoon. 2014. The relationship between growth and profit: Evidence from firm-level panel data. *Structural Change and Economic Dynamics* 28: 1–11. [CrossRef]

Li, Charlene, Miranda Mirosa, and Phil Bremer. 2020. Review of online food delivery platforms and their impacts on sustainability. *Sustainability* 12: 5528. [CrossRef]

Liu, Wenfang, and Jaewook Kim. 2021. Amid COVID-19: The impact of online food delivery service on restaurant financial performance and customer's intention to use such service. Paper presented at the APTA 2021 Conference, Chiang Mai (On-line Conference), Thailand, June 30–July 2.

Lowry, Paul Benjamin, David W. Wilson, and William L. Haig. 2014. A picture is worth a thousand words: Source credibility theory applied to logo and website design for heightened credibility and consumer trust. *International Journal of Human-Computer Interaction* 30: 63–93. [CrossRef]

Lucas, Ana, and Ana Ramires. 2022. Directions for management in small and medium hotels and restaurants companies. *GeoJournal of Tourism and Geosites* 40: 210–17. [CrossRef]

Ma, Jing, Timothy Webb, and Zvi Schwartz. 2021. A blended model of restaurant deliveries, dine-in demand and capacity constraints. *International Journal of Hospitality Management* 96: 102981. [CrossRef]

Margaritis, Dimitris, and Maria Psillaki. 2010. Capital structure, equity ownership and firm performance. *Journal of Banking & Finance* 34: 621–32. [CrossRef]

Markman, Gideon D., and William B. Gartner. 2002. Is extraordinary growth profitable? A study of Inc. 500 high–growth companies. *Entrepreneurship Theory and Practice* 27: 65–75. [CrossRef]

Menard, Scott. 2002. *Applied Logistic Regression Analysis (No. 106)*. Thousand Oaks: Sage.

Mhlanga, Oswald. 2022. 'Meal-sharing'platforms: A boon or bane for restaurants? *Current Issues in Tourism* 25: 3291–308. [CrossRef]

Mun, Sung Gyun, and SooCheong Shawn Jang. 2015. Working capital, cash holding, and profitability of restaurant firms. *International Journal of Hospitality Management* 48: 1–11. [CrossRef]

Neise, Thomas, Philip Verfürth, and Martin Franz. 2021. Rapid responding to the COVID-19 crisis: Assessing the resilience in the German restaurant and bar industry. *International Journal of Hospitality Management* 96: 102960. [CrossRef] [PubMed]

Nguyen, Chi Khanh, Anh Quang Nguyen, Nhu Quynh Nguyen, Trang Thi Minh Nguyen, Anh Ngoc Chu, and Lan Thi Mai Nguyen. 2021. Cash holding and financial stability during a crisis: A case study of Vietnamese firms in COVID-19 pandemic. In *Forum for Social Economics*. London: Routledge, pp. 1–14.

Nguyen, Hieu Thanh, and Anh Huu Nguyen. 2020. The impact of capital structure on firm performance: Evidence from Vietnam. *The Journal of Asian Finance, Economics and Business* 7: 97–105. [CrossRef]

Niu, Baozhuang, Qiyang Li, Zihao Mu, Lei Chen, and Ping Ji. 2021. Platform logistics or self-logistics? Restaurants' cooperation with online food-delivery platform considering profitability and sustainability. *International Journal of Production Economics* 234: 108064. [CrossRef]

Opstad, Leiv, Johannes Idsø, and Robin Valenta. 2022. The dynamics of the profitability and growth of restaurants; The case of Norway. *Economies* 10: 53. [CrossRef]

Peng, Yongzhang, and Changqi Tao. 2022. Can digital transformation promote enterprise performance? From the perspective of public policy and innovation. *Journal of Innovation & Knowledge* 7: 100198. [CrossRef]

Ray, Arghya, Amandeep Dhir, Pradip Kumar Bala, and Puneet Kaur. 2019. Why do people use food delivery apps (FDA)? A uses and gratification theory perspective. *Journal of Retailing and Consumer Services* 51: 221–30. [CrossRef]

Reid, Gavin C. 1995. Early life-cycle behaviour of micro-firms in Scotland. *Small Business Economics* 7: 89–95. [CrossRef]

Ribeiro-Navarrete, Samuel, Dolores Botella-Carrubi, Daniel Palacios-Marqués, and Maria Orero-Blat. 2021. The effect of digitalization on business performance: An applied study of KIBS. *Journal of Business Research* 126: 319–26. [CrossRef]

Safari, Fariba, Narges Safari, and Alireza Hasanzadeh. 2015. The adoption of software-as-a-service (SaaS): Ranking the determinants. *Journal of Enterprise Information Management* 28: 400–22. [CrossRef]

Saleem, Uzman, Muhammad Bilal, Dan Ioan Topor, and Sorinel Căpușneanu. 2022. The impact of website quality on customer satisfaction and eWOM in online purchase intention: The moderating role of gender in risk-taking. *Frontiers in Psychology* 13: 945707. [CrossRef] [PubMed]

Schwertner, Krassimira. 2017. Digital transformation of business. *Trakia Journal of Sciences* 15: 388–93. [CrossRef]

See-Kwong, Goh, NG Soo-Ryue, Wong Shiun-Yi, and Chong Lily. 2017. Outsourcing to online food delivery services: Perspective of F&B business owners. *Journal of Internet Banking and Commerce* 22: 1–13.

Shaharuddin, Sara Naquia Hanim, Radziah Mahmud, Nor Khadijah Mohd Azhari, and Widya Perwitasari. 2021. Company performance during Covid-19: Impact of leverage, liquidity and cash flows. *Environment-Behaviour Proceedings Journal* 6: 11–16. [CrossRef]

Singh, Shiwangi, Gurtej Singh, and Sanjay Dhir. 2022. Impact of digital marketing on the competitiveness of the restaurant industry. *Journal of Foodservice Business Research*, 1–19. [CrossRef]

Statista. 2022a. Year-Over-Year Daily Change in Seated Restaurant Diners Due to the Coronavirus (COVID-19) Pandemic Worldwide from February 24, 2020 to August 1, 2022. Available online: https://www.statista.com/statistics/1103928/coronavirus-restaurant-visitation-impact/ (accessed on 7 July 2023).

Statista. 2022b. Platform Delivery—Worldwide. Available online: https://www.statista.com/outlook/dmo/online-food-delivery/mealdelivery/platform-delivery/worldwide (accessed on 7 July 2023).

Statista. 2023. Número de restaurantes y puestos de comidas en España a 1 de enero de 2022, por comunidad autónoma. Available online: https://es.statista.com/estadisticas/646140/restaurantes-y-puestos-de-comida-por-cc-aa-espana/ (accessed on 29 October 2023).

Sun, Kyung-A., and Dae-Young Kim. 2013. Does customer satisfaction increase firm performance? An application of American Customer Satisfaction Index (ACSI). *International Journal of Hospitality Management* 35: 68–77. [CrossRef]

Tan, Tom Fangyun, and Serguei Netessine. 2019. At your service on the table: Impact of tabletop technology on restaurant performance. *Management Science* 66: 4496–515. [CrossRef]

Tao, Zhiying, Qinglong Gou, and Juzhi Zhang. 2020. A local seller's app channel strategy concerning delivery. *International Journal of Production Research* 58: 220–55. [CrossRef]

Teece, David J., Gary Pisano, and Amy Shuen. 1997. Dynamic capabilities and strategic management. *Strategic Management Journal* 18: 509–33. [CrossRef]

Türkes, Mirela Cătălina, Aurelia Felicia Stăncioiu, Codruța Adina Băltescu, and Roxana-Cristina Marinescu. 2021. Resilience innovations and the use of food order & delivery platforms by the Romanian restaurants during the COVID-19 pandemic. *Journal of Theoretical and Applied Electronic Commerce Research* 16: 3218–47. [CrossRef]

Van Veldhoven, Ziboud, Paulien Aerts, Sanne Lies Ausloos, Jente Bernaerts, and Jan Vanthienen. 2021. The Impact of Online Delivery Services on the Financial Performance of Restaurants. Paper presented at the 2021 7th International Conference on Information Management (ICIM), London(On-line Conference), UK, March 27–29; Piscataway: IEEE, pp. 13–17. [CrossRef]

Vial, Gregory. 2019. Understanding digital transformation: A review and a research agenda. *The Journal of Strategic Information Systems* 28: 118–44. [CrossRef]

Wieczorek-Kosmala, Monika. 2021. COVID-19 impact on the hospitality industry: Exploratory study of financial-slack-driven risk preparedness. *International Journal of Hospitality Management* 94: 102799. [CrossRef] [PubMed]

World Tourism Organization. 2020. International Tourism Highlights, 2020 Edition. Available online: https://www.e-unwto.org/doi/pdf/10.18111/9789284422456 (accessed on 13 July 2023).

Xu, Jian, and Zhenji Jin. 2022. Exploring the Impact of the COVID-19 Pandemic on Firms' Financial Performance and Cash Holding: New Evidence from China's Agri-food Sector. *Agronomy* 12: 1951. [CrossRef]

Yang, Yang, Hongbo Liu, and Xiang Chen. 2020. COVID-19 and restaurant demand: Early effects of the pandemic and stay-at-home orders. *International Journal of Contemporary Hospitality Management* 32: 3809–34. [CrossRef]

Yeo, Vincent Cheow Sern, See-Kwong Goh, and Sajad Rezaei. 2017. Consumer experiences, attitude and behavioral intention toward online food delivery (OFD) services. *Journal of Retailing and Consumer Services* 35: 150–62. [CrossRef]

Zhai, Huayun, Min Yang, and Kam C. Chan. 2022. Does digital transformation enhance a firm's performance? Evidence from China. *Technology in Society* 68: 101841. [CrossRef]

Zimon, Grzegorz, and Hossein Tarighi. 2021. Effects of the COVID-19 global crisis on the working capital management policy: Evidence from Poland. *Journal of Risk and Financial Management* 14: 169. [CrossRef]

Disclaimer/Publisher's Note: The statements, opinions and data contained in all publications are solely those of the individual author(s) and contributor(s) and not of MDPI and/or the editor(s). MDPI and/or the editor(s) disclaim responsibility for any injury to people or property resulting from any ideas, methods, instructions or products referred to in the content.

economies

MDPI

Article

Digital Economy Development, Common Prosperity, and Carbon Emissions: An Empirical Study in China

Jingke Gao [1], Wenxiao Zhou [2], Jinhua Cheng [2,3] and Ziyuan Liu [4,*]

[1] Institute of Advanced Study, China University of Geosciences (Wuhan), Wuhan 430074, China; gaojingke@cug.edu.cn
[2] School of Economics and Management, China University of Geosciences (Wuhan), Wuhan 430074, China; wenxiaozhou@cug.edu.cn (W.Z.); chengjinhua100@126.com (J.C.)
[3] Collaborative Innovation Center for Emissions Trading System Co-Constructed by the Province and Ministry, Wuhan 430205, China
[4] School of Innovation and Entrepreneurship, Wuhan Institute of Technology, Wuhan 430205, China
* Correspondence: 23091105@wit.edu.cn

Abstract: Under the new development model, the digital economy has become a new engine to promote the green development of the economy and realize the goal of "double carbon". Based on the panel data of 30 provinces in China from 2010 to 2020, this paper empirically investigates the impact of the development of the digital economy on energy and carbon emissions using a series of econometric models such as baseline regression, a mechanism test, and the spatial Durbin model, etc. Common prosperity plays an intermediary role between digital economy development and carbon emissions; digital economic development optimizes resource allocation, effectively solves the problem of uneven resource distribution, and reduces energy and carbon emissions while achieving common prosperity. In addition, green innovation, industrial structure, urbanization level, R&D intensity, and the degree of marketization also have different degrees of influence on energy and carbon emissions. Therefore, the government should accelerate the construction of new digital infrastructure and implement the digital economy development strategy according to local conditions, so as to promote the digital economy to produce a more significant carbon emission reduction effect.

Keywords: digital economy; common prosperity; energy consumption; carbon emissions; spatial spillovers; heterogeneity

1. Introduction

In the last century, human economic activities immensely relied on non-renewable resources, which led to serious emissions of CO_2 as the main greenhouse gas. This has proven to have diverse effects on the life of humankind and the threat of the deteriorating sustenance of economic growth (Pata and Isik 2021). Report number five on the Intergovernmental Panel on Climate Change (IPCC) illustrates a discernible upward trend in the global average surface temperature. Over 90% of this increase is attributed to greenhouse gases produced by human activities, with CO_2 emissions from traditional energy consumption serving as a prominent contributor to the global greenhouse effect (Pata et al. 2023; Ahmed et al. 2022). In October 2021, China made a definitive commitment that, by 2030, CO_2 emissions should come to a peak, with the ultimate goal of achieving carbon neutrality by 2060. Subsequently, the Chinese and Americans issued the "China-United States Glasgow on Enhanced Climate Action in the 21st Century 2020 Joint Declaration". This declaration signifies their commitment to strengthening climate cooperation and collaborating to uphold the outcomes of the Paris Agreement. It underscores the common responsibilities of major countries in addressing climate change (Khan et al. 2022a; Usman et al. 2022).

Based on the endowment of energy resources in China, it is imperative to strategically and progressively advance carbon peak initiatives, foster a comprehensive energy revolution, diminish reliance on traditional energy sources, enhance the utilization of coal in a clean and efficient manner, and expedite new energy system planning and implementation. Active engagement in global climate change governance is essential in this endeavor (Kamal et al. 2021a; Yang et al. 2022). Consequently, the primary focus of future advancement is based on curtailing the utilization of conventional non-renewable sources while concurrently enhancing energy efficiency. The "Made in China 2025" initiative underscores the critical necessity to expedite technological advancements, structure the optimization of energy, and propel the environmentally sustainable advancement of society. This requires profound collaboration with all industries facilitated through the digitally based economy.

The further development of the digital economy continues to give birth to new Internet technologies, and the spread of digital technology applications has effectively reduced energy intensity and energy consumption per unit of output. In addition, digitalization has promoted the disintegration and reorganization of the modern industrial chain characterized by high efficiency, high output value, and low emissions, providing new ideas and feasible paths for reducing carbon emissions and promoting the green development of the modern industrial chain. The Chinese government is actively pursuing robust measures for CO_2 reduction, encompassing the reduction in the generation of power from plants that are coal sources (Mohsin et al. 2021; Tong et al. 2018), decreased energy consumption (Soytas et al. 2007; Valadkhani et al. 2019), accelerated integration of non-fossil energy sources (Dong et al. 2018; Godil et al. 2021), increased deployment of infrastructure that charges electric-based vehicles (Liu et al. 2021a), realization of energy transition goals (Li et al. 2022), and optimization of the structure of industries (Cheng et al. 2018). Concurrently, China grapples with the challenges of the advancement of the economy and prosperity. The importance of the use of digitalization is underscored by five-year plan number fourteen in optimizing and upgrading China's future systems of economy. In accordance with the Information and Communications Technology Academy of China (CAICT) in 2021, the digitally based economy of China attained an increase rate with a percentage of 9.7 in 2020, which is equivalent to 39.2 trillion, becoming the key in driving the stable growth of China's economy (CAICT 2020). Scholars have put into analysis the correlation between digitally based economic advancement and the emission of CO_2 using various approaches. For instance, some scholars claim that the digitally based economy can reduce the emission of CO_2 effectively, a phenomenon more pronounced in China (Li et al. 2021b; Ma et al. 2022) and some third-world countries (Chen 2021). Others have explored a correlation that is not based on the digitally based economy and CO_2, arguing that the effect of reducing emissions becomes efficient as the digitally based economy of China grows to levels that are higher (Wang et al. 2023; Li et al. 2021a; Li and Wang 2022b).

Consequently, it is imperative for the Government of China to meticulously take into consideration the effects of digitally based economic advancement on the reduction in the emissions of CO_2 in its future development strategies. Based on the above research, this paper uses data from 30 provinces in China from 2011 to 2020, adopts a multi-dimensional indicator system to quantify the level of development of the digital economy, applies a variety of spatial econometric models to test the impact of the digital economy on carbon emission reduction, explores the mechanism and effect of the digital economy on carbon emission reduction, analyzes the spatial effect of the digital economy on carbon emission reduction from the spatial and temporal perspectives, and analyzes the regional heterogeneity of this impact.

This paper's contributions are manifested in three areas: Firstly, it explores the construction of indicators for the digitally based economy. The methods and standards for measuring the level of economic advancement that is digitally based have not been unified. This paper incorporates policy and talent environments into the construction of indicators of the digitally based economy for a more comprehensive assessment. Secondly, the existing literature primarily explores the correlation between the digitally based economy and the emission of carbon from aspects such as the structure of industries, structure energy, and the intensity of energy. "Common prosperity" is socialism's core requirement and the essential aspect of the modernization of China. Incorporating common prosperity into digitally based economic research and the reduction in carbon can fill research gaps. Thirdly, this paper employs baseline regression and the effects of intermediary and spatial Durbin models to study the impacts of the digitally based economy and the reduction in carbon in energy comprehensively. A heterogeneous analysis of the digitally based economy impacts on carbonic reduction in energy is also conducted.

This paper is organized into seven parts. The first part is the introduction, which provides the research background of the achievement of the goal of "dual carbon" and digitally based economy advancement. Based on this foundation, the research objectives and this paper's innovative aspects are outlined. A literature review is the second part which introduces the digitalized economy, the emissions of carbon, and the digitalized economy effects on the emissions of carbon. This report also explains the drawbacks of recent research. Thirdly, it consists of an analysis of theoretical mechanisms and research hypotheses, which makes assumptions about the correlation between the digitally based economy and emissions of carbon using three approaches. In section four, it outlines the design of the research, detailing the model, variables, and selected sources of information. In section five, it presents the empirical results, accompanied by endogeneity and robustness tests. Part six discusses mediation impacts, the impacts of spatial spillover, and analysis in a heterogenic way. Finally, the seventh section presents the conclusions and outcomes of the policy.

2. Literature Review

2.1. Research on Digital Economy

Since the advent of the digitally based economy, researchers at home and overseas have shown a growing interest in this area. Especially in the area of the urgency of the change of climate globally, academia has also been interested in the effects of the digitally based economy in terms of carbon. In current years, significant research has been conducted on the digitalized economy as a new form of economy. Studies have revealed that the digitally based economy has significant effects on the restructuring of industries and advancement of the economy in a high-quality way and is of very critical use in economic growth. Researchers have primarily looked at digitally based economic advancement from three perspectives. In terms of the indicators of digitalized economy measurement, the province-level digital economic index in China is based on the development of computerization, internetization, and the digitization of transactions (Chen and Wu 2022). Considering the new digitally based economic growth, we calculated a digitally based economic advancement index for 30 provinces of China from three aspects: infrastructure that is digitalized, digitally based industrial advancement, and digitalized leadership (Awan et al. 2022). The digital economy exerts its influence on firms at the microlevel as follows: First, it flattens the organizational structure of enterprises, makes production processes more flexible, and supports innovative and R&D model marketing (Chen et al. 2022). Secondly, the digitally based economy helps companies optimize their capital structure, and hence factor productivity increases (Pang et al. 2023), and efficiency and information acquisition are improved, which in turn contributes to the overall value of businesses (Llopis-Albert et al. 2021). At the macrolevel, researchers have demonstrated that leveraging extensive industrial data and intelligent analytics to establish networked manufacturing can genuinely transform raw data into meaningful information. This optimization of production processes enhances efficiency, thereby increasing enterprise value (Fernández-Portillo et al. 2020). Entrepreneurial activities serve as an endogenous driver of the growth of the economy, and the advancement of the digitally based economy can stimulate entrepreneurship by enriching entrepreneurs with resources, optimizing the allocation factor, and subsequently promoting the growth of the economy in a high-quality way. The digitally based economy in making energy advancements more efficient and unlocking the potential of energy savings is increasingly recognized. Against the background of the growth of the economy and management of the environment, the importance of digital information is gradually emphasized (Ozturk and Ullah 2022).

2.2. Research on Carbon Emissions

In the emissions of carbon literature context, the focus is on the emissions of carbon dioxide measurement and their consequences. For instance, standards for detecting carbon emission levels across different industries are highlighted (Khan et al. 2022b). In accordance with the elements of the consumption of energy in China, eight sources of energy, coal and coke being included, are selected to evaluate the emissions of carbon dioxide over time in China (Kong et al. 2022). The emissions of carbon are primarily influenced by policies made by the government, urbanization, the structure of the population, and air pollution. The regional emissions of carbon dioxide can be reduced by the market through structural, technological, and configurational effects in accordance with the Carbon Dioxide Emissions Trading Pilot Policy (Ma and Zhu 2022). From the perspective of auditing by the government, the initial control of resources, which is performed naturally by high officials can support the energy industry, saving, and a reduction in the emissions of carbon dioxide by increasing the use of the capacities of industry (Wu et al. 2020). Empirical research and its context have been studied and examined from a perspective focused on the development of urbanization and data use of the panel cities which is at the prefecture level. The results indicate that the implications of population and urbanization on the productivity of carbon in cities range from strong to moderate. Once a certain threshold is crossed, the urbanization of a country no longer increases the carbon productivity of cities (Visconti-Caparrós and Campos-Blázquez 2022). From a demographic standpoint, based on provincial panel data, empirical findings suggest that the increase in the proportion of the working-age population primarily leads to carbon emissions through production and consumption (Zhang and Liu 2022). The study assesses the synergistic effects of reducing emissions of carbon and pollutants in the air in different environments in accordance with empirical data; a reduction in the pollution of the air synergistically impacts reducing both emissions of carbon and air contaminants (Shi et al. 2023).

In the field of exploration of the reduction in carbon emission pathways, experts have found that the digitally based economy not only plays a crucial role in the adjustment of the structure of industries in China and high-quality economic advancement but also occupies an important role in driving the transition between old and new drivers of the economy. Old and new economies also have the ability to significantly reduce the emission of carbon dioxide. The digitally based economy's influence on carbonic discharge in Chinese cities stems from the industrial Information and Communications Technology (ICT) expansion, which is in need of large inputs of intermediate products of carbon which are carbon made from ICT sectors (Zhou et al. 2019). Scientists are delving into the carbon-reducing significance of new digital generational technologies that are ubiquitous. Geographically, the digital economy has reduced emissions of carbon in some parts and had a remarkable impact on emissions of carbon in neighboring areas (Cheng et al. 2023). Based on empirical evidence, some researchers have come to conclude that the contribution of the digitally based economy to the performance of carbon is primarily local, with minimal impacts on surrounding regions (Zhang et al. 2022). The emerging digitally based economy, created by the integration of recent digitally based technologies with the financial sector, can help in the reduction in emissions by promoting the use of technologies in industries and the use of digitalization in industry (Chen 2022). In addition, some scientists have found that Internet advancements will reduce the pollution of the environment by improving the production and efficiency of energy. However, Li and Wang (2022a) argue that the digitally based economy's effects on carbonic discharge are not a simple linear correlation of either positive contribution or negative inhibition but rather a non-linear inverted U-shaped correlation where innovation efficiency in terms of innovation serves as a crucial mediator channel for the digitally based economy's impacts on carbonic discharge. It is also pointed out that the impact of the digital economy on carbon emissions shows a U-shaped non-linear relationship that first rises and then falls, which corresponds to the fact that the digital economy empowers traditional industries and promotes transformation and upgrading (Zhu et al. 2022).

In short, digitalized economic advancement has remarkable effects on carbonic discharge reduction. However, there is still considerable scope for research on the digitalized economic effects on carbonic reduction. Currently, researchers are yet to agree on the digitalized economic indicators of measurement, and there is a lack of a comprehensive and systematic evaluation system, as indicated in Table 1. In this paper, the policy environment and talent environment are added to the construction of digital economy indicators for a more comprehensive measurement. Furthermore, achieving common wealth is an essential requirement of socialism, and the process of achieving common prosperity also involves the reduction in carbon emissions. On this basis, this study utilizes data from 30 Chinese provinces from 2010 to 2020. By constructing a system of evaluation that is comprehensive for the digitalized economy and public prosperity and employing various econometric spatial models, this study explores the techniques and the digitally based economy's effects on carbonic discharge reduction.

Table 1. Digital economy index system.

Author(s)	Digital Economy Indicators
Chen and Wu (2022)	Computerization, Internet, Digitalization
Yi et al. (2022)	Digital industrialization, Industry digitization
Cheng et al. (2023)	Digital infrastructure, Industrial structure, Digital industrial scale, Technological innovation in the digital economy
Chen et al. (2022)	Mobile phone penetration rate, Internet penetration rate, Related industry output, Related industry employees
Li et al. (2021a)	Digital infrastructure, Internet development, Digital industry, Digital finance

3. Mechanistic Theory of Analysis and Hypothetical Research

3.1. The Digitally Based Economic Impacts on Carbon Emissions

The digitalized economy leverages the collaboration and application of digitalized technologies in economic activities related to energy, environment, and other fields, playing a role in environmental leadership by promoting the conservation of energy and reduction in emissions. Relevant studies indicate that the digitally based economy, through the integration and innovation of digitalized technologies, coordinates the correlation between the supply of energy and demand, encourages technological innovation, and transforms consumption patterns, achieving both accelerated industrial digitization and reduced carbonic discharge (Han et al. 2020; Kamal et al. 2021a). The digitally based economy primarily contributes to carbonic discharge reduction as follows: First, it gives information technology support for the governance of the environment (Liu et al. 2021b). The use of huge amounts of information, cloud computing, and remote sensing technologies supports dynamic real-time monitoring by the government of air quality, emission pollution, and the carrying capacity of the environment. Secondly, the digital economy supports low-carbon technology firms, hence the enhancement of the efficiency of production factors and resource allocation (Alam et al. 2022; Li et al. 2021a). The digitally based economy can alter the products' nature, new value creation, and digitally based environmental shaping, enable businesses to gain new competitive advantages, and optimize resource allocation. Thirdly, the intrinsic advantages and basic features of the digitalized economy (Wang et al. 2021), such as the dissemination of cross-temporal information, the creation of data, and sharing, can reduce activities that are unnecessary, thereby reducing emissions of carbon. On this basis, the following hypothetic proposal was suggested:

H1: *The digitalized economy can lead to a reduction in energy-related carbonic emission intensification.*

3.2. The Digitally Based Economy's Impacts on Carbonic Discharge through Its Effect on Common Prosperity

Common prosperity is an intrinsic requirement of socialism and represents a key feature in China's context of modernization style. The "White Paper on the Facilitation of Common Prosperity through the Digital Ecological Industry" indicates that " the digitally based economic advancement is a useful path to achieve common wealth" (Li et al. 2021b). China has entered the stage of common prosperity coinciding with the era of the digitalized economy. The digitally based economy has a positive effect on common prosperity, characterized by its dynamic and non-linear nature. Achieving common prosperity requires enhanced resource allocation, reduced energy consumption, and consequent mitigation of energy-related carbon emissions (Chen and Zhang 2023). Common prosperity, possessing developmental, shareable, and sustainable attributes, necessitates the harmonious coexistence of social and natural environments, the same as the development that is balanced with production systems (Liu et al. 2023). Common prosperity can drive the advancement of a green economy, promote improvements in the environment ecologically, and encourage economic transition toward low-carbon models that can sustain the environment. Therefore, the process of achieving common prosperity inevitably influences carbon emissions (Zhao et al. 2023). High-quality economic advancement, the narrowing of income disparities, and the development of a common economy contribute to the government's better formulation of low-carbon environmental policies (Zhang and Qian 2023). On this basis, the following speculation is proposed:

H2: *The digital economy affects energy and carbon intensity by optimizing the allocation of resources, improving the structure of social wealth distribution, and contributing to the development of common prosperity.*

3.3. The Spatial Spillover Effects of the Digitally Based Economic Impacts on Carbonic Emissions

Proximity enhances the elemental flow efficiency, establishing a closer correlation in nearby regions in relation to production, operation, and economic advancement (Ren et al. 2021). An essential feature of the digitalized economy is the spreading of technology worldwide and in different geographical spaces over time. Numerous factors affect the spatial effects of the digitally based economy, including the geographical interval, information acquisition, learning capability communication and transportation, and information acquisition, impacting the spatiotemporal trajectory of digital technology adoption and dissemination (Sobaci and Eryigit 2015). The spatial diffusion speed of digital technology varies, leading to distinct adoption curves in different regions. Additionally, the technological advancement process may exhibit a siphon effect. Regions prioritizing the development of digital industry sectors might transfer low-end, high-energy-consuming industries to economically underdeveloped areas, causing lagging regions to postpone the adoption of digital technology. However, during the technology diffusion process, a demonstration effect can also emerge. When a city effectively promotes its level of advancement, carbon emissions are reduced, and it becomes a leading region through vigorous digital economic development; its development model, policy framework, and innovative experiences influence neighboring and related provinces, generating demonstration and learning effects. This contributes to the adjustment of local policies or economic activities in surrounding regions (Yi et al. 2022). On this basis, the following hypothetical research proposal is suggested by this study:

H3: *The digitally based economy's advancement has many spatial effects on carbonic emissions.*

Existing studies have provided a foundational assessment and impact analysis framework mechanisms through which the digitally based economy promotes the reduction in carbonic discharge. This study categorizes the influence of the digitally based economy on the energy-related reduction in carbon into three major types: direct effects, indirect effects, and excess spatial effects. The techniques through which the digitalized economy affects the energy-related reduction in carbon are illustrated in Figure 1.

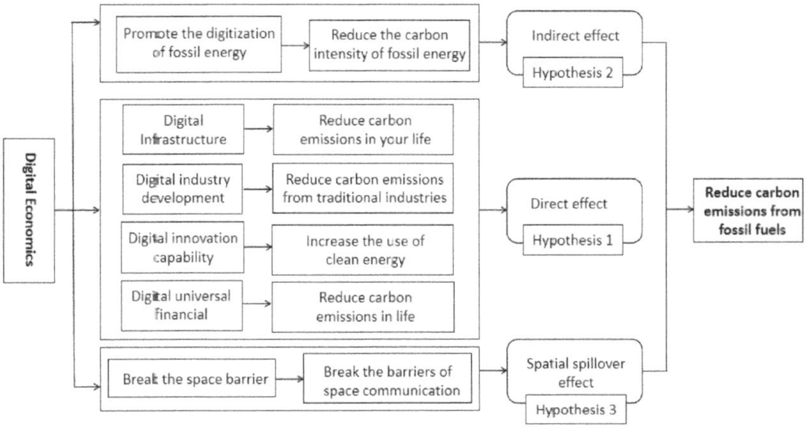

Figure 1. Conceptual framework.

4. Model and Data

4.1. Variable Description

4.1.1. Explained Variables

Energy Intensity of Carbonic Emission (CEI). CEI is indicated by the carbonic emissions (CEQ) per unit of

$$CEI = \frac{CEQ}{GDP} \quad (1)$$

This paper delves into energy-related carbon emission reduction, and energy includes eight major sources: diesel, fuel oil, liquefied petroleum gas coke, crude oil, gasoline, kerosene, and natural gas. Other energy sources are not considered due to their small proportion and data deficiencies. The method employed for calculating the emissions of carbon from the consumption of energy follows the IPCC(The Intergovernmental Panel on Climate Change)uidelines (Guo et al. 2022), and its calculation formula is as follows:

$$CEQ = \sum_{i=1}^{8} CO_{2,i} = \sum_{i=1}^{9} E_i \times NCV_i \times CEF_i \times COF_i \times \frac{44}{12} \quad (2)$$

In the equation, CEQ represents carbon emissions; E_i and NCV_i respectively denote the consumption and lower heating value of various types of energy. CEF_i stands for the oxygen content of various energy sources; COF_i is the carbon emission factor for various fossil fuels; 44 and 12 represent the chemical molecular weights of carbon dioxide and carbon, respectively.

4.1.2. Explanatory Variables

Digitally based economy (DIG). In measuring the level of digitally based economy advancement, based on mechanism analysis and incorporating previous research findings (Nicolay 1999), this study performs an assessment based on five dimensions: digitalized infrastructure, digitally based industrial advancement, digitally based innovation capability, digitally based financial inclusivity, and the digital advancement of environment. This forms platforms for evaluating the level of digitally based economy development, as indicated in Table 2. In terms of measuring the digitally based economy advancement level, the entropy weight method is employed for calculation (Zhu et al. 2022).

Table 2. Measurement index system of the digital economy.

Primary Indicators	Secondary Indicators	Description of Indicators (Units)	Index Attribute
Infrastructure	Broadband Internet infrastructure	Internet users (10,000 households)	+
	Mobile Internet fundamentals	Mobile telephone subscribers (10,000 households)	+
Industry development	E-commerce Industry development	Urban e-commerce parks (10,000)	+
	Infrastructure of the information industry	Employees in information transmission, Computer services and software (10,000 persons)	+
	Telecommunications industry output	Total telecommunication business (100 million)	+
Innovation capacity	Digital innovation factor support	Expenditure on science and technology (100 million)	+
	Level of digital Innovation output	Patents related to the digital economy (10,000)	+
	Digital Hi-Tech penetration	Degree of penetration of digital high-tech applications among listed companies (%)	+
Inclusive finance	Digital inclusive finance	Digital financial inclusion coverage breadth index (%)	+
	Depth of use	Depth of use index for digital financial inclusion (%)	+
	Degree of digitization	Digital financial inclusion digitization index (%)	+
Development environment	Talent environment	Number of graduates from general higher education institutions (10,000 persons)	+
	Policy environment	Internal expenditure on R&D personnel costs (100 million)	+

4.1.3. Intermediary Variable

Level of common prosperity (CP). The common use of "common" and "prosperity" forms the basis of common wealth. Therefore, this paper gives a measurement of the level of common prosperity in Chinese provinces from two aspects: "common" and "prosperity" (Liu et al. 2023), as indicated in Table 3. The technique of entropy is used to determine the common prosperity level.

Table 3. Common prosperity development level indicator system.

First Level Index	Second Level Index	Third Level Index	Impact
Prosperity	Resident life	GDP per capita	+
		Per capita disposable income of rural residents	+
		Per capita consumption expenditure of urban residents	+
		Per capita consumption expenditure of rural residents	+
	Education level	Per pupil education expenditure	+
	Medical level	Number of hospital beds per capita	+
	Social service level	Local fiscal general budget expenditure/GDP	+
	Cultural life level	Public library holdings per capita	+
	Science and education input	Science and education expenditure/GDP	+

Table 3. *Cont.*

First Level Index	Second Level Index	Third Level Index	Impact
Commonality	Urban–rural gap	The ratio of rural residents' income to urban residents' income	+
		The ratio of consumption expenditure of rural residents to that of urban residents	+
	Regional gap	The ratio of rural residents' income to the national average rural residents' income	+
		The ratio of urban residents' income to the national average urban residents' income	+

4.1.4. Control Variables

To evade biases in empirical test results resulting from overlooking crucial explanatory variables, the paper introduces the following five control variables into the model: (1) Green Technology Innovation (INNOV) (Zhang et al. 2023); (2) Industrial Structure (IS) (Xue et al. 2022); (3) Degree of Marketization (MAR) (Tan and Kaili 2023); (4) Research and Development Intensity (INUR) (Liu et al. 2017); and (5) Urbanization Level (UR) (Chen and Lin 2021). Table 4 provides the definitions and descriptions of the variables involved while Table 5 shows the statistics of the variables in a descriptive manner.

Table 4. Control variable selection and measure.

Variable	Symbol	Name	Measure
Dependent variable	CEI	Energy carbon intensity	Carbon emissions per unit of GDP
Explanatory variable	DIG	Development level of the digital economy	Calculated according to the index system of the digital economy
Intermediary variable	CP	Development level of the mutual enrichment	Calculated according to the index system of the common wealth
Control variables	INNOV	Green technology innovation	Number of green patents granted
	IS	Industrial structure	Ratio of tertiary to secondary sector
	MAR	Marketability	Regional marketization index
	INUR	R&D intensity	Ratio of R&D expenditure to GDP
	UR	Urbanization level	Ratio of urban population to total population

Table 5. Descriptive statistics of variables.

Variable	Obs	Min	Mean	Max	Std. Dev.
CEI	330	0.325	2.306	9.098	1.748
DIG	330	0.049	0.238	1.000	0.182
CP	330	0.187	0.763	2.245	0.436
INNOV	330	3.583	7.331	10.450	1.351
IS	330	0.518	1.218	5.296	0.695
MAR	330	0.526	6.804	11.910	2.056
INUR	330	0.004	0.016	0.011	0.064
UR	330	0.350	0.590	0.896	0.122

4.2. Model Construction

Base of Regression Test. Firstly, to examine research hypothesis H1 proposed in the analysis in terms of the theory above, the paper constructs the following baseline regression model based on the direct mechanism transmission of the digitally based economy to intensity carbonic discharge:

$$\mathrm{CEI_{it}} = \alpha_0 + \alpha_1 \mathrm{DIG_{it}} + \alpha_n \mathrm{X_{it}} + \mu_i + \delta_i + \varepsilon_{\mathrm{it}} \quad (3)$$

Baseline Regression Test. In the equation, i stands for the sample province; t denotes the annum; CEI_{it} indicates carbonic discharge intensification; DIG_{it} stands for the digitally based economy; X_{it} represents control variable series; μ_i is the individually fixed impact of the province, which does not vary over time; δ_i fixed effects of control time; and ε_{it} is the random disturbance term.

Mediation Mechanism Test. Additionally, the direct effects presented by the baseline regression model (1), to explore the potential indirect mediation techniques of the digitally based economy on the intensity of carbonic discharge, on the basis of research hypothesis H2 stated above, this study refers to the application of the mediation effects model by (Adner et al. 2019). The specific testing method is as follows: based on the significant estimation coefficients of the digitalized economy in the baseline regression model (1) for the intensity of carbon emission, we establish a regression equation for the digitally based economy on the intermediate variable (M) and a linear regression equation for the digitalized economy and the intermediate variable (M) on the intensity of carbon emission. For this purpose, the form which is specific to the mediation effect model of regression is set as follows:

$$M_{it} = \beta_0 + \beta_1 DIG_{it} + \beta_n X_{it} + \mu_i + \delta_i + \varepsilon_{it} \quad (4)$$

$$CEI_{it} = \gamma_0 + \gamma_1 DIG_{it} + \gamma_2 M_{it} + \gamma_n X_{it} + \mu_i + \delta_i + \varepsilon_{it} \quad (5)$$

Spatial Durbin Model (SDM) Test. Finally, to further explore whether the effects of a digitally based economic reduction in carbonic discharge exhibit a spatial spillover phenomenon, spatial interaction terms corresponding to a digitally based economy, the intensification of carbonic discharge, and a series of variables of control are added to the baseline regression model (1). This extends the model into an SDM (Abbas et al. 2021), with the specific form as follows:

$$CEI_{it} = \alpha_0 + \alpha_1 DIG_{it} + \alpha_n X_{it} + w_{it}(\rho_1 CEI_{it} + \rho_2 DIG_{it} + \rho_n X_{it}) + \mu_i + \delta_i + \varepsilon_{it} \quad (6)$$

ρ_1 represents the spatial autoregressive coefficient, and ρ_2 and ρ_n represent the coefficients of the spatial interaction terms for DIG and control variables; W denotes the spatial weight matrix. To ensure the effectiveness of empirical test results, the paper employs an economic geography distance matrix for regression (Elhorst 2010).

4.3. Data Sources

The article conducts an empirical study utilizing sample data from the mainland of Chinese 30 provinces, Tibet, Hong Kong, Macao, and Taiwan being excluded, spanning the years 2010 to 2020. The information utilized in this research includes digital financial data sourced from the Digital Financial Inclusivity Index published by Peking University's Digital Finance Center. Other data sources include China Environmental Yearbook, China Energy Statistics Yearbook, and National Bureau of Statistics. To mitigate potential interference from the non-stationarity of macrolevel data on empirical results, all variables employed in this paper undergo logarithmic transformations.

5. Empirical Results and Analyses

5.1. Analysis of Baseline Regression Results

According to the econometric model constructed in the previous section, the paper studies the digitally based economy's impacts on the intensification of carbonic discharge, as shown in Table 6. In the baseline regression tests, regression estimates are conducted by separately including and not including the regression model which has control variables. Simultaneously, provincial and yearly fixed effects are employed to enhance the robustness of the regression estimates (Wang et al. 2022b). The coefficient that was estimated on digitally based economy advancement on the intensification of carbonic discharge is negatively remarkable in the baseline regression, and the inclusion of control variables does not change the direction of the estimated coefficient. This indicates that the advancement of the digitalized economy has an inhibitory effect on the intensification of carbonic discharge, providing ample evidence for the digitalized economic effects on carbonic reduction, thus confirming Hypothesis 1.

Table 6. Analysis of baseline regression results.

	(1) CEI	(2) CEI	(3) 2SLS
DIG	−2.493 *** (−4.81)	−3.953 *** (−5.26)	−1.655 *** (−2.63)
INNOV		−0.317 *** (2.72)	−0.449 ** (0.072)
MAR		−0.136 ** (−2.93)	0.039 * (−0.111)
IS		0.108 (0.23)	0.395 ** (0.365)
INUR		29.835 ** (2.05)	1.186 ** (0.094)
UR		−9.625 *** (−6.51)	−0.395 (0.175)
_Cons	3.246 *** (15.89)	8.023 *** (2.72)	−14.797 ** (1.632)
Observations	330	330	300
Province FE	YES	YES	YES
Year FE	YES	YES	YES
Kleibergen-Pa ap rk LM statistics			89.833 [0.00]
Kleibergen-Pa ap Wald rk F statistics			56.473 [0.00]
R^2	0.066	0.964	0.607

Note: ***, **, and * indicate significance at the 1%, 5%, and 10% levels, respectively. T-statistics are in parentheses.

The indicators for INNOV all pass negative significance tests, suggesting that an increase in the number of applications for green patents is conducive to promoting the gradual replacement of coal and oil with clean energy, thereby reducing carbon emissions. The indicators for MAR all pass negative significance tests, indicating that an increase in marketization level improves resource allocation efficiency, reduces pollution emissions per unit output, and promotes low-carbon development. The indicators for IS all pass positive significance tests, indicating that the current industrial structure is unconducive to the discharge of carbon, possibly due to an unreasonable structure of industries. The indicators for INUR all pass positive significance tests, possibly because they focus on breakthroughs in zero-carbon industrial processes, carbon capture and utilization, and storage, reducing carbon emissions. The indicators for UR all pass negative significance tests, possibly because the urbanization level has its positive externalities, promoting carbon reduction processes through scale effects, resource allocation effects, and other pathways.

5.2. Endogeneity Test

Considering the potential endogeneity of the empirical results of the digitalized economy on the emissions of carbon which could impact the reliability of the conclusions in this study, a two-stage least squares method is employed for endogeneity testing. In addition, this study attempts to mitigate the potential reverse causality issue between the digitally based economy and energy-related emissions of carbon using the instrumental variable approach. Following the approach (Bai et al. 2023; Huang et al. 2023), the chosen instrumental variable is the distance that is spherical to Hangzhou from provincial capitals. The reasons are that the birthplace of digital financial platforms like Hangzhou and Alipay is leading the development of the digitally based financial sector. It can be expected that the smaller the geographical distance to Hangzhou, the higher the digitally based economy's advancement. Additionally, geographical interval, as a natural feature that is geographically typical, is not closely correlated to carbonic discharge, meeting the exogenic requirement. For empirical analysis, this study constructs terms of interaction between variables that are instrumental and the ones that are yearly dummies. The results are indicated in Table 5, column (3), with the coefficient of the regression being significant.

5.3. Robustness Test

5.3.1. Replace the Variables That Are Core Explanatory

Drawing on Lin and Li's (2011) study, this study selected energy-related discharge of carbon as the robustness dependent variable testing. The outcomes are shown in Table 6, column (3), with a significant regression coefficient. This indicates that, even when replacing the dependent variable, the digitally based economic advancement continues to reduce the energy-related discharge of carbon significantly in various provinces.

5.3.2. Replace the Explained Variable

In the earlier stages, empirical regression on carbon emissions was conducted using the Digitally based Economic Index based on the technique of entropy weight. In the robustness test, this index was replaced with the Digitally based Economic Index obtained through the component of principal analysis (Wang and Zhong 2023). The outcomes, tabulated in Table 6, column (4), reveal a highly significant regression coefficient. The digitally based economy reduces the discharge of carbon significantly, aligning with the regression results in the preceding sections and demonstrating robustness in the findings.

5.3.3. Replacement Sample Period

This study employs a robustness test by shortening the sample period, following the approach of Xing et al. (2023). After 2015, China experienced rapid development in the digital economy, and some literature uses 2015 as the starting year for research in the area of a digitally based economy. In this study, data were obtained from 2015 to 2020 for empirical estimation. The results, shown in Table 7, column (5), still exhibit a significantly negative regression coefficient, consistent with the baseline regression results of this study, validating the hypotheses presented in this paper.

Table 7. Robustness tests.

	(1)	(2)	(3)	(4)	(5)
DIG	−2.493 *** (−4.81)	−3.953 *** (−5.26)	−0.724 ** (−2.88)	−0.811 *** (−5.68)	−7.768 * (−2.86)
INNOV		−0.317 *** (2.72)	−0.139 *** (3.71)	−0.266 * (−2.05)	−0.253 (−0.45)
MAR		−0.136 ** (−2.93)	−0.0398 * (−2.53)	−0.125 ** (−2.70)	−0.183 (−1.93)
IS		0.108 (0.23)	−0.123 * (−2.26)	0.251 (1.50)	−1.748 ** (−3.25)
INUR		29.835 ** (2.05)	6.874 (−1.39)	37.79 * (2.54)	89.100 (1.59)
UR		−9.625 *** (−6.51)	−0.654 (1.10)	−9.495 *** (−5.73)	−21.71 (−1.64)
_Cons	3.246 *** (15.89)	8.023 *** (2.72)	9.505 *** (12.64)	7.803 *** (3.48)	25.63 (1.67)
Province FE	YES	YES	YES	YES	YES
Year FE	YES	YES	YES	YES	YES
Observations	330	330	330	330	330
R^2	0.006	0.964	0.977	0.965	0.993

Note: ***, **, and * indicate significance at the 1%, 5%, and 10% levels, respectively. T-statistics are in parentheses.

6. Discussion

6.1. Analysis of Intermediary Mechanisms

In the analysis in terms of theory in the previous section, the role of the transmission mechanism of the digitally based economy bringing effect on the intensification of carbon discharge of various provinces was analyzed from the perspective of the intensification of energy consumption. To verify this assumption of the transmission mechanism, the paper borrows the method from Tsurumi and Managi (2010) and employs a mediation effect test for empirical analysis, with the outcome of the test tabulated in Table 8. In the first column, the coefficient for DIG is significantly negative, meeting the primary condition of the mediation effect test. The results in the second column show that the digitally based economic advancement reduces the intensification of energy consumption significantly. Observing the coefficient, with control variables held constant, the digitally based economic increase by 1% can lead to a 1.817% decrease in energy consumption intensity. The results in the third column indicate that the intensity of energy consumption is correlated to the discharge of carbon intensity positively. For every 1% decrease in energy consumption intensity, the intensity of carbon discharge can be reduced by 2.553%, demonstrating the existence and significance of the mediation effect.

Table 8. Regression models for intermediate variables.

	(1) CEI	(2) CEI	(3) CEI
DIG	−2.493 *** (−4.81)	−1.817 *** (−5.29)	−1.721 (−1.49)
CP			2.553 *** (13.45)
INNOV		−0.118 *** (4.12)	−0.017 (0.18)
MAR		−0.0330 *** (−2.89)	−0.052 (−1.41)
IS		0.005 * (1.66)	−0.01 (−1.03)
INUR		15.716 *** (4.42)	−10.284 (−0.88)
UR		−3.033 *** (−8.38)	−1.883 (−1.46)
_Cons	3.246 *** (15.89)	1.743 *** (3.20)	3.573 ** (2.01)
Province FE	YES	YES	YES
Year FE	YES	YES	YES
Observations	330	330	330
R^2	0.066	0.967	0.978

Note: ***, **, and * indicate significance at the 1%, 5%, and 10% levels, respectively. T-statistics are in parentheses.

For the robustness guarantee of the mediation effect, this research conducted a bootstrap test (Wu et al. 2021), as shown in Table 9. It can be observed that the effects that are indirectly and directly correlated to energy consumption intensity are important. The 95% confidence interval for the indirect effect is [3.423–4.264], excluding 0, indicating the presence of a mediation effect.

Table 9. Bootstrap test of energy structure.

	Estimated Coefficient	Standard Error	Z Value	95% Confidence Interval	
Direct Effect	0.387 ***	0.251	0.231	0.128	0.246
Indirect Effect	3.843 ***	0.214	7.811	3.423	4.264

Note: ***, indicates significance at the 1%, 5%, and 10% levels, respectively. T-statistics are in parentheses.

6.2. Spatial Spillover Analysis of Effects

Before an analysis of economically centered spatial effects is conducted, it is necessary to separately perform an investigation on the existence of spatial effects for both the digitally based economy and the carbon discharge intensity. In this regard, Moran's I index method (Wen et al. 2020) is used to test the spatial autocorrelation on both factors, and the outcomes are tabulated in Table 10. The outcomes of the test indicate that the indices of Moran I for the digitally based economic advancement index and intensity of carbonic discharge are significant from 2010 to 2020. This indicates a clear spatial autocorrelation for the digitally based economy and carbon discharge intensity in all provinces during the study period, reflecting the spatial clustering distribution characteristics of both. The use of an economically centered spatial analysis is therefore considered reasonable and feasible. Furthermore, it is necessary to select an appropriate spatial econometric model for empirical analysis. Following the methodology described in Bai et al. (2023) to determine spatial econometric models, LM tests, Hausman tests, LR estimates, and Wald tests are performed sequentially. All outcomes of the tests indicate that the spatial model of Durbin with dual fixed impacts is optimal. Table 10 presents the outcomes of the spatial model of Durbin (SDM), which tests the effects of the digital economy on the intensity of carbon discharge within the economic geographic interval matrix of the spatial weight matrix. Examining the results, the spatial autoregressive coefficient (ρ) for discharge of carbon intensity is significantly positive at the 1% level under both matrices of spatial weights. This means that there are regional spillover effects on the discharge of carbon dioxide intensity, where the increase in the intensity of emission of neighboring counties worsens the emission intensity of the focus area. To analyze the digitally based economy's advancement impacts that are both direct and indirect on the reduction in the discharge of carbon dioxide, the partial disaggregation technique suggested by Wang et al. (2022a) is utilized in the decomposition of the overall regional effect of the digitally based economy on the intensity of carbon. The impact decomposition results presented in Table 11 below and the spatial weight matrix of economic geography show that the estimated coefficients for the indirect impact, direct impact, and total impact of the digital economy are all remarkably negative at the level of 1%. This suggests that the digitally based economy can effectively curb the intensity of the carbon dioxide discharge of the focus area and neighboring provinces, which will accelerate the growth of digitally based economic advancement and help reduce the emission intensity of carbon dioxide.

Table 10. Moran's I values of carbon emission intensity.

	2010	2011	2012	2013	2014	2015	2016	2017	2018	2019	2020
CEI	0.354 *** (3.266)	0.352 *** (3.316)	0.354 *** (3.331)	0.342 *** (3.241)	0.340 *** (3.221)	0.303 ** (2.919)	0.316 ** (3.003)	0.353 *** (3.328)	0.354 *** (3.364)	0.389 *** (3.674)	0.316 ** (3.007)
DIG	0.110 * (1.381)	0.220 ** (2.339)	0.172 ** (1.983)	0.10 * (1.722)	0.140 * (1.680)	0.143 * (1.715)	0.917 ** (2.176)	0.197 ** (2.126)	0.204 ** (2.219)	0.261 *** (2.727)	0.269 *** (2.822)

Note: ***, **, and * indicate significance at the 1%, 5%, and 10% levels, respectively. T-statistics are in parentheses.

Table 11. Spatial Durbin model regression results.

	(1) CEI	(2) Direct Effect	(3) Indirect Effect	(4) Total Effect
DIG	−3.032 *** (−4.31)	−2.899 *** (−3.60)	−1.170 (−0.50)	−4.069 ** (−1.98)
_cons	Yes	Yes	Yes	Yes
Province FE	Yes	Yes	Yes	Yes
Year FE	Yes	Yes	Yes	Yes
ρ_1	−1.374 *** (−5.56)	/	/	/
Sigma2_e	0.084 *** (12.27)	/	/	/
R^2	0.086	0.072	0.678	0.279

Note: ***, ** indicate significance at the 1%, 5% levels, respectively. T-statistics are in parentheses.

6.3. Heterogeneity Analysis

6.3.1. Heterogeneity in Different Regions

From Table 12, it is possible to observe that there is a disparity in terms of region in the digitally based economy's impacts on the emission of carbon dioxide in different parts. The reduction in carbon effects of the digitalized economy in the regions in the eastern and central parts is in line with the national level, while the emission intensity of carbon dioxide in the western areas is not remarkable. This may be due to the relatively backward development of digital infrastructure in the western region, leading to poor integration of the digital economy with green technologies, resulting in insignificant impacts on carbon reduction (Zeng and Yang (2023)). Therefore, in building China's digitalized economy, more attention must be paid to integrating regional digitalization with the aim of narrowing the gap in digitalized economic advancement between regions.

Table 12. Heterogeneity analysis.

	(1)			(2)		
	East	Central	Western	Developed	Medium Developed	Less Developed
DIG	−1.710 *** (−3.38)	−6.994 * (−4.68)	−4.951 (−2.14)	−0.913 ** (−3.62)	−1.490 * (−2.27)	−0.845 (−2.25)
Control variable	Yes	Yes	Yes	Yes	Yes	Yes
_Cons	5.759 *** (3.73)	3.599 (1.41)	6.69 ** (3.02)	7.265 *** (4.38)	0.246 (0.06)	4.140 (2.18)
Province FE	YES	YES	YES	YES	YES	YES
Year FE	YES	YES	YES	YES	YES	YES
R^2	0.972	0.982	0.962	0.993	0.944	0.981

Note: ***, **, and * indicate significance at the 1%, 5%, and 10% levels, respectively. T-statistics are in parentheses.

6.3.2. Heterogeneity in Levels of Economic Development

To examine the effects of the digitally based economy on the emission of carbon in provinces with different features of economic development, we draw on the research of scholars (Song et al. 2020). Using provincial economic advancement level as a dividing criterion and per capita GDP as a measure of economic advancement, we conducted group regression by calculating the median for the samples. The results are indicated in Table 11. The digitally based economy's effects on developed and moderately developed regions are more significant. This may be due to the scale advantages of developed regions in terms of the structure of industries, governance of environmental investment, and technological innovation, leading to certain agglomeration effects that facilitate resource optimization. In contrast, the effects are not significant in underdeveloped regions.

7. Conclusions and Policy Implications

7.1. Conclusions

On the basis of panel data from Chinese regions between 2010 and 2020, this paper focuses on typical facts indicating that the advancement of the digitally based economy can seriously affect changes in the intensity of carbon emission. Simultaneously considering the inherent attributes of the digitalized economy, the paper analytically examines the direct impacts and transmission techniques of the digitally based economy on the intensity of carbonic discharge from a theoretical perspective. By employing double fixed effects, mediating effects, and spatial Durbin models, the paper validates, from a two-dimensional to a three-dimensional perspective, the impact and mechanisms of the digitally based economy on the intensity of carbon emission. This research paper mainly concludes as follows: First of all, during the study period, China's digitalized economy achieved relatively rapid advancement, with obvious advantages in the digitally based economy's advancement in coastal areas. At the same time, the digitalized economy has a downward variation behavior in the intensity of carbon emission of each province and has more effects on the intensity of discharge of carbon of eastern and developed regions. Second, the digital economy can remarkably reduce carbon dioxide discharge intensity, and common prosperity is an important mechanism. Third, as it is viewed from the angle of spatial effects, the intensity of carbon dioxide emissions has many effects that are positive in regions, while the digitalized economic impact on the intensity of discharge of carbon dioxide shows a significant negative externality in space. This shows that the intensity of carbon can be effectively moderated by the digitalized economy in the baseline regression test. At the same time, there is still some room for improvement in this paper, mainly due to the limitations of data sources. The evaluation index system of digital economy development level and common wealth is not comprehensive enough, which leads to the final effect measurement results not being comprehensive enough. In future research, we will try to construct a more comprehensive indicator system for the level of digital economy development and common wealth. In addition, exploring the multi-scale regional heterogeneity of the impact of the digital economy on carbon emissions, especially the typical cases, is also a direction worth expanding.

7.2. Policy Implications

On the basis of the study conclusions stated above, the paper not only provides strong experiential proof for the impact of the digitally based economic reduction in the discharge of carbon energy but also puts forward the following policy suggestions: First, improve the infrastructure construction related to the digitally based economy and continue to promote the enhancement of the level of digitalized economic advancement. Networked, intelligent, service-oriented, and collaborative infrastructure layers should be continuously promoted in order to fully exploit the benefits of the digital economy in promoting deep decarbonization. Second, introduce differentiated policies for digitally based economic advancement. Intensify efforts to support and develop the digitalization level of underdeveloped regions, promote the widespread and deep penetration of digitalized technology into various fields, stimulate the use and coming up of digitally based technology, its application areas, and models of business in remote and underdeveloped areas, and balance digitally based economic advancement among regions. Third, on the basis of the mechanism of innovation and energy intensity, explore the multidimensional paths through which the digitally based economy promotes carbon emission reduction. The government should create a diversified value transmission and contribution distribution system, systematically guide the development of new employment and entrepreneurship platforms such as diverse social networks, short videos, and knowledge sharing, elevate the innovation level of regions through the digitally based economy, and thereby achieve a reduction in carbon discharge. Additionally, expedite the application of smart energy construction, promote the intelligent upgrading of energy production, transportation, consumption, and other aspects, and drive the low-carbon transformation of the energy industry. Fourth, strengthen collaborative governance of the discharge of carbon among regions and leverage the spatial "green" radiation impact of the digitally based economy. In addressing the reduction in carbon discharge, it is essential to enhance the exchange and connection of carbon emission policies among regions, establish a unified and joint platform for sharing warnings about regions exceeding emission carbon standards, advance the monitoring of statistics and systems of decision analysis on the basis of recent technologies such as block chain, artificial intelligence, and big data, formulate more flexible and effective policy measures, cultivate a new pattern of digitalized economic governance with diverse governance and coordinated development, and create a low-carbon network of digital economies across multiple regions.

Author Contributions: J.G.: Methodology, Validation, Formal analysis, Investigation, Resources. W.Z.: Software, Methodology, Validation, Formal analysis. J.C.: Formal analysis, Writing—reviewing & editing. Z.L.: Resources, Writing—reviewing & editing. All authors have read and agreed to the published version of the manuscript.

Funding: This research received no external funding.

Institutional Review Board Statement: Not applicable.

Informed Consent Statement: Informed consent was obtained from all subjects involved in the study.

Data Availability Statement: All data generated or analyzed for this study are included in this published article.

Conflicts of Interest: The authors declare that they have no competing interests.

References

Abbas, Hafiz Syed Mohsin, Xiao dong Xu, and Chun xia Sun. 2021. Role of foreign direct investment interaction to energy consumption and institutional governance in sustainable GHG emission reduction. *Environmental Science and Pollution Research* 28: 56808–21. [CrossRef] [PubMed]

Adner, Ron, Phanish Puranam, and Feng Zhu. 2019. What Is Different About Digital Strategy? From Quantitative to Qualitative Change. *Strategy Science* 4: 253–61. [CrossRef]

Ahmed, Zahoor, Mahmood Ahmad, Muntasir Murshed, Muhammad Ibrahim Shah, Haider Mahmood, and Shujaat Abbas. 2022. How do green energy technology investments, technological innovation, and trade globalization enhance green energy supply and stimulate environmental sustainability in the G7 countries? *Gondwana Research* 112: 105–15. [CrossRef]

Alam, Naushad, Nazia Iqbal Hashmi, Syed Ahsan Jamil, Muntasir Murshed, Haider Mahmood, and Shabbir Alam. 2022. The marginal effects of economic growth, financial development, and low-carbon energy use on carbon footprints in Oman: Fresh evidence from autoregressive distributed lag model analysis. *Environmental Science and Pollution Research* 29: 76432–45. [CrossRef]

Awan, Ashar, Kashif Raza Abbasi, Soumen Rej, Arunava Bandyopadhyay, and Kangjuan Lv. 2022. The impact of renewable energy, internet use and foreign direct investment on carbon dioxide emissions: A method of moments quantile analysis. *Renewable Energy* 189: 454–66. [CrossRef]

Bai, Ling, Tianran Guo, Wei Xu, Yaobin Liu, Ming Kuang, and Lei Jiang. 2023. Effects of digital economy on carbon emission intensity in Chinese cities: A life-cycle theory and the application of non-linear spatial panel smooth transition threshold model. *Energy Policy* 183: 113792. [CrossRef]

CAICT. 2020. *White Paper on China's Digital Economy Development 2020*. Beijing: China Academy of Information and Communications Technology.

Chen, Guifu, Jing Han, and Hongwei Yuan. 2022. Urban digital economy development, enterprise innovation, and ESG performance in China. *Frontiers in Environmental Science* 10: 955055. [CrossRef]

Chen, Lijuan. 2021. How CO_2 emissions respond to changes in government size and level of digitalization? Evidence from the BRICS countries. *Environmental Science and Pollution Research* 29: 457–67. [CrossRef] [PubMed]

Chen, Li, and Yuanbo Zhang. 2023. Does the development of the digital economy promote common prosperity?—Analysis based on 284 cities in China. *Sustainability* 15: 4688. [CrossRef]

Chen, Pengyu. 2022. Is the digital economy driving clean energy development? -New evidence from 276 cities in China. *Journal of Cleaner Production* 372: 133783. [CrossRef]

Chen, Wen, and Ying Wu. 2022. Does intellectual property protection stimulate digital economy development? *Journal of Applied Economics* 25: 723–30. [CrossRef]

Chen, Yu, and Boqiang Lin. 2021. Understanding the green total factor energy efficiency gap between regional manufacturing—Insight from infrastructure development. *Energy* 237: 121553. [CrossRef]

Cheng, Yue, Yue Zhang, Jingjing Wang, and Jinxing Jiang. 2023. The impact of the urban digital economy on China's carbon intensity: Spatial spillover and mediating effect. *Conservation and Recycling* 189: 106762. [CrossRef]

Cheng, Zhonghua, Lianshui Li, and Jun Liu. 2018. Industrial structure, technical progress and carbon intensity in China's provinces. *Renewable and Sustainable Energy Reviews* 81: 2935–46. [CrossRef]

Dong, Kangyin, Renjin Sun, Hongdian Jiang, and Xiangang Zeng. 2018. CO_2 emissions, economic growth, and the environmental Kuznets curve in China: What roles can nuclear energy and renewable energy play? *Journal of Cleaner Production* 196: 51–63. [CrossRef]

Elhorst, J. Paul. 2010. Applied Spatial Econometrics: Raising the Bar. *Spatial Economic Analysis* 5: 9–28. [CrossRef]

Fernández-Portillo, Antonio, Manuel Almodóvar-González, and Ricardo Hernández-Mogollón. 2020. Impact of ICT development on economic growth. A study of OECD European union countries. *Technology in Society* 63: 101420. [CrossRef]

Godil, Danish I., Zhang Yu, Arshian Sharif, Rimsha Usman, and Syed Abdul Rehman Khan. 2021. Investigate the role of technology innovation and renewable energy in reducing transport sector CO_2 emission in China: A path toward sustainable development. *Sustainable Development* 29: 694–707. [CrossRef]

Guo, Qingran, Zhou Wu, Atif Jahanger, Cuicui Ding, Bocheng Guo, and Ashar Awan. 2022. The spatial impact of digital economy on energy intensity in China in the context of double carbon to achieve the sustainable development goals. *Environmental Science and Pollution Research International* 30: 35528–44. [CrossRef]

Han, Ying, Xiaoyuan Qi, and Yuanfan Yang. 2020. Analysis of the spillover effect of energy intensity among provinces in China based on space-time lag model. *Environmental Science and Pollution Research* 27: 16950–62. [CrossRef]

Huang, Junbing, Yajun Wang, Bingjiang Luan, Hong Zou, and Jun Wang. 2023. The energy intensity reduction effect of developing digital economy: Theory and empirical evidence from China. *Energy Economics* 128: 107193. [CrossRef]

Kamal, Mustafa, Muhammad Usman, Atif Jahanger, and Daniel Balsalobre-Lorente. 2021a. Revisiting the role of fiscal policy, financial development, and foreign direct investment in reducing environmental pollution during globalization mode: Evidence from linear and nonlinear panel data approaches. *Energies* 14: 6968. [CrossRef]

Khan, Samiha, Muntasir Murshed, Ilhan Ozturk, and Khurshid Khudoykulov. 2022a. The roles of energy efficiency improvement, renewable electricity production, and financial inclusion in stimulating environmental sustainability in the Next Eleven countries. *Renewable Energy* 193: 1164–76. [CrossRef]

Khan, Yasir, Hana Oubaih, and Fatima Zahra Elgourrami. 2022b. The effect of renewable energy sources on carbon dioxide emissions: Evaluating the role of governance, and ICT in Morocco. *Renewable Energy* 190: 752–63. [CrossRef]

Kong, Haojia, Lifan Shi, Dan Da, Zhijiang Li, Decai Tang, and Wei Xing. 2022. Simulation of China's Carbon Emission based on Influencing Factors. *Energies* 15: 3272. [CrossRef]

Li, Wenjing, Xiaozhong Yu, Nan Hu, Fan Huang, Jing Wang, and Qingnan Peng. 2022. Study on the relationship between fossil energy consumption and carbon emission in Sichuan Province. *Energy Reports* 8: 53–62. [CrossRef]

Li, Xiaoyan, Jia Liu, and Peijie Ni. 2021a. The impact of the digital economy on CO_2 emissions: A theoretical and empirical analysis. *Sustainability* 13: 7267. [CrossRef]

Li, Zhiguo, and Jie Wang. 2022a. Spatial spillover effect of carbon emission trading on carbon emission reduction: Empirical data from pilot regions in China. *Energy* 251: 123906. [CrossRef]

Li, Zhiguo, and Jie Wang. 2022b. The dynamic impact of digital economy on carbon emission reduction: Evidence city-level empirical data in China. *Journal of Cleaner Production* 351: 131570. [CrossRef]

Li, Zihanxin, Nuoyan Li, and Huwei Wen. 2021b. Digital Economy and Environmental Quality: Evidence from 217 Cities in China. *Sustainability* 13: 8058. [CrossRef]

Lin, Boqiang, and Xuehui Li. 2011. The effect of carbon tax on per capita CO_2 emissions. *Energy Policy* 39: 5137–46. [CrossRef]

Liu, Da, Linlin Xu, Umma Habiba Sadia, and Hui Wang. 2021a. Evaluating the CO_2 emission reduction effect of China's battery electric vehicle promotion efforts. *Atmospheric Pollution Research* 12: 101115. [CrossRef]

Liu, Yonghong, Chaochao Gao, and Yingying Lu. 2017. The impact of urbanization on GHG emissions in China: The role of population density. *Journal of Cleaner Production* 157: 299–309. [CrossRef]

Liu, Yang, Kangyin Dong, Jianda Wang, and Farhad Taghizadeh-Hesary. 2023. Towards sustainable development goals: Does common prosperity contradict carbon reduction? *Economic Analysis and Policy* 79: 70–88. [CrossRef]

Liu, Yun, Meng Liu, Gege Wang, Lulu Zhao, and Pan An. 2021b. Effect of Environmental Regulation on High-quality Economic Development in China-An Empirical Analysis Based on Dynamic Spatial Durbin Model. *Environmental Science and Pollution Research* 28: 54661–78. [CrossRef]

Llopis-Albert, Carlos, Francisco Rubio, and Francisco Valero. 2021. Impact of digital transformation on the automotive industry. *Technological Forecasting and Social Change* 162: 120343. [CrossRef]

Ma, Dan, and Qing Zhu. 2022. Innovation in emerging economies: Research on the digital economy driving high-quality green development. *Journal of Business Research* 145: 801–13. [CrossRef]

Ma, Qiang, Muhammad Tariq, Haider Mahmood, and Zeeshan Khan. 2022. The nexus between digital economy and carbon dioxide emissions in China: The moderating role of investments in research and development. *Technology in Society* 68: 101910. [CrossRef]

Mohsin, Muhammad, Han Phoumin, Ik Joong Youn, and Farhad Taghizadeh-Hesary. 2021. Enhancing energy and environmental efficiency in the power sectors: A case study of Singapore and China. *Journal of Environmental Assessment Policy and Management* 23: 2250018. [CrossRef]

Nicolay, John. 1999. The digital economy: Promise and peril in the age of networked intelligence. *Journal of Policy Analysis and Management* 18: 156–68.
Ozturk, Ilhan, and Sana Ullah. 2022. Does digital financial inclusion matter for economic growth and environmental sustainability in OBRI economies? An empirical analysis. *Resources, Conservation and Recycling* 185: 106489. [CrossRef]
Pang, Silu, Guihong Hua, and Hui Liu. 2023. How do R&D capital market distortions affect innovation efficiency in China? Some evidence about spatial interaction and spillover effects. *Socio-Economic Planning Sciences* 90: 101739.
Pata, Ugur Korkut, and Cem Isik. 2021. Determinants of the load capacity factor in China: A novel dynamic ARDL approach for ecological footprint accounting. *Resources Policy* 74: 102313. [CrossRef]
Pata, Ugur Korkut, Sinan Erdogan, and Oktay Ozkan. 2023. Is reducing fossil fuel intensity important for environmental management and ensuring ecological efficiency in China? *Journal of Environmental Management* 329: 117080. [CrossRef]
Ren, Siyu, Y. Hao, Lu Xu, Haitao Wu, and Ning Ba. 2021. Digitalization and energy: How does internet development affect China's energy consumption? *Energy Economics* 98: 105220. [CrossRef]
Shi, Xiuyi, Yingzhi Xu, and Wenyuan Sun. 2023. Evaluating China's pilot carbon Emission Trading Scheme: Collaborative reduction of carbon and air pollutants (Dec, 10.1007/s11356-022-24685-z, 2022). *Environmental Science and Pollution Research* 30: 11357–58. [CrossRef]
Sobaci, Mehmet Zahid, and Kadir Eryigit. 2015. Determinants of E-Democracy Adoption in Turkish Municipalities: An Analysis for Spatial Diffusion Effect. *Local Government Studies* 41: 445–69. [CrossRef]
Song, Mei, Jin Wu, Mengran Song, Liyan Zhang, and Yaxu Zhu. 2020. Spatiotemporal regularity and spillover effects of carbon emission intensity in China's Bohai Economic Rim. *Science of the Total Environment* 740: 140184. [CrossRef]
Soytas, Ugur, Ramazan Sari, and Bradley T. Ewing. 2007. Energy consumption, income, and carbon emissions in the United States. *Ecological Economics* 62: 482–89. [CrossRef]
Tan, Liu, and Zhang Kaili. 2023. Effects of the digital economy on carbon emissions in China: An analysis based on different innovation paths. *Environmental Science and Pollution Research* 30: 79451–68.
Tong, Dan, Qiang Zhang, Fei Liu, Guang Geng, Yixuan Zheng, Tao Xue, Chaopeng Hong, Ruili Wu, Yu Qin, and H. Zhao. 2018. Current emissions and future mitigation pathways of coal-fired power plants in China from 2010 to 2030. *Environmental Science & Technology* 52: 12905–14.
Tsurumi, Tetsuya, and Shunsuke Managi. 2010. Decomposition of the environmental Kuznets curve: Scale, technique, and composition effects. *Environmental Economics & Policy Studies* 11: 19–36.
Usman, Muhammad, Atif Jahanger, Muhammad Sohail Amjad Makhdum, Daniel Balsalobre-Lorente, and A. Bashir. 2022. How do financial development, energy consumption, natural resources, and globalization affect Arctic countries' economic growth and environmental quality? An advanced panel data simulation. *Energy* 241: 122515. [CrossRef]
Valadkhani, Abbas, Russell Smyth, and Jeremy Nguyen. 2019. Effects of primary energy consumption on CO_2 emissions under optimal thresholds: Evidence from sixty countries over the last half century. *Energy Economics* 80: 680–90. [CrossRef]
Visconti-Caparrós, Jose Maria, and Juan Ramon Campos-Blázquez. 2022. The development of alternate payment methods and their impact on customer behavior: The Bizum case in Spain. *Technological Forecasting and Social Change* 175: 121330. [CrossRef]
Wang, Hui, Xingang Zhao, Lingzhi Ren, Jicheng Fan, and Fan Lu. 2021. The impact of technological progress on energy intensity in China (2005–2016): Evidence from a geographically and temporally weighted regression model. *Energy* 226: 120362.
Wang, Jianda, Kangyin Dong, Xiucheng Dong, and Farhad Taghizadeh-Hesary. 2022a. Assessing the digital economy and its carbon-mitigation effects: The case of China. *Energy Economics* 113: 106198. [CrossRef]
Wang, Qiang, Jiayi Sun, Ugur Korkut Pata, Rongrong Li, and Mustafa Tevfik Kartal. 2023. Digital economy and carbon dioxide emissions: Examining the role of threshold variables. *Geoscience Frontiers* 15: 101644. [CrossRef]
Wang, Xingan, and Min Zhong. 2023. Can digital economy reduce carbon emission intensity? Empirical evidence from China's smart city pilot policies. *Environmental Science and Pollution Research* 30: 51749–69. [CrossRef]
Wang, Zhijia, Lijuan Liang, Dong Cheng, Hujun Li, and Yongheng Zhang. 2022b. Emission Reduction Benefits and Economic Benefits of China's Pilot Policy on Carbon Emission Trading System. *Computational Intelligence and Neuroscience* 2022: 5280900. [CrossRef]
Wen, Le, Basil Sharp, and Erwann Sbai. 2020. Spatial Effects of Wind Generation and Its Implication for Wind Farm Investment Decisions in New Zealand. *The Energy Journal* 41: 47–72. [CrossRef]
Wu, Haitao, Yan Xue, Yu Hao, and Siyu Ren. 2021. How does internet development affect energy-saving and emission reduction? Evidence from China. *Energy Economics* 103: 105577. [CrossRef]
Wu, Xiting, Qun Cao, Xiaoping Tan, and Liang Li. 2020. The effect of audit of outgoing leading officials' natural resource accountability on environmental governance: Evidence from China. *Managerial Auditing Journal* 35: 1213–41. [CrossRef]
Xing, Zeyu, Jing Huang, and Jing Wang. 2023. Unleashing the potential: Exploring the nexus between low-carbon digital economy and regional economic-social development in China. *Journal of Cleaner Production* 413: 137552. [CrossRef]
Xue, Yan, Chang Tang, Haitao Wu, Jiamin Liu, and Yu Hao. 2022. The emerging driving force of energy consumption in China: Does digital economy development matter? *Energy Policy* 165: 112997. [CrossRef]
Yang, Bo, Minhaj Ali, Shujahat Haider Hashmi, and Atif Jahanger. 2022. Do income inequality and institutional quality affect CO_2 emissions in developing economies? *Environmental Science and Pollution Research* 29: 42720–41. [CrossRef]
Yi, Ming, Yafen Liu, Mingyue Sheng, and Le Wen. 2022. Effects of digital economy on carbon emission reduction: New evidence from China. *Energy Policy* 171: 113271. [CrossRef]

Zeng, Jingting, and Moru Yang. 2023. Digital technology and carbon emissions: Evidence from China. *Journal of Cleaner Production* 430: 139765. [CrossRef]
Zhang, Jie, and Fangbin Qian. 2023. Digital economy enables common prosperity: Analysis of mediating and moderating effects based on green finance and environmental pollution. *Frontiers in Energy Research* 10: 1080230. [CrossRef]
Zhang, Minglong, and Yin Liu. 2022. Influence of digital finance and green technology innovation on China's carbon emission efficiency: Empirical analysis based on spatial metrology. *Science of The Total Environment* 838: 156463. [CrossRef]
Zhang, Wei, Xuemeng Liu, Die Wang, and Jianping Zhou. 2022. Digital economy and carbon emission performance: Evidence at China's city level. *Energy Policy* 165: 112927. [CrossRef]
Zhang, Weike, Hongxia Fan, and Qiwei Zhao. 2023. Seeing green: How does digital infrastructure affect carbon emission intensity? *Energy Economics* 127: 107085. [CrossRef]
Zhao, Xiaochun, Laichun Long, and Shi Yin. 2023. Regional common prosperity level and its spatial relationship with carbon emission intensity in China. *Scientific Reports* 13: 17035. [CrossRef]
Zhou, Xiaoyong, Dequn Zhou, Qunwei Wang, and Bin Su. 2019. How information and communication technology drives carbon emissions: A sector-level analysis for China. *Energy Economics* 81: 380–92. [CrossRef]
Zhu, Zhichan, Bo Liu, Zhuoxi Yu, and Jianhong Cao. 2022. Effects of the Digital Economy on Carbon Emissions: Evidence from China. *International Journal of Environmental Research and Public Health* 19: 9450. [CrossRef]

Disclaimer/Publisher's Note: The statements, opinions and data contained in all publications are solely those of the individual author(s) and contributor(s) and not of MDPI and/or the editor(s). MDPI and/or the editor(s) disclaim responsibility for any injury to people or property resulting from any ideas, methods, instructions or products referred to in the content.

economies

MDPI

Article

Peruvian Agro-Exports' Competitiveness: An Assessment of the Export Development of Its Main Products

Jose Carlos Montes Ninaquispe *, Alberto Luis Pantaleón Santa María, Diego Alejandro Ludeña Jugo, William Teófilo Castro Muñoz, Juan Cesar Farias Rodriguez, Billy Heinrich Maco Elera and Kelly Cristina Vasquez Huatay

Programa de Administración y Administración de Negocios Internacionales Filial Norte, Universidad de San Martín de Porres, Chiclayo 14001, Peru; apantaleons@usmp.pe (A.L.P.S.M.); dludenaj@usmp.pe (D.A.L.J.); wcastrom@usmp.pe (W.T.C.M.); jfariasr@usmp.pe (J.C.F.R.); bmacoe@usmp.pe (B.H.M.E.); kvasquezh@usmp.pe (K.C.V.H.)

* Correspondence: jmontesn@usmp.pe; Tel.: +51-979985261

Abstract: This study analyzed the competitiveness of Peru's exports of grapes, blueberries, avocados, and asparagus from 2019 to 2023. Data were obtained from the customs declarations of all exporting companies of the analyzed products, along with data from the International Trade Center. Competitiveness was measured using the absolute revealed comparative advantage (RCA) index. The results indicate notable growth in the exports of grapes and blueberries, while asparagus and avocados face challenges in market and exporter diversification. The RCA index suggests a strong and stable specialization in these products. This study concludes with specific recommendations for institutions such as Ministerio de Desarrollo Agrario y Riego (MIDAGRI), Comisión de Promoción del Perú para la Exportación y el Turismo (PROMPERÚ), Asociación de Exportadores (ADEX), and Instituto Nacional de Innovación Agraria (INIA), aimed at enhancing competitiveness through market diversification.

Keywords: agro-exports; Peru; international competitiveness; RCA; export development

1. Introduction

The Peruvian agro-export sector has demonstrated notable growth and dynamism, especially in recent years, driven by its strategic geographical advantages, favorable climatic conditions, and dedicated efforts towards modernization and quality enhancement. This study holds significance for the Peruvian agro-export sector by providing an analysis of its four main products, serving as an indispensable tool for understanding Peru's strategic position in international business. Furthermore, the research goes beyond the mere assessment of competitiveness, venturing into the exploration of export growth over time. This approach offers a more detailed understanding as it examines the quantitative growth of exports, including market diversity expansion and the analysis of participating companies. Ultimately, it represents a significant contribution to the academic literature in the fields of international trade and agricultural economics. Its value extends beyond understanding the dynamics of the agro-export sector, as it provides a valuable resource for academics and students to grasp the complex dynamics of agro-exports in emerging economies like Peru's.

The competitiveness of agro-exports is a topic of utmost importance in the global economy (De Melo and De Carvalho 2024). Internationally, these challenges can be categorized into several fundamental aspects that affect agriculture and its product exports (Femeena et al. 2012). Climate change and environmental issues are among the most significant challenges (Bortz and Toftum 2023). Alterations in climatic patterns, including changes in rainfall and temperature regimes, have a direct impact on agricultural productivity (Liu et al. 2022). The need to adopt sustainable agricultural practices and responsible use of natural resources has become increasingly important and crucial (Laosutsan et al. 2019). Soil degradation, water scarcity, and biodiversity loss are environmental issues that not only threaten the long-term viability of the agro-export sector but also raise serious questions about the sustainability of current practices (Wang 2018). Furthermore, globalization has created a highly competitive market, requiring agricultural producers to be cost-efficient and quickly adapt to changing market demands (Morales-Marín et al. 2018). The international prices of agricultural products significantly impact the economic stability of exporting countries, underscoring the need for adaptive strategies. On the other hand, trade barriers, both tariff and non-tariff, present a considerable obstacle to the sector (Fiankor and Santeramo 2023). Additionally, protectionist policies of some countries, along with stringent sanitary and phytosanitary regulations, can limit access to key markets (Thorbecke et al. 2021). The dependence on bilateral or multi-lateral trade agreements can also affect the stability of exports (Ando et al. 2022). Moreover, technological innovation plays a crucial role in improving productivity and efficiency. However, the adoption of advanced technologies is often hindered by a lack of investment, infrastructure, and limited access to training and technical assistance (Esquivias et al. 2023).

The technological gap between developed and developing countries is a critical factor, as are logistical and supply chain processes (Peano et al. 2017). Efficiency in transportation and logistics is vital to ensure the quality and freshness of agricultural products, especially perishables (Orjuela-Castro et al. 2021). High transportation costs and inadequate infrastructure can significantly increase operational costs and affect the competitiveness of exports (Rai et al. 2022). Access to financing is another essential aspect, especially for small and medium agricultural producers, who often face difficulties in accessing credit and financing to invest in technological improvements or expand their production (Meng et al. 2023). In the social and labor sphere, working conditions and labor rights in the agricultural sector are of great concern. Issues such as labor exploitation, child labor, and inadequate working conditions not only affect the quality of life of workers but can also negatively impact the perception of products in international markets (Phan 2022). Many developing countries rely heavily on a limited number of primary products for their exports, making them vulnerable to market fluctuations and changes in global demand (Hu et al. 2023). This dependence underscores the need for strategies to diversify both production and export markets (Hossain et al. 2023). Lastly, global consumption patterns are changing, with an increasing focus on organic, ethical, and sustainable products (K. Sharma et al. 2023). Adapting to these emerging trends is a considerable challenge for producers who lack the means or knowledge to modify their productive practices according to these new market demands (Sihombing et al. 2021).

Examining the development of the main agro-export products in five specific countries, particular challenges faced by each in this sector are revealed. In Brazil, despite its prominence in soybean and sugar cane production, the critical challenge of diversifying its agricultural production arises (De Paula Junior 2020). This diversification is essential to reduce dependence on a few crops in the face of market fluctuations (Copetti et al. 2013). Additionally, environmental sustainability has become a significant concern, especially due to deforestation in the Amazon, raising serious doubts about the long-term viability of its agricultural practices (Escobar et al. 2020). Another significant obstacle in Brazil is poor logistical infrastructure, which increases operational costs and decreases the competitiveness of its agricultural exports (Figueira and de Oliveira 2023). In the United States, trade wars, particularly the conflict with China, have negatively impacted farmers, especially soy producers. The debate over agricultural subsidies and their influence on global competition continues to be a relevant discussion point (Dilawari et al. 2022). Despite being a leader in technological innovation, the challenge for the United States lies in maintaining constant adaptation to new technologies and sustainable practices to preserve its competitive edge (Ojede 2015). India faces significant challenges related to productivity and efficiency in its agricultural sector, exacerbated by dependence (Mruthyunjaya 2023). Socio-economic issues, such as rural poverty, farmer indebtedness, and small farm sizes, limit its ability to compete in international markets (Singh and Jyoti 2023). In Kenya, the economy relies heavily on a limited number of agricultural products for export, such as tea and flowers, making it vulnerable to market fluctuations (Wainaina et al. 2018).

Climatic challenges and extreme weather events disproportionately affect the country, negatively impacting agricultural production (Wanyonyi et al. 2023). Additionally, restricted access to international markets and inadequate financing represent barriers to sector growth. Australia, on the other hand, faces critical issues related to climate change and water resource management, especially in crop production like wheat (Ressia et al. 2022). Recent trade tensions with China have jeopardized important export markets for its agricultural products. Moreover, adapting to strict sanitary and phytosanitary regulations in export markets is a constant challenge for Australia (He et al. 2018). These countries illustrate the diversity of challenges faced by the agro-export sector globally. Each country exhibits a unique set of challenges, reflecting the complexity and dynamic nature of competitiveness in the field of agricultural exports. In Peru, the competitiveness of agro-exports faces a variety of complex challenges ranging from productive diversification to infrastructure and access to technology.

Despite having experienced significant growth in products like blueberries, grapes, avocados, and asparagus, the Peruvian economy still needs to expand its export portfolio to avoid excessive dependence on a few products (Pantaleón Santa María et al. 2022). This dependence could lead to economic vulnerability to demand shifts and price variations, underscoring the importance of exploring new markets and diversifying exportable products (Roja and Sánchez 2023). In terms of infrastructure and logistics, Peru has seen improvements, yet still faces challenges (Nonalaya et al. 2021). High internal transportation costs and inefficiency in ports are factors that increase export costs and decrease the competitiveness of Peruvian products in the international market (Bossio Valdivia et al. 2017). These logistical aspects are crucial to ensure that products reach international markets in optimal conditions and cost-effectively (Ramos et al. 2019). Access to technology and capital is another challenge for many agricultural producers in Peru. Limited resources restrict producers' ability to improve productivity and product quality and to adapt to the changing demands of global markets (Juarez Malaver 2022). Climate change and the need for environmental sustainability present additional challenges. The effects of climate change are impacting weather patterns and consequently agricultural production. Moreover, the growing international pressure to adopt sustainable agricultural practices requires significant investments and changes in cultivation practices (Coayla and Jiménez 2022).

This is crucial not only for the long-term viability of the agricultural sector but also to meet international expectations on sustainability (Mills-Novoa 2020). Complying with the strict sanitary and phytosanitary standards of international markets is another challenge (Leyva Morales 2023). Maintaining high-quality standards is essential for accessing and remaining in demanding markets, implying a continuous need for investment in quality and compliance with regulations (Parco Espinoza and Mallqui Cunurana 2022). Training and technical education are essential to improve competitiveness. The lack of these opportunities among farmers can limit their ability to adopt better agricultural practices and advanced technologies (Larrea-Gallegos et al. 2019), directly impacting the quality and competitiveness of their products (Carbonell Santillán 2023). Finally, Peru's international trade relations with key countries and economic blocs (Manrique Talledo and Muñoz Peláez 2021) have a significant influence on its ability to export. Successful trade negotiations and the opening of new markets are crucial for the expansion of agro-exports (Urcia Armas and Vivanco Caceres 2022).

The goal is to provide actionable recommendations for policymakers, industry leaders, and exporters to enhance Peru's competitiveness and ensure sustainable growth, contributing valuable insights to international trade and agricultural economics.

From a theoretical perspective, by exploring and analyzing theories related to the competitiveness and trade of agricultural products, this study enriches the academic understanding of these topics and offers new perspectives that can be applied in other contexts and studies. From a practical perspective, by focusing on the evaluation of the development of the main products, this study provides valuable information for producers and exporters, helping them to better understand market dynamics and optimize their strategies and operations. Socially, by encouraging improved competitiveness, higher income and employment can be generated in the agricultural sector, which in turn can contribute to poverty reduction and social development in rural areas.

Nations benefit from specializing in the production of goods where they have a comparative advantage, that is, where they are relatively more efficient than other countries (Krugman and Obstfeld 2006). In the context of agro-exports, this theory suggests that a country should specialize in the production and export of agricultural products in which it has a comparative advantage, such as in certain crops that benefit from its climate, soil, or agricultural expertise.

Competitiveness: Competitiveness refers to the ability of producers, industries, and the country to produce and export products efficiently and profitably in the international market, with aspects such as productivity, product quality, production and supply chain efficiency, market adaptability, and long-term sustainability (Esterhuizen and van Rooyen 2006). Internal factors include agricultural technology, producers' skills and knowledge, production process efficiency, the quality of inputs and natural resources (Muhamediyev 2023), and supporting infrastructure (like irrigation systems, storage, and logistics). External factors encompass global demand and consumer preferences, international market conditions (R. Zhou et al. 2023), trade policies and tariffs, and global competition. Additionally, sustainability factors related to sustainable production practices (Sharma et al. 2023), natural resource management, and adaptation to climate change are increasingly important to maintain competitiveness in the environmentally conscious global market (Saptana et al. 2023).

The Balassa model of revealed comparative advantage represents a fundamental analytical tool in the study of competitiveness in international trade applied to many studies (Das et al. 2024; Luhwago et al. 2023; De Melo and De Carvalho 2024; Nong et al. 2023; Raman et al. 2023; Saptana et al. 2023; A. Sharma et al. 2023; Shukla et al. 2023; Topcu 2023). Developed by Béla Balassa in 1965, this indicator measures a country's comparative advantage in a specific product, based on actual trade performance rather than theoretical resource endowments (Balassa 1965). Balassa's formula calculates the ratio of a product in a country's total exports relative to the ratio of that same product in total global exports. A value greater than one indicates a revealed comparative advantage, suggesting that the country is relatively more efficient in producing and exporting that product compared to other countries. The application of the revealed comparative advantage indicator in international trade analysis helps identify the products in which a country has real competitive advantages (Hidayat et al. 2023). Focusing on actual trade data, the Balassa model provides a more accurate and practical assessment of comparative advantage, which can significantly differ from predictions based solely on classic economic theory (Tarihoran et al. 2023).

Historically, Peru has undergone a significant transformation in its agricultural sector, evolving from an economy traditionally centered on domestic consumption to a more export-oriented focus. This shift has been driven by a combination of factors, including favorable government policies, investments in infrastructure, and improvements in agricultural practices.

Peru's main agro-export products have shown outstanding performance in the international market. Products like blueberries, coffee, grapes, asparagus, ginger, and avocado have not only gained significant presence in international markets but also demonstrate sustainability over time, leveraging their unique climatic conditions, biodiversity, weather, and the ability of their farmers and companies to adapt to international market demands (Arbulú Ballesteros et al. 2024; Montes Ninaquispe et al. 2024, 2023b).

Globally, the demand for agricultural products has significantly influenced the boom in Peruvian agro-exports (Montes Ninaquispe et al. 2023a). The growing preference in international markets for fresh and high-quality products has opened significant opportunities. Integrating sustainable practices in agriculture is crucial to ensure the sector's ongoing viability, addressing issues like efficient resource management, soil and water conservation, and carbon footprint reduction (Salmoral et al. 2020). This move towards sustainability not only meets ecological and social responsibilities but also aligns with global market trends, where consumers and trade partners increasingly demand products that adhere to environmental and ethical standards (Z. Zhou et al. 2024). In this regard, sustainable agricultural practices become a differentiating factor that can enhance the competitiveness of agro-exports by improving product quality, fostering innovation, and meeting international standards for sustainable production (Lan and Kien 2021). Finally, the primary objective of this study is proposed: To describe the competitiveness of Peru's agricultural exports by evaluating the export development of its main products. To achieve this, Peru's position among the world's largest exporters will be analyzed, followed by an analysis of the export reality indicators of the products, and finally, the calculation of the RCA competitiveness index.

2. Material and Methods

The research was conducted under a quantitative approach, aimed at collecting and analyzing numerical data to establish patterns and trends in the behavior of Peruvian agro-exports as in previous studies on international trade (Pantaleón Santa María et al. 2021). From this perspective, this study was approached with a descriptive scope, aimed at characterizing and detailing the fundamental properties of the involved variables, without establishing cause-and-effect relationships between them as in Monja Monja Paico's (2023) study. The methodological design adopted was non-experimental, as it was based on the observation and analysis of variables without direct manipulation or control by the researcher (Corona Lisboa 2016). This approach was consistent with the nature of the research, which did not seek to alter the natural conditions of the phenomena studied, but rather to describe them as they appeared in their real context.

In terms of its typology, the research was classified as basic. This orientation implied an approach focused on increasing theoretical knowledge regarding the export competitiveness of the selected products, without an applied focus or aimed at solving specific practical problems (Herbas Torrico and Gonzales 2018). However, the findings could lay the groundwork for future applied studies. Regarding the study population, the most exported sub-items of Peru according to SUNAT Customs records (SUNAT 2023), the official customs body of the country, were selected. The products identified for analysis were grapes, blueberries, avocados, and asparagus, corresponding to the harmonized system subheadings 080610, 081040, 080440, and 070920, respectively (Ministerio de Economía y Finanzas del Perú 2022). The study period covered five years, from 2019 to 2023, determined by the availability of data from the official source until October 2023. The source for evaluating the standardized revealed comparative advantage of these products was the International Trade Center, based on UN COMTRADE statistics and accessible through the TRADEMAP commercial tool (International Trade Center 2024), complementing information related to Peru with the web platform of Peru's customs (Sunat Customs). The sample for the study was equivalent to the population, which implied an exhaustive analysis of each of the mentioned products.

Regarding the application of the Balassa indicator, the methodological design involves a detailed analysis of the country's agricultural exports compared to global trade. There are some limitations with the Balassa indicator as it does not consider internal production capacity or governmental policies that may influence exportation. The formula is expressed as follows:

$$IB = \frac{\frac{X_k^i}{X^i}}{\frac{X_k}{X}} \quad (1)$$

where X_k^i represents the total value of exports of a specific product k from country i, while X^i expresses the total exports made by country "i". On the other hand expresses the total exports carried out by country "*i*". On the other hand, X_k indicates the total value of exports of product *k* from all over the world, while *X* represents the total exports made in the world. Based on the RCA, another much more accurate indicator was created, as evidenced when applied in some studies (Elsalih et al. 2021; Erkan and Bozduman 2022; Andrés González-Moralejo et al. 2021; Hasan et al. 2024; Saki et al. 2019; Seleka and Dlamini 2020). The formula is as follows:

$$IB = \frac{RCA_k^i - 1}{RCA_k^i + 1} \tag{2}$$

Understanding the results:
[−1,0) -> The country "*i*" does not have a revealed comparative advantage in product "*k*";
(0,1] -> The country "*i*" has a revealed comparative advantage in product "*k*".

3. Results

Table 1 presents the global grape exports in millions of USD by the major exporters from 2019 to 2023. During this period, Peru stands out as the country with the highest growth in its exports, increasing by 114.9% from USD 811.8 million in 2019 to USD 1745.5 million in 2023, with a high standard deviation of USD 353.6 million, indicating significant fluctuations. The most significant year for Chile was 2021, with an increase of 109.5% reaching USD 1732.7 million, but it also exhibited a high standard deviation of USD 386.0 million, reflecting variability. China experienced its highest export volume in 2020, with a 22.8% increase compared to 2019, showing moderate variability with a standard deviation of USD 202.0 million. In terms of the least variation, the United States of America shows a relatively stable trend, with a decrease of 10.1% from USD 855.1 million in 2019 to USD 768.4 million in 2023 and a low standard deviation of USD 39.7 million, indicating more stable export values. The average annual growth of exports across all countries shows considerable variability, with Peru having the highest average annual increase, while countries like Chile and China exhibit a decreasing trend.

Table 1. Global grape exports in millions of USD.

Exporters	2019	2020	2021	2022	2023
Chile	953.1	933.2	826.9	1732.7	811.2
Peru	811.8	991.1	1195.8	1292.4	1745.5
Italy	724.6	839.3	891.9	772.0	887.8
South Africa	521.2	520.2	708.5	764.3	615.2
United States of America	855.1	822.3	777.0	764.1	768.4
Netherlands	721.7	794.6	920.7	749.2	1029.3
China	987.2	1212.7	757.1	726.7	813.9
Spain	343.2	471.3	516.3	424.0	356.1

Note. Data taken from International Trade Center (2024).

Table 2 highlights an upward trend in Peruvian grape exports. During this period, the net weight of exports experienced a notable growth of 72.3%, with an average annual growth rate of 14.3%. Similarly, the FOB value increased by 102%, corresponding to an average annual growth rate of 19.6%. However, the number of destination countries and exporting companies showed fluctuations and a slight overall decrease, reflecting potential challenges in market diversification and the sustainability of the number of exporters. The year 2023 stood out as the best year in terms of both net weight and FOB value, while 2022 was the worst year in terms of the number of exporting companies, with a decrease of 9.4% compared to the previous year. The standard deviation of the net weight (99.5) and FOB value (358.3) indicates significant variability in these indicators over the analyzed period.

Table 2. Basic indicators of Peruvian grape exports.

Years	2019	2020	2021	2022	2023
Destination countries	59	56	58	53	55
Number of companies	157	140	149	132	140
Net weight thousand MT	376.5	442.4	513.1	554.7	648.6
FOB value million USD	877.5	1035.5	1249.8	1345.9	1772.6

Note. Data taken from the DAM registered in SUNAT (2023).

Table 3 presents the absolute revealed comparative advantage (ARCA) index in grapes. The consistent upward trend in the ARCA index indicates a strengthening of comparative advantage over this period. The highest average annual growth rate during this period was approximately 0.84%, while the lowest was around 0.21%. The average annual growth rate across the years was 0.42%, with a standard deviation of 0.0073. This steady increase reflects a positive development in the country's ability to compete in the global grape market, demonstrating enhanced efficiency and performance in grape production and export relative to other countries.

Table 3. Index of absolute revealed comparative advantage in grapes.

Year	2018	2019	2020	2021	2022	2023
Index	0.948	0.951	0.959	0.961	0.966	0.968

Note. Data taken from the DAM registered in SUNAT (2023).

Table 4 presents the global blueberry exports. Peru stands out with the highest annual percentage growth, achieving an average annual growth rate of 20.04%, accompanied by a standard deviation of 5.43, indicating moderate variability. The Netherlands shows significant growth with an average annual growth rate of 16.75% and a standard deviation of 16.53, reflecting considerable variability in its exports. Chile, on the other hand, experiences a constant decline with a negative average annual growth rate of −7.39% and a standard deviation of 10.74, indicating moderate variability in its decreases. Spain presents an average annual growth rate of 10.67% with a standard deviation of 23.69, suggesting significant fluctuations. The United States maintains relative stability with an average annual growth rate of 5.55% and a standard deviation of 11.32, indicating moderate variations. Canada records an average annual growth rate of 6.28% and a standard deviation of 15.97, reflecting considerable variability. Finally, South Africa shows an average annual growth rate of 11.86% and a standard deviation of 10.31, indicating stability with slight annual variations.

Table 4. Global blueberry exports in million USD.

Exporters	2020	2021	2022	2022	2023
Peru	809.62	1002.98	1201.36	1350.98	1675.97
Netherlands	408.73	499.84	561.61	542.31	736.41
Chile	571.19	527.01	563.61	508.64	411.97
Spain	377.94	432.31	602.74	493.45	528.01
United States of America	251.77	250.06	306.38	307.59	307.46
Canada	156.21	135.39	152.14	189.07	192.46
South Africa	106.49	125.14	152.80	150.73	164.59

Note. Data taken from International Trade Center (2024).

In Table 5, the number of destination countries had an average growth rate of 6.21% with a standard deviation of 18.23%, experiencing the highest growth in 2023 and the greatest decline in 2022. The number of companies involved grew at an average annual rate of 16.10%, with a standard deviation of 27.08%, showing the highest growth in 2023 and the greatest decline in 2021. The net weight of exports saw an average annual growth of 16.38% and a standard deviation of 27.80%, with 2022 marking the highest increase and 2023 the largest decrease. The FOB value exhibited an average annual growth rate of 19.88% and a standard deviation of 6.56%, with the highest growth in 2023 and the greatest decline in 2022. In conclusion, the indicators show an overall growth in Peruvian blueberry exports, albeit with some variability, with 2023 standing out as a year of significant growth and 2022 experiencing notable declines, especially in the number of destination countries and FOB value.

Table 5. Basic indicators of Peruvian blueberry exports.

Years	2019	2020	2021	2022	2023
Destination countries	36	35	35	33	44
Number of companies	70	84	71	78	117
Net weight thousand MT	125.04	163.83	206.38	275.66	206.61
FOB value million USD	814.56	995.67	1185.50	1319.66	1674.82

Note. Data taken from the DAM registered in SUNAT (2023).

In Table 6, the index had an average growth rate of 0.18% with a standard deviation of 0.34%. The highest growth was observed in 2020, while the greatest decline occurred in 2021. This suggests that while the comparative advantage of Peruvian blueberries has been relatively stable, there was a slight increase in 2020 followed by a minor decline in 2021. This suggests an improvement in the country's competitive standing in the global blueberry market, showcasing increased efficiency and effectiveness in blueberry production and export compared to other nations.

Table 6. Index of absolute revealed comparative advantage in blueberries.

Year	2019	2020	2021	2022	2023
Index	0.979	0.983	0.980	0.984	0.986

Table 7 presents global avocado exports. Mexico stands out with the highest annual percentage growth, achieving an average annual growth rate of 2.53%, accompanied by a standard deviation of 9.32, indicating moderate variability. The Netherlands shows significant growth with an average annual growth rate of 13.93% and a standard deviation of 29.11, reflecting considerable variability in its exports. Peru, on the other hand, experiences moderate growth with an average annual growth rate of 8.04% and a standard deviation of 22.14, indicating moderate variability in its increases. Spain presents an average annual growth rate of 3.49% with a standard deviation of 10.32, suggesting moderate fluctuations. The United States maintains relative stability with an average annual growth rate of −4.20% and a standard deviation of 8.52, indicating moderate variations. Chile records an average annual growth rate of −3.77% and a standard deviation of 17.36, reflecting moderate variability. Colombia shows substantial growth with an average annual growth rate of 25.94% and a standard deviation of 33.21, indicating significant variability. Finally, South Africa shows an average annual growth rate of 20.33% and a standard deviation of 17.00, indicating considerable growth with moderate annual variations.

In Table 8, the number of destination countries had an average growth rate of 16.10% with a standard deviation of 27.08%, experiencing the highest growth in 2023 and the greatest decline in 2021. The number of companies involved grew at an average annual rate of 16.39%, with a standard deviation of 27.81%, showing the highest growth in 2022 and the greatest decline in 2023. The net weight of exports saw an average annual growth of 19.88% and a standard deviation of 6.55%, with 2023 marking the highest increase and 2022 the largest decrease. The FOB value exhibited an average annual growth rate of 16.10% and a standard deviation of 27.08%, with the highest growth in 2023 and the greatest decline in 2021. In conclusion, the indicators show an overall growth in Peruvian avocado exports, albeit with some variability, with 2023 standing out as a year of significant growth and 2021 experiencing notable declines, especially in the number of destination countries and FOB value.

Table 7. Global avocado exports.

Exporters	2019	2020	2021	2022	2023
Mexico	2912.59	2665.85	3045.66	3143.31	3179.00
Netherlands	886.30	1059.18	1158.08	905.03	1345.91
Peru	751.33	759.05	1048.30	894.27	963.43
Spain	384.65	442.89	462.01	415.79	434.57
Chile	300.70	219.38	214.19	212.91	244.73
Colombia	89.05	146.03	204.59	179.26	200.90
United States of America	154.26	164.46	156.71	149.71	128.42
South Africa	70.76	76.87	110.49	118.14	144.17

Note. Data taken from International Trade Center (2024).

Table 8. Basic indicators of Peruvian avocado exports.

Years	2019	2020	2021	2022	2023
Destination countries	70	84	71	78	117
Number of companies	125.0	163.8	206.4	275.7	206.6
Net weight thousand MT	814.6	995.7	1185.5	1319.7	1674.8
FOB value million USD	70	84	71	78	117

Note. Data taken from the DAM registered in SUNAT (2023).

In Table 9, the index had an average growth rate of 0.16% with a standard deviation of 0.32%. The highest growth was observed in 2023, while the greatest decline occurred in 2022. This indicates that the comparative advantage of Peruvian avocados has shown a slight but consistent increase over the years, with a notable peak in 2023 and a minor setback in 2022. This trend suggests an improving competitive position in the global avocado market, reflecting increased efficiency and performance in avocado production and export relative to other countries.

Table 9. Index of absolute revealed comparative advantage in avocado.

Year	2019	2020	2021	2022	2023
Index	0.960	0.963	0.965	0.962	0.966

Table 10 presents global asparagus exports in million USD. Peru shows marginal growth with an average annual growth rate of 0.05% and a standard deviation of 7.71, indicating moderate variability. Mexico experiences a decline with an average annual growth rate of −4.09% and a standard deviation of 14.58, reflecting considerable variability. The United States maintains relative stability with an average annual growth rate of −1.93% and a standard deviation of 11.29, indicating moderate variations. Spain presents a robust growth rate with an average annual growth rate of 7.49% and a standard deviation of 22.68, suggesting significant fluctuations. The Netherlands shows minimal growth with an average annual growth rate of 0.59% and a standard deviation of 23.08, indicating high variability. Italy demonstrates substantial growth with an average annual growth rate of 21.98% and a standard deviation of 40.42, reflecting significant variability. France also shows significant growth with an average annual growth rate of 7.49% and a standard deviation of 32.34, indicating high variability. Finally, Greece exhibits a strong growth rate with an average annual growth rate of 19.29% and a standard deviation of 35.23, indicating considerable variability.

Table 10. Global asparagus exports in million USD.

Exporters	2019	2020	2021	2022	2023
Peru	394.01	377.10	400.97	366.43	391.23
Mexico	449.19	386.36	416.26	336.54	367.00
United States of America	163.57	144.45	156.27	137.98	148.34
Spain	78.84	88.54	120.26	98.33	98.40
Netherlands	83.01	75.80	97.86	73.34	78.48
Italy	31.16	41.41	60.00	37.28	55.17
France	25.78	26.15	40.20	31.58	30.39
Greece	13.69	20.09	28.75	20.22	23.65

Note. Data taken from International Trade Center (2024).

In Table 11, the number of destination countries had an average decline of −1.15% with a standard deviation of 5.71%, experiencing the highest growth in 2021 and the greatest decline in 2023. The number of companies involved showed an average annual decline of −1.26% and a standard deviation of 6.99%, with the highest growth in 2023 and the greatest decline in 2022. The net weight of exports saw an average annual decline of −6.84% and a standard deviation of 12.83%, with 2021 marking the highest increase and 2023 the largest decrease. The FOB value exhibited an average annual decline of −0.40% and a standard deviation of 6.10%, with the highest growth in 2023 and the greatest decline in 2022. In conclusion, the indicators show a general decline in Peruvian asparagus exports over the period, with some variability, highlighting 2023 as a year of recovery in some aspects and 2022 as a year of notable declines.

Table 11. Basic indicators of Peruvian asparagus exports.

Years	2019	2020	2021	2022	2023
Destination countries	40	40	41	42	38
Number of companies	89	86	82	77	84
Net weight thousand MT	133.97	128.02	135.98	129.69	97.90
FOB value million USD	400.19	387.07	399.38	369.56	391.62

Note. Data taken from the DAM registered in SUNAT (2023).

In Table 12, the index had an average growth rate of 0.10% with a standard deviation of 0.24%. The highest growth was observed in 2023, while the greatest decline occurred in 2022. This indicates a stable but slightly increasing comparative advantage of Peruvian asparagus over the years, with a significant rise in 2023 following a minor decline in 2022.

Table 12. Index of absolute revealed comparative advantage in asparagus.

Year	2021	2022	2022	2022	2023
Index	0.985	0.982	0.985	0.986	0.987

4. Discussion and Conclusions

This study has evaluated the competitiveness and export development of Peru's main agro-export products: grapes, blueberries, avocados, and asparagus, revealing several key points that contrast with the existing literature.

The results show significant growth in grape exports, which aligns with previous studies highlighting the potential of Peruvian grapes in the international market due to favorable climatic conditions and improvements in cultivation techniques (Juarez Malaver 2022). However, the high variability in exports reflects challenges in stability, indicating the need for more efficient logistics infrastructure and reduced transportation costs to maintain competitiveness (Juarez Malaver 2022; Ramos et al. 2019). This finding is consistent with observations by authors emphasizing the importance of infrastructure improvements to ensure products reach international markets in optimal conditions (Nonalaya et al. 2021).

Peru has also shown notable growth in blueberry exports, consistent with the increasing demand in international markets reported in the literature (Bossio Valdivia et al. 2017). However, significant fluctuations in the number of destination countries and exporting companies suggest challenges in market diversification and exporter sustainability. This variability indicates that despite growth, there are obstacles that need to be addressed to ensure more stable and continuous development (Carbonell Santillán 2023). This reinforces the need to diversify both the markets and the base of exporting companies to reduce dependency and improve resilience (Roja and Sánchez 2023; Urcia Armas and Vivanco Caceres 2022).

In the case of avocados, the moderate growth in exports contrasts with expectations of more robust development due to Peru's comparative advantages in avocado production (Coayla and Jiménez 2022; Mills-Novoa 2020; Salmoral et al. 2020). The observed variability suggests that factors such as market access and logistics infrastructure remain significant challenges (Nonalaya et al. 2021). Furthermore, although the revealed comparative advantage index shows a positive trend, the lower consistency compared to other products highlights the need for specific strategies to strengthen the competitiveness of avocados in the global market (Larrea-Gallegos et al. 2019; Parco Espinoza and Mallqui Cunurana 2022). This aligns with arguments by authors advocating for improvements in technology access and capital to enhance productivity and product quality (Leyva Morales 2023).

For asparagus, the results indicate marginal growth in exports, contrasting with expectations of more solid development as suggested by the literature (Esterhuizen and van Rooyen 2006; Ramos et al. 2019). The significant variability in indicators suggests that Peru faces substantial challenges in the sustainability of asparagus exports (Lan and Kien 2021). This underscores the need to improve agricultural practices and supporting infrastructure to maintain competitiveness in this sector (Bossio Valdivia et al. 2017). The literature emphasizes that adopting sustainable practices and investing in technology are crucial to overcoming these challenges (Juarez Malaver 2022). The revealed comparative advantage index shows a positive trend for grapes, blueberries, and avocados, indicating improved efficiency and performance compared to other countries (Montes Ninaquispe et al. 2021). However, asparagus presents a less consistent comparative advantage, with variations reflecting challenges in maintaining solid and continuous competitiveness (Saki et al. 2019). These findings suggest the need for adaptive and resilient strategies focused on the continuous improvement of logistics infrastructure, technology access, and market diversification to ensure sustained growth (Larrea-Gallegos et al. 2019).

The results of this study on the competitiveness and export development of Peru's main agro-export products highlight several key areas that need to be addressed to improve the sector's efficiency and sustainability.

Firstly, Peru has shown remarkable growth in grape exports, significantly increasing export volumes between 2019 and 2023. However, this growth is accompanied by high annual variability, indicating significant fluctuations in exports. Despite the growth, this variability underscores the need to improve the stability of exports through investments in logistics infrastructure and greater transportation efficiency. Modernizing roads, ports, and internal transportation systems is essential to reduce costs and ensure that products reach international markets in optimal conditions.

Conversely, blueberry exports have also shown impressive growth, with a high annual growth rate. However, variability in export destinations and the number of exporting companies suggests challenges in market diversification. Although blueberry exports are on the rise, it is crucial to address market stability and diversification to ensure sustained growth. This involves exploring new international markets and supporting more producers and companies to integrate into the export chain, thereby reducing dependency on a few markets and exporters.

Regarding avocados, exports have grown moderately, reflecting positive performance but with significant variability. This trend indicates that while Peru is improving its competitive position in the global avocado market, it still faces challenges in terms of efficiency and consistency in production and export. Adopting advanced technologies and providing technical training are fundamental to improving productivity and product quality, enabling Peruvian farmers to better meet global market demands.

In contrast to other products, asparagus exports have shown marginal growth and high variability. The revealed comparative advantage index suggests slight stability but with challenges in achieving sustained growth. The decline in the number of destination countries and exporting companies in certain years underscores the need for specific strategies to enhance the competitiveness and sustainability of asparagus exports. Adopting sustainable and efficient agricultural practices is crucial to ensure the sector's long-term viability, especially considering international pressure and the effects of climate change.

5. Recommendations

The results show a high variability in the exports of products such as grapes, which have grown significantly but exhibited large annual fluctuations. This underscores the urgent need to improve logistical infrastructure. It is essential to invest in the modernization of roads, ports, and internal transportation systems to reduce transportation costs and ensure that products reach international markets in optimal conditions. This improvement will not only increase logistical efficiency but also stabilize the observed fluctuations in exports, as seen in the export data for grapes and blueberries.

The data reveal significant fluctuations in the number of destination countries and exporting companies, especially in products such as blueberries and avocados. Although there has been notable growth in exports, these fluctuations suggest a vulnerability due to reliance on a few markets and exporting actors. It is crucial to diversify both export markets and the base of exporting companies. This involves exploring new international markets and supporting more producers and companies to integrate into the export chain, thereby reducing market fluctuation vulnerabilities and improving the stability and sustainability of Peruvian exports.

The variability in the competitiveness of products such as avocados and asparagus, which show less consistent growth, indicates the need for greater investment in agricultural technology and training for producers. The adoption of advanced technologies and technical training can significantly improve productivity and product quality, enabling Peruvian farmers to better adapt to the demands and standards of the global market. This investment in technology and training is essential to close the competitiveness gap and enhance productive efficiency, which will result in greater consistency and growth in exports.

MINAGRI must implement policies that encourage investment in infrastructure and agricultural technology, as well as training programs for farmers, focusing on improving logistical efficiency and the adoption of sustainable practices. PROMPERÚ should develop export promotion strategies that include market diversification and the enhancement of the image of Peruvian products abroad, promoting international fairs and trade missions to explore new markets and strengthen existing ones. ADEX should facilitate access to financing and technology for small and medium-sized producers, offering training and technical assistance programs to strengthen the export base and improve the competitiveness of Peruvian products. INIA should promote research and development in sustainable agricultural practices and innovative technologies, collaborating with educational institutions and the private sector to transfer advanced knowledge and technologies to farmers.

Author Contributions: Conceptualization, A.L.P.S.M.; methodology, J.C.M.N. and D.A.L.J.; formal analysis, J.C.M.N. and W.T.C.M.; investigation, J.C.M.N.; writing—original draft, J.C.M.N. and A.L.P.S.M.; visualization, J.C.F.R. and B.H.M.E.; supervision, K.C.V.H.; project administration, J.C.M.N. All authors have read and agreed to the published version of the manuscript.

Funding: The funding was provided by the Universidad de San Martín de Porres.

Institutional Review Board Statement: Not applicable.

Informed Consent Statement: Not applicable.

Data Availability Statement: The data can be found at the following link: https://drive.google.com/open?id=18dc6xkXuWF_vtZJJ9yYwQVr22LXFQSDn&usp=drive_fs (accessed on 10 May 2024).

Conflicts of Interest: The authors declare no conflict of interest.

References

Ando, Mitsuyo, Shujiro Urata, and Kenta Yamanouchi. 2022. Do Japan's Free Trade Agreements Increase Its International Trade? *Journal of Economic Integration* 37: 1–29. [CrossRef]

Andrés González-Moralejo, Silvia, Tania Marín Orantes, and Martha Flores Romero. 2021. Competitiveness Analysis of the Agri-Food Industry in Mexico. *Agroalimentaria* 27: 125–40.

Arbulú Ballesteros, Marco Agustín, Jose Carlos Montes Ninaquispe, Diego Alejandro Ludeña Jugo, Julie Catherine Arbulú Castillo, Milagros Lamadrid Aldana, Alberto Luis Pantaleón Santa María, Karol Melissa Arbaiza Godos, and Stephanie Virginia Ruiz Chacon. 2024. Diversification of Fresh Asparagus Exports from Perú. *Journal of Educational and Social Research* 14: 258. [CrossRef]

Balassa, Bela. 1965. Trade Liberalisation and "Revealed" Comparative Advantage. *The Manchester School* 33: 99–123. [CrossRef]

Bortz, Pablo G., and Nicole Toftum. 2023. Changes in rainfall, agricultural exports and reserves: Macroeconomic impacts of climate change in Argentina. *Journal of Environmental Economics and Policy* 13: 1–16. [CrossRef]

Bossio Valdivia, Miguel Ángel, Eder Eleazar Cotillo Flores, and Melissa Gloria Delgado Clemente. 2017. Optimización de costos de la logística internacional de exportación de productos peruanos como elemento de mejora en la gestión empresarial. Caso: Exportación de botellas con bebida de Maca peruana, por el grupo ALGANA. Master's thesis, UCSS Digital Institutional Repository, Lima, Peru.

Carbonell Santillán, Cinthya Elizabeth. 2023. Análisis de los factores de crecimiento y competitividad de las exportaciones de arándanos frescos en Perú, 2011–2021. Bachelor's thesis, Universidad San Ignacio de Loyola, Lima, Peru.

Coayla, Edelina, and Luis Jiménez. 2022. Financing for the climate change adaptation of organic export agriculture in Peru. *Future of Food: Journal on Food, Agriculture and Society* 10: 16–30. [CrossRef]

Copetti, Leonardo Sangoi, Kelmara Mendes Vieira, and Daniel Arruda Coronel. 2013. Transmission of exchange rates for Soya export prices: USA, Brazil and Argentina market analyses | Transmissão da variação da taxa de câmbio para os preços de exportação da soja em grão: Análise dos mercados dos Estados unidos, do Brasil e da Argentina. *Revista Em Agronegocio e Meio Ambiente* 6: 435–61.

Corona Lisboa, José. 2016. Apuntes sobre métodos de investigación. *MediSur* 14: 81–83. Available online: http://scielo.sld.cu/scielo.php?script=sci_arttext&pid=S1727-897X2016000100016&lng=es&nrm=iso&tlng=es (accessed on 10 May 2024).

Das, Sudipta, Rokibul Hasan, and Debanjan Das. 2024. Who is the next China? Comparative advantage analysis from top ten apparel exporting nations. *Competitiveness Review. ahead-of-print*. [CrossRef]

De Melo, Tatiana Massaroli, and Eneas Gonçalves De Carvalho. 2024. An analysis of the competitiveness of developing countries based on the foreign added value of exports: The use of revealed comparative advantage index for the period 1995 to 2018 | Uma análise da competitividade de países em desenvolvimento a partir do v. *Brazilian Journal of Political Economy* 44: 63–83. [CrossRef]

De Paula Junior, Amarildo. 2020. The impact of soy, coffee and sugar exports on exchange reserves: An estimation by cochrane-orcutt | O impacto das exportações de soja, café e açúcar sobre as reservas cambiais: Uma estimação por cochrane-orcutt. *Relacoes Internacionais No Mundo Atual* 1: 258–68. [CrossRef]

Dilawari, Rahul, Navneet Kaur, Nitesh Priyadarshi, Ish Prakash, Anupam Patra, Sahil Mehta, Baljinder Singh, Prateek Jain, and Aminul Islam. 2022. Soybean: A Key Player for Global Food Security. In *Soybean Improvement: Physiological, Molecular and Genetic Perspectives*. Cham: Springer. [CrossRef]

Elsalih, Osama, Kamil Sertoglu, and Mustafa Besim. 2021. Determinants of comparative advantage of crude oil production: Evidence from OPEC and non-OPEC countries. *International Journal of Finance and Economics* 26: 3972–83. [CrossRef]

Erkan, Birol, and Elif Tuğçe Bozduman. 2022. The Global Competitive Structure of ASEAN Countries in Innovative Products. In *Studies on Entrepreneurship, Structural Change and Industrial Dynamics*. Cham: Springer, pp. 53–69. [CrossRef]

Escobar, Neus, E. Jorge Tizado, Erasmus K.H.J. zu Ermgassen, Pernilla Löfgren, Jan Börner, and Javier Godar. 2020. Spatially-explicit footprints of agricultural commodities: Mapping carbon emissions embodied in Brazil's soy exports. *Global Environmental Change* 62: 102067. [CrossRef]

Esquivias, Miguel A., Akhmad Jayadi, Syahiru Shafiai, Intan M. Abd Rashid, Amirah H. Borhanordin, Kemala Sari Agusti, and Lutfi Yahwidya. 2023. The Nexus between Food Security and Investment, Exports, Infrastructure, and Human Capital Development. *Journal of Human, Earth, and Future* 4: 221–40. [CrossRef]

Esterhuizen, Dirk, and Johan van Rooyen. 2006. Determinants of competitiveness of South African agricultural export firms. *Competitiveness Review* 16: 223–32.

Femeena, Hassan, C. Jeeva, and Sangeetha K Prathap. 2012. Economics of cost of compliance with HACCP in seafood export units and its limitations for applicability in domestic markets. *Indian Journal of Fisheries* 59: 141–45.

Fiankor, Dela-Dem, and Fabio G. Santeramo. 2023. Revisiting the impact of per-unit duties on agricultural export prices. *Applied Economic Perspectives and Policy* 45: 1472–92. [CrossRef]

Figueira, Sergio Rangel Fernandes, and Galache Vinicius de Oliveira. 2023. Comparative analysis of the competitiveness of soybean exports from Brazil, the United States, and Argentina | Análise comparativa da competitividade das exportações de soja em grão do Brasil, Estados Unidos e Argentina. *Revista de Economia e Sociologia Rural* 61: e245403. [CrossRef]

Hasan, Rokibul, Ishtehar Sharif Swazan, and Debanjan Das. 2024. Beyond the seams: Evaluating competitiveness and comparative advantage in Vietnam's apparel industry. *Journal of Chinese Economic and Foreign Trade Studies. ahead-of-print*. [CrossRef]

He, Li Yu (Colly), Sue Wright, and Elaine Evans. 2018. Is fair value information relevant to investment decision-making: Evidence from the Australian agricultural sector? *Australian Journal of Management* 43: 555–74. [CrossRef]

Herbas Torrico, Boris Christian, and Erick Ariel Rocha Gonzales. 2018. Metodología científica para la realización de investigaciones de mercado e investigaciones sociales cuantitativas. *Revista Perspectivas* 42: 123–60.

Hidayat, Ariodillah, Bernadette Robiani, Taufiq Marwa, and Suhel Suhel. 2023. Competitiveness, Market Structure, and Energy Policies: A Case Study of the World's Largest Crude Palm Oil Exporter. *International Journal of Energy Economics and Policy* 13: 111–21. [CrossRef]

Hossain, Kamal, Ahmad Sufian Che Abdullah, Mohd Abd Wahab Fatoni Mohd Balwi, Asmuliadi Lubis, Noor Azlinna Azizan, Mohammad Nurul Alam, and Azni Zarina Taha. 2023. Linking entrepreneurial orientation with export performance: Mediation effects of multiple differentiation strategies. *Journal of Business and Industrial Marketing* 38: 1769–93. [CrossRef]

Hu, Xiaoqian, Boxue Sun, Chao Wang, Ming K. Lim, Peng Wang, Xinyi Geng, Cuiyou Yao, and Wei-Qiang Chen. 2023. Impacts of China's exports decline in rare earth primary materials from a trade network-based perspective. *Resources Policy* 81: 103321. [CrossRef]

International Trade Center. 2024. Trade Map—Trade Statistics for International Business Development. Available online: https://www.trademap.org/Index.aspx (accessed on 15 June 2024).

Juarez Malaver, Raysa Tatiana. 2022. Factores económicos que inciden en la participación peruana en el mercado mundial de espárrago fresco, 2010–2020. Bachelor's thesis, Universidad Privada del Norte. Facultad de Negocios, Trujillo, Peru. Available online: https://hdl.handle.net/11537/31682 (accessed on 1 May 2024).

Krugman, Paul R., and Maurice Obstfeld. 2006. *Economía Internacional: Teoría y Política*, 7th ed. Edited by Cañizal A. Pearson Educación: Available online: https://fad.unsa.edu.pe/bancayseguros/wp-content/uploads/sites/4/2019/03/Krugman-y-Obstfeld-2006-Economia-Internacional.pdf (accessed on 4 May 2024).

Lan, Ngo Thi Phuong, and Nguyen Van Kien. 2021. Back to Nature-Based Agriculture: Green Livelihoods Are Taking Root in the Mekong River Delta. *Journal of People, Plants, and Environment* 24: 551–61. [CrossRef]

Laosutsan, Pheesphan, Ganesh P. Shivakoti, and Peeyush Soni. 2019. Agricultural and natural resources adaptations to climate change: Factors influencing the adoption of good agricultural practices and export decision of thailand's vegetable farmers. *International Journal of the Commons* 13: 867–80. [CrossRef]

Larrea-Gallegos, Gustavo, Ian Vázquez-Rowe, Hugo Wiener, and Ramzy Kahhat. 2019. Applying the Technology Choice Model in Consequential Life Cycle Assessment: A Case Study in the Peruvian Agricultural Sector. *Journal of Industrial Ecology* 23: 601–14. [CrossRef]

Leyva Morales, Jhosety Alexandra. 2023. Medidas sanitarias y fitosanitarias de Estados Unidos y su efecto en las agroexportaciones de palta, arándanos y uvas de Perú, Chile y México. Bachelor's thesis, Universidad Peruana de Ciencias Aplicadas (UPC), Lima, Peru. Available online: http://hdl.handle.net/10757/670633 (accessed on 10 May 2024).

Liu, Yawen, Lingyu Yang, Jinzhu Zhang, Qi Cui, Yu Liu, Fengying Nie, and Yumeng Hu. 2022. Aggravating effects of food export restrictions under climate change on food security: An analysis of rice economy based on alternative indicators. *Climate Change Economics* 13: 2240006. [CrossRef]

Luhwago, Win, Damas Philip, Reuben Kadigi, Charles Mgeni, and Rajabu Kangile. 2023. Determinants and Competitiveness of Rice Export in Tanzania: A Vector Error Correction Model. *East African Journal of Science, Technology and Innovation* 4: 1–19. [CrossRef]

Manrique Talledo, Kelly Katsumi Odely, and Laura Eugenia Muñoz Peláez. 2021. El impacto del TLC Perú-Unión Europea en el nivel de exportaciones de palmito a Francia por la Cooperativa APROPAL Ltd.a, en el periodo 2008–2018. Bachelor's thesis, Repositorio Institucional de la UTP, Lima, Peru.

Meng, Xiangyuan, Xue Li, Wenyan Xiao, and Jie Li. 2023. The differentiated impacts of external and internal financing on export: The firm-level evidence. *International Journal of Emerging Markets* 18: 769–87. [CrossRef]

Mills-Novoa, Megan. 2020. Making agro-export entrepreneurs out of Campesinos: The role of water policy reform, agricultural development initiatives, and the specter of climate change in reshaping agricultural systems in Piura, Peru. *Agriculture and Human Values* 37: 667–82. [CrossRef]

Ministerio de Economía y Finanzas del Perú. 2022. Arancel de aduanas 2022. Available online: https://cdn.www.gob.pe/uploads/document/file/2676619/DS404_2021EF.pdf (accessed on 10 May 2024).

Monja Paico, Angie Nicolle. 2023. Diversificación de las exportaciones y el crecimiento económico peruano 2011–2021. Bachelor's thesis, Repositorio Institucional de la UTP, Lima, Peru. Available online: https://hdl.handle.net/20.500.12867/7429 (accessed on 10 May 2024).

Montes Ninaquispe, Jose Carlos, Alberto Luis Pantaleón Santa María, Marco Agustín Arbulú Ballesteros, Gabriela Lizeth Castro Ijiri, Francisco Segundo Mogollón García, Emma Verónica Ramos Farroñán, and Julio Roberto Izquierdo Espinoza. 2023a. Diversification of Peruvian Ginger exports 2012–2021. Paper presented at Leadership in Education and Innovation in Engineering in the Framework of Global Transformations: Integration and Alliances for Integral Development, Buenos Aires, Argentina, July 19–21.

Montes Ninaquispe, Jose Carlos, Alberto Pantaleón Santa María, and Iván Antonio Oblitas Vallejo. 2023b. Dinámica comercial de las exportaciones peruanas de café a la Unión Europea 2017–2021. *Revista Alfa* 7: 175–83. [CrossRef]

Montes Ninaquispe, Jose Carlos, Kelly Cristina Vasquez Huatay, Diego Alejandro Ludeña Jugo, Alberto Luis Pantaleón Santa María, Juan César Farías Rodríguez, Fernando Suárez Santa Cruz, Erik Omar Escalona Aguilar, and Marco Agustín Arbulú-Ballesteros. 2024. Market Diversification and Competitiveness of Fresh Grape Exports in Peru. *Sustainability* 16: 2528. [CrossRef]

Montes Ninaquispe, José Carlos, Alberto Luis Pantaleón Santa María, Ingrid Isabel Medina Cardozo, and Romy Mariel Palacios Díaz. 2021. Niveles de exportación de productos tradicionales y no tradicionales del Perú 2011–2020. *Revista Científica Epistemia* 5. [CrossRef]

Morales-Marín, Luis, Howard Wheater, and Karl-Erich Lindenschmidt. 2018. Potential changes of annual-averaged nutrient export in the South Saskatchewan River Basin under climate and land-use change scenarios. *Water* 10: 1438. [CrossRef]

Mruthyunjaya. 2023. Agricultural sector in India: Accelerating growth and enhancing competitiveness. In *Agricultural Sector in India: Accelerating Growth and Enhancing Competitiveness*. London: Routledge. [CrossRef]

Muhamediyev, Dilnoz. 2023. Forecasting export options for fruit and vegetable products. *AIP Conference Proceedings* 2777: 020073. [CrossRef]

Nonalaya, Estefani Caballero, StefanyCoz DelCastillo, ImeldaVeliz Huamantica, WagnerVicente Ramos, and Cinthia Galarza Balbuena. 2021. Analysis of internal logistic cost on exports of peruvian coffee in the period 2015–2019. *Acta Logistica* 8: 73–81. [CrossRef]

Nong, Tung Huu, Duong HuuNong, Nam Hai Nguyen, Dinh Thi Pham, Huyen Thi Mai, and Yanan Sun. 2023. Enhancing the Competitiveness of Tea Export of Vietnam Versus Other ASEAN Countries in the International Market. *Indian Journal of Economics and Development* 19: 515–24. [CrossRef]

Ojede, Andrew. 2015. Exchange Rate Shocks and U.S. Services and Agricultural Exports: Which Export Sector is More Affected? *International Trade Journal* 29: 228–50. [CrossRef]

Orjuela-Castro, Javier Arturo, Juan Pablo Orejuela-Cabrera, and Wilson Adarme-Jaimes. 2021. Logistics network configuration for seasonal perishable food supply chains. *Journal of Industrial Engineering and Management* 14: 135–51. [CrossRef]

Pantaleón Santa María, Alberto Luis, Ingrid Isabel Medina Cardozo, and José Carlos Montes Ninaquispe. 2021. Comportamiento de la producción e importación de arroz en el Perú 2016–2020. *TZHOECOEN* 13: 76–83. [CrossRef]

Pantaleón Santa María, Alberto Luis, Ramiro Azañero Díaz, Patricia del Rocio Chávarry Ysla, Grecia Alejandra Avarez Tello, Jose Carlos Montes Ninaquispe, and Adriana Raquel Pantaleón Zamora. 2022. *Dinamismo Exportador del Perú: Una Década de Ensueño 2012–2021*. Available online: https://a.co/d/fASHo0T (accessed on 10 May 2024).

Parco Espinoza, Ana Miqueli, and Jennifer Claudia Mallqui Cunurana. 2022. Los efectos de la normativa europea en certificación orgánica en las exportaciones peruanas de quinua orgánica en el marco del Acuerdo Comercial entre el Perú y la Unión Europea (UE) durante el periodo 2014–2019. Bachelor' thesis, Universidad Peruana de Ciencias Aplicadas (UPC), Lima, Peru. Available online: http://hdl.handle.net/10757/663400 (accessed on 10 May 2024).

Peano, Cristiana, Vincenzo Girgenti, Claudio Baudino, and Nicole Roberta Giuggioli. 2017. Blueberry Supply Chain in Italy: Management, Innovation and Sustainability. *Sustainability* 9: 261. [CrossRef]

Phan, Trang Hoai. 2022. Working Conditions, Export Decisions, and Firm Constraints-Evidence from Vietnamese Small and Medium Enterprises. *Sustainability* 14: 7541. [CrossRef]

Rai, Heleen Buldeo, Sanggyun Kang, Takanori Sakai, Carla Tejada, Quan (Jack) Yuan, Alison Conway, and Laetitia Dablanc. 2022. Proximity logistics': Characterizing the development of logistics facilities in dense, mixed-use urban areas around the world. *Transportation Research Part A: Policy and Practice* 166: 41–61. [CrossRef]

Raman, M. S., Devesh Kumar Pant, Alka Singh, and Rohit Kumar. 2023. Competitiveness of Fruits' and Vegetables' Exports from India. *Economic Affairs (New Delhi)* 68: 1379–86. [CrossRef]

Ramos, Edgar, Tamy Hinostroza, Jean Pierre Yanayaco, and Ron Mesia. 2019. Development of supply chain quality management in peruvian blueberry companies: A case study in Cañete, Peru. *International Journal of Supply Chain Management* 8: 795–808.

Ressia, Susan, Glenda Strachan, Mary Rogers, Kim Ball, and Ruth McPhail. 2022. Farm Businesswomen's Aspirations for Leadership: A Case Study of the Agricultural Sector in Queensland, Australia. *Frontiers in Sustainable Food Systems* 6. [CrossRef]

Roja, E., and P. Sánchez. 2023. Competitividad y sostenibilidad en las exportaciones peruanas. *Revista de Comercio Internacional* 15: 77–89.

Saki, Zahra, Marguerite Moore, Ivan Kilov, Lori Rothenberg, and A. Blanton Godfrey. 2019. Revealed comparative advantage for US textiles and apparel. *Competitiveness Review* 29: 462–78. [CrossRef]

Salmoral, Gloria, Araceli Viñarta Carbó, Eduardo Zegarra, Jerry W. Knox, and Dolores Rey. 2020. Reconciling irrigation demands for agricultural expansion with environmental sustainability—A preliminary assessment for the Ica Valley, Peru. *Journal of Cleaner Production* 276: 123544. [CrossRef]

Saptana, Syahrul Ganda Sukmaya, Atika Dyah Perwita, Fadhila Dhia Malihah, Irwanda Wisnu Wardhana, Atika Dian Pitaloka, Shabrina Austin Ghaisani, Bambang Sayaka, Nyak Ilham, Elna Karmawati, Mewa Ariani, and et al. 2023. Competitiveness analysis of fresh tomatoes in Indonesia: Turning comparative advantage into competitive advantage. *PLoS ONE* 18: e0294980. [CrossRef]

Seleka, Tebogo B., and Thula S. Dlamini. 2020. Competitiveness of ACP Sugar Exporters in the Global Market. *International Trade Journal* 34: 247–77. [CrossRef]

Sharma, Ashpreet, Lalit Mohan Kathuria, and Tanveen Kaur. 2023. Analyzing relative export competitiveness of Indian agricultural food products: A study of fresh and processed fruits and vegetables. *Competitiveness Review* 33: 1090–117. [CrossRef]

Sharma, Kalyani, Rajesh Kumar Vishwakarma, Shadanan Patel, Shyam Narayan Jha, and Mridula Devi. 2023. Organic production, postharvest processing, and value-added intervention of fox nuts (euryale ferox) for export. In *Transforming Organic Agri-Produce into Processed Food Products: Post-COVID-19 Challenges and Opportunities*. Abingdon: Apple Academic Press.

Sharma, Ritesh, Vivek Yadav, and Vijay Kumar Yadav. 2023. Organic Production of Basmati Rice. In *Organic Crop Production Management*, 1st ed. Abingdon: Apple Academic Press, p. 21.

Shukla, Swaraj, Sadykova Kamilla, and Jinjin Tian. 2023. Research on India-China agriculture trade dynamics: A comparative advantage analysis. *PLoS ONE* 18: e0294561. [CrossRef]

Sihombing, Fransisca Natalia, Tavi Supriana, and Sri Fajar Ayu. 2021. Identifying the Factors Contributing to the Volume of Coffee Export from North Sumatra to the United States, Malaysia and Japan. *Caraka Tani: Journal of Sustainable Agriculture* 36: 83–96. [CrossRef]

Singh, Ajay Kumar, and Bhim Jyoti. 2023. Appropriate Technology and Adaptation Strategies Mitigate the Adverse Impact of Climate Change on the Agricultural Sector. In *Handbook of Research on AI-Equipped IoT Applications in High-Tech Agriculture*. Hershey: IGI Global, pp. 389–416. [CrossRef]

SUNAT. 2023. Consulta de declaración de importación. Available online: http://www.aduanet.gob.pe/cl-ad-consdepa/FrmPrincipal.jsp (accessed on 5 May 2024).

Tarihoran, Andiga Dompak Baharaja, Musa Hubeis, Siti Jahroh, and Nimmi Zulbainarni. 2023. Competitiveness of and Barriers to Indonesia's Exports of Ornamental Fish. *Sustainability* 15: 8711. [CrossRef]

Thorbecke, Willem, Chen Chen, and Nimesh Salike. 2021. China's exports in a protectionist world. *Journal of Asian Economics* 77: 101404. [CrossRef]

Topcu, Yunus Emre. 2023. The comparative advantages in the wooden furniture industry: Does the export price matter? *Competitiveness Review* 33: 1145–60. [CrossRef]

Urcia Armas, Nataly Lucia, and Jian Carlos Vivanco Caceres. 2022. La negociación e impacto económico del tlc de Perú—Unión Europea del Sector Agrícola periodo 2017–2021. Available online: https://hdl.handle.net/20.500.12692/119354 (accessed on 10 May 2024).

Wainaina, Priscilla, Songporne Tongruksawattana, and Matin Qaim. 2018. Synergies between Different Types of Agricultural Technologies in the Kenyan Small Farm Sector. *Journal of Development Studies* 54: 1974–90. [CrossRef]

Wang, Chi-Mao. 2018. Assembling Lettuce Export Markets in East Asia: Agrarian Warriors, Climate Change and Kinship. *Sociologia Ruralis* 58: 909–27. [CrossRef]

Wanyonyi, Eileen Inyanji, W. Gathungu, and Hillary K. Bett. 2023. Drivers of competitiveness in the agricultural input sector: The case of agro-dealer businesses in Kenya. *Cogent Business and Management* 10: 2218683. [CrossRef]

Zhou, Rongrong, Hanzhou Liu, Qian Zhang, Wei Wang, Jian Mao, Xuerong Wang, and Decai Tang. 2023. Improvement of Agricultural Supply Quality in China: Evidence from Jiangsu Province. *Sustainability* 15: 11418. [CrossRef]

Zhou, Zhiyun, Haoling Liao, Hua Li, Xiao Gu, and Mohammed Moosa Ageli. 2024. The trilemma of food production, clean energy, and water: COP27 perspective of global economy. *Land Degradation and Development* 35: 1425–36. [CrossRef]

Disclaimer/Publisher's Note: The statements, opinions and data contained in all publications are solely those of the individual author(s) and contributor(s) and not of MDPI and/or the editor(s). MDPI and/or the editor(s) disclaim responsibility for any injury to people or property resulting from any ideas, methods, instructions or products referred to in the content.

economies

MDPI

Article

Learn from Whom? An Empirical Study of Enterprise Digital Mimetic Isomorphism under the Institutional Environment

Ying Chen, Haiyan Ma * and Tianyi Zhou

School of Economics and Management, China University of Geosciences, Wuhan 430074, China; chen_ying@cug.edu.cn (Y.C.); dlmzka1206@163.com (T.Z.)
* Correspondence: mahaiyan@cug.edu.cn

Abstract: The digital economy is a prevailing trend in global development, yet traditional firms still face challenges in digital transformation. Under institutional pressure, firms might imitate the digital strategy of their peers to mitigate these issues; there is still a lack of empirical research to support this. Therefore, this study, drawing on new institutional theory, focuses on investigating whether and how the institutional environment influences companies in embracing digital transformation in the digital economy era. We employ generalized least squares (GLS) regression models on a sample of 2862 non-IT listed firms in China from 2012 to 2020. In addition, we conduct a series of robustness checks. The results show that firms' mimetic isomorphism of digital transformation is related to the institutional environment. Specifically, both industrial digitalization and regional digitalization promote digital mimetic isomorphism independently; their interaction is positively related to the digital mimetic isomorphism of successful firms but negatively related to similar firms. The results provide empirical evidence for non-IT firms to converge upwards in digital transformation and achieve high-quality development.

Keywords: digital transformation; industrial digitalization; regional digitalization; mimetic isomorphism

1. Introduction

Institutions have received increasing attention as influencing factors in enterprise digitalization decisions (Sarker et al. 2019; Kern and Gospel 2023). Prior research has focused on the impact of the institutional environment on digital transformation from the perspective of individual focal firms (Chen et al. 2022; Liu et al. 2024). However, digital technologies can disrupt the existing processes and structures of non-IT firms (Hinings et al. 2018). Under institutional pressures, organizations as participants in strategic decision-making may be inclined to refer to the current practices of other entities, aiming to learn from them, thus reducing the uncertainties and risks involved in digital transformation, while maintaining their legitimacy. However, based on the "follower–leader" dyadic relation perspective, the question of whether and how the institutional environment affects the mimetic behavior of enterprise digital decision-making has not been thoroughly explored.

During the process of digital transformation, firms encounter multiple institutional pressures from their external environment. Under the influence of digital economy trends and policy orientations, specific policies and regulations have been established at both industrial and regional levels to set targets for industrial digitalization and regional digital economy development. These measures shape the digital institutional environment within the industrial and regional fields. Currently, effective measures to drive corporate digital transformation include digital cultivation within core industries and regional digital infrastructure development (Xu et al. 2023). The former leverages the institutional forces within the industrial field to stimulate digital transformation, while the latter utilizes foundational and incentivizing policy support within the regional field to promote digital transformation

(Chen et al. 2022). However, institutional pressures from different fields impose varying requirements (Greenwood et al. 2010). How do firms respond to the institutional pressures of the industrial and regional fields?

Mimetic isomorphism can reduce the uncertainty faced by firms during digital transformation, thereby alleviating institutional pressures (Cao et al. 2024). Driven by learning and risk avoidance motives, firms tend to imitate the implemented behaviors of industry peers in decision-making (Lieberman and Asaba 2006), preferring to learn from similar firms or successful firms within the same industry when selecting learning targets (DiMaggio and Powell 1983; Haveman 1993). Specifically, similar firms in the same industry exhibit comparability in their endowment structure, strategic resources, and future development perspectives, resulting in stronger interactions (Chen et al. 2016). This, to a certain extent, diminishes the barriers to imitation. Successful firms, on the other hand, serving as industry benchmarks, stand out among numerous reference companies due to their visibility and authoritative traits, making them preferred subjects for organizational learning (Lieberman and Asaba 2006; Oh and Barker 2018). Then, it becomes another major dilemma for companies to imitate similar companies or successful companies in digital transformation. However, it is not yet clearly established whether the two institutional pressures, including industrial digitalization and regional digitalization, affect a company's choice of mimetic targets like similar enterprises and successful enterprises.

To address these research questions, this study investigates (1) the impact of digitalization in different fields on firms' mimetic isomorphism behavior, (2) the selection of mimetic objects, and (3) the interactive effects of industrial and regional digitalization. Based on panel data of 2862 non-IT listed firms in China from 2012 to 2020, we test our conceptual model (see Figure 1). This study expands the research on the antecedents of mimetic isomorphism and enriches the literature of digital transformation from a dyadic perspective, providing evidence of potential imitation behavior during digital transformation.

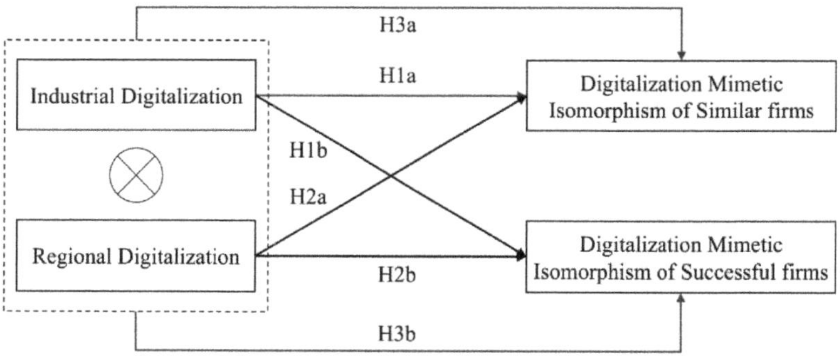

Figure 1. A conceptual model.

2. Theory and Hypothesis Development

2.1. New Institutional Theory and Mimetic Isomorphism

New institutional theory suggests that there are factors in the institutional environment that induce or constrain organizational behavior (Kostova and Zaheer 1999), causing organizations to exhibit a tendency to homogenize their behavior in order to gain legitimacy (Zimmerman and Zeitz 2002). The institutional environment exerts pressure on organizations to conform through three mechanisms, mimetic, normative, and coercive, which is seen as institutional isomorphism (DiMaggio and Powell 1983). Among these, normative and coercive pressures, while leading to organizational behavior convergence, do not lead to mimetic behavior. This is because under normative and coercive institutional pressures, the convergence of organizational behavior is not a result of the intentional imitation of other organizations but rather a consequence of organizations adopting similar behaviors to respond to institutional pressures and gain legitimacy within a similar institutional environment (Francis et al. 2009; Heugens and Lander 2009). In contrast, mimetic pressure arises when organizations, facing uncertainty, imitate the actions of more successful or legitimate organizations within their industry to guide their own decision-making (Cao et al. 2024). Therefore, mimetic isomorphism in new institutional theory is a response to uncertainty, aimed at gaining legitimacy.

For non-IT firms, digital transformation represents a break from constraints and an exploratory change, fraught with risks and uncertainties during the transformation process (Correani et al. 2020). However, imitating behaviors already undertaken by peers within the industry can reduce uncertainty risks during the transformation and effectively save on search costs (Sarrina Li and Lee 2010). Therefore, mimetic isomorphism may be a common practice for companies to gain legitimacy in response to the uncertainty of digital transformation. According to Haunschild and Miner (1997), inter-organizational imitation can be classified into the following three types: (1) trait-based imitation, which involves imitating organizations based on significant features such as scale or success, (2) frequency-based imitation, involving the replication of widely adopted behaviors, and (3) trait-based imitation, where behaviors expected to yield specific outcomes are replicated. Among them, trait-based imitation is the most common form of imitation. When there are no explicit action plans, managers often consider imitating successful peers as the best decision (Mizruchi and Fein 1999).

The current research on mimetic isomorphism is examined from various angles, such as social networks, organizational learning, and institutional theory, encompassing behaviors such as IT investments, market entry, corporate mergers, and carbon management. However, there is a lack of research on the mimetic effects on enterprise digital transformation. From a social network perspective, organizations interconnected by board members are more inclined to adopt mimetic isomorphism, primarily driven by their role in information dissemination (Palmer et al. 1993). Cheng et al. (2021) used board interlocks as a social learning channel for IT investment decisions, whereby mimicking the investment intensity of linked firms can determine the amount of corporate IT investment and increase the return on corporate investment. Viewing through the lens of organizational learning, Brookes and Altinay (2017) used franchising as an example and found that the transfer of tacit knowledge can accomplish mimetic isomorphism through opening and ongoing support. This is primarily due to open platforms that offer more learning opportunities. Meanwhile, most studies adopt an institutional theory perspective, predominantly concentrating on mimetic isomorphism observed in corporate mergers and acquisitions. To gain legitimacy, organizations tend to emulate the most commonly recurring decisions in M&A, particularly those concerning the product relatedness between acquiring and target firms, the location of target firms, and the size of acquisitions, especially under uncertainty (Haunschild and Miner 1997; Tseng and Chou 2011).

The existing research has explored the antecedents of digital transformation from different theoretical perspectives. The resource-based view posits that corporate social responsibility (CSR) can enhance a firm's human, financial, and technological resources, thereby promoting digital transformation (Nie et al. 2024). Upper echelons theory suggests that CEO characteristics, such as CEO overconfidence and international experience, can lead to a stronger digital strategic orientation (Chen et al. 2023; Saesen et al. 2024). Meanwhile, institutional theory argues that macro factors such as industrial digitalization and the regional digital economy drive digital transformation (Chen et al. 2022). From an institutional perspective, digital transformation in firms denotes a synergistic effect of digital innovations emerging from new products and services enabled by digital technologies, including big data, the internet of things, cloud computing, and artificial intelligence (Gobble 2018; Correani et al. 2020). In contrast to IT firms, non-IT firms lack inherent IT capabilities and resources, inevitably leading to the transformation process altering the internal dynamics and upending the established operational logic of the organization (Zhou et al. 2023; Ye et al. 2023). The legitimacy of an organization profoundly impacts the success of its transformation. Mimetic isomorphism facilitates organizations to gain legitimacy, referring to the process where an organization imitates other organizations within the same context to resemble them (Yang and Hyland 2012). In this paper, we define digital mimetic isomorphism as the degree of similarity in digital strategy compared to other firms in the same industry.

2.2. Industrial Digitalization and Digital Mimetic Isomorphism

Faced with digital transformation, enterprises confront a dilemma. On one hand, they aspire to optimize their existing organizational capabilities and achieve digital transformation through digital strategies (Hansen and Siew 2015). On the other hand, they also express concerns about potential challenges during the digital transformation process, such as potential disruptions to existing processes and structures (Xie et al. 2016). Industrial digitalization helps alleviate the dilemma for companies hesitant to transition in uncertain environments. Through cognitive constraints and competition-driven pressures, it encourages companies to adopt the mimicry of digital transformation, thus enhancing their legitimacy.

First, at the cognitive level, industry practices that are commonly deemed legitimate and acceptable by stakeholders within the industry (Strang and Soule 1998). Deviation from these norms results in a loss of legitimacy. Industrial digitalization has propelled industrial advancement, gradually shaping a new set of "game rules" (Correani et al. 2020). Enterprises adjust their behavior in accordance with the new industry standards and join the ranks of digital transformation (Kolomeitsev et al. 2024). According to Hinings et al. (2018), maintaining a consistent form of digital innovation in the development and promotion of new products, aligning with the existing legitimacy of digital enterprises, will assist follower enterprises in gaining legitimacy at the cognitive level.

Second, industrial digitalization drives digital homogenization among companies through competition. Digital transformation is an inevitable stage of enterprise development (Wu et al. 2021). Higher levels of industrial digitalization imply that pioneering companies within an industry have already undergone digital transformation, putting subsequent enterprises at a competitive disadvantage and accelerating investment in digital technologies. Concurrently, industrial digitalization triggers a revolution in consumer demand (Luo and Jiang 2022). Companies must continuously enhance the value of digital products through additional services and intelligent features (Khin and Ho 2018; Zhang et al. 2016). The limited market capacity intensifies competition among companies, compelling peer enterprises to undergo digital transformation. For example, Walmart's adoption of Radio-Frequency Identification (RFID) technology and its requirement for suppliers to implement this technology to save time and costs triggered imitation among other retailers (Lai et al. 2006).

Regarding focal companies, the targets of imitation comprise similar enterprises and successful firms. Whether mimicking isomorphism with similar or successful enterprises within the industry, it can signal legitimacy to the external environment. Compared to successful enterprises, the intensity of competition among similar enterprises is stronger, as are the legal constraints associated with behavioral norms. The impact of digitalization among similar enterprises introduces more potent cognitive constraints and competitive drives, significantly influencing the digital isomorphism (Chen et al. 2016). Therefore, we hypothesize that:

H1a. *Industrial digitalization is positively related to the digital mimetic isomorphism of similar firms.*

H1b. *Industrial digitalization is positively related to the digital mimetic isomorphism of successful firms.*

2.3. Regional Digitalization and Digital Mimetic Isomorphism

Regional digitalization development will boost the construction of local digital infrastructure (Shen et al. 2023), making it easier for enterprises to access policy support and resource allocations from local governments, thereby acting as a significant driver in the digitalization journey of enterprises. Enhanced regional digitalization fosters a conducive digital environment for local enterprises, offering optimal conditions to overcome the dual constraints of resources and environment (Xu et al. 2023). This, in turn, enhances their willingness and capability to adopt the digital behaviors of similar and outstanding enterprises.

Higher regional digitalization levels expand the scope of information accessible to businesses through digital infrastructure (Wernsdorf et al. 2022) and reduce information access costs (Goldfarb and Tucker 2019). This facilitates both the active and passive dissemination and penetration of information among businesses and raises the level of technological spillover absorbed by businesses (Shen et al. 2023). This surge facilitates the inflow of digital capital into firms, alleviating their financial limitations (Tang et al. 2021), thereby providing technological and financial support for inter-business emulation. Under governmental support, the formulation and implementation of digital economic policies have cultivated a thriving atmosphere for digital innovation, drawing in numerous entrepreneurs driven by digital entrepreneurship (Quinton et al. 2018). Moreover, local governments, driven by the needs of businesses, have tailored policies to fit enterprise digitalization requirements, offering governance standards and financial support so that enterprises can gain a localized advantage over other regional businesses (Anwar et al. 2020). Overall, a favorable regional digital environment advances enterprise digital transformation, encompassing technology, funding, talent, and policies (Lai and Yue 2022).

A well-established regional ecosystem stimulates the innovative vitality and latent potential of digital technology, expanding the spillover of digital knowledge and technology, enhancing its observability (Greve 2009), thus creating convenient conditions for enterprises to learn from digitalization experiences. Due to the technical and competitive features of digital products, they can be continuously adjusted and modified at a low cost, undergoing constant iterative innovations (Ni et al. 2023). Comparatively, imitating successful enterprises yields a higher performance for enterprises than imitating similar companies (Chen et al. 2016). However, imitating similar firms brings more legitimacy resources; thus, regional digitalization drives firms to imitate both similar and successful firms. Based on this, we hypothesize that:

H2a. *Regional digitalization is positively related to the digital mimetic isomorphism of similar firms.*

H2b. *Regional digitalization is positively related to the digital mimetic isomorphism of successful firms.*

2.4. Interactive Effect of Industrial Digitalization and Regional Digitalization on Digital Mimetic Isomorphism

Due to the impact of both industrial and regional digitalization in promoting the mimetic isomorphism of enterprise digitalization, non-IT firms will seize the opportunities these two factors bring, aligning their behavior with digital transformation. However, within highly digitized industrial and regional environments, enterprises face complex institutional contexts, where the aforementioned industrial and regional pressures may interplay with one another, possibly leading to conflict or mutual enhancement under certain circumstances (Greenwood et al. 2010).

In the context of imitating similar enterprises, the impacts of industry and region collide, resulting in conflicting effects. Conversely, when imitating successful firms, these influences reinforce each other. Within the same industry, similar enterprises are often considered more legitimate. Successful firms, renowned for their high visibility and comprehensive capabilities, exert an exemplary influence. Organizations improve their chances of success by imitating these successful entities (DiMaggio and Powell 1983). When companies are situated in industries and regions characterized by high levels of digitalization, regional digitalization effectively reduces the concerns about the legitimacy of digital behaviors across industries for these firms. This alleviates the pressure to passively imitate similar firms in digital initiatives, while stimulating companies to actively emulate the digital strategies of successful firms.

Optimal digital ecosystems within industries and regions promote organizations to actively emulate successful firms. Organizational learning theory suggests that companies have the capacity to reorganize external knowledge continually and repeatedly with their existing knowledge. Utilizing performance feedback mechanisms, this iterative process induces alterations in organizational practices and norms (Argote and Miron-Spektor 2011), ultimately enhancing organizational capabilities and improving business performance (Jiménez-Jiménez and Sanz-Valle 2011). Imitation is a form of organizational learning where the crucial initial step is acquiring new knowledge, and accessing it externally is a significant channel (Kesidou et al. 2023). High-level digitalization within industries and regions offers organizations a robust knowledge foundation, facilitating experiential learning from the digital behaviors of other enterprises. The affordance and self-growth of digital resources have amplified their flexibility and shareability (Huang et al. 2017), diminishing an organization's control over resources and broadening the spectrum of accessible resources (Wei et al. 2021), making digital technology easier to imitate. This facilitates enterprises acquiring a wealth of advanced digital technologies and diverse knowledge from the market (Martínez-Noya and García-Canal 2021), and enhances their dynamic and innovative capabilities by imitating successful enterprises to gain a competitive advantage (Posen et al. 2023).

High-level industrial and regional digitalization mitigates the passive imitation of similar enterprises. The current research suggests that the efficacy of imitation relies on the diversity among enterprises. Imitating similar enterprises can help organizations achieve performance levels close to industry averages (Tang et al. 2011), yet it does not guarantee above-average profits (Posen et al. 2013). The excessive imitation of similar enterprises not only leads to resource wastage and redundant development but also exacerbates inter-firm competition, compelling companies to adopt low-cost strategies, resulting in profit erosion. Additionally, in regions with high levels of digitalization, there is a loosening of the legitimacy requirements for industrial digitization. When regional digitalization provides sufficient resources for imitating enterprises, companies tend to actively imitate successful enterprises, with very few choosing to imitate similar ones. In view of this, we propose H3a and H3b.

H3a. *The interaction of industrial digitalization and regional digitalization is negatively related to the digital mimetic isomorphism of similar firms.*

H3b. *The interaction of industrial digitalization and regional digitalization is positively related to the digital mimetic isomorphism of successful firms.*

3. Reseach Design

3.1. Sample and Data

To test our conceptual model, we conduct an empirical study examining the digital strategy choices of non-IT listed firms in China from 2012 to 2020, considering the unique context of Chinese companies. China is an ideal subject for this study, as the past decade has seen steady growth in its digital economy, with increasing encouragement for companies to integrate digitalization with technological innovation, with an increasing number of firms placing greater importance on the deployment of digital technologies. The definition of the IT industry in this study is based on the "Statistical Classification of Digital Economy and its Core Industries (2021)" published by the National Bureau of Statistics of China. Following the industry classification provided by the China Securities Regulatory Commission in its 2012 version, the IT industry includes three-digit industry codes consisting of a letter representing the category and two digits representing the major group. Specifically, the following industry codes are considered part of the IT industry: C39 (Manufacture of Computers, Communication Equipment, and Other Electronic Equipment), I63 (Telecommunications, Radio, Television, and Satellite Transmission Services), I64 (Internet and Related Services), and I65 (Software and Information Technology Services).

Consequently, non-IT listed firms refer to those companies that do not fall within the IT industry category.

Our data, including company-level, regional-level, and industry-level, are sourced from multiple data channels. The revenue composition data at the company level, classified by industry, are obtained from the CCER Economic and Financial Database, while other financial and corporate governance data are sourced from the CSMAR Database. The regional-level data are derived from the China Statistical Yearbook and the Institute of Digital Finance, Peking. The industry-level data are sourced from the input–output tables (IOTs) published by the National Bureau of Statistics of China.

After identifying firms listed in the CSMAR database from 2012 to 2020, we process the initial data as follows: first, we merge the firm-level data with industry-level data based on the three-digit industry code of each listed firm, and then merge the firm-level data with regional-level data according to the city where each firm is located. Then, we exclude IT firms and those with missing values for key variables, resulting in a sample of 2862 firms with a total of 11,577 firm–year observations. Finally, we winsorize the continuous variables at the 1% level in both distribution tails to mitigate the influence of extreme values.

3.2. Variables and Measures

Dependent variables. Digital mimetic isomorphism is divided into two dimensions: similar enterprises and successful enterprises. The calculation method refers to Haveman (1993) and Chen et al. (2016). Initially, it identifies similar enterprises based on their digitalization level and then distinguishes successful enterprises through the financial performance and digitalization level of the companies, as detailed below.

First, $M1_{it}$ denotes the digital mimetic isomorphism of similar firms for firm i in year t, and Dc_{it} represents the digitalization level. Setting 0.5–1.5 times the digitalization level of this firm as the similar size window (0.5 Dc_{it}, 1.5 Dc_{it}), we can obtain the ratio of the number of other firms in the peer industry to the number of all the firms in the industry in this window. Ultimately, we used this ratio to measure similar firms' digital mimetic isomorphism.

Second, $M2_{it}$ represents the successful firms' digital mimetic isomorphism. The calculation process includes the following steps: (1) we ranked the firms in descending order of their total return on assets (ROA) by year and filtered out other firms with a higher ROA_{it} than firm i in year t, (2) firms whose digitalization level ranked in the top 1/4 of all firms in the same industry were flagged and the number of flagged firms was recorded, and (3) we calculated the number of flagged firms as a share of the total number of firms in the industry. This ratio is the successful firm's digital imitation isomorphism.

Finally, we use digital proximity to measure digitalization (Rahmati et al. 2021). Previous studies have employed questionnaire surveys (Chi et al. 2020), text analysis (Wu et al. 2021), and intangible assets (Zhang et al. 2021) measurement to assess corporate digital transformation. The first method suffers from limited research subjects, resulting in a lack of representativeness. The second method utilizes text analysis to measure the frequency of digital-related terms in the annual reports of listed companies, which may not fully reflect the actual progress in digitalization. The third method measures the proportion of intangible assets related to digitalization, but it may be influenced by firms' ostentatious investments (Triplett 1999). Digital proximity is a measurement approach that takes an outcome-oriented perspective and utilizes the concept of product space (Hidalgo et al. 2007; Hartmann et al. 2017). It is measured based on network analysis, providing a more accurate and comprehensive representation of a firm's digitalization status and its position within the digital landscape. This approach effectively addresses the limitations mentioned above. Following the measurement framework proposed by Rahmati et al. (2021), we first calculate the digital proximity at the industrial level. This involves measuring the distance from other industries to the digital industries (C39, I63, I64, I65) using Dijkstra's algorithm to calculate the average shortest path from a specific industry to all IT industries. Based on this, we compute the weighted average digital proximity for each company's business sectors, with the weights determined by the revenue generated in each industry in which the company operates.

Independent variables. To measure industrial digitalization, we use the IOTs to calculate the coefficient of complete consumption dependence to measure the digitalization level of inputs across various industries (Dai and Yang 2022). In this study, the coefficient of complete consumption represents the sum of the quantity of IT products directly and indirectly consumed by each production unit in an industry, reflecting the level of digital input fully consumed by that industry. Subsequently, we enhance the coefficient of complete consumption using the coefficient of complete dependence. The specific calculation formula is as follows:

$$Indd_{dj} = \sum_{d} \frac{Complete_{dj}}{\sum_{k=1}^{N} Complete_{kj}} \tag{1}$$

In Equation (1), d represents the IT industry, while $Complete_{kj}$ denotes the coefficient of complete consumption from industry j to industry k. Additionally, $Indd_{dj}$ represents the ratio of digital input to total input consumed by industry j. This ratio effectively characterizes the relative influence of digital input across all the intermediate sectors and provides insights into the level of digital investment inherent in each industry.

Regional digitalization. Drawing on the research by Zhao et al. (2020), we adopted principal component analysis to standardize and reduce the dimensionality of five indicators at the city level. These indicators include the number of internet broadband access users per hundred people, the proportion of employees in the computer services and software industry to urban employees, the per capita volume of telecommunications services, the number of mobile phone users per hundred people, and the China Digital Inclusive Finance Index. This approach helps alleviate the issue of substantial digital disparities between cities within the same province and contributes to addressing the problem of regional development imbalance.

Control variables. Building upon the study by Chen et al. (2022), we incorporated control variables at three levels to account for their influence on digital strategy convergence. At the industrial level, we utilized the Herfindahl index as a measure of industry concentration, where higher values indicate greater concentration. At the firm level, we included variables such as firm size, leverage ratio, cash holdings, asset return, revenue growth, firm age, and ownership. At the decision-maker level, we considered variables such as the ownership stake of the largest shareholder, the separation of ownership and control, CEO age, CEO education, and CEO tenure. Table 1 provides a description and the sources of each variable.

Table 1. Variable key.

Variables	Description	Source
Dependent variables		
M1	The level of digital mimetic isomorphism of similar firms	CCER
M2	The level of digital mimetic isomorphism of successful firms	CCER
Independent variables		
Indd	Industrial digitalization, complete dependency degree in input–output table calculations.	IOTs
Regd	Regional digitalization, the values obtained by applying principal component analysis for dimensionality reduction on the five aforementioned indicators	Statistical Yearbook et al.

Table 1. *Cont.*

Variables	Description	Source
Control variables		
Herfindahl index	Squared sum of each company's market share within an industry	CSMAR
Firm size	Natural logarithm of the sum of total assets plus one	CSMAR
Leverage ratio	Total debts divided by total assets	CSMAR
Cash holdings	Cash and cash equivalents divided by total assets	CSMAR
Asset return	Net profit divided by total assets	CSMAR
Revenue growth	The growth rate of the operating revenue	CSMAR
Firm age	Natural logarithm of the sum of the listed age plus one	CSMAR
Ownership	The dummy variable takes a value of 1 if the actual controller of the company is state-owned, and 0 otherwise	CSMAR
Board size	Natural logarithm of the number of board members	CSMAR
Shareholding No.1	Natural logarithm of the ratio of shareholding held by the largest shareholder plus one	CSMAR
Separation	Natural logarithm of the control rights ratio minus ownership rights ratio plus one	CSMAR
CEO age	Natural logarithm of CEO age	CSMAR
CEO education	Values from 5 to 1: doctorate, master's degree, bachelor's degree, associate's degree, and technical diploma or other qualifications	CSMAR
CEO tenure	Natural logarithm of the age of a CEO during their tenure (denoted in months) plus one	CSMAR

3.3. Methodology

Prior to conducting the regression analysis, this study considers the estimation methods for Model (2) and Model (3). The data in this study correspond to the category of large N, small T panel data, which necessitates a focus on the issue of heteroskedasticity. The results of the White test reveal that all p-values were below 0.000, indicating strong evidence against the null hypothesis of homoscedasticity and confirming the presence of heteroscedasticity. Consequently, the generalized least squares (GLS) method is deemed appropriate for obtaining effective parameter estimates. The GLS is ultimately selected as the estimation model for this study. Furthermore, this study employs additional methods, including variable measurement substitution, changing the window period, propensity score matching (PSM) analysis, and changing the estimation model, to ensure the accuracy and robustness of the results.

$$M_{it} = \alpha_0 + \alpha_1 Indd_{ijt} + \alpha_2 Controls + \gamma_t + \varepsilon_{it} \tag{2}$$

$$M_{it} = \beta_0 + \beta_1 Regd_{iht} + \beta_2 Controls + \gamma_t + \varepsilon_{it} \tag{3}$$

where *Controls* denotes a set of pertinent control variables, M_{it} represents $M1_{it}$ or $M2_{it}$, $Indd_{ijt}$ indicates the level of industrial digitalization for industry j for firm i in year t, $Regd_{iht}$ represents the level of regional digitalization in city h for firm i in year t, γ_t captures the year fixed effects, and ε_{it} is the error term. The values of α_1 and β_1 serve to test Hypothesis 1 and Hypothesis 2, respectively.

4. Results

4.1. Summary Statistics

Table 2 presents descriptive statistics. The mean values of digital mimetic isomorphism for similar companies (M1) and successful companies (M2) indicate that there is a higher proportion of companies resembling our enterprise in terms of digitalization within the same industry (20.9%). In contrast, the number of companies in the same industry with better profits and higher digitalization levels compared to our company is relatively lower (10.5%). The average level of industrial digitalization (Indd) stands at 0.086, indicating the average digital investment level within each industry is 0.086. As for regional digitalization (Regd), its mean and median values are proximate, suggesting a relatively even distribution. The maximum Variance Inflation Factor (VIF) among all the explanatory variables is 2.90, indicating the absence of significant multicollinearity issues in the regression model.

Table 2. Descriptive statistics.

Variables	Mean	S.D.	Median	Min	Max	VIF
M1	0.209	0.230	0.097	0.000	0.721	
M2	0.105	0.076	0.096	0.000	0.250	
Indd	0.086	0.132	0.032	0.006	0.593	1.09
Regd	0.200	0.080	0.188	0.065	0.417	1.08
Herfindahl index	0.091	0.090	0.065	0.014	0.555	1.02
Firm size	22.300	1.377	22.100	19.620	26.630	1.36
Leverage ratio	0.441	0.213	0.430	0.060	0.960	2.87
Cash holdings	0.173	0.121	0.141	0.011	0.601	1.07
Asset return	0.030	0.074	0.034	-0.362	0.201	2.90
Revenue growth	0.185	0.604	0.089	-0.661	4.429	1.00
Firm age	2.932	0.312	2.996	1.946	3.497	1.11
Ownership	0.364	0.481	0.000	0.000	1.000	1.37
Board size	2.126	0.202	2.197	1.609	2.708	1.15
Shareholding No. 1	3.468	0.449	3.495	1.162	4.511	1.13
Separation	0.972	1.210	0.000	0.000	4.013	1.06
CEO age	3.901	0.136	3.912	3.497	4.190	1.10
CEO education	3.186	1.295	4.000	0.000	5.000	1.03
CEO tenure	3.512	1.070	3.714	0.000	5.460	1.09

4.2. Baseline Results

Table 3 reports the results of the hypothesis tests. According to Table 3, the coefficients of the key explanatory variable Indd are all positive at the 1% level of significance ($\beta = 0.087$, $p < 0.01$ for M1; $\beta = 0.054$, $p < 0.01$ for M2) in Columns (1) to (2), as is the other key explanatory variable Regd ($\beta = 0.012$, $p < 0.01$ for M1; $\beta = 0.032$, $p < 0.01$ for M2) in Columns (3) to (4). The results show that both industrial digitalization and regional digitalization significantly promote firms' digital imitation isomorphism, whether of similar or successful firms. On the one hand, this confirms the views of Chen et al. (2022) and Chalmers et al. (2021) that the level of industrial and regional digitalization is conducive to facilitating firms to engage in innovative activities such as digital transformation. On the other hand, it responds to the studies of Haveman (1993) and Chen et al. (2016) that firms will choose similar firms and successful firms as imitation objects for learning. In summary, Hypothesis 1a, 1b, 2a, and 2b are valid.

Table 3. Baseline estimation results.

Variables	(1)	(2)	(3)	(4)
	M1	M2	M1	M2
Indd	0.087 ***	0.054 ***		
	(59.57)	(244.83)		
Regd			0.012 ***	0.032 ***
			(5.03)	(44.00)
Herfindahl index	−0.173 ***	0.031 ***	−0.185 ***	0.019 ***
	(−53.96)	(91.73)	(−64.81)	(27.07)
Firm size	−0.003 ***	−0.000 ***	−0.003 ***	−0.001 ***
	(−27.60)	(−3.33)	(−12.19)	(−7.32)
Leverage ratio	0.001 **	−0.011 ***	0.002 ***	−0.011 ***
	(2.39)	(−47.96)	(5.70)	(−32.63)
Cash holdings	0.022 ***	−0.093 ***	0.035 ***	−0.091 ***
	(15.38)	(−276.94)	(27.89)	(−110.80)
Asset return	0.013 ***	−0.087 ***	0.017 ***	−0.088 ***
	(5.91)	(−138.28)	(10.63)	(−97.83)
Revenue growth	−0.000	0.000	−0.000	0.000
	(−0.45)	(1.28)	(−0.42)	(1.41)
Firm age	0.003 ***	0.008 ***	−0.009 ***	0.006 ***
	(3.41)	(70.25)	(−12.69)	(40.69)
Ownership	0.006 ***	0.021 ***	0.005 ***	0.021 ***
	(7.99)	(154.46)	(7.36)	(100.04)
Board size	−0.002 *	−0.014 ***	−0.002 ***	−0.015 ***
	(−1.80)	(−65.27)	(−2.81)	(−52.82)
Shareholding No.1	0.018 ***	−0.019 ***	0.015 ***	−0.020 ***
	(41.55)	(−285.93)	(28.43)	(−171.35)
Separation	−0.001 ***	0.001 ***	−0.001 ***	0.001 ***
	(−7.65)	(23.34)	(−6.63)	(12.07)
CEO age	0.037 ***	−0.014 ***	0.030 ***	−0.015 ***
	(31.97)	(−84.98)	(26.32)	(−37.56)
CEO education	−0.002 ***	0.000 ***	−0.001 ***	0.000 ***
	(−15.88)	(11.62)	(−10.80)	(8.19)
CEO tenure	−0.002 ***	−0.002 ***	−0.002 ***	−0.002 ***
	(−12.46)	(−31.81)	(−15.87)	(−25.87)
Constant	0.051 ***	0.257 ***	0.113 ***	0.282 ***
	(9.79)	(180.07)	(17.54)	(112.25)
Year effect	Yes	Yes	Yes	Yes
Observations	11,577	11,577	11,577	11,577

Notes. Z-statistics in parentheses. * $p < 0.1$; ** $p < 0.05$; *** $p < 0.01$.

4.3. Robustness Checks

Adjusting variable measurement methods. Most of the previous studies on digital transformation were measured using text analysis based on the appearance of keywords related to digital transformation in the annual reports of listed companies. In order to avoid the problem of biased conclusions caused by the manner of data measurement, this paper refers to Wu et al. (2021), using text analysis to replace the measurement method for digitalization levels and recalculating dependent variables M1 and M2. The results, as shown in Table 4, are consistent with the conclusions of previous studies.

Changing the time frame. In order to ensure the robustness of the research findings across various sample conditions, this study altered the sample period for examination. The original sample spanned from 2012 to 2020, during which the unexpected outbreak of the COVID-19 pandemic in 2020 significantly impacted China's macroeconomic and social development. This event might have influenced the digital performance of businesses, potentially causing result biases. Hence, in the robustness testing, the regression for that year was excluded. The results, as shown in Table 5, confirm the robustness of our study's conclusions.

Table 4. Robustness check I: adjusting variable measurement methods.

Variables	(1)	(2)	(3)	(4)
	M1	**M2**	**M1**	**M2**
Indd	0.003 ***	0.003 ***		
	(86.80)	(68.47)		
Regd			0.115 ***	0.009 ***
			(180.32)	(10.59)
Controls	Yes	Yes	Yes	Yes
Constant	−0.122 ***	0.293 ***	−0.099 ***	0.298 ***
	(−72.81)	(153.56)	(−69.62)	(115.29)
Year effect	Yes	Yes	Yes	Yes
Observations	13,130	13,130	13,130	13,130

Notes. Z−statistics in parentheses. *** $p < 0.01$.

Table 5. Robustness check II: changing the time frame.

Variables	(1)	(2)	(3)	(4)
	M1	**M2**	**M1**	**M2**
Indd	0.081 ***	0.050 ***		
	(34.45)	(214.24)		
Regd			0.030 ***	0.025 ***
			(16.91)	(81.73)
Controls	Yes	Yes	Yes	Yes
Constant	0.033 ***	0.244 ***	0.059 ***	0.266 ***
	(5.85)	(134.73)	(9.61)	(158.57)
Year effect	Yes	Yes	Yes	Yes
Observations	8689	8689	8689	8689

Notes. Z-statistics in parentheses. *** $p < 0.01$.

Propensity score matching (PSM) analysis. Considering the potential endogeneity issues resulting from sample selection bias in the model, this study re-examines using PSM. The study distinguishes companies located in high-level digital industries/regions as the treatment group, setting the median as the benchmark. It utilizes propensity score matching to identify matched pairs (control group) and employs the nearest-neighbor matching method for the one-to-one non-replacement matching of the sample. For the selection of matching variables, this paper firstly selects all control variables as matching variables, and then compares the great likelihood values of different models, and then selects the matching variables to achieve the best fitting effect. When the treatment variable is industrial digitalization, the final selected matching variables are firm size, firm age, asset return, separation, ownership, CEO age, and shareholding No.1.[1] By matching the whole sample, the total number of matching successful samples is 9461, accounting for 83.27%. And the standardized deviation of the matched variables is less than 10%, and the results of the *t*-test do not reject the original hypothesis that there is no systematic difference between the treatment group and the control group, indicating that the matched samples satisfy the assumption of balance. The sample average treatment effect on the treated (ATT) between the treatment and control groups' post-matching is notably significant, with a t-value of 4.19. This signifies the continued substantial influence of industrial digitalization on fostering digital mimetic isomorphism. The treatment variable, defining regional digitalization, is not reiterated. The sample regression results' post-matching, detailed in Table 6, validates the earlier conclusions, affirming the study's findings under similar conditions.

Table 6. Robustness check III: PSM.

Variables	(1)	(2)	(3)	(4)
	M1	M2	M1	M2
Indd	0.056 ***	0.070 ***		
	(38.30)	(525.07)		
Regd			0.044 ***	0.023 ***
			(29.23)	(42.16)
Controls	Yes	Yes	Yes	Yes
Constant	0.039 ***	0.232 ***	0.018 ***	0.348 ***
	(7.14)	(181.45)	(5.34)	(137.11)
Year effect	Yes	Yes	Yes	Yes
Observations	9641	9641	9516	9516

Notes. Z-statistics in parentheses. *** $p < 0.01$.

Changing the estimation model. Furthermore, we conducted cross-sectional dependence tests, and the results indicated p-values below 0.05, confirming significant cross-sectional dependence within the panel data. Following the methods of Petersen (2009) and Brunnermeier et al. (2020), we employed two-way clustering to address dependence issues, applying the clustering of standard errors at both the firm and year levels. The regression results, as shown in Table 7, are consistent with the previous findings.

Table 7. Robustness check IV: changing the estimation model.

Variables	(1)	(2)	(3)	(4)
	M1	M2	M1	M2
Indd	0.075 *	0.047 *		
	(0.044)	(1.85)		
Regd			0.061 *	0.032 **
			(1.87)	(2.33)
Controls	Yes	Yes	Yes	Yes
Constant	−0.109	0.285 ***	−0.058	0.304 ***
	(0.173)	(10.98)	(−0.41)	(13.62)
Observations	10,916	10,916	10,916	10,916

Notes. T-statistics in parentheses. * $p < 0.1$; ** $p < 0.05$; *** $p < 0.01$.

4.4. Interaction Effect Results

Table 7 reports the results of the interaction effect. Column (1) of Table 8 provides evidence for the negative effect of the interaction of industrial digitalization and regional digitalization on the digital mimetic isomorphism of similar firms ($\beta = -0.155$, $p < 0.01$), but a positive effect on that of successful firms ($\beta = 0.218$, $p < 0.01$). The results indicate that the interaction between industrial digitalization and regional digitalization enhances firms' tendency to engage in mimetic isomorphism with successful firms, while having an opposite effect on similar firms. This finding aligns with the studies of Tang et al. (2011) and Giachetti and Torrisi (2018). When firms are situated in environments with high levels of industrial and regional digitalization, characterized by transparency and lower uncertainty, along with abundant resources, imitating similar firms can lead to fierce competition and average performance, prompting firms to imitate successful firms. Thus, H3a and H3b are both supported.

We plot moderated effects to support the interaction effect results (see Figures 2 and 3). Figure 2 reports the impact of the interaction effect on similar enterprises. From the left graph, it is evident that when the industrial digitalization level is high, the effect of low-level regional digitalization on similar enterprises is more pronounced than the effect of high-level regional digitalization. From the right graph, it is observed that when the industrial digitalization level is high, there exists a negative relationship between regional digitalization and digital mimetic isomorphism among similar enterprises. Figure 3 presents the impact of the interaction effect on successful enterprises. The left panel illustrates that, in situations with higher regional digitalization, the positive relationship between industrial digitalization and mimetic isomorphism among successful enterprises is significantly stronger than in cases with lower regional digitalization. Similar to the left panel, the results in the right panel mirror these findings. These results further confirm H3.

Table 8. Interaction effect results.

Variables	(1)	(2)
	M1	M2
Indd × Regd	−0.155 ***	0.218 ***
	(−13.90)	(36.70)
Indd	0.093 ***	0.044 ***
	(58.12)	(75.82)
Regd	−0.003	0.019 ***
	(−1.21)	(31.40)
Controls	Yes	Yes
Constant	0.048 ***	0.262 ***
	(6.57)	(100.67)
Year effect	Yes	Yes
Observations	11,577	11,577

Notes. Z-statistics in parentheses. *** $p < 0.01$. The regression process was centered on the independent and moderator variables to exclude the effect of multicollinearity.

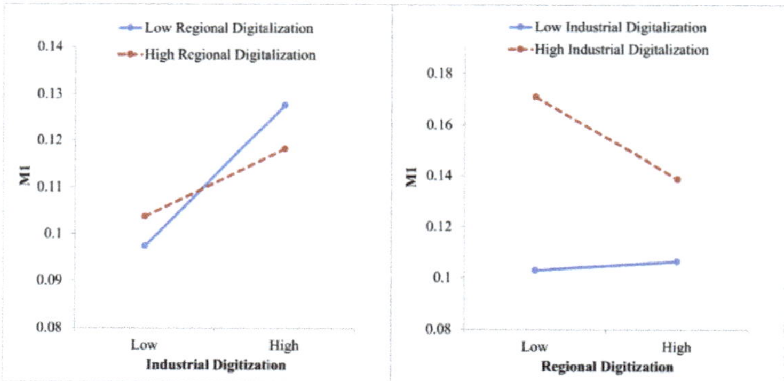

Figure 2. The moderating effect of industrial digitalization and regional digitalization on the digital mimetic isomorphism of similar firms.

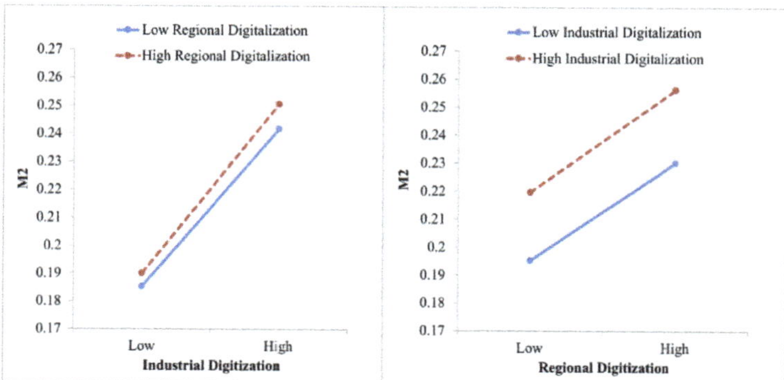

Figure 3. The moderating effect of industrial digitalization and regional digitalization on the digital mimetic isomorphism of successful firms.

5. Discussion and Conclusions

Digital transformation represents a key avenue for firms to achieve high-quality development within the digital economy. However, most non-IT firms in China are at the initial exploration stage of digital transformation, facing the dilemma of "difficulty in transformation" and "wishing to transform but hesitating to do so". Both the government and academia are highly concerned about how to drive the process of digital transformation. This study aims to investigate how industrial digitalization and regional digitalization affect firms' digital mimetic behavior, both separately and interactively, from an institutional environment perspective.

5.1. Conclusions

This study provides answers as to how firms can address the decision-making dilemmas associated with digital transformation, enriching the study from the perspective of the institutional environment. Using non-IT firms on China's A-share market from 2012 to 2020 as samples, this study provides evidence that both industrial digitalization and regional digitalization environments play crucial roles in digital strategic decision-making, encouraging the imitation of both similar and successful enterprises. Moreover, our results indicate that the interaction of industrial digitalization and regional digitalization is positively related to the digital mimetic isomorphism of successful firms but negatively related to similar firms. This extends the research of Chen et al. (2022) by further differentiating the targets of digital transformation imitation and revealing the heterogeneous responses of digital strategy choices under various institutional pressures. It also demonstrates that the diverse industrial structure and uneven regional digitalization in China present challenges for digital transformation. Firms are encouraged to make strategic decisions based on their external institutional environment. The results are valuable for promoting the digital transformation of Chinese firms, enhancing the overall quality and competitiveness of the national digital economy. Accelerating the digital transformation process will invigorate the economy, promote industrial upgrades, and create more high-value jobs, thus fostering sustainable economic growth.

5.2. Theoretical Contributions

Compared to the existing literature, this study may make several marginal contributions. First, this study extends research on mimetic isomorphism to the context of digital transformation. Previous studies have focused on mimetic isomorphism related to IT investments (Cheng et al. 2021), mergers and acquisitions (Tseng and Chou 2011), and carbon management (Liu et al. 2018). Chen et al. (2022) focuses on the impact on single entities, whereas we provide a novel perspective by focusing on the dyadic relation between followers and leaders. This study examines how institutional environments shape digital mimetic isomorphism and reveals the mechanisms driving the diffusion and spread of digital transformation.

Second, this study enriches the research on the antecedents of mimetic isomorphism. The previous literature explored various external factors, including regional cultural ties (Li et al. 2016), technological advancements and openness to international trade (Ozturk et al. 2021), uncertainty (Haunschild and Miner 1997; Sarrina Li and Lee 2010), and cultural environments (Li and Parboteeah 2015). Additionally, internal elements like organizational status (Han 1994; Durand and Kremp 2016) and experience (Ando 2011) were considered. However, this study reveals the impact of institutional environments on mimetic isomorphism from an institutional perspective and further contrasts the mimetic isomorphism towards similar firms and successful firms.

Third, this study incorporates two different types of digital institutional fields into a framework to compare their influence on promoting firms' digital transformation from the perspective of mimetic isomorphism. Extending the prior research that considers single institutional pressures as antecedents (Liu et al. 2024), our findings reveal that organizations respond differently to institutional pressures from various fields, addressing the call for applying institutional theory in strategic management (Suchman 1995).

5.3. Practical Implications

Our research has several implications. First, policymakers and related government entities provide targeted support for the digitalization of core industries and industry clusters by developing digital industry parks. Industrial digitalization serves as a critical source of institutional pressure for firms' digital transformation efforts. Shifting the focus of local government policies towards fostering the digitalization of core industries can improve the efficiency of policy implementation. Furthermore, the advancement in regional digital economies can facilitate firms' responses to pressures for industrial digitalization. By actively supporting industry clusters and prioritizing the digitalization of these clusters, local governments can maximize the policy's effectiveness and drive digital transformation among firms within the region.

Second, it is important to recognize the influence of highly visible leading firms. Under the pressures of industrial digitalization and regional digitalization, the impact of leading firms is more pronounced. National and regional governments should focus on directing and supporting leading firms in their digital transformation initiatives. By capitalizing on the positive demonstration effects of successful firms, governments can foster a positive development of digitalization.

Third, managers should fully leverage the role of the institutional environment in facilitating digital transformation. They should actively follow digitalization trends in their industry and region, including regularly reviewing relevant policies, regulations, and incentives, and participating in industry forums. By leveraging these trends, managers can formulate strategies for their digital transformation. Embracing the opportunities provided by digitalization can enhance a firm's market position and competitive advantage.

5.4. Limitations and Future Research

Although the empirical findings of this paper are consistent with the theoretical predictions, there are some limitations. First, the research context is incomplete. The analysis in this study was based on data from Chinese listed companies from 2012 to 2020, thereby restricting the overall applicability of the research conclusions. Future studies could enhance this area by conducting comparative research in other emerging or developed economies.

Second, it is suggested to employ additional research methods, including the integration of meta-analysis and structural equation modeling (MASEM), to conduct a more in-depth analysis of the factors influencing mimetic behavior. This approach could further investigate the differences in digital mimetic isomorphism and the role of environmental factors between firms in developed and emerging economies.

Third, this study concentrates on investigating mimetic isomorphism behavior. The mechanisms driving organizational homogeneity are mimetic, normative, and coercive. However, this paper primarily focuses on imitative behavior, specifically within the realm of digitalization. This concentration is due to the substantial uncertainty associated with the decision-making process of digital transformation in enterprises, leading most companies to adopt learning through imitation from their industry counterparts. Subsequent research could explore the impact of institutional environments on normative and coercive isomorphism.

Author Contributions: Conceptualization, Y.C. and H.M.; methodology, Y.C. and T.Z.; software, Y.C. and T.Z.; validation, Y.C., H.M. and T.Z.; formal analysis, Y.C. and T.Z.; investigation, H.M.; resources, T.Z.; data curation, Y.C.; writing—original draft preparation, Y.C. and T.Z.; writing—review and editing, Y.C. and H.M.; visualization, Y.C. and H.M.; supervision, H.M.; project administration, H.M.; funding acquisition, H.M. All authors have read and agreed to the published version of the manuscript.

Funding: This research was funded by the National Natural Science Foundation of China under Grant 71973130 and 72272138 and the National Social Science Foundation of China under Grant 22AZD126.

Informed Consent Statement: Not applicable.

Data Availability Statement: The data that support the findings of this study are available from the authors, upon reasonable request.

Conflicts of Interest: The authors declare no conflicts of interest.

Notes

1 When the treatment variable refers to regional digitalization, the selected matching variable are firm size, firm age, seperation, ownership, CEO education, shareholding No. 1, asset return, and CEO tenure. Moreover, all results pass the matching balance test, signifying the significant value of the ATT.

References

Ando, Naoki. 2011. Isomorphism and foreign subsidiary staffing policies. *Cross Cultural Management: An International Journal* 18: 131–43. [CrossRef]

Anwar, Muhammad, Kayhan Tajeddini, and Rizwan Ullah. 2020. Entrepreneurial finance and new venture success—The moderating role of government support. *Business Strategy & Development* 3: 408–21. [CrossRef]

Argote, Linda, and Ella Miron-Spektor. 2011. Organizational Learning: From Experience to Knowledge. *Organization Science* 22: 1123–37. [CrossRef]

Brookes, Maureen, and Levent Altinay. 2017. Knowledge transfer and isomorphism in franchise networks. *International Journal of Hospitality Management* 62: 33–42. [CrossRef]

Brunnermeier, Markus, Simon Rother, and Isabel Schnabel. 2020. Asset Price Bubbles and Systemic Risk. *The Review of Financial Studies* 33: 4272–317. [CrossRef]

Cao, Shaopeng, Xin Cui, Jing Liao, Chunfeng Wang, and Shouyu Yao. 2024. A good neighbor, a found treasure: Do local neighbors affect corporate innovation? *Journal of Product Innovation Management* 4: 1–22. [CrossRef]

Chalmers, Dominic, Russell Matthews, and Amy Hyslop. 2021. Blockchain as an external enabler of new venture ideas: Digital entrepreneurs and the disintermediation of the global music industry. *Journal of Business Research* 125: 577–91. [CrossRef]

Chen, Limin, Jingya Liu, and Shilei Zhang. 2016. Influence of Mimetic Isomorphism on Firms' Internationalization Performance Relationship-An Empirical Study Based on Legitimacy Perspective in Institutional Theory. *China Industrial Economics* 9: 127–43. [CrossRef]

Chen, Yujiao, Tiebo Song, and Jianbin Huang. 2022. Digital transformation of enterprises: Ls the company following peers in the same industry? Or in the same area? Research on decision process based on institutional theory. *Studies in Science of Science* 40: 1054–62. [CrossRef]

Chen, Yujiao, Rui Li, and Tiebo Song. 2023. Does TMT internationalization promote corporate digital transformation? A study based on the cognitive process mechanism. *Business Process Management Journal* 29: 309–38. [CrossRef]

Cheng, Zhuo, Arun Rai, Feng Tian, and Sean Xin Xu. 2021. Social Learning in Information Technology Investment: The Role of Board Interlocks. *Management Science* 67: 547–76. [CrossRef]

Chi, Maomao, Dingling Ye, Junjing Wang, and Shanshan Zhai. 2020. How Can Chinese Small-and Medium-sized Manufacturing Enterprises Improve the New Product Development (NPD) Performance? From the Perspective of Digital Empowerment. *Nankai Business Review* 23: 63–75.

Correani, Alessia, Alfredo De Massis, Federico Frattini, Antonio Messeni Petruzzelli, and Angelo Natalicchio. 2020. Implementing a Digital Strategy: Learning from the Experience of Three Digital Transformation Projects. *California Management Review* 62: 37–56. [CrossRef]

Dai, Xiang, and Shuangzhi Yang. 2022. Digital Empowerment, Source of Digital Input and Green Manufacturing. *China Industrial Economics* 9: 83–101. [CrossRef]

DiMaggio, Paul J., and Walter W. Powell. 1983. The Iron Cage Revisited: Institutional Isomorphism and Collective Rationality in Organizational Fields. *American Sociological Review* 48: 147–60. [CrossRef]

Durand, Rodolphe, and Pierre-Antoine Kremp. 2016. Classical Deviation: Organizational and Individual Status as Antecedents of Conformity. *Academy of Management Journal* 59: 65–89. [CrossRef]

Francis, John, Cong Cong Zheng, and Ananda Mukherji. 2009. An Institutional Perspective on Foreign Direct Investment: A Multi-level Framework. *Management International Review* 49: 565–83. [CrossRef]

Giachetti, C. Claudio, and Salvatore Torrisi. 2018. Following or Running Away from the Market Leader? The Influences of Environmental Uncertainty and Market Leadership. *European Management Review* 15: 445–63. [CrossRef]

Gobble, MaryAnne M. 2018. Digital Strategy and Digital Transformation. *Research-Technology Management* 61: 66–71. [CrossRef]

Goldfarb, Avi, and Catherine Tucker. 2019. Digital Economics. *Journal of Economic Literature* 57: 3–43. [CrossRef]

Greenwood, Royston, Amalia Magán Díaz, Stan Xiao Li, and José Céspedes Lorente. 2010. The Multiplicity of Institutional Logics and the Heterogeneity of Organizational Responses. *Organization Science* 21: 521–39. [CrossRef]

Greve, Henrich R. 2009. Bigger and safer: The diffusion of competitive advantage. *Strategic Management Journal* 30: 1–23. [CrossRef]

Han, Shin-Kap. 1994. Mimetic Isomorphism and Its Effect on the Audit Services Market. *Social Forces* 73: 637–64. [CrossRef]
Hansen, Rina, and Kien Sia Siew. 2015. Hummel's Digital Transformation Toward Omnichannel Retailing: Key Lessons Learned. *MIS Quarterly Executive* 14: 51–66.
Hartmann, Dominik, Miguel R. Guevara, Cristian Jara-Figueroa, Manuel Aristarán, and César A. Hidalgo. 2017. Linking Economic Complexity, Institutions, and Income Inequality. *World Development* 93: 75–93. [CrossRef]
Haunschild, R. Pamela, and Anne S. Miner. 1997. Modes of Interorganizational Imitation: The Effects of Outcome Salience and Uncertainty. *Administrative Science Quarterly* 42: 472–500. [CrossRef]
Haveman, Heather A. 1993. Follow the Leader: Mimetic Isomorphism and Entry Into New Markets. *Administrative Science Quarterly* 38: 593. [CrossRef]
Heugens, Pursey P. M. A. R., and Michel W. Lander. 2009. Structure! Agency! (And Other Quarrels): A Meta-Analysis of Institutional Theories of Organization. *Academy of Management Journal* 52: 61–85. [CrossRef]
Hidalgo, César A., Bailey Klinger, Albert-Laszlo Barabási, and Romeu Hausmann. 2007. The Product Space Conditions the Development of Nations. *Science* 317: 482–87. [CrossRef]
Hinings, Bob, Thomas Gegenhuber, and Royston Greenwood. 2018. Digital innovation and transformation: An institutional perspective. *Information and Organization* 28: 52–61. [CrossRef]
Huang, Jimmy, Ola Henfridsson, Martin J. Liu, and Sue Newell. 2017. Growing on Steroids: Rapidly Scaling the User Base of Digital Ventures Through Digital Innovaton. *MIS Quarterly* 41: 301–14. [CrossRef]
Jiménez-Jiménez, Daniel, and Raquel Sanz-Valle. 2011. Innovation, organizational learning, and performance. *Journal of Business Research* 64: 408–17. [CrossRef]
Kern, Philipp, and Howard Gospel. 2023. The effects of strategy and institutions on value creation and appropriation in firms: A longitudinal study of three telecom companies. *Strategic Management Journal* 44: 343–66. [CrossRef]
Kesidou, Effie, James H. Love, Serdal Ozusaglam, and Chee Yew Wong. 2023. Changing the geographic scope of collaboration: Implications for product innovation novelty and commercialization. *Journal of Product Innovation Management* 40: 859–81. [CrossRef]
Khin, Sabai, and Theresa Cf Ho. 2018. Digital technology, digital capability and organizational performance: A mediating role of digital innovation. *International Journal of Innovation Science* 11: 177–95. [CrossRef]
Kolomeitsev, Sergei, Kristie J. N. Moergen, Jason W. Ridge, Dan L. Worrell, and Scott Kuban. 2024. Peer Response to Regulatory Enforcement: Lobbying by Non-Sanctioned Firms. *Journal of Management* 1–24. [CrossRef]
Kostova, Tatiana, and Srilata Zaheer. 1999. Organizational Legitimacy Under Conditions of Complexity: The Case of the Multinational Enterprise. *Academy of Management Review* 24: 64–81. [CrossRef]
Lai, Kee-Hung, Christina W. Y. Wong, and T. C. Edwin Cheng. 2006. Institutional isomorphism and the adoption of information technology for supply chain management. *Computers in Industry* 57: 93–98. [CrossRef]
Lai, Xiaobing, and Shujing Yue. 2022. Do Pilot Smart Cities Promote Corporate Digital Transformation? An Empirical Study Based on a Quasi-natural Experiment. *Foreign Economics & Management* 44: 117–33. [CrossRef]
Li, Chengguang, and K. Praveen Parboteeah. 2015. The effect of culture on the responsiveness of firms to mimetic forces: Imitative foreign joint venture entries into China, 1985–2003. *Journal of World Business* 50: 465–76. [CrossRef]
Li, Xinchun, Wenping Ye, and Hang Zhu. 2016. Trapped in or Free from the Cage: The Relationship between Regional Guanxi Culture and Guanxi Strategy of Entrepreneurial Firms. *Journal of Management World* 10: 88–102. [CrossRef]
Lieberman, Marvin B., and Shigeru Asaba. 2006. Why Do Firms Imitate Each Other? *Academy of Management Review* 31: 366–85. [CrossRef]
Liu, Guanyu, Jiaqi Liu, Ping Gao, Jiang Yu, and Zhengning Pu. 2024. Understanding mechanisms of digital transformation in state-owned enterprises in China: An institutional perspective. *Technological Forecasting and Social Change* 202: 123288. [CrossRef]
Liu, Yong, Nan Wang, and Juanjuan Zhao. 2018. Relationships between isomorphic pressures and carbon management imitation behavior of firms. *Resources, Conservation and Recycling* 138: 24–31. [CrossRef]
Luo, Jianqiang, and Qianwen Jiang. 2022. Priority evolution of product and service innovation under digital transformation-Based on the case of Haier smart home. *Studies In Science of Science* 40: 1710–20. [CrossRef]
Martínez-Noya, Andrea, and Esteban García-Canal. 2021. Innovation performance feedback and technological alliance portfolio diversity: The moderating role of firms' R&D intensity. *Research Policy* 50: 104321. [CrossRef]
Mizruchi, Mark S., and Lisa C. Fein. 1999. The Social Construction of Organizational Knowledge: A Study of the Uses of Coercive, Mimetic, and Normative Isomorphism. *Administrative Science Quarterly* 44: 653–83. [CrossRef]
Ni, Jiacheng, Qian Gu, and Huajing Li. 2023. The Later, the Slower, the Better? A Study on the Relationship Between Iterative Innovation and Entrepreneurial Outcomes of Digital Startups. *Nankai Business Review* 8: 1–22. Available online: http://kns.cnki.net/kcms/detail/12.1288.F.20230831.0915.002.html (accessed on 31 August 2023).
Nie, Jun, Xin Jian, Juanjuan Xu, Nuo Xu, Tangyang Jiang, and Yang Yu. 2024. The Effect of Corporate Social Responsibility Practices on Digital Transformation in China: A Resource-Based View. *Economic Analysis and Policy* 82: 1–15. [CrossRef]
Oh, Won-Yong, and Vincent L. Barker. 2018. Not All Ties Are Equal: CEO Outside Directorships and Strategic Imitation in R&D Investment. *Journal of Management* 44: 1312–37. [CrossRef]
Ozturk, Ayse, S. Tamer Cavusgil, and O. Cem Ozturk. 2021. Consumption convergence across countries: Measurement, antecedents, and consequences. *Journal of International Business Studies* 52: 105–20. [CrossRef]
Palmer, Donald A., P. Devereaux Jennings, and Xueguang Zhou. 1993. Late Adoption of the Multidivisional Form by Large U.S. Corporations: Institutional, Political, and Economic Accounts. *Administrative Science Quarterly* 38: 100–31. [CrossRef]

Petersen, Mitchell A. 2009. Estimating Standard Errors in Finance Panel Data Sets: Comparing Approaches. *The Review of Financial Studies* 22: 435–80. [CrossRef]
Posen, Hart E., Jan-Michael Ross, Brian Wu, Stefano Benigni, and Zhi Cao. 2023. Reconceptualizing Imitation: Implications for Dynamic Capabilities, Innovation, and Competitive Advantage. *Academy of Management Annals* 17: 74–112. [CrossRef]
Posen, Hart E., Jeho Lee, and Sangyoon Yi. 2013. The power of imperfect imitation. *Strategic Management Journal* 34: 149–64. [CrossRef]
Quinton, Sarah, Ana Canhoto, Sebastian Molinillo, Rebecca Pera, and Tribikram Budhathoki. 2018. Conceptualising a digital orientation: Antecedents of supporting SME performance in the digital economy. *Journal of Strategic Marketing* 26: 427–39. [CrossRef]
Rahmati, Pouya, Ali Tafti, J. Christopher Westland, and Cesar Hidalgo. 2021. When All Products Are Digital: Complexity and Intangible Value in the Ecosystem of Digitizing Firm. *MIS Quarterly* 45: 1025–58. [CrossRef]
Saesen, Julie, Corinna Vera Hedwig Schmidt, and Steffen Strese. 2024. The more, the better: The influence of overconfident CEOs on their firms' digital orientation. *Journal of Business Research* 183: 114809. [CrossRef]
Sarker, Suprateek, Sutirtha Chatterjee, Xiao Xiao, and Amany Elbanna. 2019. The Sociotechnical Axis of Cohesion for the IS Discipline: Its Historical Legacy and its Continued Relevance. *MIS Quarterly* 43: 695–719. [CrossRef]
Sarrina Li, Shu-Chu, and Chen-Yi Lee. 2010. Market uncertainty and mimetic isomorphism in the newspaper industry: A study of Taiwan's mainstream newspapers from 1992 to 2003. *Asian Journal of Communication* 20: 367–84. [CrossRef]
Shen, Kunrong, Jianwei Lin, and Yuanhai Fu. 2023. Network Infrastructure Construction, Information Accessibility and the Innovation Boundaries of Enterprises. *China Industrial Economics* 1: 57–75. [CrossRef]
Strang, David, and Sarah A. Soule. 1998. Diffusion in Organizations and Social Movements: From Hybrid Corn to Poison Pills. *Annual Review of Sociology* 24: 265–90. [CrossRef]
Suchman, Mark C. 1995. Managing Legitimacy: Strategic and Institutional Approaches. *Academy of Management Review* 20: 571–610. [CrossRef]
Tang, Chang, Yuanyuan Xu, Yu Hao, Haitao Wu, and Yan Xue. 2021. What is the role of telecommunications infrastructure construction in green technology innovation? A firm-level analysis for China. *Energy Economics* 103: 105576. [CrossRef]
Tang, Jianyun, Mary Crossan, and W. Glenn Rowe. 2011. Dominant CEO, Deviant Strategy, and Extreme Performance: The Moderating Role of a Powerful Board. *Journal of Management Studies* 48: 1479–503. [CrossRef]
Triplett, Jack E. 1999. The Solow Productivity Paradox: What do Computers do to Productivity? *The Canadian Journal of Economics / Revue Canadienne d'Economique* 32: 309–34. [CrossRef]
Tseng, Jen-Jen, and Ping-Hung Chou. 2011. Mimetic isomorphism and its effect on merger and acquisition activities in Taiwanese financial industries. *The Service Industries Journal* 31: 1451–69. [CrossRef]
Wei, Jiang, Jialing Liu, and Yang Liu. 2021. New Trends and Problems of Innovation Strategy Theory in the Context of New Organization. *Journal of Management World* 37: 182–97+13. [CrossRef]
Wernsdorf, Kathrin, Markus Nagler, and Martin Watzinger. 2022. ICT, collaboration, and innovation: Evidence from BITNET. *Journal of Public Economics* 211: 104678. [CrossRef]
Wu, Fei, Huizhi Hu, Huiyan Lin, and Xiaoyi Ren. 2021. Enterprise Digital Transformation and Capital Market Performance: Empirical Evidence from Stock Liquidity. *Journal of Management World* 37: 130–44+10. [CrossRef]
Xie, Kang, Yao Wu, Jinghua Xiao, and Xuehua Liao. 2016. Strategic Risk Control in Organizational Change: A Multi-Case Study of Organizational Transformation towards Internet. *Journal of Management World* 2: 133–48. [CrossRef]
Xu, Qiong, Xin Li, and Fei Guo. 2023. Digital transformation and environmental performance: Evidence from Chinese resource-based enterprises. *Corporate Social Responsibility and Environmental Management* 30: 1816–40. [CrossRef]
Yang, Monica, and MaryAnne Hyland. 2012. Re-examining mimetic isomorphism: Similarity in mergers and acquisitions in the financial service industry. *Management Decision* 50: 1076–95. [CrossRef]
Ye, Dan, Meifang Yao, Baoshan Ge, and Liyi Zhao. 2023. The Mechanism of Digital Technology Driving Digital Innovation Performance in Non-Internet Enterprises: The Moderating Effect of Organizational Legitimacy. *Science & Technology Progress and Policy* 40: 11–18. [CrossRef]
Zhang, Jing A., Fiona Edgar, Alan Geare, and Conor O'Kane. 2016. The interactive effects of entrepreneurial orientation and capability-based HRM on firm performance: The mediating role of innovation ambidexterity. *Industrial Marketing Management* 59: 131–43. [CrossRef]
Zhang, Yongshen, Xiaobo Li, and Mingqiang Xing. 2021. Enterprise Digital Transformation and Audit Pricing. *Auditing Research* 3: 62–71. [CrossRef]
Zhao, Tao, Zhi Zhang, and Shangshen Liang. 2020. Digital Economy, Entrepreneurship, and High-Quality Economic Development: Empirical Evidence from Urban China. *Journal of Management World* 36: 65–76. [CrossRef]
Zhou, Yaying, Young-Seok Ock, Ibrahim Alnafrah, and Abd Alwahed Dagestani. 2023. What Aspects Explain the Relationship between Digital Transformation and Financial Performance of Firms? *Journal of Risk and Financial Management* 16: 479. [CrossRef]
Zimmerman, Monica A., and Gerald J. Zeitz. 2002. Beyond Survival: Achieving New Venture Growth by Building Legitimacy. *Academy of Management Review* 27: 414–31. [CrossRef]

Disclaimer/Publisher's Note: The statements, opinions and data contained in all publications are solely those of the individual author(s) and contributor(s) and not of MDPI and/or the editor(s). MDPI and/or the editor(s) disclaim responsibility for any injury to people or property resulting from any ideas, methods, instructions or products referred to in the content.

economies

MDPI

Article

The Use of the Data Envelopment Analysis–Malmquist Approach to Measure the Performance of Digital Transformation in EU Countries

Jarmila Horváthová and Martina Mokrišová *

Faculty of Management and Business, University of Prešov, Konštantínova 16, 080 01 Prešov, Slovakia; jarmila.horvathova@unipo.sk
* Correspondence: martina.mokrisova@unipo.sk

Abstract: Currently, the process of the digital transformation of EU countries is very important and often discussed. It will not only bring new opportunities for companies and the broader population but will also enable the transition to a more ecological economy. An important goal is to speed up the digitalization processes taking place in companies. It is very important to use already established digitalization elements more efficiently. This also resulted in the motivation for the given research. The aim of this paper is to quantify the change in the efficiency of the digital transformation of EU countries. As part of this research, the Variable Returns to Scale Data Envelopment Analysis (VRS DEA) model and the Malmquist index (MI) based on the DEA approach were applied. The results of the model made it possible to assess how the changes in technical efficiency and technological changes contributed to the changes in efficiency. The long-term theoretical added value of this paper lies in its proposal for countries and their governments to monitor not only the number of introduced digital elements, but also the efficiency of their use relative to some aggregate output; for example, GDP (Gross Domestic Product) or unemployment rate. The added value of this research is that less developed countries use digitalization elements more effectively than developed countries.

Keywords: data envelopment analysis; digital transformation; efficiency; Malmquist index; EU countries

1. Introduction

The current era is characterized by globalization, which penetrates into all areas of human life, and the economy is no exception in this regard. It is possible to point to various digital phenomena brought about by the digital economy. According to Stavytskyy et al. (2019), in general, the digital economy is not only the relationships mediated by the Internet, cellular communication and ICT (information and communication technologies). The digital economy also affects business interactions and speeds up the course of both a business itself and its various associated transactions. It also helps overcome barriers to entering the market and provides competitive advantages to companies and ultimately reduces costs. The digital economy is made up of economic activity that is the result of billions of daily online connections between people, businesses, devices, data and processes. The basis of the digital economy is hyperconnectivity, which means the growing interconnectedness of people, organizations and machines as a result of the Internet, mobile technologies and the Internet of things (Oloyede et al. 2023). The digital economy is constantly being formed and is determined by the structure and speed of the process of digitalization and digital transformation.

Nowadays, the issue of the digitalization and digital transformation of the European Union is highly topical. Differences in the digital transformation of EU countries are significant. "New" countries have difficulty catching up with the "old". This is caused by both economic and social factors, such as levels of education, the age of the population and different marginal groups within countries, but also the geographical location of the countries and the settlement of individual parts of the territory. As part of the digitalization of the business environment, the problem of falling behind is caused by a lack of funds for the introduction of digitalization elements, especially for small and medium-sized companies, but also by distrust and fear associated with the security of company data. Many studies confirm the importance of digital transformation in relation to environmental and economic growth. However, from the point of view of individual EU countries, it is again necessary to point out the different levels of this perception and understanding. In the case of lagging countries, the awareness is not as strong as in the case of "old" countries that have been dealing with this issue for longer periods of time. There was a significant shift in the digitalization process of new countries as a result of the 2020 pandemic. Since this period, the level of understanding of the need to introduce digitization elements has been growing. However, it is necessary to popularize this need more within lagging countries.

In the context of monitoring digital progress, important reports on digitalization or digital transformation have been published. In 2021, the European Commission proposed a path to the Digital Decade, which is guided by the 2030 Digital Compass. This communication of the European Commission clearly sets priorities and thus ensures Europe's successful digital transformation (Furlan 2022).

The targets and objectives of the 2030 Digital Agenda are structured according to four main areas: digital skills, digital infrastructure, digital transformation of businesses, and digitalization of public services (European Commission 2024a) (see Table 1). The core indicators of the DESI, which is one of the key tools for monitoring and measuring digital transformation in EU member countries, were aligned with these goals in 2021 (Bittner et al. 2022).

Table 1. Targets and objectives of the 2030 Digital Agenda.

Main Area	Targets and Objectives
Digital skills	ICT Specialists: 20 million + gender convergence Basic Digital Skills: min 80% of population
Digital infrastructure	Connectivity: gigabit for everyone Cutting edge Semiconductors: double EU share in global production Data—Edge and Cloud: 10,000 climate-neutral highly secure edge nodes
Digital transformation of businesses	Tech up-take: 75% of EU companies using Cloud, AI, or Big Data Innovators: grow scale-ups and finance to double EU Unicorns Late adopters: ensure more than 90% of SMEs reach at least a basic level of digital intensity
Digitalization of public services	Key Public Services: 100% online e-Health: 100% of citizens have access to medical records online Digital Identity: 100% of citizens have access to digital ID

Source: European Commission (2024b).

Another major policy initiative is the Recovery and Resilience Instrument. According to the European Commission, together with the Digital Compass, these are two main political initiatives that will have an impact on digital transformation in the EU. Through the Recovery and Resilience facility, the Commission obtains funds by borrowing from the capital markets. These funds can be used by Member States to enhance their green and digital transition in line with the EU's priorities (European Commission 2024d).

The main challenge comes within the business environments of Industry 4.0 and Industry 5.0, which represent an important motivator in the field of digitalization. In connection with this industrial revolution, it is possible to point out challenges in relation to educational institutions, which are forced to transform their programs in order to prepare quality employees for the intelligent environment. High-quality staff and high-quality software solutions are prerequisites for increasing the efficiency of the digitalization process. It is important that every person develops their digital skills and participates in the online world.

The driving force behind this research was the fact that there are not many studies (Inel 2019; Bánhidi et al. 2021; Rejman Petrovic et al. 2022; Kao et al. 2022; Georgescu et al. 2022; Lungu et al. 2022; Krstić et al. 2023) in the given area that focus on the application of the DEA method, as well as on the application of the Malmquist index (Bozkurt et al. 2022), which is based on the use of this non-parametric method. When choosing indicators to evaluate digital transformation, this research was inspired by Digital Compass indicators as well as DESI indicators. To measure the performance of the economy, the GDP per capita and unemployment rate were chosen. The relationship between digitalization indicators and GDP or labor market indicators was studied by several authors. Parra et al. (2020) studied the link between the variables of the DESI and GDP per capita. The results of their study revealed that "the implication between technology indicators and GDP per capita not only takes place but is also relevant specifically to aspects linked to the use of internet services by citizens and in the integration of digital technology by technology businesses" (Parra et al. 2020, p. 168). The influence of the DESI on labor market indicators was studied by Basol and Yalcin (2021). The results of their study confirmed that "an increase in the DESI has increased employment rate and personal earnings, which are perceived as positive labor market indicators and have decreased long-term unemployment rate and labor market insecurity, which are negative labor market indicators" (Basol and Yalcin 2021, p. 503).

Based on the above-mentioned studies, the aim of this study was to diagnose the efficiency of the digital transformation of EU countries using the MI in relation to their economic growth. In relation to this aim, we set the following research question: Is the efficiency of digitalization of developed countries higher than the efficiency of less developed countries?

The remainder of this paper is structured as follows: The "Literature Review" Section 2 defines digitalization, digital economy and digital efficiency. The "Research Methodology" Section 3 specifies the source of the data, describes the theoretical basis of the DEA and Malmquist Productivity Index based on the DEA approach and lists the applications of DEA models in the subject area or research. The "Results" Section 4 offers the results of the efficiency of EU countries in the use of digitalization elements using the VRS DEA model. It also contains the results of the change in efficiency over time calculated with the use of the Malmquist index. The "Discussion" Section 5 compares the results of the DESI with the results achieved by the VRS DEA model and the Malmquist index. The "Conclusion" Section 6 offers conclusions, limitations and future research.

2. Literature Review

The process of digitalization is essential to ensure the economic growth of EU countries. This path is particularly important for businesses in individual countries, as the economic growth of these businesses and their sustainability is a prerequisite for the growth of the country's economy. According to Sabbagh et al. (2012), digitalization offers economic growth; countries at the most advanced stage of digitalization gain 20% more economic benefits than countries at the initial stage. Digitalization has a demonstrable impact on reducing unemployment, improving quality of life and improving citizens' access to public services. Finally, yet importantly, digitalization allows governments to work with greater transparency and efficiency. In relation to digitalization and its impact on economic growth, it is appropriate to mention the term digital economy. The term "digital economy" refers to the convergence of computing and communications technologies on the Internet and the resulting flow of information and technology that is stimulating all electronic commerce and vast organizational change. No current public policy issue is more timely or has the potential to affect more people (Lane 1999). The "digital" economy is at the forefront of efficiency gains: the more customers a company has, the more "effective" it will be at attracting new customers and others to the production process, and will be able to offer better services at the same price. The benefits of a "digital" economy are many: most importantly, it will prevent shadow economies and help eliminate corruption (Jurayevich and Bulturbayevic 2020). According to Mesenbourg (2001), digital economy has three primary components: e-business infrastructure, electronic business (e-business) and electronic commerce (e-commerce). Many definitions of digital economy have arisen over time. However, many of them are simple and straightforward variants of the definition of the European Commission, which defines a digital economy as "an economy based on digital technologies" (Bukht and Heeks 2019, p. 4). Barefoot et al. (2018) understand the digital economy in terms of the introduction of the Internet and other information technologies. The digital economy is a kind of economy characterized by the active implementation and actual application of digital technologies for the collection, storage, processing, transformation and transmission of data in absolutely all areas of human activity (Borremans et al. 2018). The terminology "digital economy" mostly denotes the recent and significantly unrealized changes in various segments of the economy by the computer-assisted digitalization of data (Williams 2021). The term digital economy has been introduced "to support the improvement of the national economy and the rapid development of knowledge and technology at this time" (Limna et al. 2022, p. 3).

Measuring and comparing the level and efficiency of the digital transformations taking place in countries is a crucial issue. Therefore, the next part of this text lists studies addressing this problem.

In his research, Yalcin (2021) examined the effectiveness of the digitization of EU countries. The aim of this research was to identify countries that transformed digitalization into their growth and employment rates in the period 2015–2019. In his study, the following dimensions of the DESI of the EU-28 Member States were used as inputs: Connectivity, Human Capital, Use of Internet, Integration of Digital Technology and Digital Public Services; the GDP Growth Rate and Employment Rate were used as outputs (Yalcin 2021). The results of the study show that "in countries such as Bulgaria, Cyprus, Hungary and Romania, the effective use of DESI indicators, which are considered a measure of digitalization, has a one-on-one effect on the GDP and ER values. DESI indicators are not used effectively in the GDP and ER values of countries like Denmark, Finland, and Spain. In general, in terms of digitalization, it has been revealed that developing countries use digitalisation more effectively in terms of economic growth and job creation" (Yalcin 2021, p. 323). The correlations between digitization and economic growth in EU countries were analyzed by Georgescu et al. (2023). They applied Principal Component Analysis and neural networks to analyze the digitalization indicators obtained from Eurostat and the World Bank for the period 2019–2021. With the use of this combined approach, they intended to enhance the classification accuracy of EU countries classified according to the DESI. The results revealed an improvement in classification accuracy. The importance of building an effective digital economy infrastructure in order to improve international competitiveness was pointed out by Balcerzak and Pietrzak (2017). Their research compared the development level of digital economies in V4 countries with the application of the TOPSIS method. The results of the research confirmed relatively quick progress in building digital economies at the regional level in all V4 countries. However, the research revealed significant disparities between the analyzed regions, especially Polish regions. Małkowska et al. (2021) investigated the impact of digital transformation on EU countries. The study compared the technological development of EU countries based on three dimensions: the digitalization of society, the ability of the economy to face the challenges of technological development and the exploitation of ICT in companies. The applied methods included cluster analysis and the TOPSIS method. With the use of these methods, EU countries were grouped according to similar levels of technological development into countries with high, medium and low performance. This helped to identify the digitalization gaps between countries.

Recently, the Data Envelopment Analysis method has come to the fore in many areas of research. Emrouznejad and Yang (2018) estimate that there are up to 10,300 papers focusing on the application of DEA models in various fields. It is possible to give examples of the application of DEA models, e.g., Paradi et al. (2004) applied the DEA method to manufacturing enterprises. Feruś (2010) applied the DEA model to construction companies.

Kohl et al. (2019) applied the DEA method to hospitals. The DEA method was applied to measure the efficiency of banks by Jablonsky (2012), Sorayaei et al. (2012) and Akther et al. (2013). Paradi et al. (2014) focused on efficiency analysis in services. Sreedevi (2016) analyzed the efficiency of public service companies using the DEA model. Lim and Zhu (2019) focused on the application of DEA in the field of insurance companies. Gúčik and Uličná (2014) applied the DEA model and the Malmquist test to analyze the efficiency of hotel facilities. Kocher et al. (2006) applied the DEA method in economic research across countries. The input data consisted of the expenditure on research in the given area, the number of universities with departments of economics and, as an uncontrollable input, the number of inhabitants. The output was the number of outputs in the top 10 journals for the years 1980–1998. The research was carried out in 21 OECD countries. The USA was the most efficient country when applying a constant returns to scale (CRS) model, and the USA, New Zealand and Ireland were the most efficient when applying the BCC model (Kocher et al. 2006). Jurickova et al. (2019) used Data Envelopment Analysis to measure the technical efficiency of national innovation systems in a sample of European countries. In this study, the numbers of researchers and the expenditures on research and development were used as inputs and published scientific journal articles and applied patents were used as outputs of the DEA model. The results showed that the most efficient countries in 2016 were Cyprus, Luxembourg, Malta and Romania. Germany, which is the EU best performer in terms of patent ranking, was classified as inefficient with an efficiency score of 0.5. The authors concluded that there are differences between the innovation performance examined by various indices available in public databases and the technical efficiency measured by DEA. The impact of digitalization on economic growth explained by total factor productivity (TFP) was investigated by Bozkurt et al. (2022). They calculated TFP based on the Malmquist index using labor, capital and gross domestic capital data for 30 countries including EU Member States. To determine the impact of digitalization on TFP, they used a tobit panel estimate. The results revealed a significant and positive impact of digitalization on TFP. Therefore, the authors concluded that digitalization contributes to productivity.

Over time, DEA also began to be applied when dealing with the efficiency of digital transformation. Inel (2019) examined the efficiency of the digital transformation of EU countries using the DEA method. The data necessary for the research was taken from the Digital Transformation Scoreboard 2018. "Digital Infrastructure, Investment and Access to Finance, Supply and Demand of Digital Skills, E-leadership and Entrepreneurial Culture are considered as inputs, while ICT start-ups and Digital Transformation are considered as the output of DEA model. The results indicate that while some countries like Denmark, Italy and United Kingdom are considered relatively efficient, the Netherlands and Germany are not very efficient" (Inel 2019, p. 549). Krejnus et al. (2023) measured the efficiency of e-Government digitalization within the EU by applying DEA. For the inputs and outputs for the DEA model, they used attributes from the following digitalization and e-Government indices: GII (Global Innovation Index), Internet usage, DSGI (Digital Skills Gap Index), interaction with public administration online and e-Government benchmarks. They concluded that when comparing European regions, the countries of Northern Europe were the most efficient at e-Government digitalization. Bánhidi et al. (2021) compared the development of digitalization in Russia with EU Member States. They used data from the International Digital Economy and Society Index (I-DESI 2018) database. Their main research questions were concerned with the robustness of the EU data supply and the stability of its ranking. To answer them, they used Data Envelopment Analysis and a one-dimensional version of multidimensional scaling. Based on a comparison of the results, they suggested that the applied methods provided a similar solution, but the ranking of some countries (including Russia) showed wider variation. Rejman Petrovic et al. (2022) investigated the intensity and results of the digitization process in 2016–2019 in Serbia. They applied the DEA method in their research. The authors pointed to the fact that in Serbia, the digitization process was effective; the only drawback was the insufficient use of software packages. The authors also pointed out the lack of studies carried out in the given subject area.

Based on the above-mentioned studies, we can state that most studies have focused on the use of the DESI and the analysis of the development of digitalization from the point of view of the number of introduced digitalization elements. Other studies (Bánhidi et al. 2020; Borowiecki et al. 2021) have evaluated the static position of countries and their ranking in the field of digital transformation over one year. There are only a few articles published in the given area that have applied the DEA methodology. Moreover, according to the information currently available to the authors, the Malmquist index, which allows dynamic development to be analyzed, has only been used in the related field in the study of Bozkurt et al. (2022). This study aims to fill this research gap by comparing the development of the digital transformation of countries over time with the use of a DEA–Malmquist technique. The results of this technique make it possible to assess how the changes in technical efficiency and technology contributed to the changes in efficiency. In such a way, they differ from the results of other quantitative methodologies used to measure the efficiency of digital transformation in previous studies.

3. Research Methodology

In this empirical study, the efficiency of the use of digitalization elements in EU countries in the years 2019, 2021 and 2023 was assessed using the VRS DEA model. The change in the efficiency of the EU countries' digital transformation was calculated using the Malmquist index, which is based on the application of DEA over a period of time. The Principal Component Analysis (PCA) method was applied to graphically illustrate the position of the EU countries in the digitalization process in 2023.

DEA is a non-parametric method that can be used to measure the efficiency of a group of peer units, which are called Decision-Making Units (DMUs). This method was applied in various countries and regions to measure the efficiency and performance of various units, such as banks, universities, manufacturing enterprises, hospitals and insurance companies (Cooper et al. 2011). The DEA method is based on the efforts of Farrell (1957) to develop a better method of productivity evaluation (Cooper et al. 2011). Farrell proposed a new approach to efficiency measurement based on the use of a convex curve and functions for the measurement of the distance between the monitored enterprise and the projected point on the efficiency frontier. In this way, he proposed a new way of measuring business efficiency based on the calculation of two components of overall business efficiency: technical efficiency and allocative efficiency (Färe et al. (1984)).

The original ideas of Farrell (1957) were later reformulated by Charnes et al. (1978), who created the CCR model. The authors described DEA as a mathematical programming model that provides a new way of obtaining empirical estimates of relationships between observed data. Subsequently, this model was transformed by Banker et al. (1984) into the BCC model. The aim of the mentioned methods is to eliminate or exclude subjectivity by measuring the effectiveness of the outputs in relation to the inputs.

For research in the given area, the VRS DEA model was applied to calculate the efficiency of the digital transformation of EU countries. We solved the dual output-oriented VRS DEA model which can be defined as follows (1) (Zhu 2014):

$$
\begin{aligned}
& max\ \varnothing + \varepsilon\left(\sum_{i=1}^{m} s_i^- + \sum_{r=1}^{s} s_r^+\right) \\
& \text{subject to} \\
& \sum_{j=1}^{n} \lambda_j x_{ij} + s_i^- = x_{io} && i = 1,2,\ldots,m; \\
& \sum_{j=1}^{n} \lambda_j y_{rj} - s_r^+ = \varnothing y_{ro} && r = 1,2,\ldots,s; \\
& \sum_{j=1}^{n} \lambda_j = 1 \\
& \lambda_j \geq 0 && j = 1,2,\ldots,n,
\end{aligned}
\tag{1}
$$

where $\varnothing$ is the value of the objective function, ε is the non-Archimedean infinitesimal value, $x_{ij},\ i = 1,2,\ldots,m,\ j = 1,2,\ldots,n$ is the value of the i input for DMU_i, $y_{rj}, r = 1,2,\ldots,s$, $j = 1,2,\ldots,n$ is the value of the k output for DMU_j. DMU_0 is one of the n DMUs under evaluation, x_{i0} and y_{ro} are the i input and r output for DMU_0, respectively, m and s are the numbers of inputs and outputs, respectively, λ_j is the convex coefficient, and s_i^- and s_r^+ are the input and output slacks, respectively.

To assess countries' efficiency over time, the Malmquist index was applied. This index measures the change in the total factor productivity (TFP) between two periods based on the principle of calculating the ratio of the distances of each data point relative to a common technology. The index is based on the use of distance functions, which allow us to describe production technology with multiple inputs and outputs without the need to specify the objectives of the company's behavior. It is possible to define both input and output distance functions (Fandel 2002).

Several methods can be used to estimate distance functions, which are the starting points for calculating TFP. Linear programming is most often used, especially the Data Envelopment Analysis (DEA) method proposed by Färe, Grosskopf, Norris and Zhang in 1994 (Fandel 2002). The use of DEA models to calculate TFP is related to the assumption that homogeneous data are available over several periods. Calculating the change in efficiency requires solving four linear programming problems, assuming the use of technology with constant returns to scale (Fandel 2002).

Suppose that each $DMU_j (j = 1,2,\ldots,n)$ uses a vector of inputs $x_j^t = \left(x_{1j}^t,\ldots,x_{mj}^t\right)$ to produce the vector of the outputs $y_j^t = \left(y_{1j}^t,\ldots,y_{mj}^t\right)$ at each period of time $t, t = 1,\ldots,T$. The efficiency of DMU_0 can change or the frontier can shift, or both changes may occur at the same time. The Malmquist Productivity Index is then defined as follows (2) (Zhu 2014):

$$MI_o = \left[\frac{\theta_o^t(x_o^t,\ y_o^t)}{\theta_o^t\left(x_o^{t+1},\ y_o^{t+1}\right)}\frac{\theta_o^{t+1}(x_o^t,\ y_o^t)}{\theta_o^{t+1}\left(x_o^{t+1},\ y_o^{t+1}\right)}\right]^{\frac{1}{2}} \tag{2}$$

where MI_0 measures the change in productivity between the periods t and $t+1$. $\theta_o^t(x_o^t,\ y_o^t)$ is calculated by comparing x_o^t to the EPF (Empirical Production Frontier) at the time t with the use of the input-oriented CRS DEA model, while $x_o^t = (x_{1o}^t,\ldots\ldots\ldots\ldots x_{mo}^t)$ and $y_o^t = (y_{1o}^t,\ldots\ldots\ldots\ldots y_{so}^t)$ are the input and output vectors of DMU_0, among others. Similarly, $\theta_o^{t+1}(x_o^{t+1},\ y_o^{t+1})$ is calculated by comparing x_o^{t+1} to the EPF at the time $t+1$, $\theta_o^{t+1}(x_o^t,\ y_o^t)$ by comparing x_o^t to the EPF at time $t+1$; and $\theta_o^t(x_o^{t+1},\ y_o^{t+1})$ is calculated by comparing x_o^{t+1} to the EPF at the time t, applying the input-oriented CRS DEA model.

This model is also available in its modified form (3) (Zhu 2014):

$$MI_o = \frac{\theta_o^t(x_o^t,\ y_o^t)}{\theta_o^{t+1}\left(x_o^{t+1},\ y_o^{t+1}\right)} \times \left[\frac{\theta_o^{t+1}(x_o^{t+1},\ y_o^{t+1})}{\theta_o^t\left(x_o^{t+1},\ y_o^{t+1}\right)}\frac{\theta_o^{t+1}(x_o^t,\ y_o^t)}{\theta_o^t(x_o^t,\ y_o^t)}\right]^{\frac{1}{2}} \tag{3}$$

According to Fandel (2002), the term (4) represents a change in technical efficiency; it is the efficiency known according to Farrell (1957). The change in efficiency is equivalent to the ratio of Farrell's efficiency at time t and at time $t+1$ (technical efficiency change between the periods t and $t+1$). Usually, this term expresses the improvement, deterioration or stability of technical efficiency.

$$TECH = \frac{\theta_o^t(x_o^t,\ y_o^t)}{\theta_o^{t+1}\left(x_o^{t+1},\ y_o^{t+1}\right)} \tag{4}$$

The term (5) represents the frontier shift (FS) in the EPF between the periods t and $t+1$ (Zhu 2014).

$$FS = \left[\frac{\theta_o^{t+1}\left(x_o^{t-1}, y_o^{t+1}\right)}{\theta_o^{t}\left(x_o^{t+1}, y_o^{t+1}\right)} \frac{\theta_o^{t+1}\left(x_o^{t}, y_o^{t}\right)}{\theta_o^{t}\left(x_o^{t}, y_o^{t}\right)} \right]^{\frac{1}{2}} \tag{5}$$

The values of the indicators can be interpreted as follows:

- $TECH > 1$: the efficiency of the DMS improved, it approached the production possibility frontier and the decisions taken were correct;
- $TECH = 1$: the efficiency of the DMS did not change;
- $TECH < 1$: the efficiency of the DMS declined; the decisions taken were incorrect.

TECH informs us about a change in technical efficiency but does not inform us about a shift in the production possibility frontier as a result of technological change. This is reported by the frontier shift as follows:

- $FS > 1$: the efficiency increased and the frontier shifted outwards;
- $FS = 1$: the efficiency frontier did not shift;
- $FS < 1$: the efficiency declined and the frontier shifted inwards. This index informs us about a change within the entire EU.

Indicators representing 4 areas of the Digital Compass were selected as input data to fulfill the aim of this paper and to assess the effectiveness of the digital transformation and its impact on GDP and the unemployment rate. The following inputs were used: individuals' level of digital skills—individuals with basic or above basic overall digital skills (all five component indicators at basic or above basic level) (DG); employed ICT specialists—percentage of total employment (ICTS); households with access to the Internet at home—percentage of households (HAIHs); Internet used—percentage of individuals; cloud computing services—percentage of enterprises; enterprises using DSL or other fixed broadband connections—percentage of enterprises, small enterprises (10–49 employees and self-employed persons), without the financial sector; e-Government users—percentage of internet users (last 12 months). GDP per capita and the unemployment rate were used as outputs. The data of EU-27 Member States as well as the EU average were collected for the years 2019, 2021 and 2023. Descriptive statistics for the selected indicators for the year 2023 are presented in Table 2. The data were obtained from Eurostat (2024).

Table 2. Descriptive statistics of EU-27 Member States' indicators for the year 2023.

Variable	Descriptive Statistics				
	Mean	**Median**	**Minimum**	**Maximum**	**Std. Dev.**
Digital skills	57.89	58.95	27.73	82.70	13.05
Employed ICT specialists	4.07	3.90	2.20	6.80	1.25
Households with access to the Internet at home	93.20	93.22	86.90	99.06	3.14
Internet used	92.55	92.75	83.97	99.40	4.64
Cloud computing services	46.25	45.60	13.60	87.70	18.16
Enterprises using DSL or other fixed broadband connections	93.85	96.20	76.10	100.00	5.72
e-Government users	79.71	82.97	23.55	98.86	18.31
GDP per capita	29,080.00	25,160.00	7850.00	83,320.00	18,322.23
Total unemployment rate	5.74	5.55	2.54	12.04	2.29

Source: processed by authors in Statistica 14.1.0.8 software.

The average proportion of the EU population with basic or above basic overall digital skills in 2023 is 57.89%. In total, 4.07% of the total EU population are represented by ICT specialists. Around 7% of households still do not have an Internet connection. Cloud computing services are used on average by only 46.25% of companies in the EU. Especially in this area, it is necessary to develop activities towards increasing the use of these services.

It is also necessary to improve e-Government activities, which are at the level of 79.71% in EU countries. Another negative phenomenon is the higher average unemployment rate of EU countries.

4. Results

The starting point of this research was a comparison of the results of the implementation of seven selected indicators of the digitalization process for the year 2023. As can be seen from Figure 1, compared to the selected countries, Slovakia achieved the worst results in almost all analyzed areas, except for digital skills, employed ICT specialists and cloud computing services. It is clear from the graph that Slovakia's results reflect the EU average. The Netherlands and Finland achieved the best results in terms of digital skills, Sweden achieved the best results in terms of ICT specialists, Luxembourg achieved the best results in terms of HAIHs and Luxembourg achieved the best results in terms of Internet use. Cloud computing services were best used by Finland and Sweden. In terms of enterprises using DSL and e-Government users, Denmark dominated.

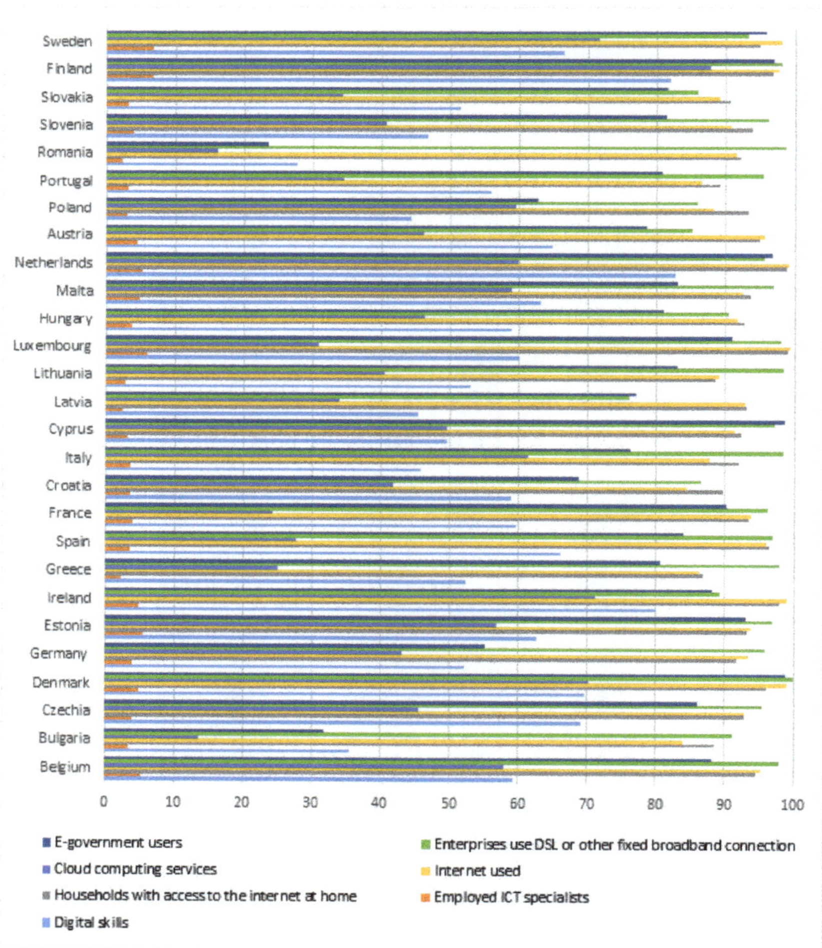

Figure 1. Selected indicators of the digitalization process for the year 2023. Source: authors.

The position of the EU countries from the point of view of the selected digital indices, GDP and unemployment rate, is shown in Figure 2. This portfolio is one of the possible graphical outputs of the PCA method, which allows a large number of indicators to be replaced with several factors. Factor 1 and factor 2 in the portfolio define a window into the K-dimensional variable space. By projecting all the observations onto the low-dimensional sub-space and plotting the results, they allow us to visualize the structure of the analyzed data set. Factor 1 is highly correlated with the indicators digital skills, employed ICT specialists, households with access to the internet at home, Internet use, cloud computing services, e-Government users and GDP per capita. Factor 2 is correlated with the indicators of enterprises using DSL or other fixed broadband connections and total unemployment rate. The portfolio consists of four quadrants. In quadrant A, the countries that report problems in the field of fulfilling criteria laid down by individual digital indices, as well as in "GDP" and "Unemployment rate", are shown. The best countries in the given field are located in quadrant B. This group includes countries like Ireland, Austria, Netherlands, Czechia and Malta. The Nordic countries Sweden, Finland and Denmark are very close to the border limits. Some of these countries show minor shortcomings in the fields "Individuals' level of digital skills", "Enterprises use DSL and other fixed broadband connection" and "Unemployment rate". Quadrant D includes the countries that are in the worst position from the point of view of not only all digital transformation indices, but also "GDP" and "Unemployment rate". These include Greece, Italy, Portugal and Cyprus.

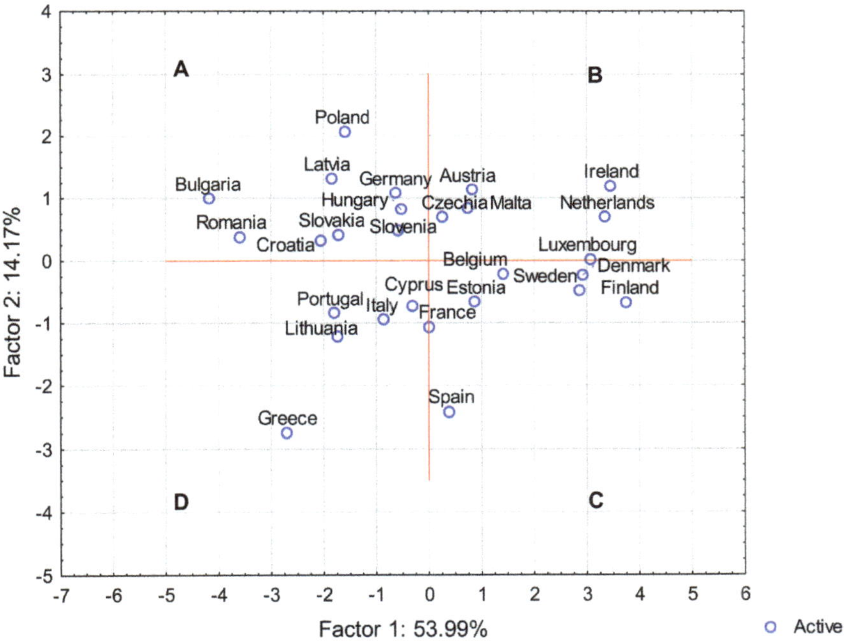

Figure 2. Position of EU countries in selected digital indices. Source: processed by authors in Statistica 14.1.0.8 software.

The results of the DEA VRS model for the years 2019, 2021 and 2023 are presented in Figure 3. From this figure, it is clear that Bulgaria, Czechia, Germany, Ireland, Greece, Italy, Latvia, Lithuania, Luxembourg, Hungary, Poland, Portugal and Romania achieved an efficiency score of 1 in each year. This shows the effective impact of the use of digitalization elements on the results of individual countries expressed by an increase in GDP and a decrease in the unemployment rate; i.e., these countries lie on the efficiency frontier. In other countries, efficiency results grow over time, and in 2023, Croatia, Malta, and Slovakia also reached the efficiency frontier. The results show that some countries that led the field in introducing digitalization elements do not lie on the efficiency frontier. This can be justified by the lower rate of introduction of individual digitalization elements, since these elements were already introduced in the given countries in a larger volume and thus their impact on GDP growth and the unemployment rate is not so significant. This mainly concerns Finland, Sweden, the Netherlands, Austria, Denmark, Belgium, etc.

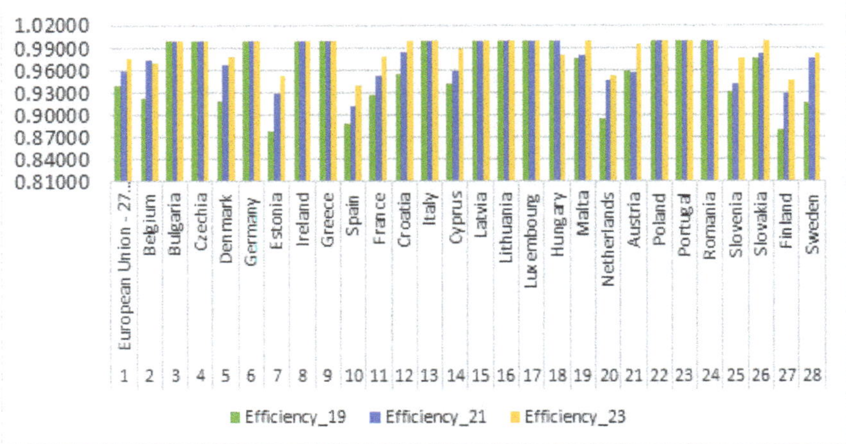

Figure 3. Results of the DEA VRS model. Source: processed by authors in DEAFrontier software.

To assess the efficiency over time, the Malmquist index for the periods 2019–2021 and 2021–2023 was applied. The results of the MI for the period 2019–2021 are presented in Table 3. Technical efficiency at the required level 1 has been achieved in almost every EU country. In our opinion, this was caused by a shift in the efficiency frontier, as a result of the technological changes that occurred in individual countries over the years. Since this is a comparison of the years 2019 and 2021, it can be assumed that these significant technological changes also occurred due to the impact of the COVID-19 pandemic. The change in the efficiency of the use of already established digitalization elements was equal to 1 only in some countries (see Table 3). When comparing the years 2019 and 2021, these countries used previously established digitalization elements very effectively (Bulgaria, Ireland, Spain, Latvia, Lithuania, Luxembourg, Hungary, Austria, Portugal, Romania).

Table 3. Results of the MI for the years 2019/2021.

No.	DMUs in Period 1	Input-Oriented CRS Malmquist Index	Efficiency Change	Frontier Shift
1	EU-27 countries	1.04773	0.98455	1.06417
2	Belgium	1.03035	0.94648	1.08861
3	Bulgaria	1.33122	1.00000	1.33122
4	Czechia	1.02675	0.93622	1.09670
5	Denmark	1.00629	0.94844	1.06099
6	Germany	1.00061	0.94839	1.05506
7	Estonia	1.03101	0.93373	1.10419
8	Ireland	0.99220	1.00000	0.99220
9	Greece	1.05749	1.00000	1.05749
10	Spain	1.06549	1.00442	1.06080
11	France	1.05456	0.97275	1.08410
12	Croatia	1.06777	0.97589	1.09415
13	Italy	1.07582	0.98751	1.08943
14	Cyprus	1.02988	0.98471	1.04587
15	Latvia	1.08555	1.00000	1.08555
16	Lithuania	1.07319	1.00497	1.06787

Table 3. *Cont.*

No.	DMUs in Period 1	Input-Oriented CRS Malmquist Index	Efficiency Change	Frontier Shift
17	Luxembourg	1.01838	1.00000	1.01838
18	Hungary	1.06959	1.00000	1.06959
19	Malta	1.05963	0.96026	1.10348
20	Netherlands	1.00471	0.94866	1.05909
21	Austria	1.05217	1.00560	1.04631
22	Poland	1.17378	0.96995	1.21015
23	Portugal	1.07369	1.00112	1.07248
24	Romania	1.17226	1.00000	1.17226
25	Slovenia	1.04205	0.96194	1.08328
26	Slovakia	1.06848	0.99875	1.06981
27	Finland	1.01587	0.94815	1.07142
28	Sweden	0.99103	0.93907	1.05533

Source: processed by authors in DEAFrontier software.

If we compare the results of the MI for the years 2021/2023, we can see that the technical efficiency in some countries fell below 1 (see Table 4). These were mainly Denmark, Greece, Spain, France, Cyprus, Latvia, Austria, Slovakia and Slovenia. This was caused both by a decrease in the efficiency of the use of already introduced digitalization elements, as well as the introduction of new digitalization elements. For example, in the case of Sweden, we can see that the MI is above 1. The change in efficiency, i.e., the use of previously introduced digitalization elements, is also above 1. However, the shift in the efficiency frontier is below 1, which means that the shift in the digitalization of this country is no longer necessary.

Table 4. Results of the MI for the years 2021/2023.

No.	DMUs in Period 2	Input-Oriented CRS Malmquist Index	Efficiency Change	Frontier Shift
1	EU-27 countries	1.00488	0.99267	1.01229
2	Belgium	1.01877	1.01833	1.00043
3	Bulgaria	1.05546	1.00000	1.05546
4	Czechia	1.04176	1.01427	1.02711
5	Denmark	0.99026	0.99636	0.99388
6	Germany	1.00010	1.00000	1.00010
7	Estonia	1.01604	0.98863	1.02773
8	Ireland	1.08906	1.00000	1.08906
9	Greece	0.96663	1.00000	0.96663
10	Spain	0.96256	0.94443	1.01920
11	France	0.98929	0.97734	1.01222
12	Croatia	1.01408	0.97246	1.04280
13	Italy	1.06680	1.00382	1.06274
14	Cyprus	0.97628	0.96336	1.01341
15	Latvia	0.95732	1.00000	0.95732
16	Lithuania	1.00459	0.99264	1.01204
17	Luxembourg	1.18784	1.00000	1.18784
18	Hungary	1.06688	1.02158	1.04434
19	Malta	1.01732	0.99684	1.02054
20	Netherlands	0.99680	0.97805	1.01916
21	Austria	0.97966	0.95902	1.02153
22	Poland	1.02660	1.00000	1.02660
23	Portugal	1.02133	0.99449	1.02699
24	Romania	1.19876	1.00000	1.19876
25	Slovenia	0.99727	0.96942	1.02873
26	Slovakia	0.99769	0.98073	1.01730
27	Finland	1.00428	0.99719	1.00711
28	Sweden	1.00628	1.00831	0.99799

Source: processed by authors in DEAFrontier software.

Figure 4 shows that the most significant changes in technical efficiency occurred when comparing the years 2019/2023, especially in Bulgaria, Italy, Hungary, Poland and Romania. These results again show that the countries that were particularly lagging behind in the digitalization process have been involved in it in recent years.

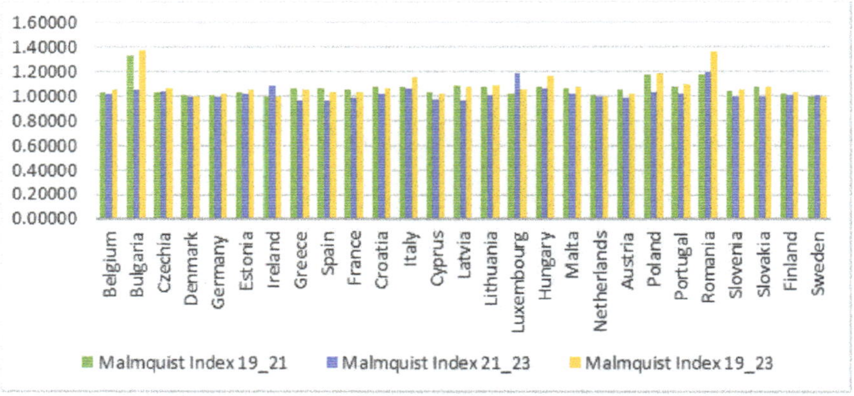

Figure 4. Results of the MI model. Source: processed by authors in DEAFrontier software.

The change in the efficiency of the use of already introduced digitalization elements was the most significant when comparing the years 2021/2023 (see Figure 5). This change was more pronounced in Belgium, Czechia, Denmark, Germany, Estonia, the Netherlands, Finland and Sweden. These countries are trying to make the most of the previously established digitalization elements and are trying to use them effectively.

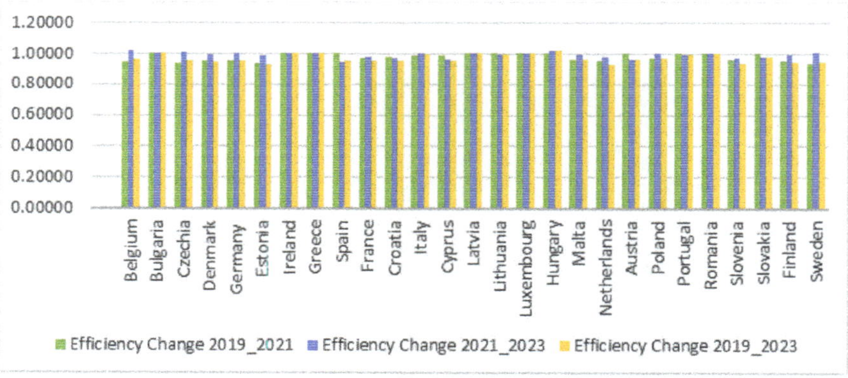

Figure 5. Results of the efficiency change. Source: processed by authors in DEAFrontier software.

The most significant changes in frontier shifts occurred when comparing the years 2019 and 2023. The largest technological changes were implemented in Bulgaria, Italy, Hungary, Poland and Romania (see Figure 6).

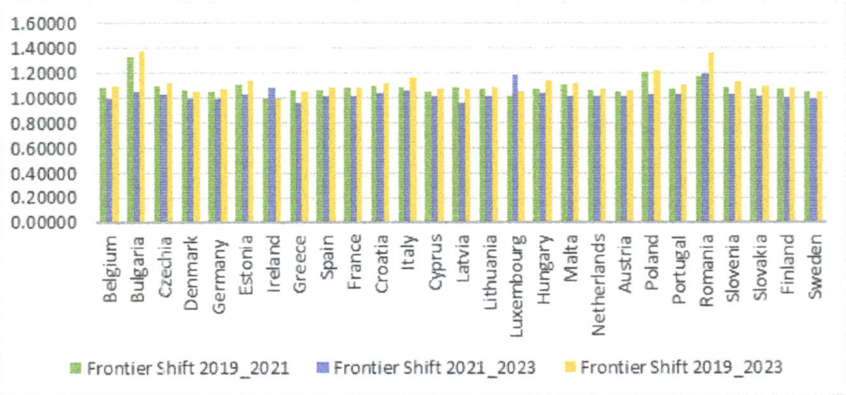

Figure 6. Results of the frontier shift. Source: processed by authors in DEAFrontier software.

The best results in introducing technological changes were achieved by Bulgaria and Romania. These results indicate that these countries are catching up with the leaders in the implementation of digitalization elements. In the field of efficiency change, several countries maintained a value of 1 (Bulgaria, Ireland, Greece, Latvia, Hungary, Romania). It is clear that the leaders in the field of introducing digitalization elements have completed this process with a high % of fulfillment of the criteria and, as a result, are not accelerating compared to other countries.

5. Discussion

Based on a review of the literature, it can be concluded that there are several approaches dedicated to the assessment of the digital transformation of EU countries. The analyzed studies use different methods and different indicators to assess this process, including methods such as TOPSIS (Balcerzak and Pietrzak 2017; Bánhidi et al. 2021), cluster analysis (Zaharia and Bălăcescu 2020; Małkowska et al. 2021; Bánhidi et al. 2020) and the fixed-effects methodology (Parra et al. 2020). The DEA method was applied to determine the efficiency of digital transformation by Inel (2019), Bánhidi et al. (2021) and Georgescu et al. (2022). Indicators based on the DESI (Zaharia and Bălăcescu 2020; Parra et al. 2020; Bánhidi et al. 2020; Georgescu et al. 2022), but also others that are not based on DESI (Balcerzak and Pietrzak 2017; Zaharia and Bălăcescu 2020; Małkowska et al. 2021) were used as input parameters. In most studies, it was mainly the annual development of digitalization indicators that was measured (Bánhidi et al. 2020; Borowiecki et al. 2021). It was also pointed out that digitalization has an impact on increases in the GDP of countries (Parra et al. 2020; Corejova and Chinoracky 2021; Olczyk and Kuc-Czarnecka 2022).

In this paper, seven digitalization inputs selected based on the Digital Compass and DESI were selected. The efficient use of these inputs was evaluated in relation to GDP and the unemployment rate, which were selected as outputs. The position of countries according to the selected inputs and outputs changed over time. Our comparison between the years 2019 and 2023 is shown in Figure 7. We can see that Ireland, Austria, the Netherlands and Czechia were placed in quadrant B in both periods. These countries were among the best ones in the analyzed years. The positions of Belgium, Denmark and Estonia, which were placed in quadrant C, slightly worsened. Even though the use of most digitalization elements in these countries increased, their unemployment rates either did not change or even increased. Germany moved from quadrant B to quadrant A, which was caused by the deterioration of the indicator "Households with access to the internet at home". Malta improved its position and moved from quadrant A to quadrant B, placing it among the best countries. This is due to a significant improvement in all digitalization indicators as well as in GDP and unemployment rate. Luxembourg moved from quadrant

C to quadrant A, so in its case there was an improvement in the unemployment rate and a deterioration in the indicator "Individuals' level of digital skills". There were slight improvements in Spain and Lithuania, especially with regard to the indicator "Enterprises use DSL or other fixed broadband connection". Some countries, for example, Greece, did not show a significant shift.

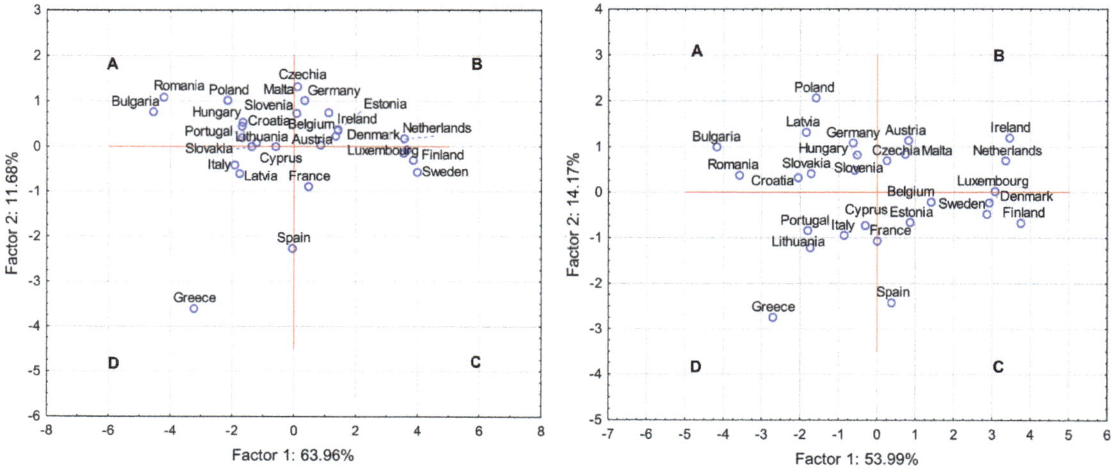

(a) (b)

Figure 7. Comparison of the position of EU countries based on selected inputs and outputs for the years (**a**) 2019 and (**b**) 2023.

In this paper, the digitalization process of individual EU countries was assessed from the point of view of changes in the efficiency of digital transformation using the MI and the VRS DEA model. Such an approach, namely the application of the MI, brings a new perspective to enhancing the digitalization process. Therefore, it is appropriate to supplement the assessment of countries and their rankings based on the quantity of introduced digitalization elements with a new perspective, which is the assessment of this process as an efficiency index. With the use of the MI, it is also possible to find out if shifts in efficiency during some periods was achieved mainly by the more effective use of previously introduced digitalization elements or by introducing new digital technologies. In the following part of the discussion, we provide some significant findings in the given area.

Based on the application of the MI, we found that the best results were achieved when comparing the years 2019/2023 in Bulgaria, Italy, Hungary, Poland and Romania. The positive results of the MI in these countries were caused mainly by introducing new digitalization elements (see Figure 6). However, it should be noted that the most important leaders from the point of view of the number of introduced digitalization elements measured by the DESI—Finland, Denmark, the Netherlands and Sweden (European Commission 2024c)—did not achieve the best results according to the MI. These countries achieved MI values close to 1 in both analyzed periods, so we can say that they maintained a high level of previously introduced digitalization elements. These results cannot be compared with previous studies because we did not find a study in which the MI was applied to analyze the efficiency of digital transformation. In the research of Bozkurt et al. (2022) mentioned in the Introduction, the MI was applied in a slightly different way. It was used to measure total factor productivity (TFP) using labor, capital and gross domestic capital data, and then the impact of digitalization on TFP was analyzed using a different method.

The VRS DEA model showed similar results. The countries that were in each year included Bulgaria, Czechia, Germany, Ireland, Greece, Italy, Latvia, Lithuania, Luxembourg,

Hungary, Poland, Portugal and Romania. Croatia, Malta and Slovakia also reached the efficiency frontier in 2023. Countries that are leaders in the implementation of digitalization elements according to the DESI 2022 like Finland, Denmark, the Netherlands and Sweden (European Commission 2024c) were evaluated as being ineffective by the VRS DEA model. This can be justified by the lower rate of introduction of individual digitalization elements, since these elements are already introduced in the given countries in a larger volume and thus their impact on GDP growth and the unemployment rate is not so significant. These results more or less confirm the findings of Inel (2019) and Yalcin (2021). Slightly different results can be found in the study by Georgescu et al. (2022). These authors found that the best results of efficiency were achieved by Denmark, Estonia, Italy, Finland, Latvia, Lithuania and Malta. The Netherlands and Sweden did not achieve efficiency. We can conclude that when analyzing countries from the point of view of their digital transformation, it is important to evaluate not only the quantity of introduced digitalization elements, but also the effectiveness of their use in relation to GDP growth and employment growth in the country.

The position of the EU countries from the point of view of the MI, TECH and FS when comparing the years 2021 and 2023 is shown in the following 3D scatterplot (Figure 8). The best results were achieved by Ireland, Italy, Hungary and Bulgaria. These countries are closely followed by Czechia and Poland. Slovakia achieved the best results in the frontier shift—a shift in the field of technological innovation. The worst MI results were achieved by Latvia, Greece and Estonia.

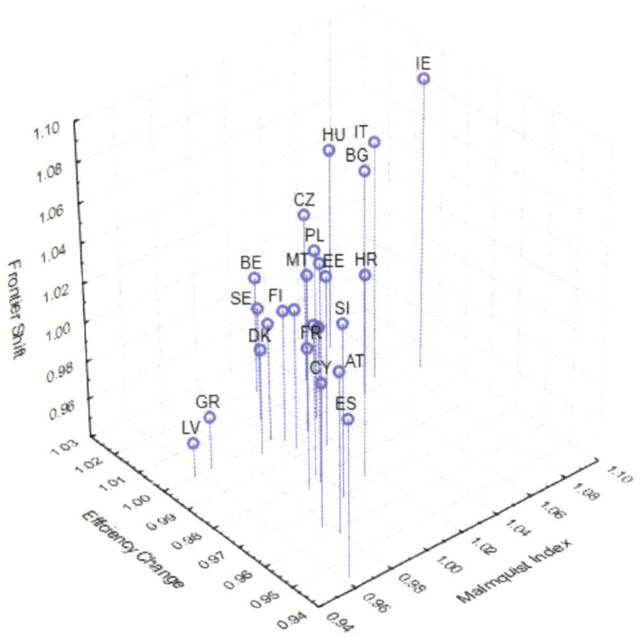

Figure 8. Three-dimensional scatterplot of Malmquist index against efficiency change and frontier shift. Source: processed by authors in Statistica 14.1.0.8 software.

6. Conclusions

The DEA model and the MI, which were applied in this study using the Digital Compass and DESI parameters for the years 2019, 2021 and 2023, provided an evaluation of the efficiency of 27 EU countries. We can conclude that the most significant changes in technical efficiency measured by MI occurred when comparing the years 2019/2023 in Bulgaria, Italy, Hungary, Poland and Romania. The positive results of the MI in these countries were caused mainly by introducing new digitalization elements. These countries were also effective in each year based on the DEA results. The change in the efficiency of the use of already introduced digitalization elements was the most significant when comparing the years 2021–2023 in Belgium, Czechia, Denmark, Germany, Estonia, the Netherlands, Finland and Sweden. Some countries like Czechia or Germany were also effective in each year based on the DEA results. However, Denmark, the Netherlands, Finland and Sweden, which are the most important leaders from the point of view of the number of introduced digitalization elements measured by the DESI 2022, were not effective based on the results of the VRS DEA model. The results from the perspective of these changes are different. This is due to the fact that some countries are at the forefront due to their better use of already established elements of digitalization and some due to the introduction of new technologies, while in the case of these countries it is a more intensive process.

The digitalization solutions using the DEA VRS and MI showed different results compared to the evaluation of the digitalization process, for example, using DESI. This finding is also confirmed by the study of Georgescu et al. (2022). This is due to the fact that the MI calculates the change in efficiency over two periods. On the other hand, most digitalization indices are based on the digital transformation data achieved in one year. Another reason for the above may be the fact that due to the limitations of the DEA model, only a limited number of digitalization elements could be used. It is also necessary to point out the limitations regarding the quantity and quality of data. Eurostat does not capture data for all years and data for some countries are also missing. That is why, for example, the year 2022 is missing from this analysis. The data must be carefully searched for in various reports and studies, and therefore only those indicators for which data can be found can be selected.

The results show that the MI has a higher informative value when it measures the effectiveness of the transformation process over time instead of for a given year. Changes over time were confirmed, especially in the countries located in the middle of the ranking. There are studies (Inel 2019; Yalcin 2021) which, using the DEA models, confirmed that some lower-ranking EU countries already established digital processes with more efficiency than the ranking leaders (also in terms of the impact on economic growth and employment). This statement was also confirmed in this study by the VRS DEA model and MI and answered the set research question. However, it is obvious that lower-ranking EU countries are still lagging behind in the introduction of new digitalization elements. The main pillar of the countries' digital policies is the possibility of equal access to technologies and innovative possibilities. This is the only way to ensure equality within EU countries. Currently, the world is approaching the end of the introduction phase of the "ICT age", and the introduction phase of a new paradigm, including Industry 4.0 technologies, is beginning. It is necessary to prevent these technologies from further exacerbating inequalities within countries. Much will depend on whether countries catch up, advance or fall behind, which will depend on national policies. EU policy makers should encourage greater knowledge exchange across the EU, with structured programs that allow for the sharing of best practices and digital solutions between EU countries.

The results of this study significantly enrich the knowledge in the methodology of investigating the efficiency of digitalization of EU-27 countries, and from this point of view they represent a significant theoretical contribution to the given issue. In addition, the findings of this study provide theoretical as well as practical applications, especially in terms of building an innovative knowledge economy. They point to the diversity of the EU-27 countries in digitalization and suggest ways to eliminate it, either by better use of the existing digitalization elements or by intensifying the introduction of new ones. Diagnosing the level of digitalization and established levels of the use of innovative technologies among EU-27 enterprises can ensure a comprehensive approach to the digital transformation process, taking into account the differences between these countries. Within this process it is necessary to focus on more consistent data collection and to introduce new ways and methods of evaluating the achieved results, especially by applying mathematical programming as well as artificial intelligence; namely, the implementation of artificial intelligence tools lags behind in both developed as well as less developed countries. Therefore, governments, institutions and organizations that deal with the given issue should tackle it more consistently and take into account the results of scientific research. A comprehensive approach to solving this issue could include the MI score—an innovative index of the digital transformation of EU countries over time, which will take into account the level as well as the efficiency of the digitalization of EU countries. This could also be a challenge within the governments of individual countries to focus not only on the introduction of digitalization elements, but also their effective use. The benefit of this research for practice is the finding that digitalization is beneficial for increasing the performance of countries and businesses, but it is necessary to take into account the increase in expenses at the beginning of the introduction of individual digitalization elements.

Future research will be aimed at confirming the finding that less developed EU countries use elements of the digitalization process more effectively than developed countries. The goal is also to assess the effectiveness of the digitalization process of businesses in EU countries, the impact of this process on the performance of businesses' and averting the risk of their bankruptcy.

Author Contributions: Conceptualization, J.H.; methodology, M.M.; software, J.H.; validation, J.H.; formal analysis, M.M.; investigation, J.H. and M.M.; resources, M.M.; data curation, J.H. and M.M.; writing—original draft preparation, J.H. and M.M.; writing—review and editing, J.H. and M.M.; visualization, J.H. and M.M.; supervision, J.H.; project administration, J.H. and M.M.; funding acquisition, J.H. and M.M. All authors have read and agreed to the published version of the manuscript.

Funding: This research was supported by the grant scheme VEGA No. 1/0449/24—Design of an integrated system for measuring the sustainable businesses' performance in the era of digitalization and by the Slovak Research and Development Agency under the contract No. APVV-20-0338.

Informed Consent Statement: Not applicable.

Data Availability Statement: Data are contained within this article.

Conflicts of Interest: The authors declare no conflicts of interest.

References

Akther, Syed, Hirofumi Fukuyama, and William L. Weber. 2013. Estimating two-stage network slacks-based inefficiency: An Application to Bangladesh banking. *Omega* 41: 88–96. [CrossRef]

Balcerzak, Adam P., and Bernard M. Pietrzak. 2017. Digital economy in Visegrad countries. Multi-criteria decision analysis at regional level in the years 2012 and 2015. *Journal of competitiveness* 9: 5–18. [CrossRef]

Banker, Rajiv D., Abraham Charnes, and William W. Cooper. 1984. Some models for estimating technical scale inefficiencies in Data Envelopment Analyresis. *Management Science* 30: 1078–92. [CrossRef]

Barefoot, Kevin, Dave Curtis, William Jolliff, Jessica R. Nicholson, and Robert Omohundro. 2018. Defining and Measuring the Digital Economy. Working Paper No. 3/15/2018. Available online: https://www.bea.gov/sites/default/files/papers/defining-and-measuring-the-digital-economy.pdf (accessed on 6 November 2023).

Bánhidi, Zoltán, Imre Dobos, and András Nemeslaki. 2020. What the overall Digital Economy and Society Index reveals: A statistical analysis of the DESI EU28 dimensions. *Regional Economics* 10: 42–62. [CrossRef]

Bánhidi, Zoltán, Imre Dobos, and Madina Tokmergenova. 2021. Russia's Place Vis-à-Vis the EU28 Countries in Digital Development: A Ranking Using DEA-Type Composite Indicators and the TOPSIS Method. In *Digitalization, Digital Transformation and Sustainability in the Global Economy*. Springer Proceedings in Business and Economics. Edited by Tim A. Herberger and Jörg J. Dötsch. Berlin/Heidelberg: Springer, pp. 135–46. [CrossRef]

Basol, Oguz, and Esin C. Yalcin. 2021. How does the Digital Economy and Society Index (DESI) affect labor market indicators in EU countries? *Human Systems Management* 40: 503–12. [CrossRef]

Bittner, Beáta, Tünde Kovács, and András Nábrádi. 2022. The Integration of Digital Technologies in the European Union based on the DESI Index. *ENTRENOVA—ENTerprise REsearch InNOVAtion* 8: 337–49. [CrossRef]

Borowiecki, Ryszard, Barbara Siuta-Tokarska, Jolanta Maroń, Marcin Suder, Agnieszka Thier, and Katarzyna Żmija. 2021. Developing digital economy and society in the light of the issue of digital convergence of the markets in the European Union countries. *Energies* 14: 2717. [CrossRef]

Borremans, Alexandra D., Irina M. Zaychenko, and Oksana Y. Iliashenko. 2018. Digital economy. IT strategy of the company development. *MATEC Web of Conferences* 170: 01034. [CrossRef]

Bozkurt, Eda, Özlem Topçuoğlu, and Ali Altiner. 2022. Relationship between productivity and digitalization with Tobit model based on Malmquist index. *Journal of Productivity*, 67–78. [CrossRef]
Bukht, Rumana, and Richard Heeks. 2019. Defining, Conceptualising and Measuring the Digital Economy. Development Informatics Working Paper No. 68. Available online: https://ssrn.com/abstract=3431732 (accessed on 13 July 2024).
Charnes, Abraham, William W. Cooper, and Edwardo Rhodes. 1978. Measuring the efficiency of decision making units. *European Journal of Operation Research* 2: 429–44. [CrossRef]
Cooper, Willam W., Lawrence M. Seiford, and Joe Zhu. 2011. Data Envelopment Analysis: History, models and interpretations. In *Handbook on Data Envelopment Analysis*. Edited by Willam W. Cooper, Lawrence M. Seiford and Joe Zhu. New York: Springer, pp. 1–39. [CrossRef]
Corejova, Tatiana, and Roman Chinoracky. 2021. Assessing the Potential for Digital Transformation. *Sustainability* 13: 11040. [CrossRef]
Emrouznejad, Ali, and Guo-liang Yang. 2018. A survey and analysis of the first 40 years of scholarly literature in DEA: 1978–2016. *Socio-Economic Planning Sciences* 61: 4–8. [CrossRef]
European Commission. 2024a. DESI 2023 Dashboard for the Digital Decade. Available online: https://digital-decade-desi.digital-strategy.ec.europa.eu/datasets/desi/indicators (accessed on 23 May 2024).
European Commission. 2024b. Europe's Digital Decade: Digital Targets for 2030. Available online: https://commission.europa.eu/strategy-and-policy/priorities-2019-2024/europe-fit-digital-age/europes-digital-decade-digital-targets-2030_en (accessed on 15 May 2024).
European Commission. 2024c. Questions and Answers: Digital Economy and Society Index (DESI) 2022. Available online: https://ec.europa.eu/commission/presscorner/detail/en/qanda_22_4561 (accessed on 1 July 2024).
European Commission. 2024d. The Recovery and Resilience Facility. Available online: https://commission.europa.eu/business-economy-euro/economic-recovery/recovery-and-resilience-facility_en (accessed on 10 June 2024).
Eurostat. 2024. Database. Available online: https://ec.europa.eu/eurostat/web/main/data/database (accessed on 10 April 2024).
Fandel, Peter. 2002. Intertemporal efficiency measures in wheat production industry. In *Quantitative Methods in Economics (Multiple Criteria Decision Making XI)*. Nitra: Slovak Agricultural University, pp. 40–49. Available online: https://fhi.euba.sk/www_write/files/katedry/kove/zborniky/QME_2002.pdf#page=41 (accessed on 28 June 2023).
Farrell, Michael J. 1957. The Measurement of productive efficiency. *Journal of the Royal Statistical Society, Series A* 120: 253–90. [CrossRef]
Färe, Rolf, Shawna Grosskopf, and C. A. Knox Lovell. 1984. The Structure of Technical Efficiency. In *Topics in Production Theory. Scandinavian Journal of Economics*. Edited by Finn R. Førsund. London: Palgrave Macmillan. [CrossRef]
Feruś, Anna. 2010. The Application of DEA Method in Evaluating Credit Risk of Companies. *Contemporary Economics* 4: 109–18. [CrossRef]
Furlan, Martina. 2022. Our guide to the 2030 Digital Compass: The European Way to the Digital Decade. Available online: https://89initiative.com/our-guide-to-the-2030-digital-compass-the-european-way-to-the-digital-decade/ (accessed on 14 June 2023).
Georgescu, Irina, Ane-Mari Androniceanu, and Irina V. Drăgulănescu. 2023. A Deep Learning Approach to Digitalization and Economic Growth. In *Digital Economy and the Green Revolution. ICBE 2022. Springer Proceedings in Business and Economics*. Edited by Mihail Busu. Cham: Springer. [CrossRef]
Georgescu, Mircea R., Eduard A. Stoica, Ioana A. Bogoslov, and Anca E. Lungu. 2022. Managing Efficiency in Digital Transformation—EU Member States Performance during the COVID-19 Pandemic. *Procedia Computer Science* 204: 432–9. [CrossRef] [PubMed]
Gúčik, Marián, and Katarína Uličná. 2014. Using Malmquist index in evaluating hotel efficiency. *Journal of Economics and Social Research* 15: 159–68. Available online: https://www.ekonomikaaspolocnost.umb.sk/wp-content/uploads/2020/07/2_2014.pdf#page=39 (accessed on 18 May 2022).
Inel, Mehmet N. 2019. An empirical study on measurement of efficiency of digital transformation by using data envelopment analysis. *Management Science Letters* 9: 549–56. [CrossRef]
Jablonsky, Josef. 2012. Multicriteria approaches for ranking of efficient units in DEA models. *Central European Journal of Operations Research* 20: 435–49. [CrossRef]
Jurayevich, Mahmudov B., and Mullabayev B. Bulturbayevic. 2020. The impact of digital economy on economic growth. *International Journal of Business, Law and Education* 1: 4–7. [CrossRef]
Jurickova, Eva, Michal Pilik, and Michael A. Kwarteng. 2019. Efficiency measurement of national innovation systems of the European Union countries: DEA model application. *Journal of International Studies* 12: 286–299. [CrossRef]
Kao, Ling J., Chih C Chiu, Hung T. Lin, Yun W. Hung, and Cheng C. Lu. 2022. Evaluating the digital transformation performance of retail by the DEA approach. *Axioms* 11: 284. [CrossRef]
Kocher, Martin G., Mikulas Luptacik, and Matthias Sutter. 2006. Measuring productivity of research in economics: A cross-country study using DEA. *Socio-Economic Planning Sciences* 40: 314–32. [CrossRef]
Kohl, Sebastian, Jan Schoenfelder, Andreas Fügener, and Jens O. Brunner. 2019. The use of Data Envelopment Analysis (DEA) in healthcare with a focus on hospitals. *Health Care Management Science* 22: 245–86. [CrossRef] [PubMed]
Krejnus, Matej, Jana Stofkova, Katarina Repkova Stofkova, and Vladimira Binasova. 2023. The Use of the DEA Method for Measuring the Efficiency of Electronic Public Administration as Part of the Digitization of the Economy and Society. *Applied Sciences* 13: 3672. [CrossRef]

Krstić, Ana, Dragana Rejman-Petrović, Ivana Nedeljković, and Predrag Mimović. 2023. Efficiency of the use of information and communication technologies as a determinant of the digital business transformation process. *Benchmarking* 30: 3860–83. [CrossRef]

Lane, Neal. 1999. Advancing the Digital Economy into the 21st Century. *Information Systems Frontiers* 1: 317–20. [CrossRef]

Lim, Sungmook, and Joe Zhu. 2019. Primal-dual correspondence and frontier projections in two-stage network DEA models. *Omega* 83: 236–48. [CrossRef]

Limna, Pongsakorn, Tanpat Kraiwanit, and Supaprawat Siripipatthanakul. 2022. The growing trend of digital economy: A review article. *International Journal of Computing Sciences Research* 6: 1–11. [CrossRef]

Lungu, Anca E., Mircea R. Georgescu, and Vasile Işan. 2022. An entrepreneurial appraisal of the COVID-19 pandemic: Measuring digitalization efficiency. Paper presented at FEB Zagreb International Odyssey Conference on Economic and Business, Zagreb, Croatia, June 1–4.

Małkowska, Agnieszka, Maria Urbaniec, and Malgorzata Kosała. 2021. The impact of digital transformation on European countries: Insights from a comparative analysis. *Equilibrium. Quarterly Journal of Economics and Economic Policy* 16: 325–55. [CrossRef]

Mesenbourg, Thomas L. 2001. Measuring the Digital Economy, US Bureau of the Census, Suitland, MD. Available online: https://www.census.gov/content/dam/Census/library/working-papers/2001/econ/umdigital.pdf (accessed on 15 July 2023).

Olczyk, Magdalena, and Marta Kuc-Czarnecka. 2022. Digital transformation and economic growth—DESI improvement and implementation. *Technological and Economic Development of Economy* 28: 775–803. [CrossRef]

Oloyede, Abdulkarim A., Nasir Faruk, Nasir Noma, Ebinimi Tebepah, and Augustine K. Nwaulune. 2023. Measuring the impact of the digital economy in developing countries: A systematic review and meta- analysis. *Heliyon* 9: e17654. [CrossRef] [PubMed]

Paradi, Joseph C., D'Andre Wilson, and Xiaopeng Yang. 2014. Data Envelopment Analysis of Corporate Failure for Non-Manufacturing Firms Using a Slacks-Based Measure. *Journal of Service Science and Management* 7: 277–90. [CrossRef]

Paradi, Joseph C., Mette Asmild, and Paul C. Simak. 2004. Using DEA and worst practice DEA in credit risk evaluation. *Journal of Productivity Analysis* 21: 153–65. [CrossRef]

Parra, Javier, María-Eugenia Pérez-Pons, and Jorge González. 2020. Study based on the incidence of the Index of Economy and Digital Society (DESI) in the GDP of the Eurozone economies. In *Distributed Computing and Artificial Intelligence: Proceedings of International Symposium on Distributed Computing and Artificial Intelligence*. Berlin/Heidelberg: Springer International Publishing, pp. 164–68. [CrossRef]

Rejman Petrovic, Dragana, Ana Krstic, Ivana Nedeljković, and Predrag Mimovic. 2022. Efficiency of digital business transformation in the Republic of Serbia. *VINE Journal of Information and Knowledge Management Systems, ahead-of-print*. [CrossRef]

Sabbagh, Karim, Roman Friedrich, Bahjat El-Darwiche, Milind Singh, and Sandeep Ganediwalla. 2012. Maximizing the Impact of Digitization. The Global Information Technology Report. Available online: https://www3.weforum.org/docs/GITR/2012/GITR_Chapter1.11_2012.pdf (accessed on 2 December 2022).

Sorayaei, Ali, Fariborz Kalashi, and Masoumeh S. Divkolaii. 2012. Evaluating Efficiency of SEPAH Bank Branches in Mazandaran Province by Using Data Envelopment Analysis. *Australian Journal of Basic and Applied Sciences* 6: 335–40. Available online: http://www.ajbasweb.com/old/ajbas/2012/Nov%202012/335-340.pdf (accessed on 14 June 2022).

Sreedevi, Rayadurgam. 2016. A Case Study of Minority Institutions by Using BCC Model-DEA Approach. *Journal of Mathematics* 12: 66–8. [CrossRef]

Stavytskyy, Andriy, Ganna Kharlamova, and Eduard A. Stoica. 2019. The analysis of the digital economy and society index in the EU. *TalTech Journal of European Studies* 9: 245–61. [CrossRef]

Williams, Luyanda D. 2021. Concepts of Digital Economy and Industry 4.0 in Intelligent and information systems. *International Journal of Intelligent Networks* 2: 122–9. [CrossRef]

Yalcin, Esin C. 2021. Efficiency measurement of digitalization on EU countries: A study based on data envelopment analysis. *International Journal of Management, Knowledge and Learning* 10: 323–33. [CrossRef]

Zaharia, Marian, and Aniela Bălăcescu. 2020. Digital Economy and Society. *Comparative Cluster Analysis of EU States. Journal of Applied Computer Science & Mathematics* 14: 30–6. [CrossRef]

Zhu, Joe. 2014. *Quantitative Models for Performance Evaluation and Benchmarking: Data Envelopment Analysis with Spreadsheets*, 3rd ed. Cham: Springer. [CrossRef]

Disclaimer/Publisher's Note: The statements, opinions and data contained in all publications are solely those of the individual author(s) and contributor(s) and not of MDPI and/or the editor(s). MDPI and/or the editor(s) disclaim responsibility for any injury to people or property resulting from any ideas, methods, instructions or products referred to in the content.

economies

MDPI

Article

The Impact of AI on International Trade: Opportunities and Challenges

Ozcan Ozturk

College of Public Policy, Hamad bin Khalifa University, Doha P.O. Box 34110, Qatar; oozturk@hbku.edu.qa

Abstract: This study aims to explore the transformative potential of Artificial Intelligence (AI) in international trade, focusing on its key roles in optimizing trade operations, enhancing trade finance, and expanding market access. In trade optimization, AI leverages advanced machine learning and predictive analytics to enhance demand forecasting, route optimization, and customs procedures, leading to more efficient logistics and inventory management. In trade finance, AI can automate document processing and risk assessment, increasing access to finance and enhancing transactional transparency, particularly through integration with blockchain technology. In terms of market access, AI-driven analytics can identify consumer trends and competitive dynamics, enabling personalized marketing and overcoming linguistic and cultural barriers. Due to the lack of quantitative data, this study employed qualitative research methods, specifically a multiple-case-study approach. The case studies of leading companies such as Alibaba, DHL, and Maersk showcase how they leverage AI to optimize their trade operations, improve customer service, and achieve greater efficiency. These real-world examples demonstrate AI's practical applications and significant benefits in the global trade landscape. However, the adoption of AI in international trade is not without challenges. These include issues around data quality, ethical concerns, technological complexity, and public perception. Policy recommendations highlight the need for a robust data infrastructure, establishing ethical AI guidelines, and fostering international cooperation to align data protection regulations.

Keywords: artificial intelligence; AI; international trade; AI Case Studies; AI-driven logistics; trade operations optimization

1. Introduction

Artificial Intelligence (AI) is transforming industries worldwide, and its impact on international trade is particularly significant. As countries and companies navigate the complexities of global markets, AI presents new opportunities to optimize trade operations, enhance market access, and streamline trade finance. This study seeks to explore the diverse role AI plays in reshaping international trade, offering a comprehensive analysis of how AI technologies are transforming trade dynamics, as well as identifying the key challenges and opportunities ahead. The central research question guiding this study is as follows: What is the role of AI in international trade, and how can its potential be fully harnessed while addressing the associated challenges? While this study seeks to contribute to a broader understanding of AI's transformative impact on international trade, it also aims to offer practical insights and recommendations for stakeholders in this evolving field. Given the limited availability of quantitative data, we adopted a multiple-case-study approach as our research design. Future studies may build on this work by utilizing more extensive data as they become available.

Section 2 of this study provides a brief overview of AI, its various types, and its technological underpinnings, setting the stage for understanding its applications in trade. Section 3 develops a framework to analyze the literature. Section 4 provides three case studies of leading companies—Alibaba, DHL, and Maersk—showcasing how they leverage AI to enhance their trade operations. Section 5 discusses the significant challenges that need to be addressed to fully realize AI's potential in international trade. Section 6 provides actionable recommendations for policymakers to foster AI adoption in international trade and address the identified challenges. The last section concludes by summarizing the key insights and outlines the future direction of AI in international trade.

2. Definition and Types of AI

Artificial intelligence is a pivotal technological advancement that seeks to replicate human cognitive functions through machines and data analysis. AI has permeated various aspects of life, including healthcare, finance, entertainment, and academia, revolutionizing how we interact with technology and make decisions. Despite its widespread application, providing a precise definition of AI can be challenging due to its broad scope. However, the core feature of AI is its ability to simulate human intelligence.

The term "artificial intelligence" was first coined in the 1950s, when pioneers like Alan Turing proposed the idea of machines being able to emulate human thought processes (Anyoha 2020). Allen (2020) traces the origins of AI back to the 1940s, highlighting its evolution from a theoretical concept to a practical tool used in various fields today. Britannica defines AI as the capability of a computer or robot to perform tasks typically requiring human intelligence, such as learning, reasoning, problem-solving, perception, and language understanding (Copeland 2024). Du-Harpur et al. (2020) describe AI as a simulation of human intelligence, emphasizing its capacity to learn from and adapt to new information

Despite significant advancements, AI still falls short of fully replicating human cognitive abilities. AI lacks the nuanced reasoning, deep understanding, and common sense inherent in human intelligence. One of the primary limitations of AI systems is their reliance on large datasets to function effectively, which introduces challenges related to data quality and biases. Moreover, AI systems often struggle with context-specific decision-making and abstract thinking, which are areas where human cognition excels. Nevertheless, ongoing research and development aim to address these limitations and progressively enhance AI's capabilities, moving closer to more sophisticated and adaptable systems (Firt 2023). This continuous improvement is driven by advancements in machine-learning algorithms, computational power, and the integration of multidisciplinary approaches to better simulate human-like intelligence (Firt 2023; Chollet 2017).

2.1. *Types of AI*

AI is a complex and multifaceted field encompassing various types and capabilities. Based on its capabilities, AI is categorized into two primary types: Narrow AI and General AI.

Narrow AI: Narrow AI, also referred to as weak AI, is designed to perform specific tasks or a limited range of functions with high proficiency. These systems are highly specialized, excelling in language translation, voice recognition, and data analysis. For instance, virtual assistants like Siri and Alexa are prime examples of narrow AI, proficiently handling tasks such as setting reminders, answering queries, and managing smart home devices (Labbe and Wigmore 2023).

The advantages of narrow AI are substantial, including faster decision-making processes and the automation of mundane tasks, thereby relieving humans from repetitive duties. Virtual assistants, for example, can streamline daily activities by managing routine inquiries and transactions. Moreover, narrow AI systems can outperform humans in certain tasks, such as detecting anomalies in medical images, exemplified by the enhanced accuracy of cancer detection from X-rays (Kanade 2022a).

However, narrow AI has inherent limitations. It relies heavily on specific datasets, which can introduce biases and affect the accuracy of its outcomes. This dependency on data not only limits the generalizability of narrow AI systems but also makes them susceptible to errors when encountering data outside their training scope. Consequently, while narrow AI can perform certain tasks exceptionally well, it lacks the adaptability and broader understanding that characterize human intelligence (Chollet 2017; Firt 2023).

General AI: General AI, also known as Artificial General Intelligence (AGI) or strong AI, aims to replicate human cognitive abilities comprehensively. Unlike narrow AI, general AI can understand, learn, and implement knowledge across various domains and contexts (Kanade 2022b). The goal of general AI is to mimic the full range of human cognitive functions, including reasoning, problem-solving, creativity, and self-awareness.

A truly general AI system would be capable of learning new skills independently, adapting to different environments, and performing tasks with the same efficiency and flexibility as humans (Heath 2019). While general AI remains largely theoretical, ongoing research in this area holds the potential to transform how we interact with machines and automate complex decision-making processes.

AI technologies can also be categorized based on the underlying technologies they utilize. The five main types of AI technologies include the following:

2.1.1. Machine Learning

Machine learning is a subset of AI focused on developing algorithms that allow computers to learn from data and make decisions or predictions without explicit programming (Naqa and Murphy 2022). Machine-learning algorithms can identify patterns and relationships in data, enabling computers to make informed decisions. There are three main types of machine learning:

Supervised Learning: The machine is trained using labeled examples, learning to perform specific tasks based on the provided data.

Unsupervised Learning: The machine identifies patterns and relationships in data without labeled examples, finding its way to categorize or predict outcomes.

Semi-Supervised Learning: A combination of supervised and unsupervised learning, where labeled data helps guide the machine in making predictions or classifications.

Machine learning has a wide range of applications, from search engines and recommendation systems such as those used by Amazon and Netflix to complex fields such as medical diagnostics (Heath 2020).

2.1.2. Deep Learning

Deep learning is a specialized branch of machine learning that uses multi-layered neural networks to model and extract intricate patterns from large datasets (Chollet 2017). Each layer of the neural network processes data at varying levels of abstraction, allowing deep-learning algorithms to generate hierarchical representations of information. The applications of deep learning include natural language processing, image recognition, and advanced virtual assistants like ChatGPT (Diaz 2024).

2.1.3. Natural Language Processing (NLP)

Natural Language Processing (NLP) focuses on the interaction between computers and human languages. NLP enables computers to understand, interpret, and generate human language in a meaningful way (Investopedia 2021). Applications of NLP include language translation, sentiment analysis, text analytics, and chatbots. NLP technologies are integral to improving communication between humans and machines, making them more accessible and user-friendly (Roldós 2021).

2.1.4. Robotics

Robotics is a multidisciplinary field that involves robot design, construction, and operation. It integrates elements of AI, mechanical engineering, and electrical engineering to create machines capable of performing tasks autonomously or semi-autonomously (Tripathi 2023). Robotics applications range from industrial automation and manufacturing to healthcare and space exploration.

2.1.5. Expert Systems

Expert systems are AI programs that mimic the decision-making abilities of a human expert in a specific domain. These systems use a knowledge base of facts and heuristics to reason through complex problems and provide recommendations or solutions (Tripathi 2023). Expert systems are widely used in fields such as medicine, engineering, finance, and troubleshooting, where they assist in decision support and problem-solving.

3. AI and International Trade: Conceptual Framework

AI is increasingly recognized as a transformative force in global trade, influencing areas from supply chain management to trade finance. In this section, to better analyze AI's role, we developed a **conceptual framework** that highlights its impact across three key areas: (1) **trade operations**, (2) **trade finance**, and (3) **market access**. This framework provides a structured approach to understanding how AI influences international trade, offering solutions that streamline processes, reduce costs, and enhance overall efficiency.

3.1. AI Optimizes Trade Operations

AI can optimize trade operations by reducing costs and increasing efficiency. AI enhances supply chain management through machine learning and predictive analytics, which help businesses anticipate demand by analyzing historical data and market trends. This predictive capability minimizes overstock and stockouts, ensuring that inventory levels are aligned with market needs (Praveenadevi et al. 2023; Ferencz et al. 2022). For example, Oyewole et al. (2024), Ferencz et al. (2022), and Cannas et al. (2024) demonstrated how AI-based predictive models can reduce overstock and stockouts by adjusting inventory levels in real-time based on external factors such as market demand and shipping conditions. This ability to adapt to dynamic global markets allows businesses to minimize costs and optimize their logistics.

AI-powered route optimization is another area where significant advancements are being made. Algorithms that consider traffic patterns, weather conditions, and geopolitical risks help companies reduce shipping times and costs (Vaka 2024). This is especially relevant for firms dealing with perishable goods or just-in-time inventory systems.

Moreover, customs processes have benefitted from AI-driven automation. By analyzing large shipping documents, identifying compliance issues, and ensuring proper classification process, AI reduces human errors, accelerates custom clearance, and minimizes delays, enhancing overall efficiency (Garg et al. 2022). The World Trade Organization (WTO) estimates that implementing trade-facilitation measures, such as more efficient customs processes, could lower trade costs by approximately 14.3%. In this context, AI is poised to act as a transformative technology, driving further advancements in streamlining these processes (WTO 2020). Furthermore, AI automates repetitive tasks such as customer inquiries, inventory management, and order processing. This automation frees up human resources for more strategic tasks, leading to higher productivity, shorter processing times, and lower operating costs (Makar 2023; Vijayakumar 2023). Moreover, AI systems improve risk management by identifying and responding to potential risks such as political instability, natural disasters, and economic fluctuations (M. D. Wang 2023; Ozturk 2017; Ozturk et al. 2024). By providing early warnings and actionable insights, AI enables businesses to develop contingency plans and adjust strategies, ensuring trade stability (Tjoa et al. 2022).

In logistics and transportation, AI aids in predictive maintenance by monitoring machinery and vehicles using sensors and Internet of Things (IoT) devices. This proactive approach reduces downtime, increases equipment longevity, and ensures seamless trade operations (Rojek et al. 2023). Additionally, AI enhances customer experience by providing personalized recommendations and improving service standards. In e-commerce, AI analyzes consumer data to recommend products based on personal interests and responds to inquiries around the clock, improving customer satisfaction (Pal et al. 2023).

AI also assists companies in navigating international trade laws by accurately computing tariffs and taxes, automatically classifying companies, and ensuring regulatory compliance. This reduces penalties, hold-ups, and legal issues, thereby enhancing business efficiency (Chinen 2023; Chow et al. 2022).

3.2. *AI Improves Trade Finance*

In the realm of trade finance, AI is transforming processes by automating document processing, risk assessment, and verification. These tasks are traditionally time-consuming and prone to human error. AI-powered platforms streamline these processes by scanning, validating, and organizing documents efficiently, significantly reducing costs and the likelihood of human errors (Garg et al. 2022; Rajagopal et al. 2023). This automation accelerates transaction times and reduces administrative costs.

In terms of risk assessment, AI enhances trade finance risk evaluation by analyzing vast amounts of data from various sources, including financial statements, transaction histories, and market conditions. AI identifies patterns and trends that indicate potential risks, such as unstable finances or fraudulent activity, leading to better loan decisions and more accurate risk profiles (Pathak et al. 2023). Additionally, AI-driven platforms facilitate trade finance access by analyzing non-traditional data points, supply chain data, and payment histories. These platforms provide more inclusive and accurate credit assessments, benefiting underrepresented businesses such as SMEs and closing the financing gap (Rajagopal et al. 2023). Moreover, AI provides predictive insights for companies to manage cash flow more effectively. By analyzing historical data and financial trends, AI systems estimate future cash flows and identify potential deficits, enabling companies to plan wisely and secure necessary funding (Rajagopal et al. 2023). Furthermore, AI improves trade credit insurance by enhancing risk evaluations and claims handling. AI expedites claim processing, accelerates payouts, and reduces the administrative burden on insurers (Tjoa et al. 2022). When combined with blockchain technology, AI enhances trade finance transparency and reliability by allowing accurate verification of transactions, reducing disagreements, and fostering trust between trading partners through a secure, unchangeable record (Aruna et al. 2023; Aysan et al. 2024).

3.3. *Improve Market Access*

AI has a significant impact on improving market access by providing insights into consumer behavior, analyzing market dynamics, and improving market strategies. Saha et al. (2023) highlight how AI-driven analytics help businesses process large volumes of data from various sources, including social media, online reviews, market reports, and customer behavior statistics. These tools identify new trends, consumer preferences, and regional competitive dynamics, helping companies determine which markets have the greatest potential for their goods or services and the most effective entry strategies (Saha et al. 2023). Moreover, AI enables personalized marketing strategies by utilizing machine-learning algorithms to analyze consumer data, segment audiences, and tailor messages based on demographics, interests, and actions. This enhances engagement and conversion rates, attracting and retaining clients (Pal et al. 2023).

In addition, AI-driven Natural Language Processing (NLP) and translation solutions enable businesses to effectively communicate with their target market, overcoming linguistic and cultural barriers. AI translates marketing materials, product descriptions, and consumer communications while also assessing consumer sentiment and cultural nuances (Kunst and Bierwiaczonek 2023; Khurana et al. 2022). Additionally, AI enhances e-commerce platforms by optimizing pricing, search results, and product recommendations, delivering personalized shopping experiences. AI-driven logistics solutions improve cross-border commerce by enhancing supply chain management, enabling companies to meet demand in new markets, prevent overstocking and stockouts, optimize inventory, and reduce costs and shipping times (Praveenadevi et al. 2023). AI systems monitor competitors' actions, product launches, price adjustments, and advertising campaigns in real time. This enables companies to adjust their strategies, identify opportunities and risks in new markets, and enhance their competitiveness (Borges 2021).

Additionally, AI-driven chatbots provide round-the-clock assistance to clients across various time zones and languages, enhancing customer satisfaction and loyalty. These chatbots also analyze interactions to identify common issues, enabling companies to improve their products and services based on customer feedback (Singh et al. 2024). Finally, AI helps companies identify and mitigate the risks associated with entering new markets by analyzing economic data, political stability, and market conditions. This enables informed decision-making and strategies to mitigate risks like supply chain disruptions and geopolitical challenges (Chinen 2023).

In short, AI is fundamentally transforming international trade by optimizing operations, improving trade finance, and enhancing market access. By leveraging AI technologies, businesses can make informed decisions, streamline processes, and enhance customer experiences, leading to increased efficiency and competitiveness in the global market. The subsequent sections will provide case studies of companies successfully leveraging AI to achieve these benefits.

4. Case Studies

In this study, we adopt a multiple-case-study research design approach to investigate real-world applications of AI in international trade. This method enables us to examine AI's role in specific companies within their natural operational context, making it well-suited for analyzing complex, contemporary trade issues (Yin 2018). The selected cases—Alibaba, DHL, and Maersk—provide both individual insights and comparative analysis, allowing us to identify patterns and generate context-specific conclusions about AI's impact on trade operations. However, as with most case-study approaches, there are limitations regarding generalizability. The findings from these specific companies are exploratory and may not fully represent AI applications across different sectors or regions. Therefore, while the case studies offer valuable qualitative insights, their applicability to the broader landscape of international trade may be limited (Flyvbjerg 2006).

4.1. Case Study 1: Alibaba

Alibaba is a B2B e-commerce platform that was established in 1999 by 18 people in China with the belief of making it easy for businesses and consumers. This platform brings businesses together, connects them to manufacturers and distributors, and offers them a virtual platform to reach customers as well as facilitate shopping for them. As Alibaba grows and is now one of the biggest e-commerce platforms, it has many divisions and departments, and one of them is Alibaba Cloud, a special division related to technology and innovation.

Alibaba Cloud is leading the way in AI innovation, providing a variety of cutting-edge AI services that let retailers fully utilize this game-changing technology (Enda 2023).

Alibaba Cloud uses advanced algorithms used by computer vision services to identify objects, spot trends, and extract insightful information from photos and videos (Enda 2023). The services offered by NLP facilitate human–machine communication, such as text analysis, sentiment analysis, language translation, and chatbot development (X. Wang 2023). In this way, businesses on the Alibaba platform can improve customer service, automate procedures, and facilitate multilingual communication.

Alibaba Cloud AI makes individualized product suggestions, improves shopping experiences, and increases consumer engagement and loyalty by utilizing machine learning to assess user behavior, purchase history, and preferences (X. Wang 2023). Alibaba Cloud AI analyses past sales data, market trends, and outside variables to help retailers with supply chain management (M. D. Wang 2023). To guarantee product availability, lower stockouts, and increase efficiency, it anticipates demand, optimizes inventory, and simplifies logistics (Enda 2023).

4.2. Case Study 2: DHL

One of the leading shipping companies in the world, DHL, uses AI to boost productivity, improve operations, and provide consumers with better services. At DHL, supply chain optimization is one important use of AI. Predictive analytics powered by AI helps reduce delays and cut costs by managing inventory levels, forecasting demand, and addressing supply chain interruptions (DHL 2021). Furthermore, by examining traffic patterns, meteorological data, and other factors, AI algorithms optimize delivery routes, leading to quicker deliveries, less fuel usage, and cheaper operating expenses (DHL 2021).

DHL uses AI-powered robots in warehouse automation to help with packing, moving, and sorting products (DHL 2022). These robots expedite order processing times and increase accuracy and production when used in collaboration with human workers. DHL has recorded a 40% increase in sorting capacity, 99% sorting accuracy, and 1000 parcels sorted per hour (DHL 2022). AI systems are also essential for inventory management since they automate reordering procedures and provide real-time stock level monitoring, which keeps inventory levels in line with demand. Lastly, DHL uses AI-powered chatbots and virtual assistants for customer care to improve the customer experience by promptly and accurately answering questions, providing real-time tracking information, and resolving common difficulties (DHL n.d.).

4.3. Case Study 3: Maersk

Maersk is a prominent international shipping and logistics enterprise that utilizes AI to optimize its operations, increase efficiency, and elevate customer satisfaction. Maersk uses AI extensively for supply chain optimization. Their AI-driven predictive analytic model uses real-time and historical data analysis to forecast demand, identify possible interruptions, and optimize cargo routes (Iqbal 2023). This enhances the planning and decision-making processes. In order to identify the most cost-effective shipping routes and minimize travel times, fuel expenses, and carbon emissions, AI algorithms also examine variables like weather, port traffic, and fuel usage (Raj 2024).

Maersk uses AI in fleet and equipment management to track the state of ships and machinery in real time and perform predictive maintenance (Maersk n.d.). By analyzing sensor data, predictive maintenance algorithms can forecast when maintenance is required, increasing asset lifespan, averting malfunctions, and cutting downtime. By evaluating data on ship performance, weather, and sea conditions, AI also optimizes fuel usage (Maersk n.d.). AI improves port operations by managing traffic and providing automated terminals. By controlling cranes and other equipment, AI-driven automation at Maersk's port facilities increases container handling efficiency and decreases turnaround times (Maersk n.d.). These developments increase the overall efficiency of logistics by streamlining port operations.

5. Challenges in AI Adoption

While AI holds immense potential for transforming international trade, several significant challenges must be addressed to fully harness its benefits. These challenges span across data quality, ethical considerations, technological complexity, public perception, and other specific issues related to international trade. Understanding and mitigating these challenges is crucial for successful AI integration in international trade.

5.1. Data Quality and Availability

AI systems rely on large volumes of high-quality data to operate effectively. When data are inaccurate, biased, or incomplete, it can lead to flawed conclusions and reinforce existing biases, undermining the reliability of AI outputs (Quaresmini and Primiero 2023). However, access to comprehensive and relevant data is often limited due to privacy concerns, proprietary ownership, and regulatory restrictions. These barriers make it challenging for AI systems to learn and adapt, particularly in diverse and rapidly changing trade environments. Integrating data from multiple sources—such as supply chain databases, market reports, and customer feedback—also presents technical difficulties. Ensuring that data is consistent and compatible across different platforms and formats is crucial for AI to deliver accurate analysis.

5.2. Ethical and Regulatory Considerations

AI algorithms can unintentionally, and sometimes intentionally, perpetuate biases present in training data, leading to unfair outcomes (Carlos González De Villaumbrosia 2024). This raises ethical concerns regarding transparency, accountability, and fairness in AI decision-making (Perc et al. 2019; Simplilearn 2024; Katah and Ozturk 2024). Additionally, AI systems often handle sensitive information, making data privacy and security top priorities. Protecting against cyberattacks and preventing data misuse are critical challenges that require strong, effective solutions. Additionally, navigating the complex regulations surrounding AI and data usage can be difficult, especially since different countries have their own standards and regulations. This makes it hard to implement a consistent AI strategy across borders (Chinen 2023). Lastly, determining liability when AI systems make errors or cause harm is another complicated issue. There is a need for clear legal frameworks and guidelines to ensure accountability and build trust.

5.3. Technological Complexity and Implementation

Developing, implementing, and maintaining AI systems require specialized knowledge and skills. The shortage of skilled professionals in AI and related fields can hinder the adoption and effective use of AI technologies (Hagendorff and Wezel 2019). Moreover, implementing AI solutions often demands substantial investments in infrastructure, including high-performance computing resources and data storage systems. These costs can be prohibitive, especially for Small and Medium-sized Enterprises (SMEs). Many organizations operate on legacy systems that are not compatible with modern AI technologies. Integrating AI with these existing systems can be technically challenging and costly, requiring significant upgrades or complete overhauls.

5.4. Public Perception and Societal Impact

The fear of job displacement due to AI automation is a significant concern. Workers across various sectors worry about losing their jobs to machines, leading to resistance against AI adoption (Ahmed 2023; Katah and Ozturk 2024). Building public trust in AI systems is critical, and it requires transparency in how AI decisions are made and clear communication about the benefits and limitations of AI. Promoting the ethical use of AI involves ensuring that AI applications adhere to societal values and norms, including respecting privacy, ensuring fairness, and preventing the misuse of AI technologies. Addressing the societal impact of AI requires programs for reskilling and upskilling the workforce, providing opportunities for workers to acquire new skills and transition to roles that complement AI technologies.

5.5. Other Challenges Specific to International Trade

International trade faces unique challenges, particularly when it comes to the transfer of data across borders, where different data protection laws and regulations apply. Ensuring compliance with these regulations while maintaining seamless data flow is a significant hurdle for businesses operating globally. Moreover, AI systems must navigate diverse customs regulations and trade barriers, which differ across countries

Another critical challenge involves managing language and cultural differences. The AI systems used in international trade need to handle multiple languages and cultural nuances to ensure accurate translations and context-aware communication. This is particularly important for maintaining clear and effective interactions between global stakeholders.

Geopolitical risks—such as trade wars, sanctions, and political instability—also add complexity to international trade. AI systems must be capable of predicting and mitigating these risks by using advanced models that incorporate real-time data analysis. Such models help businesses adjust their strategies in response to volatile geopolitical landscapes.

Furthermore, international trade involves complex, multi-stakeholder supply chains. AI systems must integrate and coordinate data from various sources, including suppliers, logistics providers, and customs authorities. Achieving seamless collaboration across these entities is critical for optimizing trade operations.

Currency exchange rate fluctuations are yet another factor that AI systems must account for when optimizing international trade activities. These fluctuations can significantly impact profit margins, making it crucial for AI models to incorporate real-time financial data to provide accurate forecasts and recommendations.

Lastly, the legal and ethical standards for AI usage vary across countries. Ensuring that AI systems comply with these diverse standards while maintaining operational efficiency is a major challenge. Businesses must ensure that their AI systems are designed to adapt to different regulatory and ethical frameworks, balancing compliance with effectiveness.

6. Policy Recommendations

Based on the analysis of AI's role in international trade and the challenges identified, several policy recommendations are proposed to enhance AI integration and maximize its benefits while addressing potential obstacles.

6.1. Enhance Data Quality and Accessibility

Governments and international organizations should invest in robust data infrastructures to ensure high-quality, accessible data. This includes creating standardized data formats and encouraging data sharing among stakeholders in the trade ecosystem. Public–private partnerships can help create comprehensive data repositories that AI systems can leverage for more accurate analysis. Additionally, developing and enforcing data privacy regulations that protect sensitive information without stifling innovation can build trust among businesses and consumers.

6.2. Foster Ethical and Fair AI Usage

Formulating clear ethical guidelines for AI in international trade is crucial for ensuring responsible use. These guidelines need to address critical issues like bias, fairness, transparency, and accountability, making sure AI systems function within established ethical boundaries. It is essential to implement policies that promote fairness and inclusivity in AI algorithms, along with regular audits to detect and reduce biases. Moreover, establishing a clear framework for accountability in AI decision-making is key. This should include defining who is responsible for errors or harm caused by AI systems, ensuring that there are mechanisms for compensation and remedy when things go wrong.

6.3. Address Technological Complexity and Implementation

Investing in education and training programs to develop a skilled workforce capable of developing, implementing, and maintaining AI systems is critical. This includes providing scholarships, grants, and incentives for students and professionals pursuing AI-related fields. Financial incentives such as tax breaks, grants, and low-interest loans can help businesses offset the high initial costs of AI implementation, encouraging wider adoption.

6.4. Enhance Public Perception and Societal Impact

Launching public awareness campaigns to educate people about both the benefits and limitations of AI is essential for building trust and widespread acceptance. Transparent communication about how AI systems function, as well as their potential impacts on society, is critical to ensuring informed public discourse. Additionally, establishing reskilling and upskilling programs for workers affected by AI-driven automation can help them transition into new roles that complement these emerging technologies. Equally important is promoting the development and use of AI systems that align with societal values and norms. This includes supporting research and initiatives focused on ethical AI practices, ensuring that AI operates within frameworks that prioritize fairness, transparency, and accountability.

6.5. International Cooperation

Harmonizing data protection and privacy regulations across countries is essential for facilitating smooth cross-border data transfers. International cooperation and agreements can help establish a standardized regulatory framework for AI in trade. By implementing AI-friendly customs and regulatory processes, countries can reduce delays and complexities in cross-border trade operations. In addition, encouraging the development of AI-powered natural language processing tools that handle multiple languages and cultural nuances is equally important, as these can improve communication and reduce misunderstandings in international trade transactions. Furthermore, developing AI models capable of predicting and managing geopolitical risks—such as trade disruptions due to political instability—is crucial. Governments and businesses should collaborate to establish contingency plans and strategies to mitigate these risks.

Promoting policies that support the integration of AI across the supply chain is another key area. Initiatives that facilitate data sharing and collaboration among suppliers, logistics providers, and customs authorities can greatly enhance efficiency. Lastly, aligning legal and ethical standards for AI usage across countries is necessary to ensure consistent and fair practices globally. International bodies and trade organizations should take the lead in developing guidelines that uphold these standards and promote the responsible use of AI in trade.

7. Conclusions

In this study, we have explored the transformative potential of AI in international trade. We provide a comprehensive analysis of AI's applications in optimizing trade operations, enhancing trade finance, and expanding market access. Through the case studies of Alibaba, DHL, and Maersk, we have seen how AI can fundamentally reshape the logistics, financial, and operational landscapes of global trade. These real-world examples highlight the significant opportunities AI presents in terms of improving efficiency, reducing costs, and enabling more agile responses to market demands.

However, while the potential of AI is vast, this study has also highlighted the challenges that remain. Issues surrounding data quality, privacy concerns, ethical use, and technological complexity require careful consideration to ensure that AI is implemented responsibly and effectively. Moreover, regulatory inconsistencies across borders add another layer of complexity, particularly in maintaining data privacy and compliance.

This research suggests that a collaborative approach between businesses, policymakers, and international organizations is essential for maximizing AI's benefits in trade. Robust data infrastructures, clear ethical frameworks, and targeted reskilling programs will be vital in mitigating the risks associated with AI adoption while ensuring that the technology can drive sustainable economic growth and innovation.

While this study offers a thorough analysis of AI's impact on international trade, it does come with certain limitations. Given the rapidly evolving nature of AI technologies, some findings may quickly become outdated as new developments emerge. Moreover, while the case studies provide valuable insights, they may not fully capture the diversity of AI applications and their varying effects across different regions and industries. Additionally, more extensive and diverse case studies are necessary to understand the nuanced impacts of AI across various contexts. Future research should consider longitudinal studies to examine the long-term effects of AI integration in international trade. Moreover, this study's multiple-case-study approach—examining how companies like Alibaba, DHL, and Maersk utilize AI—offers practical examples but cannot serve as the basis for generalizing conclusions. Future research could benefit from broader datasets and a wider range of case studies to validate and expand upon these findings. Lastly, quantitative analysis could provide more robust insights into the measurable impacts of AI on trade.

By incorporating quantitative methods, future studies could assess the broader trends and causal relationships between AI adoption and trade performance across different sectors and regions.

Funding: This research received no external funding.

Informed Consent Statement: Not applicable.

Data Availability Statement: Publicly available data have been used in this research.

Acknowledgments: We would like to thank the two anonymous reviewers for their valuable and insightful feedback.

Conflicts of Interest: The authors declare no conflicts of interest.

References

Ahmed, Ali. 2023. The Impact of AI on Job Markets: Challenges and Opportunities. Datafloq. Available online: https://datafloq.com/read/the-impact-of-ai-on-job-markets-challenges-and-opportunities/ (accessed on 15 October 2024).

Allen, C. Gregory. 2020. *Understanding AI Technology*. Washington, DC: DoD Joint Artificial Intelligence Center (JAIC). Available online: https://www.ai.mil/docs/Understanding%20AI%20Technology.pdf (accessed on 15 October 2024).

Anyoha. 2020. The History of Artificial Intelligence. *Science in the News*. Available online: https://sitn.hms.harvard.edu/flash/2017/history-artificial-intelligence/ (accessed on 7 March 2024).

Aruna, S., S. Mohana Priya, K. Reshmeetha, E. Salai Sudhayini, and A. Ajay Narayanan. 2023. Blockchain Integration with Artificial Intelligence and Internet of Things Technologies. Paper presented at 2023 7th International Conference on Intelligent Computing and Control Systems (ICICCS), Madurai, India, May 17–19.

Aysan, Ahmet, Ozcan Ozturk, and Noha Selim. 2024. Local power, global reach: The rise and impact of domestic payment networks in the financial landscape. *Journal of Science and Technology Policy Management, ahead-of-print*. [CrossRef]

Borges, Georg. 2021. AI systems and product liability. Paper presented at Eighteenth International Conference on Artificial Intelligence and Law, Online, June 21–25.

Cannas, V. Giada, Maria P. Ciano, Mattia Saltalamacchia, and Rafaele Secchi. 2024. Artificial intelligence in supply chain and operations management: A multiple case study research. *International Journal of Production Research* 62: 3333–60. [CrossRef]

Carlos González De Villaumbrosia. 2024. AI Implementation for Business Leaders. Available online: https://productschool.com/blog/artificial-intelligence/ai-implementation? (accessed on 15 October 2024).

Chinen, Mark. 2023. AI and international law. In *The International Governance of Artificial Intelligence*. Cheltenham: Edward Elgar Publishing, pp. 178–202. [CrossRef]

Chollet, Francois. 2017. *Deep Learning with Python*. New York: Simon and Schuster. Available online: http://books.google.ie/books?id=wzozEAAAQBAJ&printsec=frontcover&dq=Deep+Learning+With+Python&hl=&cd=1&source=gbs_api (accessed on 15 October 2024).

Chow, Peter, Ozcan Ozturk, and Henry Thompson. 2022. Short-Run Adjustments in Taiwan to Free Trade in a Multisector Specific Factors Model. *The International Trade Journal* 37: 595–607. [CrossRef]

Copeland, B. Jack. 2024. *Artificial intelligence (AI) | Definition, Examples, Types, Applications, Companies, & Facts*. Edinburgh: Encyclopedia Britannica. Available online: https://www.britannica.com/technology/artificial-intelligence (accessed on 15 October 2024).

DHL. 2021. How Digitalization Has Transformed Dhl Express' Operations. Available online: https://www.dhl.com/discover/en-global/about-dhl/reports-and-press-releases/digitalization-has-transformed-operations (accessed on 31 May 2024).

DHL. 2022. We, Robot: How Humans and AI Are Working Together in Logistics. Available online: https://www.dhl.com/global-en/delivered/digitalization/ai-in-logistics.html (accessed on 31 May 2024).

DHL. n.d. Interactive AI. Available online: https://www.dhl.com/us-en/home/innovation-in-logistics/logistics-trend-radar/gen-ai.html (accessed on 15 October 2024).

Diaz, Maria. 2024. What Is Deep Learning? Everything You Need to Know. *ZDNET*. Available online: https://www.zdnet.com/article/what-is-deep-learning-everything-you-need-to-know/#google_vignette (accessed on 15 October 2024).

Du-Harpur, Xinyi, Fiona Watt, Nicholas Luscombe, and Magnus Lynch. 2020. What is AI? Applications of artificial intelligence to dermatology. *British Journal of Dermatology* 183: 423–30. [CrossRef] [PubMed]

Enda, Maya. 2023. Exploring Alibaba Cloud's Cutting-Edge Artificial Intelligence Services. Available online: https://www.alibabacloud.com/blog/exploring-alibaba-clouds-cutting-edge-artificial-intelligence-services_600114 (accessed on 1 June 2024).

Ferencz, Janos, Javier López-González, and Irene Oliván García. 2022. *Artificial Intelligence and International Trade*. OECD Trade Policy Papers. Paris: OECD Publishing. [CrossRef]

Firt, Erez. 2023. Artificial understanding: A step toward robust AI. *AI & SOCIETY* 39: 1653–65. [CrossRef]

Flyvbjerg, Bent. 2006. Five Misunderstandings About Case Study Research. *Qualitative Inquiry* 12: 219–45. [CrossRef]

Garg, Seema, Nativa Mahajan, and Jayanta Ghosh. 2022. Artificial Intelligence as an Emerging Technology in Global Trade. In *Research Anthology on Macroeconomics and the Achievement of Global Stability*. Hershey: IGI Global, pp. 604–23. [CrossRef]

Hagendorff, Thilo, and Katharina Wezel. 2019. 15 challenges for AI: Or what AI (currently) can't do. *AI & Society* 35: 355–65. [CrossRef]

Heath, Nick. 2019. What Is Artificial General Intelligence? *ZDNET*. Available online: https://www.zdnet.com/article/what-is-artificial-general-intelligence/ (accessed on 15 October 2024).

Heath, Nick. 2020. What Is Machine Learning? Everything You Need to Know. *ZDNET*. Available online: https://www.zdnet.com/article/what-is-machine-learning-everything-you-need-to-know/ (accessed on 15 October 2024).

Investopedia. 2021. Natural Language Processing (NLP): What It Means, How It Works. Available online: https://www.investopedia.com/terms/n/natural-language-processing-nlp.asp (accessed on 8 March 2024).

Iqbal, Raja. 2023. Here's How 3 Global Giants Improve the Supply Chain with AI. Built In. Available online: https://builtin.com/articles/artificial-intelligence-supply-chain#:~:text=Real-time%20insights%20into%20supply,optimize%20the%20flow%20of%20goods (accessed on 15 October 2024).

Kanade. 2022a. Narrow Artificial Intelligence Definition, Challenges, Best Practices. *Spiceworks*. Available online: https://www.spiceworks.com/tech/artificial-intelligence/articles/what-is-narrow-ai/ (accessed on 7 March 2024).

Kanade. 2022b. What Is General Artificial Intelligence (AI)? Definition, Challenges, and Trends. *Spiceworks*. Available online: https://www.spiceworks.com/tech/artificial-intelligence/articles/what-is-general-ai/ (accessed on 8 March 2024).

Katah, Iman, and Ozcan Ozturk. 2024. Smart Cities and Sustainability: Comparative Analysis and Strategic Insights for Qatar. *Preprints*, 2024101106. [CrossRef]

Khurana, Diksha, Aditya Koli, Kiran Khatter, and Sukhdev Singh. 2022. Natural language processing: State of the art, current trends and challenges. *Multimedia Tools and Applications* 82: 3713–44. [CrossRef]

Kunst, Jonas, and Kinga Bierwiaczonek. 2023. Utilizing AI questionnaire translations in cross-cultural and intercultural research: Insights and recommendations. *International Journal of Intercultural Relations* 97: 101888. [CrossRef]

Labbe, Mark, and Ivy Wigmore. 2023. Narrow AI (Weak AI). *Enterprise AI*. Available online: https://www.techtarget.com/searchenterpriseai/definition/narrow-AI-weak-AI (accessed on 15 October 2024).

Maersk. n.d. Technology at Maersk. maersk.com. Available online: https://www.maersk.com/about/technology (accessed on 31 May 2024).

Makar, Katarina. 2023. Driven by Artificial Intelligence (AI)—Improving Operational Efficiency and Competitiveness in Business. Paper presented at 2023 46th MIPRO ICT and Electronics Convention (MIPRO), Opatija, Croatia, May 22–26.

Naqa, E. Isam, and Martin J. Murphy. 2022. *Machine and Deep Learning in Oncology, Medical Physics and Radiology*. Cham: Springer Nature. Available online: http://books.google.ie/books?id=mJxcEAAAQBAJ&printsec=frontcover&dq=Machine+Learning+in+Radiation+Oncology?&hl=&cd=3&source=gbs_api (accessed on 15 October 2024).

Oyewole, Aadedoyin, Chinwe Okoye, Onyeka Ofodile, and Emuesiri Ejairu. 2024. Reviewing predictive analytics in supply chain management: Applications and benefits. *World Journal of Advanced Research and Reviews* 21: 568–74. [CrossRef]

Ozturk, Ozcan. 2017. Effects of price transmission and exchange rate elasticities of three developing countries on the world cotton trade. *Applied Economics and Finance* 5: 91. [CrossRef]

Ozturk, Ozturk, Akturk Ergun, and Gultekin Sena. 2024. An empirical examination of trade policy and food security in MENA countries: Evidence from quantile regressions. *Global Business and Economics Review* 31: 259–72. [CrossRef]

Pal, Suraj, Shubham Halder, and Prof A. D. Talware. 2023. Artificial Intelligence Tools for Enhancing Customer Experience. *International Journal for Research in Applied Science and Engineering Technology* 11: 7040–47. [CrossRef]

Perc, Matjaz, Mahmut Ozer, and Janja Hojnik. 2019. Social and juristic challenges of artificial intelligence. *Palgrave Communications* 5: 61. [CrossRef]

Pathak, Soham, Antara Pawar, Shruti Taware, Sarthak Kulkarni, and Afsha Akkalkot. 2023. A Survey on Machine Learning Algorithms for Risk-Controlled Algorithmic Trading. *International Journal of Scientific Research in Science and Technology* 10: 1069–89. [CrossRef]

Praveenadevi, D., S. Sreekala, B. Girimurugan, K. V. R. Krishna Teja, G. Naga Kamal, and A. C. Chandra. 2023. An Enhanced Method on Using Deep Learning Techniques in Supply Chain Management. Paper presented at 2023 International Conference on Disruptive Technologies (ICDT), Greater Noida, India, May 11–12.

Quaresmini, Camilla, and Giuseppe Primiero. 2023. Data quality dimensions for fair AI. *arXiv*. [CrossRef]

Raj, Anita. 2024. AI in Transportation and Logistics. ThroughPut Inc. Available online: https://throughput.world/blog/ai-in-transportation-and-logistics/#:~:text=The%20world%E2%80%99s%20largest%20shipping%20company,for%20each%20of%20its%20shipments (accessed on 15 October 2024).

Rajagopal, Manikandan, Keyurkumar M. Nayak, K. Balasubramanian, Irfan A. Shaikh, Sunil Adhav, and Monika Gupta. 2023. Application of Artificial Intelligence in the Supply Chain Finance. Paper presented at 2023 Eighth International Conference on Science Technology Engineering and Mathematics (ICONSTEM), Chennai, India, April 6–7.

Rojek, Izabela, Malgorzata Jasiulewicz-Kaczmarek, Mariusz Piechowski, and Dariusz Mikołajewski. 2023. An Artificial Intelligence Approach for Improving Maintenance to Supervise Machine Failures and Support Their Repair. *Applied Sciences* 13: 4971. [CrossRef]

Roldós. 2021. 10 Examples of Natural Language Processing in Action. *MonkeyLearn Blog*. Available online: https://monkeylearn.com/blog/natural-language-processing-examples/ (accessed on 8 March 2024).

Saha, Chandra, Reshmi Menon, Sudha M. Paulin, Santosh Yerasuri, Hasi Saha, and Padam Dongol. 2023. The Impact of Artificial Intelligence on Business Strategy and Decision-Making Processes. *European Economic Letters* 13: 926–34. [CrossRef]

Simplilearn. 2024. Top 15 Challenges of Artificial Intelligence in 2024. *Simplilearn.com*. Available online: https://www.simplilearn.com/challenges-of-artificial-intelligence-article (accessed on 15 October 2024).

Singh, Deepti, Manju, and Aman Jatain. 2024. Artificial Intelligence and Natural Language Processing Inspired Chabot Technologies. *Recent Advances in Computer Science and Communications* 17: 11–20. [CrossRef]

Tjoa, Simon, Peter K. Marlies Temper, Marlies Temper, Jakob Zanol, Markus Wagner, and Andreas Holzinger. 2022. AIRMan: An Artificial Intelligence (AI) Risk Management System. Paper presented at 2022 International Conference on Advanced Enterprise Information System (AEIS), London, UK, December 2–4.

Tripathi, Archit S. 2023. The Subsets of Artificial Intelligence. *Scaler Topics*. Available online: https://www.scaler.com/topics/artificial-intelligence-tutorial/subsets-of-ai/ (accessed on 15 October 2024).

Vaka, Dilip K. 2024. From Complexity to Simplicity: AI's Route Optimization in Supply Chain Management. *Journal of Artificial Intelligence, Machine Learning and Data Science* 2: 386–89. [CrossRef]

Vijayakumar, Harsha. 2023. Transforming service operations with ai: A case for business value. *International Journal of Managing Information Technology* 15: 19–31. [CrossRef]

Wang, Michael D. 2023. Artificial Intelligence Techniques for Political Risk Management: An NLP Analysis of the 2019 US-China Trade War. In *Machine Learning and Data Mining Annual Volume 2023*. London: IntechOpen. [CrossRef]

Wang, Xun. 2023. Exploring the Power of Alibaba Cloud AI: Revolutionizing Industries. Medium. Available online: https://medium.com/@wangxun37851/exploring-the-power-of-alibaba-cloud-ai-revolutionizing-industries-a4178571dbf1 (accessed on 15 October 2024).

WTO. 2020. Annual Report 2020. Available online: https://www.wto-ilibrary.org/content/books/9789287050458 (accessed on 15 October 2024). [CrossRef]

Yin, Robert K. 2018. *Case Study Research and Applications. Design and Methods*, 6th ed. Thousand Oaks: COSMOS Corporation, Sage.

Disclaimer/Publisher's Note: The statements, opinions and data contained in all publications are solely those of the individual author(s) and contributor(s) and not of MDPI and/or the editor(s). MDPI and/or the editor(s) disclaim responsibility for any injury to people or property resulting from any ideas, methods, instructions or products referred to in the content.

economies

MDPI

Article

The Impact of Trade Openness and ICT on Technical Efficiency of Township Economies in South Africa

Brian Tavonga Mazorodze

Department of Accounting and Economics, Faculty of Economic and Management Sciences, Sol Plaatje University, Kimberley 8301, South Africa; brian.mazorodze@spu.ac.za

Abstract: While the impact of trade openness on economic growth has been widely studied, its effect on township economies remains underexplored. In view of this empirical gap, this study examines the impact of trade openness proxied by export intensity on the technical efficiency of five major township economies in South Africa—Soweto, Khayelitsha, Alexandra, Tembisa, and Soshanguve—while considering the moderating role of information and communication technology (ICT). This aim speaks to the ongoing quest to unravel factors limiting the transformation of South African townships since the advent of democracy in 1994. The analysis uses an instrumental variable stochastic frontier model and annual panel data covering the 1995–2023 period. On average, the five townships were found to have operated 19% below their full potential during the sampling period, with Soweto being the least efficient. Holding constant factors peculiar to township economies, such as crime rates and informality, the main results show that ICT plays a positive moderating role in reducing trade-related technical inefficiencies of these townships. This finding underscores the importance of targeted policy interventions, such as investments in digital infrastructure and digital literacy programs, to ensure that township economies benefit from global markets and achieve their full potential.

Keywords: trade openness; technical efficiency; townships

1. Introduction

Township economies in South Africa have long been characterized by informality, constrained market access, and limited integration into the broader national and global economy. Historically marginalized under apartheid-era spatial planning, these economies continue to face structural barriers that hinder their growth and competitiveness. Despite various policy interventions aimed at fostering inclusive economic development, townships remain economically isolated, with low levels of formal investment and technological adoption. Given these persistent challenges, trade openness and information and communication technology (ICT) present two avenues for enhancing productivity and efficiency in these underdeveloped areas that the majority of the country's poor people call home.

Trade openness has the potential to unlock new market opportunities for township businesses by facilitating access to international markets, fostering competition, and encouraging innovation. The theoretical and empirical literature suggests that increased trade exposure can drive economic growth by improving resource allocation and enabling firms to benefit from economies of scale. However, it is argued that the extent to which township economies can capitalize on trade liberalization depends on their ability to overcome structural inefficiencies and leverage complementary factors such as technological adoption. In this regard, information and communication technology (ICT) plays a crucial role in modernizing production processes, improving access to market information, and reducing transaction costs. Digital platforms, mobile banking, and e-commerce solutions have the potential to integrate township enterprises into regional and global value chains, mitigating the disadvantages of geographical and economic marginalization.

Despite the growing recognition of trade openness and ICT as key drivers of economic development, limited empirical research has examined their combined effects within the context of township economies. Most existing studies focus either on the impact of trade openness at a national or sectoral level or on ICT adoption in urban and formal business settings. Consequently, there is a gap in understanding how these factors interact in the unique setting of township economies, where informality, infrastructure deficits, and institutional constraints present unique challenges. This study seeks to fill this gap by probing the moderating role of ICT in the relationship between trade openness and economic growth in five major township economies in South Africa: Khayelitsha, Soshanguve, Soweto, Alexandra, and Tembisa.

Prominent studies on the growth effects of international trade (Dollar, 1992; Frankel & Romer, 1999) have largely demonstrated a positive and significant impact of trade openness on economic growth. While the evidence is, to a large extent, supportive of a positive link between openness and growth, the extent to which the benefits of trade openness accrue to township economies remains underexplored. In addition, very few studies have considered the moderating effect of ICT, which is surprising given the growing prominence of digitalization and its potential role in increasing market access. Against this background, this study contributes to the empirical evidence by examining the impact of trade openness on the technical efficiency of township economies in South Africa while considering the moderating role of ICTs. It defines technical efficiency as the ability of townships to produce at full potential.

Examining the impact of trade openness on the technical efficiency of township economies in South Africa and understanding the moderating role of ICTs is important for several reasons. First, township economies have failed to transform into cities since the advent of democracy in 1994 despite South Africa being a more open economy today than it was thirty years ago. It is generally understood from the literature that township economies face a myriad of factors that inhibit them from achieving their full potential (Moos & Sambo, 2018). Second, the majority of previously disadvantaged populations reside in township economies, where key drivers of economic activity—such as informal businesses, shebeens, and Spaza shops—operate on the margins of global markets due to poor connectivity and limited network coverage (Bvuma & Marnewick, 2020b). It is necessary, against this background, to shed light on whether improvements in ICT infrastructure can help township economies integrate into the global economy and reap the benefits of international trade.

Drawing from existing literature, there is strong evidence to suggest that trade openness and ICT adoption can serve as catalysts for economic transformation by enhancing access to global markets and fostering growth within townships. Trade openness and ICTs can particularly enhance the competitiveness of township economies by reducing transaction costs and enhancing access to information. It is additionally argued that digital technologies facilitate trade participation by lowering entry barriers, enabling e-commerce, and improving market linkages. Despite this potential, the extent to which ICTs moderate the trade-growth relationship in these economies is less known, and understanding this link could be key to unlocking the growth potential of township economies. This paper specifically tests the hypothesis that low ICT infrastructure may impede the ability of township economies to capitalize on trade opportunities.

The study contributes to the literature in the following four ways. First, it provides empirical evidence on the link between trade openness and technical efficiency in township economies, an area that remains underexplored in the existing literature. Second, it assesses the role of ICT as a potential enabler of efficiency gains, shedding light on the importance of ICT investments and their implications for township development. Third, given the current absence of a model that addresses both heterogeneity endogeneity and idiosyncratic endogeneity, this study uses an ad hoc procedure in which a within transformation is applied on frontier inputs based on the Karakaplan (2022) model. This procedure yields inefficiency scores that are not contaminated with unobserved factors specific to each township while at the same time circumventing the bias in frontier and inefficiency specifications. Fourth, it offers policy insights into how township economies can harness globalization and technological progress to enhance their competitiveness.

Given South Africa's ongoing efforts to promote economic transformation and digital inclusion, the findings of this study have important implications for policymakers. In addition, townships are characterized by high levels of poverty and economic stagnation, exacerbated by geographical marginalization. Therefore, targeting these areas from a research perspective could yield policies that may help the government to achieve Sustainable Development Goals (SDGs) 1 (No Poverty) and 2 (Zero Hunger).

Within the literature, this study is closely related to two strands of inquiry. The first strand comprises studies focusing on factors that hinder the growth and development of township economies (Mbonyane & Ladzani, 2011; Moos & Sambo, 2018; Bvuma & Marnewick, 2020b; Wiid & Cant, 2021). A central conclusion reached in these studies is that township economies are constrained by the lack of government support, poor infrastructure, and lack of access to funding. The second strand of the literature comprises studies focused on the impact of trade openness on cities (Karayalcin & Yilmazkuday, 2015; Munir & Ameer, 2018; Fang et al., 2020). A common finding in these studies is that trade openness is associated with the expansion of cities and urbanization. While these conclusions shed important insights, they do not reveal much about how trade openness and ICTs affect the growth and development of township economies. This study, therefore, differs from the first strand of the literature by specifically focusing on the impact of trade openness and limited access to global markets. It differs from the second strand of the literature by exclusively focusing on township economies whose place in the trade-growth literature is yet to receive its fair share of scholarly attention.

The primary objective of this study is to empirically examine whether trade openness improves the technical efficiency of township economies in South Africa and whether ICT moderates this relationship. The specific problem motivating this analysis is the persistence of structural inefficiencies in township economies despite decades of economic liberalization. Specifically, the analysis poses the following question: do township economies benefit from trade openness, and can ICT help them overcome the structural barriers to global integration? This analysis seeks to contribute to the literature by combining trade, ICT, and efficiency analysis at a township level, which is a terrain rarely addressed in the existing literature.

The results corroborate the notion that township economies in South Africa operate below their full potential. On average, a typical township is found to have operated 19% below its full potential between 1995 and 2023. Evidence demonstrates the critical role of ICT in reducing inefficiencies associated with the participation of township economies in global trade. In particular, in the absence of adequate ICT infrastructure, exporting is associated with higher technical inefficiencies, highlighting the need for digital transformation for townships to maximize the benefits of participating in global markets. This conclusion aligns with endogenous growth theory, which emphasizes the role of technology and knowledge diffusion in enhancing efficiency when participating in global trade. From a policy perspective, the results raise the need for targeted interventions such as the expansion of digital infrastructure, subsidies for ICT adoption, and digital literacy programs aimed at enhancing the integration of township economies into global markets.

The rest of the study is organized as follows. Section 2 reviews the theoretical and empirical literature. Section 3 provides the methodology. Section 4 presents and interprets the empirical results. Section 5 discusses the findings, while Section 6 provides the conclusion and policy implications and suggests areas for further study.

2. Literature Review

Township economies in South Africa have their roots in the country's apartheid era when racially segregated urban areas were created to enforce spatial inequality. They were primarily established as residential areas for black South Africans, who were denied access to better opportunities in productive cities. As a result, township economies remained underdeveloped, with limited infrastructure and resources. The apartheid government's policy of economic exclusion meant that these areas were largely isolated from global markets, with the majority of businesses being small, informal, and reliant on local demand.

In the post-apartheid period, where trade liberalization and market access have opened new avenues for growth, township economies are still struggling to compete on an international scale due to persistent barriers such as low productivity, inadequate infrastructure, and a lack of skills. Global market forces, coupled with the challenges of operating in a highly competitive environment, have made it difficult for township businesses to break into international supply chains. The lack of digital infrastructure and the slow adoption of ICTs have further hindered their ability to engage with global markets, leaving many township economies at the margins of South Africa's broader economic growth and limiting their capacity to benefit from globalization.

This section reviews the existing literature on three key areas: (1) the impact of trade openness on economic growth and efficiency, with a focus on developing and marginalized economies; (2) the role of ICT in economic transformation, particularly in improving productivity and market integration; and (3) the intersection of trade openness and ICT in driving economic development.

2.1. Theoretical Framework

This study is grounded in endogenous growth theory, particularly the models developed by Romer (1990) and Grossman and Helpman (1991), which emphasize the role of technological progress and knowledge diffusion in driving long-term economic growth. Romer's (1990) framework posits that technological advancements, facilitated by knowledge spillovers and innovation, enhance productivity and efficiency. In the context of township economies, ICTs serve as a conduit for these spillovers by enabling firms to access, absorb, and implement new knowledge and production techniques. The adoption of digital technologies reduces transaction costs, facilitates market access, and improves business processes, all of which improve technical efficiency. However, the extent of these efficiency gains may be contingent upon the level of digital infrastructure and firms' ability to leverage ICTs effectively.

Grossman and Helpman's (1991) open economy endogenous growth model further provides a theoretical lens through which to examine the role of trade openness in shaping efficiency outcomes. Their framework suggests that exposure to international markets enhances productivity by fostering technology diffusion, competitive discipline, and learning-by-doing effects. In township economies, trade openness creates opportunities for firms to integrate into global value chains, adopt foreign technologies, and improve their production efficiency. However, without adequate ICT adoption, these benefits may not be fully realized, as firms may struggle to engage in digital trade, optimize supply chains, or absorb external knowledge efficiently. The interaction between ICTs and trade openness is thus conceptualized as a moderating mechanism that determines the extent to which township firms can enhance their technical efficiency. This study, therefore, situates itself within the broader discourse on endogenous growth and technological diffusion, examining how the synergistic effects of ICTs and trade openness shape efficiency dynamics in township economies.

In line with these theories, this study assumes that township economies produce output (Y) using capital stock (K), labor (L), and human capital (H). Further assumed is that, as a result of inefficiencies, the actual observed output deviates from the potential frontier output. The production function is specified as

$$Y = AF(K, L, H) \tag{1}$$

where A represents total factor productivity proxying efficiency in the use of K, L, and H. Assuming a Cobb–Douglas technology, we have

$$Y = AK^{\alpha}L^{\beta}H^{\theta} \tag{2}$$

where α, β, and θ are output elasticities with respect to capital stock, labour, and human capital. Trade openness and ICT are hypothesized to affect Y indirectly by influencing technical inefficiency. With this hypothesis, A can be specified as

$$A = e^{v-u} \tag{3}$$

where v captures deviations of observed output from potential frontier output due to factors beyond the control of township economies, and u is a term capturing deviations of observed output due to technical inefficiency. The final specification is given by

$$u = f(z) \tag{4}$$

where z captures the sources of technical inefficiency, including trade openness, ICT, and their interaction. It is hypothesized that ICT facilitates the benefits of participating in global trade; hence, townships that invest more in ICT are expected to benefit more from trading in global markets. This hypothesis is plausible given the widely documented role of ICT as a complement to international trade. ICT facilitates trade by reducing transaction costs, improving market access, and enhancing business productivity through digital platforms. In township economies, where structural impediments such as poor infrastructure and limited financial access constrain growth, ICT serves as a catalyst for local economic growth. Theoretically, as derived from open economy endogenous growth theories, ICT can enhance the benefits of trade openness by improving firms' ability to integrate into broader markets, access price information, and optimize production. In the context of this study, the interaction between ICT and trade openness is therefore expected to influence the technical efficiency of township economies, as firms that leverage ICT are likely to overcome traditional barriers to market entry and global competition.

2.2. Empirical Literature

Empirical studies examining the relationship between trade openness, ICT, and technical efficiency have largely focused on either macro, sectoral, or firm-level effects. A substantial body of literature highlights the role of trade openness in enhancing firm-level productivity by exposing producers to competitive pressures, encouraging technological upgrading, and facilitating knowledge spillovers from international markets (Yasin, 2022; Mazorodze, 2020; Wenlong et al., 2023). Similarly, research on the use of ICT emphasizes its contribution to efficiency gains through improved information flows, reduced transaction costs, and enhanced production processes (Adeleye et al., 2021; Ndubuisi et al., 2022). However, the combined effect of trade openness and ICT on technical efficiency, particularly within the context of township economies, remains less understood.

Given the structural constraints and historical legacies of township economies, understanding how ICT adoption moderates the efficiency gains from trade openness is critical. Some studies suggest that ICTs enhance the absorptive capacity of producers, allowing them to capitalize on trade-induced efficiency gains (Suatmi et al., 2017), while others indicate that the benefits of trade liberalization may be limited in the absence of sufficient digital infrastructure (Adeleye et al., 2021). In addition, research has shown that factors such as crime and informality can also hamper the ability of townships to achieve their full potential. The following subsections review key empirical findings on these relationships, with a focus on studies that analyze their implications in developing economies and marginalized areas.

2.2.1. Trade Openness and Growth

A significant strand of the literature examines the relationship between trade openness and economic growth at a macro-economic level, with early contributions such as Dollar (1992) and Frankel and Romer (1999) demonstrating a positive and sizeable effect of trade openness on economic growth. Dollar (1992) argues that trade openness enhances growth by improving resource allocation and facilitating technology diffusion. Using cross-country data, he finds outward-oriented policies facilitating growth compared to restrictive trade policies. Similarly, Frankel and Romer (1999) provide empirical evidence that greater trade integration leads to higher income, primarily through increased specialization, economies of scale, and knowledge spillovers using an instrumental variable approach to pin down causality.

These studies largely suggest that trade liberalization promotes economic growth by expanding market access, encouraging investment, and accelerating technological progress. However, the magnitude of these effects depends on complementary factors such as institutional quality, infrastructure, and human capital. While trade openness creates opportunities for efficiency improvements, its benefits are not automatic, particularly in economies with structural constraints. Recent studies supportive of a positive causal effect of trade openness on economic growth include but are not limited to Jalil and Rauf (2021), Ibrahim and Abdulmalik (2023), and Abdulkarim (2023). A key methodological caveat raised and addressed in these studies relates to the endogeneity of trade openness. Most studies in this area use the panel Generalized Method of Moments (GMM), which uses lagged values of endogenous regressors as instruments.

2.2.2. ICT and Growth

Several studies have explored the impact of ICT on economic growth. These studies emphasize the role of ICT in enhancing productivity, innovation, and knowledge diffusion. Early studies, such as Röller and Waverman (2001), establish a positive relationship between ICT infrastructure and economic performance, arguing that digital connectivity facilitates efficiency gains by reducing transaction costs and improving access to information. More recently, using the partial least squares, Fernández-Portillo et al. (2020) similarly demonstrate that ICT contributes positively to economic growth, particularly in developed economies where digital adoption is widespread.

Some of the studies, including Pradhan et al. (2021), have differentiated between long-run and short-run effects. Pradhan et al. particularly focus on the role played by ICT in economic growth using data on 20 Indian states observed between 1991 and 2018. The results from their analysis demonstrated a causal effect of ICT on economic growth. This result is similarly documented in D. Wang et al. (2021), Dumor et al. (2024), and Saba et al. (2024). Particularly confirmed by Dumor et al. (2024) is that ICT and infrastructural growth have provided the East African Community (EAC) with opportunities to boost intra-regional trade. These findings, therefore, collectively suggest that ICTs are a catalyst for economic growth and could be vital for township economies where the participation of firms in global markets is impeded by structural barriers and geographical marginalization.

2.2.3. Trade Openness, ICT and Growth

Recent studies have considered the moderating effect of ICT on trade openness. These studies are mainly premised on the notion that ICTs improve trade efficiency by reducing information asymmetries, lowering transaction costs, and expanding market access. These effects are particularly pronounced in developing economies, where digital infrastructure enables producers to integrate into global supply chains and capitalize on international trade opportunities. Notable studies include Awad and Albaity (2022), who cite openness as one of the factors through which ICT penetration indirectly promotes per capita income growth. Others include Clarke and Wallsten (2006) and Freund and Weinhold (2004). Within this literature, common proxies for ICT include internet penetration, mobile phone subscriptions, fixed broadband subscriptions, ICT investment, telecommunication infrastructure, and ICT service exports.

2.2.4. Summary and Empirical Gap

From the above brief review, it is clear that a well-established body of literature has explored the relationship between trade openness and economic growth, with seminal studies such as Dollar (1992) and Frankel and Romer (1999) demonstrating that trade liberalization enhances economic performance. Parallel to this, the role of ICT in economic growth has been widely examined, with studies such as Röller and Waverman (2001) and Fernández-Portillo et al. (2020) highlighting ICT's ability to reduce transaction costs, enhance productivity, and foster innovation. Additionally, growing research explores how ICT moderates the trade-growth nexus, arguing that digital infrastructure strengthens the efficiency gains from trade, particularly in developing economies (Clarke & Wallsten, 2006; Awad & Albaity, 2022).

Despite these insights, little attempt has been made to examine the relationship between trade openness, ICT, and economic efficiency at the township level, where structural constraints may limit firms' ability to fully capitalize on trade liberalization. Existing studies primarily focus on macro or industry-level analyses, overlooking the unique challenges and opportunities within township economies. This study extends the approach of Abdulkarim (2023) by incorporating an inefficiency term to account for deviations from frontier output due to technical inefficiency. By applying a stochastic frontier model, this research provides a more nuanced understanding of how ICT and trade openness jointly influence efficiency in township economies, something that has been overlooked in the literature.

3. Methodology

The empirical framework of this study uses the stochastic frontier model pioneered by Aigner et al. (1977). This approach is preferred over its alternative, the data envelopment approach (DEA), due to its ability to separate random noise from technical inefficiencies (Aigner et al., 1977). Township economies are generally confronted by adverse environmental factors that are beyond their control, making the stochastic frontier analysis (SFA) more appealing. The analysis follows Abdulkarim (2023), who extended a Cobb-Douglas specification to accommodate the effect of trade openness. This study improves Abdulkarim's specification by adding an inefficiency term within a stochastic frontier framework to suit the context of the analysis. The application of a stochastic frontier model in analyzing township economies is particularly justified by the need to measure not only the productive capacity of these economies but also the extent of inefficiency that hinders their growth. Township economies operate in unique environments characterized by resource constraints and systemic inefficiencies. Unlike the traditional production function model applied in Abdulkarim (2023), which assumes that all deviations from the frontier are purely random, the stochastic frontier model explicitly accounts for inefficiency, making it a suitable framework for assessing productivity in these settings. By decomposing output deviations into inefficiency and statistical noise, the model allows for a more nuanced understanding of the constraints faced by township economies. In addition, given the role of ICT and trade openness as potential drivers of efficiency, the chosen framework provides a relevant empirical approach to analyze how these environmental factors interact with inefficiency.

3.1. Model Specification

Building on the theoretical framework presented earlier, the starting point empirically is specifications that take the following form:

$$Y_{it} = f(X_{it}\beta) + \varepsilon_{it} \tag{5}$$

$$\varepsilon_{it} = v_{it} - u_{it}$$

$$u_{it} = f(z_{it}) \tag{6}$$

where subscripts i and t denote township and year, respectively, Y is output, X is a vector of inputs (labour, human capital, and physical capital stock), β is a vector of frontier parameters, and ε_{it} is an error term composed of the random component (v_{it}) and the inefficiency term (u_{it}). The inefficiency term (u_{it}) specifically measures the distance between each township's level of output and its full potential. Equation (6) is then specified to identify the sources of inefficiency. In this equation, z is a vector of variables that affect efficiency. With the actual variables, the econometric specifications in this study take the following form.

$$\log(y)_{i,t} = \gamma_0 + \gamma_1 \log(L)_{i,t} + \gamma_2 \log(K)_{i,t} + \gamma_3 EDU_{i,t} + \varepsilon_{i,t} \tag{7}$$

$$\begin{aligned} u_{i,t} = \alpha_0 + \alpha_1 OP_{i,t} + \alpha_2 \log(ICT)_{i,t} + \alpha_3 OP_{i,t} \times \log(ICT)_{i,t} + \alpha_4 \log(C)_{i,t} \\ + \alpha_5 INF_{i,t} + \epsilon_{ii,t} \end{aligned} \tag{8}$$

$$i = 1, \ldots, 5; t = 1995, \ldots, 2023$$

where $y_{i,t}$ is the level of local GDP in township i year t; L is labor captured by the number of employed workers; K is fixed capital stock; EDU is education, which is the share of literate population capturing the quality of labor; OP signifies trade openness; ICT captures the stock of information and communication technologies; C captures crime measured by the total number of reported crimes; and INF is informality measured as the number of informal workers as a share of total employment proxying the informal sector. The inclusion of the interaction term (OP $*$ ICT) is motivated by the hypothesis that the impact of trade openness on technical efficiency in township economies is conditional upon the level of ICT infrastructure. That is, while trade openness theoretically enhances efficiency through exposure to global markets and technology spillovers, these benefits may not materialize in contexts where townships lack the technological capacity to engage effectively with international markets.

This interaction term allows the model to capture the moderating role of ICT, consistent with the framework of open economy endogenous growth models (Grossman & Helpman, 1991), which emphasize the importance of absorptive capacity often facilitated by technology in realizing the gains from trade. Specifically, ICT facilitates access to market information, reduces transaction costs, and improves supply chain management, which ultimately enables producers in marginalized township economies to better participate in global markets.

The inclusion of crime and informality is driven by the need to account for factors that are peculiar to township economies. A potential criticism of these controls, however, is that both variables are likely to be measured with error. Crimes tend to suffer from underreporting, and the share of informal workers may not accurately reflect the true size of the informal sector. A mitigating factor is that the stochastic frontier method accounts for measurement error and noise in data (Aigner et al., 1977; Meeusen & van Den Broeck, 1977).

In terms of the channels, it is important to note that output growth in the empirical model above is achievable through the accumulation of physical capital, human capital, and labor (Mankiw et al., 1992). Trade openness and ICTs, therefore, affect output growth through raising productivity. Since $u_{i,t}$ is technical inefficiency, a negative slope coefficient in Equation (4) implies a positive relationship with technical efficiency. Negative and significant estimates of α_1, α_2, and α_3 would support the hypothesis that trade openness moves township economies closer to their full potential and that the effect increases with ICTs.

A key econometric concern in this analysis is endogeneity, which arises when explanatory variables are correlated with the error term. In the context of township economies, factors such as labor input, capital investment, trade openness, and ICT infrastructure may respond to unobserved shocks or be jointly determined with output, violating the exogeneity assumption. If not addressed, endogeneity leads to biased and inconsistent parameter estimates, undermining the reliability of the results. For example, if more efficient townships attract higher ICT investments or export more due to unobservable managerial quality, the model will overstate the true effect of ICT or trade openness on efficiency. Labor may also be endogenous since producers in townships often adjust employment based on productivity and wages. Capital, on the other hand, is likely endogenous since investment decisions are normally based on expected profits. To address this potential econometric challenge, the study adopts an instrumental variable (IV) stochastic frontier model, which instruments endogenous regressors with their lagged values.

The study specifically follows an approach proposed by Karakaplan (2022). Compared to other panel stochastic frontier models, such as the true-fixed effects of Greene (2005) and the frontier model of Battese and Coelli (1995), this approach accounts for the endogeneity of both frontier inputs and the sources of inefficiency. Using Karakaplan's (2022) approach, against the background of these endogeneity concerns, this study instruments labor, capital, openness, and ICT using their lagged values. The validity of these instrumental variables hinges on their relevance (strong correlation with the endogenous regressors) and exogeneity (uncorrelated with the error term). To establish relevance, first-stage regression results ought to have a strong predictive power of the instruments for the endogenous variables, typically assessed using the F-statistical test from the weak instrument test (Karakaplan, 2022). In the present case, using lagged values assumes that past values of labor, capital,

OP, and ICT can only affect output by influencing current employment levels, capital stock, openness, and ICT. This is plausible since lagged values of labor, capital, openness, and ICT capture the dynamic adjustment process inherent in production decisions while remaining exogenous to contemporaneous efficiency shocks. In addition to this intuition, a formal weak instrument test was performed post-estimation.

An important limitation of Karakaplan's (2022) approach is, however, that it contaminates technical inefficiency with unobserved heterogeneity, which makes it susceptible to overstating the levels of inefficiency. To circumvent this problem, this study applies the within transformation on frontier inputs to eliminate time-invariant factors specific to each township (such as historical, institutional, or geographic characteristics that may influence both output and inefficiency) as recommended by H. J. Wang and Ho (2010). The within transformation, commonly used in panel data analysis, involves de-meaning each variable by subtracting its time average for each cross-sectional unit (i.e., township). This essentially removes any township-specific fixed effects that do not vary over time, allowing for a cleaner identification of the relationships between explanatory variables and the dependent variable. In the context of the stochastic frontier model, this helps isolate the inefficiency effects from confounding township-level factors that are constant over time.

The frontier equation and the inefficiency specification can be estimated using either the two-step approach or the one-step approach. In the two-step approach, the frontier equation is first estimated using the maximum likelihood estimator. The sources of inefficiency are then estimated in the second step. It has long been demonstrated, however, that this traditional approach is biased (H. J. Wang & Schmidt, 2002). Therefore, this study uses the one-step approach in which the frontier equation and the inefficiency specification are simultaneously estimated, as recommended by H. J. Wang and Schmidt (2002) to prevent this bias. The empirical estimation is performed using Stata 17 implemented using the xtsfkk command developed by Karakaplan (2022). The within-transformation of frontier inputs is performed using the command: egen X_mean = mean(X), by(id), where X is the frontier variable. This is followed by the command: gen X_within = educ − X_mean. For readers interested in replication, the specific codes are available upon request.

3.2. Data and Variable Description

The analysis uses an annual panel dataset comprising 5 major townships in South Africa (Khayelitsha, Soshanguve, Soweto, Alexandra & Tembisa) covering the 1995–2023 period. The use of panel data is justified by the need to account for unobserved factors specific to each township. While the panel dimensions of T = 29 and N = 5 yield 145, the ultimate sample size reported later in the regression table is 140 observations since the use of lagged values as instruments implies a loss of one observation for each township.

The 5 townships are selected due to their history, economic significance, and population size. Soweto, the largest and most economically active township, is essentially a microcosm of township economic activities in Johannesburg. Khayelitsha is one of the fastest-growing townships in terms of population size in Cape Town, which remains characterized by high unemployment and informal sector reliance. Alexandra, located near Sandton, one of the richest residential areas in South Africa, highlights the stark economic disparities between affluent and underdeveloped urban areas. Tembisa, with its rapidly urbanizing and growing middle-class population, sheds light on the evolving nature of township economies. Soshanguve, located near Pretoria, is home to a diverse population, which mainly includes the Sotho, Shangani, Nguni, and Venda tribes, hence the name SO-SHA-NGU-VE. These townships collectively provide a diverse and representative sample for understanding how trade openness and ICTs can drive township economic growth in South Africa. The sampling period is 1995–2023. The selection of this period is guided by the desire to focus on the democratic era, as South Africa was under economic sanctions prior to 1995.

In terms of measurement, there is currently no consensus on the appropriate measure of trade openness. Common measures applied in literature are tariffs and trade shares. Although tariffs are usually more appealing, they are measured at the macro level and, therefore, do not vary across townships. This makes them inappropriate for this analysis. Trade shares are more appealing for this study since they vary both over time and across townships. For this reason, trade openness was proxied in this study by the share of exports on total output expressed as a percentage. This is referred to in the literature as export intensity. A high value indicates high intensity, which often reflects a more open trade policy stance. While import penetration is an alternative, the use of export intensity measures is consistent with the idea that development is more achievable through outward orientation (Dollar, 1992). ICT is a stock variable expressed in logarithm form so that its effect can be interpreted as an elasticity. Both variables are expected to correlate positively with technical efficiency. Crime and informal labor are included to control some of the peculiar features of township economies. Table 1 contains variable descriptions and data sources.

Table 1. Variable description and sources.

Variable	Notation	Description	Measurement	Source
Output	Y	Local GDP	Log units	Statistics South Africa
Labour	L	Employment	Log units	Quarterly Labour Force Surveys
Capital	K	Fixed capital stock	Log units	Statistics South Africa
ICT	ICT	Stock of ICT	Log units	Statistics South Africa
Trade openness	OP	Export intensity	% of output	Statistics South Africa
Human capital	EDUC	Functional literacy	% of total population	Statistics South Africa
Informal sector	INF	Informal workers	% of total employment	Statistics South Africa
Crime	C	Number of cases	Log units	South African Police Service

The stock of ICT is measured by Statistics South Africa using the perpetual inventory method, which captures the cumulative value of ICT-related infrastructure and services (e.g., broadband penetration, mobile subscriptions, telecommunications investment) within a township. It is log-transformed to ensure scale comparability and to allow for elasticity-based interpretation. This proxy is widely used in the ICT-growth literature (e.g., Adeleye et al., 2021; D. Wang et al., 2021) and reflects the enabling environment for digital engagement in economic activities.

Human capital, while a broad theoretical concept, is operationalized using the percentage of the population that is functionally literate, a widely accepted and observable proxy in development studies. This aligns with prior research, including Mankiw et al. (1992), that treats literacy as a basic determinant of labor quality.

Labor input is proxied by the number of employed individuals, as reported in the Quarterly Labour Force Surveys (QLFS). It is essentially the number of paid employees and includes casual, seasonal, and informal workers. The QLFS is a nationally representative household survey designed to collect detailed information on labor market dynamics, including employment, unemployment, labor force participation, and characteristics of workers. Employment figures reported in the QLFS include individuals aged 15–64 years who, during the reference week, performed any work for pay, profit, or family gain or who had a job or business but were temporarily absent. This broad definition aligns with International Labour Organization (ILO) standards.

Capital input is proxied by fixed capital stock. According to Statistics South Africa, this refers to the value of all capital goods in a township at the beginning of a period. Fixed capital stock consists of buildings and construction works, transport equipment, machinery, and other equipment and transfer costs. The methodology employed by Statistics South Africa to calculate this stock variable is based on the perpetual inventory method.

Informal employment data are derived from two principal official datasets produced by Statistics South Africa, namely the Quarterly Employment Statistics (QES) and the Quarterly Labour Force Survey (QLFS). The QES, based on enterprise-level surveys, measures formal employment in non-agricultural sectors but excludes domestic workers, while the QLFS, based on household surveys, captures total employment across both formal and informal sectors, including agriculture and domestic work. To reconcile the differences between these sources, Statistics South Africa constructs a harmonized employment dataset by taking the formal employment figures from the QES and augmenting them with formal agricultural workers and domestic workers identified in the QLFS. Informal employment is then calculated residually as the difference between total employment reported in the QLFS and the adjusted formal employment estimate.

Output is measured by goods and services used or consumed by individuals, households, general government, and firms and is not processed further or resold within a township. It is essentially represented by the following equation: Final output = Expenditure on GDP = Gross domestic expenditure + Net exports = Gross domestic product (GDP) at market prices.

Crime is measured by the number of reported criminal cases compiled from administrative records maintained by the South African Police Service (SAPS). Reported crime data are disaggregated geographically, which allows one to match the crime incidents to township-level economic indicators. At the data source, crime figures are grouped into two categories, namely crimes reported by the community and crimes detected by police. In this study, the total of the two is used to represent crimes committed in each township.

To ensure the robustness of the results, several diagnostic checks were performed. These include tests for functional form, the presence of inefficiencies, and weak instruments.

4. Results

The results section proceeds as follows. First, it presents descriptive statistics to obtain a preliminary feel of the data and identify an anomaly prior to estimation. This is followed by a correlation matrix, which seeks to measure the degree of collinearity among the regressors. Subsequently, regression results are presented. Finally, diagnostic test results are presented to ensure the reliability of the main results. Following this chronology, Table 2 contains summary statistics. On average, exports accounted for only 8.4% of local output annually between 1995 and 2023, which falls short of the national average. This low average export intensity confirms the general concerns that township economies are marginalized from global markets. Education literacy averaged 66% of the total population, which is not surprising given how the government has invested in education since 1994. Informal workers accounted for 21% of total employment. Reported cases averaged 34,070 annually, which translates to roughly 93 cases per day.

Tables 3–7 present disaggregated summary statistics across the five townships. Alexandra and Tembisa stand out with the highest average export shares (16.6% and 14.3%, respectively), surpassing the national average and suggesting stronger integration into global markets, unlike Khayelitsha and Soweto, where exports remain below 3%. Education levels vary, with Alexandra leading at nearly 70% literacy, while Soshanguve lags at 61.3%.

Informal employment is particularly high in Khayelitsha and Soweto, both exceeding 22%, reinforcing the precarious nature of township labor markets. Crime rates differ remarkably, with Khayelitsha experiencing the highest average annual cases (57,391), over twice that of Alexandra and Soshanguve.

Table 2. Overall summary statistics.

Variable	Obs	Mean	Std. Dev.	Min	Max
logoutput	145	11.675	0.291	10.997	12.131
loglabour	145	12.47	0.252	11.937	12.882
logcapital	145	11.617	0.23	11.11	12.041
logict	145	6.46	1.047	4.478	8.083
exports share	145	8.414	6.372	1.333	23.826
educ	145	66.022	5.757	50.941	73.862
informal share	145	21.132	4.319	12.83	29.926
crime	145	34,070.313	14,545.315	17,701	77,628

Table 3. Summary statistics—Khayelitsha.

Variable	Obs	Mean	Std. Dev.	Min	Max
logoutput	29	11.62	0.276	11.075	11.917
loglabour	29	12.687	0.15	12.442	12.88
logcapital	29	11.437	0.23	11.11	11.751
logict	29	6.324	1.058	4.509	7.757
exports share	29	2.804	0.52	1.612	3.833
educ	29	62.794	5.383	51.898	68.998
informal share	29	22.535	4.178	15.899	29.461
crime	29	57,391.002	13,753.95	32,126.7	77,628.33

Table 4. Summary statistics—Tembisa.

Variable	Obs	Mean	Std. Dev.	Min	Max
logoutput	29	11.804	0.294	11.175	12.131
loglabour	29	12.372	0.195	12.051	12.629
logcapital	29	11.684	0.22	11.347	11.971
logict	29	6.459	1.078	4.614	7.947
exports share	29	14.312	2.654	9.636	19.168
educ	29	68.997	4.983	57.762	73.384
informal share	29	19.871	4.042	13.601	26.607
crime	29	22,492.007	3178.46	17,701.42	29,053.93

Table 5. Summary statistics—Soweto.

Variable	Obs	Mean	Std. Dev.	Min	Max
logoutput	29	11.721	0.235	11.25	11.946
loglabour	29	12.716	0.13	12.521	12.882
logcapital	29	11.644	0.165	11.441	11.861
logict	29	6.521	1.016	4.756	7.883
exports share	29	2.306	0.317	1.333	2.663
educ	29	67.068	4.091	58.248	71.029
informal share	29	22.624	4.211	15.862	29.926
crime	29	36,483.987	4276.827	28,424.15	43,316.79

Table 6. Summary statistics—Alexandra.

Variable	Obs	Mean	Std. Dev.	Min	Max
logoutput	29	11.726	0.317	11.058	12.042
loglabour	29	12.218	0.167	11.937	12.435
logcapital	29	11.78	0.211	11.429	12.041
logict	29	6.648	1.057	4.756	8.083
exports share	29	16.566	4.308	10.513	23.826
educ	29	69.972	3.84	59.677	73.862
informal share	29	18.53	3.676	12.83	24.929
crime	29	29,803.701	5478.619	17,812.58	37,763.73

Table 7. Summary statistics—Soshanguve.

Variable	Obs	Mean	Std. Dev.	Min	Max
logoutput	29	11.504	0.246	10.997	11.732
loglabour	29	12.358	0.143	12.14	12.539
logcapital	29	11.542	0.166	11.329	11.764
logict	29	6.348	1.067	4.478	7.775
exports share	29	6.08	1.044	3.633	7.89
educ	29	61.281	4.966	50.941	66.364
informal share	29	22.099	4.113	15.663	29.068
crime	29	24,180.866	3488.476	18,493.28	30,664.65

The empirical results are presented in Table 8. Model EX ignores endogeneity, while Model EN serves as the baseline model, accounting for endogeneity. The upper section of the table reports frontier estimates, while the lower section presents results from the inefficiency specification. Two key findings emerge from the frontier equation. First, output growth is primarily driven by labor, with a 1% increase in labor associated with a 0.4% increase in output, holding capital and literacy rates constant. The inelastic response of output is typical in township economies where capital constraints limit the productivity gains from additional labor. In the literature, an inelastic coefficient of labor has similarly been observed in Coelli et al. (2003) (0.1%) and is comparable to the 0.59 reported in Bragagnolo et al. (2010). Second, capital has no statistically significant effect on output, while the impact of literacy rates is modest. The insignificance of capital suggests that township economies may be operating in environments where investments in physical capital are suboptimal and inadequate to sufficiently generate productivity gains. The marginal effect of human capital, on the other hand, could reflect the lack of employment opportunities for skilled workers in township economies. With limited employment opportunities, skilled workers often end up trapped in economic activities where their productivity is low.

In the inefficiency specification, the coefficient of log ICT is negative and statistically significant, indicating that ICT enhances efficiency. Export intensity shows up with a positive and significant coefficient, suggesting that exporting is associated with technical inefficiencies. While this result is not as expected theoretically, it is not particularly surprising considering that firms in townships operate on a small scale and lack the necessary resources and infrastructure to efficiently manage the demands of international markets. As theoretically expected, however, the interaction between export intensity and ICT is negative, demonstrating the crucial role of ICT in mitigating the inefficiencies associated with exporting.

Table 8. Trade openness, ICT, and technical efficiency.

Frontier Equation	Model EX	Model EN
Dependent var = Log Output		
Log Labour	0.489 *** (0.067)	0.418 *** (0.114)
Log Capital	0.055 (0.054)	0.031 (0.068)
Literacy (%)	0.003 *** (0.0004)	0.004 *** (0.0004)
Inefficiency equation		
Dependent var: ln (σ_u^2)		
Constant	17.227 *** (2.727)	15.384 *** (2.035)
Log ICT	−1.183 *** (0.116)	−1.196 *** (0.107)
Exports/Output (%)	0.101 *** (0.029)	0.046 ** (0.023)
Exports/Output (%) × Log ICT	−0.027 *** (0.006)	−0.018 *** (0.004)
Informal workers/total employment (%)	0.011 (0.011)	0.014 (0.012)
Log Crime	−1.277 *** (0.235)	−1.021 *** (0.172)
Dependent var = Dependent var: ln (σ_v^2)		
Constant	−7.555 *** (0.122)	
Dependent var = Dependent var: ln (σ_w^2)		
Constant		−7.989 *** (0.125)
Eta1 (Log ICT)		−0.288 *** (0.042)
Eta2 (Exports/Output (%))		−0.019 *** (0.005)
Eta3 (Log Labour)		0.047 (0.151)
Eta4 (Log Capital)		0.848 *** (0.315)
Observations	140	140
Log Likelihood	312.91	1275.33
Mean Technical Efficiency	0.8318	0.8089
Median Technical Efficiency	0.8786	0.8580

*** and ** denote significance at 1% and 5%, respectively. Figures in parentheses are standard errors. In the specification, labor, capital, OP, and ICT are treated as endogenous, and they are instrumented by their first lag (i.e., t − 1).

With respect to the control variables, the evidence shows no significant link between informality and technical inefficiencies. Worrisomely, the crime variable is significantly negative, suggesting that criminality has a positive effect on economic activity in these townships. The average technical efficiency based on the preferred model is 0.8089, suggesting that a typical township municipality produced about 81 percent of its potential output. Thus, a typical township economy operated about 19 percent below its full potential. When decomposed by township, Soweto was found to be the least efficient, operating 21% below its full potential. This illustrates a sizeable scope for economic transformation in these townships. It is necessary to mention that the trend variable was excluded from the specification to avoid unnecessary model overfitting, as it turned out to be highly insignificant. Its insignificance demonstrated the absence of technical changes or frontier shifts, which is not surprising given the low levels of innovation at the township level.

Diagnostic Tests

This subsection presents the results from diagnostic tests conducted to ensure the reliability of the results presented above. It was necessary to justify the Cobb–Douglas functional form in particular compared to its flexible counterpart, the Translog specification. It was also necessary to test the presence of technical inefficiencies as their absence would reduce the stochastic frontier model into a normal production function estimable using the standard ordinary least squares method. Lastly, the analysis tested for endogeneity as an instrumental variable approach when the variables are exogenous can be worse than the OLS method (Sturm, 1998). Accompanying this was a test for weak instruments.

Table 9 presents the results from functional form and inefficiency tests. The likelihood (LR) test statistic that compares the restricted OLS regression and the unrestricted stochastic frontier model is significant at a 1% level. This implies that the townships are technically inefficient and that a stochastic frontier model is justified over the standard OLS regression with normal errors. The Wald test was performed to determine the joint significance of interactions and higher-order terms in the frontier specification. As Table 9 shows, the test yielded an insignificant probability value, suggesting that the Cobb–Douglas specification was an adequate representation of the data. Table 10 presents the skewness of the residuals generated from an OLS regression. For a production-type stochastic frontier model, the presence of inefficiencies is normally reflected in negatively skewed residuals (Kumbhakar et al., 2015). The results in Table 6 validate this proposition, lending further support to a stochastic frontier model over a normal OLS regression. Table 11 presents the results of an endogeneity test. The test returns a low probability value, justifying the correction of endogeneity in the model. This result confirms that the true-fixed effects of Greene (2005) and other stochastic frontier models that ignore idiosyncratic endogeneity would be biased.

Table 9. Pre-estimation tests.

Test	Test Statistic	Conclusion
LR Test for technical inefficiencies	$-2 \times$ (H0) − L(Ha) = 2218 ***	$u_{it} \neq 0$
Functional Form (Wald test)	Chi^2 = 3.52, p-value = 0.1724	Cobb–Douglas

*** denotes significant at 1%.

Table 10. Skewness of OLS residuals.

Variables	Obs	Mean	Std. Dev.	Min	Max	Skew.	Kurt.
OLS residuals	145	0	0.077	−0.22	0.203	−0.135	3.336

Table 11. Endogeneity and weak instrument test.

Test	Test Statistic	p-Value
eta Endogeneity Test	$X^2 = 64.89$	0.000
Weak instrument test	$Chi^2 = 478$	0.000

Lastly, to test the strength of the instruments, the study applied the approach proposed by Karakaplan (2022). In Stata 17, this is achievable through the command est res ModelEN followed by the command test iv, where iv is a vector of instruments used in the model. As Table 11 shows, the corresponding probability of the test is low, which, as argued by Karakaplan (2022), suggests that the instruments are not weak.

In summary, the diagnostic tests justify the methodology used in the study. The LR test confirms the presence of technical inefficiency, validating the use of a stochastic frontier model over a conventional OLS regression. The Wald test for functional form adequacy reveals that the Cobb–Douglas specification is a suitable representation of the data, as higher-order terms and interactions were found to be statistically insignificant. Additionally, the skewness of OLS residuals aligns with the expectations of a production-type stochastic frontier model, reinforcing the choice of model. The endogeneity test reveals significant evidence of endogeneity, justifying the use of an instrumental variable approach to avoid biased estimates, while the weak instrument test confirms that the instruments employed are valid. Overall, the baseline results presented in this study can be deemed reliable based on these diagnostic checks.

5. Discussion

The main hypothesis of this study was that low ICT infrastructure may limit the ability of township economies to capitalize on trade opportunities. The evidence supports this claim as the interaction between ICT and export intensity is significantly negative. As argued in the literature, township businesses typically operate in localized and informal markets, limiting their ability to integrate into regional or global trade networks. ICT facilitates market expansion by enabling firms to access market information, connect with international buyers, and optimize supply chain logistics. This enhanced market access allows township firms to capitalize on export opportunities and reduce inefficiencies associated with exporting. The positive coefficient of export intensity is not surprising as it suggests that exporting is associated with technical inefficiencies when ICT is held constant. This result demonstrates the important complementary role of ICT if township economies are to take advantage of global market opportunities and achieve their full potential.

With respect to other variables, the weak positive effect of literacy on local output can be explained by the lack of employment opportunities for skilled workers in townships. The insignificant link between capital stock and local output, on the other hand, may reflect a suboptimal allocation of capital in townships, which limits the productivity of capital. This explanation is plausible considering Cant's (2017) proposition that South Africa's townships are confronted by suboptimal infrastructure.

The negative effect of crime on technical inefficiency suggests that criminality drives economic activity in townships. Although surprising at first glance, this result is consistent with the notion that criminality can be a source of livelihood when income inequality is high, and the labor market has limited employment opportunities. Therefore, crime may act as an informal livelihood strategy in contexts where formal employment is scarce. In such cases, illicit economic activity, although undesirable from a legal and ethical standpoint, might support household income and enable continued economic participation, thereby masking inefficiencies at the aggregate level. Another potential interpretation lies in the entrepreneurial resilience of township economies. In high-crime environments, firms may be compelled to adopt efficiency-enhancing practices (e.g., digital payment systems, security infrastructure, and localized supply chains). These adaptations may inadvertently improve productivity. A third possible explanation may relate to data limitations. Crime reporting is often higher in better-resourced areas due to stronger institutional capacity, which are also the townships with relatively better economic activity. In this view, the negative relationship may be spurious, reflecting administrative efficiency rather than a causal economic link.

To explore this further, a sensitivity analysis was conducted using the one-year lag of crime to reduce the possibility of reverse causality. The direction and statistical significance of the coefficient remained robust, reinforcing the observed relationship. Nevertheless, given the complexity of crime's socio-economic impacts, this result should be interpreted with caution, and future research is encouraged to unpack this relationship more closely.

The finding that informality does not have a statistically significant effect on technical inefficiency is noteworthy, especially given the centrality of informal economic activity in township economies. One possible explanation is the heterogeneity within the informal sector. Informal businesses range from micro-enterprises with high entrepreneurial capacity to survivalist operations. These divergent characteristics may offset each other in aggregate analysis, resulting in no net effect on inefficiency.

A second consideration relates to measurement challenges. Informality is proxied by the share of informal workers in total employment, which may not fully capture the intensity or productivity of informal enterprise activity. Moreover, informality statistics often underreport actual activity due to definitional ambiguities and data collection constraints.

Lastly, it is plausible that informal businesses operating outside formal regulatory frameworks may already be operating near their efficiency frontier, constrained by limited capital, low overheads, and simplified production processes. In such cases, while these businesses may be small in scale, they might still exhibit technical efficiency within their operational context. These interpretations highlight the complexity of the informal sector's role in local productivity dynamics and suggest that a micro-econometric approach that distinguishes between types of informal activity may be needed in future research.

From a theoretical perspective, the main results of the study align with endogenous growth theory (Romer, 1990; Grossman & Helpman, 1991), which highlights the role of technological progress and knowledge diffusion in driving productivity and economic growth. ICT adoption facilitates knowledge spillovers, reduces transaction costs, and improves coordination, thereby increasing the efficiency of exporting firms in township economies. Empirically, the main results agree with Bvuma and Marnewick (2020a), whose results demonstrated the need to address ICT issues with SMMEs operating in South African townships. Makena et al. (2015) also highlight the positive role of ICT usage on businesses in township economies in the context of Zambia. The complementary role of ICT in exporting is in line with previous studies such as those of Kneller and Timmis (2016) and Adeleye et al. (2021). The analysis of Adeleye et al. (2020) particularly found that ICT enhances the impact of trade on growth in Africa. The current study has contributed to this understanding by presenting estimates drawn at the township level. Such a granular approach is important as it provides localized insights that are more applicable to the realities of townships, bridging the gap between macroeconomic findings and micro-level experiences.

It is important to mention the limitations of this study at this stage. First, the modeling approach employed in this analysis ignored spatial effects. Townships are not isolated economic units and may potentially interact with each other through supply chains, migration, and shared infrastructure. It is possible that technical efficiency improvement in one township could have positive externalities for nearby townships. Neglecting such spatial dependence may, therefore, paint an incomplete picture of inefficiency dynamics in townships. A mitigating factor, however, is that the five townships included in this analysis are hardly close to each other, making spatial spillovers arising from geographical proximity less problematic. In addition, incorporating spatial effects within a stochastic frontier framework remains a developing area of research, and the properties of many emerging spatial stochastic frontier estimators are not yet well understood. Another limitation of the study relates to data constraints on some of the key challenges affecting the transformation of township economies, such as income inequality and limited access to funding.

Lastly, the study was based on a relatively small sample, which might hinder generalization beyond the five townships analyzed in this study. This sample reflected the best possible number of observations given current data availability and the need to focus on major townships. Township-level annual economic data are only systematically available from 1995 onwards, and extending the sample period further was not feasible. Similarly, data coverage across townships is highly uneven, and only five major township economies had sufficiently complete data to support the analysis. While recognizing the sample size limitation, the use of small-N panel econometric techniques and diagnostics tests performed provides reasonable confidence in the validity of the empirical findings. Future research could expand the scope as more township-level data become available over time.

6. Conclusions

This study set out to examine the impact of trade openness on the technical efficiency of township economies in South Africa and to assess whether ICT acts as a moderating factor in this relationship. Using an instrumental variable stochastic frontier model applied to a balanced panel of five major townships from 1995 to 2023, the results provide clear empirical support for the hypothesis that ICT significantly enhances the efficiency benefits of trade openness. The findings of this study particularly provide strong empirical evidence that inadequate ICT infrastructure constrains township economies from fully capitalizing on trade opportunities. The significant negative interaction between ICT and export intensity underscores ICT's critical role in facilitating market access, optimizing logistics for townships, and reducing inefficiencies. Without sufficient ICT infrastructure in place, exporting is linked to technical inefficiencies, highlighting the urgent need for digital transformation to maximize the benefits of trade liberalization. This conclusion aligns with endogenous growth theory, which emphasizes technology and knowledge diffusion as key drivers of efficiency and long-term economic growth.

These findings contribute to economic theory by extending the application of endogenous growth models to subnational township economies, a domain typically excluded from the macro trade-growth empirical literature. The study introduces new empirical insights to understand productivity dynamics in marginalized urban contexts by demonstrating that the interaction between ICT and trade openness significantly affects technical efficiency.

From a practical perspective, the results carry important implications for policymakers. Targeted interventions to expand digital infrastructure, promote digital literacy, and subsidize ICT adoption can unlock significant efficiency gains in township economies, particularly by enabling informal and small businesses to engage more effectively with global markets. The results essentially highlight the pressing need for policies that strengthen ICT infrastructure in South African townships to ensure that firms reach the full potential of global market participation. Given that ICT mitigates inefficiencies associated with exporting, government interventions may need to, as alluded to shortly above, focus on expanding digital access, subsidizing ICT adoption for small businesses, and implementing digital literacy programs. These initiatives would empower township enterprises to integrate more effectively into regional and global markets, improving efficiency and boosting local economic output.

A key limitation of this study is its inability to account for spatial dependencies, which may influence efficiency spillovers across township economies. Future research could explore recent advancements in spatial stochastic frontier models to capture the potential interdependence of township economies. Additionally, future studies could apply the indirect production function approach to examine the combined effects of ICT and trade openness on technical efficiency in the presence of borrowing constraints.

Funding: This research received no external funding.

Institutional Review Board Statement: Not applicable.

Informed Consent Statement: Not applicable.

Data Availability Statement: The dataset supporting the results of the study was submitted to the journal. The dataset is also available upon request from the author.

Conflicts of Interest: The author declare no conflict of interest.

References

Abdulkarim, Y. (2023). Reevaluating the linkage between trade openness and economic growth in Nigeria. *SN Business & Economics*, *3*(7), 125.

Adeleye, B. N., Adedoyin, F., & Nathaniel, S. (2021). The criticality of ICT-trade nexus on economic and inclusive growth. *Information Technology for Development*, *27*(2), 293–313. [CrossRef]

Adeleye, B. N., Gershon, O., Ogundipe, A., Owolabi, O., Ogunrinola, I., & Adediran, O. (2020). Comparative investigation of the growth-poverty-inequality trilemma in Sub-Saharan Africa and Latin American and Caribbean Countries. *Heliyon*, *6*(12). [CrossRef]

Aigner, D. J., Lovell, C. A. K., & Schmidt, P. (1977). Formulation and estimation of stochastic frontier production functions. *Journal of Econometrics*, *6*(1), 21–37. [CrossRef]

Awad, A., & Albaity, M. (2022). ICT and economic growth in Sub-Saharan Africa: Transmission channels and effects. *Telecommunications Policy*, *46*(8), 102381. [CrossRef]

Battese, G. E., & Coelli, T. J. (1995). A model for technical inefficiency effects in a stochastic frontier production function for panel data. *Empirical Economics*, *20*, 325–332. [CrossRef]

Bragagnolo, C., Spolador, H. F., & Barros, G. D. C. (2010). Regional Brazilian agriculture TFP analysis: A stochastic frontier analysis approach. *Revista Economia*, *11*(4), 217–242.

Bvuma, S., & Marnewick, C. (2020a). An information and communication technology adoption framework for small, medium and micro-enterprises operating in townships South Africa. *The Southern African Journal of Entrepreneurship and Small Business Management*, *12*(1), 12. [CrossRef]

Bvuma, S., & Marnewick, C. (2020b). Sustainable livelihoods of township small, medium and micro enterprises towards growth and development. *Sustainability*, *12*(8), 3149. [CrossRef]

Cant, M. C. (2017). The availability of infrastructure in townships: Is there hope for township businesses? *International Review of Management and Marketing*, *7*(4), 108.

Clarke, G. R., & Wallsten, S. J. (2006). Has the internet increased trade? Developed and developing country evidence. *Economic Inquiry*, *44*(3), 465–484. [CrossRef]

Coelli, T., Rahman, S., & Thirtle, C. (2003). A stochastic frontier approach to total factor productivity measurement in Bangladesh crop agriculture, 1961–92. *Journal of International Development: The Journal of the Development Studies Association*, *15*(3), 321–333. [CrossRef]

Dollar, D. (1992). Outward-oriented developing economies really do grow more rapidly: Evidence from 95 LDCs, 1976–1985. *Economic Development and Cultural Change*, *40*(3), 523–544. [CrossRef]

Dumor, K., Shurong, Z., Dumor, H. K., Ampaw, E. M., Amouzou, E. K., Okae-Adjei, S., & Boadi, E. K. (2024). Evaluating the effect of ICT on trade and economic growth from the perspective of Eastern African belt and road countries. *Information Technology for Development*, *30*(3), 452–471. [CrossRef]

Fang, Z., Huang, B., & Yang, Z. (2020). Trade openness and the environmental Kuznets curve: Evidence from Chinese cities. *The World Economy*, *43*(10), 2622–2649. [CrossRef]

Fernández-Portillo, A., Almodóvar-González, M., & Hernández-Mogollón, R. (2020). Impact of ICT development on economic growth. A study of OECD European union countries. *Technology in Society*, *63*, 101420. [CrossRef]
Frankel, J. A., & Romer, D. H. (1999). Does trade cause growth? *American Economic Review*, *89*(3), 379–399. [CrossRef]
Freund, C. L., & Weinhold, D. (2004). The effect of the Internet on international trade. *Journal of International Economics*, *62*(1), 171–189. [CrossRef]
Greene, W. (2005). Reconsidering heterogeneity in panel data estimators of the stochastic frontier model. *Journal of Econometrics*, *126*(2), 269–303. [CrossRef]
Grossman, G. M., & Helpman, E. (1991). Trade, knowledge spillovers, and growth. *European Economic Review*, *35*(2–3), 517–526. [CrossRef]
Ibrahim, A., & Abdulmalik, M. R. (2023). Do trade openness and governance matter for economic growth in Africa? A case of EAC and WAEMU countries. *International Economics and Economic Policy*, *20*(3), 389–412. [CrossRef]
Jalil, A., & Rauf, A. (2021). Revisiting the link between trade openness and economic growth using panel methods. *The Journal of International Trade & Economic Development*, *30*(8), 1168–1187.
Karakaplan, M. U. (2022). Panel stochastic frontier models with endogeneity. *The Stata Journal*, *22*(3), 643–663. [CrossRef]
Karayalcin, C., & Yilmazkuday, H. (2015). Trade and cities. *The World Bank Economic Review*, *29*(3), 523–549. [CrossRef]
Kneller, R., & Timmis, J. (2016). ICT and exporting: The effects of broadband on the extensive margin of business service exports. *Review of International Economics*, *24*(4), 757–796. [CrossRef]
Kumbhakar, S. C., Wang, H. J., & Horncastle, A. P. (2015). *A practitioner's guide to stochastic frontier analysis using Stata*. Cambridge University Press.
Makena, J. C., Kimwele, M. W., & Guyo, W. (2015). The effect of ICT services on business performance in the informal sector in Kenya—A case of informal enterprises in Mlolongo township. *ICTACT Journal on Management Studies*, *1*(3), 118–128. [CrossRef]
Mankiw, N. G., Romer, D., & Weil, D. N. (1992). A contribution to the empirics of economic growth. *The Quarterly Journal of Economics*, *107*(2), 407–437. [CrossRef]
Mazorodze, B. (2020). Trade and efficiency of manufacturing industries in South Africa. *The Journal of International Trade & Economic Development*, *29*(1), 89–118.
Mbonyane, B., & Ladzani, W. (2011). Factors that hinder the growth of small businesses in South African townships. *European Business Review*, *23*(6), 550–560. [CrossRef]
Meeusen, W., & van Den Broeck, J. (1977). Efficiency estimation from Cobb-Douglas production functions with composed error. *International Economic Review*, *18*, 435–444. [CrossRef]
Moos, M., & Sambo, W. (2018). An exploratory study of challenges faced by small automotive businesses in townships: The case of Garankuwa, South Africa. *Journal of Contemporary Management*, *15*(1), 467–494.
Munir, K., & Ameer, A. (2018). Effect of economic growth, trade openness, urbanization, and technology on environment of Asian emerging economies. *Management of Environmental Quality: An International Journal*, *29*(6), 1123–1134. [CrossRef]
Ndubuisi, G., Otioma, C., Owusu, S., & Tetteh, G. K. (2022). ICTs quality and technical efficiency: An empirical analysis. *Telecommunications Policy*, *46*(10), 102439. [CrossRef]
Pradhan, R. P., Arvin, M. B., Nair, M. S., Hall, J. H., & Bennett, S. E. (2021). Sustainable economic development in India: The dynamics between financial inclusion, ICT development, and economic growth. *Technological Forecasting and Social Change*, *169*, 120758. [CrossRef]
Romer, P. M. (1990). Endogenous technological change. *Journal of Political Economy*, *98*(5, Part 2), S71–S102. [CrossRef]
Röller, L. H., & Waverman, L. (2001). Telecommunications infrastructure and economic development: A simultaneous approach. *American Economic Review*, *91*(4), 909–923. [CrossRef]
Saba, C. S., Ngepah, N., & Odhiambo, N. M. (2024). Information and communication technology (ICT), growth and development in developing regions: Evidence from a comparative analysis and a new approach. *Journal of the Knowledge Economy*, *15*(3), 14700–14748. [CrossRef]
Sturm, R. (1998). Instrumental variable methods for effectiveness research. *International Journal of Methods in Psychiatric Research*, *7*(1), 17–26. [CrossRef]
Suatmi, B. D., Bloch, H., & Salim, R. (2017). Trade liberalization and technical efficiency in the Indonesian chemicals industry. *Applied Economics*, *49*(44), 4428–4439. [CrossRef]
Wang, D., Zhou, T., Lan, F., & Wang, M. (2021). ICT and socio-economic development: Evidence from a spatial panel data analysis in China. *Telecommunications Policy*, *45*(7), 102173. [CrossRef]
Wang, H. J., & Ho, C. W. (2010). Estimating fixed-effect panel stochastic frontier models by model transformation. *Journal of Econometrics*, *157*(2), 286–296. [CrossRef]
Wang, H. J., & Schmidt, P. (2002). One-step and two-step estimation of the effects of exogenous variables on technical efficiency levels. *Journal of Productivity Analysis*, *18*, 129–144. [CrossRef]

Wenlong, Z., Tien, N. H., Sibghatullah, A., Asih, D., Soelton, M., & Ramli, Y. (2023). Impact of energy efficiency, technology innovation, institutional quality, and trade openness on greenhouse gas emissions in ten Asian economies. *Environmental Science and Pollution Research, 30*(15), 43024–43039. [CrossRef] [PubMed]

Wiid, J. A., & Cant, M. C. (2021). The future growth potential of township SMMEs: An African perspective. *Journal of Contemporary Management, 18*(1), 508–530. [CrossRef]

Yasin, M. Z. (2022). Technical efficiency and total factor productivity growth of Indonesian manufacturing industry: Does openness matter? *Studies in Microeconomics, 10*(2), 195–224. [CrossRef]

Disclaimer/Publisher's Note: The statements, opinions and data contained in all publications are solely those of the individual author(s) and contributor(s) and not of MDPI and/or the editor(s). MDPI and/or the editor(s) disclaim responsibility for any injury to people or property resulting from any ideas, methods, instructions or products referred to in the content.

economies

MDPI

Article

Are Nations Ready for Digital Transformation? A Macroeconomic Perspective Through the Lens of Education Quality

Roman Chinoracky, Natalia Stalmasekova , Radovan Madlenak * and Lucia Madlenakova

Faculty of Operation and Economics of Transport and Communications, University of Zilina, Univerzitná 8215/1, 010 26 Žilina, Slovakia; roman.chinoracky@gmail.com (R.C.); natalia.stalmasekova@uniza.sk (N.S.); lucia.madlenakova@uniza.sk (L.M.)

* Correspondence: radovan.madlenak@uniza.sk

Abstract: The global shift toward digital transformation presents both opportunities and challenges for national economies, particularly in terms of workforce readiness. While many studies assess digital readiness via infrastructure or technological adoption, fewer investigate the preparedness of countries' future labor forces. This article addresses this research gap by examining how quality of education relates to job automation risk across OECD countries. The goal is to identify which nations are least prepared for digital disruption due to weak educational foundations and high automation exposure. Using data on education expenditure, PISA scores, and the Education Index, compared to the percentage of jobs at high risk of automation, this study applies correlational analysis and a quadrant overview to assess national readiness. Findings show that countries such as Slovakia, Poland, and Greece are least prepared, combining low investment in education and high exposure to automation. Conversely, nations like Finland, Norway, Sweden, and New Zealand exhibit strong readiness, characterized by robust education systems and lower automation risks. This study contributes to the literature by integrating automation vulnerability into national readiness assessments and offers actionable insights for policymakers focused on education reform and workforce development.

Keywords: digitalization; job automation; education; technological change

1. Introduction

Digital transformation—the widespread adoption of digital technologies—has emerged as a defining trend of the 21st century. It is fundamentally altering how individuals live and work, businesses operate, and how governments deliver services (Mikalef & Parmiggiani, 2022; Verhoef et al., 2021). The importance of studying countries' readiness for digital transformation lies in the profound economic and social implications of this shift. Nations that effectively harness digitalization can achieve higher productivity, innovation, and competitiveness, whereas those that lag risk widening development gaps and losing out on growth opportunities. As digital tools become ubiquitous, countries must be prepared to integrate these tools into their industries. Understanding which countries are ready (and which are not) is critical for international development and policy making, as digital transformation is now closely linked to economic prosperity and social well-being (Corejova & Chinoracky, 2021; Arıkan Kargı, 2022; Cisco Systems, 2019; OECD, 2019b; Aleksandrova et al., 2022; Tudose et al., 2023).

A key insight from comparative studies is that multiple factors influence a country's digital transformation readiness, cutting across technology, human capital, governance, and economic conditions. Robust ICT infrastructure is a foundational requirement—widespread internet access, reliable electricity, and modern telecommunications networks enable digital connectivity. Equally important is human capital, including education quality and digital skills in the workforce, since people must be able to use and develop new technologies. The business environment and investment climate shape how readily firms can adopt digital innovation; factors such as R&D expenditure, entrepreneurship, and ease of doing business all contribute to readiness for digital transformation (Cisco Systems, 2019). Effective government policies and institutions—from national digital strategies and e-government services to legal frameworks for data and intellectual property—create an enabling environment for digital transformation. As the United Nations Development Programme notes, an inclusive digital transformation requires coordinated efforts across five pillars: people, connectivity, government, regulation, and economy (United Nations Development Programme [UNDP], 2023). In sum, readiness is multidimensional, reflecting a country's technical capacity, skill base, and policy support for leveraging digital technology.

Within this context, an important and under-examined question rises: Which countries are least prepared for the changes brought about by digitalization, based on the potential of their future workforce? The "future workforce" refers to the upcoming generation of workers—today's students and young people—who will drive and sustain digital transformation in the years ahead.

This aspect is especially critical because even if a country builds infrastructure, it cannot fully benefit from digitalization without a skilled workforce to use and innovate on those technologies. Countries with a well-educated, adaptable youth population may leapfrog in readiness despite lower income levels (Arntz et al., 2016; OECD, 2022; World Economic Forum, 2024; United Nations Development Programme [UNDP], 2023). Yet, relatively few studies have explicitly focused on the intersection of workforce development and national digital readiness. Many existing indices emphasize current infrastructure or institutional metrics, while giving less attention to whether the educational system and labor force are equipped for rapid technological change. This is a notable research gap: for instance, global assessments have pointed out that low-skilled and low-educated workers are the most vulnerable to job automation, and that without sufficient retraining, countries will face rising inequality as automation accelerates (Arntz et al., 2016). Even high-skilled workers are not immune—recent evidence shows that non-routine analytical tasks performed by highly educated professionals are increasingly susceptible to AI-driven automation, with significant variation in wage outcomes and job redesign implications (Ozgul et al., 2024; OECD, 2022). Translating this insight into a country-level readiness perspective—identifying which countries' future labor workforce face the greatest risk—remains an open challenge.

This article addresses this gap by examining global digital transformation readiness through the lens of workforce education and automation risk. In particular, it investigates which countries appear already prepared and least prepared for digital disruption due to limitations in their future workforce's skills and the susceptibility of their jobs to automation. This focus on the human capital dimension complements prior work and is crucial for policymakers: if a country's next-generation workforce lacks digital skills, or if a large share of its jobs are poised to be replaced by technology, then that country's digital future is uncertain despite other favorable factors. Identifying such nations can inform targeted interventions (such as educational reforms, upskilling programs, or labor market policies) to support preparedness for the coming wave of digitalization.

The remainder of this article is organized as follows: first, we present a review of the relevant literature, clarifying key concepts (digitization vs. digital transformation), the economic benefits of digitalization, the concept of national readiness and its drivers, and prior findings on workforce readiness and automation. We then outline the research gap and contribution of this study in detail, before proceeding to the methodological approach and analysis that address the research question. The last part of the article is dedicated to a discussion and conclusion. Section 5 sums up the research and subsequently points to the policy implications. Section 6 outlines research limitations and lists opportunities for future research.

2. Literature Review

Robert Wachal, in his essay addressing the social consequences of societal changes in the context of evaluating the potential of computer-based research in the humanities, was the first to use the term digitalization (Wachal, 1971). The term digitalization is often incorrectly confused with the term digitization. While digitization is the conversion of information flows from analogue to digital in a form of a combination of zeros and ones within one process, digitalization is the conversion of all information flows within the entire process. Digitalization simply refers to the use and implementation of specific digital technology by a company, an entire industry, or even society as a whole within the scope of a single project (Mikalef & Parmiggiani, 2022; Wachal, 1971; Brennen & Kreiss, 2016).

A company may carry out a series of projects aimed at digitalization: from the automation of production processes, the implementation of information systems managing various elements of supply chains, to the creation of ecommerce platforms and the training of employees to work with artificial intelligence. The set of such digitalization projects is collectively referred to as digital transformation, which is a strategic transformation based not only on the implementation of digital technologies, but also on changes in corporate culture, cross-organizational shifts, and adjustments in business models (Vial, 2019; Vrana & Singh, 2021).

Digitization is about bits and bytes—converting analog to digital. Digitalization is about processes—using digital technologies to do what we already do, but better. Digital transformation is about strategy and paradigm shifts—doing what we never could before, or doing fundamentally new things, enabled by digital technology (Mikalef & Parmiggiani, 2022; Wachal, 1971; Brennen & Kreiss, 2016; Vial, 2019; Vrana & Singh, 2021).

At the national level, a country may start by building internet infrastructure (digitization), then promote online services and e-commerce (digitalization), and eventually see its economy transformed with new digital industries and innovations (digital transformation). Clarifying these terms is not just semantic, it helps in scoping what "readiness" entails. A country might be well-equipped for digitization (e.g., having the hardware to convert analog systems) but not yet ready for deeper digital transformation (which requires talent, innovation ecosystems, and adaptable institutions) (Schreckling & Steiger, 2017). Thus, in assessing readiness, we must consider not only technology deployment but also the capacity for strategic, transformative change.

Digital transformation is widely seen as a positive force for economic development. For example, firms that digitalize their operations (through enterprise software, automation, AI, and so forth) can produce more with the same inputs, innovate faster, and serve customers in new ways, thereby expanding their market share and profitability.

On a larger scale, when many firms in an economy become more productive thanks to digital tools, the aggregate economic output (GDP) of that country is expected to rise. Empirical research supports these expectations:

- A cross-country econometric analysis by Tudose et al. (2023) finds that higher digital readiness correlates with higher GDP per capita. Using the Network Readiness Index (NRI) as a measure of nations' digital transformation status, they show that the NRI has a positive and significant impact on GDP per capita across a sample of 46 countries.

In other words, countries that score better on infrastructure, technology adoption, skills, and other digital criteria tend to enjoy stronger economic performance, even after controlling for their income group. This suggests that digital transformation is a driver of growth: better networked, more digital-savvy economies can produce more goods and services or higher-value outputs, boosting average incomes (Tudose et al., 2023; Dutta & Lanvin, 2023).

- Similarly, Cisco's global digital readiness study reported a strong relationship between digital readiness and GDP per capita, underscoring that investing in digital capacity yields tangible economic value. One reason is that digitalization can spur innovation and entrepreneurship, creating entirely new industries (such as fintech, e-commerce, digital entertainment) and job opportunities that did not exist before. For example, the rise of the mobile app economy or digital content creation has contributed significantly to employment and GDP in countries that have embraced these trends (Cisco Systems, 2019).
- From the perspective of work-related processes, routine tasks can be automated, reducing labor costs or freeing workers for higher-value activities; supply chains can be synchronized in real time, minimizing inventories and downtime; and data analytics can optimize everything from energy use to marketing strategies. Historical evidence shows that major technological adoptions—steam power, electricity, etc.—boosted productivity, and digital technology is no exception (Corejova & Chinoracky, 2021). Corejova and Chinoracky (2021) further note that the effects of digital technologies are associated with growth in efficiency and output, often leading to increased revenues and profits for businesses that successfully integrate them.

Digital transformation also tends to enhance a country's competitiveness and efficiency in global markets. By adopting advanced technologies (like robotics in manufacturing or digital finance in banking), countries can increase the productivity of their industries, making their exports more competitive. It enables cost reductions and quality improvements that can expand a nation's trade potential. Digitalization often improves service delivery in both private and public sectors, which can raise the overall productivity of the economy. For example, digital banking and e-payments make financial transactions faster and more secure, supporting commerce; e-government services reduce bureaucratic hurdles, saving time for businesses and citizens. These efficiency gains collectively improve what economists call total factor productivity, a key ingredient of long-term growth (Arıkan Kargı, 2022; Tudose et al., 2023). The OECD and World Bank have documented that digital adoption boosts productivity and growth, particularly when combined with complementary investments in skills and organizational change (OECD, 2019a; Cusolito et al., 2020).

Another benefit of digital transformation is the potential for inclusive growth, though this is not automatic. Digital platforms can empower small entrepreneurs to reach wider markets (think of artisans selling on global e-commerce platforms) and can provide new job opportunities such as gig work or IT-enabled services in regions where formal jobs are scarce. This means that digital technologies can help overcome geographic barriers—for instance, allowing remote education and telemedicine in rural areas—thereby contributing to human capital development and health, which feed back into economic growth. (Aleksandrova et al., 2022) A study by Suntsova (2024), on the global digital economy, argued that while digitalization is a "two-edged sword", the opportunities for economic growth, innovation, and improved services are significant if managed well. However, it must be noted that the benefits of digital transformation can be uneven if parts of the population or certain regions are left behind; hence, many scholars and international organizations stress the need for policies to bridge the digital divide so that the gains from digitalization are broadly shared (Suntsova, 2024).

In summary, digital transformation can drive a country's economy forward by increasing productivity, fostering innovation, creating new markets and industries, and improving efficiency in existing sectors. Countries that successfully embrace digitalization often experience faster economic growth and improved competitiveness. For example, Estonia's economy has benefited from its early adoption of e-government and digital services (often cited as "e-Estonia") (Vassil, 2015; e-Estonia, 2022), and China's rapid digital economy expansion (e.g., in e-commerce and fintech) has contributed to its GDP growth and global trade presence (McKinsey & Company, 2021; ING Think, 2022). These examples illustrate the general finding that digital readiness is tied to economic performance. However, realizing these benefits is contingent on having the necessary conditions in place—which brings us to the concept of digital transformation readiness at the national level.

Readiness for digital transformation at the national economic level refers to a country's capacity to adopt, implement, and leverage digital technologies for its development and growth. It is a holistic concept that encompasses the state of infrastructure, human capital, institutions, and other foundational elements that determine how well positioned a country is to undergo digital transformation. In simple terms, a nation that is "digitally ready" has the prerequisites needed to successfully integrate advanced technologies into its economy and society, whereas a less ready nation faces significant gaps or barriers in doing so. Several frameworks and indices have been developed to measure digital readiness across countries, including the following:

- The Network Readiness Index (NRI) (Tudose et al., 2023; Dutta & Lanvin, 2023),
- The IMD World Digital Competitiveness Ranking (IMD, 2024),
- The Digital Adoption Index of the World Bank (World Bank, 2016),
- Industry-backed measures like the Cisco Digital Readiness Index (Cisco Systems, 2019).

These typically aggregate various indicators into a composite score meant to benchmark countries' digital capabilities. Common to these assessments is the understanding that readiness spans multiple dimensions.

One useful example is Cisco's model, which uses seven components to gauge digital readiness: (1) Basic Needs, (2) Business and Government Investment, (3) Ease of Doing Business, (4) Human Capital, (5) Start-up Environment, (6) Technology Adoption, and (7) Technology Infrastructure (Arıkan Kargı, 2022; Cisco Systems, 2019):

- The "Basic Needs" (1) component acknowledges that general socio-economic development (health, education, basic services) sets the stage—if basic needs are not met, a country will struggle to focus on digital advancement (Arıkan Kargı, 2022).
- The "Technology Adoption and Infrastructure" (6) (7) components measure the availability of digital networks (like broadband and mobile) and the extent to which people and businesses are actually using digital services.
- The "Human Capital" (4) component captures education levels, digital skills, and labor force participation, indicating whether the workforce can support and sustain digital initiatives.
- The "Business environment and government investment" (2) (3) (5) components reflect whether firms have the freedom, incentives, and support to innovate and invest in technology (for instance, ease of starting a business, R&D spending, venture capital availability). When all these factors are favorable, countries create a virtuous cycle that attracts tech investment and enables widespread tech adoption, thus being highly "ready".

Apart from dimensions, the literature identifies a broad array of factors that impact these dimensions. These factors are often interlinked and reinforce one another. The factors are categorized as follows:

- *Infrastructure and Connectivity:* A fundamental requirement for any digital activity is physical and digital infrastructure. This includes telecommunications networks (broadband internet, mobile 4G/5G coverage, fiber optic networks), data centers and cloud services, electricity supply, and access to devices (smartphones, computers). High-quality, ubiquitous connectivity is consistently associated with greater digital uptake. For instance, the expansion of broadband infrastructure has been linked to increases in economic growth and online business activity (Röller & Waverman, 2001). Countries that have invested in nationwide high-speed internet (like South Korea's early adoption of broadband or Estonia's public Wi-Fi and digital ID system) enjoy a head start in digital readiness. In contrast, infrastructure gaps—whether rural communities without the internet or frequent power outages—severely hinder digital progress. Thus, metrics like internet penetration rate, broadband speed, and network reliability are core indicators in readiness indices (Arıkan Kargı, 2022; Cisco Systems, 2019).
- *Human Capital and Skills*: Arguably the most critical factor is the education and skill level of the population, particularly the workforce. Digital transformation is not self-acting; it requires people who can develop, implement, and utilize new technologies. A country with a high level of general education, strong STEM (science, technology, engineering, mathematics) training, and widespread digital literacy will be far more ready to innovate and adapt. Indicators such as the literacy rate, average years of schooling, share of graduates in STEM fields, and proficiency in ICT skills are regularly used to evaluate this (Arıkan Kargı, 2022; Cisco Systems, 2019). It is not just technical skills—adaptability, problem solving, and continuous learning are vital in a fast-changing digital environment. The World Economic Forum often emphasizes "reskilling and upskilling" the workforce as a pillar of future readiness (World Economic Forum, 2024). Empirical studies reinforce the importance of human capital: countries that score higher on education indices tend to have greater technology adoption and innovation output. Conversely, nations where large portions of the workforce have low educational attainment may struggle; indeed, research on automation risk finds that workers with low education face greater threats from displacement by technology, which can hamper a country's overall readiness to transition to a digital economy. A digitally ready country invests heavily in its people—through quality basic education, digital skills training, vocational IT programs, and lifelong learning (Arntz et al., 2016).
- *Policy and Regulatory Environment*: Government policies and the regulatory framework can significantly enable or impede digital transformation. Proactive government investment in digitalization (for example, funding broadband rollout, smart city pilots, or R&D in tech) can jumpstart progress (Digital Regulation Project, 2023). Clear and forward-looking regulations (such as data protection laws, cybersecurity frameworks, electronic transaction laws) build trust and stability, encouraging businesses and consumers to participate in the digital economy (United Nations Capital Development Fund, 2023). For instance, a country that quickly establishes a legal basis for fintech and digital payments may experience rapid growth in those services. On the other hand, uncertain regulations can suppress innovation. The presence of a national digital strategy or an e-government agenda also signals readiness—many of the top-ranked countries have comprehensive plans (e.g., Singapore's Smart Nation initiative or the EU's Digital Decade targets) (Government of Singapore, 2024; European Commission, 2021). Additionally, ease of doing business and governance quality matter: if it is easier to start a business, register intellectual property, or engage in trade, then digital entrepreneurs can flourish (Beier et al., 2018). In summary, an enabling institutional environment—characterized by political support for digital initiatives, effective public

administration, and inclusive digital policies—is a key factor. This includes public-sector readiness too: governments that themselves adopt digital tools (for tax collection, service delivery, etc.) not only become more efficient but also drive demand for digital solutions in society (Ha, 2022; Lindgren et al., 2019).

- *Economic Factors and Investment Climate*: A country's overall economic development and openness to investment shape its digital readiness. Wealthier countries naturally have more resources to invest in technology and education, but beyond income, the allocation of investment matters. High R&D spending (public or private), a vibrant start-up ecosystem, and availability of venture capital or financing for tech projects all contribute to readiness (de Lucas Ancillo & Gavrila Gavrila, 2023). For example, Israel's strong venture capital scene and government support have made it one of the leading tech hubs (the "Startup Nation") despite its small size (Senor & Singer, 2009). Trade openness can facilitate access to new technologies and expertise from abroad (Škare & Ribeiro Soriano, 2021). A culture of innovation also plays a role: societies that encourage experimentation, entrepreneurship, and have a tolerance for risk and failure often adapt faster to technological shifts (Butt et al., 2024). On the flip side, countries with rigid economic structures, monopolistic markets, or low competition may see slower digital adoption. The presence of large tech companies or industries can also help—for instance, Taiwan's semiconductor industry or India's IT services sector have spillover effects on the country's digital capabilities (Raj, 2024; Chen & Shih, 2007). In essence, a dynamic economy that invests in future technologies and fosters business innovation will be more ready to transform digitally.
- *Social and Cultural Factors:* These are sometimes less quantified but still important. Public attitudes towards technology (e.g., trust in digital services, willingness to adopt new products) influence uptake. In some countries, fear of job loss or privacy concerns might impede things like AI or data sharing unless addressed. Demographics can matter too—a younger population might be more tech-savvy and quick to embrace digital lifestyles, whereas aging societies may have more difficulty retraining workers (Kiser & Washington, 2015). Additionally, inequality and the digital divide within a country affect readiness: if certain groups (rural, lower income, women) have less access to technology or education, that country's overall readiness is hampered by an underutilized segment of talent (Barra et al., 2024). Therefore, inclusive policies that bring marginalized groups into the digital fold can improve a nation's readiness profile.

These factors often interact. For example, improving broadband infrastructure (technology factor) might be of limited use if the education system is not producing IT-proficient graduates (human capital factor)—both need to progress in tandem. Likewise, even a highly educated workforce may innovate elsewhere if the domestic business climate is poor (policy/economic factors). This suggests that foundational socio-economic development and proactive investments create the fertile ground upon which specific digital advancements grow.

In practice, countries need to address all these areas to varying degrees to boost their readiness. For developing nations, international organizations often recommend starting with infrastructure and skills (as basics) but also modernizing regulatory frameworks to not fall behind. For advanced nations, the focus might be on frontier innovations and continuously updating skillsets through lifelong learning. The literature emphasizes that digital readiness is not a static end-state but a continuous process of capacity building (United Nations Development Programme [UNDP], 2023).

Policies such as improving STEM education, incentivizing ICT infrastructure expansion, ensuring affordable internet access, encouraging tech startups, and protecting digital rights are all levers to enhance readiness. If these policies are neglected, it may evolve into a key barrier to progress. For instance, if a country fails to invest in education, it may face a talent shortage that leaves expensive new infrastructure underutilized.

The readiness of a country's future workforce—essentially the supply of young talent and the adaptability of its labor force—is increasingly viewed as a key driver of digital transformation success. While research, studies and indices have measured nations' digital infrastructure and current usage extensively, fewer have closely analyzed how the education system and occupational structure of a country prepare it (or not) for impending digital disruptions.

Digital transformation, especially in its next phase involving artificial intelligence and robotics, is expected to bring about substantial changes in the labor market. Many tasks will be automated, some jobs will decline, new jobs will emerge, and almost all jobs will require a higher baseline of digital competency. Therefore, a country's capacity to educate, train, and retrain its people is absolutely critical for ensuring that digitalization leads to broadly shared prosperity rather than unemployment or polarization. The literature strongly indicates that countries investing in education and skills development are better positioned to absorb technological shocks (Arntz et al., 2016).

Workers with lower educational attainment are disproportionately at risk from automation (Arntz et al., 2016; Chang & Huynh, 2016). Low-wage, routine jobs—often held by less-educated workers—are easier to automate than high-skill jobs that involve creativity, complex problem solving, or human interaction (Chang & Huynh, 2016; OECD, 2019a). Thus, countries with a large share of employment in low-skill routine occupations (for example, assembly line manufacturing or basic clerical work) face a double challenge: these jobs might be lost to machines, and the workers may not have the education needed to shift into new roles. The International Labour Organization (ILO) and other bodies have warned that without significant upskilling, automation could worsen inequality between high-skill and low-skill workers, and between countries that have skilled labor versus those that do not (United Nations & International Labour Organization, 2024).

Although research points to the risk of automation of work based on routine tasks performed by low-skilled workers, recent studies point to the fact that high-skilled workers are not immune to disrupting changes. Advances in artificial intelligence and machine learning enable automation of non-routine cognitive tasks traditionally thought to be the domain of highly educated professionals (Ozgul et al., 2024; OECD, 2022). While some highly skilled workers benefit from task augmentation, others experience wage stagnation or erosion, particularly in occupations where routine elements are susceptible to automation (Acemoglu & Restrepo, 2018). Brynjolfsson and McAfee (2014) emphasize that this wave of "digital disruption" has introduced a new form of skill-biased technological change, where both low- and mid-skill jobs are hollowed out while high-skill roles become more competitive. This suggests that inequality risks are not only vertical (low- vs. high-skill) but also horizontal—cutting across sectors and job types depending on their specific task structures.

While policymakers talk about the future of work, traditional readiness metrics do not directly account for how threatened a country's existing jobs are by automation. A country might score reasonably on infrastructure and current usage, but if a large fraction of its workforce is in automatable jobs and the country lacks retraining programs, its future readiness is shaky. The Economist Intelligence Unit's Automation Readiness Index (ARI) in 2018 was a pioneering effort to qualitatively assess how prepared countries are for automation, examining education policies, labor market programs, and innovation strategies. The ARI found that even leading nations had much room for improvement—for example, few countries had updated their education policies significantly to address AI and automation (The Economist Intelligence Unit, 2018). South Korea, Germany, and Singapore topped that index because they had started initiatives like curriculum reforms and vocational training updates, whereas many others had barely begun. This suggests that policy proactiveness in workforce development is a differentiator. The ARI also highlighted that middle-income countries (like Malaysia, Indonesia) aiming to industrialize via automation face severe hurdles due to weaknesses in basic education and skills, implying they are at risk of being caught unprepared. However, the ARI was more of a policy checklist and did not directly quantify the state of the workforce or education outcomes. Thus, there is room for academic research to incorporate metrics like the percentage of workforce in high-risk jobs, or the effectiveness of training systems, into evaluations of digital readiness. We can conclude that the research gap is in considering automation risk as a component of national readiness for digital transformation.

While conceptual links between education, skills, and digital readiness are acknowledged, they have not been the primary focus of most empirical cross-country analyses. Researchers have thoroughly studied the impacts of infrastructure and digital technology adoption on economic outcomes (Corejova & Chinoracky, 2021; Arıkan Kargı, 2022; Tudose et al., 2023; Cisco Systems, 2019; OECD, 2019b; Cusolito et al., 2020; Suntsova, 2024; Dutta & Lanvin, 2023; Röller & Waverman, 2001; de Lucas Ancillo & Gavrila Gavrila, 2023; Senor & Singer, 2009; Škare & Ribeiro Soriano, 2021; Butt et al., 2024; Aleksandrova et al., 2022; Ha, 2022; Lindgren et al., 2019), but fewer studies systematically rank countries by the skill readiness of their population for digital disruption (Tudose et al., 2023; Cisco Systems, 2019; Arntz et al., 2016; IMD, 2024; World Bank, 2016; World Economic Forum, 2024).

This article aims to contribute by examining the workforce dimension of digital transformation readiness. Workforce dimension and its readiness for digital transformation was examined by quantifying the relationship between measures related to risk of job automation and measures related to education quality. Final measurements point out which countries are least prepared for digitalization-driven change. This addresses the identified research gap.

The concept of education is operationalized through three widely recognized indicators. First, expenditure on educational institutions as a percentage of GDP reflects a country's investment in developing its human capital. Second, PISA overall scores, combining results in mathematics, science, and reading, provide a standardized measure of student learning outcomes and cognitive readiness. Third, the Education Index, part of the UN's Human Development Index, captures average and expected years of schooling, thus offering a broader view of educational attainment. These indicators were selected based on their international comparability and together they form a composite representation of education quality, enabling a data-driven analysis of how educational factors relate to national exposure to job automation and future workforce vulnerability.

3. Methodology

Based on the literature review conducted and the identified research gap, it is possible to summarize and formulate the following research question: Which countries, by the potential of their future workforce, are the least prepared for the changes resulting from digitalization?

For the purpose of addressing the formulated research question, and as mentioned at the end of the literature review section, specific variables were identified.

On the basis of study by Frey and Osborne (2017), Nedelkoska and Quintini published a study in 2018 in which they identified the percentages of jobs at risk of automation, specifically the "Jobs at high risk of automation" metric (Nedelkoska & Quintini, 2018). This study is based on data from the 2012 PIAAC survey. Thirteen years have passed since that year, and more recent data are not available. If the aim is to analyze the readiness of countries for the changes resulting from the development of digital technologies, it is necessary to examine the data in the time range closest to year 2025.

The anchor point for the research presented in this article is 2012. In this year, the values by which the risk of job automation were measured are set. In our research, we applied a research approach from Georgieff and Milanez, and their study "What happened to jobs with high risk of automation?" (Georgieff & Milanez, 2021) conducted for the OECD. As part of the study, the authors examined how employment has changed over time since the risk of automation of jobs was identified in 2012. They examined employment as a percentage of the average change in employment rates for selected years from 2012 to 2019.

Building on the measurement essence of the Georgieff and Milanez study, this study provides an analysis of how the values of selected education-related indicators change over time in selected countries compared to the risk of job automation in 2012. The selected countries can be understood as OECD countries for which, in the measurement framework, data are available.

The dimension of education was quantified using selected indicators:

- The first is the share of education expenditure in GDP. By education expenditure we mean the share of expenditure of both public and private institutions. This metric is important because it is an indicator of the quality of education in a country. Higher investment in education can improve school infrastructure, provide better salaries for teachers, support modern teaching aids and technology, and fund research and innovation in education. Data for the calculation of this metric ("Expenditure on educational institutions as a percentage of GDP") were obtained from the OECD database (OECD, 2025).

The question is whether this indicator alone is indicative of the quality of education. Therefore, to make the measurements more accurate and comprehensive, two other indicators in the calculations were included:

- The second indicator is the PISA overall score metric. PISA overall scores provide data on students' basic skills in reading, math, and science. It is calculated as an average of math, reading, and science scores. High scores indicate that students in a given country have good academic skills and are able to apply them in a variety of contexts, in a variety of subject areas. Conversely, low scores may indicate problems in basic skills. The data on the value of the metric ("PISA overall score") were obtained directly from the database (OECD, 2019c, 2023).
- The third metric is the Education Index. This index is a part of the HDI (Human Development Index). The Education Index basically measures the average of the expected number of years a young person spends in school and the average number of years a young person spends in school. A high score on the Education Index implies that a country has strong educational outcomes and broad access to education. The data related to the metrics ("Expected years of schooling" and "mean years of schooling") from which Education Index was calculated were obtained from the UN Human Development Reports database (United Nations Development Programme [UNDP], 2024).

To assess the dependence of the selected metrics, this article uses metrics that determine the statistical significance of the observed relationships (using a hypothesis test of correlation significance) to help us determine whether the observed relationship between the variables is real or coincidental:

- The first metric is the correlation coefficient, which measures the strength and direction of the relationship between two variables. Depending on the linear dependence of the variables, the correlation can be positive, negative, or zero. For the purpose of performing the calculations, we chose Pearson's correlation coefficient, as all analyzed variables are continuous and measured on an interval or ratio scale. In addition, visual inspection of scatterplots confirmed that the relationships between the variables are approximately linear, and the data do not exhibit extreme deviations or significant non-linear trends. Pearson's correlation coefficient is therefore appropriate for capturing the strength of linear associations in this context. The correlation coefficient itself does not provide information about the statistical significance of the relationship.

- Therefore, to assess the statistical significance of the correlation coefficients, we applied a standard hypothesis testing procedure. Specifically, we used the t-statistic derived from the Pearson correlation coefficient, which allows us to determine whether the observed correlation could have occurred by chance. Based on the t-statistic, a p-value is calculated to evaluate whether the correlation is statistically significant.
- The hypothesis test follows the conventional logic: if the p-value is less than the alpha level of significance (0.05), the null hypothesis (that there is no statistically significant correlation) is rejected, and the alternative hypothesis (that there is a statistically significant correlation between the two variables) is accepted. This approach enables us to distinguish between relationships that are likely to exist in the population and those that may result from sampling variability.

The results of the measurements are intended primarily for policymakers concerned with the issue of countries' readiness for changes related to the digital transformation. In addition, the results of the measurements represent an information basis for strategic planning aimed at shaping education policies.

4. Results

Based on the measurements reported by Nedelkoska and Quintini, the proportion of jobs at high risk of automation (metric A "Jobs at high risk of automation") significantly varies across the countries studied (see Chart 1). The percentage of such jobs ranges from 5.7% in Norway to 33.7% in Slovakia. Generally, Northern Europe (including Scandinavian countries and the United Kingdom), North America (Canada and the United States), and New Zealand exhibit relatively low levels of risk. Conversely, Eastern and Southern European countries face a much higher risk of automation. The publication notes that these differences are not due to sectoral variations in the economies but rather to how jobs are organized in these countries. Jobs in Southern and Eastern Europe are more likely to involve automatable tasks compared to similar job categories in other countries. For instance, in one country, assembly line workers might only perform manual tasks with a high risk of automation, whereas, in another country, workers in the same role might also monitor industrial robots and carry out quality control measures. Consequently, jobs in the second country are much less at risk than those in the first.

Considering the values of metric A (jobs at high risk of automation), we identified values for metrics B (expenditure on educational institutions as a percentage of GDP), C (PISA testing overall score) and D (Education Index). Based on the research and measurement logic (outlined in the methodology section of the paper and derived from measurements in the Georgieff and Milanez study (2021)), metrics B, C, and D are the average of the values measured over the years (see Table 1). For metric C, it is an average of average overall values of metric. The selection of years was affected by availability of the data.

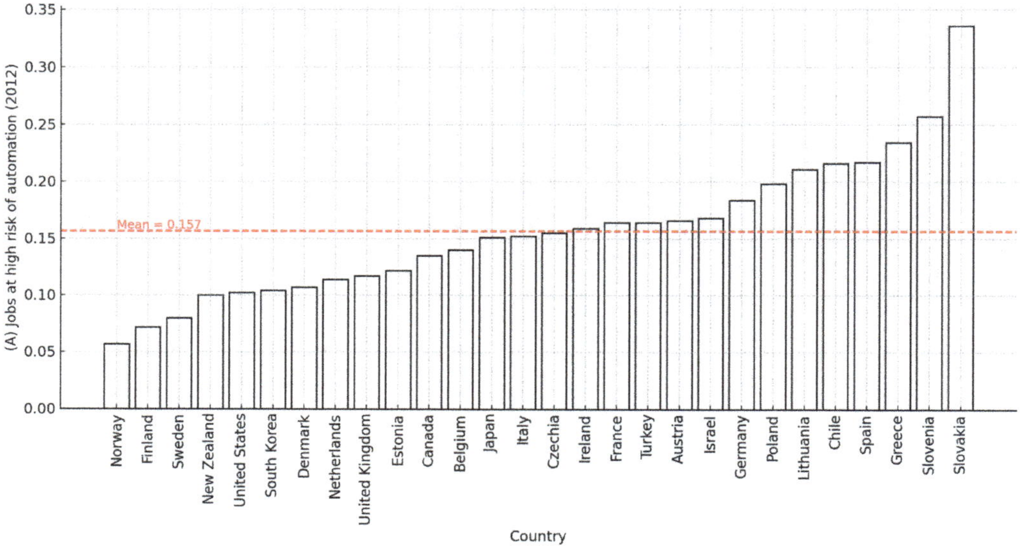

Chart 1. Jobs at high risk of automation by country.

Table 1. Summarization of values identified for metrics A, B, C, and D.

Country	(A) Jobs at High Risk of Automation (2012)	(B) Expenditure on Educational Institutions as a Percentage of GDP Average (2012–2020)	(C) Average Overall PISA Testing Score (2012–2022)	(D) Education Index Average (2012–2022)
Austria	16.60%	4.83%	494	0.85
Belgium	14.00%	5.73%	502	0.94
Canada	13.50%	5.83%	517	0.90
Czechia	15.50%	3.97%	438	0.88
Denmark	10.70%	5.84%	493	0.95
Estonia	12.20%	4.70%	499	0.90
Finland	7.20%	5.48%	523	0.95
France	16.40%	5.24%	516	0.82
Germany	18.40%	4.30%	492	0.95
Greece	23.40%	3.73%	501	0.88
Chile	21.60%	6.13%	453	0.81
Ireland	15.90%	4.00%	508	0.90
Israel	16.80%	6.09%	469	0.85
Italy	15.20%	3.93%	482	0.80
Japan	15.10%	4.12%	531	0.85
South Korea	10.40%	5.15%	526	0.87
Lithuania	21.10%	3.87%	479	0.90
Netherlands	11.40%	5.28%	502	0.92

Table 1. *Cont.*

Country	(A) Jobs at High Risk of Automation (2012)	(B) Expenditure on Educational Institutions as a Percentage of GDP Average (2012–2020)	(C) Average Overall PISA Testing Score (2012–2022)	(D) Education Index Average (2012–2022)
New Zealand	10.00%	5.63%	503	0.97
Norway	5.70%	6.48%	493	0.93
Poland	19.80%	4.57%	508	0.88
Slovakia	33.60%	3.87%	466	0.84
Slovenia	25.70%	4.46%	499	0.90
Spain	21.70%	4.41%	485	0.82
Sweden	8.00%	5.40%	492	0.93
Turkey	16.40%	5.13%	453	0.78
United Kingdom	11.70%	6.29%	498	0.92
United States	10.20%	6.11%	491	0.91

The first metric (B) that is examined is the expenditure on educational institutions as a percentage of GDP metric (Figure 1). The slope of the trend line resulting from the graph tells us that this is a negative relationship. As the values of metric A decrease, the values of metric B decrease. This means that if a country is measured to have a high risk of job automation, then that country has a lower share of spending on education as a proportion of the country's total GDP.

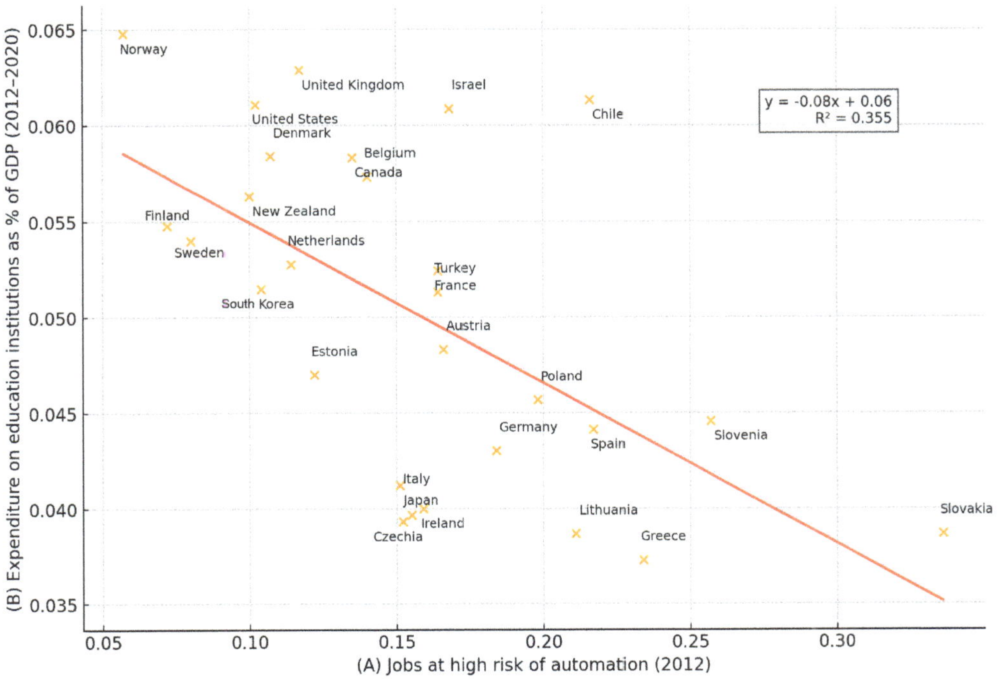

Figure 1. Automation risk vs. education expenditure.

The second metric we examined is the overall PISA score for the domains of math, science, and reading (Figure 2). The graphical results presented in the graph suggest a possible same dependency as in the previous case. The higher risk of automation is in those countries where lower PISA scores were recorded. What should be noted is that if there is a dependency even between the metrics, it is a dependency with very low intensity.

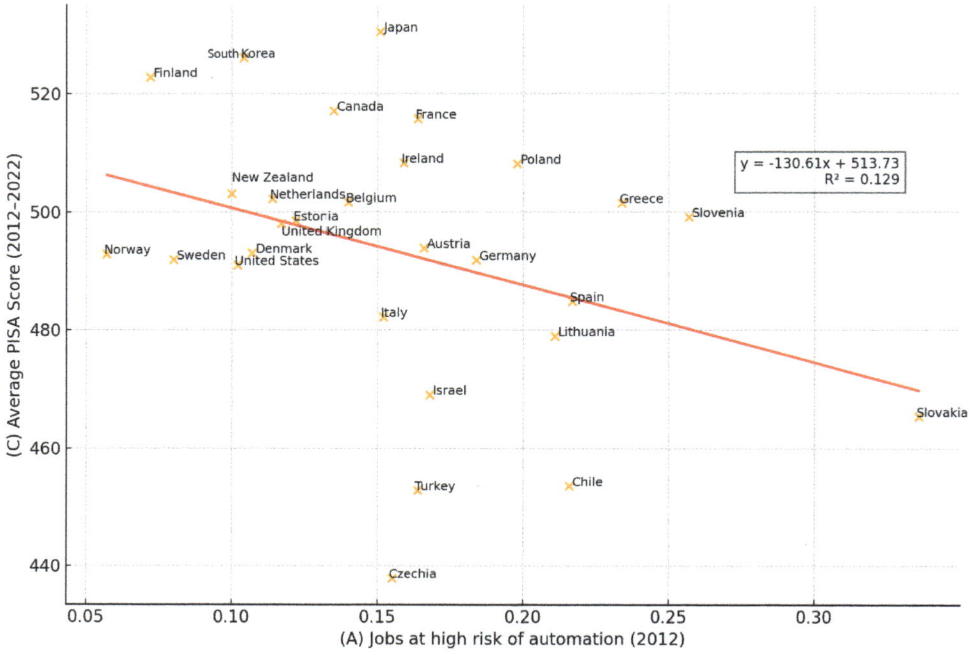

Figure 2. Automation risk vs. PISA score.

The third metric we examined is the value of the Education Index, which is part of the HDI measurements (Figure 3). As in the previous cases—the graphical visualization suggests a negative relationship. The higher the risk of automation of jobs in a given country is, the lower is the value of the Education Index.

Even if certain dependencies between metrics were measured. They need to be further statistically investigated. The table below presents the findings, which provide a more detailed picture of how the metrics are interdependent. For each variable, it is indicated what combination of metrics (A to D) is under investigation.

If we look at the correlation coefficients (Table 2), none of the observed relationships can be classified as strong. In two cases—between metrics B and A, and between D and A—the correlations are moderate and negative. In the third case—between C and A—the correlation is weak and negative.

To evaluate the statistical relevance of these correlations, we examined the *p*-values associated with each Pearson correlation coefficient. In the case of the first correlation (B–A), the *p*-value is below 0.05, which indicates that the observed negative correlation is statistically significant. We can therefore reject the null hypothesis of no correlation.

For the second correlation (C–A), the *p*-value is 0.06, which exceeds the standard threshold of 0.05. This means that we do not have sufficient evidence to reject the null hypothesis, and the observed weak negative correlation may not be statistically significant. Consequently, this relationship is not subject to further interpretation or analysis in the following sections.

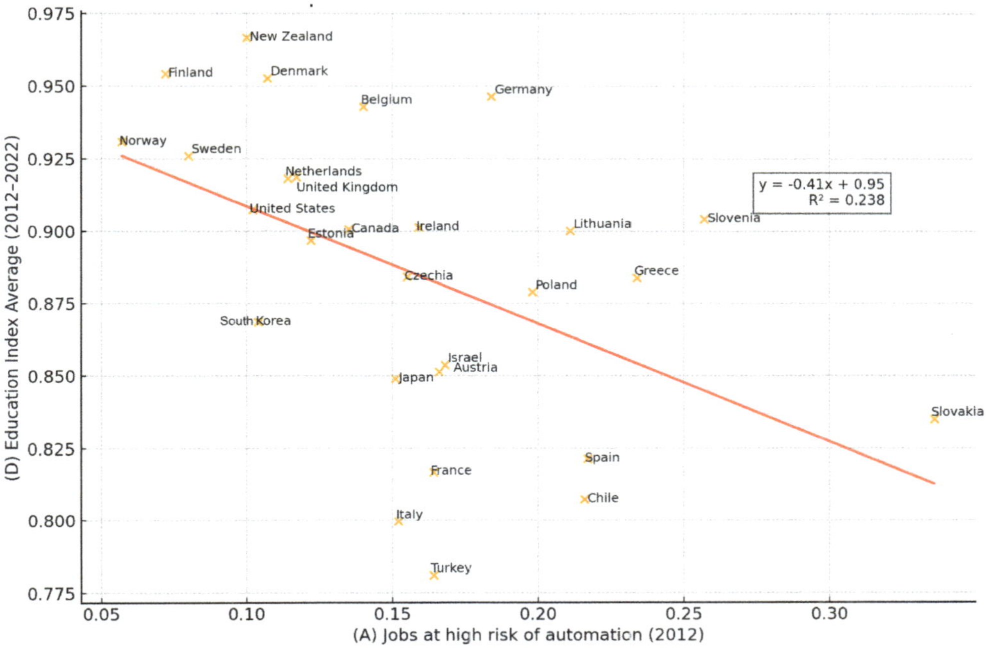

Figure 3. Automation risk vs. Education Index.

Table 2. Statistical significance of measurements.

B and A	C and A	D and A
Correlation	Correlation	Correlation
−0.5959752068	−0.3594763521	−0.4876465918
p-value	*p*-value	*p*-value
0.0008182403957	0.06027140363	0.008481857593

In the third case (D–A), the *p*-value is again below 0.05, confirming a statistically significant negative correlation between metrics D and A.

It is important to note that while the strength and direction of the relationship are described by the correlation coefficient, the *p*-value is used to determine whether the observed correlation is statistically unlikely to have occurred by chance. In line with this criterion, only those correlations with *p*-values below 0.05 are considered further in the analysis.

If we form clusters grouping countries by metric A, it is possible to see a pattern in the values of metrics B and D (Tables 3 and 4). The clusters, according to Metric A, are formed with 5% numeric intervals. That is, the groups are distributed as 0–5%, 5–10%, 10–15%, 15–20%, and 20–25%. The pattern is expressed using a heat map. Using the color scales relationships, deviations and extreme values are identified. Metric B values above 5% are highlighted with a darker shade of green. Values below 5% are highlighted by lighter shades of green. For metric D, the darkest shades of green are applied to those values that are in closest proximity to 1. Further upgrading the clarity of Tables 3 and 4, Figures 4 and 5 show quadrants where we can group countries according to the degree of risk of work automation and average spending on education or average values of the Education Index. Quadrants are numbers from 1 to 4 (top left is 1, top right is 2, bottom right is 3, bottom left is 4).

Table 3. Heat map of patterns between metrics A and B.

Country	(A) Jobs at High Risk of Automation (2012)	(B) Average Expenditure on Educational Institutions as a Percentage of GDP (2012–2020)
Norway	5.70%	6.48%
Finland	7.20%	5.48%
Sweden	8.00%	5.40%
New Zealand	10.00%	5.63%
United States	10.20%	6.11%
South Korea	10.40%	5.15%
Denmark	10.70%	5.84%
Netherlands	11.40%	5.28%
United Kingdom	11.70%	6.29%
Estonia	12.20%	4.70%
Canada	13.50%	5.83%
Belgium	14.00%	5.73%
Japan	15.10%	4.12%
Italy	15.20%	3.93%
Czechia	15.50%	3.97%
Ireland	15.90%	4.00%
Turkey	16.40%	5.13%
France	16.40%	5.24%
Austria	16.60%	4.83%
Israel	16.80%	6.09%
Germany	18.40%	4.30%
Poland	19.80%	4.57%
Lithuania	21.10%	3.87%
Chile	21.60%	6.13%
Spain	21.70%	4.41%
Greece	23.40%	3.73%
Slovenia	25.70%	4.46%
Slovakia	33.60%	3.87%

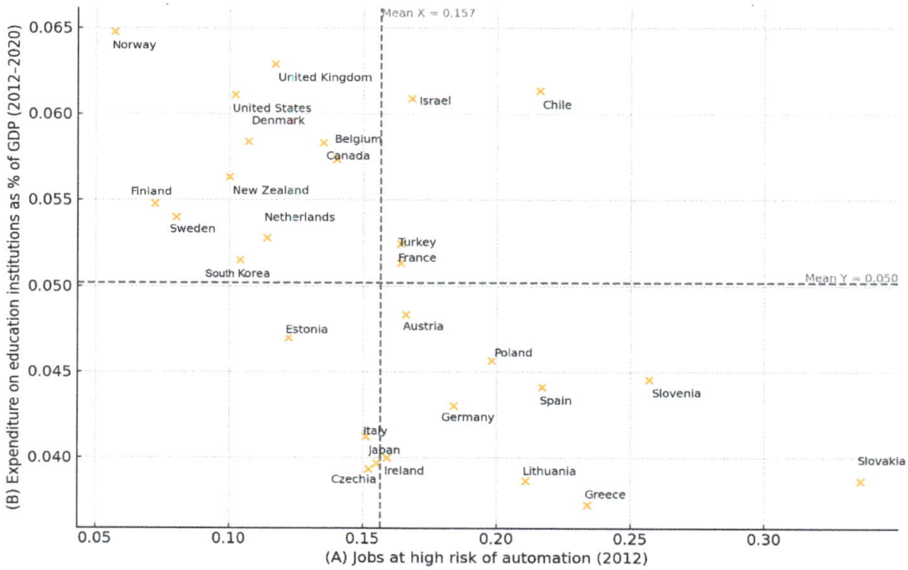

Figure 4. Quadrant view—automation risk vs. education expenditure.

Table 4. Heat map of patterns between metrics A and D.

Country	(A) Jobs at High Risk of Automation (2012)	(D) Average Value of Education Index (2012–2022)
Norway	5.70%	0.93
Finland	7.20%	0.95
Sweden	8.00%	0.93
New Zealand	10.00%	0.97
United States	10.20%	0.91
South Korea	10.40%	0.87
Denmark	10.70%	0.95
Netherlands	11.40%	0.92
United Kingdom	11.70%	0.92
Estonia	12.20%	0.90
Canada	13.50%	0.90
Belgium	14.00%	0.94
Japan	15.10%	0.85
Italy	15.20%	0.80
Czechia	15.50%	0.88
Ireland	15.90%	0.90
Turkey	16.40%	0.78
France	16.40%	0.82
Austria	16.60%	0.85
Israel	16.80%	0.85
Germany	18.40%	0.95
Poland	19.80%	0.88
Lithuania	21.10%	0.90
Chile	21.60%	0.81
Spain	21.70%	0.82
Greece	23.40%	0.88
Slovenia	25.70%	0.90
Slovakia	33.60%	0.84

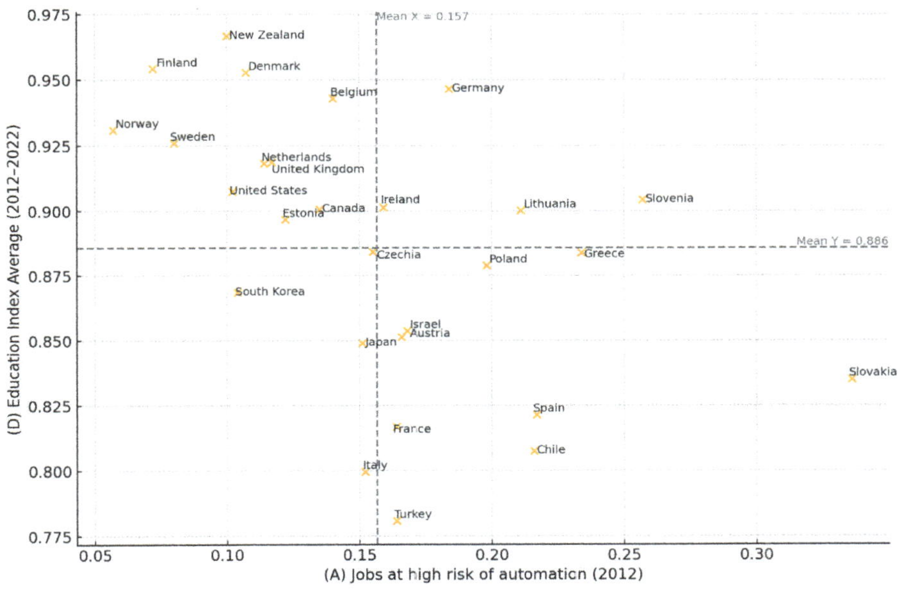

Figure 5. Quadrant view—automation risk vs. Education Index.

Looking at Table 3, average share of jobs at high risk of automation is 15.65%, with the lowest value 5.7% and the highest reaching 33.6%. As for spending on educational institutions, the average is 5.02% of GDP, with values ranging from 3.73% to 6.48%. These data point to a relatively wide dispersion in the intensity of public investment in education, reflecting different political and economic strategies of individual countries. The heat map of Table 3 clearly shows that the upper part of the table representing those countries, whose risk of job automation is lower than average, have higher expenditures in education. The bottom part of the table does not give us a clear answer.

Figure 4 further elaborates and groups countries as follows:

- Quadrant 1: Countries with above-average education expenditures as a % of GDP (>0.05) have a below-average % of jobs at high risk of automation (<0.157). These are Norway, Finland, Sweden, New Zealand, United States, South Korea, Denmark, Netherlands, United Kingdom, Canada, and Belgium.
- Quadrant 2: Countries with above-average education expenditures as a % of GDP (>0.05) have an above-average % of jobs at high risk of automation (>0.157). These are Israel, Chile, Turkey, and France.
- Quadrant 3: Countries with below-average education expenditures as a % of GDP (<0.05) have an above-average % of jobs at high risk of automation (>0.157). These are Ireland, Austria, Germany, Poland, Spain, Slovenia, Lithuania, Greece, and Slovakia.
- Quadrant 4: Countries with below-average education expenditures as a % of GDP (<0.05) have a below-average % of jobs at high risk of automation (<0.157). These are Estonia, Italy, Japan, and Czechia.

In terms of the Education Index (Table 4), the average value is 0.886, with a minimum value of 0.78 and a maximum value of 0.97. These data again indicate significant diversity between countries in terms of exposure to automation risk and years spent schooling in education systems. Again, as is the case with data in Tables 3 and 4, using heat map coloring, it is split into two parts. The upper part again clearly shows that countries that have a high Education Index are less susceptible to job automation. The lower part of the table is not so clear. Clarity again provides a scatter plot graph divided into quadrants (Figure 5) where quadrants are again grouped into four categories:

- Quadrant 1: Countries with above-average average values of the Education Index (>0.886) have a below-average % of jobs at high risk of automation (<0.157). These are Norway, Finland, Sweden, New Zealand, Denmark, Belgium, Netherlands, United Kingdom, United States, Estonia, and Canada.
- Quadrant 2: Countries with above-average average values of the Education Index (>0.886) have an above-average % of jobs at high risk of automation (>0.157). These are Ireland, Germany, Lithuania, and Slovenia.
- Quadrant 3: Countries with below-average average values of the Education Index (<0.886) have an above-average % of jobs at high risk of automation (>0.157). These are Turkey, France, Austria, Israel, Poland, Greece, Spain, Chile, and Slovakia.
- Quadrant 4: Countries with below-average average values of the Education Index (<0.886) have a below-average % of jobs at high risk of automation (<0.157). These are Czechia, Japan, Italy, and South Korea.

5. Discussion

The findings of this study reveal substantial disparities in countries' readiness for digital transformation in terms of human capital and the risk of job automation. We identified a group of best-prepared countries that systematically invest significantly in education and demonstrate high educational performance (e.g., Education Index), while simultaneously exhibiting a relatively low share of jobs at high risk of automation. These include economically advanced countries such as New Zealand, Canada, Sweden, Norway, Denmark, and Finland, which consistently develop human capital and whose labor forces possess the competencies required to mitigate the disruptive effects of automation. At the opposite end of the spectrum are least-prepared countries—for example, Slovakia, Poland, and Greece—with below-average investment in education and weaker educational outcomes, which also show a high proportion of jobs susceptible to automation. This combination of insufficient human capital and high technological vulnerability suggests significant exposure to labor market shocks.

While the Automation Readiness Index (ARI) (The Economist Intelligence Unit, 2018) qualitatively highlighted that many countries had not sufficiently updated their education policies in response to the rise of AI and automation, our study quantitatively reinforces this perspective. It shows that countries with underdeveloped or underfunded education systems already exhibit higher vulnerability, with larger proportions of automatable jobs. Thus, policy recommendations include implementing large-scale upskilling programs and lifelong learning strategies targeting workers in the most exposed sectors. If neglected, automation may exacerbate regional and social inequalities—for instance, through rising long-term unemployment or the decline of entire economic sectors. Governments should prioritize increasing education investment, which includes not only raising education expenditure as a share of GDP but ensuring the effective allocation of these resources. Examples of such allocation can be focused on modernizing curricula (with emphasis on digital skills, STEM disciplines, and adaptability), improving teaching quality, and preparing educators for the digital era.

For moderately prepared countries, our findings indicate the need for better policy alignment. Nations like France or Israel, where education spending is high yet automation risk remains elevated, should assess whether resources are used effectively—for instance, whether education systems respond to labor market needs in the digital era. These countries may benefit from reforms linking education and practice (e.g., dual education, partnerships with tech firms) and promoting transferable digital skills. Others, such as Germany and Ireland, with high-quality education outcomes but persistent automation risk, should examine their economic structures. A large share of routine-intensive industrial sectors may render even well-educated workforces vulnerable. Hence, policy priorities include innovation support and job creation in sectors resilient to automation, alongside reskilling workers from industries negatively impacted by digital transformation.

Best-prepared countries should not be complacent. While currently leading, rapid technological change (e.g., AI, robotics, platform economy) may reveal future weaknesses. These countries should continue investing in human capital, regularly update educational content, and promote a culture of lifelong learning. They may serve as models of best practice for less-prepared countries. Less-prepared countries could adopt successful policies, such as early digital literacy education, investment in R&D, and active labor market policies.

From the broader literature perspective, this study extends and complements prior research on digital transformation readiness, especially by emphasizing the role of human capital and automation risk. Many existing indices (Network Readiness Index (NRI) (Dutta & Lanvin, 2023), IMD World Digital Competitiveness Ranking (IMD, 2024), Digital Adoption Index of the World Bank (World Bank, 2016), Cisco Digital Readiness Index (Cisco Systems, 2019)) emphasize current infrastructure or usage but underrepresent the future workforce dimension. Results of this research advance this perspective by linking education quality indicators with automation risk estimates. Thus, this study addresses a gap previously noted in the literature: the need to integrate automation vulnerability into national readiness assessments. Our findings from a certain point of view confirm on a macro level what previous studies (Corejova & Chinoracky, 2021; Arntz et al., 2016; Frey &

Osborne, 2017; Nedelkoska & Quintini, 2018) suggested on an individual level—that the workforces of countries with a lower quality of education and thus, with lower education, face a higher automation risk. Unlike the qualitative ARI (The Economist Intelligence Unit, 2018), this study uses quantitative data to identify the most vulnerable countries. The resulting typology creates a more comprehensive picture of readiness that merges technological and human capital dimensions.

6. Conclusions

This study contributes to understanding how countries are prepared for changes driven by digital transformation from the perspective of their future workforce. By quantifying the relationship between education quality indicators and job automation risk, we identified which OECD countries are best and least prepared for impending technological changes. The analysis showed that inadequate educational investment and weak learning outcomes correlate with greater automation vulnerability. This has implications for both research and policymaking.

The study and analysis have several methodological limitations to which directions for further research are suggested:

- The study is based on risk estimates from 2012 by Nedelkoska and Quintini, 2018. Technological advances since 2012—particularly in AI and robotics—have likely shifted both the nature and scale of automatable tasks. The direction of further research should build on the study by Nedelkoska and Quintini and should produce an updated list of countries categorized according to the risk of automation of work in those countries.
- Data for the other indicators, which are PISA scores, Education Index and Average Education Expenditure as % of GDP, are from previous years. This can be seen as a form of limitation of the research, which is a suggestion for further research: depending on the availability of more recent data, the measurements need to be updated to best reflect the current situation.
- The sample of countries was limited to those with available standardized data (OECD countries). Future research should examine datasets from other countries or organizations that use similar or complementary metrics.
- Due to the availability of data for a selected sample of countries, the indicators used to measure human capital were limited to three: education expenditure, PISA scores, and the Education Index. While relevant, these metrics do not fully capture the dimensions necessary to provide a comprehensive overview of education quality. Therefore, future research could delve deeper by clustering countries based on complementary indicators specifically designed to assess the quality of education.

In conclusion, this study highlights the importance of future workforce preparedness as a key pillar of national digital readiness. Countries with weak investment in education and a vulnerable labor structure may struggle to adapt to rapid technological change. For policymakers, the findings offer a clear directive: invest in human capital, promote skill adaptability, and foster resilient labor markets to secure the benefits of digital transformation and mitigate its risks.

Author Contributions: Conceptualization, R.C. and N.S.; methodology, R.C.; validation, R.M.; formal analysis, R.C. and N.S.; investigation, R.C.; resources, R.C.; data curation, R.C.; writing-original draft preparation, R.C.; writing-review and editing, R.C., N.S. and L.M.; visualization, R.C.; funding acquisition, R.M. All authors have read and agreed to the published version of the manuscript.

Funding: This research was funded by a grant provided by the scientific research project 2020-1-MT01-KA203-074215: Integrated RPL & APEL Level 6 Accredited Online Programme for Entrepreneurs.

Institutional Review Board Statement: Not applicable.

Informed Consent Statement: Not applicable.

Data Availability Statement: The data that support the findings of this study are derived from publicly available sources (OECD, 2019c, 2023, 2025; United Nations Development Programme [UNDP], 2024) and were processed by the authors.

Conflicts of Interest: The authors declare no conflicts of interest.

References

Acemoglu, D., & Restrepo, P. (2018). Low-skill and high-skill automation. *Journal of Human Capital, 12*(2), 204–232. [CrossRef]

Aleksandrova, A., Truntsevsky, Y., & Polutova, M. (2022). Digitalization and its impact on economic growth. *Brazilian Journal of Political Economy, 42*(2), 424–441. [CrossRef]

Arıkan Kargı, V. S. (2022). Determining digital readiness levels of the OECD countries with CRITIC-Based ARAS method. *Akademik Yaklaşımlar Dergisi, 13*(2), 363–376. [CrossRef]

Arntz, M., Gregory, T., & Zierahn, U. (2016). *The risk of automation for jobs in OECD countries: A comparative analysis*. OECD Social, Employment and Migration Working Papers No. 189. OECD.

Barra, C., Grimaldi, M., Muazzam, A., Troisi, O., & Visvizi, A. (2024). Digital divide, gender gap, and entrepreneurial orientation: How to foster technology adoption among Pakistani higher education students? *Socio-Economic Planning Sciences, 93*, 101904.

Beier, G., Niehoff, S., Ziems, T., & Xue, B. (2018). Sustainability aspects of a digitalized industry—A comparative study from China and Germany. *International Journal of Precision Engineering and Manufacturing-Green Technology, 4*(2), 227–234. [CrossRef]

Brennen, J. S., & Kreiss, D. (2016). Digitalization. In K. B. Jensen, R. T. Craig, J. D. Pooley, & E. W. Rothenbuhler (Eds.), *The international encyclopedia of communication theory and philosophy*. Wiley-Blackwell.

Brynjolfsson, E., & McAfee, A. (2014). *The second machine age: Work, progress, and prosperity in a time of brilliant technologies*. W.W. Norton & Company. ISBN 978-0393239355.

Butt, A., Imran, F., Helo, P., & Kantola, J. (2024). Strategic design of culture for digital transformation. *Long Range Planning, 57*(2), 102415. [CrossRef]

Chang, J.-H., & Huynh, P. (2016). *ASEAN in transformation: The future of jobs at risk of automation*. Bureau for Employers' Activities, Working Paper No. 9. International Labour Office. ISBN 9789221309659.

Chen, M.-L., & Shih, H.-Y. (2007). Patent citations, R&D spillover and Tobin's Q: Evidence from the semiconductor industry in Taiwan. *Review of Quantitative Finance and Accounting, 28*, 123–140.

Cisco Systems. (2019). *Cisco digital readiness index*. Cisco Systems.

Corejova, T., & Chinoracky, R. (2021). Assessing the potential for digital transformation. *Sustainability, 13*(19), 11040. [CrossRef]

Cusolito, A. P., Lederman, D., & Peña, J. (2020). *The effects of digital-technology adoption on productivity and factor demand: Firm-level evidence from developing countries*. Policy Research Working Paper 9333. World Bank Group.

de Lucas Ancillo, A., & Gavrila Gavrila, S. (2023). The impact of research and development on entrepreneurship, innovation, digitization and digital transformation. *Journal of Business Research, 157*, 113580. [CrossRef]

Digital Regulation Project. (2023). *National digital transformation strategy: Mapping the digital journey*. DigitalRegulation.org.

Dutta, S., & Lanvin, B. (Eds.). (2023). *Network readiness index 2023: Trust in a network society—A crisis of the digital age?* Portulans Institute.

e-Estonia. (2022). *How digital signatures save 2% of GDP annually*. e-Estonia Briefing Centre.

European Commission. (2021). *Europe's digital decade: Digital targets for 2030*. European Commission.

Frey, C. B., & Osborne, M. A. (2017). The future of employment: How susceptible are jobs to computerisation? *Technological Forecasting and Social Change, 114*, 254–280. [CrossRef]

Georgieff, A., & Milanez, A. (2021). *What happened to jobs at high risk of automation?* OECD Social, Employment and Migration Working Papers, No. 255. OECD Publishing.

Government of Singapore. (2024). *Smart nation and digital government office. Smart nation Singapore: Transforming the future today*. Government of Singapore.

Ha, L. T. (2022). Effects of digitalization on financialization: Empirical evidence from European countries. *Technology in Society, 68*, 101851. [CrossRef]

IMD. (2024). *World digital competitiveness ranking 2024*. IMD World Competitiveness Center.

ING Think. (2022). *China's digital economy: Divided but growing. ING economic and financial analysis*. Available online: https://think.ing.com/articles/china-digital-economy-divided-but-growing/ (accessed on 15 May 2025).

Kiser, A. I. T., & Washington, R. (2015). The information gap amongst the generations and the implications for organizations. *International Journal of Digital Literacy and Digital Competence, 6*(2), 36–63. [CrossRef]

Lindgren, I., Madsen, C. Ø., Hofmann, S., & Melin, U. (2019). Close encounters of the digital kind: A research agenda for the digitalization of public services. *Government Information Quarterly, 36*(3), 427–436. [CrossRef]

McKinsey & Company. (2021). *The future of digital innovation in China: Megatrends shaping one of the world's fastest evolving digital ecosystems*. McKinsey & Company.

Mikalef, P., & Parmiggiani, E. (Eds.). (2022). *Digital transformation in Norwegian enterprises*. Springer.

Nedelkoska, L., & Quintini, G. (2018). *Automation, skills use and training*. OECD Social, Employment and Migration Working Papers. No. 202. OECD Publishing.

OECD. (2019a). *Getting skills right: Future-ready adult learning systems*. OECD Publishing.

OECD. (2019b). *Going digital: Shaping policies, improving lives*. OECD Publishing.

OECD. (2019c). *PISA 2018 database*. OECD Publishing.

OECD. (2022). *What skills and abilities can automation technologies replicate and what does it mean for workers?* OECD Social, Employment and Migration Working Papers. OECD Publishing.

OECD. (2023). *PISA 2022 database*. OECD Publishing.

OECD. (2025). *OECD data explorer—Education and skills*. OECD.Stat.

Ozgul, P., Fregin, M.-C., Stops, M., Janßen, S., & Levels, M. (2024). High-skilled human workers in non-routine jobs are susceptible to AI automation but wage benefits differ between occupations. *arXiv*, arXiv:2404.06472.

Raj, R. (2024). National digital development strategy and its implementation in India. In D. Maiti, F. Castellacci, & A. Melchior (Eds.), *Digitalization and development: India and beyond* (pp. 95–112). Springer.

Röller, L.-H., & Waverman, L. (2001). Telecommunications infrastructure and economic development: A simultaneous approach. *American Economic Review*, *91*(4), 909–923. [CrossRef]

Schreckling, E., & Steiger, C. (2017). Digitalize or drown. In O. Gassmann, P. Sutter, & K. Frankenberger (Eds.), *Digitalization cases* (pp. 1–17). Springer.

Senor, D., & Singer, S. (2009). *Start-up nation: The story of Israel's economic miracle*. Twelve.

Suntsova, O. (2024). Digital transformation of the global economy: Challenges and opportunities. *Financial and Credit Systems: Prospects for Development*, *3*(14), 87–100. [CrossRef]

Škare, M., & Ribeiro Soriano, D. (2021). How globalization is changing digital technology adoption: An international perspective. *Journal of Innovation & Knowledge*, *6*(4), 222–233.

The Economist Intelligence Unit. (2018). *The automation readiness index: Who is ready for the coming wave of automation?* ABB Group.

Tudose, M. B., Georgescu, A., & Avasilcăi, S. (2023). Global analysis regarding the impact of digital transformation on macroeconomic outcomes. *Sustainability*, *15*(5), 4583. [CrossRef]

United Nations Capital Development Fund. (2023). *Brief: Data protection and the digital economy*. UNCDF Policy Accelerator.

United Nations Development Programme [UNDP]. (2023). *From vision to action: Explaining UNDP's digital transformation framework*. UNDP.

United Nations Development Programme [UNDP]. (2024). *Human development reports—Data center: Documentation and downloads*. UNDP Human Development Data Center.

United Nations & International Labour Organization. (2024). *Mind the AI divide: Shaping a global perspective on the future of work*. ILO.

Vassil, K. (2015). *Estonia's e-government ecosystem: Foundation, applications, outcomes*. World Bank Group Background Paper for the World Development Report 2016: Digital Dividends. World Bank.

Verhoef, P. C., Broekhuizen, T., Bart, Y., Bhattacharya, A., Dong, J. Q., Fabian, N., & Haenlein, M. (2021). Digital transformation: A multidisciplinary reflection and research agenda. *Journal of Business Research*, *122*, 889–901. [CrossRef]

Vial, G. (2019). Understanding digital transformation: A review and a research agenda. *The Journal of Strategic Information Systems*, *28*(2), 118–144. [CrossRef]

Vrana, J., & Singh, R. (2021). Digitization, digitalization, and digital transformation. In N. Meyendorf, N. Ida, R. Singh, & J. Vrana (Eds.), *Handbook of nondestructive evaluation 4.0*. Springer.

Wachal, R. (1971). Humanities and computers: A personal view. *The North American Review*, *5*(2), 65–71.

World Bank. (2016). *World development report 2016: Digital dividends*. World Bank.

World Economic Forum. (2024). *The future of jobs report 2025*. World Economic Forum.

Disclaimer/Publisher's Note: The statements, opinions and data contained in all publications are solely those of the individual author(s) and contributor(s) and not of MDPI and/or the editor(s). MDPI and/or the editor(s) disclaim responsibility for any injury to people or property resulting from any ideas, methods, instructions or products referred to in the content.

economies

MDPI

Article

Tokenomics and Digital Economy in China: Analyzing the Influence of Blockchain Technology Integration on Traditional Business Models

Fadi Ghosn [1], Mohamad Zreik [2,*], Hala Koleilat Al Dilby [3], Caroline Dib Kassably Fakhry [4] and Fida Ragheb Hassanein [5]

1 Banking and Finance Department, Lebanese International University, Bekaa 1803, Lebanon; fadi.ghosn@liu.edu.lb
2 Institute of International and Regional Studies, Sun Yat-sen University, No. 2 Daxue Road, Xiangzhou District, Zhuhai 519082, China
3 Marketing Department, Lebanese International University, Beirut 146404, Lebanon; hala.koleilat@liu.edu.lb
4 School of Business, Lebanese International University, Bekaa 1803, Lebanon; caroline.kassably@liu.edu.lb
5 School of Business, Lebanese International University, Beirut 146404, Lebanon; fida.hassanein@liu.edu.lb
* Correspondence: zreik@sysu.edu.cn

Abstract: This study investigates the impact of tokenomics and the integration of blockchain technology on China's digital economy, focusing on how blockchain adoption influences traditional business models. As China becomes a global leader in digital transformation, understanding the role of the blockchain in economic modernization is critical. The aim of this research is to quantify the effects of blockchain adoption on key economic indicators such as GDP growth, investment levels, and business innovation. Using panel data analysis and regression models, this study provides empirical evidence on the positive correlation between blockchain integration and improved economic performance. Key results reveal that a 1% increase in blockchain adoption is associated with a 0.3% rise in GDP growth, while tokenization contributes significantly to investment levels and business innovation. These findings emphasize the transformative potential of the blockchain in enhancing economic stability, increasing liquidity, and fostering new business opportunities. In conclusion, this research highlights the critical role of the blockchain and tokenomics in driving economic modernization in China, offering valuable insights for policymakers, business leaders, and investors aiming to leverage digital technologies for sustainable growth. Future research should explore the broader global implications of blockchain adoption and tokenomics in emerging markets.

Keywords: tokenomics; blockchain technology; digital economy; China; econometric analysis

1. Introduction

The advent of blockchain technology and its associated economic principles, commonly referred to as tokenomics, has introduced a transformative potential for economies worldwide (Freni et al., 2022; Kher et al., 2021). In particular, China has been at the forefront of integrating blockchain technology into its digital economy, driven by the need for innovation and enhanced economic performance (Tseng et al., 2023). While many studies have examined the blockchain's impact on global economies, the specific role of tokenomics in China's digital transformation has not been sufficiently explored. The concept of tokenomics encompasses the creation, distribution, and management of digital tokens, which represent various assets and can be used in numerous applications, from cryptocurrencies

 https://doi.org/10.3390/economies13070189

to tokenized physical assets (Lo & Medda, 2020; Blemus & Guégan, 2020; Sazandrishvili, 2020). As China continues to evolve into a digital powerhouse, understanding the role of tokenomics in its economic landscape becomes increasingly critical.

This paper aims to explore the influence of tokenomics on China's digital economy and the integration of blockchain technology into traditional business models. The primary objectives are to quantify the effects of blockchain adoption on key economic performance metrics, such as GDP growth, investment levels, and business innovation, and to provide empirical evidence on how digital tokens can reshape traditional business practices. What is novel about this research is the use of econometric analysis to provide evidence-based insights on how blockchain adoption directly impacts China's economy, beyond the conceptual or theoretical discussion. By employing econometric analysis, this study seeks to identify the underlying factors that contribute to the successful integration of blockchain technology and its potential to drive economic modernization in China.

The significance of this study lies in its potential to offer a comprehensive understanding of the economic implications of blockchain technology in one of the world's largest economies. This paper rigorously quantifies the impact of blockchain adoption in China's diverse sectors, providing policymakers, business leaders, and investors with actionable insights on how to harness blockchain technology for sustainable growth. By emphasizing the economic outcomes of the blockchain, this research uniquely focuses on the integration of digital tokens in traditional sectors, a novel contribution to the discourse on digital innovation. Moreover, the empirical evidence presented in this paper will serve as a foundation for future research and policy formulation, aimed at leveraging blockchain technology to achieve sustainable economic growth in China and beyond.

2. Literature Review

Tokenomics, a portmanteau of "token" and "economics," refers to the economic systems and models that underpin the creation, distribution, and utilization of digital tokens. According to Freni et al. (2022), tokenomics represents a paradigm shift in the digital economy, enabling new forms of value exchange and economic interaction. Tokens can be categorized into utility tokens, security tokens, and asset-backed tokens, each serving different purposes within the blockchain ecosystem. Utility tokens, as discussed by Lee (2019), provide access to specific services or products within a blockchain network, while security tokens represent ownership in an underlying asset, akin to traditional securities. Asset-backed tokens, highlighted by Hines (2020), are pegged to real-world assets such as commodities, real estate, or precious metals, providing a stable value base and reducing the volatility commonly associated with cryptocurrencies.

The rise of tokenomics has facilitated the development of decentralized finance (DeFi) platforms, which leverage blockchain technology to offer financial services without intermediaries. This democratization of finance, noted by Blemus and Guégan (2020), has opened up new investment opportunities and has the potential to enhance financial inclusion globally. The tokenization of assets, as explored by Nestarcova (2018), allows for fractional ownership and the increased liquidity of traditionally illiquid assets, such as real estate or fine art. This innovation has profound implications for investment strategies and asset management.

China has emerged as a global leader in blockchain technology, driven by strong governmental support and significant investments in research and development. In 2019, the Chinese government formally recognized the blockchain as a critical component of its national strategy for technological innovation. The People's Bank of China (PBOC) has been at the forefront of this initiative, developing the Digital Currency Electronic Payment (DCEP) system, which aims to digitize the Chinese yuan (Kshetri, 2023). This state-backed digital currency is designed to enhance the efficiency and security of the financial system, reduce transaction costs, and combat money laundering and tax evasion.

Chinese enterprises have also been proactive in adopting blockchain technology across various industries. Alibaba and Tencent, two of China's largest tech companies, have implemented blockchain solutions in supply chain management, healthcare, and finance (Hasan et al., 2021). Alibaba's Ant Financial, for example, has developed a blockchain-based platform for tracking the provenance of goods, ensuring transparency and authenticity in supply chains (Balzarova, 2021). Tencent has launched blockchain applications in areas such as digital identity verification and intellectual property protection (Chen et al., 2020).

The integration of blockchain technology in China's public and private sectors underscores its potential to transform the economic landscape. However, this rapid adoption has also raised concerns about regulatory oversight and data privacy. According to Sigley and Powell (2023), the Chinese government has implemented strict regulations to ensure that blockchain applications comply with national security standards and protect user data. These regulatory measures aim to balance innovation with security, fostering a stable environment for blockchain development.

The integration of blockchain technology into traditional business models has been a significant area of research and practice. The blockchain's decentralized, immutable ledger offers numerous advantages, including enhanced transparency, reduced fraud, and improved efficiency. As noted by Werbach (2018), the core principle of the blockchain is to provide a trustless system where transactions can be verified without the need for intermediaries. This capability has profound implications for industries that rely on trust and verification, such as finance, supply chain management, and healthcare.

In the finance sector, the blockchain has been used to streamline processes such as cross-border payments, trade finance, and securities settlement. According to Tsai et al. (2020), the blockchain can significantly reduce the time and cost associated with these processes by eliminating the need for intermediaries and enabling real-time settlement. For example, the use of smart contracts—self-executing contracts with the terms directly written into code—can automate and enforce contract conditions without the need for manual intervention (Mik, 2017).

Supply chain management is another area where the blockchain has shown substantial promise. By providing a transparent and immutable record of transactions, the blockchain can enhance the traceability and accountability of goods as they move through the supply chain. As highlighted by Azzi et al. (2019), this capability is particularly valuable in industries such as food and pharmaceuticals, where ensuring the authenticity and safety of products is critical. The blockchain can help track the origin and journey of products, reducing the risk of counterfeit goods and improving consumer trust.

In healthcare, blockchain technology has been used to secure patient data, streamline medical records, and enhance interoperability between different healthcare providers. According to Zaabar et al. (2021), the blockchain can address many of the challenges associated with data privacy and security in healthcare by providing a decentralized and secure platform for storing and sharing medical information. This capability can improve the efficiency and accuracy of medical care, reducing the risk of errors and enhancing patient outcomes.

Empirical studies on the digital economy and blockchain technology have provided valuable insights into their impact on various economic and business outcomes. According to Javaid et al. (2022), the adoption of blockchain technology has been associated with increased efficiency and reduced costs in financial transactions. This finding is supported by empirical evidence from case studies of blockchain implementations in banking and finance, which have shown significant reductions in transaction times and costs (Patki & Sople, 2020).

In the context of supply chain management, empirical research by Centobelli et al. (2022) has demonstrated that blockchain technology can enhance the transparency and traceability of supply chains, leading to improved operational efficiency and reduced fraud. These benefits have been observed in various industries, including food, pharmaceuticals, and luxury goods. For example, a study by Li et al. (2023) found that blockchain implementation in the food supply chain resulted in the faster and more accurate traceability of products, reducing the risk of contamination and enhancing consumer trust.

In healthcare, empirical studies have highlighted the potential of the blockchain to improve data security and interoperability. According to Attaran (2022), blockchain technology can provide a secure and decentralized platform for storing and sharing patient data, addressing many of the challenges associated with data privacy and security. Empirical evidence from pilot projects in healthcare has shown that the blockchain can improve the accuracy and efficiency of medical records, enhancing patient care and outcomes (Tanwar et al., 2020).

The impact of tokenomics on the digital economy has also been a focus of empirical research. According to Nestarcova (2018), the tokenization of assets can increase liquidity and provide new investment opportunities, particularly for traditionally illiquid assets such as real estate and fine art. This finding is supported by empirical evidence from studies of tokenized asset platforms, which have shown increased liquidity and reduced transaction costs compared to traditional asset markets (Ciriello, 2021).

Although previous research has highlighted the potential of blockchain technology to transform industries such as finance, supply chain, and healthcare, much of the existing literature has focused on theoretical frameworks and isolated sectoral applications. While the blockchain's advantages in enhancing transparency, reducing costs, and improving efficiency have been well documented (e.g., Tsai et al., 2020; Azzi et al., 2019), there is a notable gap in empirical studies that examine the comprehensive economic impact of blockchain adoption, particularly in the context of emerging economies like China. Furthermore, while tokenomics has gained significant attention as a driver of innovation, there remains a lack of research on how the integration of digital tokens affects broader economic performance metrics, such as GDP growth, investment levels, and business innovation. This study aims to fill these gaps by providing a comprehensive empirical analysis of the role of blockchain technology and tokenomics in driving China's digital economy, offering new insights into the transformation of traditional business models in this rapidly developing market.

3. Methodology

The data for this study were collected from a combination of sources to ensure a comprehensive analysis of the impact of tokenomics on China's digital economy and the integration of blockchain technology into traditional business models. Data were mainly sourced from reputable databases, government reports, industry publications, and academic journals. Key indicators such as GDP growth, investment levels, blockchain adoption rates, and business innovation metrics were extracted for analysis. Data for blockchain adoption rates were primarily sourced from the China Blockchain Application Research Center (CBARC) and industry reports published by organizations such as Deloitte and PwC. Tokenization metrics were obtained from blockchain-specific financial databases such as CoinMarketCap (CoinMarketCap LLC, Dover, Delaware, USA), TokenAnalyst (TokenAnalyst Ltd., London, United Kingdom), and Blockchain.info (Blockchain Luxembourg S.A., Luxembourg City, Luxembourg).

Panel data analysis is particularly suited for this study as it allows for the examination of multiple entities over time, capturing both cross-sectional and time-series dimensions. This approach enables the analysis of the dynamic effects of blockchain adoption and tokenomics on economic performance in China. The panel data will consist of annual observations from various sectors within the Chinese economy over a period of 10 years, from 2013 to 2023. The sectors included in the analysis were selected based on their relevance to the digital economy in China, including finance, supply chain management, healthcare, real estate, and manufacturing, which were chosen to represent both traditional and emerging industries impacted by blockchain technology. This timeframe captures the period of significant blockchain innovation and adoption in China.

The panel data model will be specified as follows:

$$Yit = \alpha + \beta Xit + \gamma Zit + \mu i + \lambda t + \epsilon it$$

where the variables are defined as follows:

- Yit is the dependent variable representing economic performance metrics (e.g., GDP growth, investment levels) for sector i at time t.
- Xit represents the main independent variables of interest, including blockchain adoption rate and tokenization metrics.
- Zit includes control variables such as labor force, capital investment, and technological infrastructure.
- μi captures the unobserved individual effects (e.g., year dummies), which account for events or factors affecting all sectors in the same year, such as national policy changes or economic crises.
- λt captures the time-specific effects.
- ϵit is the error term.

To estimate the effects of blockchain technology and tokenomics on China's digital economy, multiple regression models will be employed. The primary model will be a fixed effects regression, which controls for time-invariant unobserved heterogeneity across sectors. The fixed effects model is specified as follows:

$$Yit = \alpha + \beta Xit + \gamma Zit + \mu i + \epsilon it$$

Additionally, a random effects model will be estimated to account for both within-entity and between-entity variations. The Hausman test will be conducted to determine which model is more appropriate, as the test compares the consistency of the fixed and random effects models.

For robustness checks, this study will also utilize dynamic panel data models, such as the Generalized Method of Moments (GMM) estimator, to address potential endogeneity issues arising from the inclusion of lagged dependent variables and other endogenous regressors. The instruments used in the GMM model include lagged values of blockchain adoption rates and tokenization metrics, as well as sectoral lagged GDP and investment levels. The GMM model is specified as follows:

$$\Delta Yit = \alpha + \beta \Delta Xit + \gamma \Delta Zit + \epsilon it$$

The dependent variable in this study is the economic performance of China's digital economy, measured through various indicators such as GDP growth rate, investment levels, and business innovation indices. These indicators provide a comprehensive view of the economic impact of blockchain technology and tokenomics.

The key independent variables include the following:

- Blockchain Adoption Rate: measured as the percentage of businesses and sectors adopting blockchain technology, sourced from industry reports and surveys.
- Tokenization Metrics: measured through the number of tokenized assets, the market value of these assets, and the volume of transactions involving digital tokens, obtained from blockchain databases and financial reports.

Control variables include the following:

- Labor Force: measured as the total number of employed individuals in each sector, sourced from national labor statistics.
- Capital Investment: measured as the total capital expenditure in each sector, sourced from financial reports and investment databases.
- Technological Infrastructure: measured through indicators such as internet penetration rate, availability of high-speed broadband, and technological readiness index, obtained from government and industry reports.

To ensure comparability across sectors, the data were standardized by adjusting for the sector-specific economic output and scale. For example, GDP growth was normalized by sector-specific growth rates, and investment levels were adjusted for capital intensity in each sector.

To ensure the accuracy and reliability of the data, rigorous data cleaning and preprocessing steps were undertaken. Missing values were addressed through appropriate imputation methods, and outliers were identified and managed using statistical techniques. Missing data were handled using the Multiple Imputation by Chained Equations (MICE) method, which is appropriate for panel data. The percentage of missing data was found to be low (approximately 3–5%) across key variables. Descriptive statistics and correlation analysis were performed to understand the data distribution and relationships among variables. Multicollinearity was assessed using the Variance Inflation Factor (VIF), and no variables showed problematic multicollinearity (VIF > 10). Heteroskedasticity was addressed by using robust standard errors, and serial correlation was tested using the Wooldridge test for autocorrelation in panel data.

4. Results

4.1. Descriptive Statistics

The descriptive statistics provide an initial understanding of the data distribution and the central tendencies of the key variables used in this study. The analysis covers the period from 2013 to 2023, encompassing various sectors within China's digital economy. The panel data in this study are based on sectors within China's digital economy, rather than individual firms. This approach allows for an analysis of sector-level economic performance and the integration of blockchain technology across different industries.

The mean GDP growth rate for the sectors under study was found to be 6.5%, with a standard deviation of 1.2%, indicating moderate variability around the average growth rate. The minimum GDP growth rate observed was 3.2%, while the maximum was 9.1%, reflecting the diverse economic performance across different sectors during the study period.

The blockchain adoption rate, measured as the percentage of businesses integrating blockchain technology, had a mean value of 15%, with a significant standard deviation of 10%. This high variability suggests that while some sectors have rapidly embraced blockchain technology, others are still in the early stages of adoption. The adoption rate ranged from a low of 2% to a high of 45%.

Tokenization metrics, including the number of tokenized assets and the volume of transactions, also exhibited considerable variation. The mean number of tokenized assets was 120 per sector, with a standard deviation of 50. The minimum number of tokenized assets recorded was 30, and the maximum was 300. The volume of transactions involving digital tokens had a mean value of USD 2 billion, with a standard deviation of USD 1 billion, ranging from USD 500 million to USD 4.5 billion.

Control variables such as labor force, capital investment, and technological infrastructure were also analyzed. The average labor force size was 1.2 million individuals per sector, with a standard deviation of 200,000. Capital investment averaged USD 500 million per sector, with a standard deviation of USD 100 million. Technological infrastructure, measured by the technological readiness index, had a mean value of 70, with a standard deviation of 10.

The correlation analysis revealed significant positive correlations between the blockchain adoption rate and GDP growth rate (r = 0.45), indicating that sectors with higher blockchain adoption tended to experience greater economic growth. Tokenization metrics also showed positive correlations with investment levels and business innovation indices, supporting the hypothesis that tokenomics contributes to enhanced economic performance. The descriptive statistics for the key variables are summarized in Table 1.

Table 1. Descriptive statistics for key variables.

Variable	Mean	Standard Deviation	Min	Max
GDP Growth Rate	6.5%	1.2%	3.2%	9.1%
Blockchain Adoption Rate	15%	10%	2%	45%
Tokenized Assets (per sector)	120	50	30	300
Volume of Digital Token Transactions (USD)	USD 2 B	USD 1 B	USD 500 M	USD 4.5 B
Labor Force (per sector, millions)	1.2	0.2 million	0.9	1.6
Capital Investment (USD million)	500	100	300	700

Source: Authors' work.

As shown in Table 1, the mean GDP growth rate for the sectors was 6.5%, with a standard deviation of 1.2%. These descriptive statistics provide a foundational understanding of the data and set the stage for more advanced econometric analyses to further explore the relationships between tokenomics, blockchain technology, and economic outcomes in China's digital economy.

4.2. *Econometric Analysis*

The econometric analysis utilizes panel data regression models to examine the impact of blockchain adoption and tokenomics on economic performance indicators across various sectors in China from 2013 to 2023. Both fixed effects and random effects models were estimated to capture the effects while controlling for unobserved heterogeneity. The panel data for this study are aggregated at the sector level, not at the individual firm level. This allows for the exploration of blockchain adoption and tokenomics' impact on economic performance at a broader industry scale, rather than focusing on firm-specific outcomes.

The fixed effects regression model results indicate a significant positive relationship between blockchain adoption and GDP growth rate. Specifically, a 1% increase in the blockchain adoption rate is associated with a 0.3% increase in GDP growth ($\beta = 0.003$, $p < 0.01$). This finding underscores the transformative potential of blockchain technology in driving economic growth by enhancing efficiency and innovation in traditional business models.

The random effects model, confirmed by the Hausman test as appropriate for this analysis ($\chi^2 = 12.34$, $p < 0.05$), also supports these findings, showing a consistent positive impact of blockchain adoption on GDP growth. Additionally, the random effects model highlights the significant influence of tokenization metrics on investment levels. A higher volume of transactions involving digital tokens is associated with increased sectoral investments ($\beta = 0.25$, $p < 0.05$), suggesting that tokenization enhances liquidity and attracts more capital into the economy.

Dynamic panel data models using the GMM were employed to address potential endogeneity issues. The GMM results confirm the robustness of the previous findings, indicating that blockchain adoption and tokenization significantly contribute to economic performance. The coefficient for blockchain adoption remains positive and significant ($\beta = 0.004$, $p < 0.01$), while tokenization metrics show a strong positive effect on business innovation indices ($\beta = 0.45$, $p < 0.01$).

Control variables such as labor force, capital investment, and technological infrastructure were also significant in the models, demonstrating their importance in driving economic outcomes. For instance, capital investment showed a positive relationship with GDP growth ($\beta = 0.002$, $p < 0.05$), emphasizing the role of financial resources in fostering economic development.

4.3. Regression Results

The regression analysis, employing both fixed effects and random effects models, reveals significant insights into the impact of blockchain adoption and tokenomics on economic performance indicators across various sectors in China from 2013 to 2023.

The fixed effects regression model results indicate a significant positive relationship between blockchain adoption and GDP growth rate. Specifically, a 1% increase in the blockchain adoption rate is associated with a 0.3% increase in GDP growth ($\beta = 0.003$, $p < 0.01$). This suggests that sectors with higher levels of blockchain adoption experience greater economic growth, likely due to improved efficiency, reduced transaction costs, and enhanced transparency.

Additionally, the fixed effects model shows that tokenization metrics, such as the volume of transactions involving digital tokens, positively impact investment levels. A higher transaction volume is associated with a 0.2% increase in sectoral investments ($\beta = 0.002$, $p < 0.05$), indicating that tokenization enhances liquidity and attracts more capital.

The random effects model, validated by the Hausman test ($\chi^2 = 12.34$, $p < 0.05$), corroborates these findings. The model confirms the positive impact of blockchain adoption on GDP growth ($\beta = 0.003$, $p < 0.01$) and highlights the significant influence of tokenization on investment levels ($\beta = 0.25$, $p < 0.05$). The random effects model also reveals that blockchain adoption significantly improves business innovation indices ($\beta = 0.35$, $p < 0.05$), suggesting that blockchain technology fosters innovative business practices.

The GMM estimator addresses potential endogeneity issues and further supports the robustness of the results. The GMM results show that blockchain adoption has a significant positive effect on GDP growth ($\beta = 0.004$, $p < 0.01$) and business innovation indices ($\beta = 0.45$, $p < 0.01$). This confirms that blockchain technology and tokenomics drive economic performance and innovation.

Control variables such as labor force, capital investment, and technological infrastructure were significant in the models. For example, capital investment showed a positive relationship with GDP growth ($\beta = 0.002$, $p < 0.05$), highlighting the importance of financial resources in economic development.

The econometric analysis reveals significant insights into the impact of blockchain adoption and tokenomics on economic performance in China. The fixed effects regression model shows that a 1% increase in blockchain adoption rate is associated with a 0.3% increase in GDP growth, indicating that sectors with higher blockchain integration experience enhanced economic performance. This positive relationship suggests that blockchain technology improves efficiency, reduces transaction costs, and increases transparency, thereby driving economic growth.

The results of the fixed effects regression model in Table 2 show that blockchain adoption significantly impacts GDP growth.

Table 2. Regression results for fixed effects model.

Variable	Coefficient	Standard Error	*p*-Value
Blockchain Adoption Rate	0.003	0.001	<0.01
Tokenization Metrics (Volume)	0.002	0.001	<0.05
Labor Force	0.0002	0.0001	<0.05
Capital Investment	0.002	0.001	<0.05
Technological Infrastructure	0.001	0.0005	<0.10

Source: Authors' work.

The random effects model further validates these findings, highlighting the substantial influence of tokenization metrics on investment levels. A higher volume of transactions involving digital tokens correlates with increased sectoral investments, demonstrating that tokenization enhances liquidity and attracts more capital into the economy. This effect underscores the role of digital tokens in providing new investment opportunities and improving asset liquidity.

Dynamic panel data models, using the GMM estimator, address potential endogeneity issues and confirm the robustness of the results. The GMM analysis reveals that blockchain adoption has a significant positive effect on both GDP growth and business innovation indices. This indicates that blockchain technology not only boosts economic performance but also fosters innovative business practices. The empirical evidence from the GMM model underscores the transformative potential of blockchain and tokenomics in driving economic modernization in China.

Control variables, such as labor force, capital investment, and technological infrastructure, also play crucial roles in determining economic outcomes. Capital investment shows a positive relationship with GDP growth, emphasizing the importance of financial resources in fostering economic development. These findings collectively highlight the significant impact of blockchain technology and tokenomics on enhancing economic stability, investment levels, and business innovation in China's digital economy. The results provide valuable insights for policymakers, business leaders, and investors aiming to leverage blockchain technology for sustainable economic growth.

5. Discussion

5.1. Implications for China's Digital Economy

The findings from the econometric analysis underscore the transformative potential of blockchain technology and tokenomics in shaping China's digital economy. The positive relationship between blockchain adoption and GDP growth indicates that integrating blockchain technology can significantly enhance economic performance. This enhancement is attributed to blockchain's ability to improve efficiency, reduce transaction costs, and increase transparency across various sectors (Javaid et al., 2022). As China continues to position itself as a leader in digital innovation, the widespread adoption of blockchain technology could further solidify its status in the global digital economy.

Moreover, the significant impact of tokenization metrics on investment levels highlights the crucial role of digital tokens in fostering new investment opportunities. By increasing liquidity and providing fractional ownership, tokenization allows for greater capital influx into the economy, particularly in traditionally illiquid asset classes such as real estate and fine art (Nestarcova, 2018). This increased liquidity can stimulate economic activity and drive further innovation.

The implications extend to the democratization of finance through decentralized finance (DeFi) platforms. Blockchain technology, by eliminating intermediaries, opens up financial services to a broader population, promoting financial inclusion. This democratization can lead to a more inclusive and resilient economy, where access to financial services is not limited by traditional barriers.

5.2. Impact on Traditional Business Models

Blockchain technology's integration into traditional business models has far-reaching implications. The decentralized and immutable nature of the blockchain can fundamentally alter how businesses operate, ensuring greater transparency and trust in transactions. In supply chain management, for example, blockchain can provide an immutable record of a product's journey from origin to consumer, reducing fraud and ensuring authenticity (Azzi et al., 2019). This capability is particularly valuable in industries such as food and pharmaceuticals, where the integrity of the supply chain is critical.

In the financial sector, blockchain technology can streamline processes such as cross-border payments, trade finance, and securities settlement. By reducing the need for intermediaries, the blockchain can lower costs and expedite transactions (Javaid et al., 2022). Smart contracts, which are self-executing contracts with terms directly written into code, can automate and enforce contractual agreements without manual intervention (Mik, 2017). This automation can significantly reduce the time and cost associated with traditional contract management.

The healthcare sector can also benefit from blockchain technology through improved data security and interoperability. By providing a secure platform for storing and sharing patient data, the blockchain can address many of the challenges associated with data privacy and security. This capability can enhance the accuracy and efficiency of medical care, reducing errors and improving patient outcomes.

5.3. Comparison with the Existing Literature

The findings of this study align with and expand upon the existing literature on the economic implications of blockchain technology and tokenomics. Previous research has highlighted the blockchain's potential to increase efficiency and reduce costs in financial transactions (Javaid et al., 2022; Patki & Sople, 2020). This study corroborates these findings, showing that blockchain adoption is significantly associated with GDP growth and investment levels.

In the context of supply chain management, prior studies have demonstrated the blockchain's ability to enhance transparency and traceability (Centobelli et al., 2022; Li et al., 2023). The present research supports these conclusions, providing empirical evidence that blockchain integration can improve operational efficiency and reduce fraud in supply chains.

The healthcare sector has also been a focal point of blockchain research, with studies indicating its potential to improve data security and interoperability (Attaran, 2022; Tanwar et al., 2020). This study reinforces these findings, showing that blockchain technology can significantly enhance business innovation indices, which include measures of technological advancement and efficiency improvements in healthcare.

This research also contributes to the literature on tokenomics by empirically demonstrating the positive impact of tokenization on investment levels and business innovation. While previous studies have explored the theoretical benefits of tokenomics (Nestarcova, 2018; Ciriello, 2021), this study provides concrete evidence of its economic impact, particularly in the context of China's digital economy.

5.4. Policy Recommendations

Based on the findings, several policy recommendations can be made to further leverage blockchain technology and tokenomics for sustainable economic growth in China. Policymakers should continue to encourage the adoption of blockchain technology across various sectors. This can be achieved through incentives such as tax breaks, grants, and subsidies for businesses implementing blockchain solutions. Additionally, public awareness campaigns highlighting the benefits of blockchain technology can help accelerate its adoption. Establishing clear and supportive regulatory frameworks is crucial for fostering innovation while ensuring security and compliance. Regulations should address issues such as data privacy, security standards, and anti-money laundering measures. A balanced approach that promotes innovation while mitigating risks will be essential.

Supporting the development of tokenization platforms and initiatives is another critical area. The government should create legal frameworks for tokenized assets and ensure the protection of investors. By facilitating the tokenization of traditionally illiquid assets, policymakers can enhance liquidity and attract more investment into the economy (Tian et al., 2020). Investing in technological infrastructure, such as high-speed internet and blockchain research and development, is also vital. Improving technological readiness will ensure that businesses and consumers can fully leverage the benefits of blockchain technology.

Fostering public–private partnerships can drive blockchain innovation and adoption (Toufaily et al., 2021). Collaboration between the public and private sectors can facilitate the sharing of resources, expertise, and best practices, accelerating the integration of blockchain technology into traditional business models. Additionally, developing a skilled workforce capable of understanding and implementing blockchain technology is essential. Policymakers should support educational programs and training initiatives focused on blockchain and digital economy skills. This will ensure a steady supply of talent to drive the digital transformation.

The continuous monitoring and evaluation of blockchain initiatives will be important to understand their impact and make necessary adjustments. Policymakers should establish mechanisms for tracking the adoption and performance of blockchain technology, gathering data to inform future policy decisions. Engaging in international collaboration and knowledge exchange can enhance China's blockchain ecosystem. By participating in global blockchain initiatives and sharing insights with other countries, China can stay at the forefront of blockchain innovation and adoption.

5.5. Limitations of This Study

While this research provides valuable insights into the impact of blockchain adoption and tokenomics on China's digital economy, there are several limitations to consider.

The data used in this study, particularly for blockchain adoption and tokenization metrics, were obtained from industry reports and blockchain-specific databases, which may not always be comprehensive or entirely accurate. The reliance on publicly available data means that certain sectors or regions may be underrepresented, potentially affecting the generalizability of the findings.

The analysis is based on sector-level data, not firm-level data, which may limit the ability to draw conclusions about how individual firms are affected by blockchain adoption. Sector-level analysis aggregates heterogeneity within each sector, which could overlook variations in blockchain adoption at the firm level.

Although dynamic panel data models, such as the GMM, were employed to address potential endogeneity, there may still be unobserved factors influencing both blockchain adoption and economic performance that were not captured in the models. This could potentially introduce bias into the estimates.

This study covers the period from 2013 to 2023, which captures a phase of significant blockchain adoption in China. However, blockchain technology is still evolving, and the long-term effects of blockchain adoption on the digital economy may differ from the short-term effects observed in this study.

The results may also be influenced by external factors such as government policies, global economic conditions, and technological advancements unrelated to the blockchain. Although time fixed effects were included to control for some of these factors, there may still be other unaccounted-for variables that influence the results.

Despite these limitations, this study provides valuable insights into the role of blockchain technology in reshaping China's digital economy, offering directions for future research to explore these issues in greater depth.

6. Conclusions

This paper provides a comprehensive analysis of the impact of blockchain technology and tokenomics on China's digital economy and traditional business models. Through advanced econometric techniques, including fixed effects and random effects models, as well as the GMM estimator, this study quantifies the significant positive effects of blockchain adoption on GDP growth, investment levels, and business innovation. The empirical evidence demonstrates that integrating blockchain technology enhances economic performance by improving efficiency, reducing transaction costs, and increasing transparency across various sectors.

This research highlights the transformative potential of digital tokens in fostering new investment opportunities and increasing liquidity in traditionally illiquid asset classes. Tokenization, by allowing fractional ownership and facilitating smoother transactions, plays a critical role in attracting more capital into the economy. These findings underscore the importance of blockchain and tokenomics in driving economic modernization and innovation, positioning China as a global leader in the digital economy.

Policy recommendations derived from this study emphasize the need for continued promotion of blockchain adoption through incentives and public awareness campaigns. Establishing clear regulatory frameworks that balance innovation with security, supporting tokenization initiatives, investing in technological infrastructure, and fostering public–private partnerships are crucial steps to leverage the full potential of blockchain technology. Additionally, developing a skilled workforce through education and training programs, the continuous monitoring and evaluation of blockchain initiatives, and engaging in international collaboration will further enhance China's blockchain ecosystem.

The integration of blockchain technology and tokenomics offers significant opportunities for economic growth and innovation in China. By adopting supportive policies and strategic investments, China can harness the transformative power of the blockchain to achieve sustainable economic development and maintain its competitive edge in the global digital landscape. The insights from this study provide a valuable foundation for future research and policy formulation aimed at leveraging blockchain technology for long-term economic prosperity.

Author Contributions: Conceptualization: F.G. and M.Z.; methodology: M.Z.; software: M.Z.; validation: F.G., M.Z. and H.K.A.D.; formal analysis: M.Z.; investigation: M.Z.; resources: F.G.; data curation: C.D.K.F.; writing—original draft preparation: F.G.; writing—review and editing: H.K.A.D., F.G. and M.Z.; visualization: F.G.; supervision: H.K.A.D. and F.R.H.; project administration: H.K.A.D.; funding acquisition: H.K.A.D. All authors contributed equally to this work. All authors have read and agreed to the published version of the manuscript.

Funding: This research has received no external funding.

Institutional Review Board Statement: Not applicable.

Informed Consent Statement: Not applicable.

Data Availability Statement: No new data were created or analyzed in this study. Data sharing is not applicable to this article.

Conflicts of Interest: The authors declare no conflict of interest.

References

Attaran, M. (2022). Blockchain technology in healthcare: Challenges and opportunities. *International Journal of Healthcare Management, 15*(1), 70–83. [CrossRef]

Azzi, R., Chamoun, R. K., & Sokhn, M. (2019). The power of a blockchain-based supply chain. *Computers & Industrial Engineering, 135*, 582–592.

Balzarova, M. A. (2021). Blockchain technology—A new era of ecolabelling schemes? *Corporate Governance: The International Journal of Business in Society, 21*(1), 159–174. [CrossRef]

Blemus, S., & Guégan, D. (2020). Initial crypto-asset offerings (ICOs), tokenization and corporate governance. *Capital Markets Law Journal, 15*(2), 191–223. [CrossRef]

Centobelli, P., Cerchione, R., Del Vecchio, P., Oropallo, E., & Secundo, G. (2022). Blockchain technology for bridging trust, traceability and transparency in circular supply chain. *Information & Management, 59*(7), 103508.

Chen, W., Zhou, K., Fang, W., Wang, K., Bi, F., & Assefa, B. (2020). Review on blockchain technology and its application to the simple analysis of intellectual property protection. *International Journal of Computational Science and Engineering, 22*(4), 437–444. [CrossRef]

Ciriello, R. F. (2021). Tokenized index funds: A blockchain-based concept and a multidisciplinary research framework. *International Journal of Information Management, 61*, 102400. [CrossRef]

Freni, P., Ferro, E., & Moncada, R. (2022). Tokenomics and blockchain tokens: A design-oriented morphological framework. *Blockchain: Research and Applications, 3*(1), 100069. [CrossRef]

Hasan, M. R., Deng, S., Sultana, N., & Hossain, M. Z. (2021). The applicability of blockchain technology in healthcare contexts to contain COVID-19 challenges. *Library Hi Tech, 39*(3), 814–833. [CrossRef]

Hines, B. (2020). *Digital finance: Security tokens and unlocking the real potential of blockchain*. John Wiley & Sons.

Javaid, M., Haleem, A., Singh, R. P., Suman, R., & Khan, S. (2022). A review of blockchain technology applications for financial services. *BenchCouncil Transactions on Benchmarks, Standards and Evaluations, 2*(3), 100073. [CrossRef]

Kher, R., Terjesen, S., & Liu, C. (2021). Blockchain, Bitcoin, and ICOs: A review and research agenda. *Small Business Economics, 56*, 1699–1720. [CrossRef]

Kshetri, N. (2023). China's digital yuan: Motivations of the Chinese government and potential global effects. *Journal of Contemporary China, 32*(139), 87–105. [CrossRef]

Lee, J. Y. (2019). A decentralized token economy: How blockchain and cryptocurrency can revolutionize business. *Business Horizons, 62*(6), 773–784. [CrossRef]

Li, K., Lee, J. Y., & Gharehgozli, A. (2023). Blockchain in food supply chains: A literature review and synthesis analysis of platforms, benefits and challenges. *International Journal of Production Research, 61*(11), 3527–3546. [CrossRef]

Lo, Y. C., & Medda, F. (2020). Assets on the blockchain: An empirical study of Tokenomics. *Information Economics and Policy*, 53, 100881. [CrossRef]

Mik, E. (2017). Smart contracts: Terminology, technical limitations and real world complexity. *Law, Innovation and Technology, 9*(2), 269–300. [CrossRef]

Nestarcova, D. (2018). A critical appraisal of initial coin offerings: Lifting the "digital token's veil". *Brill Research Perspectives in International Banking and Securities Law, 3*(2–3), 1–171. [CrossRef]

Patki, A., & Sople, V. (2020). Indian banking sector: Blockchain implementation, challenges and way forward. *Journal of Banking and Financial Technology, 4*(1), 65–73. [CrossRef]

Sazandrishvili, G. (2020). Asset tokenization in plain English. *Journal of Corporate Accounting & Finance, 31*(2), 68–73.

Sigley, G., & Powell, W. (2023). Governing the digital economy: An exploration of blockchains with Chinese characteristics. *Journal of Contemporary Asia, 53*(4), 648–667. [CrossRef]

Tanwar, S., Parekh, K., & Evans, R. (2020). Blockchain-based electronic healthcare record system for healthcare 4.0 applications. *Journal of Information Security and Applications, 50*, 102407. [CrossRef]

Tian, Y., Lu, Z., Adriaens, P., Minchin, R. E., Caithness, A., & Woo, J. (2020). Finance infrastructure through blockchain-based tokenization. *Frontiers of Engineering Management, 7*(4), 485–499. [CrossRef]

Toufaily, E., Zalan, T., & Dhaou, S. B. (2021). A framework of blockchain technology adoption: An investigation of challenges and expected value. *Information & Management, 58*(3), 103444.

Tsai, W. T., Luo, Y., Deng, E., Zhao, J., Ding, X., Li, J., & Yuan, B. (2020). Blockchain systems for trade clearing. *The Journal of Risk Finance*, *21*(5), 469–492. [CrossRef]

Tseng, F. M., Liang, C. W., & Nguyen, N. B. (2023). Blockchain technology adoption and business performance in large enterprises: A comparison of the United States and China. *Technology in Society*, *73*, 102230. [CrossRef]

Werbach, K. (2018). Trust, but verify: Why the blockchain needs the law. *Berkeley Technology Law Journal*, *33*(2), 487–550.

Zaabar, B., Cheikhrouhou, O., Jamil, F., Ammi, M., & Abid, M. (2021). HealthBlock: A secure blockchain-based healthcare data management system. *Computer Networks*, *200*, 108500. [CrossRef]

Disclaimer/Publisher's Note: The statements, opinions and data contained in all publications are solely those of the individual author(s) and contributor(s) and not of MDPI and/or the editor(s). MDPI and/or the editor(s) disclaim responsibility for any injury to people or property resulting from any ideas, methods, instructions or products referred to in the content.

economies

MDPI

Article

Digital Transformation and Competitive Advantage in Manufacturing: The Role of Business Model Innovation

Shanqiang Zheng * and Yaodong Zhou

School of Economics and Management, Beijing Jiaotong University, Beijing 100044, China; ydzhou@bjtu.edu.cn
* Correspondence: 22110161@bjtu.edu.cn

Abstract: In the era of the digital economy, how digital transformation (DT) contributes to economic development has become a topic of growing interest. This study focuses on business model innovation (BMI) driven by DT in the manufacturing sector. From this perspective, we aim to explore how DT can reshape the fundamental connotation of economic development. To this end, we construct a mathematical model grounded in a Multi-Structural Economic System framework and employ econometric models focusing on fixed effects, mediation effects, and moderation effects. We also compile a panel dataset using data from China spanning from 2008 to 2024. The empirical findings reveal that BMI serves as a mediation mechanism between the DT and competitive advantage (CA) of manufacturing enterprises. However, competitive imitation of BMI by peer enterprises partially offsets this effect, weakening the relationship between DT and enhanced CA. These findings offer evidence-based insights into the role of BMI in the digital era. For policymakers and industry regulators, this study provides practical implications for promoting knowledge spillovers from BMI, thereby fostering market dynamism and enabling structural transformation in the manufacturing industry.

Keywords: manufacturing; competitive advantage; digital transformation; business model innovation; competitive imitation

1. Introduction

Digital transformation (DT) enables data to transcend time and space and integrate with traditional production factors, driving extensive enterprise-level change. Such transformation has proven effective in facilitating the upgrading and restructuring of manufacturing enterprises (Fu, 2022; Johns, 2022). These changes are not merely technological adoptions but reflect profound shifts in overall business models, offering crucial support for enterprises to remain competitive in the digital era (Omidvar et al., 2025). As traditional modes of production and operation struggle to meet the demands of the digital economy, DT has become a pressing necessity for the future development of manufacturing enterprises (Johns, 2022; Y. Zhou et al., 2019; Banga, 2022). Therefore, to better understand how manufacturing enterprises leverage digital technologies to enhance their performance, it is essential to examine the impact of business model innovation (BMI).

BMI refers to the process by which enterprises improve or redesign the methods through which they create value. It is considered a key mechanism for helping enterprises adapt to market changes or gain competitive advantages (Dewan & Kraemer, 2000). By understanding market demands, enterprises adjust and innovate their business models to build market power, which is widely recognized as an essential way for both enterprises and industries to enhance competitiveness (Hanelt et al., 2021; Mikalef & Pateli, 2017;

Scuotto et al., 2021). With the advent of the digital economy, BMI has become an extensively discussed topic in the survival and development of the manufacturing sector. Typically, enterprises utilize digital technologies to strengthen network effects with upstream and downstream partners, improve market performance, and consolidate their market position. This view has been supported by the widespread adoption of digital technologies among global enterprises (Ibarra et al., 2018; Zott & Amit, 2007). Moreover, some scholars argue that dominant enterprises in the digital era are more likely to achieve economies of scale, resulting in the phenomenon of winner takes all among enterprises (Brettel et al., 2012; Forkmann et al., 2017).

However, the resource allocation patterns and value creation logic of manufacturing enterprises are undoubtedly different from those of platform enterprises. These differences present challenges to enterprises that are seeking to establish competitive advantage (CA) through DT. This issue remains underexplored in existing research on manufacturing. The resource allocation and production models of manufacturing enterprises are rooted in the physical economy, making their digital investments highly asset specific (Riordan & Williamson, 1985). Once such specific assets are formed, they become locked into particular forms and production or transaction models, resulting in high switching costs during transformation (Kermani & Ma, 2023). To cope with the lock-in effect and the risk of opportunism associated with asset specificity, enterprises often adopt conservative investment and management strategies. They may reduce or even cancel investments in high-risk projects and take a cautious stance toward further DT and innovation (Joskow, 1988; Kim, 2018). As a result, DT in these enterprises often yields benefits only within niche sectors or product categories, which contrasts with findings in studies on digital platform enterprises (Abrell et al., 2016; X. Sun et al., 2024).

Traditional value creation logic also brings security and privacy risks to the DT of manufacturing enterprises. In market competition, platform enterprises that create value through supply and demand matching can leverage digital networks and Metcalfe's Law to achieve monopoly over supply chains and sales chains by expanding their user base (Cutolo & Kenney, 2021; Pan et al., 2023). However, manufacturing enterprises primarily rely on semi-standardized industrial production; consequently, they cannot rely solely on scale advantages to build market exclusivity. As digital integration deepens, the exposure of sensitive information in areas such as product design, production processes, and supply chains becomes more likely (Tilson et al., 2010; Y. Chen & Zeng, 2022). Competitive imitation by peer enterprises can also undermine the positive effects of DT (Kiveu et al., 2019; Mahesh et al., 2020). Furthermore, uncertainties in production technologies, product development, and market responses can elevate operational risks for these enterprises (Chavez et al., 2023; Björkdahl, 2020; Buer et al., 2021).

These challenges contribute to the ongoing debate over the impact of DT on enterprise competitiveness. Some scholars posit that DT helps reduce transaction costs (Dewan & Kraemer, 2000; Hanelt et al., 2021), automate and enhance production processes (Mikalef & Pateli, 2017), strengthen capital spillovers (Horvat et al., 2019; S. Chen & Zhang, 2021), and improve innovation performance (J. Zhou, 2013; Trabucchi & Buganza, 2019). All of them can enhance the competitiveness of enterprises (Y. Q. Wu et al., 2021; Wen et al., 2022; Gao et al., 2023). However, opposing views highlight that the complex production systems of manufacturing enterprises make DT costly and time-consuming (Vasylyshyna et al., 2022; Chavez et al., 2023), potentially leading to structural unemployment or production stagnation due to workforce adjustments (Bertschek & Kaiser, 2004; Black & Lynch, 2001). Others, from a cybersecurity perspective, warn that DT exposes sensitive data, which may result in the leakage of production technologies and supply chain resources (Björkdahl, 2020; Buer et al., 2021). This not only boosts the capabilities of potential competitors but also creates legal risks associated with privacy breaches, potentially damaging reputation and social capital (Choi et al., 2019). Therefore, it is of both theoretical and practical significance to investigate the mechanisms through which DT influences CA in the manufacturing sector.

Although most studies acknowledge that digital technologies can enable manufacturing enterprises to build competitive advantage, few are grounded in formal mathematical models (Hanelt et al., 2021). Moreover, limited attention has been given to the role of business model innovation and competitive imitation in this process (Z. Zhang et al., 2022). The study addresses this gap by focusing on the role of BMI. Specifically, it investigates how digital technology investment influences enterprise competitiveness in manufacturing and elucidates the underlying mechanisms, providing both theoretical insight and empirical evidence for evaluating the performance outcomes of DT.

To be specific, (a) the study develops a theoretical framework based on a Multi-Structural Economic System (MSES) Model, which explains how DT promotes BMI and enhances the competitiveness of production-oriented enterprises. It also incorporates industrial organization theory to examine the impact of competitive imitation. (b) We construct a panel dataset using data from Chinese listed enterprises between 2008 and 2024, covering 50 sub-industries. A series of econometric models, including fixed-effects models and chain mediation models, are developed to test the effect of DT on the market competitiveness of manufacturing enterprises, with a particular focus on the mediating role of BMI. (c) We further incorporate the moderation effects of market competition by using moderation models, in order to examine the impact of imitation by competitors.

This paper consists of seven sections. Section 2 reviews the relevant literature on BMI, the benefits of DT in enterprises, and competitive imitation. Section 3 constructs a theoretical analysis framework based on the MSES model and derives research hypotheses through theoretical modeling. In Section 4, we describe the data sources, measurement methods, and analytical methods. Section 5 presents the empirical results validated through econometric models. In Section 6, we discuss the main findings and propose theoretical and practical implications. Section 7 summarizes the main conclusions, contributions, and directions for future research.

2. Literature Review

2.1. Digital Technology and Business Model Innovation

Research on BMI driven by DT in enterprises has developed relatively recently. Most scholars agree that DT has a positive effect on enterprises' exploration of new approaches and logics to create value. Given the different focal points of DT, enterprises exhibit diverse paths toward realizing BMI (Han & Zhang, 2022). Early studies argued that DT enables enterprises to identify patterns in customer behavior from data, thereby facilitating value matching for consumers or downstream supply chains (Zott & Amit, 2010). This represents a demand-driven model of innovation for value creation (Gu & Zhang, 2024). Some scholars emphasize the role of digital technologies in internal business operations, suggesting that DT helps optimize internal business structures, operational processes, and work patterns (Soukhoroukova et al., 2012; Ancillai et al., 2023; Mittra et al., 2015). This reflects a supply-side innovation mechanism. In addition, other studies highlight digital technologies in promoting value interaction between enterprises and customers, arguing that DT improves the ability to capture customer needs and to adjust operations accordingly (Ciampi et al., 2021), showcasing interactive innovation based on supply–demand interplay.

The relationship between DT and BMI in manufacturing enterprises can be illustrated as shown in Figure 1. Digital technologies impact enterprises through efficiency enhancement and product innovation across three dimensions: the supply side, the demand side, and supply–demand alignment. These impacts serve to refine or reconstruct the value creation logic of enterprises (S. Z. Wang & Nie, 2011; Picciotti, 2017), thereby achieving BMI.

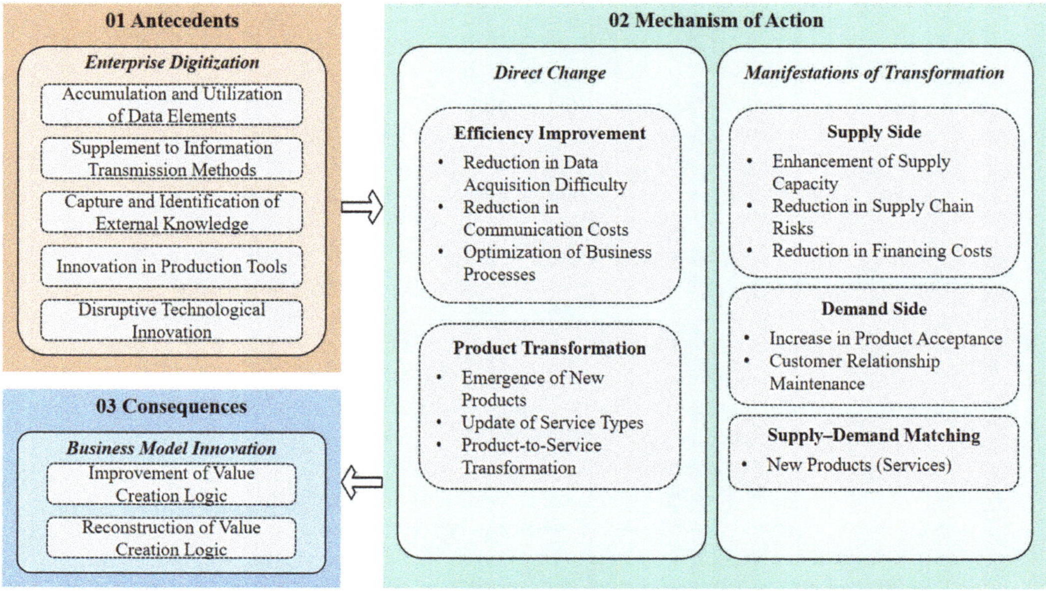

Figure 1. Logic of digitalization and business model innovation in manufacturing enterprises in the literature.

Some scholars have analyzed the relationship between the enterprise life cycle and BMI. They argue that the growth stage is the phase with the greatest freedom for BMI (Trimi & Berbegal-Mirabent, 2012; Taran et al., 2015). In the maturity stage, the impact of DT on BMI in manufacturing enterprises weakens (Freisinger et al., 2021), while in the decline stage, BMI in manufacturing enterprises is more reflected in thorough business transformation (Meier & Massberg, 2004; Chandler et al., 2014).

2.2. The Impact of Enterprises Adopting Digital Technology

Tracing the theoretical lines of performance research on enterprise DT, it is evident that most studies are based on the breakthrough of technological revolutions in the scale boundaries of enterprises. Classical economic theory posits that economies of scale are the primary drivers of enterprise growth. The intrinsic motivation behind enterprise growth lies in the pursuit of scale economies, wherein enterprises continuously adjust and optimize to achieve an optimal scale (Xiao & Huang, 2006; Morroni, 2007; Valerdi et al., 2008). In contrast, new institutional economics views enterprise growth not only as functional expansion but also as boundary expansion. As enterprises expand boundaries, they internalize transactions previously handled through markets to minimize market transaction costs (Gulbrandsen et al., 2017). Technological revolutions lead to economic revolutions (Gawer, 2021), and each technological revolution results in the modernization of the entire production system, ultimately generating new production practices (Foresman, 2016).

Most studies on the impact of DT in manufacturing on CA focus on the optimization of production and operations through the basic characteristics of DT, such as real-time capability, connectivity, and replicability. These studies argue that DT helps break down information silos between business systems within enterprises, reducing transaction costs in operations and improving management efficiency (Peng & Tao, 2022). DT is beneficial for automating and intelligentizing production processes in manufacturing enterprises, thereby enhancing the predictability of production risks and improving production efficiency (D. Wang & Shao, 2024; Rangaswamy et al., 2020). It also helps strengthen the spillover effects of knowledge and human capital, promoting the integration of innovation resources and improving innovation capabilities, thereby enhancing innovation performance (Bielig, 2023; Bhandari et al., 2023). There is a positive impact on enterprises forming CA (Di Silvestre et al., 2018; Oliveira et al., 2021), or affirming the positive role of DT from the perspective of improving financing capabilities and avoiding entrepreneurial myopia (Zaman et al., 2025). However, some studies suggest that the complex production processes in manufacturing enterprises increase the difficulty of digitalizing production, while the asymmetry of production data and supply chain information pose challenges for complex data integration. The need for updating equipment and infrastructure puts financial and time pressures on enterprises, and even adjusting human resource structures may lead to structural unemployment or production stagnation risk (Black & Lynch, 2001), thus bringing the risk of failure to DT in manufacturing enterprises (Sandulli et al., 2014).

2.3. *The Dynamics of Competitive Advantage and Competitive Imitation*

Competitive advantage refers to the relative position of an enterprise in the market, representing the level and stance of the enterprise leadership in value creation, such as resource development, integration, and utilization, compared with its competitors. Existing research explains the sources of competitive advantage from perspectives such as resource exclusivity, cost advantage, differentiation strategy, technological innovation, economies of scale, brand advantage, and network effects (Cantwell & Vertova, 2004; Amir & Lazzati, 2011; Shim & Lee, 2012; Fast et al., 2023). The establishment of competitive advantage is not static; it is influenced by factors such as competitor behavior, business environment, customer demand, and technological innovation. As a result, the competitive ability of an enterprise in the market evolves dynamically (L. L. Wang & Gao, 2021).

Among these factors, the influence of competitor behavior has always been present, directly affecting the establishment of the competitive advantage (Rivkin, 2001). Research on competitive imitation originates from the Herding Effect Theory. Industrial organization theory constructs theoretical frameworks, such as the Cournot model, the Bertrand model, the Stackelberg model, and the Beloff model. In these models, regardless of the game strategy employed by enterprises, the response decisions of competing enterprises always cause enterprise profits to deviate from expectations, corroborating the significant impact of competitor behavior on the establishment of CA. Some scholars, starting from the innovation behavior of enterprises, construct game models to analyze the decision-making logic of innovation and imitation, suggesting that in highly competitive markets, the innovation efforts and business model optimization of the enterprise may become a reference for other competitors to maintain competitive balance (L. Wang et al., 2024; Li, 2025). This phenomenon is more evident in platform enterprises (Duffy & Ralston, 2020; Park & Yi, 2024), which challenges the CA of first-mover enterprises.

3. The Theoretical Framework and Hypotheses

We construct the theoretical framework in three main steps. First, we develop an MSES model to analyze the relationship between DT and BMI. Our theoretical contribution lies in introducing digital technology as a tradable service, which serves as the starting point for modeling DT. Changes in the production and consumption structures of economic agents across products X, Y, and the digital service DT reflect the emergence of BMI. Second, we examine how BMI contributes to CA. This part builds upon the Cournot model and the Bertrand model, in which we solve for the impact of BMI on firm-level equilibrium output under monopolistic competition. Third, we incorporate the effect of competitive imitation by analyzing dynamic responses from rival enterprises within a Stackelberg competition framework.

3.1. The Relationship Between Digital Technology and Business Model Innovation

This section focuses on the mechanistic research of how DT leads to BMI. Based on the MSES model of neoclassical economics (Miller, 2004), we incorporate information technology elements into the analysis of production growth (Huang et al., 2019) and examine how the increasing level of DT in production-oriented enterprises alters their business models and the potential productivity incentives and competitive advantages brought by innovations in value creation methods.

First, the MSES model is constructed. It is assumed that there are two products, X and Y, in the economic system, with economic agents producing and consuming these two products. Labor endowment serves as the production factor, and the scale of economic agents is sufficiently large, with production following the law of diminishing marginal returns. In the context of DT, resources are not only used for the production of products X and Y, but also flow into the production of DT or the trade of digital services, such that the production functions and budget constraints faced by economic agents are as shown in Equations (1) and (2).

$$\begin{gathered} x + x^s = L_x^a \\ y + y^s = L_y^a \\ D + D^s = L_D^b \\ L_x + L_y + L_D = 1 \end{gathered} \tag{1}$$

$$p_x(x^s - x^d) + p_y(y^s - y^d) + p_D(D^s - D^d) = 0 \tag{2}$$

In this context, x represents the quantity of product X produced and sold by the economic agent, x^s represents the quantity of product X supplied to the market by the economic agent as a producer, and L_x represents the share of productivity spent on producing product X. The same economic meanings apply to y, y^s, and L_y for product Y, and a represents the degree of specialization, which in turn indicates the efficiency of labor resource transformation in producing products X and Y. As the degree of specialization increases, the production transformation efficiency gradually increases ($a > 1$). The character D indicates the economic agent's self-supply of DT, and D^s represents the provision of digital services by the economic agent to the market. The D^d represents the digital services obtained by the economic agent from market transactions, and L_D represents the share of productivity invested in DT. The codability of DT makes a high level of expertise a key factor in improving production efficiency. It is still assumed that the accumulation of labor skills has a positive impact on production transformation efficiency ($b > 1$). The characters p_x, p_y, and p_D represent the prices of products X, Y, and digital services in the market.

Then, the influence of DT is introduced. The theoretical derivation primarily focuses on the ability of DT to solve information asymmetry problems, using the Cobb–Douglas utility function to measure the utility of economic agents, as shown in Equation (3). To make the utility model more aligned with the market transaction environment, the Iceberg Cost paradigm is borrowed to introduce the concept of transaction costs, assuming that there are transaction costs between economic agents, and r can be understood as market transaction efficiency. As the integration of DT with economic agents deepens, the degree of information asymmetry in the market decreases, and transaction efficiency improves.

Therefore, market transaction efficiency is positively influenced by the level of DT. This can be characterized by $r = (D + D^d)^{\lambda}$.

$$U = [x + (D + D^d)^{\lambda} x^d]^{\alpha} * [y + (D + D^d)^{\lambda} y^d]^{1-\alpha} \tag{3}$$

Furthermore, the potential business models of economic agents and their conditions are derived. For different economic agents, their business models can be summarized into three categories: the first category of economic agents adopts a fully self-sufficient business model (M^1). The second category adopts a partially market-divided business model (M^2), engaging in market transactions for certain products and services while maintaining the ability to produce and sell most products and services internally. The third category adopts a fully market-participating business model (M^3), participating in the market division of labor as part of a multi-structured market. These business models can be represented by Equation (4).

$$K \times M = K \times \begin{bmatrix} x & x^s & x^d \\ y & y^s & y^d \\ D & D^s & D^d \end{bmatrix} \tag{4}$$

where K is the coefficient matrix, representing the shares of products X, Y, and DT in the equilibrium state, and M_{ij} indicates the production and transaction status of products or services under the respective business model. Value 1 is assigned to the first column if the economic agent produces a given product or service; otherwise, it is 0. The second column reflects the sales status of the corresponding product, and the third column indicates whether the product is purchased from the market. For example, in the first row, the entry x denotes whether the agent produces product X, x^s indicates whether the agent supplies product X to the market, and x^d shows whether the agent purchases product Y from the market.

These economic agents make decisions regarding their business models, optimizing constraints around the utility function (Equation (3)), production function (Equation (1)), and budget constraint (Equation (2)) under the respective constraints of each business model (M^i). Assuming equivalence of preferences for products X and Y across economic agents ($\alpha = 0.5$), the optimal responses of economic agents under each business model, along with the equilibrium utility conditions and transaction efficiency thresholds, are shown in Table 1.

The study then analyzes the relationship between DT in enterprises and BMI. In Table 1, when the degree of DT is low, market transaction efficiency conforms to $r^* \in \left(0, 4/(2I)^{2a}\right]$. In this scenario, economic agents face high transaction costs. The cost for economic agents to acquire products and services through market transactions is much higher than self-production, leading to the adoption of a self-sufficient business model (M^1). As DT deepens, the digital services acquired by economic agents ($D + D^d$) continuously increase, and market transaction efficiency improves to $r^* \in \left(4/(2I)^{2a}, T\right]$. It is suggested that the decline in transaction costs leads to greater utility from market-acquired products than from internal production using equivalent labor input; however, due to residual information asymmetry, economic agents may still lack sufficient incentive for full market participation. At this point, the optimal business model is partial market division (M^2). As the integration of DT and the economy deepens further ($D + D^d \geq 0.5$), market transaction efficiency increases to a higher level ($r^* > T$), and the labor input required by economic agents to produce both products begins to exceed the need for market transactions to achieve the same utility. At this stage, the business model of the economic agent gradually evolves into a fully market-participating business model (M^3). In summary, DT reduces TC among economic agents, promotes more efficient market specialization, and drives the evolution and innovation of business models.

Table 1. Multi-structural economy model solution results.

Business Model	Production and Transaction	Optimal Response	Condition of Equal Utility	Transaction Efficiency
M^1	$M_{ij} = \begin{bmatrix} 1 & 0 & 0 \\ 1 & 0 & 0 \\ 0 & 0 & 0 \end{bmatrix}$	$L_x = \frac{1}{2}, L_y = \frac{1}{2}$ $x = \left(\frac{1}{2}\right)^a, y = \left(\frac{1}{2}\right)^a$	-	$r^* \in \left(0, \frac{4}{(2I)^{2a}}\right]$
M^2	$M_{ij} = \begin{bmatrix} 1 & 1 & 0 \\ 0 & 0 & 1 \\ 1 & 0 & 0 \end{bmatrix}$	$L_x = I, L_D = 1 - I$ $x = \left(\frac{e^{\ln I}}{2}\right)^a, x^s = I^a - \left(\frac{e^{\ln I}}{2}\right)^a$ $y^d = \frac{p_x}{p_y}\left(\frac{e^{\ln I}}{2}\right)^a, D = (1 - I)^b$ $r = (1 - I)^{\lambda b}$	$p_x = p_y$	$r^* \in \left(\frac{4}{(2I)^{2a}}, T\right]$
	$M_{ij} = \begin{bmatrix} 0 & 0 & 1 \\ 1 & 1 & 0 \\ 1 & 0 & 0 \end{bmatrix}$	$L_y = I, L_D = 1 - I$ $y = \left(\frac{e^{\ln I}}{2}\right)^a, y^s = I^a - \left(\frac{e^{\ln I}}{2}\right)^a$ $x^d = \frac{p_y}{p_x}\left(\frac{e^{\ln I}}{2}\right)^a, D = (1 - I)^b$ $r = (1 - I)^{\lambda b}$		
M^3	$M_{ij} = \begin{bmatrix} 1 & 1 & 0 \\ 0 & 0 & 1 \\ 0 & 0 & 1 \end{bmatrix}$	$L_x = 1$ $x = \frac{1}{2} - \frac{p_D}{4p_x}, x^s = \frac{1}{2} + \frac{p_D}{4p_x}$ $y^d = \frac{2p_x - p_D}{4p_y}, D^d = \frac{1}{2}$ $r = (\frac{1}{2})^\lambda$	$p_D = \frac{p_x}{\frac{1}{2} + \left(\frac{1}{2}\right)^\lambda}$ $p_D = \frac{p_y}{\frac{1}{2} + \left(\frac{1}{2}\right)^\lambda}$	$r^* \in (T, 1]$
	$M_{ij} = \begin{bmatrix} 0 & 0 & 1 \\ 1 & 1 & 0 \\ 0 & 0 & 1 \end{bmatrix}$	$L_y = 1$ $y = \frac{1}{2} - \frac{p_D}{4p_y}, y^s = \frac{1}{2} + \frac{p_D}{4p_y}$ $x^d = \frac{2p_y - p_D}{4p_x}, D^d = \frac{1}{2}$ $r = (\frac{1}{2})^\lambda$		
	$M_{ij} = \begin{bmatrix} 0 & 0 & 1 \\ 0 & 0 & 1 \\ 1 & 1 & 0 \end{bmatrix}$	$L_D = 1$ $D = \frac{1}{2}, D^s = \frac{1}{2}$ $x^d = \frac{p_D}{2p_x}, y^d = \frac{p_D}{2p_y}$ $r = (\frac{1}{2})^\lambda$		

Notes: $I = \frac{2a}{\lambda b + 2a}$, $T = \min\left(2^{-a} - 2^{1-0.5\lambda-a}, \frac{I^a}{2}(1 - I)^{0.5\lambda b}(1 + 2^{1-0.5\lambda})\right)$. The production–transaction status is expressed mathematically by M_{ij} in Equation (4), representing whether the economic agent produces and transacts in products X, Y, and digital services.

3.2. The Establishment of Enterprise Market Competitive Advantage

Further analysis is conducted on how enterprise DT enhances competitiveness and expands CA through BMI. Enterprises with different levels of DT have varying abilities to overcome information asymmetry, resulting in differentiated business models under optimal decision making. The study on the formation of competitive advantage focuses primarily on enterprises involved in market transactions. Taking the market for product X as an example, when the DT level of an enterprise is low, the optimal business model is M^2. At this point, the average cost of production can be understood as the labor input required to produce a unit of the product, as shown in Equation (5). As DT progresses, the optimal business model gradually evolves into M^3, and the average cost of production is shown in Equation (6).

$$AC_{M2\_x} = \frac{L_x}{x + x^s} = (\frac{2a}{\lambda b + 2a})^{1-a} \quad (5)$$

$$AC_{M3\_x} = \frac{L_x}{x + x^s} = 1 \quad (6)$$

Assume there are two enterprises in the market for product X, Enterprise 1 and Enterprise 2, both of which only produce product X and are homogeneous except for their DT levels. Market demand is understood as a linear relationship, as shown in Equation (7).

$$P = A - B(x_1 + x_2) \tag{7}$$

When the two enterprises engage in price competition, each enterprise will attempt to lower its price to gain a larger market share. Under the assumption of homogeneity, the competitive advantage of the enterprises is based on the optimization of production costs due to DT. The price competition outcomes for Enterprise 1 and Enterprise 2 at different levels of DT are solved using the Bertrand model, and the results are shown in Table 2.

Table 2. Equilibrium supply solution for two enterprises under price competition.

		En. 2		
	Business Model	M^1	M^2	M^3
En. 1	M^1	$(0,0)$	$\left(0, \frac{A(\lambda b+2a)^{1-a}-(2a)^{1-a}}{2B(\lambda b+2a)^{1-a}}\right)$	$\left(0, \frac{A-1}{2B}\right)$
	M^2	$\left(\frac{A(\lambda b+2a)^{1-a}-(2a)^{1-a}}{2B(\lambda b+2a)^{1-a}}, 0\right)$	(x_1, x_2)	$\left(0, \frac{A(\lambda b+2a)^{1-a}-(2a)^{1-a}}{2B(\lambda b+2a)^{1-a}}\right)$
	M^3	$\left(\frac{A-1}{2B}, 0\right)$	$\left(\frac{A(\lambda b+2a)^{1-a}-(2a)^{1-a}}{2B(\lambda b+2a)^{1-a}}, 0\right)$	(x_1', x_2')

Notes: When both enterprises are at the same business model stage, $x_1 + x_2 = \left[A(\lambda b + 2a)^{1-a} - (2a)^{1-a}\right]/B(\lambda b + 2a)^{1-a}$, $x_1' + x_2' = (A-1)/B$. The table reports equilibrium outputs (X_1, X_2) under a duopolistic competition setting, where X_1 denotes the equilibrium output of Enterprise 1 and X_2 that of Enterprise 2.

From Table 2, it can be seen that when a price competition strategy is adopted, regardless of the DT level of Enterprise 2, as the DT level of Enterprise 1 increases, the business model of Enterprise 1 shifts toward M^3, which will increase its market supply of product X; in other words, the DT of Enterprise 1 expands its market share in the equilibrium state, benefiting the expansion of its CA. When Enterprise 2 has an extremely low level of DT, its optimal business model is M^1. At this point, the equilibrium supply of Enterprise 1 at different levels of DT is 0, $\frac{A(\lambda b+2a)^{1-a}-(2a)^{1-a}}{2B(\lambda b+2a)^{1-a}}$ and $\frac{A-1}{2B}$. Since $\frac{A-1}{2B} > \frac{A(\lambda b+2a)^{1-a}-(2a)^{1-a}}{2B(\lambda b+2a)^{1-a}}$, the equilibrium output of Enterprise 1 gradually increases with DT. This conclusion holds when the business model of Enterprise 2 is M^2 or M^3, indicating that DT still positively impacts its CA.

Considering market share competition, the impact of DT on its CA is examined. The market share competition outcomes for Enterprise 1 and Enterprise 2 at different levels of DT are solved using the Cournot model, and the results are shown in Table 3.

Table 3. Equilibrium supply solution for two enterprises under market share competition.

		En. 2	
	Business Model	M^2	M^3
En. 1	M^2	$\left(\frac{A(\lambda b+2a)^{1-a}-(2a)^{1-a}}{3B(\lambda b+2a)^{1-a}}, \frac{A(\lambda b+2a)^{1-a}-(2a)^{1-a}}{3B(\lambda b+2a)^{1-a}}\right)$	$\left(\frac{(A+1)(\lambda b+2a)^{1-a}-2(2a)^{1-a}}{3B(\lambda b+2a)^{1-a}}, \frac{(A-2)(\lambda b+2a)^{1-a}+(2a)^{1-a}}{3B(\lambda b+2a)^{1-a}}\right)$
	M^3	$\left(\frac{(A-2)(\lambda b+2a)^{1-a}+(2a)^{1-a}}{3B(\lambda b+2a)^{1-a}}, \frac{(A+1)(\lambda b+2a)^{1-a}-2(2a)^{1-a}}{3B(\lambda b+2a)^{1-a}}\right)$	$\left(\frac{A-1}{3B}, \frac{A-1}{3B}\right)$

Notes: The table reports equilibrium outputs (X_1, X_2) under a duopolistic competition setting, where X_1 denotes the equilibrium output of Enterprise 1 and X_2 that of Enterprise 2.

From Table 3, it can be seen that as both enterprises adjust their supply to compete for market share, with the deepening of DT, BMI increases the equilibrium market supply of both enterprises, thereby forming competitive advantages and promoting the expansion of their CA. Specifically, when Enterprise 2 has a low level of DT and is in M^2, equilibrium supply at different DT levels of Enterprise 1 is $\frac{A(\lambda b+2a)^{1-a}-(2a)^{1-a}}{3B(\lambda b+2a)^{1-a}}$, $\frac{(A-2)(\lambda b+2a)^{1-a}+(2a)^{1-a}}{3B(\lambda b+2a)^{1-a}}$. Due to the assumption of the model ($a > 1$, $b > 1$, $\lambda > 0$), it can be proven that $\frac{(A-2)(\lambda b+2a)^{1-a}+(2a)^{1-a}}{3B(\lambda b+2a)^{1-a}} > \frac{A(\lambda b+2a)^{1-a}-(2a)^{1-a}}{3B(\lambda b+2a)^{1-a}}$ holds. As DT progresses, Enterprise 1 gradually establishes an advantage in market competition with Enterprise 2. Similarly, when Enterprise 2 has a higher level of DT and is in M^3, Enterprise 1 can still increase its market share gradually to 50% through DT, indicating that enterprise DT has a positive impact on expanding CA.

In summary, our theoretical framework clarifies how DT in manufacturing reduces TC, facilitates BMI, and enhances CA. Based on the analyses in Sections 3.1 and 3.2, we propose the following hypotheses:

Tables 2 and 3 consistently indicate that DT in manufacturing significantly contributes to the expansion of market power, thereby fostering CA.

H1. *Digital transformation of manufacturing enterprises is beneficial for establishing competitive advantages.*

Section 3.1 explores the relationship between DT, TC, and BMI. The application of digital technologies helps alleviate information asymmetry and reduce TC between economic agents. As the degree of DT increases, the utility of obtaining intermediate goods or services via market exchange begins to exceed that of internal production, leading to deeper market specialization and driving BMI. Section 3.2 discusses how BMI enhances CA. The evolution of business models is accompanied by increasing returns to unit input. This improvement allows enterprises to achieve lower production costs in price-based competition or stronger economies of scale in quantity-based competition, thereby strengthening CA.

These findings suggest that digital transformation in manufacturing can reduce transaction costs and promote business model innovation. And the BMI helps enhance enterprise competitiveness. This implies the existence of a chain transmission mechanism linking DT to CA, leading to the formulation of the following hypothesis:

H2. *Digital transformation enhances competitive advantage in manufacturing firms through a chain mechanism of reduced transaction costs and improved business model innovation.*

3.3. *The Impact of Competitive Imitation*

In a highly competitive market, technological innovation and business model optimization may be imitated by other competitors, eroding the competitive advantage established by the first mover and forming a new market equilibrium. Research on CA must consider the impact of competitors. To further analyze the impact of imitation on market structure under the security and privacy risks of DT, the perspective of the Stackelberg model is incorporated into the analysis. It is assumed that Enterprise 2 has established strong CA and has become the leading enterprise in market production decisions, while Enterprise 1 is the market follower. The BMI and imitation effects are shown in Table 4.

Table 4. Equilibrium supply solution for two enterprises under competitive imitation.

		En. 2	
	Business Model	M^2	M^3
En. 1	M^2	$\left(\frac{A(\lambda b+2a)^{1-a}-(2a)^{1-a}}{4B(\lambda b+2a)^{1-a}}, \frac{A(\lambda b+2a)^{1-a}-(2a)^{1-a}}{2B(\lambda b+2a)^{1-a}}\right)$	$\left(\frac{(A+2)(\lambda b+2a)^{1-a}-3(2a)^{1-a}}{4B(\lambda b+2a)^{1-a}}, \frac{(A-2)(\lambda b+2a)^{1-a}+(2a)^{1-a}}{2B(\lambda b+2a)^{1-a}}\right)$
	M^3	$\left(\frac{(A-3)(\lambda b+2a)^{1-a}+2(2a)^{1-a}}{4B(\lambda b+2a)^{1-a}}, \frac{(A+1)(\lambda b+2a)^{1-a}-2(2a)^{1-a}}{2B(\lambda b+2a)^{1-a}}\right)$	$\left(\frac{A-1}{4B}, \frac{A-1}{2B}\right)$

Notes: The table reports equilibrium outputs (X_1, X_2) under a duopolistic competition setting, where X_1 denotes the equilibrium output of Enterprise 1 and X_2 that of Enterprise 2.

Considering DT led by the leading enterprise, from Table 4, it can be seen that when the DT level of Enterprise 2 increases, its business model evolves to M^3, and the market equilibrium output increases from $\frac{A(\lambda b+2a)^{1-a}-(2a)^{1-a}}{2B(\lambda b+2a)^{1-a}}$ to $\frac{(A-2)(\lambda b+2a)^{1-a}+(2a)^{1-a}}{2B(\lambda b+2a)^{1-a}}$. DT leads to BMI, effectively promoting the leading enterprise to form a competitive advantage. As a competitor, Enterprise 1 recognizes the improvements in transaction efficiency and production efficiency brought about by DT, and similarly undertakes DT to imitate Enterprise 2. Under the new competitive framework, as Enterprise 1 deepens its DT, its business model gradually transitions from M^2 to M^3. The imitation reduces the equilibrium supply of Enterprise 2 from $\frac{(A-2)(\lambda b+2a)^{1-a}+(2a)^{1-a}}{2B(\lambda b+2a)^{1-a}}$ to $\frac{A-1}{2B}$. It indicates that in a DT led by the leading enterprise, the imitation behavior of the follower enterprise constrains the expansion of CA through DT.

We then consider DT led by the follower enterprise in Table 4. It can be seen that when Enterprise 1 undertakes DT and achieves BMI, its equilibrium output increases from $\frac{A(\lambda b+2a)^{1-a}-(2a)^{1-a}}{4B(\lambda b+2a)^{1-a}}$ to $\frac{(A-3)(\lambda b+2a)^{1-a}+2(2a)^{1-a}}{4B(\lambda b+2a)^{1-a}}$, and its market share increases from $\frac{1}{3}$ to $\frac{(A-3)(\lambda b+2a)^{1-a}+2(2a)^{1-a}}{(3A-1)(\lambda b+2a)^{1-a}-2(2a)^{1-a}}$, thus facilitating the expansion of its CA. Enterprise 2, as the leading enterprise, may imitate Enterprise 1 to maintain its market advantage, evolving from M^2 to M^3. The equilibrium output of Enterprise 1 then decreases from $\frac{(A-3)(\lambda b+2a)^{1-a}+2(2a)^{1-a}}{4B(\lambda b+2a)^{1-a}}$ to $\frac{1}{3}$, while the market share gradually shrinks from $\frac{(A-3)(\lambda b+2a)^{1-a}+2(2a)^{1-a}}{(3A-1)(\lambda b+2a)^{1-a}-2(2a)^{1-a}}$ to $\frac{1}{3}$. This means that in a DT led by the followers, the imitation by the leading enterprise also constrains the ability of the followers to expand CA.

In summary, in a static competitive relationship, enterprises use DT to eliminate the negative impact of information asymmetry and achieve business model optimization and innovation, establishing a competitive advantage in the market and benefiting from the positive effects of DT. From a dynamic perspective, however, both leading and follower enterprises have incentives to imitate competitors' DT and BMI to establish or maintain market dominance. Competitive imitation causes the effects of DT to spill over within the industry, improving the production efficiency of competitors within the industry. It also opens up the black box of manufacturing production, lowering entry barriers for external enterprises, intensifying industry competition, and constraining enterprises from expanding their CA through DT.

H3. *Business model innovation has become the subject of observation and imitation by competitors, and the imitation has a negative impact on the effectiveness of enterprise DT, constraining enterprises from achieving competitive advantage through DT.*

Based on the above analysis, our research framework is shown in Figure 2.

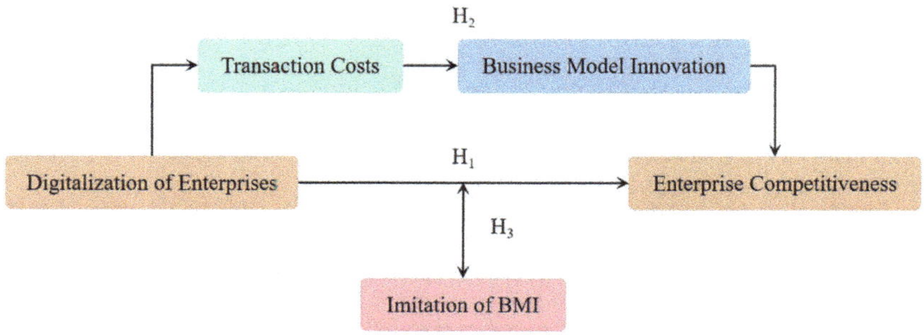

Figure 2. The research model.

4. Methodology

4.1. Data Sources

This study selects Chinese publicly listed manufacturing enterprises from 2008 to 2024 as the primary research subjects. A panel dataset is constructed, covering 50 sub-industries and comprising a total of 29,131 samples. The dataset includes several categories of core variables. Enterprise-level operational data are obtained from the CSMAR database. Industry-level data are derived from Chinese official business registration records and macroeconomic statistical yearbooks. Regional economic indicators related to the locations of enterprises are collected from the statistical yearbooks of Chinese cities.

4.2. Variable Measurement

4.2.1. Dependent Variable

Competitive Advantage (CA). The competitive advantage of enterprises in the market is calculated using the price markup to avoid the issues of missing data for non-listed companies and difficulties in marginal cost estimation that exist in methods such as HHI and the Lerner Index. Referring to the approach by Loecker and Warzynski (2012), the price markup is calculated using the ratio of variable cost elasticity to the share of variable input in production under the condition of minimizing production cost.

The methodological steps are as follows:

(1) Firms are first grouped according to their respective industries.

(2) A Translog production function is then constructed, as shown in Equation (8), where l_{it} denotes the price of labor input for firm i in year t, proxied by the average employee compensation. k_{it} represents the price of capital input, proxied by the long-term return on capital. ω_{it} and ε denote the total factor productivity estimated using the Olley–Pakes (OP) method and the error term.

$$y_{it} = \beta_1 l_{it} + \beta_2 k_{it} + \beta_3 l_{it}^2 + \beta_4 k_{it}^2 + \beta_5 l_{it} * k_{it} + \omega_{it} + \varepsilon \tag{8}$$

(3) Equation (8) is estimated separately for each industry sample, yielding the regression coefficients β_1, β_2 and β_5.

(4) They are then substituted into Equation (9) to compute the elasticity of variable costs θ_{it}^X for firm i in year t.

$$\hat{\theta}_{it}^X = \hat{\beta}_1 + 2\hat{\beta}_2 l_{it} + \hat{\beta}_5 k_{it} \tag{9}$$

(5) The share of variable input in total output α_{ir}^X is calculated, with the numerator and denominator represented by operating costs and total operating revenue, respectively.

(6) Finally, we obtain the CA indicator for sub-sectors, as shown in Equation (10).

$$PI_{it} = \theta_{it}^X / \alpha_{ir}^X \tag{10}$$

The data are summarized in Table 5.

Table 5. Definitions and explanations of core variables.

Item	Variable Definitions
Dependent Variable	
Competitive Advantage (CA)	The CA of enterprises in sub-sectors is calculated using the price markup, which is represented as the ratio of variable cost elasticity to the share of variable input.
Independent Variable	
Digital Transformation (DT)	The actual investment made by enterprises in digital transformation is represented by the number of intangible assets that include DT.
Mediation and Moderation Variables	
Transaction Costs (TCs)	The efforts made by enterprises to ensure smooth production and operation processes, both internally and externally, are represented by the sum of operating expenses and administrative expenses of listed companies.
Business Model Innovation (BMI)	Changes in business models of enterprises are represented by a six-dimensional vector of revenue models, value propositions, and cost structures, with the cosine distance to the corresponding sub-sector.
Competitive Imitation (I_BMI)	The recognition and imitation of BMI by competing enterprises in relation to digital transformation are represented by the average of BMI in the sub-sector.
Control Variables	
Control Variables_enterprise	Nature of Equity Concentration of Power Firm Size Labor Cost Capital Cost Total Asset Growth Rate Years in Business Since Founding
Control Variables_city	GDP Population at Year-End Administrative Level Market Segmentation Index Foreign Investment Amount

4.2.2. Independent Variable

Digital Transformation (DT). The number of intangible assets associated with digital technologies is used as the indicator for digital transformation, where the definition of digital technology intangible assets refers to the treatment of Fan et al. (2023). When measuring DT at the enterprise level, existing studies have gradually developed three main methods of calculation: digital system applications (Z. Sun & Hou, 2019), annual report disclosure keyword frequency (F. Wu et al., 2021), and the proportion of digital assets. The characteristics of DT make DT in enterprises have relatively low marginal costs (J. Zhang & Li, 2023). The cost of the digital economy primarily arises from the high threshold for technology adoption, meaning that the relationship between the investment in DT and the production scale is not linear. Using the proportion of intangible assets associated with DT to measure the degree of DT will underestimate the transformation level of larger enterprises, as listed companies tend to be larger in scale; therefore, the number of intangible assets associated with DT should be used to measure the DT of enterprises.

4.2.3. Mediation and Moderation Variables

Transaction Costs (TC). The study focuses on the internal and external organizational efforts enterprises expend to maintain smooth business operations. From the perspective of external transactions, some scholars argue that selling expenses reflect the costs incurred in the process of product sales or service delivery and can thus serve as a proxy for transaction costs (Cai et al., 2024). Others further include administrative expenses—those incurred by corporate administrative departments for organizing and managing production activities—as part of transaction costs. This broader view regards both selling and administrative expenses as relevant indicators (Huang et al., 2019). We align with the latter view, using the sum of operating expenses and management expenses as the indicator for TC.

Business Model Innovation (BMI). The BMI indicator is constructed based on the approach of Guo et al. (2018), using a multi-dimensional vector of the revenue model, value proposition, and cost structure, and measuring the cosine distance to the industry vector. Although the paths and forms of BMI in each module vary, the changes brought by a new business model are directly reflected in the revenue model, value proposition, and cost structure. Therefore, BMI is measured by the differences in these three aspects between the enterprise and the industry. The revenue model is represented by the proportion of service revenue to total revenue and the proportion of current assets to total revenue. The value proposition is represented by the proportion of purchases from the top five suppliers and the proportion of sales to customers. The cost structure is represented by the proportion of sales expenses and the operating cycle. These indicators are normalized at the industry level, and then the cosine similarity between the business model vector of enterprises and that of the sub-sector is calculated. The indicator for BMI is set based on the cosine distance, as shown in the shaded area of Figure 3.

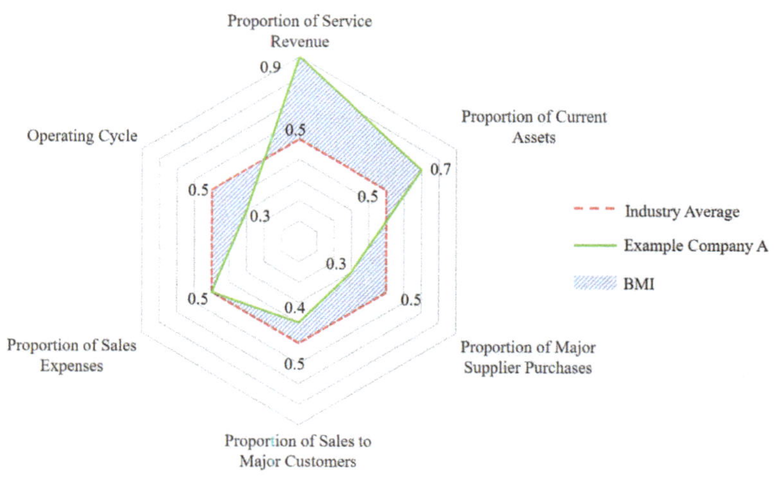

Figure 3. Example of business model innovation variable calculation.

Competitive Imitation. Market behavior evolves dynamically. When digital enterprises emerge in the market, the digital economy generates technological spillovers to the traditional economy, promoting the transformation and upgrading of other enterprises within the industry (Li et al., 2024; Montemari et al., 2024). Changes in business models are more direct (Climent et al., 2024) and more easily recognized by competitors than other DT measures. Thus, the study measures the spillover effect within the industry using the average BMI level in the sub-sector (I_BMI).

4.2.4. Control Variables

Control variables are incorporated to account for two categories of factors influencing enterprise CA: enterprise-specific characteristics and city-level contextual variables (Y. Zhang et al., 2024; Xie & Wu, 2024; Sui et al., 2024). At the enterprise level, resource exclusivity is measured using the ownership structure and power concentration of the enterprise, controlling for the competitive advantage brought by policy assistance and entrepreneurial resources. The scale of the enterprise is used to control for the positive impact of economies of scale on establishing CA, measured as the natural logarithm of the total assets. Labor costs, capital costs, and operational conditions represent the cost advantages established by the enterprise, with operational conditions measured by the total asset growth rate. The founding year variable is also controlled. At the city level, the GDP of the location city is used to control for the advantages gained from local economic development. The development potential and orientation are represented by the total population at the end of the year and the administrative level. The market segmentation index and actual foreign investment are used to control the impact of the business environment.

4.3. Model Building

We construct econometric models based on the results of the theoretical framework, aiming to investigate the impact of DT on the CA of manufacturing enterprises. Since CA is inevitably influenced by year-specific and industry-specific characteristics, we adopt a fixed-effects (FE) model to control for these unobserved heterogeneities. A Hausman Test is also conducted to ensure the validity of the model selection, as shown in Equation (11):

$$CA_{ijt} = \beta_0 + \beta_1 DT_{ijt} + \Phi X_{ijt} + \Psi X'_{jt} + u_i + \delta_t + \varepsilon_{i,t} \quad (11)$$

Here, i, j, and t represent a specific manufacturing enterprise, the industry category of the enterprise, and the year of the sample, respectively. X_{ijt} represents the enterprise-level control variables, X'_{jt} represents the city-level control variables, and Φ and Ψ are the coefficient vectors of the control variables. The model controls individual fixed effects (μ_i) and time fixed effects (δ_t).

$$\begin{aligned} M^{\lambda}_{ijt} &= \beta_0 + a^{\lambda} DT_{ijt} + \Phi X_{ijt} + \Psi X'_{jt} + \varepsilon_{i,t} \\ CA_{ijt} &= \beta_0 + c' DT_{ijt} + \sum_{\lambda=1}^{2} b^{\lambda} M^{\lambda}_{ijt} + \Phi X_{ijt} + \Psi X'_{jt} + \varepsilon_{i,t} \\ CA_{ijt} &= \beta_0 + c DT_{ijt} + \Phi X_{ijt} + \Psi X'_{jt} + \varepsilon_{i,t} \end{aligned} \quad (12)$$

We propose that DT reduces TC and promotes BMI in H2, suggesting a mediation pathway among the core variables. To examine the underlying causal mechanisms, we employ a mediation analysis framework. Referring to the method of Gelbach (2016), a chain mediation effect model that includes DT, TC, BMI, and CA is constructed (Equation

(12)). In this model, M_{ijt}^{λ} represent the variables for TC or BMI. Sobel Tests are used to assess the significance of the decomposed indirect effects.

$$CA_{ijt} = \beta_0 + \beta_1 DT\_O_{ijt} + \beta_2 I\_BMI_{ijt} + \beta_3 I\_BMI_{ijt} \times DT_{ijt} + \Phi X_{ijt} + \Psi X_{jt}' + \mu \quad (13)$$

Finally, we explore the moderating role of competitive imitation in shaping the relationship between DT and CA. As shown in the theoretical analysis in Section 3, competitive advantage is dynamic. The BMI may be subject to observation and imitation by rival enterprises, leading to new competitive equilibria. In this context, the relationship between competitive imitation and DT is not strictly causal but reflects complex interactions and strategic motivations. Since Hypothesis 3 focuses on how competitive imitation influences the effectiveness of DT in establishing CA, we construct a moderation model (Equation (13)) to empirically test this interaction effect.

Before conducting the empirical analysis, all continuous variables were standardized using Z-score standardization.

5. Empirical Results and Analysis

5.1. Benchmark Regression

Panel regression of Equation (11) was conducted using a sample of listed manufacturing companies to study the impact of DT on the CA of manufacturing enterprises. The results are shown in Table 6. Columns (1) to (4) of Table 6 display the random effects without control variables, the random effects with control variables, and the results with fixed effects. In all these results, the coefficient of DT is significantly positive, indicating that there is a positive correlation between DT and price markup. By applying DT to address information asymmetry, enterprises break the information silo effect, effectively reduce the circulation costs of information and products within departments, between departments, and between enterprises, and improve the management and production efficiency of manufacturing enterprises. This enables enterprises to better utilize economies of scale in output competition, facilitating the expansion of CA. H1 is thus confirmed.

Table 6. Benchmark regression results.

	(1) *CA*	(2) *CA*	(3) *CA*	(4) *CA*
DT	1.128 * (0.613)	2.238 *** (0.705)	1.335 * (0.701)	2.124 *** (0.707)
Controls	NO	YES	NO	YES
μ_i_FE	NO	NO	YES	YES
δ_t_FE	NO	NO	YES	YES
Constant	2.149 *** (0.083)	2.432 *** (0.614)	1.570 *** (0.324)	4.523 *** (1.422)
N	29,131	29,131	29,131	29,131
R^2_{adj}	0.226	0.281	0.218	0.294

Notes: * and *** indicate significance at 10% and 1% levels, respectively. The numbers in parentheses are standard errors.

5.2. The Endogenous Test

Some studies suggest that enterprises with competitive advantages may be more likely to implement DT (Rangaswamy et al., 2020). Considering the possible reverse causality between DT and competitive advantage, as well as potential omitted variable bias, we conduct an endogenous analysis using the Two-Stage Least Squares (2SLS) model and design two instrumental variables. The first one is the average DT investment of other enterprises in the same industry, as there is a network externality in technological diffusion within the industry. The DT of other enterprises in the same industry influences the DT decisions of the target enterprise through supply chains, competitive pressure, or knowledge spillovers (Y. Chen & Guo, 2024), while the characteristics of a single enterprise are unlikely to affect the DT level of the entire industry or region. The second instrumental variable is the internet infrastructure level of these locations, calculated using a weighted entropy method based on the number of internet users per 100 people, the proportion of workers in computer services and software, per capita telecom business volume, the number of mobile phone users per 100 people, and the annual Peking University Digital Financial Inclusion Index of the city. Since regional internet infrastructure is a necessary condition for enterprise DT, it directly impacts the cost and feasibility of adopting digital technologies, and the DT level is clearly the primary path through which regional digital infrastructure affects its development, thus meeting the relevance and exogeneity requirements.

Columns (1) and (2) of Table 7 show the results using the instrumental variables. It is found that, whether using the industry instrumental variable or the regional instrumental variable, the first-stage estimated coefficients of IV_I and IV_C are significantly positive, indicating a positive correlation between the DT levels of the same region or the same industry and the DT of the enterprise. The relevance between the instrumental variables and the explanatory variables is confirmed. In the second-stage results, the coefficients remain significant, and the Anderson LM statistic is significant at the 1% level. The Cragg–Donald Wald F-statistic is greater than 10, indicating the validity of the instrumental variables. After addressing the endogeneity issue, the conclusion that DT in manufacturing enterprises promotes the enhancement of their competitive ability remains valid.

Table 7. Instrumental variable regression results.

	(1)		(2)	
	First_Stage *DT*	*First_Stage* *CA*	*First_Stage* *DT*	*First_Stage* *CA*
IV_I	0.121 *** (0.007)			
IV_C			0.002 *** (0.001)	
$\hat{DT}$		16.387 *** (6.348)		0.491 ** (0.247)
$Controls$	YES	YES	YES	YES
μ_i_FE	YES	YES	YES	YES
δ_t_FE	YES	YES	YES	YES
$Constant$	0.024 *** (0.002)	1.8883 *** (8.22)	0.008 *** (0.002)	2.068 *** (0.384)
N	29,131	29,131	29,131	29,131
R^2_{adj}	0.271	0.368	0.185	0.264
$AndersonLM$	268.270 ***		11.850 ***	
$Cragg-Donald\ Wald\ F$	270.630		18.530	

Notes: ** and *** indicate significance at 5% and 1% levels, respectively. The numbers in parentheses are standard errors.

5.3. The Mediation Effect of Business Model Innovation

We examine the chain mediation effect of TC and BMI in the relationship between DT and CA, based on the model specified in Equation (12). Specifically, we apply the

Baron–Kenny approach to test the causal relationships among the four core variables in a stepwise manner. We then compute the corresponding Sobel statistics for each step. The results are presented in Table 8, columns (1) through (4). Based on the confirmed causal paths, we further construct a chain mediation effect model and estimate the path coefficients for TC and BMI, as reported in column (5) of Table 8.

Table 8. Mediation effect test results.

	c	c'	a	b	Sobel
Result (1): Mediation Variable BMI					
$Y: CA$	2.341 ***	2.318 ***	0.485 ***	0.047 *	0.023 *
$X: DT$	(0.391)	(0.391)	(0.089)	(0.029)	(0.013)
Result (2): Mediation Variable TC					
$Y: CA$	2.341 ***	2.206 ***	−0.029 ***	−4.655 ***	0.135 ***
$X: DT$	(0.391)	(0.389)	(0.007)	(0.380)	(0.033)
Result (3): Mediation Variable TC					
$Y: BMI$	0.295 ***	0.286 ***	−0.028 ***	−0.304 ***	0.008 **
$X: DT$	(0.094)	(0.094)	(0.007)	(0.094)	(0.003)
Result (4): Mediation Variable BMI					
$Y: CA$	−5.048 ***	−5.031 ***	−0.312 ***	0.053 *	−0.016 *
$X: TC$	(0.391)	(0.391)	(0.094)	(0.027)	(0.010)
Result (5): Chain Mediation Effect					
$r(Direct)$	$r(TC)$	$r(BMI)$	$r(TC \times BMI)$	$r(Total)$	
1.395	0.176 **	0.057	0.364 **	1.792 **	
(0.916)	(0.090)	(0.038)	(0.148)	(0.895)	

Notes: *, ** and *** indicate significance at 10%, 5% and 1% levels, respectively. The numbers in parentheses are standard errors.

The results in Result (1) of Table 8 show the mediation effect of BMI in the DT of enterprises. The coefficient a is significantly positive, indicating a positive correlation between DT and IBM. The coefficient b is positive, suggesting that BMI plays a positive role in the expansion of CA. In the independent variable model, the coefficient c is significantly positive and greater than c' after including the mediator variable. The Sobel value is 0.023, indicating that BMI plays a positive mediating role in the process of CA expansion through enterprise DT.

In the results of Result (2), where TC is the mediator variable, the Sobel value is 0.135, indicating that DT reduces TC both internally and externally, thereby promoting the expansion of CA. The chain mediation effect tests the interaction between TC and business model paths, and the results show that the TC path coefficient and the interaction path coefficient are significantly positive, while the path coefficient for BMI and the direct effect are no longer significant. This suggests that BMI in manufacturing enterprises is primarily driven by the reduction in TC. There is a sequential relationship between the reduction in TC and BMI. The application of DT in the design, production, and sales processes of enterprises can optimize the organization of certain production factors, reduce internal and external TC, promote BMI, and improve management and production efficiency, thereby facilitating the expansion of CA and forming a chain mediation path between TC and business models.

5.4. The Moderation Effect of Competitive Imitation

To test the effect of competitor imitation behavior, a regression analysis of the Moderation Effect model in Equation (13) is conducted; the results are presented in Table 9. The estimated coefficient of the competitive imitation is significantly negative, indicating a negative correlation between the level of industry BMI and the competitiveness of enterprises within the industry. This suggests that due to the presence of competitive imitation, the outcomes of BMI may quickly spill over to other enterprises in the industry, eroding the competitive advantage that the enterprise has established. The interaction coefficient is significant and opposite to the coefficient of DT, indicating that competitive imitation plays a negative moderating role in the process of expanding CA through DT. This means that DT makes the new business model easier to recognize and imitate, weakening the market barriers formed by technology and information resources, intensifying the market competition faced by enterprises undergoing DT, and constraining the establishment of competitive advantages in the industry.

Table 9. Moderation effect test results.

	(1)	(2)	(3)
	CA	*CA*	*CA*
DT	2.124 *** (0.707)	2.165 *** (0.707)	2.156 *** (0.707)
I_BMI		−0.349 ** (0.145)	−0.320 ** (0.154)
I_BMI × *DT*			−5.652 ** (2.839)
Controls μ_i_*FE* δ_t_*FE*	YES YES YES	YES YES YES	YES YES YES
Constant	4.523 *** (1.422)	−4.726 *** (1.424)	−4.727 *** (1.424)
N R^2_{adj}	29,131 0.294	29,131 0.283	29,131 0.223

Notes: **, and *** indicate significance at 5% and 1% levels, respectively. The numbers in parentheses are standard errors.

5.5. The Robustness Test

Rationale for FE Model Selection. We tested the validity of using an FE model in Equation (11); the results of the Hausman test are presented in Table 10. The Hausman_Chi in the results is 407.06, and the Hausman_P is below 1%, indicating that there are significant differences between the FE model and the RE model, with the FE model better capturing individual differences.

Table 10. Robustness test results of the regression model.

Equation	N	Parms	Hausman_Chi	VIF_mean	VIF_max	Wooldridge_F	Wooldridge_P
Equation (11)	29,131	14	407.06 ***	1.68	4.46	0.621	0.531

Notes: *** indicate significance at 1% level.

Collinearity and Autocorrelation Issues. The impact of DT on enterprise competitive advantage involves multiple pathways, and the establishment of competitive advantage is not solely reliant on the application of digital technologies, meaning that it is systematically influenced by multi-dimensional factors. To overcome potential issues such as heteroscedasticity and endogeneity, the benchmark model and path analysis included as many enterprise-level and city-level control variables as possible, and an FE model was constructed. However, the broad selection of control variables has, to some extent, increased the risk of multicollinearity in the regression model and does not directly reduce the possibility of residual autocorrelation. Therefore, the multicollinearity and autocorrelation issues in the regression model are tested. The Variance Inflation Factor (VIF) is used to check for multicollinearity, and the Wooldridge test is applied to analyze serial autocorrelation in the residuals. The results are shown in Table 10. It was found that in the results of Equation (11), the average VIF of the variables ranges from 1.5 to 2, with all variables, including control variables, having VIF values less than 5. Additionally, the p-value of the Wooldridge test is greater than 10%, indicating that there are no issues of multicollinearity or autocorrelation in the regression model.

Core Variable Representation Issues. Considering that the benchmark regression uses the original value of intangible assets containing digital technology as the DT indicator, the approach overcomes potential biases inherent in word frequency statistical methods and asset ratio methods. However, it may reduce the credibility of the results in traditional samples. Using the price markup to calculate enterprise competitive advantage, we avoid the issue of missing data for non-listed companies and difficulties in estimating marginal costs in methods such as the industry concentration approach and the Lerner index. However, it may weaken the direct representation of competitive advantage. Therefore, the explanatory variables are replaced by the proportion of intangible assets associated with digital technology in the enterprise, the frequency of digital technology-related keywords in the annual report[1], and the explained variable is replaced by the market share calculated from the main business income and from the total assets at the end of the year. The robustness of the benchmark regression model is tested. The results are shown in Table 11. Columns (1) and (2) present the robustness results when replacing the DT indicator, and Columns (3) and (4) present the results when using the new indicators to measure enterprise competitive advantage. The positive correlation between DT and enterprise competitive advantage remains valid through the robustness test of replacing the core variables.

Table 11. Robustness test of replaced core variables and the regression model.

	(1)	(2)	(3)	(4)	(5)	(6)
	CA	*CA*	*HHI_r*	*HHI_a*	*CA*	*CA*
DT			0.021 ** (0.011)	0.022 ** (0.009)	0.390 *** (0.066)	0.237 *** (0.026)
DT_p	163.479 *** (54.429)					
DT_w		1.024 *** (0.345)				
Controls	YES	YES	YES	YES	YES	YES
μ_i_FE	YES	YES	YES	YES	YES	YES
δ_t_FE	YES	YES	YES	YES	YES	YES
Constant	4.666 *** (1.422)	5.467 *** (1.449)	0.187 *** (0.022)	0.178 *** (0.019)	1.170 *** (0.024)	2.549 *** (0.209)
N	29,131	29,131	29,131	29,131	29,131	28,975
R^2_{adj}	0.276	0.314	0.213	0.258	0.174	0.250

Notes: ** and *** indicate significance at 5% and 1% levels, respectively. The numbers in parentheses are standard errors.

Extreme Value Issues. The median regression and truncated regression methods are used for testing. Although the data have been standardized, a small number of extremely large or small values exist in the sample, which means that regression models based on mean regression may be affected by extreme values, leading to bias in the results. Therefore, median regression and a method of removing the extreme values of the CA indicator at the 1% threshold are used for robustness testing. The results are shown in Columns (5) and (6) of Table 11. The conclusions of the benchmark regression remain robust after removing the influence of extreme values in the objective data.

6. Discussion

6.1. Key Findings

This study constructed a theoretical model and three econometric models to analyze the role of BMI in the DT process of manufacturing enterprises from both a theoretical framework and an empirical evidence perspective. (a) We explored the theoretical mechanisms based on the inferences from the MSES model. The model illustrates the mechanism through which DT in manufacturing enterprises reduces transaction costs, facilitates BMI, and ultimately enhances CA. (b) We constructed an FE model and applied econometric methods to study the impact of DT on the competitiveness of manufacturing enterprises. The findings indicate that the DT significantly increases the markup of enterprises. (c) We used a chain mediation effect model to test the role of BMI in this process. The results show a sequential relationship between the reduction in transaction costs and the emergence of BMI. (d) We considered the spillover of BMI between enterprises (Park & Yi, 2024). The findings show that the rapid spillover of BMI across enterprises may constrain the enhancement of competitive advantage.

The study focused on the role of BMI in the DT process of manufacturing enterprises. We found that BMI is a crucial mediating factor in how DT enhances CA. DT improves transaction efficiency and reduces TC. The reduction in TC leads to improvements or restructuring of value creation methods, achieving BMI. The BMI, in turn, enhances market competitiveness, promoting the CA of the enterprises. This viewpoint can be corroborated by recent studies (X. Sun et al., 2024; Mikalef & Pateli, 2017), which affirm the significant role of BMI in the development of enterprises in the digital age.

The study further suggests that competitive imitation by other enterprises of BMI may limit the expansion of the enterprise. This conclusion implies that, although enterprises can maintain the exclusivity of DT results in the short term, the improvements in production organization and supply chain optimization brought about by BMI will be observed and imitated (Climent et al., 2024). This imitation behavior can weaken entry barriers for external enterprises and intensify cross-industry competition (Li et al., 2024), negatively impacting the effectiveness of enterprise DT. However, when viewed from an industry-wide perspective, this finding also implies that BMI can serve as a conduit for knowledge spillovers, ultimately contributing to the collective advancement of the industry (Posen et al., 2023). As such, our study offers a novel perspective on business model innovation in the digital era and provides policy insights for governments and industry regulators seeking to promote innovation diffusion and sustainable industrial transformation.

In terms of overall effects, despite the various challenges faced by the DT of manufacturing enterprises (Chavez et al., 2023) digital technologies continue to play an important role in the pursuit of competitive advantage (Johns, 2022). This finding aligns with existing research (Omidvar et al., 2025), which has affirmed the role of digital technologies in the growth and development of manufacturing enterprises. However, this does not imply that the observed pattern will remain unchanged. It is important to note that DT in most manufacturing enterprises remains at a relatively early stage (Zhao & Li, 2024). At this stage, the spillover effects of digital achievements such as BMI across industries are not yet prominent. As DT progresses, two issues may become increasingly salient: whether enterprises can sustain a high return on digital investment, and whether enhanced information flow will intensify the negative impacts of competitive imitation. Both issues may shape the direction and evolution of future research.

6.2. Theoretical Implications

The study has certain theoretical significance. First, it supplements and refines a possible theoretical framework for analyzing the growth of manufacturing economies or enterprises in the digital age. Most existing studies remain at the level of literature reviews, case summaries, or empirical descriptions (Hanelt et al., 2021). By contrast, this study develops a formal mathematical model. Existing research has proposed many insights and views on the pathways through which DT affects enterprises, such as production efficiency, management efficiency, and innovation performance (Peng & Tao, 2022; Omidvar et al., 2025). However, we argue that these pathways have complex interdependencies. Including all such factors in a theoretical model may result in logical inconsistencies. Therefore, the model focuses only on the ability of DT to eliminate information asymmetry. This modeling strategy reduces the impact of excessive assumptions on theoretical inference.

Second, the study explores the mathematical and econometric aspects of BMI in manufacturing enterprises. Many studies affirm the positive role of DT in updating the value creation methods of enterprises (X. Sun et al., 2024). However, the relationship between BMI and CA remains unclear; thus, we addressed whether the BMI brought by DT improves enterprise performance. The results confirm the mediating role of BMI between DT and CA. We conclude that digital technologies enhance CA by lowering transaction costs and promoting BMI. This viewpoint enriches theoretical perspectives on the growth and development of manufacturing enterprises in the context of the digital economy.

The study also offers a new understanding of the role of BMI in the digital economy era. Existing research has pointed out that DT in enterprises brings risks associated with privacy issues (Björkdahl, 2020; Buer et al., 2021). These risks may enhance the competitive capabilities of potential competitors. Based on these points, the study further focuses on the demonstration effect of BMI (Climent et al., 2024). We find that BMI is more easily observed and imitated compared with other changes. This means the BMI can become a window for knowledge spillovers in manufacturing. Although imitation of BMI may impose some constraints on the development of the first innovating enterprises, this phenomenon could drive the overall transformation and vitality enhancement of the industry.

6.3. Practical Implications

The study reveals the distinctive features of DT in the manufacturing sector. The BMI provides an entry point for competitors to observe and imitate successful practices (Posen et al., 2023). This imitation may accelerate knowledge spillovers across the industry and intensify market competition; in other words, competitive imitation constrains the sustained expansion of CA for any single firm. Therefore, to foster the development of manufacturing, governments should not only support firm-level digital investment but also recognize the strategic role of BMI in promoting sector-wide progress.

In terms of enterprises, more effort should be made to direct DT outcomes toward production and operational scenarios. Our findings indicate that manufacturing enterprises expand CA by reducing transaction costs through DT and implementing BMI. Thus, breakthroughs in production and operational scenarios should be prioritized to form new growth momentum. Policies such as subsidies for digital equipment can accelerate the digital upgrade of production assets. Additionally, governments may support short-term financing and leasing solutions to promote lightweight industrial platform software among manufacturing enterprises, thereby lowering the cost of experimentation and transition.

In terms of market governance, special attention should be paid to facilitating entry and exit mechanisms in the manufacturing sector. The imitation of BMI by competitors can stimulate market vitality. A key condition for this process is the existence of smooth entry and exit mechanisms (Yang & Deng, 2024). Governments should thus focus on removing outdated barriers to market access and withdrawal in the manufacturing sector. This includes establishing clear and fair access rules as well as streamlining approval processes. At the same time, a flexible exit mechanism should be established to prevent non-competitive enterprises from inefficiently occupying production resources.

7. Conclusions, Contributions, and Future Research

This study investigates the role of BMI in the digital era by integrating theoretical modeling and empirical analysis. A theoretical framework linking DT to CA is developed based on an MSES model. Using fixed-effects, mediation-effects, and moderation-effects models, we confirm the existence of a transmission mechanism whereby DT reduces TC, thereby enabling BMI. This mechanism mediates the establishment of CA from DT. In addition, we find that competitive imitation by peer enterprises can weaken the CA achieved through DT.

The study makes three main contributions. First, it enriches the theoretical understanding of the economic benefits of DT for manufacturing enterprises by incorporating digital technologies into the MSES model. This provides a theoretical foundation for explaining how DT fosters BMI and enhances CA. Second, it clarifies the relationship between business model innovation and competitive advantage. BMI in manufacturing enterprises is identified and quantified by analyzing changes across production, transaction, and pricing functions, and its mediating role between DT and CA is empirically tested. Third, we propose a new perspective on BMI in the digital age by incorporating the observation and imitation behavior of competitors. This imitation helps explain the failure of DT in certain manufacturing contexts and suggests that BMI may serve as a channel for knowledge spillover. This perspective offers a novel lens for understanding the broader implications of BMI.

However, the study has some limitations, providing areas for future research. First, the study focuses on listed companies. However, under the strict Initial Public Offering (IPO) policies in China, listed companies are more likely to reflect oligopolistic monopolies within their respective sub-sectors. There remains untapped potential in the vast number of small enterprises (M. Chen et al., 2024). Future researchers could consider conducting field studies targeting small enterprises. Second, the construction of the BMI indicator primarily relies on the use of proxy variables. Because of limitations in data disclosure by listed companies, we have to determine the degree of BMI from the operational outcomes results. Future studies may improve upon this by using more detailed firm-level data. Additionally, future research could benefit from the perspective of Life Cycle Theory. As DT progresses, the returns on digital investment may exhibit diminishing marginal productivity or other nonlinear effects.

Author Contributions: Conceptualization, S.Z. and Y.Z.; methodology, S.Z.; software, S.Z.; validation, S.Z. and Y.Z.; formal analysis, S.Z.; investigation, S.Z.; resources, S.Z.; data curation, S.Z.; writing—original draft preparation, S.Z.; writing—review and editing, S.Z.; visualization, S.Z.; supervision, Y.Z.; project administration, Y.Z.; funding acquisition, Y.Z. All authors have read and agreed to the published version of the manuscript.

Funding: This research was funded by the National Social Science Fund of China (24BJY018) and the Fundamental Research Funds for the Central Universities of China (2023JBWB001).

Institutional Review Board Statement: Not applicable.

Informed Consent Statement: Not applicable.

Data Availability Statement: The original data presented in the study are openly available in [data-for-me] at [https://github.com/zheng3qiang666/data-for-me.git] (accessed on 9 June 2025).

Conflicts of Interest: The authors declare no conflicts of interest.

Abbreviations

The following abbreviations are used in this manuscript:

BMI	Business Model Innovation
CA	Competitive Advantage/Advantages
DT	Digital Transformation
2SLS	Two-Stage Least Squares
MSES	Multi-Structural Economic System
TC	Transaction Costs

Notes

1 Referring to the method of F. Wu et al. (2021), we use the proportion of digital technology-related nouns in the annual report to the total nouns as an indicator, then apply Min–Max Normalization to the variable.

References

Abrell, T., Pihlajamaa, M., Kanto, L., Vom Brocke, J., & Uebernickel, F. (2016). The role of users and customers in digital innovation: Insights from B2B manufacturing firms. *Information & Management*, *53*(3), 324–335. [CrossRef]

Amir, R., & Lazzati, N. (2011). Network effects, market structure and industry performance. *Journal of Economic Theory*, *146*(6), 2389–2419. [CrossRef]

Ancillai, C., Sabatini, A., Gatti, M., & Perna, A. (2023). Digital technology and business model innovation: A systematic literature review and future research agenda. *Technological Forecasting and Social Change*, *188*, 122307. [CrossRef]

Banga, K. (2022). Digital technologies and product upgrading in global value chains: Empirical evidence from Indian manufacturing firms. *The European Journal of Development Research*, *34*(1), 77–102. [CrossRef]

Bertschek, I., & Kaiser, U. (2004). Productivity effects of organizational change: Microeconometric evidence. *Management science*, *50*(3), 394–404. [CrossRef]

Bhandari, K. R., Zámborský, P., Ranta, M., & Salo, J. (2023). Digitalization, internationalization, and firm performance: A resource-orchestration perspective on new OLI advantages. *International Business Review*, *32*(4), 102135. [CrossRef]

Bielig, A. (2023). The propensity to patent digital technology: Mirroring digitalization processes in Germany with intellectual property in a European perspective. *Journal of the Knowledge Economy*, *14*(3), 2057–2080. [CrossRef] [PubMed]

Björkdahl, J. (2020). Strategies for digitalization in manufacturing firms. *California Management Review*, *62*(4), 17–36. [CrossRef]

Black, S. E., & Lynch, L. M. (2001). How to compete: The impact of workplace practices and information technology on productivity. *Review of Economics and Statistics*, *83*(3), 434–445. [CrossRef]

Brettel, M., Strese, S., & Flatten, T. C. (2012). Improving the performance of business models with relationship marketing efforts—An entrepreneurial perspective. *European Management Journal*, *30*(2), 85–98. [CrossRef]

Buer, S. V., Strandhagen, J. W., Semini, M., & Strandhagen, J. O. (2021). The digitalization of manufacturing: Investigating the impact of production environment and company size. *Journal of Manufacturing Technology Management*, *32*(3), 621–645. [CrossRef]

Cai, J., Sharkawi, I., & Taasim, S. I. (2024). How does digital transformation promote supply chain diversification? From the perspective of supply chain transaction costs. *Finance Research Letters*, *63*, 105399. [CrossRef]

Cantwell, J., & Vertova, G. (2004). Historical evolution of technological diversification. *Research Policy*, *33*(3), 511–529. [CrossRef]

Chandler, G. N., Broberg, J. C., & Allison, T. H. (2014). Customer value propositions in declining industries: Differences between industry representative and high-growth firms. *Strategic Entrepreneurship Journal*, *8*(3), 234–253. [CrossRef]

Chavez, C. A. G., Unamuno, G., Despeisse, M., Johansson, B., Romero, D., & Stahre, J. (2023). Analyzing the risks of digital servitization in the machine tool industry. *Robotics and Computer-Integrated Manufacturing*, *82*, 102520. [CrossRef]

Chen, M., Sui, Y., & Liu, Y. (2024). Regional development and its spatial structure in the information age. In *The transforming spatial organization in the information age*. Springer Nature. [CrossRef]

Chen, S., & Zhang, H. (2021). Does digital finance promote manufacturing servitization: Micro evidence from China. *International Review of Economics & Finance*, *76*, 856–869. [CrossRef]

Chen, Y., & Guo, H. (2024). Corporate performance: Green supply chain management, digital transformation and carbon neutrality. *Management Decision*, *63*, 2432–2451. [CrossRef]

Chen, Y., & Zeng, F. (2022). Dark side of digitalisation: Discussion on digital assets leakage and its protection mechanisms in operations and supply chain research. In *responsible innovation management* (pp. 65–78). Springer Nature. [CrossRef]

Choi, J. P., Jeon, D. S., & Kim, B. C. (2019). Privacy and personal data collection with information externalities. *Journal of Public Economics*, *173*, 113–124. [CrossRef]

Ciampi, F., Demi, S., Magrini, A., Marzi, G., & Papa, A. (2021). Exploring the impact of big data analytics capabilities on business model innovation: The mediating role of entrepreneurial orientation. *Journal of Business Research*, *123*, 1–13. [CrossRef]

Climent, R. C., Haftor, D. M., & Staniewski, M. W. (2024). AI-enabled business models for competitive advantage. *Journal of Innovation & Knowledge*, *9*(3), 100532. [CrossRef]

Cutolo, D., & Kenney, M. (2021). Platform-dependent entrepreneurs: Power asymmetries, risks, and strategies in the platform economy. *Academy of Management Perspectives*, *35*(4), 584–605. [CrossRef]

Dewan, S., & Kraemer, K. L. (2000). Information technology and productivity: Evidence from country-level data. *Management Science*, *46*(4), 548–562. [CrossRef]

Di Silvestre, M. L., Favuzza, S., Sanseverino, E. R., & Zizzo, G. (2018). How Decarbonization, Digitalization and Decentralization are changing key power infrastructures. *Renewable and Sustainable Energy Reviews*, *93*, 483–498. [CrossRef]

Duffy, J., & Ralston, J. (2020). Innovate versus imitate: Theory and experimental evidence. *Journal of Economic Behavior & Organization*, *177*, 727–751. [CrossRef]

Fan, H. J., Wu, T., & He, S. (2023). Research on the industrial chain linkage effect of enterprise digitalization. *China Industrial Economics*, *3*, 115–132. [CrossRef]

Fast, V., Schnurr, D., & Wohlfarth, M. (2023). Regulation of data-driven market power in the digital economy: Business value creation and competitive advantages from big data. *Journal of Information Technology*, *38*(2), 202–229. [CrossRef]

Foresman, T. W. (2016, July 7–8). Beyond Moore's law: Harnessing spatial-digital disruptive technologies for digital earth. In *IOP conference series: Earth and environmental science* (Vol. 46, No. 1, p. 012055). IOP Publishing. [CrossRef]

Forkmann, S., Ramos, C., Henneberg, S. C., & Naudé, P. (2017). Understanding the service infusion process as a business model reconfiguration. *Industrial Marketing Management*, *60*, 151–166. [CrossRef]

Freisinger, E., Heidenreich, S., Landau, C., & Spieth, P. (2021). Business model innovation through the lens of time: An empirical study of performance implications across venture life cycles. *Schmalenbach Journal of Business Research*, *73*(3), 339–380. [CrossRef]

Fu, Q. (2022). How does digital technology affect manufacturing upgrading? Theory and evidence from China. *PLoS ONE*, *17*(5), e0267299. [CrossRef] [PubMed]

Gao, J., Zhang, W., Guan, T., Feng, Q., & Mardani, A. (2023). The effect of manufacturing agent heterogeneity on enterprise innovation performance and competitive advantage in the era of digital transformation. *Journal of Business Research*, *155*, 113387. [CrossRef]

Gawer, A. (2021). Digital platforms' boundaries: The interplay of firm scope, platform sides, and digital interfaces. *Long Range Planning*, *54*(5), 102045. [CrossRef]

Gelbach, J. B. (2016). When do covariates matter? And which ones, and how much? *Journal of Labor Economics*, *34*(2), 509–543. [CrossRef]

Gu, L., & Zhang, X. (2024). Motivations, mechanisms, and paths of business model innovation driven by the digital economy. *Frontiers of Business Research in China*, *18*(2), 83–94. [CrossRef]

Gulbrandsen, B., Lambe, C. J., & Sandvik, K. (2017). Firm boundaries and transaction costs: The complementary role of capabilities. *Journal of Business Research*, *78*, 193–203. [CrossRef]

Guo, B., Pang, X., & Li, W. (2018). The role of top management team diversity in shaping the performance of business model innovation: A threshold effect. *Technology Analysis & Strategic Management*, *30*(2), 241–253. [CrossRef]

Han, X., & Zhang, J. (2022). Business model innovation paths of manufacturing oriented towards green development in digital economy. *International Journal of Environmental Research and Public Health*, *19*(24), 16454. [CrossRef] [PubMed]

Hanelt, A., Firk, S., Hildebrandt, B., & Kolbe, L. M. (2021). Digital M&A, digital innovation, and firm performance: An empirical investigation. *European Journal of Information Systems*, *30*(1), 3–26. [CrossRef]

Horvat, D., Kroll, H., & Jäger, A. (2019). Researching the effects of automation and digitalization on manufacturing companies' productivity in the early stage of industry 4.0. *Procedia Manufacturing*, *39*, 886–893. [CrossRef]

Huang, Q., Yu, Y., & Zhang, S. (2019). The development of the internet and the improvement of manufacturing productivity: The intrinsic mechanism and Chinese experience. *China Industrial Economics*, *8*, 5–23. [CrossRef]

Ibarra, D., Ganzarain, J., & Igartua, J. I. (2018). Business model innovation through Industry 4.0: A review. *Procedia Manufacturing*, *22*, 4–10. [CrossRef]

Johns, J. (2022). Digital technological upgrading in manufacturing global value chains: The impact of additive manufacturing. *Global Networks*, *22*(4), 649–665. [CrossRef]

Joskow, P. L. (1988). Asset specificity and the structure of vertical relationships: Empirical evidence. *The Journal of Law, Economics, and Organization*, *4*(1), 95–117. [CrossRef]

Kermani, A., & Ma, Y. (2023). Asset specificity of nonfinancial firms. *The Quarterly Journal of Economics*, *138*(1), 205–264. [CrossRef]

Kim, J. H. (2018). Asset specificity and firm value: Evidence from mergers. *Journal of Corporate Finance*, *48*, 375–412. [CrossRef]

Kiveu, M. N., Namusonge, M., & Muathe, S. (2019). Effect of innovation on firm competitiveness: The case of manufacturing SMEs in Nairobi County, Kenya. *International Journal of Business Innovation and Research*, *18*(3), 307–327. [CrossRef]

Li, Y. (2025). Literature review on business model innovation: Digital technology perspective and suggestions for future research. *SAGE Open, 15*(2), 21–58. [CrossRef]

Li, Y., Cui, L., Wu, L., Lowry, P. B., Kumar, A., & Tan, K. H. (2024). Digitalization and network capability as enablers of business model innovation and sustainability performance: The moderating effect of environmental dynamism. *Journal of Information Technology, 39*(4), 687–715. [CrossRef]

Loecker, J. D., & Warzynski, F. (2012). Markups and firm-level export status. *American Economic Review, 102*(6), 2437–2471. [CrossRef]

Mahesh, P., Tiwari, A., Jin, C., Kumar, P. R., Reddy, A. N., Bukkapatanam, S. T., Gupta, N., & Karri, R. (2020). A survey of cybersecurity of digital manufacturing. *Proceedings of the IEEE, 109*(4), 495–516. [CrossRef]

Meier, H., & Massberg, W. (2004). Life cycle-based service design for innovative business models. *CIRP Annals, 53*(1), 393–396. [CrossRef]

Mikalef, P., & Pateli, A. (2017). Information technology-enabled dynamic capabilities and their indirect effect on competitive performance: Findings from PLS-SEM and fsQCA. *Journal of Business Research, 70*, 1–16. [CrossRef]

Miller, S. M. (2004). New classical versus neoclassical frameworks: A review of Yang. *Journal of Economic Behavior & Organization, 55*(2), 175–185. [CrossRef]

Mittra, J., Tait, J., Mastroeni, M., Turner, M. L., Mountford, J. C., & Bruce, K. (2015). Identifying viable regulatory and innovation pathways for regenerative medicine: A case study of cultured red blood cells. *New Biotechnology, 32*(1), 180–190. [CrossRef] [PubMed]

Montemari, M., Taran, Y., Schaper, S., Nielsen, C., Thomsen, P., & Sort, J. (2024). Business model innovation or business model imitation–That is the question. *Technology Analysis & Strategic Management, 36*(3), 393–407. [CrossRef]

Morroni, M. (2007). Complementarities among capability, transaction and scale-scope considerations in determining organizational boundaries. *Technology Analysis & Strategic Management, 19*(1), 31–44. [CrossRef]

Oliveira, L., Fleury, A., & Fleury, M. T. (2021). Digital power: Value chain upgrading in an age of digitization. *International Business Review, 30*(6), 101850. [CrossRef]

Omidvar, M., Confetto, M. G., & Palazzo, M. (2025). Business model innovation: A bridge between corporate social responsibility and successful performance for Medium-Size Enterprises (SMEs) in the digital era. *Systems, 13*(5), 378. [CrossRef]

Pan, X., Wang, Y., Zhang, C., Shen, Z., & Song, M. (2023). The impact of platform economy on enterprise value mediated by technological innovation. *Journal of Business Research, 165*, 114051. [CrossRef]

Park, G., & Yi, S. (2024). Why do leaders help followers follow? *Technology Analysis & Strategic Management, 36*(12), 4084–4097. [CrossRef]

Peng, Y., & Tao, C. (2022). Can digital transformation promote enterprise performance?—From the perspective of public policy and innovation. *Journal of Innovation & Knowledge, 7*(3), 100198. [CrossRef]

Picciotti, A. (2017). Towards sustainability: The innovation paths of social enterprise. *Annals of Public and Cooperative Economics, 88*(2), 233–256. [CrossRef]

Posen, H. E., Ross, J. M., Wu, B., Benigni, S., & Cao, Z. (2023). Reconceptualizing imitation: Implications for dynamic capabilities, innovation, and competitive advantage. *Academy of Management Annals, 17*(1), 74–112. [CrossRef]

Rangaswamy, A., Moch, N., Felten, C., Van Bruggen, G., Wieringa, J. E., & Wirtz, J. (2020). The role of marketing in digital business platforms. *Journal of Interactive Marketing, 51*(1), 72–90. [CrossRef]

Riordan, M. H., & Williamson, O. E. (1985). Asset specificity and economic organization. *International Journal of Industrial Organization, 3*(4), 365–378. [CrossRef]

Rivkin, J. W. (2001). Reproducing knowledge: Replication without imitation at moderate complexity. *Organization Science, 12*(3), 274–293. [CrossRef]

Sandulli, F. D., Baker, P. M., & López-Sánchez, J. I. (2014). Jobs mismatch and productivity impact of information technology. *The Service Industries Journal, 34*(13), 1060–1074. [CrossRef]

Scuotto, V., Nicotra, M., Del Giudice, M., Krueger, N., & Gregori, G. L. (2021). A microfoundational perspective on SMEs' growth in the digital transformation era. *Journal of Business Research, 129*, 382–392. [CrossRef]

Shim, S., & Lee, B. (2012). Sustainable competitive advantage of a system goods innovator in a market with network effects and entry threats. *Decision Support Systems, 52*(2), 308–317. [CrossRef]

Soukhoroukova, A., Spann, M., & Skiera, B. (2012). Sourcing, filtering, and evaluating new product ideas: An empirical exploration of the performance of idea markets. *Journal of Product Innovation Management, 29*(1), 100–112. [CrossRef]

Sui, X., Jiao, S., Wang, Y., & Wang, H. (2024). Digital transformation and manufacturing company competitiveness. *Finance Research Letters*, *59*, 104683. [CrossRef]

Sun, X., Wang, H., Zhan, Y., & He, J. (2024). Mechanism of digital business model innovation driven by big data in manufacturing enterprises. *Frontiers of Business Research in China*, *18*(2), 95–120. [CrossRef]

Sun, Z., & Hou, Y. L. (2019). How does industrial intelligence reshape the employment structure of Chinese labor force. *China Industrial Economics*, *5*, 61–79. [CrossRef]

Taran, Y., Boer, H., & Lindgren, P. (2015). A business model innovation typology. *Decision Sciences*, *46*(2), 301–331. [CrossRef]

Tilson, D., Lyytinen, K., & Sørensen, C. (2010). Research commentary—Digital infrastructures: The missing IS research agenda. *Information Systems Research*, *21*(4), 748–759. [CrossRef]

Trabucchi, D., & Buganza, T. (2019). Data-driven innovation: Switching the perspective on big data. *European Journal of Innovation Management*, *22*(1), 23–40. [CrossRef]

Trimi, S., & Berbegal-Mirabent, J. (2012). Business model innovation in entrepreneurship. *International Entrepreneurship and Management Journal*, *8*(4), 449–465. [CrossRef]

Valerdi, R., Nightingale, D., & Blackburn, C. (2008). Enterprises as systems: Context, boundaries, and practical implications. *Information Knowledge Systems Management*, *7*(4), 377–399. [CrossRef]

Vasylyshyna, L., Popova, O., Hoholieva, N., Lyzunova, O., Medvedieva, M., Laskavets, K., Mykytenko, T., Diachenko, V., Yemets, A., & Shevchenko, S. (2022). Assessment of the impact of digitalized management on the financial risks of industrial enterprises. *Eastern-European Journal of Enterprise Technologies*, *6*, 87–95. [CrossRef]

Wang, D., & Shao, X. (2024). Research on the impact of digital transformation on the production efficiency of manufacturing enterprises: Institution-based analysis of the threshold effect. *International Review of Economics & Finance*, *91*, 883–897. [CrossRef]

Wang, L., Zhang, W., White, S., & Fan, H. (2024). Digital technology-based business model design and innovation to address grand challenges: A process model. *Strategic Entrepreneurship Journal*, *4*, 1–28. [CrossRef]

Wang, L. L., & Gao, Y. (2021). Competition network as a source of competitive advantage: The dynamic capability perspective and evidence from China. *Long Range Planning*, *54*(2), 102052. [CrossRef]

Wang, S. Z., & Nie, R. (2011, May 13–15). *Paths of business model innovation for manufacturing enterprises based on value chain*. 2011 International Conference on Business Management and Electronic Information, Guangzhou, China. [CrossRef]

Wen, H., Zhong, Q., & Lee, C. C. (2022). Digitalization, competition strategy and corporate innovation: Evidence from Chinese manufacturing listed companies. *International Review of Financial Analysis*, *82*, 102166. [CrossRef]

Wu, F., Hu, H. Z., Lin, H. Y., & Ren, X. Y. (2021). Digital transformation of enterprises and capital market performance: Empirical evidence from stock liquidity. *Management World*, *37*(07), 130–144. [CrossRef]

Wu, Y. Q., Lu, H. X., Liao, X. L., & Zhu, J. M. (2021). Research on the digitization of manufacturing will enhance the competitiveness of the value chain based on advantage comparison. *Complexity*, *2021*(1), 9917772. [CrossRef]

Xiao, Z., & Huang, B. (2006, October 5–7). *Discussion on the nature of the enterprise and boundary model*. 2006 International Conference on Management Science and Engineering, Lille, France. [CrossRef]

Xie, Y., & Wu, D. (2024). How does competition policy affect enterprise digitization? Dual perspectives of digital commitment and digital innovation. *Journal of Business Research*, *178*, 114651. [CrossRef]

Yang, G., & Deng, F. (2024). The impact of digital transformation on enterprise vitality–evidence from listed companies in China. *Technology Analysis & Strategic Management*, *36*(11), 3955–3972. [CrossRef]

Zaman, S. A. A., Vilkas, M., Zaman, S. I., & Jamil, S. (2025). Digital technologies and digitalization performance: The mediating role of digitalization management. *Journal of Manufacturing Technology Management*, *36*(2), 307–333. [CrossRef]

Zhang, J., & Li, H. (2023). Business models and the performance of Chinese high-tech service firms: The role of the technological innovation mode and technological regimes. *Heliyon*, *9*(7), e17797. [CrossRef] [PubMed]

Zhang, Y., Pang, J., & Li, H. (2024). Research on the influence of digitalization on competitive advantage of manufacturing enterprises. *Managerial and Decision Economics*, *45*(5), 3316–3334. [CrossRef]

Zhang, Z., Zhang, J., Ye, B., & Chen, Y. (2022). The impact of digital transformation on business model innovation. *Science & Technology Progress and Policy*, *39*(11), 114–123. [CrossRef]

Zhao, R., & Li, L. (2024). Does digitalization always benefit cultural, sports, and tourism enterprises quality? Unveiling the inverted U-shaped relationship from a resource and capability perspective. *Humanities and Social Sciences Communications*, *11*(1), 1066. [CrossRef]

Zhou, J. (2013). Digitalization and intelligentization of manufacturing industry. *Advances in Manufacturing*, *1*(1), 1–7. [CrossRef]

Zhou, Y., Zang, J., Miao, Z., & Minshall, T. (2019). Upgrading pathways of intelligent manufacturing in China: Transitioning across technological paradigms. *Engineering*, *5*(4), 691–701. [CrossRef]

Zott, C., & Amit, R. (2007). Business model design and the performance of entrepreneurial firms. *Organization Science*, *18*(2), 181–199. [CrossRef]

Zott, C., & Amit, R. (2010). Business model design: An activity system perspective. *Long Range Planning*, *43*(2–3), 216–226. [CrossRef]

Disclaimer/Publisher's Note: The statements, opinions and data contained in all publications are solely those of the individual author(s) and contributor(s) and not of MDPI and/or the editor(s). MDPI and/or the editor(s) disclaim responsibility for any injury to people or property resulting from any ideas, methods, instructions or products referred to in the content.

economies

MDPI

Article

Digital Transformation, New Quality Productive Forces, and Corporate Environmental Investment: Empirical Evidence from Chinese A-Share Listed Companies

Yunsong Xu * and Qian Ao

School of Business, Beijing Language and Culture University, Beijing 100083, China; yian2727ao@163.com
* Correspondence: xuyunsong@blcu.edu.cn

Abstract: Amplifying corporate environmental investments is a pivotal strategy for achieving the "carbon peak and carbon neutral" objectives of China's green development initiative. The digital transformation has the potential to generate new quality productive forces by leveraging data, thereby promoting green technology innovation, enhancing technology efficiency, and leveraging the impact of resource reallocation. Consequently, this transition enables enterprises to transition from a "passive compliance" model to a "proactive enhancement" model, thereby achieving a significant quality leap forward in their environmental investment. The present study utilises a sample of Chinese A-share companies from 2011 to 2023 to innovatively construct a multifaceted data model to quantitatively analyse the impact of digital transformation on corporate environmental investment. This analysis incorporates the intermediary effects of enhanced new quality productive forces, the intermediary effects of data application, and the threshold effects of environmental uncertainty, as well as the non-linear effects of industry, property rights, regional differences, policy, and the intensity of production factors. The study's findings are as follows: (1) Digital transformation significantly promotes corporate environmental investment, and this conclusion is robust. (2) The new quality productive forces have a positive intermediary effect on corporate environmental investment during digital transformation. (3) The application of big data has been demonstrated to moderate the intermediary effects of "digital transformation-new quality productive forces-enterprise environmental investment." (4) The impact of environmental uncertainty on corporate environmental investment during the digital transformation process is characterised by a "barrier effect," exhibiting a "border effect" that is non-linear in nature. (5) In the context of the lightweight pollution industry, non-state-owned enterprises, the eastern region, and the implementation of environmental policies, the efficacy of digital transformation in enhancing corporate environmental investment is particularly pronounced. In light of the aforementioned, the present study puts forth four specific recommendations, offering invaluable insights for the contemporary Chinese enterprise to navigate the process of transformation and achieve sustainable, high-quality growth.

Keywords: digital transformation; corporate environmental investment; new quality productive forces; big data applications; environmental uncertainty

1. Introduction

As global climate change continues to intensify and resource and environmental constraints grow increasingly stringent, the People's Republic of China, as the world's second-largest economy, faces unprecedented challenges in environmental governance. The report of the 20th National Congress of the Communist Party of China clearly stated that green development should be promoted and harmony between man and nature should be fostered, and established accelerating the green transformation of the development model as a key path to achieving modernization with Chinese characteristics. The report also emphasises actively and steadily promoting carbon peaking and carbon neutrality, pointing out that achieving the "dual carbon" goals is an inherent requirement of implementing the new development philosophy, building a new development pattern, and promoting high-quality development. This represents a broad and profound transformation of the economic and social system (Communist Party of China, 2022). The Third Plenary Session of the 20th Central Committee of the Communist Party of China further emphasized "driving high-quality development through digital transformation," "accelerating the establishment of institutional mechanisms to promote digital economic development, and improving the policy framework to promote digital industrialization and industrial digitalization." It also proposed "establishing institutional mechanisms to develop new productive forces in accordance with local conditions" and "improving the ecological and environmental governance system (Communist Party of China, 2024)." However, despite significant economic growth, shortcomings in environmental governance remain significant, and environmental quality has not improved at the same pace. According to data released by the Chinese Ministry of Ecology and Environment in 2024, high-energy-consuming industries in China emitted approximately 82 million tons of hazardous waste, accounting for 63.3% of the country's total hazardous waste production. Industrial wastewater emissions amounted to 244.999 million tons, also accounting for a high proportion of total wastewater emissions (MEE, 2024). In light of the prevailing circumstances, the strategic allocation of financial resources towards environmentally sustainable and energy-efficient investments has become imperative. The digital transformation offers a novel approach to address the challenges associated with environmental investment. The process of digitization has the potential to enhance an enterprise's capacity for technological innovation, thereby unlocking the full value of digital technology. This, in turn, can lead to an improvement in the overall effectiveness of new quality productive forces, which, in turn, can encourage companies to increase their investment in environmental protection initiatives.

Consequently, in this novel stage of development where digital transformation is increasingly valued and breakthroughs in new quality productive forces are being accelerated, it is imperative to explore the driving effects of digital transformation on corporate environmental investment and further analyse the intrinsic connections and mechanisms between digital transformation, new quality productive forces, and corporate environmental investment. This will facilitate a more profound comprehension of the contemporary significance of the deep integration of sustainable development and new quality productive forces. This initiative is poised to provide strategic support for enhancing corporate environmental investment and promoting China's green and low-carbon transformation. It possesses far-reaching theoretical significance and practical value.

Numerous domestic and international studies have analysed the direct mechanisms and effects of digital transformation. Tao et al. (2023) found that digital transformation significantly improved corporate productivity in some companies. F. Li (2025) examined digital transformation from the perspective of controlling shareholder equity pledges and found that it significantly enhanced green innovation capabilities. Jin et al. (2022) used Chinese manufacturing listed companies as a sample and pointed out that digital transformation can improve information transparency and optimize resource allocation, significantly enhancing the level of green innovation in enterprises. Additionally, some studies have analysed the impact of digital transformation on different fields, such as promoting strategic and organizational change (Hanelt et al., 2021), enhancing corporate

ESG responsibility performance (F. Y. Liu & Wu, 2024), and promoting corporate product innovation (Babina et al., 2020), among others. Currently, the direct impacts of digital transformation are primarily concentrated in areas such as green innovation levels, organizational change, ESG responsibility performance, and product innovation. Furthermore, the effects of digital transformation on corporate environmental investment are largely theoretical analyses, with limited empirical research available.

Some domestic and international studies have examined the indirect effects of digital transformation. From the perspective of technological innovation, Pan and Hu (2025) found that digital transformation significantly promotes the formation of new quality productive forces by enhancing enterprises' technological innovation capabilities. J. Li and Zhou (2024) analyzed the annual reports of Chinese manufacturing listed companies and pointed out that the indirect impact of digital transformation has significantly enhanced corporate environmental performance. Research on the indirect effects of digital transformation primarily focuses on pathways related to technological innovation, governance efficiency, and financing costs within enterprises. However, from a transmission pathway perspective, no existing research reveals the indirect relationship between digital transformation and corporate environmental investment in terms of new quality productive forces. Furthermore, new quality productivity indicators are currently constructed in a relatively single-dimensional and incomplete manner. Existing studies have also paid limited attention to the moderating and mediating effects of big data applications in the relationship between digital transformation and corporate environmental investment.

In recent years, a number of scholars have conducted in-depth research on the barriers to digital transformation. Liang et al. (2022) demonstrated that there is a "U" shaped curve relationship between the process of enterprise digital transformation and long-term financial performance. It was found that the management and operational costs of the enterprise were a significant barrier to this relationship. Following the transition period, the management and operational costs of the enterprise will decrease in a step-like manner, thereby promoting financial performance from stagnation to growth. You et al. (2023) discovered that the digital transformation of companies that use a lot of resources has a positive effect on their productivity. This effect is not linear and increases with the level of specialisation in the professional division. Sun (2024) found that digital transformation had a positive effect on supply chain integration, which in turn led to an improvement in the innovation performance of enterprises. However, it was also noted that supply chain integration was subject to certain barriers. Although the extant literature has begun to explore the effects of digital transformation on the barriers to entry, it has yet to comprehensively address the non-linear characteristics of digital transformation in terms of corporate financial performance, overall manufacturing efficiency, and supply chain integration. A critical aspect that has been overlooked is the role of environmental uncertainty as a pivotal barrier to digital transformation. The literature has yet to comprehensively elucidate the differential effects of digital transformation in various environments characterised by uncertainty.

Some studies have examined the heterogeneous effects of digital transformation. Based on empirical evidence from listed companies in China, Peng et al. (2024) found that the effect of digital transformation on the improvement of new productive forces is more significant in state-owned enterprises, small-scale enterprises, and non-physical enterprises. F. Y. Liu and Wu (2024) proposed that the impact of digital transformation on corporate ESG performance is heterogeneous, with state-owned enterprises, mature enterprises, and heavily polluting enterprises experiencing more significant effects from digital transformation. J. Li and Zhou (2024) found that the impact of digital transformation on environmental performance improvement is subject to heterogeneous effects related to property rights, enterprise size, industry attributes, and regional environmental regulation intensity. Current heterogeneous studies on digital transformation mainly focus on property rights, industry attributes, enterprise growth cycles, environmental regulations, and other aspects, but related research is relatively scattered. Furthermore, these studies have not examined the heterogeneous effects of digital transformation on environmental investment in enterprises across industries, property rights, regions, policy contexts, and levels of production factor intensity.

A comprehensive review of the extant domestic and international literature reveals the following findings: Firstly, despite the considerable research achievements in the field of digital transformation in recent years, the majority of this research has focused on the direct and indirect impact mechanisms and effects of digital transformation, as well as the non-linear effects and heterogeneous effects. However, there has been a paucity of research exploring the direct inclusion of environmental investment in the economic benefits of digital transformation. Secondly, the establishment of a comprehensive system of indicators for the digital transformation, new quality productive forces and corporate environmental investment; the relationship between multiple dimensions; the role of the driving mechanism and the effectiveness of the transmission process; and the evaluation of the results is lacking. Thirdly, there is a conspicuous absence of research on the impact of digital transformation on environmental investment in enterprises, as well as any recommendations for solutions, in the area of experience and lessons learned. In view of the aforementioned, the present article makes the following four contributions: Firstly, the present study proposes a novel framework for understanding the relationship between digital transformation and corporate environmental investment, building upon the theories of information asymmetry and agency theory. The findings of this study contribute to the existing body of knowledge by addressing a significant gap in the literature on the subject. Secondly, the new quality productive forces, the application of big data, and the uncertainty of the environment were incorporated as key variables. The multifaceted effects of digital transformation on corporate environmental investment were analysed quantitatively, with the effects of fixed, intermediary, and regulatory intermediary, as well as threshold effects and non-homogeneous effects being thoroughly revealed. The direct and indirect effects, linear and non-linear effects, and the research levels were expanded, and the existing literature's lack of depth was addressed. Thirdly, a comprehensive index system is established through the entropy method and text analysis method, thus providing a more systematic, comprehensive and rational reflection of enterprise digital transformation, new quality productive forces and big data application levels. This enriches the levels of variables in the index system and the overall evaluation system, enabling more precise consideration of the differences between enterprises in these areas, and consequently deriving more stable conclusions. For example, in contrast to the existing literature, this paper constructs indicators from the following five dimensions: artificial intelligence technology, big data technology, cloud computing technology, blockchain technology and digital technology. The degree of enterprise digital transformation is measured using the text analysis method. The level of new quality productive forces is measured using the entropy weighted TOPSIS method from the perspectives of labour, physical, technology, soft and hard technology. The application level of big data is measured using the text analysis method from the perspectives of data centre, data, information asset, data and computing power. Fourthly, the measures recommended to promote the digital transformation of enterprises, enhance their new quality productive forces, and improve their application of big data, as well as establish a comprehensive risk management system for enterprises, offer valuable insights into how enterprises can respond to the call of the 20th National Congress. These measures will accelerate the development of new quality productive forces, facilitate the breakthrough of green and low-carbon technologies, and promote the upgrade of industries, thereby aligning with the new development concept.

2. Theoretical Mechanisms and Research Hypotheses

In the contemporary business environment, enterprises function as both major contributors to environmental pollution and significant consumers of energy resources. To address the challenges posed by environmental pollution and the inadequate level of corporate environmental investment, a multifaceted approach is required. The present study suggests that enterprises can address these issues by accelerating their digital transformation, promoting the development of new quality productive forces, and enhancing their application of big data. Furthermore, enterprises should recognise the impact of environmental uncertainty on their operations and take measures to mitigate it. By adopting these practices, enterprises can demonstrate their commitment to the principles of sustainable development in the current era, contributing to the creation of a new development paradigm.

2.1. Direct Impact Effects of Digital Transformation on Corporate Environmental Investments

The ongoing process of digitisation within enterprises has created a new strategic opportunity for the expansion of environmental investment and the enhancement of efficiency. Firstly, in accordance with the theory of information asymmetry, environmental investments are characterised by elevated costs, extended return periods and uncertain outcomes, which collectively diminish enterprises' propensity to assume environmental stewardship responsibilities. Digital transformation facilitates the real-time acquisition and comprehensive analysis of extensive environmental data, thereby providing enterprises with valuable information support and mitigating the information asymmetry inherent in environmental investment decision-making, thereby enhancing the scientific and precise nature of investment decision-making. In the second instance, the digital transformation has led to a significant enhancement in the effectiveness of the company's governance. Firstly, the establishment of an intelligent supervision system has effectively resolved internal conflicts arising from the use of external management, thereby improving the scientific nature of decision-making and the efficiency of implementation. Secondly, the digital governance platform enables stakeholders to obtain real-time information regarding management decisions and to monitor the progress of investments, effectively preventing the misuse of power by management and the concealment of information, and thereby promoting transparency and compliance in environmental investment decisions. Based on the above analysis, this paper proposes the following hypothesis:

H1. *Digital transformation contributes to corporate environmental investments.*

2.2. Mediating Effects of Digital Transformation on the Impact of Corporate Environmental Investments

The advent of new quality productive forces characterised by their capacity to drive technological advancement, efficiency and effectiveness, finds expression in the contemporary development paradigm. The impetus for this transformation stems from a confluence of technological breakthroughs, optimised resource allocation and the imperative for industrial transformation. The crux of this paradigm shift lies in the enhancement of overall production efficiency (Y. Lu et al., 2024b). The process of digital transformation has been shown to have a significant impact on the ability of companies to innovate, thereby enhancing their overall new quality productive forces. This, in turn, has been demonstrated to encourage companies to increase their investment in environmental protection. New quality productive forces play a key intermediary role between digital transformation and environmental protection investment, and its mechanism is mainly reflected in the following aspects: Firstly, the new quality productive forces of enterprises to produce new products and services is enhanced by technological innovation, thereby increasing their environmental capabilities. The digital transformation has provided significant support for technological innovation, enabling enterprises to develop green processes and optimise their pollution control technologies, thus strengthening their core competitiveness in the field of environmental management. Secondly, the enhancement of production efficiency is contingent upon the optimisation of the configuration of production elements, thereby facilitating the augmentation of environmental investment efficiency. For instance, the implementation of a digital supply chain management system enables the precise tracking of logistics processes' carbon emissions, thereby achieving significant improvements in resource utilisation and environmental performance. In conclusion, the emergence of new quality productive forces has engendered novel investment opportunities in the field of environmental protection. The rapid development of clean energy technologies and circular economic models has resulted in the creation of new market spaces for enterprises, thereby reinforcing their intrinsic motivation for environmental investment. Based on the above analysis, this paper puts forward the following hypotheses:

H2. *Digital transformation drives the development of new quality productive forces, which in turn drives corporate environmental investments.*

2.3. Moderating Mediating Effects of Digital Transformation on the Impact of Corporate Environmental Investment

The implementation of digital transformation in enterprises has been proven to enhance their new quality productive forces, thereby exerting a favourable influence on their environmental investment. In this process, big data plays a pivotal role in data-driven decision-making, optimising resource allocation and enhancing management efficiency. Consequently, it significantly amplifies the intermediary effect of new quality productive forces in the digital transformation and environmental investment nexus. Firstly, the application of big data has been demonstrated to enhance the new quality productive forces. The digital transformation has been achieved by the introduction of advanced technologies, thereby facilitating the establishment of new quality productive forces. The application of big data has been shown to provide the necessary data support and analysis capabilities. By collecting, storing and analysing large amounts of data, companies can more accurately identify environmental risk factors, thus enhancing the promotion of new quality productive forces by environmental investment. Secondly, big data applications can optimize the resource allocation efficiency of new-quality productive forces. The core of new-quality productive forces lies in achieving efficient allocation of production factors through technological means. As a new type of production factor, big data serves as the core driving force of new-quality productive forces by optimizing resource allocation and enhancing total factor productivity (B. Zhang & Li, 2024). Data elements, with big data as a key means, provide technical support to enterprises, helping them make more scientific environmental investment decisions and reduce resource misallocation and environmental governance costs. Finally, the application of big data can enhance our new quality productive forces. The creation of new quality productive forces relies on technological innovation, and the application of big data can significantly boost our capacity for technological innovation by providing a wealth of data resources and advanced analysis tools. The mechanism for regulating the effects of intermediaries is shown in Figure 1. Based on the above analysis, this paper puts forward the following hypotheses:

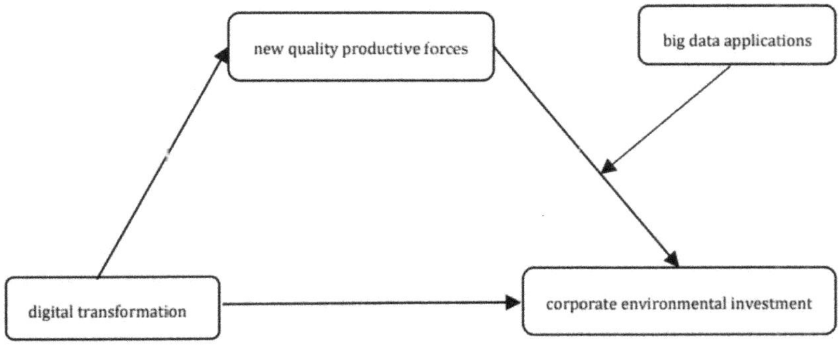

Figure 1. Mechanisms for regulating the transmission of mediating effects.

H3. *Big data applications can moderate the mediating effect of new quality productive forces between digital transformation and corporate environmental investment, and this mediating effect is more pronounced at higher levels of big data application.*

2.4. Threshold Effects of Digital Transformation on the Impact of Corporate Environmental Investments

The concept of environmental uncertainty pertains to the extent and unpredictability of external environmental fluctuations. From an economic perspective, environmental uncertainty exerts a non-linear regulatory influence on the relationship between digital transformation and environmental investment. When the environment is less uncertain, companies can invest more in digital technology to help with environmental protection. But when the uncertainty is higher, this effect is weaker. This is called the "limited effect that gets smaller the more you go" effect. First, in a less uncertain environment, companies can make the most of digital technology. They can spot environmental risks and organise their resources better. But as the uncertainty becomes higher, it becomes harder for companies to use digital technology to help with environmental protection. This makes the effect weaker. Second, the uncertainty affects how well companies can deal with risk. In a less uncertain environment, companies are more likely to take risks and use digital technology to help with environmental protection to achieve an advantage over their competitors. But as the uncertainty becomes higher, companies are more likely to avoid high risks and focus on short-term gains and how to deal with risk. Based on this analysis, this paper proposes the following hypotheses:

H4. *The impact of digital transformation on corporate environmental investment is non-linear with a "diminishing marginal effect" depending on the degree of environmental uncertainty.*

2.5. Heterogeneous Effects of Digital Transformation on Corporate Environmental Investments

The impact of digital transformation on corporate environmental investment is characterised by industry-specific heterogeneity. Enterprises can be categorised into two groups: those with high pollution levels and those with low pollution levels. Firstly, enterprises with low pollution levels tend to demonstrate a stronger environmental consciousness and responsibility, and they are aware of the importance of environmental protection. They are also more likely to take proactive measures to improve their environmental performance. These enterprises have more financial resources and stronger motivation to pursue digital transformation. Their aim is to enhance their environmental performance and increase their environmental investment. However, compared to enterprises with low pollution levels, those with high pollution levels face greater environmental protection responsibilities. This makes it more challenging for them to allocate sufficient funds to environmental investment.

Consequently, the effectiveness of digital transformation in stimulating environmental investment is more pronounced for enterprises with low pollution levels. Based on the above analysis, this paper proposes the following hypotheses:

H5-1. *Digital transformation is a more significant driver of environmental investments among light polluters than among heavy polluters.*

The impact of digital transformation on corporate environmental investment is influenced by the ownership structure of the company. This impact is particularly pronounced in non-state-owned enterprises. Firstly, non-state-owned enterprises are subject to fewer rigid policies, and they are more motivated by market reputation to disclose environmental information and increase environmental investment. Secondly, non-state-owned enterprises have greater market adaptability in technology application. Through intelligent monitoring and process optimisation, they can achieve energy consumption reduction and emission reduction, which in turn increases environmental investment. In contrast, state-owned enterprises are subject to more rigid policies, and their environmental investment is often passive and driven by compliance. The potential for digital transformation is limited for state-owned enterprises. They face the 'dual surplus problem', which refers to the low level of integration of digital technology into their production systems. Environmental investment is often overshadowed by other objectives, resulting in the 'resource competition effect'. Based on the above analysis, this paper puts forward the following hypotheses:

H5-2. *The digital transformation of non-state-owned enterprises (NSOEs) is a more prominent driver of environmental investments than state-owned enterprises (SOEs).*

The impact of digital transformation on corporate environmental investment is also characterised by regional heterogeneity. According to the development strategy of China, the country can be divided into four primary regions: the eastern, central, western, and northeastern regions. First, the eastern developed regions have implemented the "dual carbon" pilot project and the digital new infrastructure policy, resulting in the establishment of a "digital supervision platform + environmental credit evaluation" rigid regulatory mechanism. This mechanism forces companies to upgrade their environmental facilities through digital transformation. Second, the eastern regions possess a complete digital value chain (e.g., the Yangtze River industrial internet platform) and a specialised environmental service market. Companies can reduce the cost of environmental protection through technology such as cloud monitoring and AI diagnosis. However, in less developed eastern regions, environmental enforcement tends to be "competitive", and digital transformation is difficult to achieve. In addition, the data infrastructure in these regions is lagging, and the compatibility between technology and data infrastructure is insufficient. This hinders the conversion of digital investment into environmental performance. Therefore, the digital transformation of companies in the eastern regions has a more significant effect on environmental investment than that in the less developed regions. Based on this analysis, the following hypotheses are proposed in this paper:

H5-3. *Compared to less developed regions, digital transformation in developed eastern regions has a more significant role in promoting corporate environmental investment.*

It has been demonstrated that the formulation of environmental policies has a significant impact on the effectiveness of digital transformation in the field of environmental investment. Firstly, the promulgation of the 'Environmental Quality Standards (2012)' has led to the government strengthening its oversight of corporate environmental pollution, establishing clearer and more stringent environmental standards and requirements. This is the 'green barrier'. It explores the relationship between corporate social responsibility and the exploration of diversified pathways for the transition towards a green economy. It is evident that enterprises are increasingly aware of their environmental responsibility and are seeking to enhance their green technology output through digital transformation. This is achieved by optimising production processes, increasing efficiency in resource usage, and reducing energy consumption and emissions. Consequently, there is an increase in the scale of environmental investment. Secondly, prior to the announcement of environmental policies, the regulatory intensity of environmental pollution behaviour by enterprises was minimal, resulting in a lack of environmental awareness among enterprises. The pursuit of profit by enterprises often supersedes environmental considerations, as the cost of environmental compliance is low. Based on this analysis, this paper puts forward the following hypotheses:

H5-4. *Digital transformation has a more significant role in promoting corporate environmental investments after environmental protection policies are formulated.*

The digital transformation of enterprises also exhibits heterogeneity in terms of the intensity of production factors. According to the intensity of production factors, the digital transformation can be categorised as follows: technology-intensive, labour-intensive, and asset-intensive. Notably, the impact of the digital transformation on environmental investment is particularly pronounced in capital-intensive enterprises. Firstly, capital-intensive enterprises typically have a high proportion of fixed assets. Through the utilisation of IoT devices to monitor energy consumption data, the digital transformation can accurately identify the timing of environmental equipment upgrades, thereby generating a strong economic effect. Secondly, compared to capital-intensive enterprises, technology-intensive and labour-intensive enterprises are characterised by a lower asset base, which hinders the formation of a scale effect in environmental investment. In addition, technology-intensive enterprises allocate their research resources primarily to their core technical innovation activities, while labour-intensive enterprises face constraints in their human capital structure. Consequently, both of these enterprises prioritise the control of short-term production costs, resulting in the digital transformation of environmental investment being of low strategic priority. Based on the above analysis, this paper proposes the following hypotheses:

H5-5. *Compared to technology- and labour-intensive industries, digital transformation is more effective in driving environmental investments in capital-intensive firms.*

3. Research Design

3.1. Data Sources

Since 2011, there has been an acceleration in the digital transformation of enterprises, with the accumulation of new quality productive forces and an increasing focus on environmental protection. Given the need to consider the timeliness and accessibility of data, this study utilised a sample set of Chinese companies listed on the A-share market from 2011 to 2023 as the initial research sample. To ensure the quality and reliability of the research findings, a rigorous screening process was employed to select the sample, adhering to the following principles:

(1) Excluding financial enterprises.
(2) Excluding the sample of ST, *ST and financial anomalies companies with gearing ratio over 100%.
(3) Samples containing missing values for other variables were excluded.

In order to ensure the reliability of the study's findings and to minimise the impact of abnormal values on the analysis, the study implemented a 1% and 99% quantile truncation procedure for all variables. This method is a more common approach in the field of measurement economics for dealing with abnormal values than direct deletion or truncation. The selection of 1% and 99% quantile boundaries effectively eliminates the influence of extreme values while preserving as much sample information as possible. Following this step, the subsequent stage involved the selection and processing of samples. The study obtained 18,434 observation data points, all of which were sourced from the CSMAR and Wind databases.

3.2. Description of Variables

3.2.1. Explained Variable

The dependent variable in this study is the firm's environmental investment (Epinvest), which is measured in terms of the natural logarithm of the efficiency ratio. In comparison to the other common indicators in the literature, the advantage of the indicator selected for this study is as follows: Firstly, compared with Y. Y. Liu et al. (2021), who used the scale of corporate environmental protection investment as an indicator, the scale of energy conservation and emission reduction investment can more comprehensively capture various types of corporate environmental protection investment activities. Secondly, in comparison with the environmental tax indicators used by Chen et al. (2021), this approach directly measures the actual investment amount rather than the indirect tax burden, thereby ensuring a higher measurement accuracy. Thirdly, in contrast to the ESG ratings and other comprehensive indicators, the data on environmental protection investment is more objective and precise. This study draws on the methods employed by Cui et al. (2021), where the investment amount is calculated by taking the natural log of the total investment and standardising it. This method effectively eliminates the influence of differences in enterprise size, while also addressing the issue of biased data distribution, thereby ensuring the comparability of environmental investment across enterprises of different sizes.

3.2.2. Explanatory Variable

The explanatory variable in this study is enterprise digital transformation (Dig). Y. K. Zhang et al. (2021) use the proportion of intangible assets accounted for by digital technology to measure digital transformation. Wu et al. (2021), Yuan et al. (2021) used text analysis and digital characteristics keyword frequency as measurement indicators. Zhao et al. (2021) used annual report text analysis and expert scoring to construct digital transformation indicators for manufacturing enterprises. The present study employs the methods of Yuan et al. (2021), Wu et al. (2021), and Zhao et al. (2021), with the consideration of the compatibility of artificial intelligence, big data, cloud computing, and blockchain with the business operations of heavily polluting enterprises. The selection of these dimensions for the assessment of the digital transformation of heavily polluting enterprises is both reasonable and effective. The specific procedure is outlined below. Initially, the Python (version 3.9.x) web crawling technique is employed to collect the annual reports of all A-share listed companies in Shanghai and Shenzhen, with the assistance of Java the PDFbox library extracts text information, thereby establishing a data set for subsequent use in feature selection. Secondly, the Python programme was employed to search, match and count words in the data set of annual reports of listed companies, in accordance with pre-defined features. The final count and frequency of words in key technological areas were obtained, and the frequency of features was visualised in a feature frequency graph, as shown in Figure 2. Finally, the indicators for the digital transformation of enterprises were established, and the total frequency was standardised after the addition of the total frequency. The procedure is shown in Figure 3.

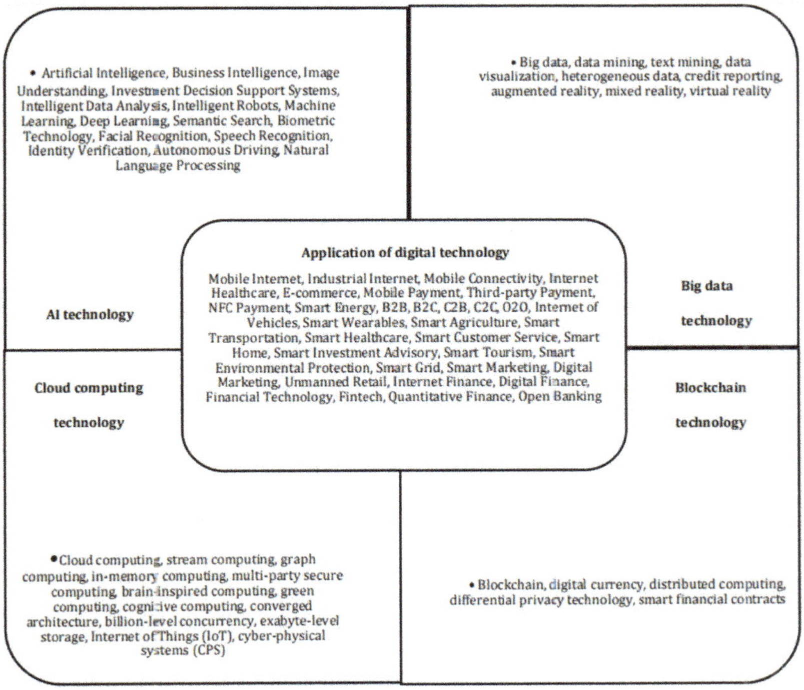

Figure 2. Structured feature word mapping for enterprise digital transformation.

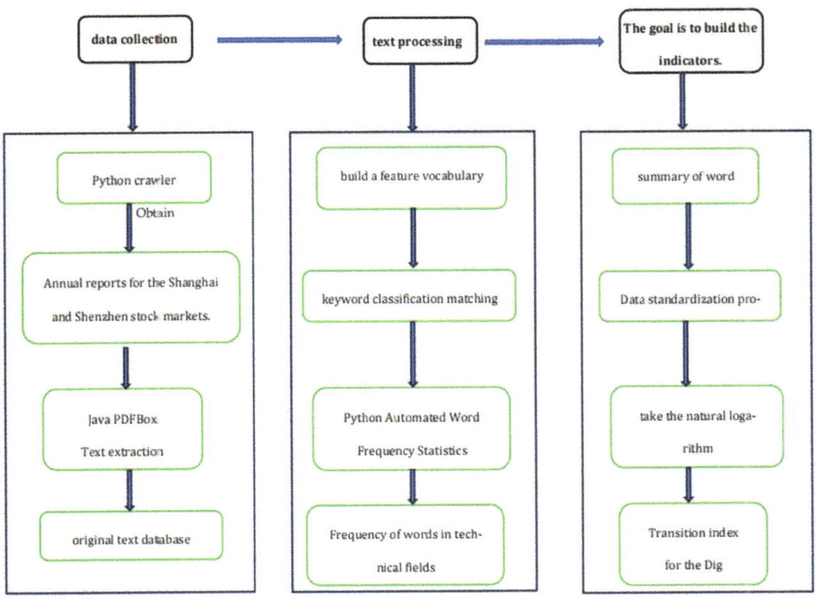

Figure 3. Steps for creating the index to measure digital transformation.

3.2.3. Mediating Variables

The mediating variable is new quality productive forces (Npro). The existing literature adopts diverse measurement approaches: J. Lu et al. (2024a) developed a trinity composite index system encompassing scientific, digital, and green productivity, with further refinements to tertiary and quaternary indicators for comprehensive assessment. Song et al. (2024) incorporated labour object value based on the two-factor productivity theory, employing entropy weighting for quantification. To achieve industrial adaptability, systematic indicators, and data-driven advantages while precisely capturing the dynamic transition characteristics of new quality productive forces, this study integrates and adapts the evaluation metrics from Song et al. (2024) and X. E. Zhang et al. (2024) considering data availability. The construction process involves three steps: First, we select firms in future-oriented and strategic emerging industries as the sample set, given their intrinsic alignment with new quality productive forces. Second, building upon the two-factor productivity theory, we construct a four-dimensional indicator system spanning living labour, materialised labour, hard technology, and soft technology. Third, entropy weighting is applied to determine indicator weights and aggregate scores. This method automatically assigns weights by analysing data dispersion—higher weights are given to indicators with greater variability (lower information entropy), effectively capturing dimensional importance heterogeneity while mitigating subjective bias. The synthesised NPRO index holistically reflects firms' performance in technological innovation and efficiency enhancement, where higher values indicate superior new quality productive forces. Table 1 presents the detailed weighting results.

Table 1. Indicators of new quality productive forces.

<table>
<tr><th>Considerations</th><th>Subfactor</th><th>Norm</th><th>Description of Indicator Values</th><th>Weights</th></tr>
<tr><td rowspan="5">labour force</td><td rowspan="3">labour</td><td>Percentage of R&D salaries</td><td>Research and development expenses − salaries and wages/operating income</td><td>28</td></tr>
<tr><td>Percentage of R&D staff</td><td>Number of R&D staff/Number of employees</td><td>4</td></tr>
<tr><td>Percentage of highly educated personnel</td><td>Number of people with bachelor's degree or above/Number of employees</td><td>3</td></tr>
<tr><td rowspan="2">materialised labour (objects of labour)</td><td>Fixed assets as a percentage</td><td>Fixed assets/total assets</td><td>2</td></tr>
<tr><td>Manufacturing costs as a percentage</td><td>(Subtotal of cash outflows from operating activities + depreciation of fixed assets + intangible assets
Amortisation + Provision for impairment − Cash paid for purchases of goods and services − Expenses
Cash paid to and on behalf of employees)/(Cash outflow from operating activities + depreciation of fixed assets + Amortisation of intangible assets + provision for impairment)
Subtotal cash outflow from operating activities + depreciation of fixed assets + amortization of intangible assets + provision for impairment)</td><td>1</td></tr>
</table>

Table 1. *Cont.*

Considerations	Subfactor	Norm	Description of Indicator Values	Weights
production tool	hard technology	R&D depreciation and amortisation as a percentage of	R&D expenses − depreciation and amortisation/operating income	27
		R&D lease payments as a percentage of	Research and development expenses − lease payments/operating income	2
		R&D direct investment as a percentage	R&D expenses − direct inputs/operating income	28
		Intangible assets as a percentage	Intangible assets/total assets	3
	soft technology	Total asset turnover	Operating income/average total assets	1
		Inverse equity multiplier	Owners' equity/total assets	1
new mass productivity				100

3.2.4. Moderating Variables

The moderating variable is big data applications (Bigdata). Compared with the questionnaire survey method used by K. Xie et al. (2020), this paper refers to the research of Y. Q. Zhang et al. (2021) and Wu et al. (2021) and uses a keyword frequency analysis method based on annual report texts. This method has the following advantages: firstly, the keywords are selected based on a literature review, policy documents and industry standards, ensuring content validity; secondly, annual reports are mandatory and regulated, and the data is objective; and thirdly, the frequency of keywords can reflect the extent to which companies use big data, capturing their actual technological applications. The following methods are proposed: Firstly, the Python programming language is employed to analyse the annual reports of A-share listed companies in order to calculate the frequency of specific words and phrases. These include "cloud computing" and "big data", which are core keywords that have been reviewed by experts and have been confirmed as applicable to the application of big data in enterprises. The results of this analysis are then processed to create an index of the extent to which big data is applied. Keywords and definitions related to "big data" are in the Table 2.

Table 2. Keywords and definitions related to "big data".

Byword	Define
big data	Meet the massive, high-speed, diversified elements or assets collected, processed and utilised by the enterprise.
huge volume of data	According to Goldner's definition of Big Data, massive scale is one of the key characteristics of Big Data.
data centre	Data centres, as facilities housing computer systems and their related components, assume the functions of delivering, accelerating, displaying, computing and storing data and information on the network infrastructure. In the information age, big data storage, calculation and exchange are highly dependent on safe, reliable and efficient data centres.
information asset	According to a report by Goldner, Big Data is essentially an information asset, i.e., an information resource that is owned and controlled by an organisation and can generate future economic benefits for it.
digitization	Granularization and structuring of uniformly and continuously distributed digital bits are implemented to create standardised, open-ended, non-linear, and versatile data objects. Relying on these different forms and categories of data objects, we can promote the practical application of big data.
arithmetic power	Also known as the hash rate, it is a unit used to measure the processing power of the Bitcoin network, which reflects the speed of a computer's output when performing hash function operations.

3.2.5. Threshold Variables

The threshold variable is environmental uncertainty (Eu). The article employs the industry-adjusted abnormal sales revenue volatility metric, with the primary considerations being the following: firstly, the method was proposed by Ghosh and Olsen (2009) and subsequently validated by Shen et al. (2012) in the Chinese context, thus becoming the predominant method for measuring environmental uncertainty; secondly, abnormal sales fluctuations often reflect market demand variability, policy adjustments, and other uncontrollable factors, thus effectively capturing the external environmental challenges faced by enterprises; and thirdly, in comparison to other methods, the data used is objective, can be obtained, and reflects the unique characteristics of enterprises, and after adjustment by the industry, it possesses excellent comparability. The specific steps are as follows: first, the OLS model (1) is employed to obtain the abnormal sales revenue deviation ε, and then the enterprise in order to calculate the standard deviation of sales revenue over a five-year period, the mean of the sales revenue must first be calculated. The standard deviation is then calculated as the mean of the sales revenue divided by the mean of the sales revenue. This is an unadjusted, or 'unknown' value. Finally, the standard deviation is adjusted using the industry standard deviation mean. This is achieved by dividing the standard deviation by the mean of the standard deviation. The result is the standard deviation of the industry.

$$Sale = \varphi_0 + \varphi_1 \times Year + \varepsilon \tag{1}$$

In Equation (1), *Sale* revenue is Sale, and the starting point for annual variables is the current year, denoted by *Year*.

3.2.6. Control Variables

The selection of control variables is informed by the research of Q. Zhang et al. (2019) and D. M. Xie (2020), follows the "resource-governance-environment" multi-dimensional driving framework for corporate environmental protection investment decisions. The present study employs a multifaceted framework to explore the impact of environmental factors on corporate financial resources, organisational structures, and external institutional environments. This approach enables a comprehensive and representative examination of the existing literature, while ensuring the completeness and representativeness of the system. In terms of financial structure, the asset-liability ratio (Dar) is employed to analyse the extraneous effects of financing constraints on environmental investment. In the operational capacity domain, the revenue generation capability (Oc), profit generation capability (Pa), and the proportion of fixed assets (Fixed) are utilised to assess an enterprise's capacity for resource allocation. The revenue growth rate (Tagr) is employed to examine the regulatory influence of environmental strategy on corporate growth. In the governance layer, the concentration of ownership (Top1) is employed to analyse the environmental oversight motivations of major shareholders. The proportion of independent directors (Indep) and the presence of a dual-class share structure (Dceo) are employed to assess the impact of internal control mechanisms on environmental investment decisions. The regional GDP level is employed to measure the regulatory pressure and resource allocation differences. The definitions of all variables are presented in Table 3.

Table 3. Variable definitions.

Variant Type	Variable	Variable Name	Variable Definition
explanatory variable	Epinvest	environmental investment	Take the natural logarithm of "current year's energy saving and emission reduction inputs".
explanatory variable	Dig	digital transformation	Digital Transformation Related Keywords Frequency Plus One Taking Logarithms
intermediary variable	Npro	new quality productive forces	Calculated by the entropy weight method
moderator variable	Bigdata	big data applications	The number of times big data-related keywords appear in the annual report is added to one and then logarithmised
Threshold variables	Eu	Environmental uncertainty	Coefficient of variation in operating income over the past five years, adjusted for industry
control variable	Dar	gearing	Total liabilities at year-end/total assets at year-end
	Oc	operating ability	Operating income/total assets closing balance
	Pa	profitability	Net profit/total assets closing balance
	Fixed	Fixed assets as a percentage	Net fixed assets/total assets closing balance
	Tagr	Development capacity	(Closing value of total assets for the period − Opening value of total assets for the period)/Opening value of total assets for the period
	Top1	Concentration of property rights	Shareholding ratio of the company's largest shareholder
	Indep	Proportion of independent directors	Number of independent directors/directors
	GDP	Regional economic level	Measured by logarithm of GDP
virtual variable	Dceo	two jobs in one	If the chairman of the board and the general manager are the same person, the value will be set to 1; if they are different persons, the value will be 0.
	Year	particular year	Year dummy variable
	Pollute	Nature of pollution by industry	Take 1 if it is a heavy polluting industry, otherwise take 0

3.3. *Modelling*

3.3.1. Basic Regression Model

In this model, log of environmental investment by firm i in period t is represented by $Epinvest_{it}$; α_0 is the intercept term; are coefficients; is the degree of digital transformation of firm i in period t; $\sum Controls_{it}$ are control variables; μ_i are individual fixed effects; θ_t is the time fixed effect; ε_{it} is the random error term. This model is used to study the impact of digital transformation on environmental investment. This model is used to study how digital transformation affects environmental investment. This model is used to study how digital transformation affects environmental investment.

$$Epinvest_{it} = \alpha_0 + \alpha_1 Dig_{it} + \alpha \sum Controls_{it} + \mu_i + \theta_t + \varepsilon_{it} \quad (2)$$

3.3.2. Mediating Effects Model

Among them, $Npro_{it}$ represents the level of new quality productive forces of Enterprise i in period t; β_0, γ_0 are the intercept terms; β_1, γ_1, γ_2, β, γ are the coefficients; Based on the three-step method proposed by Wen and Ye (2014), this paper constructs a mediation effect analysis model. On this basis, the Sobel test is used to verify the robustness of the mediation effect of the model, thereby ensuring the reliability and validity of the research results. Then, the Bootstrap method is used to measure the strength of the mediation effect. This model is used to study how digital transformation affects environmental investment.

$$Npro_{it} = \beta_0 + \beta_1 Dig_{it} + \beta \sum Controls_{it} + \mu_i + \theta_t + \varepsilon_{it} \tag{3}$$

$$Epinvest_{it} = \gamma_0 + \gamma_1 Dig_{it} + \gamma_2 Npro_{it} + \gamma \sum Controls_{it} + \mu_i + \theta_t + \varepsilon_{it} \tag{4}$$

3.3.3. Moderating the Mediating Effect

Among them, the moderating effect is $a_1(b_2{+}b_4 Bigdata_{it})$. $Bigdata_{it}$ is the moderating variable, representing the logarithm of the big data application level of enterprise i in period t; $Npro_{it} \times Bigdata_{it}$ is the product term of new quality productive forces and big data application level; a_0 and b_0 are the intercept terms, a_1, a, b_1, b_2, b_3, b_4 and b are the coefficients. This model looks at how digital transformation affects environmental investment.

$$Npro_{it} = a_0 + a_1 Dig_{it} + a \sum Controls_{it} + \mu_i + \theta_t + \varepsilon_{it} \tag{5}$$

$$\begin{aligned} Epinvest_{it} = b_0 + \quad & b_1 Dig_{it} + b_2 Bigdata_{it} + b_3 Npro_{it} + b_4 Npro_{it} \times Bigdata_{it} + \\ & b \sum Controls_{it} + \mu_i + \theta_t + \varepsilon_{it} \end{aligned} \tag{6}$$

3.3.4. Threshold Effect Model

Among them, δ_0 is the intercept term; $\delta_1 \ldots \delta_n$ and δ are coefficients; Eu_{it} represents the environmental uncertainty faced by enterprise i in period t; $\Omega_1 \ldots \Omega_n$ are the threshold value; $I(\cdot)$ represents an indicator function, which takes a value of 1 when the condition is met and 0 otherwise. This model explores the impact of digital transformation on environmental investment under different environmental uncertainty thresholds. Model (7) assumes that there is only one threshold value, while model (8) assumes that there are multiple threshold values. This model looks at how digital transformation affects the cost of environmental investment. This model looks at how digital transformation affects the cost of environmental investment.

$$\begin{aligned} Epinvest_{it} = \delta_0 + \quad & \delta_1 Dig_{it} I(Eu_{it} \le \Omega_1) + \delta_2 Dig_{it} I(Eu_{it} < \Omega_1) + \delta \sum Controls_{it} + \mu_i + \\ & \theta_t + \varepsilon_{it} \end{aligned} \tag{7}$$

$$\begin{aligned} Epinvest_{it} = \delta_0 + \quad & \delta_1 Dig_{it} I(Eu_{it} \le \Omega_1) + \delta_2 Dig_{it} I(\Omega_1 < Eu_{it} \le \Omega_2) + \ldots + \\ & \delta_n Dig_{it} I(Eu_{it} > \Omega_n) + \delta \sum Controls_{it} + \mu_i + \theta_t + \varepsilon_{it} \end{aligned} \tag{8}$$

3.4. Descriptive Statistics

Table 4 presents descriptive statistical results, with 18,434 data points for each variable. The maximum value for corporate environmental investment was 18.959, the minimum value was 0, and the standard deviation was 3.140. The minimum value for digital transformation was 0, the maximum value was 1.798, and the standard deviation was 0.597, indicating significant differences between companies in terms of digital transformation and environmental investment.

Table 4. Results of descriptive statistics.

Variant	Sample Number	Mean Value	Median Value	Standard Deviation	Minimum Value	Maximum Values
Epinvest	18434	0.620	0.000	3.140	0.000	18.959
Dig	18434	0.745	0.870	0.597	0.000	1.798
Npro	18434	0.123	0.116	0.071	0.011	0.373
Bigdata	18434	0.632	0.000	1.005	0.000	4.234
Eu	18434	2.330	1.909	3.045	0.002	290.331
Dar	18434	0.427	0.422	0.202	0.051	0.921
Oc	18434	0.615	0.521	0.424	0.064	2.469
Pa	18434	0.034	0.033	0.059	−0.285	0.200
Fixed	18434	0.205	0.171	0.157	0.002	0.680
Tagr	18434	0.153	0.078	0.340	−0.305	2.521
Top1	18434	33.549	31.100	14.854	8.380	74.820
Indep	18434	0.266	0.333	0.171	0.000	0.556
Dceo	18434	0.234	0.000	0.424	0.000	1.000
GDP	18434	10.142	10.402	1.003	5.965	11.818

3.5. Correlation Analysis and Multicollinearity Test

Firstly, the investigation of correlation is essential to ensure the reliability of the empirical results. To this end, the present study conducted a correlation analysis of the variables. The results, as illustrated in Table 5, demonstrate a positive correlation between digital transformation and environmental investment in enterprises.

Table 5. Correlation analysis.

Variant	Epinvest	Dig	Npro	Bigdata	Eu	Dar	Oc
Epinvest	1						
Dig	0.025 ***	1					
Npro	0.080 ***	0.368 ***	1				
Bigdata	−0.010	0.662 ***	0.340 ***	1			
Eu	−0.019 **	−0.033 ***	−0.015 **	−0.027 ***	1		
Dar	0.029 ***	−0.019 ***	0.010	−0.010	−0.035 ***	1	
Oc	0.031 ***	0.050 ***	−0.034 ***	−0.026 ***	−0.039 ***	0.153 ***	1
Pa	0.020 ***	−0.045 ***	−0.003	−0.075 ***	−0.021 ***	−0.320 ***	0.117 ***
Fixed	0.094 ***	−0.283 ***	−0.047 ***	−0.248 ***	−0.015**	0.025 ***	0.022 ***
Tagr	−0.022 ***	−0.014 *	0.004	−0.013 *	0.171 ***	−0.026 ***	−0.027 ***
Top1	0.050 ***	−0.162 ***	−0.096 ***	−0.169 ***	0.011	0.062 ***	0.050 ***
Indep	0.001	0.006	0.017 **	0.015 **	0.003	0.016 **	−0.001
Dceo	−0.039 ***	0.082 ***	0.053 ***	0.073 ***	0.021 ***	−0.104 ***	−0.031 ***
GDP	0.009	0.015 **	0.010	0.023 ***	0.016 **	−0.043 ***	−0.033 ***
	Pa	**Fixed**	**Tagr**	**Top1**	**Indep**	**Dceo**	**GDP**
Pa	1						
Fixed	−0.017 **	1					
Tagr	0.231 ***	−0.093 ***	1				
Top1	0.162 ***	0.095 ***	0.058 ***	1			
Indep	0.002	0.016 **	−0.001	0.008	1		
Dceo	−0.007	−0.075 ***	0.048 ***	−0.093 ***	−0.012	1	
GDP	−0.003	−0.028 ***	0.012	0.034 ***	0.333 ***	0.001	1

Note: *, **, *** represent 10%, 5%, and 1% significance levels, respectively.

Secondly, we must perform a multiple collinearity test. Although the correlation coefficients among the variables are relatively low, one coefficient, 0.662, is relatively high. To circumvent the potential influence of collinearity, we must perform a VIF test. As shown in Table 6, the VIF values for all variables are less than 5, which indicates that the model does not exhibit significant collinearity.

Table 6. VIF test.

Variant	VIF	1/VIF
Dig	1.950	0.513
Bigdata	1.850	0.539
Pa	1.280	0.781
Dar	1.210	0.830
Npro	1.190	0.837
GDP	1.130	0.883
Indep	1.130	0.887
Fixed	1.120	0.891
Tagr	1.110	0.898
Top1	1.090	0.921
Oc	1.080	0.928
Eu	1.040	0.962
Dceo	1.030	0.970
Mean VIF		1.250

4. Empirical Testing and Analysis of Results

4.1. Benchmark Regression Analysis

To ensure the reliability and validity of the regression results, this study employs a mixed-effects regression model, an individual fixed-effects model, a time fixed-effects model, and a two-way fixed-effects panel model for empirical testing.

The results are presented in Table 7. The coefficients for corporate digital transformation are 0.339, 0.680, 0.128, and 0.329, respectively. These discrepancies arise primarily because the individual fixed-effects model captures the micro-level heterogeneous impacts of digital transformation across firms, whereas the time fixed-effects model reflects the macro-level average effect along the temporal dimension. The decrease in the coefficient from 0.680 to 0.128 suggests that macroeconomic fluctuations partially offset the positive effect of digital transformation. Meanwhile, the two-way fixed-effects model, which controls for both individual and time effects, yields a coefficient of 0.329—intermediate between 0.680 and 0.128 and close to the pooled regression result. These results clearly demonstrate that digital transformation exerts a statistically significant and positive impact on corporate environmental investment behaviour, effectively incentivising firms to increase their environmental expenditures. Thus, Hypothesis H1 is supported

Table 7. Benchmark regression test results.

Variant	Epinvest	Epinvest	Epinvest	Epinvest
Dig	0.339 *** (7.331)	0.680 *** (10.223)	0.128 *** (2.632)	0.329 *** (4.584)
Dar	0.460 *** (3.191)	−0.702 *** (−2.802)	0.274 * (1.894)	−1.071 *** (−4.243)
Oc	0.105 (1.599)	−0.140 (−1.252)	0.200 *** (2.991)	0.110 (0.972)
Pa	1.621 *** (3.092)	−0.501 (−1.073)	2.260 *** (4.264)	0.165 (0.353)
Fixed	2.086 *** (8.452)	0.214 (0.553)	2.007 *** (8.251)	0.603 (1.543)

Table 7. *Cont.*

Variant	Epinvest	Epinvest	Epinvest	Epinvest
Tagr	−0.170 *** (−3.464)	−0.122 ** (−2.311)	−0.055 (−1.072)	−0.054 (−0.992)
Top1	0.009 *** (3.431)	0.002 (0.594)	0.011 *** (4.352)	0.015 *** (3.552)
Indep	−0.136 (−0.851)	−0.138 (−0.894)	−0.099 (−0.632)	−0.091 (−0.598)
Dceo	−0.211 *** (−3.33)	−0.127 * (−1.76)	−0.177 *** (−2.80)	−0.122 * (−1.72)
GDP	0.044 (1.212)	0.119 (0.511)	0.042 (1.182)	0.144 (0.631)
Constant	−0.997 *** (−2.599)	−0.720 (−0.299)	−0.924 ** (−2.432)	−1.258 (−0.542)
Company FE	No	Yes	No	Yes
Year FE	No	No	Yes	Yes
N	18434	18434	18434	18434
R^2	0.016	0.117	0.056	0.155

Note: ***, **, and * indicate significant at 1%, 5%, and 10% confidence levels, respectively; T-values are in parentheses.

4.2. Analysis of Mediating Effects

The present study employs a mediation model to investigate the impact of digital transformation on enterprises' environmental investment, facilitated by new quality productive forces. Table 8 presents the results of the Bootstrap test, which examines the mediation effect of new quality productive forces on digital transformation and enterprises' environmental investment. The results indicate that the indirect effect of digital transformation on enterprises' environmental investment is [0.126, 0.192] does not include 0, thereby confirming that the new quality productive forces have a mediating effect on the digital transformation and environmental investment of enterprises. Digital technology has the capacity to enhance green innovation capabilities, optimise the environment, improve efficiency, and create new investment opportunities. Consequently, enterprises can achieve growth in environmental investment through the intermediary effect of new quality productive forces.

As illustrated in Table 8, the results of the intermediary effect test conducted using the stepwise regression method are presented. The model (2) (3) (4) corresponds to the intermediary effect equation. The model (2) employs the degree of digital transformation in the listed company as the explanatory variable, and the investment in environmental protection by the enterprise as the dependent variable. The regression analysis was conducted. The results indicate that the digital transformation coefficient α_1 is 0.329, suggesting a positive influence of digital transformation on environmental protection investment. In the model (3), the adoption of digital transformation by the enterprise is employed as the explanatory variable, with the new quality productive forces (Npro) serving as the dependent variable. The findings indicate that the impact of digital transformation on the new quality productive forces is represented by the coefficient $\beta_1 = 0.027$. The results of the study indicate a significant increase in the level of production efficiency, with a 1% rise being observed. This suggests that the digital transformation of businesses has a considerable impact on the enhancement of their production efficiency. Firstly, as businesses progress through their digital transformation, they are able to utilise a wider range of digital technologies that are conducive to the development of new quality productive forces. Secondly, the advancement of digital technologies in businesses has encouraged innovation, thereby enhancing their technological capabilities. Consequently, this has led to an improvement in the efficiency of resource allocation, resulting in the attainment of enhanced production quality. In the model (4), the digital transformation (Dig) and the new quality productive forces (Npro) are considered concurrently in order to analyse their combined effect on the environmental investment (Epinvest) of the enterprise. Following the incorporation of the new quality productive forces as a mediating variable, the intermediary coefficient γ_2 is found to be 1.212 at a 5% level, which indicates that an enhancement in the new quality productive forces can, to a certain extent, result in an increase in the environmental investment of the enterprise. It is also noteworthy that the digital transformation coefficient γ_1 is found to be 0.296 in this model. The regression coefficient is significant at the 1% level, indicating a direct impact of digital transformation on corporate environmental investment. This result suggests the presence of a partial mediating effect. Lastly, the Sobel test p-value is less than 0.01, confirming that the mediating effect passes the test. These results validate Hypothesis H2.

Table 8. Results of the mediation effect test.

Variant	Model (2)	Models (3)	Models (4)
	Epinvest	**Npro**	**Epinvest**
Dig	0.329 *** (4.581)	0.027 *** (20.653)	0.296 *** (4.197)
Npro			1.212 ** (2.142)
Controls	Yes	Yes	Yes
Constant	−1.258 (−0.542)	0.109 *** (3.521)	−1.389 (−0.593)
Company FE	Yes	Yes	Yes
Year FE	Yes	Yes	Yes
N	18434	18434	18434
R^2	0.155	0.643	0.155
Bootstrap test results 95% confidence interval [0.126, 0.192]		Sobel test results 0.158 ***	

Note: ***, **, and * indicate significant at 1%, 5%, and 10% confidence levels, respectively; T-values are in parentheses.

4.3. Analysis of the Mediating Effect of Regulation

We further analysed the magnitude and significance of the effect of the mediating variable, new quality productive forces (Npro), under the moderation of big data applications (Bigdata) using the Bootstrap method to test for moderated mediation effects. We used the mean of big data application plus or minus one standard deviation as the grouping criterion, resulting in three groups: low, mean, and high levels of big data application. Table 9 corresponds to Models (5) and (6), respectively. The coefficient of the interaction term Npro×Bigdata in the dependent variable model is significantly positive, indicating a significant moderating effect of enterprise big data application, which validates the technology synergy enhancement mechanism. Subsequently, the mean of the standardised deviation of the application of big data is employed as a standard for the categorisation of the data. This process yields three groups: low, medium and high levels of big data application. As demonstrated in Table 9, the indirect effect coefficient has increased from 0.242 to 0.409 as the level of application of big data has been elevated. This indicates that as the level of data utilisation improves, the capacity for data-driven decision-making, optimising resource allocation and enhancing management efficiency also increases. Consequently, the intermediary effect of new quality productive forces in the digital transformation and environmental investment is significantly reinforced. However, the negative coefficient of the standalone big data application term reveals its non-linear moderating characteristics. This contradictory phenomenon can be explained from two perspectives. First, in the short term, the high sunk costs of data governance may crowd out enterprises' liquidity resources, leading to an immediate inhibitory effect on environmental protection investment. Second, applying big data technology requires breaking existing organisational norms, and management frictions during the initial phase of technology integration may weaken the actual effectiveness of productivity transformation. The findings indicate that the application of big data can achieve a symbiotic integration of "data-technology-governance" systems, thereby facilitating the harmonious progression of enhanced new quality productive forces and environmental management. Finally, based on the results of the bootstrap test, the interval values do not include 0 within the 90% confidence interval, passing the significance test. Therefore, Hypothesis H3 is supported.

Table 9. Moderated mediation effect test results.

	Regression Coefficient	Standard Deviation	Z-Value	Significance
multivariate model				
Dig	0.045 ***	0.001	53.360	0.000
Constant	−0.083 *	0.005	15.320	0.093
model of dependent variable				
Dig	0.329 ***	0.054	6.080	0.000
Npro	3.217 ***	0.425	7.570	0.000
Bigdata	−0.235 ***	0.062	−3.820	0.000
Npro× Bigdata	0.627 **	0.319	1.960	0.049
Constant	−1.253 ***	0.260	−4.830	0.000
Moderating the mediating effect test				
Bigdata (Npro)	indirect effect	significance	Bootstrap method 90% confidence interval	
minus one standard deviation	0.242 ***	0.000	[0.163, 0.321]	
average value	0.326 ***	0.001	[0.167, 0.485]	
Add one standard deviation	0.409 ***	0.005	[0.169, 0.650]	
Controls			Yes	
Company FE			Yes	
Year FE			Yes	
N			18,434	

Note: ***, **, and * indicate significant at 1%, 5%, and 10% confidence levels, respectively.

4.4. Analysis of Threshold Effects

The present study posits that environmental uncertainty is an indispensable element in the context of digital transformation and its subsequent impact on corporate environmental investment. This study aims to elucidate the characteristics and implications of this phenomenon. Refer to Table 10 for the results of the single-barrier test. The p-values obtained from the single-barrier test are statistically significant. Therefore, this study will employ a single-barrier model for analysis. The results of the single-barrier model are particularly evident; therefore, this model will be utilised in subsequent analyses. The results of the analysis indicate that environmental uncertainty significantly impacts enterprises' digital transformation. The threshold estimation results are reported in Table 11. The threshold value for corporate environmental investment is 2.047, with a confidence interval of [1.977, 2.064]. Figure 4 shows that environmental uncertainty has been successfully overcome, as demonstrated by the results of the single-threshold regression analysis presented in Table 12. Digital transformation has been observed to significantly influence enterprise environmental investment, exhibiting a 'border effect' that intensifies in the presence of environmental uncertainty. In the context of uncertain environmental conditions, the digital transformation of enterprises is positively influenced by the coefficient of 0.756. This indicates that enterprises can enhance their investment in environmental protection by transitioning to digital formats, even in environments characterised by low environmental uncertainty. Conversely, in environments characterised by high environmental uncertainty, the coefficient declines to 0.544. This suggests that enterprises operating in such environments experience diminished efficiency and risk aversion in resource allocation, leading to a reduction in long-term environmental investment. Thus, Hypothesis H4 is supported.

Table 10. Threshold effect self-sampling test.

Threshold Number	F-Value	*p*-Value	Bootstrap Count	Threshold Value		
				1%	5%	10%
single-threshold test	16.39 **	0.013	300	16.422	11.865	10.234
Double Threshold Test	5.43	0.513	300	14.515	12.688	10.839
Triple Threshold Test	6.10	0.527	300	24.292	16.620	14.421

Note: ***, **, and * indicate significant at 1%, 5%, and 10% confidence levels, respectively.

Table 11. Threshold estimate and its confidence interval.

Threshold Variable	Threshold Value	95% Confidence Interval
single-threshold	2.047	[1.977, 2.064]

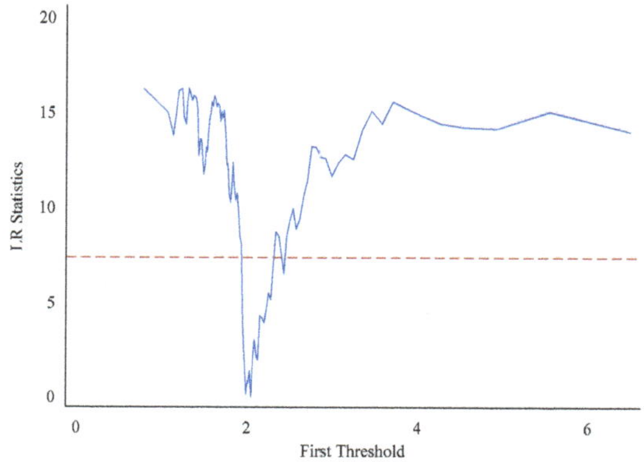

Figure 4. Environmental uncertainty threshold value test. The red line represents the significance critical value, usually a horizontal line, while the blue line represents the curve of the LR statistic changing with the threshold value.

Table 12. Threshold effect test results.

Variant	Models (6)		
	Coefficient Estimate	*p*-Value	T-Value
Dig (Eu ≤ 2.047)	0.756 ***	0.000	10.592
Dig (Eu > 2.047)	0.544 ***	0.000	8.353
Controls		Yes	
Constant		0.121 ***	
Company FE		Yes	
Year FE		Yes	
N		18,434	
R2		0.183	

Note: ***, **, and * indicate significant at 1%, 5%, and 10% confidence levels, respectively.

4.5. Endogeneity Tests and Robustness Tests

4.5.1. Endogeneity Test

First is the instrumental variable method. This paper refers to the research method used by Xiao et al. (2021) and selects the "average digital transformation degree of provinces, industries, and years" (IV_Dig) as the instrumental variable. This variable reflects the group's overall digital trend and does not have a direct causal relationship with individual enterprises' environmental protection investment. Thus, it can effectively avoid reverse causality and meet the requirements of relevance and exclusion. Second, the study uses the two-stage least squares (2SLS) method to address over-identification issues effectively. The results of the regression analysis are presented in Table 13. After incorporating the instrumental variable, the digital transformation of enterprises significantly increases environmental investment. The LM statistic test results of the Kleibergen-Paap rk test are significant, rejecting the assumption of insufficient identification. Additionally, the Wald F statistic results reject the assumption of weak identification. Together, these results indicate that the positive impact effect is robust and reliable.

Table 13. Endogeneity test results.

Variant	Instrumental Variable Approach		Dynamic Panel Analysis	
	Phase I	Phase II	Differential GMM	System GMM
L. Epinvest			0.101 *** (2.933)	0.110 *** (4.412)
Dig		0.361 *** (4.390)	0.184 * (1.822)	0.108 * (1.691)
iv_Dig	0.917 *** (169.130)			
Controls	Yes	Yes	Yes	Yes
Constant	−0.051 (−0.567)	−0.477 (−0.344)	−1.024 *** (−3.534)	−1.144 *** (−2.696)
Company FE	Yes	Yes	Yes	Yes
Year FE	Yes	Yes	Yes	Yes
AR(1)			0.000	0.000
AR(2)			0.643	0.771
Hansen			0.588	0.609
N	18,434	18434	15598	17016
R^2	0.897	0.221		
Kleibergen-Paap rk LM		4361.880 ***		
Kleibergen-Paap rkWald F		31,043.20 (16.381)		

Note: ***, **, and * indicate significant at the 1%, 5%, and 10% confidence levels, respectively; T-values in parentheses. Values in parentheses in Kleibergen-Paap rkWaldF are critical values for the Stock-Yogo test at the 10% level; AR(1), AR(2), and Hansen report are *p*-values for the statistic.

Second is dynamic panel analysis. Since the dependent variable, Epinvest, has endogeneity issues—meaning corporate environmental investment has a cumulative effect—the lagged term (L. Epinvest) of the dependent variable was included among the explanatory variables to construct a difference GMM model. The results are shown in Table 13, where the Dig regression coefficient is positively significant at the 10% level. Subsequently, a system GMM model was constructed for further testing. The Dig regression coefficient is positively significant at the 10% level, indicating that corporate digital transformation has a significant promotional effect on environmental investment. Additionally, the Hansen test confirmed the validity of the instrumental variables, and the AR(2) test results showed that the second-order differences in the disturbance terms in the model are not autocorrelated. This further validates the robustness of the benchmark regression.

Third is propensity score matching. This study used PSM to eliminate sample selection bias from the research results. First, the treatment and control groups were clearly defined. Companies with a measurement value of digital transformation greater than the mean were classified as the treatment group (Treat = 1). Conversely, companies were classified as the control group (Treat = 0). Next, the appropriate covariates were selected for the PSM calculations, and k-nearest neighbour matching (k = 2, radius = 0.05) was used for sample matching. The results of the balance test are shown in Table 14. The mean deviation of the standard deviation of the covariates has been significantly reduced, indicating that the differences between the two groups of samples in terms of covariates have been effectively controlled within a small range. Figure 5 shows that the standardised deviations of all variables decreased significantly before and after matching, proving the matching method's effectiveness in balancing data distribution and reducing variable deviations. Additionally, Figure 6 shows the range of common values of the samples, with only 20 samples failing to be matched successfully. This suggests that the number of samples lost during the matching process is minimal and will not cause significant bias in the final conclusions of the research. To eliminate potential interference from the matching method on the estimation results, two additional matching methods, kernel matching and Mahalanobis matching, were employed for estimation analysis. The results are detailed in Table 15. The average treatment effects (ATT) of the three methods are highly consistent and significant at the 1% level, which validates the robustness of the estimation results. Finally, after screening the sample, the main hypothesis was tested via regression analysis, and the results are presented in Table 15. The regression coefficients for digital transformation were 0.366, 0.329, and 0.404, respectively; all were significant at the 1% level. This confirms the significant promotional effect of digital transformation on environmental protection investment and the robustness of the conclusions after overcoming the issue of sample self-selection.

Table 14. Balance test results.

Variant	Match Before/After	Average Value		Standard Error (%)	Error Reduction (%)	T-Value	*p*-Value
		Process Group	Control Subjects				
Oc	prematch	0.639	0.591	11.500		7.821	0.000
	after matching	0.636	0.642	−1.500	86.700	−0.932	0.353
Pa	prematch	0.032	0.036	−5.400		−3.651	0.000
	after matching	0.033	0.033	−0.100	98.200	−0.072	0.948
Fixed	prematch	0.168	0.242	−48.800		−33.143	0.000
	after matching	0.168	0.170	−1.300	97.400	−0.963	0.336
Tagr	prematch	0.149	0.157	−2.300		−1.592	0.112
	after matching	0.149	0.145	1.200	48.600	0.841	0.399
Top1	prematch	31.663	35.447	−25.700		−17.442	0.000
	after matching	31.697	31.506	1.300	95.000	0.902	0.366
Indep	prematch	0.266	0.265	0.700		−1.141	0.646
	after matching	0.266	0.269	−1.700	−147.200	−0.674	0.252
GDP	prematch	10.157	10.127	3.000		−11.541	0.044
	after matching	10.156	10.166	−1.000	65.800	−0.702	0.484

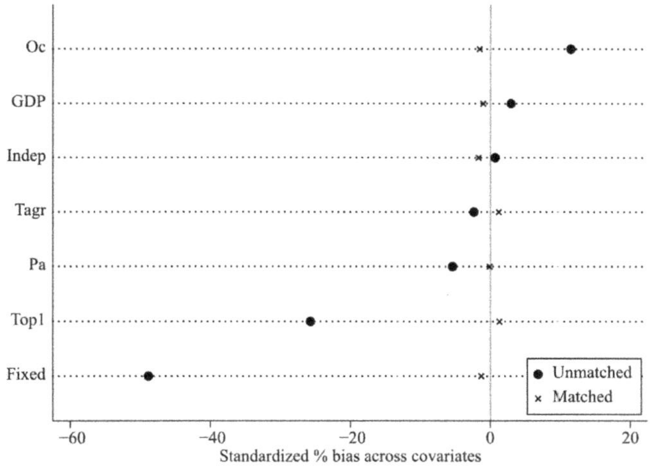

Figure 5. Plot of standardised deviations for each variable.

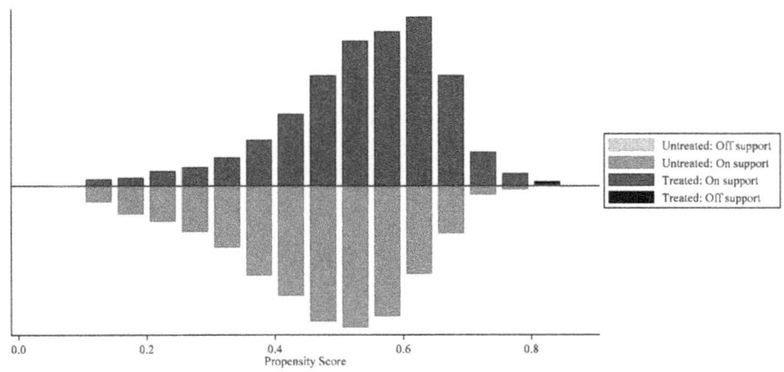

Figure 6. Common range of values for the propensity score.

Table 15. PSM test results.

Variant	k Nearest Neighbour Matching Within Callipers	Nuclear Matching	Martensitic Match
Dig	0.366 ***	0.329 ***	0.404 ***
	(4.698)	(4.583)	(4.662)
Controls	Yes	Yes	Yes
Constant	−2.501	−1.265	−7.812
	(−0.841)	(−0.542)	(−1.374)
Company FE	Yes	Yes	Yes
Year FE	Yes	Yes	Yes
N	13,500	18,414	9160
R^2	0.250	0.221	0.184
ATT	0.371 ***	0.343 ***	0.317 ***
	(6.721)	(6.901)	(5.164)

Note: ***, **, and * indicate significant at 1%, 5%, and 10% confidence levels, respectively; T-values are in parentheses.

4.5.2. Robustness Tests

Firstly, replace the explanatory variables. The present study draws upon the research methodology and approaches proposed by Zhen et al. (2023), leveraging the CSMAR framework. The Digital trans index was developed to measure the extent of the digital transformation of Chinese companies. It is based on CSMAR database, which integrates multiple sources of data, such as annual reports, fundraising announcements, and certification announcements. This integrated approach ensures consistency with the regression analysis and enhances the comprehensibility of the index. It also overcomes the limitations of single-source data. The index can effectively verify the robustness of the regression results and mitigate potential measurement errors caused by single-source data. In conclusion, the index is a valuable tool for evaluating the digital transformation of Chinese companies. Digital Trans (DT) serves as a substitute for core explanatory variables, conducting a cautious verification process. The regression results in Table 16 show that the regression coefficient between digital transformation and corporate environmental investment still presents a significant positive correlation, with a value of 0.081, indicating that the previous research conclusions are robust.

Secondly, replace the dependent variable. The discrepancy in measurement methods has the potential to yield divergent results. Given the path dependency of corporate environmental investment, it is recommended that the proportion of corporate environmental investment to total assets be adopted as a metric for corporate environmental investment. This metric effectively mitigates the issues associated with the size effect, and not only validates the robustness of the primary regression result, but also enhances the credibility of the study's conclusions through the use of multiple measurement dimensions. The regression results are presented in Table 16. The relationship between digital transformation and corporate environmental investment remains significant at the 5% level, supporting the conclusions previously discussed. The conclusions of this study remain unaltered despite the modification of the metric for measuring corporate environmental investment.

Thirdly, high-dimensional fixed effects. This paper tests the robustness of the core conclusions using a triple fixed effects combination. First, we control for time, province, and industry fixed effects (Year × Province × Industry) to eliminate the confounding effects of cross-regional industrial policy differences and fluctuations in the timing of technological evolution on digital transformation and environmental protection investment. Second, we control for time, province, and ownership type fixed effects (Year × Province × SOE) to eliminate the interference of differences in the timing of digital transformation among enterprises of different ownership types across provinces with environmental protection investment. Third, we control for time, industry, and SOE fixed effects (Year × Industry × SOE) to eliminate the interference caused by differences in technology adoption rhythms and responses to environmental regulations among enterprises of different ownership types. Finally, we control for industry, province, and SOE fixed effects (Industry × Province × SOE) to mitigate estimation bias caused by the interaction between regional resource endowments, industry pollution intensity, and ownership structure. As demonstrated in Table 16, the regression coefficients are 0.313, 0.126, 0.318 and 0.553, respectively. This indicates that the digital transformation has a significant positive effect on environmental investment in the three models, which indicates that the research conclusions are not significantly influenced by changes in the fixed-effects structure and have reliable causal inferential properties.

Table 16. Robustness test results.

Variant	(1)	(2)	(3)			
			Higher Dimensional Fixed Effect			
	Substitution of Explanatory Variables	**Substitution of Explanatory Variables**	**Control Time Province Industry**	**Control of Property Rights in Time Provinces**	**Control Time Industry Property Rights**	**Control of Property Rights in Industrial Provinces**
Dig		0.001 ** (2.387)	0.313 *** (5.178)	0.126 *** (2.583)	0.318 *** (5.098)	0.553 *** (9.862)
Digitaltrans	0.081 ** (2.53)					
Controls	Yes	Yes	Yes	Yes	Yes	Yes
Constant	−1.134 (−0.482)	0.000 (0.544)	−1.154 *** (−3.082)	−0.848 ** (−2.181)	−1.131 *** (−3.000)	−1.219 *** (−3.163)
Company FE	Yes	Yes	No	No	No	No
Year FE	Yes	Yes	Yes	Yes	Yes	No
Province Fe	Yes	No	Yes	Yes	No	Yes
Industry FE	No	No	No	No	Yes	Yes
Soe FE	No	No	Yes	Yes	Yes	Yes
N	18434	18434	18108	18110	18108	18108
R^2	0.220	0.232	0.072	0.060	0.068	0.035

Variant	(4)	(5)	(6)
	Replacement of the Test Model	**Replacement Sample Interval**	**1% Inden-tation**
Dig	0.329 *** (5.062)	0.366 *** (4.634)	0.323 *** (4.551)
Controls	Yes	Yes	Yes
Constant	−0.460 (−0.332)	−1.975 (−0.893)	−2.099 (−0.626)
Company FE	Yes	Yes	Yes
Year FE	Yes	Yes	Yes
Province Fe	No	No	No
Industry FE	No	No	No
Soe FE	No	No	No
N	18,434	15,598	18,434
R^2		0.226	0.221
var(e.EPInvest)	7.684 *** (96.053)		

Note: ***, **, and * indicate significant at 1%, 5%, and 10% confidence levels, respectively; T-values are in parentheses.

Fourthly, change the estimation model. To ensure the reliability and stability of the research conclusions, this paper uses the Tobit model for regression analysis instead of the original estimation model. This approach effectively addresses potential truncation issues in corporate environmental investment data and improves regression analysis with constrained dependent variables. Table 16 shows that, after applying the Tobit model, the coefficient is 0.329, which is significant at the 1% level. This indicates that the positive promotional effect of digital transformation on corporate environmental investment remains stable and is unaffected by the model replacement.

Fifth, change the sample interval. Drawing on the approach of N. J. Li et al. (2023), this paper excludes the impact of special events by removing data from 2015 and 2020. China's financial markets experienced a stock market crash in 2015, which significantly impacted the entire market and severely disrupted corporate operational decisions and investment strategies. 2020 was the year the pandemic first erupted, plunging corporate operations into extreme uncertainty. By 2021, companies had adapted to the pandemic and refocused on long-term development strategies. The analysis results, as shown in Table 16, indicate that the coefficient of digital transformation is positive and significant, which suggests that the conclusions of this study remain robust after excluding the impact of special events. The digital transformation's significance in influencing enterprises' environmental investments remains consistent with the fundamental regression coefficient. This suggests that the conclusions of this study remain robust, even when considering the impact of outliers.

Sixth, 1% tail trimming was performed. The present study employs a 1% 'smoothed' treatment of the sample, with the objective of eliminating the potential impact of extreme values. As demonstrated in Table 16, the digital coefficient (Dig) is found to be 0.323, and is observed to be at a 1% level, thereby confirming the hypothesis that there is a significant positive correlation between digital transformation and environmental investment.

4.6. Further Analysis

First, industry heterogeneity effects. To this end, the study employs a sample of enterprises categorised into two groups based on their pollution levels: high- and low-pollution enterprises. The regression analysis, the results of which are presented in Table 17, revealed a significant discrepancy in the impact of digital transformation on environmental investment between high- and low-pollution enterprises. Specifically, the regression coefficient for the high-pollution enterprises was 0.326, and it was not significant at the 1% level. In contrast, for the low-pollution enterprises, the coefficient was not significant, indicating that digital transformation has a differential impact on environmental investment based on the extent of pollution. These findings support Hypotheses H5-1.

Table 17. Results of the test for industry heterogeneity effects.

Variant	Heavily Polluting Industries	Lightly Polluting Industries
	Epinvest	Epinvest
Dig	0.382	0.326 ***
	(1.394)	(4.391)
Controls	Yes	Yes
Constant	7.616 ***	−0.177
	(−7.273)	(−0.072)
Company FE	Yes	Yes
Year FE	Yes	Yes
N	1916	16,500
R^2	0.140	0.157

Note: ***, **, and * indicate significant at 1%, 5%, and 10% confidence levels, respectively; T-values are in parentheses.

Second, the heterogeneous effect of property rights. According to property rights, enterprises can be divided into state-owned enterprises and non-state-owned enterprises. As shown in Table 18, the digital transformation coefficient of non-state-owned enterprises is 0.406 and significant, while that of state-owned enterprises is negative and insignificant. The above test results verify Hypothesis H5-2.

Table 18. Results of the test for heterogeneous effects of property rights.

Variant	Nationalised Business	Non-State Enterprise
	Epinvest	Epinvest
Dig	−0.050	0.406 ***
	(−0.332)	(5.032)
Controls	Yes	Yes
Constant	−3.123	2.556
	(−1.398)	(0.624)
Company FE	Yes	Yes
Year FE	Yes	Yes
N	3089	15,270
R^2	0.177	0.163

Note: ***, **, and * indicate significant at 1%, 5%, and 10% confidence levels, respectively; T-values are in parentheses.

Third, the regional heterogeneity effect. According to the standard of the four regional divisions (east, central, west, and northeast) in the national development plan, the selected samples were divided and analysed. As shown in Table 19, the digital transformation coefficient of eastern enterprises is 0.305 and significant, while the coefficients of other regions are not significant. This indicates that the digital transformation of eastern enterprises has a more significant impact on environmental investment. The above test results verify the Hypothesis H5-3.

Table 19. Results of the test for regional heterogeneous effects.

Variant	The East	Central Section	Western Part	Northwest
	Epinvest	Epinvest	Epinvest	Epinvest
Dig	0.305 ***	0.353	0.446	0.062
	(4.794)	(1.553)	(0.579)	(0.198)
Controls	Yes	Yes	Yes	Yes
Constant	−1.109 ***	−0.775	−9.256	−0.924
	(−2.694)	(−0.843)	(−0.852)	(−0.844)
Company FE	Yes	Yes	Yes	Yes
Year FE	Yes	Yes	Yes	Yes
N	14547	2626	176	755
R^2	0.074	0.075	0.234	0.122

Note: ***, **, and * indicate significant at 1%, 5%, and 10% confidence levels, respectively; T-values are in parentheses.

Fourthly, the policy's differential impact is evident. This study adopts the research methods of Q. Zhang et al. (2019) and Zhu et al. (2022), utilising the 2012 Environmental Quality Standard (EQS) as the policy reference series. The study employs a sample verification method to explore the external policy constraints on the digital transformation of enterprises and their impact on environmental investment. The regression analysis results in Table 20 show that before the official implementation of this standard, the regression coefficient of enterprise digital transformation on environmental protection investment was 0.158, which was not statistically significant; however, after the implementation of the standard, this coefficient jumped to 0.406, showing a prominent significance at the 1% level. This shows that updated and enforced environmental policies encourage businesses to take more proactive and effective environmental measures to comply with regulations. The results of this test have confirmed the Hypothesis H5-4.

Table 20. Before and after policy Heterogeneous Effectiveness test results.

Variant	Prior to Policy Implementation	After Policy Implementation
	Epinvest	Epinvest
Dig	0.158 (1.184)	0.406 *** (4.732)
Controls	Yes	Yes
Constant	17.958 (1.143)	−0.733 (−0.294)
Company FE	Yes	Yes
Year FE	Yes	Yes
N	236	15598
R^2	0.130	0.165

Note: ***, **, and * indicate significant at 1%, 5%, and 10% confidence levels, respectively; T-values are in parentheses.

Fifth, the heterogeneous effect of production factor intensity. This article categorises enterprises based on the density of production factors into three types: technology-intensive, labour-intensive, and asset-intensive. The analysis results under this classification framework are shown in Table 21, with respective regression coefficients of 0.251, 0.300, and 0.621. These results indicate that digital transformation has the greatest positive impact on environmental investment in capital-intensive firms. These results validate H5-5 Hypothesis.

Table 21. Results of the test for heterogeneous effects of production factor intensity.

Variant	Technology-Intensive	Labour-Intensive	Capital-Intensive
	Epinvest	Epinvest	Epinvest
Dig	0.251 ** (2.321)	0.300 *** (2.985)	0.621 ** (2.453)
Controls	Yes	Yes	Yes
Constant	4.684 (0.943)	−2.883 (−1.421)	−5.776 *** (−2.704)
Company FE	Yes	Yes	Yes
Year FE	Yes	Yes	Yes
N	8064	6965	3081
R^2	0.160	0.120	0.173

Note: ***, **, and * indicate significant at 1%, 5%, and 10% confidence levels, respectively; T-values are in parentheses.

5. Conclusions and Recommendations

5.1. Conclusions

The present study is based on data collected from 2011 onwards. This paper sets out to explore the impact of digital transformation on corporate environmental investment in Chinese A-share companies from multiple perspectives. Naturally, the study could be further expanded in several directions. Firstly, as data sets and samples increase over time, it would be worthwhile to consider conducting a more detailed study of corporate data.

Secondly, given the heterogeneity of China's digital transformation, future research could explore the development of different digital transformation indicators for different regions, ownership structures, industries and production factors. Thirdly, it would be beneficial to further examine the relationship between new quality productive forces and corporate environmental investment.

The study's findings indicate that, in the context of achieving the "dual carbon" targets, addressing environmental pollution and the insufficient scale of corporate environmental investment can be facilitated by digital transformation. This conclusion is supported by empirical evidence and is considered to be reliable. The impact of digital transformation on corporate environmental investment is mediated by new quality productive forces. The application of big data can regulate digital transformation and environmental investment. The present study investigates the intermediary effects of the new quality productive forces and environmental investment, and the impact of environmental uncertainty on the digital transformation of enterprises. The results of the study indicate that the digital transformation has a significant positive effect on environmental investment in enterprises with low pollution, non-state-owned enterprises, and those located in developed regions. The study also found that the digital transformation has a more pronounced effect on environmental investment in enterprises with a high density of capital.

5.2. Policy Recommendations

5.2.1. Gradual Drive for Enterprise Digital Transformation

To respond to national policies and achieve the "dual carbon" goals, the government should encourage and support enterprises in enhancing their return on investment through digital technologies. This will guide them toward a win-win outcome of economic development and environmental protection. Considering the significant differences among enterprises in terms of ownership structure, geographical location, and industry type, the government should formulate differentiated strategies to ensure targeted policies. First, policies should be tailored to the extent of pollution in different industries. High-polluting industries should implement mandatory digital environmental compliance monitoring systems that incorporate real-time pollutant monitoring data into enterprise credit ratings. For low-polluting industries, the focus should be on guiding policies that encourage enterprises to optimise green supply chain management through digital tools. Second, state-owned enterprises should incorporate digital transformation and environmental protection investment into their performance evaluation systems to strengthen the exemplary role of their leaders in the industry. For non-state-owned enterprises, optimise tiered tax policies to encourage digital transformation and expand coverage of special loans for green technologies. Third, adopt a tailored approach based on regional conditions. In developed eastern regions, prioritise the application of advanced digital technologies, and support the development of regional smart environmental protection cloud platforms. In less developed regions, increase central government fiscal transfers for digital infrastructure, prioritising the deployment of 5G base stations and industrial internet infrastructure. Fourth, take a tailored approach based on industry density. Provide subsidies for digital transformation skill training for labour-intensive enterprises. Develop low-threshold digital environmental management tools and offer social insurance premium rate discounts to enterprises that hire green workers. Strengthen intellectual property protection for technology-intensive enterprises. Improve the fast-track review process for green patents and encourage industry-academia-research collabouration to establish digital environmental protection technology labouratories. For capital-intensive enterprises, optimise green asset securitization policies to guide long-term capital toward upgrading digital environmental protection equipment. Establish industry-level environmental information disclosure platforms to strengthen investor ESG evaluation constraints.

5.2.2. Promoting the Development of New Quality Productive Forces in Enterprises

New quality productive forces are a key bridge between digital transformation and environmental protection investment. Therefore, enterprises should become the main body of innovation, and the government needs to optimise policies to support them. On the one hand, the government should strengthen the supply of innovation-driven policies. Enterprises that adopt digital green technologies such as AI pollution monitoring and blockchain carbon traceability should be given preferential treatment in the form of increased deductions for research and development expenses, so that enterprises have more incentive to empower new quality productive forces through technological innovation. At the same time, the government should promote the innovation of green financial instruments and guide enterprises to optimise industrial upgrading. Special bonds for new quality productive forces should be issued to raise funds to support enterprises' digital environmental protection projects, so that enterprises have more capital to develop new quality productive forces and provide endogenous momentum for enterprises' environmental protection investment. Emerging industries such as clean energy should be supported, and a database of environmental protection industry projects should be established.

On the other hand, enterprises themselves need to increase investment in digital technology research and development, build joint digital green laboratories with universities, cultivate 'digital + industry' composite talents, solve the problem of the disconnect between technology application and business, and enhance the digital capabilities of enterprises to empower the development of new quality productive forces. At the same time, enterprises should deepen the digital transformation of production factors. They should introduce intelligent management systems, build enterprise-level industrial Internet platforms, and promote real-time analysis and intelligent scheduling of production data. This will enable enterprises to develop in the direction of 'high technology, high efficiency, and high quality,' ultimately achieving a virtuous cycle of environmental protection investment and enterprise development, and promoting the sustainable development of new quality productive forces.

5.2.3. Comprehensively Enhance the Level of Enterprise Big Data Application

In order to achieve a comprehensive enhancement in the application of big data by enterprises, both the government and the private sector must exert concerted effort. The digital transformation process has been shown to facilitate the transmission of the positive influence of big data on environmental investment through the enhancement of new quality productive forces. To this end, the government is required to strengthen its guidance and service functions, thereby optimising the environment for big data application. This can be achieved by means of a staged subsidy policy that provides differentiated subsidies to enterprises at different stages of big data application, thereby reducing their investment costs. In addition, the establishment of a collaborative platform for big data industry should be considered, with leading enterprises being encouraged to share their experience, thereby facilitating the exchange of data between enterprises in the upstream and downstream sectors. This will accelerate the application of big data technology in areas such as environmental protection, among others, and will assist enterprises in achieving a symbiotic relationship between big data application and environmental management.

On the other hand, enterprises should focus on reducing costs and improving efficiency to lower the initial costs of big data application. By cooperating with universities and research institutions to introduce mature big data technologies and models, they can reduce independent research and development costs, rapidly improve big data analysis capabilities, accurately identify environmental risks, and optimise environmental protection investment decisions. At the same time, they should establish cross-departmental data sharing mechanisms to integrate production, operation, environmental protection and other data, improve data utilisation efficiency, avoid duplicate collection and storage, reduce data management costs, and enhance the effectiveness of big data in environmental protection investment decisions.

5.2.4. Establishment of a Sound Early Warning Mechanism for Environmental Risks in Enterprises

Under high environmental uncertainty, the role of enterprise digital transformation in promoting environmental protection investment has weakened. Therefore, it is imperative to establish and improve an environmental risk early warning mechanism for enterprises. On the one hand, the government should play a leading role in building a macro-level environmental risk early warning platform. By integrating environmental monitoring data, information on policy and regulatory changes, and industry trends, and utilising digital tools, the government can provide enterprises with precise environmental risk early warning information, helping them prepare in advance and mitigate the impact of high environmental uncertainty on their operations. At the same time, governments should also improve relevant policies and regulations. They should provide tax incentives and financial subsidies to companies that continue to invest in environmental protection despite high environmental uncertainty, thereby reducing the risks associated with such investments. Additionally, governments should strengthen supervision and penalties for companies that neglect environmental investments, encouraging them to actively utilise digital transformation technologies to enhance their environmental investment levels even in complex environments.

On the other hand, enterprises should actively utilise digital technologies to proactively build internal environmental risk early warning systems. They should increase investment in environmental risk monitoring equipment and use big data analysis technologies to collect and analyse environmental data from enterprise production and operations in real time. When environmental risk indicators approach or exceed thresholds, early warnings should be issued in a timely manner so that enterprises can adjust their production strategies in advance to reduce environmental risks and improve the efficiency of digital transformation resources in highly uncertain environments. At the same time, enterprises should enhance their external risk resistance capabilities. They should establish comprehensive environmental risk response plans, clarify measures to be taken under different risk scenarios, overcome the tendency to avoid risks in high-uncertainty environments, and reasonably increase environmental protection investments.

Author Contributions: Writing—original draft, Y.X. and Q.A.; Writing—review and editing Y.X. and Q.A.; Funding acquisition, Y.X. All authors have read and agreed to the published version of the manuscript.

Funding: This work was supported by the Fundamental Research Funds for the Central Universities (Grant Number: 24QN40).

Institutional Review Board Statement: Not applicable.

Informed Consent Statement: Not applicable.

Data Availability Statement: The data presented in this study are available upon request from the corresponding author. The data are not publicly available due to privacy and confidentiality restrictions.

Conflicts of Interest: The authors declare no conflicts of interest.

References

Babina, T., Fedyk, A., He, A., & Hodson, J. (2020). Artificial intelligence, firm growth, and product innovation. *Journal of Financial Economics, 151,* 103745. [CrossRef]

Chen, J. T., Wu, Y. Y., & Chen, J. D. (2021). Impacts of the environmental protection taxation on the environmental protection investment of the high pollution industry. *Taxation Research, (11),* 44–49. (In Chinese) [CrossRef]

Cui, X. M., Wang, J. Y., & Wang, M. (2021). Environmental investment, CEOs with overseas experiences and the value of enterprises: Increase or decrease? An analysis from the perspective of imprinting theory. *Journal of Audit & Economics, 36*(5), 86–94. (In Chinese)

Ghosh, D., & Olsen, L. (2009). Environmental uncertainty and managers' use of discretionary accruals. *Accounting, Organizations and Society, 34*(2), 188–205. [CrossRef]

Hanelt, A., Bohnsack, R., Marz, D., & Antunes Marante, C. (2021). A systematic review of the literature on digital transformation: Insights and implications for strategy and organizational change. *Journal of Management Studies, 58*(5), 1159–1197. [CrossRef]

Jin, Y., Wen, W., & He, Y. (2022). Impact of digital transformation on corporate green innovation: Evidence from China's manufacturing listed companies. *Finance and Trade Research, 33*(7), 69–83. (In Chinese) [CrossRef]

Li, F. (2025). Pledge of controlling shareholder's equity, digital transformation, and green innovation. *Finance Research Letters, 76,* 106999. [CrossRef]

Li, J., & Zhou, M. Y. (2024). Environmental governance effects of digital transformation: Evidence from textual analysis of annual reports of listed manufacturing enterprises in China. *Journal of Lanzhou University (Social Sciences), 52*(1), 52–65. (In Chinese) [CrossRef]

Li, N. J., Peng, Q., & Shu, C. L. (2023). Enterprise digital transformation and green innovation differentiation. *Journal of Shanxi University of Finance and Economics, 45*(10), 97–112. (In Chinese) [CrossRef]

Liang, L. N., Zhang, G. Q., Li, H., & Yang, Y. Y. (2022). The economic effects of corporate digital transformation: An analysis based on market performance and financial performance. *Modern Management Science, (5),* 146–155. (In Chinese)

Liu, F. Y., & Wu, Y. L. (2024). Digital transformation and esg performance of enterprise under the "double carbon" goal: Effect and impact mechanism. *Science & Technology Progress and Policy, 41*(5), 40–49. (In Chinese) [CrossRef]

Liu, Y. Y., Huang, Z. Y., & Liu, X. X. (2021). Environmental regulation, management's compensation incentive and corporate environmental investment—Evidence from the implementation of the environmental protection law in 2015. *Accounting Research, (5),* 175–192. (In Chinese)

Lu, J., Guo, Z. A., & Wang, Y. P. (2024a). Levels of development of new quality productivity, regional differences and paths to enhancement. *Journal of Chongqing University (Social Science Edition), 30*(3), 1–17. (In Chinese) [CrossRef]

Lu, Y., Pan, H., & Tang, J. R. (2024b). Digital transformation accelerates the formation of new quality productive forces in industries: Connotation and characteristics. *China Tendering, (11),* 44–51. (In Chinese)

MEE. (2024). *Bulletin on the state of ecology and environment in China.* Ministry of Ecological Environment. Available online: https://www.mee.gov.cn/hjzl/sthjzk/zghjzkgb/202506/P020250604527010717462.pdf (accessed on 21 July 2025).

Pan, H. L., & Hu, G. F. (2025). Can enterprise facilitate new quality productive forces through digital transformation? Empirical study based on the perspective of technological innovation. *Journal of Technology Economics, 44*(2), 31–42. (In Chinese) [CrossRef]

Peng, J. Z., Wu, W. B., & Ling, J. J. (2024). Digital transformation and the development of new quality productivity—Based on empirical evidence from listed companies in China. *Journal of Industrial Technology and Economy, 43*(9), 33–43. (In Chinese) [CrossRef]

Shen, H. H., Yu, P., & Wu, L. S. (2012). State ownership, environment uncertainty and investment efficiency. *Economic Research Journal, 47*(7), 113–126. (In Chinese)

Song, J., Zhang, J. C., & Pan, Y. (2024). Research on the impact of ESG development on New quality productive forces of enterprises—Empirical evidence from chinese a-share listed companies. *Contemporary Economic Management, 46*(6), 1–11. (In Chinese) [CrossRef]

Sun, L. (2024). Digital transformation, supply chain integration, and innovation performance in retail enterprises. *Journal of Commercial Economics, (10),* 156–159. (In Chinese)

Tao, F., Wang, X. R., Xu, Y., & Zhu, P. (2023). Digital transformation, resilience of industrial chain and supply chain, and enterprise productivity. *China Industrial Economics, (5),* 118–136. (In Chinese) [CrossRef]

The Central People's Government of the People's Republic of China. (2022). *Xi jinping: Hold high the great banner of socialism with chinese characteristics and strive in unity to build a modern socialist country in all respects—Report to the 20th national congress of the communist party of china.* Available online: https://www.gov.cn/xinwen/2022-10/25/content_5721685.htm (accessed on 21 July 2025).

The Central People's Government of the People's Republic of China. (2024). *The decision of the central committee of the communist party of China on further comprehensively deepening reform and promoting Chinese-style modernization.* Available online: https://www.gov.cn/zhengce/202407/content_6963770.htm?slb=true (accessed on 21 July 2025).

Wen, Z. L., & Ye, B. J. (2014). Analyses of mediating effects: The development of methods and models. *Advances in Psychological Science, 22*(5), 731–745. (In Chinese) [CrossRef] ı, F., Hu, H. Z., Lin, H. Y., & Ren, X. Y. (2021). Enterprise digital transformation and capital market performance: Empirical evidence from stock liquidity. *Journal of Management World, 37*(7), 130–144. (In Chinese) [CrossRef]

ao, H. J., Yang, Z., & Liu, M. Y. (2021). The promotion effect of corporate digitalization on corporate social responsibility: A test of internal and external dual paths. *Business and Management Journal, 43*(11), 52–69. (In Chinese) [CrossRef]

e, D. M. (2020). Local supervision, vertical supervision and corporate environmental protection investment—an empirical study based on listed A—Share heavily polluting enterprises. *Accounting Research, (11)*, 170–186. (In Chinese)

e, K., Xia, Z. H., & Xiao, J. H. (2020). The enterprise realization mechanism of big data becoming a real production factor: From the product innovation perspective. *China Industrial Economics, (5)*, 42–60. (In Chinese) [CrossRef]

u, B. Y., Zheng, M. G., Hu, Z. L., & Wang, X. Y. (2023). The impact of digital transition on total factor productivity of resource-based enterprises. *Resources Science, 45*(3), 536–548. (In Chinese) [CrossRef]

ıan, C., Xiao, T. S., Geng, C. X., & Sheng, Y. (2021). Digital transformation and division of labor between enterprises: Vertical specialization or vertical integration. *China Industrial Economics, (9)*, 137–155. (In Chinese) [CrossRef]

hang, B., & Li, L. (2024). "Data Element×" driving new quality productive forces: Intrinsic logic and implementation path. *Contemporary Economic Management, 46*(8), 1–10. (In Chinese) [CrossRef]

hang, Q., Zheng, Y., & Kong, D. M. (2019). Local Environmental governance pressure, executive's working experience and enterprise investment in environmental protection: A quasi-natural experiment based on China's "Ambient Air Quality Standards 2012". *Economic Research Journal, 54*(6), 183–198. (In Chinese)

hang, X. E., Wang, W., & Yu, Y. B. (2024). Research on the influence of digital intelligence transformation on the new quality productivity of enterprises. *Studies in Science of Science, 43*(5), 943–954. (In Chinese) [CrossRef]

hang, Y. K., Li, X. B., & Xing, M. Q. (2021). Enterprise digital transformation and audit pricing. *Auditing Research, (3)*, 62–71. (In Chinese)

hang, Y. Q., Lu, Y., & Li, L. Y. (2021). Effects of big data on firm value in china: Evidence fromtextual analysis of chinese listed firms' annual reports. *Economic Research Journal, 56*(12), 42–59. (In Chinese)

hao, C. Y., Wang, W. C., & Li, X. S. (2021). How does digital transformation affect the total factor productivity of enterprises? *Finance & Trade Economics, 42*(7), 114–129. (In Chinese) [CrossRef]

hen, H. X., Wang, X., & Fang, H. X. (2023). Administrative protection of intellectual property rights and corporate digital transformation. *Economic Research Journal, 58*(11), 62–79. (In Chinese)

hu, L. N., Zhang, Z. Y., & Gao, H. (2022). Green performance feedback and corporate environmental investment. *Journal of Finance and Economics, 48*(7), 94–108. (In Chinese) [CrossRef]

Disclaimer/Publisher's Note: The statements, opinions and data contained in all publications are solely those of the individual author(s) and contributor(s) and not of MDPI and/or the editor(s). MDPI and/or the editor(s) disclaim responsibility for any injury to people or property resulting from any ideas, methods, instructions or products referred to in the content.

MDPI AG
Grosspeteranlage 5
4052 Basel
Switzerland
Tel.: +41 61 683 77 34

Economies Editorial Office
E-mail: economies@mdpi.com
www.mdpi.com/journal/economies

Disclaimer/Publisher's Note: The title and front matter of this reprint are at the discretion of the Guest Editor. The publisher is not responsible for their content or any associated concerns. The statements, opinions and data contained in all individual articles are solely those of the individual Editor and contributors and not of MDPI. MDPI disclaims responsibility for any injury to people or property resulting from any ideas, methods, instructions or products referred to in the content.

www.ingramcontent.com/pod-product-compliance
Lightning Source LLC
Chambersburg PA
CBHW061823210926
51850CB00006B/794